FORENSIC SCIENCE UNDER SIEGE

FORENSIC SCIENCE UNDER SIEGE

THE CHALLENGES OF FORENSIC LABORATORIES
AND THE MEDICO-LEGAL DEATH INVESTIGATION SYSTEM

Kelly M. Pyrek

AMSTERDAM • BOSTON • HEIDELBERG • LONDON
NEW YORK • OXFORD • PARIS • SAN DIEGO
SAN FRANCISCO • SINGAPORE • SYDNEY • TOKYO

Academic Press is an imprint of Elsevier

Elsevier Academic Press
30 Corporate Drive, Suite 400, Burlington, MA 01803, USA
525 B Street, Suite 1900, San Diego, California 92101-4495, USA
84 Theobald's Road, London WC1X 8RR, UK

This book is printed on acid-free paper.

Library of Congress Cataloging-in-Publication Data
APPLICATION SUBMITTED

British Library Cataloguing in Publication Data
A catalogue record for this book is available from the British Library

ISBN 13: 978-0-12-370861-8
ISBN 10: 0-12-370861-3

For all information on all Elsevier Academic Press publications visit our Web site at www.books.elsevier.com

Printed in The United States of America
07 08 09 10 9 8 7 6 5 4 3 2 1

To the outstanding individuals in the crime labs and medico-legal offices who seek justice for the living and for the dead.

To Judi and Tony, with love and gratitude.

CONTENTS

CHAPTER 11   DNA: CONVICTING THE GUILTY, EXONERATING THE INNOCENT

CHAPTER 12   THE EVIDENCE TRILOGY AND FORENSIC SCIENCE

CHAPTER 13   THE STAKEHOLDERS IN COURT: JUDGES, JURIES, EXPERTS, AND ATTORNEYS

FOREWORD

Kelly Pyrek is a passionate person. She is passionate about forensic science and understands the importance of timely, high-quality forensics to the criminal justice system. More specifically, she understands how science and technology can be used to help the police, prosecutors and the courts to make certain that guilty people are convicted of crimes and innocent ones are not harmed.

I had the great pleasure to have met Kelly several years back. She edits a forensic nursing magazine which I've contributed to and I've spoken at a seminar she helped coordinate. During that time and later we discussed a wide variety of forensic science issues and the ways in which forensic science in the United States could be improved. From those very preliminary discussions came the idea to write a book on the topic and interview many people to get their opinions on the issue at hand. Kelly's enthusiasm for forensic science and its potential contribution to the criminal justice made this book a reality.

In 16 chapters, Kelly covers the scope and breadth of forensic science from a public policy point of view. Through in-depth interviews of knowledgeable people, she explores the field and examines the problems, real and imaginary, facing this profession and explores some of the bright spots on the horizon.

Kelly deserves kudos for taking on this complex field and for her enthusiastic support of those who daily labor in the trenches to help forensic science meet its potential to improve the criminal justice system in our country.

Barry A.J. Fisher
Los Angeles, California

"There is nothing more deceptive than an obvious fact."—*Sherlock Holmes*

Forensic science is under siege. If you are a practitioner in the field currently, you already know this. If you are a stakeholder in the criminal justice system, you already suspect this. And if you are an interested layperson, you are about to discover this.

Forensic science is so ubiquitous that its terminology has become a part of our everyday lexicon and its images burnished into our collective consciousness. Forensic science is familiar because we are voyeurs at heart; weekly, we tune in to watch the fictional character Gil Grissom collect evidence at crime scenes and Jordan Cavanaugh conduct autopsies. For a dose of reality, we dial up Dr. Henry Lee or Dr. Michael Baden providing commentary on a high-profile crime on cable news. And for a nice session of armchair sleuthing, we turn to the case re-enactment shows that allow us to try our hand at solving crimes like the professionals.

Forensic science is approachable, like a de-clawed cat, because it has been reduced to the lowest common denominator. Stripped of its complicated science and mundane technical details, and sexed-up for the cameras, forensic science for the masses is a slick, sophisticated, manufactured commodity, heavy on soundbites and stereotypes, and light on substance.

Forensic science is a look-but-don't-touch proposition. We are allowed to leer, through splayed fingers in front of our eyes, at the horrors of man's inhumanity to man, but it is a sanitized peep-show; the gore and the grit have been removed, leaving a sheen and a sparkle that simultaneously dazzles and deceives.

A steady diet of this forensic science fact and fiction creates a real-life conundrum. Unrealistic expectations are fostered, misperceptions fester unchecked, and assumptions about what forensic science can and cannot achieve are negatively impacting the provision of forensic science services and, ultimately, hampering the operations of the U.S. criminal justice system.

The next 16 chapters will escort you on a journey through the inner workings of forensic science, introducing you to how and why this field is under siege, and why it matters so greatly to the future of the adjudication of criminal cases. Forensic science affects deeply every individual alive—and dead—on the planet today. In life, forensic science can condemn, acquit, or exonerate; in death it can help determine and explain causation. For this reason, it is imperative that every individual understand how forensic science and its practitioners truly function, and why the outcome of this contentious, win-at-all-costs war over forensic science has direct implications for all members of society.

As we will see in subsequent chapters, engaged in battle most frequently are social scientists and legal scholars vs. forensic practitioners in a tussle over, if you will, ownership rights: Who owns forensic science, who has the right to dictate to it, and who will ultimately assume leadership over a field with immense power and strategic access to all three levels of U.S. government—legislative, judicial, and executive. The feud is triggered by allegations of errors, fraud, and malfeasance on the part of forensic service providers that undermine criminal justice, and fueled by disagreements over a diverse plank of issues ranging from the very definition of science and its purpose, to the admissibility of forensic evidence in a court of law, to the effects of a significant paradigm shift some commentators say is occurring at the nexus of law and science—the place where forensic science lives.

One very important argument that we will explore is the allegation by critics that forensic science is deficient in scientific methodology and rigor—with the extremists asserting that it is utterly lacking in science altogether—and the response from forensic practitioners, stunned by the charges, that forensic science was born from and is steeped in the traditional sciences. Both sides sputter at each other's stances, incredulous that the other would make such naïve, "unsubstantiated" claims, totally devoid of empirical data and ridiculously reasoned. In Chapter 10, we explore these claims and try to offer various perspectives on the definition and purpose of science in whatever iteration exists these days—applied, natural, pseudo, or pure.

I wonder, as we call into question the very science that presumably explains our world, do we also question the meaning of truth? If science is the ultimate pursuit of truth, are we only hurting ourselves if we decimate one of the foundations of reason and rationalism? And are we getting into dangerous territory when we, with prescience, decide that one thing is science and the other is not? While science lays one mystery to rest, it creates still others to ponder. Are we guilty of pigeon-holing and packaging science to our liking, as a social construct and a byproduct of a consumer-driven country, so that it more easily explains the world that we have crafted and subjugated to our will? I believe the very nature of science perpetuates ongoing discovery; and that science is not a finite entity capable of being restrained. I believe further that science is the ongoing building of knowledge, a journey instead of a destination. But that is an upsetting concept to some commentators who expect finiteness and certainty from their favorite brand of science.

Another issue going to the heart of this book is the fact that members of the public—potential jurors—are confused and upset when more of science in general, and forensic science in particular, is demanded from it that it can rightly yield. Consumers of popular culture and the mass media expect absolutes in certainty, validity and reliability; however, as Cohn and Cope (2001) observe, "The first thing to understand about science is that it is almost always uncertain." The uninformed place science on a pedestal, assuming it is neutral and objective when it is inherently political, a commodity used to prove or disprove almost any hypothesis. Science is relied upon to help us explain the mysteries of our world, but can it be trusted implicitly? We hear about conflicting studies, fraudulent research, bias, and errors, and dubious assumptions and conclusions. Science is a slippery slope; as one scientist remarked, "Is science always right, or is it increasingly less wrong?" Sort of turns your world upside down, doesn't it?

Not only must forensic science operate on this belligerent scientific plane, but it also must survive the medico-legal turbulence created in the courtroom. Much of this book examines the symbiotic relationship of the law and forensic science, two dissimilar entities co-existing in an intimate association that mimics the six relationships found in the biological incarnation of this scientific term symbiosis: Parasitism, in which the association is disadvantageous or destructive to one of the entities and beneficial to the other; mutualism, in which the association is advantageous to both entities; commensalism, in which one member of the association benefits while the other is not affected; amensalism, in which the association is disadvantageous to one member while the other is not affected; neutralism, in which both entities are unaffected, and competition, in which both organisms are harmed.

You may draw your own analogies, but for example, to me, parasitism occurs when a defendant is wrongful accused, while mutualism occurs when there is proper adjudication of a criminal case and justice is served. There are varying degrees of commensalism and amensalism throughout the criminal justice process; while neutralism is generally rejected, and competition seems to be the order of the day. Kudos to Rudin and Inman (2001) for recognizing that the adversarial nature of the U.S. legal system, rife with personal attacks, very much throws symbiotic relationships out the window: "Often it is much easier for an attorney to try to discredit the testifying expert than the evidence itself. It is a sad commentary on both professions when much of the discussion is focused on either perpetrating or defending oneself from attacks, rather than attempting to understand what the evidence is telling us. We are invited participants in the judicial process; without the lawyers, none of us would have a job. Yet, to best assist the judicial system in analyzing, interpreting, and understanding physical evidence, we must maintain our objectivity, autonomy, and identity; we cannot become simply a pawn of either side of the system."

Going to the heart of much of the debate addressed in this book is the controversy of the autonomy of forensic service providers; while the forensic science community wants self-determination, critics assert that forensic science is a veritable Wild West, complete with rogue cowboys and hired guns, and that the field is completely lacking in oversight and quality control mechanisms. A better system of checks and balances is needed, commentators assert, to prevent analyst and examiner bias, curtail and prevent errors, expose fraud, and in general, optimize the field. Most forensic practitioners would agree that this is a mutual goal, but they bristle at the way in which they and their work is denigrated and dismissed by commentators in ivory towers and not in the trenches. It is the blanket indictment of forensic science that causes so many practitioners to become hostile and defensive, even when they have no reason to be; it is a defense mechanism cultivated after years of accusations that may or may not actually bear any legitimate weight.

Like the physician taking the Hippocratic Oath of "First, do no harm," the forensic practitioner takes his or her own pledge; as the American Academy of Forensic Sciences (AAFS) notes, "The forensic scientist's goal is the evenhanded use of all available information to determine the facts and, subsequently, the truth. Some place their faith in forensic science to the degree that they are under the impression that it is absolute, infallible and unassailable. In truth, it is a manmade construct, dependent upon manmade machinery, man-calibrated accuracy, man-led action under manmade protocols, and analyzed by man—an altogether human construct." Instead of a reckless community playing God, it is a thoughtful, concerned group of professionals searching for the same kind of answers—but in their own way. As Inman and Rudin (2001) observe, "The reputation of forensic science has been significantly tarnished in recent years. A number of unethical, unprofessional, and immoral acts have been clearly perpetrated and we condemn them. However, because of the public impact of forensic investigations and analyses, they often become fodder for journalists, the most well intentioned of whom has little or no scientific expertise and likely no forensic background. We cannot allow the media or political bodies to police our profession, especially in the forum of public opinion. We must enforce standards from within the profession; if we are unwilling to monitor analyst integrity on our own, it will be done for (and to) us."

As philosopher John Locke once remarked, "It is one thing to show a man that he is in error, and another to put him in possession of the truth." As we will see throughout this book, forensic service providers and critics are locked in a battle for the truth, each determined to take the other down the road to redemption they see fit to pursue. It is a journey fraught with the same kind of tension to be found in the adversarial nature of the law and traversed with the same spirit of contemplation that should characterize all medico-legal endeavors. In Chapter 9 we discuss the oft-cited paradigm shift affecting forensic science, a concept suggested by social scientists, watched keenly by legal practitioners, and debated by forensic professionals. Rudin and Inman (2005) opine, "The forensic science paradigm has already shifted. Both the profession and the practice have changed significantly over the last decade, for more reasons than merely the introduction of DNA typing into the forensic lexicon. The question is, will we, as a profession, actively determine the direction of shift as it continues, or will we sit passively while others make those decisions for us."

It is grossly unfair to depict all forensic practitioners as deceitful, biased, careless individuals with hidden agendas. Yes, there are a few people who have given the field a bad name, but to classify an entire profession as liars and cheats is undignified and incredibly disingenuous. What I have come to realize about the forensic science community is that it is filled with individuals too dignified to stoop to the level of those who would attempt to engage them in mud-slinging. Not only are they much too busy to be caught up in a round of finger-pointing, they know they must conserve and direct their energy toward the one thing that matters: The evidence that must be analyzed, or the decedent on the autopsy table. In both cases, the task at hand will yield valuable information used to answer the questions that arise. Anything else is subjugated, and rightly so. However, it seems to me that on occasion, it would benefit the forensic science community to respond to the intellectual and scientific taunts, if only to use it as an opportunity to correct the misperceptions, clarify the issues, and resolve the disputes whenever possible. To this end, I was gratified to find the following passage penned by Rudin and Inman (2006): "While the many observers of forensic science comment vociferously and frequently, the forensic community is comparatively silent. We must understand that we invite reinvention by leaving a vacuum; if we do not take positive action, the consumers of forensic science will fill the void and define our profession for us. Although input from both the consumers of forensic science and from the academic disciplines from which it is derived should be welcomed, we cannot let others define our practice and our profession."

Forensic practitioners simply want to be respected for their knowledge, abilities, and contributions. For far too long they have been misunderstood, unappreciated, and expected to accomplish their goals without adequate resources, infrastructure, and support. They want to be understood, and they want the stakeholders in the criminal justice system to appreciate their limitations. They also want these stakeholders to have realistic expectations for the caseloads they handle, and the immense pressures they experience daily. As we will see in Chapters 4 and 7, the attacks on these forensic science professionals are numerous, and as we will see in Chapters 5 and 8, the grim realities faced by forensic laboratories and medico-legal offices only add to the pressure-cooker environment.

Forensic service providers need and deserve increased, reliable sources of local, state and federal funding. It's the only way they can add the personnel and equipment necessary to clear cases, address backlogs, and function efficiently, let alone keep up with the increasing demands of the future. Funding is the engine that drives everything related to quality assurance and improvement in forensic science.

Forensic service providers need and deserve adequate infrastructure in order to perform their duties. So much of it is crumbling, inadequate, or downright dangerous. There is a frightening lack of parity among forensic laboratories and medico-legal offices when it comes to the quality of physical facilities, equipment, and available technology.

Forensic service providers need and deserve improved access to top-notch education and training for veterans as well as those who are new to the field. They need to stay sharp, and they must keep pace with the advancing technology that will only increase with each decade.

Forensic service providers need and deserve a system of quality control and improvement that is neither overly punitive nor inadequate to address any cases of true malfeasance or fraud that occur. It needs to be a system that they can live with, enhancing their work but one that is not overly limiting or constraining. They want a partner in improvement, not another taskmaster.

Forensic service providers need and deserve an environment in which they can practice good science. They are accused of trafficking in junk science, when they desperately need funding for research to bolster the science associated with specific forensic disciplines under attack, such as latent fingerprint examination.

Forensic service providers need and deserve improved communication along the entire spectrum of the criminal justice continuum, with all stakeholders involved and with buy-in from key decision-makers and legislators who hold the power and the purse-strings.

Forensic service providers need and deserve a safe haven to air their grievances and concerns without censure. Don't make them jeopardize their futures and their pensions if they identify areas of concern but are afraid to speak up. Create for them an environment that is conducive to improvement without repercussions or professional penalties.

Forensic science providers need and deserve to be added to the top of this country's lengthy list of priorities, especially in light of their relevance to public health and homeland security in addition to criminal justice.

* * *

If you couldn't tell, I feel very strongly about the need to champion forensic science because it is a crucial underpinning of the entire criminal justice system, because it is a pillar supporting the heavy weight of democracy, and because it is a vital component of so many liberties and rights we have come to alternately expect, demand, and forfeit. I also feel very strongly about the need to tell the whole story of forensic science, and not just the one-sided snippets and soundbites that constitute the mass media in an unfortunate era of tiny attention spans. I am bothered by the shallow depth of the majority of coverage of forensic science in the mainstream media. With very few exceptions, reporters crank out versions of the same tired lists of offenders and issues that have been promulgated everywhere for years. A prime example of this is the mileage the media has gotten from the so-called "CSI effect" that is explored in Chapter 13 as part of a larger look at the stakeholders in the criminal justice system; run a search of "CSI effect" on Google, and you'll run out of time before you run out of hits. There is nothing wrong with the exposure to forensic science that the popular culture has facilitated, but I am distressed by the resistance the media has shown to fully understand the deeper issues related to forensic laboratories and medico-legal offices and translate these issues for its consumers. I can criticize the media in this way because I am a member of its ranks. As a seasoned journalist, I understand the need for telling a story beyond the obvious, and for digging a little deeper to expose the undercurrents of any issue. Every time news of a lab scandal or a botched autopsy breaks, the report is inevitably formulaic, and that is disappointing to me. Some commentators have made their names and fortunes solely by riding the media merry-go-round, supplying a requisite soundbite but never really adding to and expanding the dialogue. I suspect we can do much, much better than this. It's a ratings game, and scandals make good ink, but I fear that in the stampede to cover the story, forensic science gets trampled underfoot.

Forensic science is indeed under siege, and it is a death by a thousand cuts. Those inflicting the most damage are the individuals who refuse to become educated about the issues.

The problem is, there are few opportunities for erudition because very few of the debates taking place occur within national forums and even fewer present the issues with meaningful context preserved. Critics and commentators snipe at the forensic science community under the cover of white papers and journal articles with amusing headlines, such as, "Oops! We forgot to put it in the refrigerator: DNA identification and the state's duty to preserve evidence." (I swear I did not make this one up; it came from a law review journal.) All very amusing, but it does nothing to advance productive dialogue about the issues, let along resolve the problems. Instead, it fans the flames of hostility between the very individuals who stand the best chance to finally effecting real change. The sniping and the finger-pointing must stop, replaced by peace talks that facilitate agenda-building and conflict resolution.

One member of the forensic science community told me that what is desperately needed is a single song sheet from which the assembled choir could sing; meaning that to achieve the goal of improving forensic science, there must be clear, unwavering consensus, not just among a few, but among all of stakeholders. This book is designed to serve as a critical mass of information, opinions, and perspectives about what is wrong about forensic science, what is right about forensic science, and what is very much mistaken about forensic science. It is meant to serve as a vehicle for discussion, whether it is practitioner to practitioner, practitioner to lawmaker, or practitioner to critic. This book enumerates the issues, presents suggestions for improvement, and most of all, challenges the assumptions that forensic science is broken. This is not to say that there are not elements of the profession that need fixing; however, I object to the assumption that the field is too far gone. The challenge of writing this kind of book is that there is no definitive ending to the debate; the issues are shifting sands but the principles involved are enduring. Instead of serving as a definitive tome that has all of the answers, it asks more questions. This book is a springboard to further inquiry, as it was designed to be.

It also endeavors to bring the issues of two pillars of the criminal justice system together for the first time. Much attention has been focused on crime labs, but medico-legal offices housing medical examiners, coroners, and medico-legal death investigators, have had less time in the spotlight. Not surprisingly, their issues are very similar, if not identical, and create exciting parallel opportunities for improvement. There is a disconnect, however, between many forensic laboratories and medico-legal offices at the local, state and federal level, which hinders both systems, and this is perpetuated, I suspect, by a lack of understanding of how the systems are symbiotic and dependent upon one another. Not until an event such as 9/11 do we comprehend how the various forensic and medico-legal disciplines come together to identify the deceased, investigate the cause of the disaster, and provide answers for the living and the dead. For too long this link between the living and the dead, and the appreciation that forensic professionals serve dual constituencies have not been recognized by the general public and by legislators, the two groups most affected by and influential upon, respectively, the forensic community. It is my hope that these connections can be made, and a better understanding of the interaction between forensic laboratories and medico-legal offices is fostered.

Most of all, I wrote this book to show the forensic science community that it must take a more proactive stance if it is to weather its time under siege. The community has been silent for a very long time, and when it does respond, it has done so in a largely reactive and defensive manner, which instantly triggers renewed bouts of criticism. As we will see in Chapter 14, the forensic science community has only very recently created a consortium that can act as an entity of like-mindedness and represent the diverse and occasionally divergent interests of its eight forensic service provider organizations. These are honorable people with good intentions, a passion for their work, and the overriding desire to get it right. They are distressed by accusations that they are anything less than disciplined, capable, objective fact finders for the medico-legal system. But they have kept a low profile, and it is incumbent upon them to assume responsibility for the protection of their reputations, the preservation of justice, and the upholding of accurate forensic analyses. They must achieve this through advocacy work, through interaction with the media and with lawmakers, and through diligence in academic-based research and empirical data make their forensic disciplines bulletproof. When this happens, everyone wins because quality is actualized, communication is achieved, and forensic science is validated. The forensic science community must continue to endeavor to voice its concerns and galvanize the appropriate responses to charges laid against the forensic disciplines.

*   *   *

In 2001 I embarked on one of the most fascinating and rewarding journeys I have ever taken as a journalist who is closing in on a quarter-century of inquiry about the world in which I live. That was when I first discovered forensic nursing. Mind you, I have been a forensic science fan since discovering Sir Arthur Conan Doyle when I was eight; that appreciation has only grown as fate—and a few strategic work assignments—led me down a very fortuitous path. As I started observing, interacting with, and writing about the forensic nursing field I quickly learned how these amazing nurses interact with the larger forensic science community, and that is how I first met an extraordinary group of individuals comprised of crime lab directors, medical examiners, and medico-legal death investigators. Through exploration of the world of forensic nursing I discovered the bigger-picture needs and issues of the forensic science community. I began attending meetings of the American Academy of Forensic Sciences (AAFS), reading journals, and talking to the people in the trenches in forensic laboratories and medico-legal offices across the country. I began seeing a pattern relating to legislative undercurrents, and dire infrastructure and budgetary needs. Being expected to do too much with too little was a constant among the numerous variables facing this field. I am exceedingly fortunate to know a number of remarkable practitioners who are tireless in their devotion to the field and in the sacrifices they make in order to advocate for their profession, serve as a role model for their peers, and in general champion the cause of forensic science at a time when it is very much under siege.

Barry A.J. Fisher has become a professional associate, ally, and friend. His many kindnesses over the years have included encouragement, referrals, long discussions about the state of the field, and earnest dialogue about what must change in order for forensic science to work as effectively as it should. His tutelage has been of tremendous assistance to me as I continue to be an earnest and eager student. Barry is joined by a long list of stellar individuals who were gracious in sharing their time and their expertise with me for this book as well as many other projects.

Not everyone I contacted for an interview for this book wanted to speak to me. Many declined my invitation to talk about the issues because they feared professional repercussions, or felt that everything that could be said about the issues had been already. Several individuals felt there wasn't much merit in the project, and while I won't name names, I am frustrated by their near-sightedness and their declining of an opportunity to add their perspective to the mix. One individual taunted me about my ability to garner honest, open opinions on difficult topics, much less offer anything new to the dialogue. Again, while I would never presume to be the authority on the issues facing the forensic science community, my motivation for writing this book was to create a critical mass of information that would summarize the issues and articulate in some meaningful way the need for greater consensus-building both internally and externally of the field, as well as the importance of communicating a progressive agenda to the decision-makers who determine the future of forensic science within the criminal justice system. In the several years leading up to this project, it appeared to me that commentators were not only asking the questions, but supplying the answers, and the practitioners themselves had very little to say; not because they had nothing to offer, but because they relegated their opinions to the few small opportunities to provide comment in the press. And quite often it was a defensive tactic in the midst of attack, not a proactive stance when battle was not being waged in the media.

Rudin and Inman (2006) perhaps say it best when they comment, "Observers feel justified in commenting . . . that the field is not sufficiently self-critical. Historically, we tend to justify, explain, and rationalize before we agree to make substantive changes. Why is this? Much of the problem lies in the very fact that our job is to defend our work on a daily basis. It is easy to confuse defending our work with defending ourselves. There exists an underlying fear that human fallibility is not an option. This very real fear is fueled in large part by the vociferous and condescending attacks of legal observers, often through the public channel of the media. Sometimes, this unfortunately has been the only way to force a wayward lab to open itself to independent review, providing a justification on which the critics can hang their hats. However, as a general approach, it is not an effective tool to promote openness, transparency, and positive change."

Throughout this book you will be presented with the strong views of critics, commentators, and champions of forensic science. I don't think that all critics are evil, and in fact, many of them have made well-reasoned arguments and valid statements that should be considered carefully. Some of the critics are full of bluster and bother, and while they are buoyant on their own cloud of hot air for now, they have to come back down to earth—and to reality—at some point. A few critics expressed to me their sincere desire to improve the forensic science community, and I believe them. But they don't have to win me over; they have to win over the forensic practitioners they may have alienated with their collective tirades. I think that if everyone can come to the peace-talks, open minds will abound and overcome.

If there is one overriding thought I would like you to take away from this book, it is that the sky is not falling. Don't read and digest the headlines without discernment because isolated incidents occur in every profession; mishaps are isolated and not systemic, and certainly not exclusive to forensic science. Do they signal the need for attention? Most definitely, and the forensic science community is very aware of the necessity for a deeper foray into the issues. While Rudin and Inman (2006) insist that the forensic science community must define its own agenda, they recognize that it is not a solo endeavor: "We must accept that practicing criminalists are not going to single-handedly solve many of the challenges facing the forensic profession today. We simply do not have the time, monetary resources, academic resources, or, in many cases, adequate education and training. We must actively solicit assistance from and seek partnerships with our clients, those in the legal profession, and from our roots, the academic 'feeder' disciplines that form the basis of our applied science. Furthermore, forensic science needs to be an ongoing and formalized academic endeavor, supported with concomitant funding, human resources, and competent direction. If we cannot develop and support our opinions based on science, rather than policy, then those who like to refer to working criminalists as technicians will be entirely justified."

As we will see in Chapter 16, there are numerous new opportunities to study these imperatives, share perspectives, and draw conclusions that will gain traction in the real world. Instead of pointing fingers, within the next several years we can hope for productive, proactive approaches to resolving the issues that for far too long have been allowed to undermine the great strides taken in forensic science. After all, isn't a dialogue is much better than a monologue when it comes to determining the future of something as important as forensic science?

REFERENCES

Cohn V and Cope L. *News and Numbers: A Guide to Reporting Statistical Claims and Controversies in Health and Other Fields.* Second edition. Blackwell Publishing Professional. 2001.

Rudin N and Inman K. The shifty paradigm. *CAC News.* 2006.

Inman K and Rudin N. *Principles and Practice of Criminalistics: The Profession of Forensic Science.* Boca Raton, Fla.: CRC Press. 2001.

ACKNOWLEDGEMENTS

The list of individuals interviewed for this book reads like a veritable Who's Who of the forensic science, forensic pathology, legal, and social science communities. I extend to them my heartfelt gratitude for sharing their wisdom with me: Michael Baden, Jan Burke, Michael Dobersen, Mary Fran Ernst, David Faigman, Paul Ferrara, Marcella Fierro, Barry Fisher, Randy Hanzlick, Carol Henderson, Randy Jonakait, Terrence Kiely, Lawrence Kobilinsky, Beth Lavach, Henry Lee, Kurt Nolte, Joseph Polski, Janet Reno, Richard Saferstein, Michael Saks, Allan Sobel, Jami St. Clair, Brent Turvey, William Webster, Cyril Wecht, Victor Weedn, Earl Wells, and Don Wyckoff. I am also indebted to numerous other individuals whose work I perused and sampled for this project—your perspectives are the beacon that will light the way to the truth.

I also acknowledge the terrific members of the Elsevier team for their dedication to making this book a reality. A special thank you to acquisitions editor Mark Listewnik, who "got it" from the get-go.

CHAPTER 1

FORENSIC SCIENCE: CELEBRATED
AND VILIFIED

Wherever he steps, whatever he touches, whatever he leaves, even unconsciously, will serve as silent evidence against him. Not only his fingerprints or his footprints, but his hair, the fibers from his clothes, the glass he breaks, the tool mark he leaves, the paint he scratches, the blood or semen that he deposits or collects—all these and more bear mute witness against him. This is evidence that does not forget. It is not confused by the excitement of the moment. It is not absent because human witnesses are. It is factual evidence. Physical evidence cannot be wrong; it cannot perjure itself; it cannot be wholly absent. Only its interpretation can err. Only human failure to find it, study and understand it, can diminish its value.
—Paul L. Kirk, Ph.D.

Just as Locard's principle of exchange—alluded to by Kirk—has defined one of the quintessential processes of forensic science, this prescient discipline is making its mark on the worlds of science, the law, and medicine in ways that we are just beginning to comprehend and appreciate. Concurrently, the awesome power of forensic science to deliver a conviction or an acquittal in the court of law is being questioned, challenged, and scrutinized as never before. Forensic science is simultaneously celebrated and vilified to the point where the constant torrent of kudos and the criticism blur to create a confusing, muddled picture. It is akin to a smeared canvas bearing an abstract design upon which many painters have dabbled and from which observers with varying perspectives draw vastly different opinions. As beauty is in the eye of the beholder, so it would seem is forensic science. As we will see in Chapter 2, the numerous stakeholders in the criminal justice system extract from forensic science what they need to perpetuate their positions. One's stance on forensic science depends on what is at stake—the tearing down of a reputation or the building up of a career perhaps, as well as a conviction or an exoneration, and the repercussions of the final disposition of a case. No matter how forensic science is used and abused as a commodity within the science and legal communities, one thing is certain: It remains a tantalizing, fascinating subject for the layperson, perhaps the most important arbiter of all. To the forensic practitioner, forensic science is not a conundrum, an enigma, a paradox, or an oxymoron; it is a straightforward application of scientific principles to arrive at a logical, appropriate, verifiable conclusion. It is not magic, and there is no smoke and mirrors despite the insistence of a few commentators. Why then, is forensic science still shrouded in mystery?

Inman and Rudin (2001) observe, "From its inception, forensic science has evoked an air of mystery and intrigue. It is probably both the least understood and most misunderstood of all scientific disciplines. Because speculation immediately expands to fill an informational void, rumor and gossip have become the stuff upon which the lay public judges the forensic profession. Certainly, forensic practitioners have historically contributed to the perception that the reconstruction of a criminal event from limited evidence can only be achieved by a few talented individuals with a special aptitude for such work. Even those whose methods were scientifically defensible could not resist encouraging the bit of celebrity and notoriety that seems to follow those known for solving difficult crimes. The accordance of these attributes, combined with the understandable inability of legal professionals to separate true experts from charlatans, has unfortunately also encouraged a proliferation of self-appointed experts whose motives are based solely in greed and infamy."[1]

The pressure exerted on forensic science and its practitioners in forensic laboratories and in medico-legal offices is immense. No other science is responsible for playing a role in the determination of an individual's guilt or innocence. Because the stakes are so high, the expectations of forensic science are enormous and the scrutiny is razor sharp and appropriately microscopic in nature.

Forensic science is celebrated in numerous ways. Forensic evidence is frequently considered to be the single most important tool in the adjudication of most criminal cases and an increasing number of civil cases. For the victim and/or the decedent's family, forensic science is viewed as the great equalizer and is equated with the swift delivery of justice and vindication. Conversely, for the defendant, forensic science represents an opportunity for deliverance from a wrongful conviction hovering like a specter over the courtroom. In an age of televised trials and verdicts conveyed instantly thanks to the 24/7 news outlets, forensic science is a celebrity in itself, fawned over and feted. It is congratulated, commended, and consecrated by those who place absolute faith in its power.

Forensic science is appealing because there are so many recognizable and lovable characters—fictional and real—associated with it. It takes a cold heart to not warm to the likes of Sherlock Holmes, the quintessential symbol of all things deductive and rational. A creation of the fertile imagination of British physician Sir Arthur Conan Doyle, Holmes embodies everything we want our sleuth of a forensic scientist to be: calculating, uncannily observant, brilliantly eccentric, and completely trustworthy when not lying in a lethargic, opium-induced haze. As a consulting detective, the detached Holmes enjoyed tweaking the noses of bumbling law enforcement officers, confounding his detractors, and astounding mere mortals devoid of his superhuman powers of deduction. The denizen of 221B Baker Street, could crack a case without leaving the cozy confines of his London study, eschewing legwork and the contrivances of the scientific lab. Holmes was equal parts bravado and humility, alternately gregarious and withdrawn, and consummately a perplexing puzzle unto himself. Holmes has had a profound impact on the armchair sleuth, and to some extent, Doyle has left his mark on the face of medico-legal issues. More than a few laypersons and even some members of the forensic community concede that Holmes could have been a literary foreshadowing of the developments in forensic science taking place in the late 19th century. For example, in "A Case of Identity" Holmes used typewritten letters to expose a fraud; deduced that a homicide had occurred from examining two pieces of human remains in "The Adventure of the Cardboard Box"; observed gunpowder residue on a victim in "The Adventure of the Reigate Squire"; studied bullets from the murder weapon obtained from two crime scenes in "The Adventure of the Empty House"; and used a fingerprint to free an innocent man in "The Adventure of the Norwood Builder." Holmes' unique brand of deductive reasoning consisted of drawing inferences based on careful observation and inductive study. Doyle had been inspired by surgeon and forensic expert Dr. Joseph Bell, a professor at the University of Edinburgh Medical School. Doyle picked up on Bell's ability to deduce substantial information simply from looking at a patient. Bell is purported to have commented, "The student must be taught to observe . . . he can discover in ordinary matters information such as the previous history, nationality and occupation."

Logicians, scientists, and criminalists alike may cringe, but this tactic was good enough to earn Holmes the distinction of being named as an honorary fellow of the Royal Society of Chemistry in appreciation of his contributions to forensic science—pretty impressive, again, for a fictional character.

Therein lies the problem, one could argue, that fictional characters take on a persona that is as alive and vivid as the layperson who brings this character to life and is an accepted by-product of hero worship in the halls of popular culture. Holmes' legacy is a lasting one, and his imitators are many, including another iconoclastic literary sleuth, Agatha Christie's Hercule Poirot, as well as a long list of television gumshoes with varying degrees of conviction. In Chapter 13, we explore the modern-day incarnations of the small-screen pathologist and criminalist and how their dramatized exploits are affecting jurisprudence, so mankind has had no lack of highly fictionalized personages that are seen by impressionable consumers as infallible role models above reproach. The general public prefers to take a voyeuristic romp through medicine, law, pathology, toxicology, anatomy, and chemistry through the safety of its fictional heroes, leaving the messy real-world issues to the scientist toiling away in the lab, safely removed and forgotten. The problem is that real-world scientists have a funny way of popping out of nowhere, reminding us that real science isn't glossy, glamorous, or grandiose.

Forensic science is both celebrated and vilified for its contributions to traditional science. Koertge et al. (2000) argue that science is "politics by other means," essentially asserting that the results of scientific inquiry are significantly shaped by the ideological agendas of powerful elites and that there has been a systematic intrusion of sexist, racist, capitalist, and special interests into science. These commentators argue that scientific results tell us more about social context than they do about the natural world.

To its supporters, forensic science observes and upholds the scientific inquiry when its practitioners properly observe patterns of objects and events, use scientific tools for classification, make inferences based on observations, and predict the results of actions based on patterns in data and experiences. Forensic scientists contribute to collective scientific thought by thinking critically and logically to make relationships between evidence and explanations and by reviewing data to demonstrate cause-and-effect relationships in their experiments.

Criminalist Henry Lee, Ph.D., chief emeritus of the Connecticut State Police, and founder and professor of the forensic science program at the University of New Haven, argues that over the years, forensic practitioners have made notable contributions to science: "The public recognizes forensics as a field; they understand better what it is. They used to think we were in forestry or involved in foreign affairs. We've made a tremendous contribution to the forensic literature. There used to only be one book on criminalistics, and today there are so many more good forensic scientists contributing to the research and to making better textbooks for younger people to study. We used to be afraid of putting down information because if we taught everyone else, we might be out of a job. Now more scientists share their results. People are more interested in forensics and more good students are getting inspired to major in forensics. That might get the justice department to put more resources into forensics, which will bring more justice to our society" (Ramsland, 2006).

Ribaux et al. (2006) assert, "The debate in forensic science concentrates on issues such as standardization, accreditation, and de-contextualization, in a legal and economical context, in order to ensure the scientific objectivity and efficiency that must guide the process of collecting, analyzing, interpreting, and reporting forensic evidence. At the same time, it is recognized that forensic case data is still poorly integrated into the investigation and the crime analysis process, despite evidence of its great potential in various situations and studies. A change of attitude is needed in order to accept an extended role for forensic science that goes beyond the production of evidence for the court. To stimulate and guide this development, a long-term intensive modeling activity of the investigative and crime analysis process that crosses the boundaries of different disciplines has been initiated. A framework that fully integrates forensic case data shows through examples the capital accumulated that may be put to use systematically."

WHAT IS FORENSIC SCIENCE, ANYWAY?

For being so ubiquitous, forensic science is frequently the subject of varied misconceptions. The National Institute of Justice (NIJ, 1998) defines forensic science as "the application of scientific knowledge to the legal system." Thornton (1997) observes, " 'Forensic' comes to us from the Latin *forensus* meaning 'of the forum.' In ancient Rome, the forum was where governmental debates were held, but it was also where trials were held. It was the courthouse. So, forensic science has come to mean the application of the natural and physical sciences to the resolution of conflicts within a legal setting."

The American Academy of Forensic Sciences observes, "The single feature that distinguishes forensic scientists from any other scientist is the certain expectation that they will appear in court and testify to their findings and offer an opinion as to the significance of those findings. The forensic scientist will testify not only to what things are, but to what things mean. Forensic science is science exercised on behalf of the law in the just resolution of conflict."

James and Nordby (2003) state, "The forensic sciences uniquely share their applications to legal issues for resolution in a public forum. Without courts of law, there could be no forensic sciences; without the *Polis*, there could be no law. Forensic sciences operate inextricably in the service of the public, represented through the rule of the law by the courts. Different functions, but all necessary for the common good."[2] Forensic science is a wondrous intersection where science, medicine, and the law meet, with a final disposition being the adjudication of criminal cases. Saferstein (2001) states, "Forensic science in its broadest definition is the application of science to law. As our society has grown more complex, it has become more dependent on rules of law to regulate the activities of its members. Forensic science applies the knowledge and technology of science for the definition and enforcement of such laws."

Forensic science is most often identified with the discipline known as criminalistics. According to the NIJ, criminalistics is "the science and profession dealing with the recognition, collection, identification, individualization, and interpretation of physical evidence, and the application of the natural sciences to law-science matters." The term originated from the 1898 book, *Handbuch fur Untersuchungsrichter als System der Kriminalististik*, by Hans Gross, an investigating magistrate and professor of criminology at the University of Prague. He described the need for a scientifically trained investigator who could undertake certain technical aspects of an investigation and could also serve as liaison between the scientific specialists who were consulted on a case. The concept was popular in Europe, where a number of forensic science institutes were developed to apply the tools and techniques of the natural sciences to the investigation of inquiries. Criminalistics encompasses a number of scientific specialties: forensic biology (in DNA analysis); forensic chemistry; forensic toxicology; forensic microscopy; analysis of controlled substances, fire debris, explosive residues, hairs, fibers, glass, soil, paint, and other materials, and fingerprints and other impressions (such as footwear, tire tracks, and tool marks); forensic document examination; and crime scene reconstruction. But there is much more to forensic science; one should not forget the role played by forensic pathology and medico-legal death investigation, as well as the subspecialties of forensic odontology, forensic anthropology, forensic toxicology, and forensic psychology.

Forensic science is multidisciplinary, encompassing a wide spectrum of subspecialties that are steeped in the traditional sciences, yet it is criticized for being a renegade field that is more fringe than fundamental in terms of practices reflecting validated methods and original research that yields empirical data.

NATURAL SCIENCE VS. APPLIED SCIENCE

Members of the forensic science community say that science and forensic science are recipro-cal, an inherent relationship denied by many critics who charge that forensic science somehow denigrates the traditional sciences. The fact that forensic science *is* a multidisciplinary entity—from questionable origins, the critics assert—is precisely what creates so much angst among the scientific, legal, and humanities communities when debating its role and purpose. Because it is born of these three disciplines, forensic science inherits characteristics that serve it well but also create opportunities for purists to question its heritage and its lineage.

Forensic science is grounded in the traditional sciences of biology, chemistry, physics, and, more recently, genetics because DNA typing is rooted in genetics. These sciences are fixed, resolute, tried and true, trusted, respected; however, forensic science is still viewed as the interloper, depending on social constructs instead of universal truths (as we will see in an upcoming section addressing the science wars).

Some commentators battle over the status of whether forensic science is a pure, more tra-ditional science or an applied, inherently less prestigious science. Inman and Rudin (2001) state, "The realm of science can be divided into pure science, or research, and applied science. Basic research seeks to understand the physical world for its own sake; in applied science we seek to use the physical principles discovered to obtain a desired goal. Like medicine or engineering, the forensic analysis of physical evidence is an applied science, resting firmly on a foundation of the basic scientific principles of physics, chemistry, and biology."[1]

Perhaps the problem is that forensic science has always been equal parts art and science. Inman and Rudin (2001) remark, "Scientific breakthroughs stand on the bedrock of many small, insignificant advances; but the final solution is often rooted in an intuition that is not fully understandable based simply on previous data. We do not mean to imply that a forensic analysis is an act of genius, only that the boundaries between art and science are perhaps less distinct than is commonly understood. The nature of forensic science lends itself to an artistic and intuitive approach. Facts are often in short supply, analytical results are rarely textbook, and human nature prompts us to fill in the gaps. The very recognition of this proclivity, however, and the institution of rigorous review procedures, serves as an effective counter to our natural tendencies."[1]

Regarding the subjectivity of an applied science, Inman and Rudin (2001) note, "At the same time that we strive to maintain scientific objectivity, however, we must realize that the comparison between evidence and reference, regardless of whether the items of interest are two fingerprints or two spectra, is not free of human subjectivity. Nor should it be. . . . The question before the forensic scientist is not, as the uninitiated might assume, are these two items the same, but rather, can we exclude the possibility that they originate from the same source? Even the most sophisticated instrumentation cannot overcome imperfections in the samples themselves; analysts must rely on their education, training, and experience to deter-mine whether small differences observed between evidence and reference samples qualify as significant or explainable."[1] They add that even though there is a set of ground rules, or protocol, "No matter how clear and well reasoned the guidelines, and no matter how conscientiously applied, two competent scientists may still ultimately disagree about the interpretation of a result. This is simply the nature of science. One could program a computer with all the interpretation guidelines in the world, but a human being still must designate and input the guidelines."[1]

As an applied science, forensic science must be prepared for challenges under the ever-evolving standard of admissibility of evidence, as well as closer scrutiny of all forensic disciplines. Inman and Rudin (2001) ponder, "Some criminalists debate whether any useful purpose would be served by demanding a more scientific treatment of disciplines that have traditionally relied on the experience and expertise of each examiner."[1] Thornton (1997) notes, "To master statistical models to explain much of our evidence may be a slow, reluctant march through enemy territory, but we must begin to plan for that campaign." To which Inman and Rudin (2001) add, "We agree that, at least for physical evidence, providing a statistical justification for the analyst's opinion should be a goal. . . . The discussion within the forensic community remains heated and current."[1]

Koppl and Kobilinsky (2005) insist that science is a social process in which the truth emerges from a rule-governed competitive process (Merton, 1957; Polanyi, 1962; Koppl and Butos, 2003; McQuade and Butos, 2003): "It is a competitive process in which knowledge is public, the idiosyncrasies of individual researchers are checked by the results of other workers, and results are subject to criticism, review, and reproduction. As it is practiced today, forensic science departs needlessly from this model. Forensic analysis often depends too much on the personal qualities of each individual forensic scientist. Idiosyncrasies of individual forensic scientists may determine the final result, and there is limited criticism, review, and reproduction. A competitive process of self-regulation is constantly at work eliminating errors in pure science. No such process is at work in forensic science. Pure science is self-regulating, forensic science is not."

Koppl and Kobilinsky (2005) go on to say that the differences between "pure" science and forensic science can be most readily demonstrated within the context of an institutional structure: "Forensic science is sometimes unreliable because the larger environment of knowledge seeking is not appropriately structured. Most forensic scientists are skillful and diligent practitioners of their trade. They find themselves in an environment, however, that does not encourage the sort of institutional self-criticism characterizing pure science. They are in an environment that can induce unconscious bias and even give the unscrupulous an incentive to lie. If competitive self-regulation has value, it is because it provides a better institutional structure for truth seeking and knowledge production." We explore the concept of competitive self-regulation as a plank of the current reform initiatives addressed in Chapter 15.

Inman and Rudin (2001) observe, "It appears that the science part of forensic science is what instigates so much consternation. Why should this be? Perhaps a partial answer may be found in modern society's perception of science. Science is believed by the average person to offer hard facts, definite conclusions, and uncompromised objectivity. Therefore, any discipline called a science gains a certain legitimacy and credibility in society's (the judge's? the jury's?) view. . . . Science is an oft-misused term, frequently employed to lend credibility to an idea or statement as if the aura of science automatically confers trustworthiness. Just as often, it is used to discredit a concept, as if ideas outside the realm of science have no merit. The reality lies in understanding that science is a process not a truth."[1]

Inman and Rudin (2001) observe further that forensic science is damaged by the presumption that science embraces immutable truths: "In fact, nothing could be further from reality.

At any point in time, science provides us with our best estimate of how the universe works. But soon enough, an idea or discovery comes along either to refine or refute what we once 'knew to be true.' This is simply the nature of scientific discovery; our understanding changes with new information. This revelation can be somewhat disconcerting to the layperson who perceives that science can provide hard and fast, black and white, irrefutable answers to questions about the physical realm. All science can provide is the best answer based on all the information available at that point in time."[1]

WITHSTANDING THE TEST OF TIME

Whether or not it is an applied or a natural science, or whether it teeters on the brink of pseudo-science in the minds of critics, commentators have groused that forensic science has not withstood the test of time. To many members of the forensic science community, such statements come off as naïve. Modern laboratory-driven forensic science owes a significant debt of gratitude to the traditional sciences but also to forensic medicine and pathology. Spitz (2006) says that the earliest association between law and medicine dates back to the Egyptian culture around 3000 B.C., while more obvious medico-legal associations can be found in codes of law ranging from 1700 to 1400 B.C. Ancient Greece had the work of Hippocrates, who studied medical and ethical issues and presented these opinions in court, while the ancient Roman civilizations employed *amicus curiae* (friend of the court) to provide expert testimony. Spitz (2006) points to Roman physician Antistius who in 44 B.C. "was asked to examine the slain body of Julius Caesar and render an opinion as to how he died. Antistius concluded that of the 23 wounds on Caesar's body, the only fatal wound was one in his chest." Spitz (2006) observes, "Developments involving medico-legal investigations continued throughout the middle ages with greater reliance on medical testimony in cases of physical injury, infanticide, rape, and bestiality." Medico-legal autopsies were performed as early as 1300 on victims of homicides and suicides and those individuals executed for their crimes. Spitz (2006) reports, "One of the first documents pertaining to post-mortem examinations was a Chinese handbook published in 150 titled *His Yuan Lu*. It contained simple autopsy techniques, proposed general post-mortem guidelines, and discussed injuries caused by blunt and sharp instruments. It also offered comments on the determination of whether an individual in water had drowned or died prior to submersion and whether a burned victim was alive or dead at the onset of the fire."

Early statutes that boosted the value of legal medicine began to appear with increasing speed in the 16th century, as did more scholarly writings that further developed the concept of forensic science. Paulo Zacchias (1584–1659) came to be called the father of legal medicine for his comprehensive work on the characteristics of wounds and questionable deaths. By the mid-17th century, formal lectures in forensic medicine were being held in Western Europe; Spitz (2006) explains: "During this period, Germany had the most advanced court system in Europe and it was routine for physicians to render opinions in criminal proceedings regarding injuries and cause of death. Judicial authorities all over Europe were now using forensically knowledgeable physicians in criminal and civil trials. At this time, physicians had a limited role in regard to crime scene investigation which was typically carried out by the police; however, in complicated cases police investigators occasionally consulted a physician to discuss crime scene evidence."

As we will explore more fully in subsequent chapters, the concept of medico-legal institutes through which medico-legal principles could be practiced began to spread throughout much of Europe in the 18th and 19th centuries. Spitz (2006) observes, "Continued research in forensic medicine and toxicology laid the foundation for the future of forensic pathology in Europe and the United States." The rise of the ancient coroner system in England in the 12th century set the stage for the modern coroner and medical examiner office, and further set the wheels in motion for a more sophisticated approach to medico-legal death investigation and the practice of forensic science and criminalistics. In 1898, one of the first treatises describing the application of science to criminal investigation, penned by Austrian prosecutor and judge Hans Gross (1847–1915), explained how the fields of physics, chemistry, microscopy, anthropometry, and fingerprinting could assist in criminal investigations. Perhaps the individual most known for advancing thought in criminalistics was Edmond Locard (1877–1966), who established the principle that every contact leaves a trace, meaning that trace evidence is deposited by the perpetrator at the crime scene, and conversely, the perpetrator takes with him minute elements of the crime scene. It was Locard who also established the Institute of Criminalistics at the University of Lyons, one of the preeminent aforementioned medico-legal institutes in Europe at the time.

Saferstein (2001) observes, "Forensic science owes its origins first to those individuals who developed the principles and techniques needed to identify or compare physical evidence, and second to those who recognized the necessity of merging these principles into a coherent discipline that could be practically applied to a criminal justice system." A number of individuals made significant contributions to the body of knowledge that was shaping up to be the field of forensic science. Mathieu Orfila (1787–1853) published one of the first treatises on the detection of poisons, and many consider him to be the one who established forensic toxicology as a scientific endeavor, according to Saferstein (2001). Alphonse Bertillon (1853–1914) created the study of anthropometry, a system of taking body measurements to distinguish one individual from another. Saferstein (2001) notes, "For nearly two decades, this system was considered the most accurate method of personal identification. Although anthropometry was eventually replaced by fingerprinting in the early 1900s, Bertillon's early efforts have earned him the distinction of being known as the father of criminal identification." Francis Galton (1822–1911) was the first to undertake a comprehensive study of fingerprints and established an early classification of prints to be used as proof of personal identification. From a forensic serology point of view, a milestone was reached in 1901 when Karl Landsteiner discovered that human blood can be typed; however, in 1915, Leone Lattes (1887–1954) created a procedure for determining the classification of blood from a dried bloodstain, with important implications for the field of criminalistics.

Readers who are interested in a more comprehensive timeline of forensic science history may wish to access http://www.forensicdna.com/Timeline020702.pdf

THE SCIENCE WARS

With the history of forensic science more clearly established, the argument against forensic science frequently turns to the concept of theory change. Since the earliest days of Aristotle, Galen, and Ptolemy, science has always been marked by upheaval as it evolves and transforms itself through discovery. The beginning of the most intense period of scientific revolution is assigned to the year 1543, when *De Revolutionibus*, penned by the astronomer Nicolas Copernicus, was first printed; the treatise asserted that the earth rotated around the sun. This period was further advanced while scientists like Galileo pioneered the use of experiment to validate physical theories, a key idea in scientific method. The period culminated with the publication of the *Philosophiae Naturalis Principia Mathematica* in 1687 by Isaac Newton. Scientific discovery kept pace with development in philosophy, and these new ways of thinking about the natural sciences (and placing emphasis on experimentation and empirical reasoning) were the earliest tenets of the scientific method. Many historians say that the Scientific Revolution established science as the preeminent source for the growth of pure knowledge; several centuries later, during the 19th century, the practice of science became professionalized and institutionalized in ways that would continue through the 20th century, as the role of scientific knowledge grew and became incorporated into social constructs such as the law. Quantum physics and quantum mechanics fostered new avenues of discovery, as did biochemistry, which further integrated these important natural sciences and laid the foundation for stunning new discoveries in science and medicine, including genetics. In the late 20th century, the possibilities of genetic engineering became practical for the first time, and a massive international effort began in 1990 to map out an entire human genome. Advances in DNA typing, of course, are the building blocks for modern forensic science. The evolution of the natural sciences has been aided in the 20th century by developments in emerging disciplines such as telecommunications, computer science, discrete mathematics, electrical engineering, artificial intelligence, and materials science and by advancements in technology and equipment.

The philosophy of science triggers controversy and debate when the issue of theory change is discussed. The three critical thinkers in this arena were Karl Popper, who argued that scientific knowledge is progressive and cumulative; Thomas Kuhn, who argued that scientific knowledge transitions through "paradigm shifts" and is not necessarily progressive; and Paul Feyerabend, who argued that scientific knowledge is not cumulative or progressive and that there can be no demarcation between science and any other form of investigation. Until the mid-20th century, the pervading philosophy of science had concentrated on the viability of scientific method and knowledge, proposing justifications for the truth of scientific theories and observations and attempting to discover on a philosophical level why science worked. During this time there were some philosophers and scientists who believed that logical models of pure science did not apply to actual scientific practice. Since the publication of Kuhn's 1962 work, *The Structure of Scientific Revolutions,* there has been much debate in the academic and scientific communities on the meaning and objectivity of science. Frequently, a conflict relating to the truth of science has split commentators into two camps along the lines of those in the scientific community and those in the social sciences and humanities, triggering the "science wars."

The science wars consisted of a series of intellectual battles in the 1990s between postmodernists and realists regarding the nature of scientific theories. In general, postmodernists questioned the objectivity of science and have critiqued a vast amount of the current body of scientific knowledge and methodology. Realists asserted that objective scientific knowledge exists, and that postmodernists did not fully understand the science they were criticizing. This attack by the social sciences and humanities communities on the validity and reliability of science in general alarmed scientists who were observing this flight from science, reasoning, and empirical evidence.

McConnell and March (2001) call for peace talks in the science wars, "the series of contentious and vitriolic disputes between some members of the scientific community and a faction within the group of humanists who study science, particularly those in science and technology studies." McConnell and March explain, "Science and technology studies was born as a field in the 1940s, with the laudable goal of enhancing public understanding of science in a society increasingly defined by rapidly evolving technology. From the outset, it paid particular attention to the process by which scientific knowledge comes into being."

Proponents of a method of studying science based on sociological methodology created what McConnell and March (2001) describe as "a major break from the tradition in science and technology studies of explaining science to the lay public in terms scientists would approve." This led sociologists, philosophers, and historians of science to treat the process of science as well as the knowledge content of science as "social constructs."

As the science wars persist within the scientific communities, some experts believe that the current atmosphere of antagonism is harmful to science, and potentially catastrophic for science and technology studies. Others insist that the science wars are being waged by a small (albeit vocal) minority in science and technology studies against a similarly small (equally vocal) minority within the scientific community. Then there are those whose belief in science as a social institution ultimately dictates that its findings inevitably qualify as social constructs. Some wonder if the science wars simply equate to a breakdown in communication between the two communities. Still others assert that we must not succumb to the view that science is "the product of the rational and selfless efforts of dispassionate humans," McConnell and March state, adding that "Everyone who has participated in research knows that it is an untidy process, guided as much by intuition as by logic, the work of reasonably intelligent beings with all the incumbent faults and frailties. Its objectivity is far from perfect, residing not in the individuals who practice it but in the scientific community, and especially in its systems of communication," referred to by some researchers as "collective skepticism."

McConnell and March (2001) point to the gradual emergence of what some believe to be "post-academic science" or "the convergence of academic and industrial modes of research." They explain further: "University research is increasingly supported by industrial sponsors and mission-oriented government agencies that exercise control of the research agenda and restrict the dissemination of findings that is so essential to the process of science. This potential bias is likely to further erode public confidence in science. . . . Scientists must find new modalities to maintain their collective integrity. Scientists, sociologists, philosophers, and historians alike would be better served paying attention to the issues surrounding post-academic science than continuing the petty battles of the science wars."

While the overall nature of science, as context for the forensic sciences, is explored more fully in Chapter 10, we now turn to the many ways in which forensic science is both celebrated and vilified.

HOW FORENSIC SCIENCE IS CELEBRATED AND VILIFIED

Forensic science is the mechanism by which some amount of certainty in the guilt or innocence of an individual accused of a crime is determined and the case adjudicated. However, some may ask, has the pace of the advancement in theory and practice of forensic science outpaced our human understanding of its limitations and parameters?

Kelly and Wearne (1998) observe, "In the past 25 years forensic science has been transformed, growing up so fast that even the most sophisticated researchers cannot keep up."

One of the ways in which forensic science is vilified is that it is considered to be only as good as its practitioners, the quality of the evidence being analyzed, and the soundness of the greater context of the criminal justice system in which forensic science is used. Forensic science is subjected to the axiom of "garbage in, garbage out," and the critics are justified in their insistence that any systemic issues related to quality be ferreted out and addressed. Forensic science is also subjected to political agendas when it becomes a pawn at the hands of law enforcement, attorneys, judges, and jurors looking to extract from it a specific outcome contrary to the best interests of justice. And it is vilified for a number of high-profile cases in which presumed error, fraud, bias, or malfeasance on the part of practitioners became central to the defense's argument that the science was not sound. For example, a New York man was sentenced to 50 years to life for a double murder, having been convicted largely on a fingerprint lifted by a New York State Police investigator who testified he found it on a Formica counter at the murder scene. This trooper, one of three troopers found guilty of criminal misconduct in what later became a New York State Police fingerprint scandal, later conceded no fingerprints were found at the scene. He said he obtained the print from a cabinet frame the suspect leaned against when he was booked. Or consider the case in which a man was convicted of abducting and raping a woman at gunpoint in Virginia. She identified him from a photo lineup. A police forensic expert found sperm in the seminal fluid collected at the scene, but the suspect had undergone a vasectomy years earlier and did not produce sperm.

While very few members of the forensic community find these examples of unethical behavior to be defensible, most of them believe that the way these cases have come to represent the field in totality is unwarranted, unfair, and disingenuous. Much of the criticism of forensic science is carried out in an exceedingly public forum, facilitated by the mass media as well as through various journals that promulgate a particular point of view. Forensic science is ubiquitous, it is life altering, it is sexy, it is woven into the very fabric of the criminal justice system, and so any criticism automatically places the field in the cultural crosshairs. Forensic science makes for good press, so why *wouldn't* it be used to sell newspapers, drive Internet traffic, win Nielsen's ratings, and sway public opinion? Because forensic science is such a willing subject, it is used for purposes detrimental to its livelihood but advantageous for those who stand to profit from its downfall or, at the very least, its injury. And because forensic practitioners are dutiful and dogged, they—and not the evidence—become subjects of target practice for the media, for social scientists, for legal scholars, for anyone whose career can be vaulted by the vilification of forensic science.

In 2001 testimony before Congress, Senator Orrin G. Hatch, committee chairman of the Senate Judiciary Committee, had kind words for the forensic science community: "As any reader of a Patricia Cornwell novel or any viewer of the television program 'CSI: Crime Scene Investigation' knows, the work performed by our nation's forensic scientists is truly fascinating. These are the people who, by analyzing fingerprints, DNA samples, fibers, hair, ballistics, and other crime scene evidence, help solve some of our most difficult crimes. The work performed by these scientists carries with it an awesome responsibility. Because of their expertise, the testimony of forensic scientists often carries great weight with the jury in a criminal trial. In that regard, we are all troubled by allegations that mistakes by a police chemist in Oklahoma helped send innocent people to prison. This isolated situation should not be used unfairly to indict the thousands of forensic scientists who perform their work professionally and responsibly. It should, however, remind us that those who work in our criminal justice system have an obligation to be diligent, honest, and fair-minded. And we, as public policy leaders, have the obligation to ensure that our forensic scientists have the resources necessary to carry out their critical work."

As we will see in various chapters, a deficiency in resources, funding, and infrastructure as referred to by Hatch has plagued the forensic laboratory and medico-legal communities, but many of the criticisms of forensic science ignore the physical deficiencies of forensic science and instead zero in on more philosophical issues.

One of the strongest criticisms levied against forensic science is that it is not a science in its purest form. As we have seen, many regard forensic science to be an applied science at best, but not in the same league as the natural sciences; critics charge that certain forensic disciplines are lacking in scientific rigor and empirical data. The forensic science community counters with the argument that forensic science is not a pristine discipline, and is required to engage in the kind of scientific inquiry that cannot be modeled after the traditional natural sciences. James and Nordby (2003) observe, "Currently, legal challenges to many established forensic science techniques, such as fingerprint and hair comparison, are being made. The law is questioning whether such evidence is truly scientific. The natural sciences from this adversarial position remain theoretical, while the forensic sciences remain pejoratively practical. The forensic scientist must work to counteract this misguided view without appearing defensive."[2] For example, James and Nordby point out, while the natural sciences are said to be, among other things, theoretical, orderly, controlled, pristine, certain, and consist of pure knowledge, the forensic sciences are said to be practical and applied, disorderly, contaminated, chaotic, uncertain, and comprised of conjectures on the part of its practitioners.

James and Nordby (2003) add, "Unlike the carefully controlled experiment set up in a laboratory, consider the slightly smudged half fingerprint on a glass. If forensic science is conjectural, operating in chaotic situations where data are likely to become contaminated, can we trust the fingerprint as evidence? The so-called covering law model of natural science accounts for expectations of scientific certainty which no forensic science allegedly approximates: epistemically certain laws of nature cover and, thereby, through deduction, explain cases."[2]

These deductions, such as Newton's law for shearing force, James and Nordby (2003) say, "assume that a single cause explains a single specific given effect. Laboratory conditions or observational situations artificially manipulate phenomena to fall within the parameters of the law under investigation. Hence they are *ceteris paribus* laws, that is, they hold only with 'other things being equal' such as with situations in an artificially controlled laboratory environment. In contrast, the crime scene is anything but a controlled setting."[2] James and Nordby continue, "Of course, almost all cases requiring explanation in the forensic setting involve many combinations of so-called causes all mixed together in the world existing outside of the laboratory. . . . The search for some single covering law becomes sheer myth. Until we discover some such law, it is up to science to supply acceptable explanations in the absence of any so-called certain knowledge. In practice, the forensic sciences have an important element in common with the natural sciences. While their scientific goals obviously differ, their scientific common ground rests within an identical method of inquiry."[2]

James and Nordby (2003) assert, "The aims of the so-called scientific method remain solidly within a procedural scope, focusing on scientific reliability. Follow these steps and the results will be consistent. With this methodological focus, illusive certainty becomes attainable reliability; natural laws and causes disappear in favor of explanatory connections, and the quest for comprehensive theory is replaced by relevant experience."[2]

James and Nordby (2003) say that there is no generalized abstraction available to describe the scientific method, and that at best, certain features of reliable methods can be enumerated, such as the fact that reliable scientific methods help distinguish evidence from coincidence without ambiguity, disallow hypotheses more extraordinary than the facts themselves, pursue testing by breaking hypotheses into their smallest logical components, risking one part at a time; and allow tests to prove or to disprove alternative explanations. "The aims of forensic science and medicine rest with developing justified explanations. . . . Some involve entirely appropriate statistical assessments and degrees of error suitably dependent on accurate mathematical models and accurate population studies. . . . However, not all forensic scientific explanations involve such statistical issues. Instead, individual, non-repeatable events with no statistical characteristics may demand scientific explanation."[2]

Nordby (2003) states, "Scientifically reliable methods help forensic scientists develop reasoned opinions, views that may not be proved conclusively true, but views toward which the explanatory patterns emerging from the evidence, together with the evidence itself, most unambiguously point. Reasoned opinions developed from scientifically acceptable methods avoid subjective, unsupported, and untested hunches and guesses. While the observation may be correct, its truth is merely coincidental. Since truth often hides among the debris of coincidence, a method, one that reveals the truth more often than not, earns the mantle of reliability."[2]

As we will see in subsequent chapters, critics assert that forensic science is not resolute, is not based on empirical reasoning and evidence, and that statements of certainty relating to analyses and hypotheses are unfounded and should not be made by forensic scientists in a court of law. Starrs (2003) states, "Forensic science, being a branch of scientific inquiry, must often reconcile itself to affirmations that sometimes are only a hen's kick away from categorically positive positions, but are, nonetheless, marked by uncertainty to a greater or lesser degree. But that is the lot of any pursuit of knowledge when verging on the ultimate." Starrs says that the "legions of uncertainties in the forensic sciences" manifest themselves constantly, but adds, "That is not said in criticism of the forensic sciences, but in recognition that forensic science is bottomed on a combination of rest and motion. The many accomplishments of the forensic sciences can give it just cause for encomiums, but, being scientific in nature, it cannot rest on its laurels. It must ever be in motion seeking new pathways to the scientific truths that will emerge only from innovative scientific inquiries into those uncertainties that demand attention."

Regarding these uncertainties, Starrs (2003) asserts that "guesstimates" abound in forensic science. For example, time-dating, which he calls a "perturbing complexity," is a challenge in the forensic discipline of fingerprinting and ballistics. (Was the print left at the time the crime was committed? Was the gun fired at the time of the crime?) Starrs also points to forensic pathologists who are "constantly besieged to provide more exact statements on the time of a person's death" or asked to determine the precise sequence of the creation of stab wounds or bullet holes. (Can the wounds be sequenced so that the first wound can be differentiated from the last wound? Can the bullets be chronologically timed in order, with respect to the other wounds?) Starrs notes, "The interest of the public, fed by the media, in forensic science and concomitantly, the belief that forensic science has all the answers, has risen in a geometric progression, but forensic science moves more lumberingly in its research and development according to an arithmetic formulation. Soon, if we are not exceedingly careful to rein in the public portrayals of the forensic sciences to a more realistic scientific level, the forensic sciences will be found to be wanting in credibility by juries failing to measure up to public image. Worse yet, forensic scientists, to keep pace with this public misperception of forensic science, will render opinions as experts in the courts by expressing more scientific assurance that they should or can."

James and Nordby (2003) emphasize, "How one's opinion is constructed determines its certainty. The certainty of forensic explanations is measured by assessing their explanatory justifications. This, in turn, involves showing first that the explanation is justified, and second, that the explanation is better justified than any available alternative explanation. In this forensic setting, certainty assessments address the scientific explanation's rational justification, leaving the question of the explanation's truth and role in legal deliberations of the court. This allows for a clearer understanding of requests for certainty assessments when scientists are asked by attorneys to attach some degree of certainty to their work product."[2]

Nordby (2003) recognizes the challenges inherent in the criminal justice system when cases come down to mere semantics: "Scientific opinions involve interpretations of and inferences from data which can be subject to challenge on scientific grounds. The argument must be developed in the spirit of rational disagreement in either science or the law." Nordby sees scientific disagreements as scientific process, but these arguments and opinions must have purpose: "Forensic scientists have a scientific obligation to present their reasoning as clearly as possible, showing how their conclusions follow from the scientific work applied to a given case." Nordby adds, "Good science, and good forensic science, produces reasoned opinions." Nordby also states that when the court asks for a statement of certainty, "it must remain solidly within the methodological realm of forensic science." Nordby adds, ". . . Scientists shouldn't navigate scientific waters with an eye fixed solely on conclusions. Instead we must navigate with a critical eye focused firmly on the methods dictated by logic."

James and Nordby (2003) say that opinions should be held with what scientist Charles Sanders Peirce called "contrite fallibilism." James and Nordby explain, "By this is meant an awareness of how much we do not know, and the humility to acknowledge the possibility of making mistakes. . . . Forensic scientists must develop an intellect not too sure of what must remain uncertain, not too uncertain about what must remain sure. In the spirit of intellectual honesty and judicial prudence, the best advice for the forensic scientist to carry from the scene to the lab and into court throughout a long career comes from a 20th century Viennese philosopher, Ludwig Wittgenstein: 'Whereof one cannot speak, thereof one must remain silent.'"[2]

Forensic scientists are expected to demonstrate logical acumen in applying the scientific method and they are expected to explain their application of science to the problem at hand clearly, accurately, and responsibly. In essence, Nordby (2003) admonishes the forensic scientist to own his or her conclusions: "Once you, as a forensic scientist, write something in a report, or say something under oath, you own that forever, good, bad, or indifferent." With this comes two scenarios; Nordby explains that forensic scientists' statements may either appear to be "overly definitive or precise" or appear "overly inconclusive or imprecise." Nordby adds, "When a degree of precision expressed by a conclusion fails to mirror the available precision among the data, red flags ought to fly." Going back to the issue of semantics within the context of expressions of certainty, forensic scientists face danger in using pejorative language when using words such as *likely* or *indicates*—the implication is that there is some degree of probability or even certainty to these claims. Nordby admonishes, "When couching claims with these words, the forensic scientist must be prepared to supply a foundation for the probabilistic nature of the attendant opinion." The absence of this foundation will, of course, open the scientist up to attack by the defense and cause counsel to probe for underlying scientific weaknesses, whether real or imagined.

"My fear is that in the courtroom, some of those who testify may have a mentality of, 'You are either with us or you are against us,' and that colors how the person delivers his or her testimony," says Carol Henderson, J.D., director of the National Clearinghouse for Science, Technology, and the Law at Stetson University, and a visiting professor at George Washington University. "If you are a forensic scientist, you cannot be an advocate for one side or the other; you are there because you have examined the evidence and you are going to testify to exactly what the evidence tells you, no more and no less."

Kiely (2003) states that proving facts in litigation increasingly focuses on inferences flowing from the application of one or more natural sciences. Kiely remarks, "The important aspect of this increasing dependence on the scientific method as a basis for determining dispositive facts is the fact generated, not the method used to generate it. The existence or nonexistence of a matter of fact depends largely on the theory of fact-finding used by the fact seekers. The antagonism between forensic scientists and the courts can be encapsulated in two questions: How far can forensic scientists go in making definitive statements about crime scenes and/or linking a suspect to them because they have a microscope? How far do we let them go because we have a constitution? The importance of these questions lies in the recognition of how far and on what empirical basis such statements can be made at all, and the impact they may have on a jury in causing such match testimony, albeit given in a qualified manner, to be taken as true by a jury. The concern has always been that a scientist's testimony that a hair or fiber obtained from a suspect was consistent in all respects or not dissimilar will be internalized by jurors as statement of a definitive match. It is important to realize that . . . the opinions of most forensic experts are routinely couched in such qualified terms."

The presentation of expert testimony is one of the primary ways in which forensic science and the law clash and create difficulties for jurors who must decipher intimidating, complex technical data proffered by seemingly bulletproof scientific titans. Scientists and attorneys do not speak the same language and uphold polar-opposite approaches to reasoning, and therein is the challenge of the reconciliation of divergent techniques to search for the truth. Starrs (2003) notes, "Even though forensic scientists may be respectful of the limits of their own scientific inquiries, they may nevertheless chomp at the legal bit which curbs them in the legal forum. The law proceeds at a pace moved by restraint and conservatism. Indeed the law's detractors in the scientific community often perceive the snail's pace of the law's acceptance of science to be a bone of much contention. Science, on its part, can and does make gigantic strides with new insights and almost magisterial new-found instrumentation." Starrs continues, "The law's methodical pace, therefore, is seen as pitted against the rapidity of scientific advances, while forensic scientists are seemingly left to grouse and muddle through their discomfiture with the legal rules that bind them. . . . The last thing forensic scientists should extol is the lifting of the barriers to the admission of what Peter Huber has aptly and tellingly termed 'junk science.' . . . A syncretic frame of mind is necessary to reconcile the divergent views of science and the law so that forensic scientists can function advantageously and harmoniously with two masters, one in science, and the other in law." James and Nordby (2003) state, "Lawyers and forensic scientists enjoy a close, yet often uneasy relationship. Forensic scientists must not forget that lawyers have moral and legal obligations that often generate conflict and misunderstanding among those with scientific minds."

James and Nordby (2003) observe, "Without the underpinnings of high ethical standards, forensic scientists may become what is known in the profession as hired guns. The student considering this profession should resist the temptation of selling whatever opinion is needed by defense or prosecution. Not all hired guns become forensic frauds merely through nonexistent or meaningless credentials. Properly educated, experienced scientists may also act as gunslingers through ignorance or misapplication of method. This might involve purposely omitting relevant tests or suppressing relevant results. Many such experts may develop an entirely unjustified sense of their own scientific abilities and observational powers. Generally, such experts offer firm, certain, and conclusive opinions designed to fit the relevant courtroom advocate's agenda. Such a forensic expert may even resort to defining scientific error as any interpretation that disagrees with his or her own."[2]

James and Nordby (2003) add that celebrity is not part of the equation: "In the real forensic sciences, individual scientists always work as members of a larger team, perhaps with other specialized scientists, law enforcement investigators, prosecutors, defense attorneys, judges, juries, and the media, each contributing his or her efforts toward the bigger picture of a public trial, or an investigation capturing the public interest. The job of a forensic scientist is not one of glamorous celebrity."[2]

But the cult of celebrity is difficult to avoid. Whether it is the expert witness who is larger than life in the minds of jurors, or the glamorization of forensic science as the Hollywood starlet in its own right, the perception of the public is becoming increasingly significant to the legal and forensic science communities. Forensic science is vilified through the so-called "*CSI* effect," a modern-day crucible in which the very tenets of forensic disciplines and the criminal justice system are reworked like alchemy of old. James and Nordby (2003) state, "Forensic scientists must be prepared to battle dubious cultural expectations, either inappropriately elevating or denigrating the powers of science. Such expectations are usually generated through crime novels, popular theatre, movies, and television. These inappropriate expectations, when found among jurors, lawyers, and even judges, can negate conservative scientific testimony."[2]

Forensic science is frequently vilified for the connection between the proximity to law enforcement and the margin for error related to potential for conflict of interest and examiner bias. The very nature of forensic science is rooted in law enforcement (although it is with some amusement that members of the forensic science community point to their fictional hero Sherlock Holmes' distaste for and distrust of the meddlesome police in the classic tales from the brilliant mind of Sir Arthur Conan Doyle). As Saferstein (2001) notes, "Forensic science is the application of science to those criminal and civil laws that are enforced by police agencies in a criminal justice system." As we will see in subsequent chapters, critics have gotten much mileage out of the debate over undue influence by law enforcement.

James and Nordby (2003) observe, "The philosophical foundation of the criminal justice system remains to protect the innocent and to ensure that the truth emerges for any matter before the court, thereby ensuring that justice is done. Given the number of cases to be heard, however, the criminal justice system has the potential to sacrifice values of truth and justice to organizational efficiency. While crime laboratory scientists may pride themselves as being independent finders of fact, most operate under police jurisdiction or administration, and many scientists, perhaps unconsciously, develop the attitude that they work exclusively for the best interest of the police or the prosecutor. When emotions overcome reason, a zealous forensic scientist may intentionally or inadvertently deny real justice. Results are misinterpreted, or worse, falsified. Such flawed science may not be easy to spot, since it can only appear through the results of the scientific investigation. While no one can attain anything close to a perfect harmony of reason with emotion, forensic scientists at least have a duty to strike the best balance possible under life's most difficult circumstances. Of course, completely satisfying this duty remains both difficult and elusive."[2]

IS FORENSIC SCIENCE BROKEN? EXPERTS HAVE THEIR SAY

One of the most vehement ways in which forensic science has been vilified of late has to do with the alleged uptick in incidences of malfeasance and fraud on the part of forensic scientists. James and Nordby (2003) state, "The commitment to ethics should be stressed in the education of a forensic scientist. The values inherent in good science . . . should be a part of official forensic science curricula."[2] Forensic science and its practitioners are being maligned without meaningful context, and so it is the hope of many that the United States stands poised to reconsider everything it knows and assumes about forensic laboratory science and medicolegal death investigation and to rededicate attention, time, money, and resources to taking an objective, rational look at what needs fixing, what is not broken, and having the wisdom to understand the difference between the two. If one were to read the newspaper headlines only, one could quite easily come away with the notion that forensic science is a "broken" discipline, marred by malfeasance, rattled by fraud, and riddled with errors. But without context or challenge by the practitioners themselves, these allegations ring hollow. Throughout this book you will be treated to the perspectives of various members of the medico-legal community, including forensic practitioners and scientists, educators, social scientists, legal scholars, and other commentators who are pushing for reform in the way the business of forensic science is conducted and how it is used in the adjudication of criminal cases.

Joseph Polski, chief operations officer for the International Association for Identification and chairman of the Consortium of Forensic Science Organizations, remarks, "There certainly are instances where mistakes have been made in forensic science, and you can't deny there are people who have done some very egregious things. However, I don't think there is a general feeling among the members of the forensic science community that we're losing the battle. I think that, to some extent, this give and take and discussion about how we can improve forensic science is healthy. In the next few years at the national level there will be some fairly high-level reviews of the field, and out of that, I think, will come the identification of areas that need more research and probably a much more solid basis for conclusions, especially in the pattern evidence arena." Having said that, however, Polski says one must consider the source of the criticism. "Much of the negative commentary on forensic science comes from the scientific research community, which sees applied science as sort of a poor stepchild. With the increasing visibility of forensic science, the field is a target for that kind of criticism. Some of the people saying that the system is broken are in a lofty position and can expound upon their views, but I am not sure that they want to participate in improving the field."

Henderson says that many critics haven't kept up with the times. "They either don't see the bigger picture or they haven't seen what strides have been made in forensic science over the years," she says. "Many positive developments, such as the accreditation of forensic laboratories, have occurred and made a difference. I don't think forensic science is broken, even though there have been a few major problems along the way. But problems were identified, and systems were reviewed to see how changes could be implemented."

Henderson says that a few high-profile white papers criticizing forensic science have inflicted some damage: "Randolph Jonakait wrote and published an article many years ago, and I actually wrote a letter to the editor in response to it. He was analyzing the situation by referring to a study conducted in 1978, and I'm thinking, 'We have to look at what has been going on since then.' Yes, a case could be made on all the things that are presumably wrong about forensic science, but on the other hand, as learned people, we can't ignore the strides that have been made in the field. The issues are that we need more funding, not just for DNA analysis, but for medical examiners' offices and other units of the crime labs, which are woefully underfunded. There must be a concerted, coordinated effort among all those involved in the forensic science and legal communities. We can't just say forensic science is broken, or say that it's impossible to fix it."

"I'm always somewhat concerned when things are not perfect, but in life nothing is perfect, so my concern is somewhat limited," says author and forensic science media consultant Lawrence Kobilinsky, Ph.D., a professor and science adviser to the president of John Jay College of Criminal Justice. "In my opinion, science has become much more important in the criminal justice system, and what has brought that about, of course, is DNA. People are much more cognizant of what science, especially DNA, can do and that has been brought about by the more than 25 forensic science programs on television right now. Problems don't happen every day, but when you hear about them, it goes against the grain of what people expect from forensic science and it gets publicized. Suddenly everyone is saying, well, now we have a science that helps us make decisions in the criminal justice arena, but if there are questions about ethics and people who are not doing their jobs and making mistakes, can we still trust this science? I hear that, and I understand that reaction, but we must look at the bigger picture and the tremendous progress we have made using forensic science correctly. We must be vigilant about problems when they do occur, but we also need to face these problems head on, address the issues in question, and figure out ways to resolve the problems so they are avoided in the future."

Many forensic service providers wish that observers would notice the many contributions forensic science and forensic pathology make to society. Michael Dobersen, M.D., Ph.D., coroner for Arapahoe County in Colorado and president of the Colorado Coroner Association, notes, "When something good happens, you don't necessarily hear about it. The regular day-to-day practice of forensic pathology and how we are tied into the criminal justice system is just as important as news about the big cases that are solved. On the other hand, perhaps our best legacy is that we are *not* making headlines all of the time. We're an integral part of the system, and the system is working, contrary to popular belief. It's only when headlines are made do people pay attention, and it's negative attention. Practitioners must hang onto the quiet determination they have toward their jobs, knowing that the behind-the-scenes efforts that we put into the system do pay off. Every day we see the good in what we do, even if it's a seemingly little thing like comforting a decedent's family member, but that's not what is promulgated to the public. They are more interested in hearing about that high-profile murder case."

Henry Lee acknowledges the existence of detractors, as well as the increased duress under which so many forensic practitioners work. "I have been in the field almost 40-some years now and forensic scientists are under the most pressure I have ever seen," Lee remarks. "In the early days, the police and the prosecutors had very few expectations of forensic laboratories and medico-legal offices. It was basic stuff, like comparing fingerprints, bullets, or tool marks, but in recent years, forensic science has seen tremendous advances in technology that has enhanced the concept of individualization. So everyone expects more of the forensic laboratories in particular. But at the same time that we face so much pressure, we have too many forensic scientists who are not as prepared or as adequately trained and educated as they should be. And yes, there are scientists like Fred Zain who did not actually do the experiments they testified to in court. But sometimes it is not the forensic scientist's fault that the lawyers misinterpret things. My concern is that there are scientists on the witness stand who do not have the guts or integrity to say, 'Wait a second, that is not what I am saying,' and instead, they let an erroneous or misleading interpretation be presented. There are unintentional errors, and then there are those errors where a scientist knows a result is a mistake and allows a misleading conclusion to be accepted as truth. That type of inexcusable mistake should not be made." Lee is quick to condemn the pseudo-scientists that give the profession a bad name. "Just like in any other field, we may have a few bad apples who are not genuine, and who provide interpretations beyond scientific principles. They are not forensic scientists, but they claim they are, and the public doesn't know the difference."

Lee also points to the so-called "*CSI* effect" as having an impact on the perceptions and expectations of forensic science: "Jurors watch *CSI* and they think every case should work like *CSI*—by the second commercial we should have all of the answers. Or they think, 'Well, just spray a chemical, shine a light source, and the forensic evidence should just pop out in plain view.' But in reality, it doesn't work that way, and when it doesn't, of course the public gets upset; they entertain the perception that the forensic scientist is incompetent or that forensic science is working the way it should. Forensic scientists should have the professional integrity to call it as it is, no more and no less. Let the evidence show us and tell us the facts."

Lee continues, "Unfortunately, forensic scientists are being squeezed by an adversarial legal system; the prosecution, of course, wants us to link the suspect while the defense lawyer wants us to exonerate the suspect. When the prosecution uses us as expert witnesses, the defense instantly says we're biased. It doesn't matter how fair we are, if you become a defense expert, the prosecution says we're prostitutes, or that we are hired guns," Lee says. "When you give your testimony, each side will accuse you, try to beat on you, and try to discredit you, and that's why I made the suggestion that forensic evidence should be the neutral, objective friend of the court. In other words, it must become a court-appointed expert witness, and not for the prosecution of the defense; it should be independent. Maybe that would relieve some of the pressure on forensic scientists."

Lee says he is bothered by critics who assert that forensic science is broken because it is not akin to the sterile confines of a clinical laboratory and thus is somehow less rigorous. "Forensic science is not a pure or pristine scientific discipline," Lee emphasizes. "We have no control over the samples that come into the forensic laboratory. It's a different ball game than clinical laboratories where you can go to the stockroom and get a fresh, clean sample of unlimited quantity to test or analyze. When we go to a crime scene, we find the victim lying in questionable surroundings, the body decomposing. There is no such thing as a clean sample at a crime scene. For example, you have the dirty, blood-stained clothes of a suspect retrieved from a garbage dump. That's all you have to work with, so it's unfair of anyone to say you did not meet scientific principles because this sample tested is contaminated; of course it is contaminated. But what can the forensic scientist do about it? Nothing. Some scientists don't understand that; they say every experiment demands controls. For example, I was working on an investigation related to a possible homicide aboard a cruise ship. I wanted to conduct an experiment by using a mannequin, and people probably criticized me, saying, why don't you use real people? Sure, how many of you want to volunteer? Let me see how many times I can push a live person off of a balcony! There is no way to replicate a sample. Critics say we lack scientific principles and controls, but they don't understand the nature of forensic science." Lee continues, "The beauty of forensic science is that it uses scientific principles as well as things like logic, intuition, and the ability to put the pieces of the puzzle together to solve the case. I have been involved in six or seven thousand major cases, and no two cases are alike. That's why when forensic science is criticized, it is by the people who really don't understand it. They think everything should be black and white, but unfortunately, in our profession, many times it is gray."

Lee says he has identified three critical areas of need in forensic science related to the underlying criticisms of the field. The first area is related to the need for greater autonomy of and involvement by forensic practitioners in their own field. Lee explains, "Currently, the utilization of forensic science and forensic evidence is not controlled by forensic scientists but by police detectives; whatever they collect from the crime scene they send to the crime lab, and the crime lab doesn't have any say in the matter of what is collected or how it is collected and preserved. Very few forensic scientists like me go to the actual crime scene to investigate—it's not like *CSI*. Most forensic scientists stay in the laboratory and accept whatever is given to them. In the adjudication process, it's the same thing; prosecutors decide which evidence to introduce in the case, and the judge decides what to accept into the courtroom, so forensic scientists really don't have any say in the entire process from crime scene to court. There should be a better team approach and more involvement from the forensic field."

The second area of improvement is funding, Lee emphasizes: "Proper funding is not just for buying a piece of equipment for the crime lab, it's also for the education and training of forensic scientists and also for the detectives because they are part of the forensic team; they must be trained on how to properly recognize, collect and preserve forensic evidence. We also need funding for the education and training of lawyers and judges, teaching them about the expectations and limitations of forensic science."

The third area of improvement, Lee says, is creating opportunities for and funding additional research in forensic science: "We need practical, applied research as well as theory. Yes, we can do a lot of statistical calculations, but what do they mean? Everyone wants a number and a bullet-proof interpretation attached to it, but sometimes we don't have that. For example, in a hit-and-run case we find a big chunk of skin from the hairline that matches biological samples from the car, and it's a match. Now, attorneys want a statistical value attached to it, and we just don't have a value. People in other professions have to understand this, but it would help to have more research in forensic science to improve our conclusions."

Richard Saferstein, Ph.D., a forensic science consultant and author, says that with a higher profile comes greater scrutiny and criticism, but that the field of forensic science is strong enough to handle it. "Given the high-profile nature of many cases, particularly with the advent of DNA, the forensic community has moved to the forefront of investigations," Saferstein says. "Years ago, forensic science was seen as simply a way to confirm police leads, and now it is generating leads and suspects, through DNA, for the police; then when the police do produce a suspect, the courts expect that the evidence we analyze would add a level of objectivity to the case that might be missing with conventional evidence. The level of service is quite high, but there are always going to be issues and mistakes that arise. While it's the function of the press to report these situations, it does not report the other 99 percent of cases that go right. People must bear in mind that there is no national crisis, and there is no evidence that the forensic science community is deficient. Problems do arise every now and again, and things fall through the cracks; do I like saying that? No. But it happens, and the question is, how can we address these problems? You can't ever avoid problems, but you can have systems in place with which to address the source of the problems."

"Errors in forensic science, as well as the criticism they trigger, undoubtedly compromise and diminish the overall effectiveness of the profession," notes forensic pathologist and law professor Cyril Wecht, M.D., J.D. "It harms the criminal justice system in many ways, but the field is also fighting unrealistic expectations. We're never going to achieve the exaggerated fictional status of television forensic shows, where crimes are solved in a matter of minutes and all the manpower and equipment in the world is available to the crime lab. However, we should have the wherewithal to address crime labs' backlogged cases and workloads. There's no good reason why thousands of rape kits are sitting on the shelves of forensic labs around the country, and not being tested. It's symbolic of what's wrong with the system. Not to politicize the issue further, but in a country as affluent as ours, billions of dollars can be spent on warfare but what about the importance of criminal justice?"

Wecht continues, "Of course, if health and education can be shortchanged, then you can bet that criminal justice also will be shortchanged, and that undermines and delays the effective delivery of justice in this country. Funding is so essential, and what the forensic science community needs is mere chicken feed compared to the defense budget; we're not talking about billions and billions of dollars to get it right. People must understand that investing in criminal justice and forensic science can save the country money. If you can quickly solve a murder case because the forensic science community has what it needs, think of what the system has saved by way of manpower hours and overtime pay, not to mention the cost of the trial that can be obviated when definitive scientific evidence shows where guilt lies. From an economic standpoint, there is no question that giving the forensic community what it needs and helping it resolve its problems, benefits everyone."

THE NEEDS OF THE FORENSIC SCIENCE COMMUNITY

The bulk of this book explores the needs of the forensic science community and makes a loose association between a lack of manpower, education and training, funding, and infrastructure, and the ways in which forensic science is coming under siege from its stakeholders. While subsequent chapters will explore these points of contention in depth, it is helpful to review the critical issues facing forensic science here.

The 2004 Consolidated Appropriations Act required the NIJ to submit to Congress a report addressing the needs of forensic service providers beyond the Advancing Justice Through DNA Technology initiative. The act directed the NIJ, in conjunction with the professional societies serving the field—the American Society of Crime Lab Directors (ASCLD), the American Academy of Forensic Sciences (AAFS), the International Association for Identification (IAI), and the National Association of Medical Examiners (NAME)—to develop a plan to address the issues deemed critical for the forensic laboratories and medical examiner community. Each organization presented its formal comments at a summit held in Washington, D.C., in May 2004 (NIJ, 2004).

The NIJ (2004) reports that forensic laboratories face several important challenges, the most notable being personnel needs, as well as education and training for new and veteran forensic scientists: "Although it is difficult to quantify these needs, every forensic discipline believes that it faces shortfalls of personnel qualified to replace retiring examiners or meet increasing case workloads. In addition, examiners should be required to meet minimum training and proficiency standards in all disciplines."

The forensic community reports that training needs are significant across all disciplines, including training of novices and continuing education for experienced professionals. In particular disciplines there are a declining number of qualified experts, according to the AAFS. The AAFS Technical Working Group on Education and Training recommended that between 1 and 3 percent of the total forensic science laboratory budget be allocated for training and continuing professional development.

Data reported by the Bureau of Justice Statistics (BJS) from its census of forensic laboratories showed that the training and continuing education budgets of the largest 50 laboratories in the United States were actually less than one-half of 1 percent of their total budgets. To close this gap, according to the forensic science organizations, the federal government should provide grants for continuing education or training academies for the forensic sciences. Some options to address the training needs of forensic examiners and managers include traditional face-to-face or hands-on training, collaborations, and alternative delivery systems such as electronic media. Regional centers would be suited for expanding the scope and delivery of training programs. Also, professional models for training and establishing competency should be encouraged. According to the NIJ (2004), the forensic science community should consider methods to encourage quality graduate education in forensic science. ASCLD suggested that a program to eliminate or forgive student loans for graduates who obtain full-time employment in public forensic science laboratories be considered.

In addition, the forensic service organizations recognize the need to improve the understanding of the scientific foundations of specific disciplines. DNA analysis has a fully characterized statistical and scientific basis, in that the uniqueness of one individual's DNA profile can be quantified and presented with great accuracy. Scientific research and the publication of best practices guides can improve the practice and acceptance of the forensic disciplines.

Although Congress did not specifically ask for input concerning research and development needs, each of the forensic science organizations outlined specific needs for improved scientific understanding and technology to serve the forensic community. In particular, forensic service providers report that basic research is needed into the scientific underpinning of impression evidence, questioned documents, and firearms/tool mark examination. The forensic science organizations believe the federal government should sponsor research to validate forensic science disciplines to address basic principles, error rates, and standards of procedure. In addition, forensic laboratories need tools to improve speed and efficiency, extend forensic analysis to more difficult samples, and support the full range of forensic techniques. Technology is needed to improve evidence collection, crime scene analysis, and field testing of drugs and other material for investigative purposes.

The NIJ (2004) states that these issues should be addressed more fully by a forensic science commission, which was authorized by the Justice for All Act. The creation of this commission was also part of the president's DNA Initiative, and the entity is charged with the responsibilities of developing recommendations for long-term strategies to maximize the use of current forensic technologies to solve crimes and protect the public, and identifying potential scientific breakthroughs that may be used to assist law enforcement.

According to the NIJ (2004), each forensic service organization supports the creation of this commission to review the needs of the forensic science community in the long term at the federal, state, and local levels. The commission is viewed by the organizations as a mechanism to identify issues and needs of particular disciplines and provide national leadership to improve the practice of forensic science. But, the future of this commission is uncertain, and a number of other initiatives are under way that may supplant the commission or support the commission should it be established. These endeavors are discussed in Chapter 16.

A manpower shortage is one of the biggest concerns of the forensic community and directly impacts the ability of forensic laboratories and medico-legal offices to address casework backlogs. According to a BJS report on the 50 largest crime labs, by the end of 2002, forensic laboratories reported a backlog of about 270,000 forensic analysis requests. (For the purpose of the census, a backlog was defined as any request that remained unanalyzed in the laboratory for more than 30 days.) The laboratories, which employed 4,300 full-time equivalent personnel, reported that they would need approximately 930 additional full-time equivalents (at an estimated cost of approximately $36 million), to achieve a 30-day turnaround for 2002 requests. All member organizations reported equipment shortages as a limiting factor in processing forensic casework. Specifically, ASCLD estimated that equipment needs for the 50 largest crime laboratories in the disciplines of controlled substances, trace evidence, firearms, questioned documents, latent prints, toxicology, and arson exceeded $18 million. ASCLD also recommended that a reliable process be established to monitor the manpower and equipment needs of the forensic community on an ongoing basis.

The forensic community reports even more acute manpower shortages for the death investigation system. NAME reports that the United States requires at least 850 board certified forensic pathologists, roughly double the current number. Many autopsies are now performed by individuals without needed training in general pathology and forensic pathology. Equipment is lacking in some basic areas of need, such as histology, microbiology, clinical lab testing, and genetic and metabolic services. The forensic science community's concerns include improving its capacity, an issue that relates to manpower and equipment. The organizations support the continuation or expansion of Coverdell Act funding to support specific needs, including fingerprint identification systems, alternate light sources, vehicles, training, accreditation and certification, and photo and digital imaging equipment.

Regarding issues relating to professionalism, each of the forensic science organizations supports the exploration of mandatory accreditation of organizations and certification of practitioners. Accreditation is a voluntary program through which a laboratory demonstrates that its management, operations, personnel, procedures, equipment, physical plant, security, and health and safety procedures meet established standards. Certification is a process of peer review through which an individual practitioner is recognized as having attained the professional qualifications needed to practice in one or more disciplines. The organizations also support funding to support quality assurance programs that can help labs attain accreditation. Maintaining and increasing professionalism within the forensic science community are critical to the delivery of quality services. Professionalism is enhanced by demonstrating compliance with quality assurance measures such as laboratory accreditation and practitioner certification. Unfortunately, many laboratories are confronted with budgets that are insufficient to meet caseload demands and at the same time support participation in accreditation and certification programs. Costs associated with accreditation and certification programs include proficiency testing and inspection fees, at a minimum. Dedicated personnel are needed to support participation in such programs, and examiners need to be given the time away from casework to participate in proficiency testing programs.

Another important issue facing the forensic science community is fostering greater collaboration among federal, state, and local forensic service providers. Federal laboratories collaborate with state and local forensic service providers in many ways. They provide leadership and resources for research, training, and technology transfer. Federal laboratories also maintain and support investigative databases for firearms, fingerprints, and DNA. The FBI has provided onsite training and online training via its Virtual Academy; however, over the years, the forensic science organizations have asserted that the FBI has decreased training available to state and local agencies. The forensic community would like the federal forensic science training programs expanded to meet current and future needs.

The bottom line is that the forensic sciences community needs additional attention and improved resources to address its deficits and advance its ability to contribute to the criminal justice process. Saferstein (2001) notes, "... Science cannot offer final and authoritative solutions to problems that stem from a maze of social and psychological factors. However ... science does occupy an important and unique role in the criminal justice system, a role that relates to the scientist's ability to supply accurate and objective information that reflects the events that have occurred at a crime ... a good deal of work remains to be done if the full potential of science as it is applied to criminal investigations can be realized."

REFERENCES

Bureau of Justice Statistics. 50 Largest Crime Labs, 2002. September 2004. Available at http://www.ojp.usdoj.gov/bjs/abstract/50lcl02.htm.

Inman K and Rudin N. *Principles and Practice of Criminalistics: The Profession of Forensic Science*. Boca Raton, Fla.: CRC Press, 2001.

James SH and Nordby JJ. *Forensic Science: An Introduction to Scientific and Investigative Techniques*. Boca Raton, Fla.: CRC Press, 2003.

Kelly JF and Wearne PK. Tainting Evidence: Inside the Scandals at the FBI Crime Lab. New York: The Free Press, 1998.

Kiely T. Forensic science and the law. In: *Forensic Science: An Introduction to Scientific and Investigative Techniques,* James SH and Nordby JJ, Eds. Boca Raton, Fla.: CRC Press, 2003.

Kirk P. *Crime Investigation*. New York: John Wiley & Sons, 1953.

Koertge N. *A House Built on Sand: Exposing Postmodernist Myths about Science*. New York: Oxford University Press, 2000.

Koppl R and Butos WN. Science as a Spontaneous Order: An Essay in the Economics of Science. In: Jensen HS, Vendeloe M, and Richter L, Eds. The Evolution of Scientific Knowledge. Cheltenham, UK: Edward Elgar. 2003.

Koppl R and Kobilinsky L. Forensic Science Administration: Toward A New Discipline. 2005. Available at http://alpha.fdu.edu/~koppl/fsa.doc.

McConnell C and March RH. Bringing reason and context to the science wars. *Physics Today*, May 2001.

McQuade TJ and Butos WN. Order-dependent knowledge and the economics of science. The Review of Austrian Economics. Springer Netherlands. Vol. 16, No. 2–3. Pp. 133–152.

Merton RK. Science and the Social Order. In: Social Theory and Social Structure, revised edition. New York: The Free Press, 1957.

National Institute of Justice. National Law Enforcement and Corrections Technology Center Bulletin. March 1998. Available at http://www.nlectc.org/txtfiles/12575-5.html.

Nordby JJ. Countering chaos: Logic, ethics, and the criminal justice system. In: *Forensic Science: An Introduction to Scientific and Investigative Techniques,* James SH and Nordby JJ, Eds. Boca Raton, Fla.: CRC Press, 2003.

Polanyi M. The Republic of Science: Its Political and Economic Theory. Minerva. Vol. 1. Pp. 54–74. 1962. Available at http://www.compilerpress.atfreeweb.com/Anno%20Polanyi%20Republic%20of%20Science%201962.htm.

Ramsland K. Henry C. Lee interview about forensic science. Accessed July 12, 2006, at http://www.crimelibrary.com/criminal_mind/forensics/lee/4.html.

Ribaux O, Walsh SJ, and Margot P. The contribution of forensic science to crime analysis and investigation: Forensic intelligence. *Forensic Science International*, 156(2–3):171–181, January 27, 2006.

Saferstein R. Introduction. In: *Criminalistics: An Introduction to Forensic Science,* 7th ed. Upper Saddle River, N.J.: Prentice Hall, 2001.

Spitz DJ. History and development of forensic medicine and pathology. In: *Medico-Legal Investigation of Death: Guidelines for the Application of Pathology to Crime Investigation*, 4th ed., WU. Spitz, Ed. Springfield, Ill.: Charles C Thomas Publisher, 2006.

Starrs JE. Foreword. In: *Forensic Science: An Introduction to Scientific and Investigative Techniques,* James SH and Nordby JJ, Eds. Boca Raton, Fla.: CRC Press, 2003.

Thornton J. The DNA statistical paradigm vs. everything else. *Journal of Forensic Science,* 42(4):758, 1997.

RECOMMENDED READING

Fisher BAJ. *Techniques of Crime Scene Investigation,* 7th ed. Boca Raton, Fla.: CRC Press, 2003.

Houck MM and Siegel JA. *Fundamentals of Forensic Science*. Boston: Elsevier Academic Press, 2006.

ENDNOTES

1. *Principles and Practice of Criminalistics: The Profession of Forensic Science* by Inman and Rudin. Copyright 2007 by Taylor & Francis Group LLC—Books. Reproduced with permission of Taylor & Francis Group LLC—Books in the format Other Book via Copyright Clearance Center.

2. *Forensic Science: An Introduction to Scientific and Investigative Techniques, Second Edition* by James and Nordby. Copyright 2007 by Taylor & Francis Group LLC—Books. Reproduced with permission of Taylor & Francis Group LLC—Books.

CHAPTER 2

THE STAKEHOLDERS IN FORENSIC SCIENCE: ROLES, PERSPECTIVES, AND EXPECTATIONS

The criminal justice system has a number of stakeholders—defendants, judges, jurors, expert witnesses, and attorneys—each with different expectations of the criminal justice system and forensic science. To members of the legal community, including attorneys, judges, and jurors, forensic science is frequently viewed as a means to an end. After all, the physical forensic evidence and the scientific principles used to analyze the samples collected from a crime scene are the mechanisms through which many criminal cases are tried. To the prosecutor, forensic science is the apparatus used to inculpate a defendant. To the defense attorney, forensic science is the adversary to whom a fatal blow must be struck. To the judge, forensic science is the scale on which guilt or innocence is weighted. To jurors, forensic science is the critical tool for decision making. To members of the law enforcement community, forensic science is the vehicle through which leads and theories are confirmed.

That being said, there are two other important stakeholders in the criminal justice system whose perspectives often shape the outcome of trials. To the forensic science community, the discipline represents many things: It is the end to the means, although forensic practitioners represent only a small segment of the criminal justice continuum; it is an instrument used to link evidence with a perpetrator; and it is a tool with which to search for the truth. Finally, to the members of the general public (who represent potential jurors, no less), forensic science is a complicated collection of technicians, tools, and technology designed to catch the bad guy. To the general populace, forensic science represents all aspects of that nebulous crime-fighting machine that delivers justice in a manner that is swift, mighty, and resolute. As we saw in Chapter 1, forensic science is both celebrated and vilified, and it also means many different things to many people.

Commentators suggest that forensic science is becoming so controversial because it is an important player in a high-stakes game. After all, the bottom line of the adjudication of cases through trials and the employment of forensic evidence is convictions—winning them, or avoiding them. According to the Bureau of Justice Statistics (BJS, 2006), 85 percent of all trials result in a guilty verdict. BJS statistics also show that the highest felony conviction rates (80 percent) were for defendants charged with a homicide, and murder defendants (44 percent) were the most likely to have their case adjudicated by trial. In 2002, the date for the most recent statistics available from the BJS, state and federal courts convicted a combined total of nearly 1.1 million adults of felonies, state courts convicted an estimated 1 million adults, and federal courts convicted about 63,000 adults (accounting for 6 percent of the national total). As we will see in various chapters throughout this book, the margin for error in criminal trials, ranging from faulty forensic science to wrongful convictions, raises the stakes even higher for defendants and places an even heavier burden on stakeholders to ensure that forensic science works as it should.

THE STAKEHOLDERS

We now review the role and perspective of each stakeholder in the criminal justice system to gain a better understanding of why and how forensic science is under siege in today's courtroom.

The Defendant

The defendant is the individual who is accused of and indicted for a crime, and whose legal guilt or innocence will be determined at the end of the trial's proceedings. According to Kurland (1997), "If acquitted, the defendant will go free and cannot be tried for the same crime again. If found guilty, the defendant may be deprived of his or her liberty or, in a capital case (his or her) life."

The defendant expects the legal system to operate under the presumption that the defendant is innocent and that the burden is on the prosecution to prove guilt beyond a reasonable doubt. The defendant also expects that his or her constitutionally guaranteed rights will not be compromised by the criminal justice system. The Fifth Amendment to the U.S. Constitution provides that a defendant cannot "be compelled in any criminal case to be a witness against himself." Essentially, the defendant cannot be forced to speak; if the defendant chooses to remain silent, the prosecutor cannot call the defendant as a witness, nor can a judge or defense attorney force the defendant to testify. Among the clauses of the Fifth Amendment is the provision: "nor shall any person be subject for the same offense to be twice put in jeopardy of life or limb." This provision, known as the double jeopardy clause, protects defendants from harassment by preventing them from being put on trial more than once for the same offense. One important exception to the rule against double jeopardy is that defendants can properly be charged for the same conduct by different jurisdictions. For example, a defendant may face charges in both federal and state court for the same conduct if some aspects of that conduct violated federal laws while other elements ran afoul of the laws of the state. Furthermore, the double jeopardy clause forbids more than one criminal prosecution growing out of the same conduct. A defendant can be brought once to criminal court (by the government) and once to civil court (by members of the public) for the same crime. The Sixth Amendment to the U.S. Constitution provides the bulk of a defendant's legal rights. The "confrontation clause" of the Sixth Amendment gives defendants the right to be "confronted by the witnesses against" them. This gives defendants the right to cross-examine witnesses, or to "look the defendant in the eye," and subject themselves to questioning by the defense. The Sixth Amendment also prevents secret trials and, except for limited exceptions, forbids prosecutors from proving a defendant's guilt with written statements from absent witnesses. The Sixth Amendment gives the defendant the right to be tried by a jury. In most cases, a unanimous verdict is required to convict. In most states, a lack of unanimity is called a hung jury, and the defendant will go free unless the prosecutor decides to retry the case. Finally, the Sixth Amendment provides that in all criminal prosecutions, "the accused shall enjoy the right . . . to have the assistance of counsel for his defense." If a defendant is indigent, a judge must appoint an attorney at government expense (but only if the defendants might be actually imprisoned for a period of more than six months for the crime). The U.S. Supreme Court has ruled that both indigent defendants who are represented by appointed counsel and defendants who hire their own attorneys are entitled to adequate representation. The Sixth Amendment gives defendants a right to a speedy trial; but because it does not specify precise time limits, judges usually decide on a case-by-case basis whether a defendant's trial has been so delayed that the case should be thrown out. In making this decision, judges look at the length of the delay, the reason for the delay, and whether the delay has prejudiced the defendant's position. Every jurisdiction has enacted statutes that set time limits for moving cases from the filing of the initial charge to trial. While these statutes are very strict in their wording, most defendants cannot get their convictions reversed on the ground that these statutes were violated.

To the defendant, forensic science can be both an incriminator and an ally. Defendants expect that the forensic evidence used to adjudicate their case has been properly analyzed by an experienced forensic scientist who has been properly educated and trained; conversely, the defendant also expects that his or her legal counsel is prepared to launch an attack on this forensic evidence that results in an acquittal.

The Defense Attorney

Frequently, the person charged with violating a state or federal criminal statute is unable to pay for the services of a defense attorney. In some areas a government official known as a public defender bears the responsibility for representing indigent defendants. Thus, the public defender is a counterpart of the prosecutor. Unlike the district attorney, however, the public defender is usually appointed rather than elected. In some parts of the country, there are statewide public defender systems; in other regions the public defender is a local official, usually associated with a county government. Like the district attorney, the public defender employs assistants and investigative personnel. In criminal cases in the United States, the defendant has a constitutional right to be represented by an attorney. Some jurisdictions have established public defender's offices to represent indigent defendants. In other areas, some method exists of assigning a private attorney to represent a defendant who cannot afford to hire one. Those defendants who can afford to hire their own lawyers will do so. When a private lawyer must be appointed to represent an indigent defendant, the assignment usually is made by an individual judge on an ad hoc basis. Local bar associations or lawyers themselves often provide the courts with a list of attorneys who are willing to provide such services. Some attorneys in private practice specialize in criminal defense work. Although the lives of criminal defense attorneys may be depicted as glamorous on television and in movies, the average real-life criminal defense lawyer works long hours for low pay and low prestige.

The American Bar Association's (ABA's) Model Rules of Professional Conduct outline a number of important tenets of responsibility and professional conduct for attorneys, including "A lawyer shall provide competent representation to a client. Competent representation requires the legal knowledge, skill, thoroughness and preparation reasonably necessary for the representation" and "A lawyer shall act with reasonable diligence and promptness in representing a client."

To the defense attorney, forensic science represents the barrier to acquittal for his or her client, a juggernaut of the prosecution that must be dismantled, piece by piece, to reveal the weakest link that can be exploited.

The Prosecutor

The prosecutor represents the state, and therefore the people of a jurisdiction, in the pursuit of justice against the person accused and indicted of committing a crime. According to the Center for Professional Responsibility of the ABA, "A prosecutor has the responsibility of a minister of justice and not simply that of an advocate. This responsibility carries with it specific obligations to see that the defendant is accorded procedural justice and that guilt is decided upon the basis of sufficient evidence. Precisely how far the prosecutor is required to go in this direction is a matter of debate and varies in different jurisdictions."

Attorneys working in the prosecutorial role function at all levels of the judicial process, from trial courts to the highest state and federal appellate courts. Each federal judicial district has one U.S. attorney and one or more assistant U.S. attorneys. They are responsible for prosecuting defendants in criminal cases in the federal district courts and for defending the

United States when it is sued in a federal trial court. U.S. attorneys are appointed by the president and confirmed by the Senate. Nominees must reside in the district to which they are appointed and must be lawyers. They serve a formal term of four years but can be reappointed indefinitely or removed at the president's discretion. The assistant U.S. attorneys are formally appointed by the U.S. attorney general, although in practice they are chosen by the U.S. attorney for the district, who forwards the selection to the attorney general for ratification. Assistant U.S. attorneys may be fired by the attorney general.

In their role as prosecutors, U.S. attorneys have considerable discretion in deciding which criminal cases to prosecute. They also have the authority to determine which civil cases to try to settle out of court and which ones to take to trial. U.S. attorneys, therefore, are in a very good position to influence the federal district court's docket. Also, because they engage in more litigation in the district courts than anyone else, the U.S. attorneys and their staffs are vital participants in policy making in the federal trial courts.

Those who prosecute persons accused of violating state criminal statutes are commonly known as district attorneys. In most states they are elected county officials; however, in a few states they are appointed. The district attorney's office usually employs a number of assistants who do most of the actual trial work. Most of these assistant district attorneys are recent graduates of law school, who gain valuable trial experience in these positions. Many later enter private practice, often as criminal defense attorneys. Others will seek to become district attorneys or judges after a few years. The district attorney's office has a great deal of discretion in the handling of cases. Given budget and personnel constraints, not all cases can be afforded the same amount of time and attention. Therefore, some cases are dismissed, others are not prosecuted, and still others are prosecuted vigorously in court. Most cases, however, are subject to plea bargaining. This means that the district attorney's office agrees to accept the defendant's plea of guilty to a reduced charge or to drop some charges against the defendant in exchange for pleas of guilty to others.

The prosecutor leans heavily on forensic science for its ability to link the physical evidence collected from the crime scene to the person charged with committing the crime, and also depends on the evidence to make the case bulletproof against the defense team.

SIDEBAR 2.1 SPECIAL CHALLENGES FOR THE PROSECUTOR

The National Research Council (2001) states that not only are prosecutors faced with technological and scientific advances that can serve as new prosecutorial tools, they must meet new challenges to the way in which prosecutions are conducted. They must handle complex matters of law and justice, issues that may be "further convoluted by competing community attitudes and local politics" in addition to their engagement in the U.S. adversarial legal culture.

Perhaps the most significant technological advancement impacting prosecutors is DNA profiling. According to the National Research Council (2001), "The development of DNA profiling has revolutionized 20th century forensic science as well as the criminal justice system. It frequently enables prosecutors to conclusively establish the guilt of a defendant, particularly in sexual assault and homicide cases, where an offender is most likely to leave his genetic signature, in the form of skin, hair, or bodily fluids, at the crime scene. Moreover, DNA evidence is even more likely to exonerate a wrongly accused suspect than to identify a guilty one. This helps prosecutors to avoid unjust prosecutions that may carry high human, financial, and political costs. In recent years, DNA profiling has proven valuable in exonerating wrongly convicted persons whose trials took place before DNA profiling became available. By 1996, it had been instrumental in correcting injustices in 28 convictions, obtained by using less discriminating identification methods that failed to exclude the defendant as the guilty party (National Institute of Justice, 1999)."

More than a decade after its introduction, DNA profiling is still used only selectively. The costs of DNA testing remain high, and case-processing backlogs in the relatively few laboratories currently qualified to conduct DNA tests number in the tens of thousands. This can be expected to change, however, as research develops less costly and time-consuming DNA evidence collection and profiling methods. According to the National Research Council (2001), the prosecutor's chief responsibilities in the use of this valuable, new forensic tool are traditional ones that involve both case and administrative management: "Prosecutors need a detailed understanding of DNA technology and its appropriate uses so that DNA evidence is both credible and clearly presented at trial. Several recent cases, most notably the O.J. Simpson trial, have established the importance of implementing clear and specific evidence collection, storage, and chain-of-evidence guidelines and procedures for investigators. Prosecutors have a responsibility to ensure that DNA profiling is accessible to defendants in cases where its use will serve justice. Social science research can improve the human interface with the technical capabilities of DNA profiling by developing information on the kinds and number of cases where the use of DNA evidence benefits the prosecution or the defense. It is also important to document the non-technical reasons for success or failure, for example, by tying procedures to collect and preserve DNA evidence to case outcomes."

A WORD ABOUT ACCOUNTABILITY AND PROSECUTORS

Forst and Brosi (1977) observe that prosecutors are "insulated by the virtual absence of a system of measured public accountability" and explain further: "Public perceptions of effectiveness are shaped almost entirely by a few high-profile cases in the news and by occasional public pronouncements by prosecutors asserting toughness. Conviction rates are not reported to a national agency or even locally by most prosecutors' offices, as arrest rates are by the police, for example. Such data, while susceptible to misinterpretation, nevertheless would make the performance of prosecutors more transparent to those who rely on their work, especially the police, courts, and victim assistance organizations, and to the public." Forst and Brosi (1977) suggest the annual reporting and publication of uniform office performance statistics. Professional associations such as the National District Attorney's Association and the American Prosecutor's Research Institute might be enlisted to help design such a system. The researchers emphasize that data also could be collected on the problems reported by prosecutors that may impede successful prosecution of cases, such as heavy caseloads, and more recently reported phenomena such as the true extent of witness intimidation, failure to appear at trial, or jury nullification. In addition, they suggest that a formal survey could be conducted of the stakeholders who depend on prosecutors, including victims, witnesses, judges, police, the defense bar, and the general public.

Continues on next page

Closely linked with accountability is the transparency of prosecutors' actions and their compliance with codes of ethics. Abuse of discretion is an issue identified by the National Research Council (2001) as a potential problem; Liebman et al. (2000) discovered that misconduct by prosecutors was a factor in approximately 16 percent of erroneous convictions. At issue, according to the National Research Council (2001), is "whether there is adequate recognition of a shifting role between neutral fact-finding, as the state's representative, and active advocacy as a prosecutor at different stages of a case. What, if any, kind of information would help prosecutors determine the appropriate balance between the quality of the evidence in a case and other factors, such as heinousness of the offense, or demonstrable bad character of the suspect, in deciding to bring charges or agree to a plea? Do the stakes in high-profile cases more frequently lead to greater care on the part of a prosecutor or do they foster an atmosphere where misconduct may occur? What part do training or individual characteristics of prosecutors play in ethically questionable behavior? Are the rules of conduct and the expectations for the behavior of prosecutors clear in most offices?" The National Research Council (2001) suggests that these questions could be addressed through periodic, objective, and thorough reviews of case files and court decisions on randomly selected cases, which might then be compared to targeted cases. The targeted cases would be selected from convictions that subsequently have been proven erroneous, from cases where ethical complaints were filed, and from cases where jurors have recanted their vote to convict, in order to develop information on who com-mits ethical errors or engages in misconduct, and under what circumstances. Social sci-entists and legal scholars working together on these reviews also may be able to uncover patterns or circumstances where such errors or misconduct are most likely to occur.

In a workshop conducted by the National Research Council (2001), participants asked themselves to what degree the potential exists for misjudgments or errors made by prosecutors. According to the National Research Council (2001), "Largely unfettered discretion can also provide a milieu for misconduct, which, even if only occasional, can raise serious doubts about the legitimacy of the criminal justice system." Dwyer et al. (2000) report that prosecutorial misconduct played a role in 26 out of 62 cases in which convicted defendants were later exonerated based on analysis of DNA evidence. Liebman et al. (2000) examined rates of reversible error in more than 5,000 death penalty cases and found that prosecutorial suppression of exculpatory evidence (that the defendant was either innocent or not deserving of the death penalty) or other forms of law enforcement misconduct were responsible for appellate reversal of convictions in 16 to 19 percent of the reversed cases, although this did not necessarily lead to subsequent acquittals. In 22 of the 5,760 cases, retrial resulted in an acquittal.

The Judge

A judge or justice is an appointed or elected official who presides over a court; the powers, functions, and training of judges vary widely from jurisdiction to jurisdiction. According to the ABA's Model Code of Judicial Conduct, "Anyone, whether or not a lawyer, who is an officer of a judicial system and who performs judicial functions, including an officer such as a magistrate, court commissioner, special master or referee, is a judge." The ABA's Model Code of Judicial Conduct outlines a number of important tenets of responsibility and professional conduct for judges, including the following canons: "A judge shall uphold the integrity and independence of the judiciary," "A judge shall avoid impropriety and the appearance of impropriety in all of the judge's activities," "A judge shall perform the duties of judicial office impartially and diligently," "A judge shall so conduct the judge's extra-judicial activities as to minimize the risk of conflict with judicial obligations," and "A judge or judicial candidate shall refrain from inappropriate political activity." It is the responsibility of the judge to act objectively, acknowledging that even though he is shaped by the society in which he or she lives, he or she must govern the courtroom with fairness and neutrality. Barak notes, "Clearly, the purpose of judicial objectivity is not to amputate the judges from their surroundings. In fact, the opposite is true: the goal is to permit judges to set forth and express the basic values of their epoch. The purpose of judicial objectivity is not to free the judges from their past, from their education, experience, convictions and values. Instead, it seeks to prompt them to make use of all these tools in an effort to reflect the nation's basic democratic values, in the clearest, most accurate manner possible." Ungs and Bass (1972) conducted a study of trial court judges and created five categories of role orientations for judges:

1. *The Law Interpreter:* emphasizes adherence to judicial restraint
2. *The Adjudicator:* emphasizes concern for social consequences of decisions
3. *The Administrator:* emphasizes procedural goals and precedent only if they expedite case resolution
4. *The Trial Judge:* emphasizes a concern for timeliness, justice in individual cases, and precedent
5. *The Peacekeeper:* emphasizes a balancing of contending principles and does not consider *stare decisis* to be the working rule of law.

As we will see in Chapters 9, 10, 12, and 13, judges also must serve as gatekeepers in the determination of the admissibility of forensic, scientific, and technical evidence. To this end, the judge views forensic science with a wary eye, and must examine it against various criteria to evaluate the validity, reliability, and soundness of the science.

The Jury

A jury is a small group of citizens, chosen at random, who are asked to gather together and hear the case against an accused, to weight the evidence presented during the trial, and to make a determination of guilt or innocence. Jurors are unbiased members of the community who have a duty to keep an open mind and must not form or express an opinion until they have heard all the evidence, the arguments of counsel, and the final instruction as to the law from the court. To this end, jurors must take an oath to honestly, justly, and impartially hear a case. Jurors are the exclusive judges of the evidence, the credibility of the witnesses, and the weight to be given to the testimony. In weighing the testimony to determine what or who is to be believed, the jury should use its own knowledge, experience, and common sense as a guide. The jury of 12 people selected to hear the evidence in the case must unanimously agree beyond a reasonable doubt that the defendant is guilty in order to convict. The jury in a criminal case will consider all aspects of the case in private for as long as is needed in order to come to a unanimous decision. Once a verdict is reached, it is presented to the defendant in court. A jury may find a person guilty of all, some, or none of the crimes charged. In some cases, depending on the evidence presented and the nature of the instructions given by the court to the jury, a jury may convict a defendant of a lesser crime than that charged in the indictment. If the jury presents a not guilty verdict, then the proceedings are over and the jury verdict may not be overturned. If the verdict is guilty, then the defense may appeal the decision.

While many Americans consider jury duty to be a fate worse than an IRS audit, some jurors believe it represents the opportunity to help the system deliver justice that is essential to a free society. In addition, some jurors believe that through jury duty, they can contribute as a citizen to the political good of the country, short of serving as an elected official. Some jurors also expect that they will be able to serve the legal system without being manipulated by attorneys or subjected to undue pressure to cast a vote.

The jury selection process is one fraught with potential difficulties, and it can create a first impression of the legal system in the potential juror's mind. The clerk of the court maintains a list of potential jurors using, for example, lists of registered voters or licensed drivers, or a combination of the two. When a case is set for trial by jury, the clerk uses this list to provide the court with a *venire* of potential jurors representing a fair cross section of the community. The jurors who will actually hear the case are then chosen by the attorneys for each side in a process known as *voir dire*. Each attorney and/or the judge asks the potential juror questions designed to discover any potential bias or prejudice for or against the parties or issues in the case. If the juror concedes such a bias or if evidence suggests he or she may have one, the attorney may ask the court to strike the juror "for cause" and remove him or her from the pool of potential jurors in that case. If the judge refuses to remove the potential juror "for cause," the attorney will consider whether to use one of his or her *peremptory strikes* to remove the juror. In federal civil trials, each party can make up to three peremptory strikes to remove a juror without providing a reason.

Voir dire is a powerful process, and an increasing number of attorneys are sharpening their skills to determine juror candor, ensuring that jurors are not allowed to hide their true feelings on issues relating to the case that could prove to be damaging at the trial deliberation stage. Most jurors endeavor to serve to the best of their ability, with good intentions to act as an objective fact-finding body. While there are certainly horror stories of hung juries, jury tampering, and undue pressure on jurors to vote a certain way, most jurors simply want to see what they believe is justice being served. And most understand and take to heart that they bear a heavy burden of deciding the fate of another human being. As we will see in Chapter 13, jurors seem to be promulgating what has become known as the "*CSI* effect," which may be shaping the way attorneys present and explain forensic evidence in particular.

COLLABORATION IN ACTION: THE COURTROOM WORKGROUP

Carp and Stidham (2001) state that "Rather than functioning as an occasional gathering of strangers who resolve a particular conflict and then go their separate ways, lawyers and judges who work in a criminal courtroom become part of a workgroup. The most visible members of the courtroom workgroup—judges, prosecutors, and defense attorneys—are associated with specific functions: Prosecutors push for convictions of those accused of criminal offenses against the government, defense attorneys seek acquittals for their clients, and judges serve as neutral arbiters to guarantee a fair trial. Despite their different roles, members of the courtroom workgroup share certain values and goals and are not the fierce adversaries that many people imagine. Cooperation among judges, prosecutors, and defense attorneys is the norm."

The importance of the interaction of stakeholders in the criminal justice system is not lost on the NIJ (1998), which states, "The lab can do nothing without the physical evidence gathered by police and evidence technicians; it is the fuel that runs a forensic laboratory. The quality of this evidence must be as secure as the crime scene itself." To this end, the NIJ states that "Forensic science must apply only those scientific techniques and procedures that are solidly grounded through previous experimentation; standards for qualifying technicians and scientists must be followed; and standard procedures must be adhered to during evidence collection and analysis. If the forensic science methods and technologies are untested, unstandardized, or misapplied, or if the examiner's qualifications are shaky or blemished, the value of the evidence can be diminished to the point where the evidence might as well never have been collected, analyzed, or presented in court." The NIJ (1998) adds further, "The more scientifically grounded the evidence, the more prosecutors will be willing to use the evidence to strengthen a case. Police and evidence technicians, laboratory analysts, and attorneys must cooperate with each other to ensure proper use of this evidence. Cooperation requires knowing how one action affects another, how not collecting a certain type of evidence will preclude using a certain forensic technique, or how collecting a certain type of evidence requires using a particular forensic test rather than any other. Knowing how one action affects another in the long chain of events leading toward the presentation of scientific evidence and expert testimony requires communication among the involved parties."

Carp and Stidham (2001) assert that the most important goal of the courtroom workgroup is to handle cases expeditiously: "Judges and prosecutors are interested in disposing of cases quickly to present a picture of accomplishment and efficiency. Because private defense attorneys need to handle a large volume of cases to survive financially, resolving cases quickly works to their advantage. And public defenders seek quick dispositions simply because they lack adequate resources to handle their caseloads." Another goal is to maintain group cohesion. Carp and Stidham (2001) add, "Conflict among the members makes work more difficult and interferes with the expeditious handling of cases." A third goal of the workgroup is to reduce or control uncertainty. Carp and Stidham (2001) explain: "In practice this means that all members of the workgroup strive to avoid trials. Trials, especially jury trials, produce a great deal of uncertainty given that they require substantial investments of time and effort without any reasonable guarantee of a desirable outcome. To attain these goals, workgroup members employ several techniques. Although unilateral decisions and adversarial proceedings occur, negotiation is the most commonly used technique in criminal courtrooms."

THE OVERLOOKED STAKEHOLDER?

While criminalists and forensic laboratory personnel are the most common forensic professionals on the witness stand, as portrayed on television, one must not forget the vital role that medico-legal practitioners, including medical examiners, coroners, and death investigators, play in criminal trials. Forensic pathologist Randy Hanzlick, M.D., chief medical examiner for Fulton County in Georgia, explains that death investigations carry broad societal importance for criminal justice. "Death investigations provide evidence to convict the guilty and protect the innocent, whether they are accused of murder, child maltreatment, neglect, or other crimes."

Kaye (2003) asserts that one of the most significant issues facing the U.S. legal system is the development of a credible and objective process to determine which deaths to investigate, how to investigate them, what constitutes a thorough investigation, and how to keep suspicious deaths and homicides from being overlooked. Kaye observes, "Accurate evidence from a death investigation should be used in court to convict the guilty and protect the innocent. Our current legal system has two problems. The first is its adversarial nature: expert witnesses can be pressured, or selected, to take one-sided positions. The courtroom can be turned into a battle of experts, which is highly confusing to a jury. How can the system be structured to produce objective evidence that will not produce such battles?" Kaye continues, "A second problem arises from the disparity in resources between criminal prosecution and defense. It is a rarity for the defense to mount its own death investigation with the same resources as the prosecution. If the prosecution's coroner or medical examiner is negligent, biased, or inept, miscarriages of justice are inevitable. In an egregious example, a pathologist in Texas single-handedly performed 450 autopsies a year for 40 Texas counties. Exhumations of some of the corpses revealed an absence of marks on the bodies, indicating that no autopsy had been performed. The system needs to be structured in such a way as to prevent miscarriages of justice or to capture them early in the process."

Medico-legal practitioners' skills and contributions are vital to the prosecution's case, explains Dusek (2003): "A prosecutor looks to the medical examiner's office for accuracy, promptness, and the ability to state opinions clearly in court. Accuracy must prevail as to the manner of death, the cause of death, and the time of death. . . . The prosecutor's advice to the medical examiner is to simplify the investigation for the jury, make it understandable, and make it persuasive. Visual aids and diagrams are valuable. It is also important for medical examiners to restrict their testimony to what they are comfortable with without extending themselves in a way that leaves them open to cross-examination by a defense lawyer."

Dusek (2003) recalls a case in San Diego which the medical examiner played a critical role in securing a conviction: "All the features of a strong and credible medical examiner's office were on display in the notorious case of child abduction. A suspect was charged even before the child's body was found. When the body was found several days later, the death investigation had to proceed quickly during the 10-day window before a preliminary hearing. The medical examiner, presented with a badly decomposed body, summoned the on-call forensic entomologist and dentist. The dentist was able to identify the victim and ruled that suffocation was the cause of death; some of the victim's teeth were missing, and the forensic dentist attributed that to their falling out from the pressure of suffocation. The case was successfully prosecuted on the basis of the quality of the medical examination. The only testimony that the jury requested be reread was that of the medical examiner and the entomologist. When asked why they concluded as they did, the jurors responded that 'the medical examiners were the objective fact finders in the case. We relied upon them.' "

From the defense camp's perspective, medico-legal practitioners who serve as expert witnesses should demand the highest of standards in science—an expectation that should be shared by every stakeholder in the criminal justice system. Scheck (2003) asserts, "The field of medico-legal death investigation should work to widen as much as possible what the legal profession calls 'scientific facts.' Scientific facts are observations that do not require interpretation, such as the position of the body, identifying marks, and results of analysis of blood and other physical evidence. There should be no differences between the defense perspective and the prosecution perspective on scientific facts."

The unspoken question on many stakeholders' minds is, therefore, "Is forensic science somehow defined differently in court than it is elsewhere?" Houck (2003) asserts there is a "demarcation problem in the philosophy of science (distinguishing science from pseudoscience) and how it relates to forensic science." Houck explains, "Forensic science offers a new wrinkle to the demarcation problem in the requirement of science to be defined in legal, not scientific, settings. Legal rulings . . . threaten to reduce forensic science to a technical specialty and this must be avoided for the benefit of the discipline. In the philosophy of science, the demarcation problem is the decision between what constitutes science, say, astronomy, and distinguishes it from pseudoscience, astrology, for example. This has a direct bearing on forensic science inasmuch as certain disciplines are still considered scientifically borderline by some and it is important to sort out the science from the junk." (For a more in-depth discussion of junk science, see Chapter 10.)

As we will see in Chapter 12, forensic science takes on new meaning when scrutinized through filters handed down by the U.S. Supreme Court, including general acceptability by the relevant scientific community, knowledge of the actual or potential rate of error for the practice, subjection of the practice to peer review, and actual or potential testability of the method's results. Houck (2003) comments, "Forensic science adds a novel wrinkle to the demarcation problem because, not only must it adhere to the definitions of science as understood by philosophers and practicing scientists, its science is applied in the legal arena where the home field provides a distinct advantage. . . . Courts act as gatekeepers, allowing 'good' science to pass while barring the door to 'bad' pseudo science." The crux of the issue, then, according to Houck, is that "This legal interpretation of what constitutes acceptable science . . . may or may not have any grounding in what scientists consider 'good science' to be."

Forensic evidence and the techniques used to study these samples make up the gist of forensic knowledge presented in a criminal trial, and they are considered by its practitioners to be routine casework. However, Houck (2003) points out that "These results are not used, however, solely to further the growth of science but to reconstruct past events to determine causes, sources, and effects in crimes. This and other information is presented in court to assist the trier of fact. Of the possible competing hypotheses offered by the involved parties, one will be selected as more plausible by judge or jury, based in part on scientific conclusions and interpretations, leading to a legal decision. This duality of identity, empirical and historical, has probably led to the perception that forensic science is a lesser science or even merely a technique with no guiding philosophy. Historical disciplines have been derided as unscientific. Legal rulings . . . encourage this perception by reducing scientific disciplines with potentially sufficient supporting research to technical specialties that are unscientific and simply applications of 'real' scientific principles. Forensic science as a discipline is cheapened by the promulgation and reinforcement of this perception; resources of all kinds, from grants to budgets to public confidence, are reduced by the devaluing of the science in forensic science."

Houck (2003) further beseeches stakeholders in the criminal justice system to "seek more education on the nature of science and the underlying philosophy of forensic science. Forensic scientists should eschew the implications of current legal rulings and pursue research that will integrate the forensic science literature into a cohesive scientific foundation that will exceed the . . . framework. The information exists, the requirements are known, and the only obstacle that remains is our perception of forensic science as a lesser discipline."

ON COMMON GROUND: THE COURTROOM TRIAL

Regardless of the perspective of the stakeholder, they all meet on the common ground of the court of law. According to the ABA, "American courtroom procedures are based on historical precedent, modified by the needs and experience of lawyers and judges. When two parties cannot agree on their respective rights and obligations, or even on what gave rise to the dispute, the system provides each side with an equal opportunity to present its case (and to point out the weaknesses in its opponent's case) to a neutral judge or jury. Each side is championed by a lawyer following the same statutes, case law, and rules of procedure. The system is designed to permit the truth to emerge whether the case is criminal or civil in nature."

According to the U.S. State Department (2004), the adversarial model is based on the assumption that every case or controversy has two sides to it; in criminal cases the government claims a defendant is guilty while the defendant contends innocence; in civil cases the plaintiff asserts that the person he or she is suing has caused some injury while the respondent denies responsibility. In the courtroom each party provides his or her side of the story as he or she sees it. The theory underlying this model is that the truth will emerge if each party is given unbridled opportunity to present the full panoply of evidence, facts, and arguments before a neutral and attentive judge (and jury). The lawyers representing each side are the major players in this courtroom drama. The judge acts more as a passive, disinterested referee whose primary role is to keep both sides within the accepted rules of legal procedure and courtroom decorum. The judge eventually determines which side has won in accordance with the rules of evidence, but only after both sides have had a full opportunity to present their case.

Kurland (1997) observes, "For sheer human interest, the ability to catch public attention and cleave to it from start to finish, nothing else in real life equals a good murder trial. A prominent victim, or, even better, a prominent defendant; a bit of mystery surrounding the facts of the case; two prides of high-powered attorneys facing each other across the courtroom; a cluster of witnesses, each contributing a few tantalizing facts to a tale of human fallibility; a bevy of expert witnesses to explain the unexplainable; a man or woman's life or freedom hanging in the balance—these are the makings of high drama." Kurland also describes the components of an "ideal trial" as an independent judge, an adversary trial, an unbiased jury, established legal precedent, and a just verdict. In reality, many trials are impacted by fallible individuals in an imperfect system, as Kurland notes: "Circumstantial evidence is suspect, eyewitnesses are unreliable, forensic evidence is only as good as the laboratory that (analyzed) it. On the other hand, circumstantial evidence, if properly interpreted, can tell the story of the crime; eyewitnesses can be good observers; and a professionally run forensic laboratory can (analyze) evidence that is trustworthy." Equally so, individuals who have committed murder and have been tried, are acquitted "due to inadequate evidence, incompetent prosecution, a brilliant defense, or a jury not disposed to convict," Kurland adds.

A trial is not as common as most laypersons assume. Goodale (1995) reports that less than 5 percent of criminal trials in metropolitan areas actually go to trial. Johnson (1996) says that despite the justice system's presumption of innocence, the state has a remarkably high conviction rate. According to the Justice Council of California's 1995 annual report, in fiscal year 1993–1994, for example, 93.7 percent of the 147,269 felony filings resulted in a guilty plea or conviction. Of the 9,348 cases resulting in acquittal or dismissal, 305 were acquitted by a court trial and 932 by jury trial. Rueben (1995), citing a U.S. Department of Justice study, reports that similarly, just 2 percent of the 762,000 civil cases in the 75 most populous counties in the nation were decided by juries; plaintiffs won 52 percent of the time.

Although trials are the exception, not the norm, in the criminal justice system, the ones that do reach the courtroom often leave an indelible mark on the U.S. legal system. Increasingly, these kinds of trials also make their mark on forensic science as a discipline.

If so few trials are decided by juries these days, it stands to reason that the trials which do go to court trigger considerable interest—particularly if they involve a high-profile defendant.

REFERENCES

American Bar Association. *How the Legal System Works. Family Legal Guide.* Accessed at http://www.abanet.org/publiced/practical/books/family_legal_guide/chapter_2.pdf.

Barak A. The role of a judge in a democracy. *Justice in the World,* online edition, No. 3. Accessed at http://www.justiceintheworld.org/info/rj_barak.htm.

Bureau of Justice Statistics. State Court Processing Statistics: Felony Defendants in Large Urban Counties, 2002. February 2006. Available at http://www.ojp.usdoj.gov/bjs/pub/ascii/fdluc02.txt.

Bureau of Justice Statistics. *Prosecutors in State Courts, 1996.* Washington, D.C.: U.S. Department of Justice, 1998.

Carp RA and Stidham R. *Judicial Process in America,* 5th ed. Washington, D.C.: Congressional Quarterly Press, 2001.

Dusek J. The prosecutor's perspective. In: *Institute of Medicine's Medico-Legal Death Investigation System: Workshop Summary.* Washington, D.C.: National Academic Press, 2003.

Dwyer J, Neufeld P, and Scheck B. *Actual Innocence: Five Days to Execution and Other Dispatches from the Wrongly Convicted.* New York: Doubleday, 2000.

Forst B and Brosi K. A theoretical and empirical analysis of the prosecutor. *Journal of Legal Studies,* 6:177–191, 1977.

Goodale G. Dollars and sense of the Simpson trial. *The Christian Science Monitor,* May 16, 1995.

Houck MM. The cheapening of forensic science: How philosophical, practical and legal definitions of science shape our discipline. Poster abstract presented at Promega Corporation 14th International Symposium on Human Identification, 2003.

Johnson E. Effect of the O.J. trial on the access to justice. San Francisco: UC Hastings College of the Law, Public Law Research Institute, 1996. Accessed at http://w3.uchastings.edu/plri/fal95tex/ojacc.html#F34.

Judicial Council of California. *1995 Annual Report,* p. 93.

Kaye DH. How the MEs are viewed. Scientific evidence in the courtroom: Introductory comments. In: *Institute of Medicine's Medico-Legal Death Investigation System: Workshop Summary.* Washington, D.C.: National Academic Press, 2003.

Kiely T. Forensic science and the law. In: *Forensic Science: An Introduction to Scientific and Investigative Techniques,* James SH and Nordby JJ, Eds. Boca Raton, Fla.: CRC Press, 2003.

Kirk PL and Lowell WB. *The Crime Laboratory: Organization and Operation.* Springfield, Ill.: Charles C Thomas Publishers, 1965, pp. 22–23.

Kurland M. *How to Try a Murder.* New Jersey: Castle Books, 1997.

Liebman J, Fagan J, and West V. A broken system: Error rates in capital cases, 1973–1995, 2000. Accessed at http://justice.policy.net/jpreport/.

National Institute of Justice. *What Every Law Enforcement Officer Should Know about DNA Evidence.* Washington, D.C.: U.S. Department of Justice, 1999.

National Institute of Justice. *The National Institute of Justice and Advances in Forensic Science and Technology Series: National Law Enforcement and Corrections Technology Center Bulletin.* Washington, D.C.: U.S. Department of Justice, March 1998.

National Research Council. *What's Changing in Prosecution: Report of a Workshop. Commission on Behavioral and Social Sciences and Education,* Heymann P and Petrie C., Eds. Washington, D.C.: National Academic Press, 2001.

Rueben RC. Plaintiffs rarely win punitive, study says. *ABA Journal,* October 1995.

Scheck B. The defense's perspective. In: *Institute of Medicine's Medico-Legal Death Investigation System: Workshop Summary.* Washington, D.C.: National Academic Press, 2003.

Ungs TD and Bass LR. Judicial role perceptions: A technique study of Ohio judges. *Law and Society Review,* 6:343, 1972.

U.S. Department of State. Outline of the U.S. legal system. Accessed at http://usinfo.state.gov/products/pubs/legalotln/criminal.htm.

RECOMMENDED READING

Cleland CE. Historical science, experimental science, and the scientific method. *Geology,* 29:987–990, 2001.

Faigman DL. Science and the law: Is science different for lawyers? *Science,* 297:339–340, 2002.

Jasanoff S. The eye of everyman: Witnessing DNA in the Simpson trial. *Social Studies of Science,* 28(5/6): 1997.

CHAPTER 3

AN INTRODUCTION TO THE U.S. FORENSIC LABORATORY SYSTEM

In the last four decades, forensic laboratories have evolved from a collection of fewer than 100 state and local agencies scattered in various jurisdictions around the country to the present day's approximately 400 sophisticated scientific operations. The growth of the forensic laboratory system has been propelled in part by increasing reliance on scientific evidence and the resulting demand for analysis and examination (American Society of Crime Laboratory Directors [ASCLD], 2004).

St. Clair (2003) states, "From the collection of evidence through the sentencing of the convicted, the crime laboratory plays an integral role in the criminal justice process."

St. Clair adds that there are a number of stakeholders to which forensic laboratories are beholden, including the general public, law enforcement, prosecutors, victims, and suspects. St. Clair observes, "Regardless of a crime laboratory's role or level of involvement, they have a responsibility to perform services in a manner responsive to the demands of their stakeholders. While these demands may vary between segments of the population, many elements remain the same. For example, forensic scientists are expected to approach every situation in an objective, scientific manner with a high degree of integrity. A crime laboratory's challenge is to meet the various expectations of its stakeholders with the same high level of responsiveness.

The typical forensic laboratory consists of separate analytical sections, referred to as disciplines. Each of the disciplines concentrates on different evidence types and has specific personnel, training, equipment, and facility requirements. Differences exist among the crime laboratories in the United States, with various factors contributing to the uniqueness of the facilities, including variance among laws that impact how laboratories adjust their procedures to answer legal questions and varying evidence types with different analytical and laboratory needs. According to the ASCLD (2004), 86 percent of accredited forensic laboratories have sections that analyze for controlled substances, 60 percent have firearms/tool marks sections, 57 percent have sections that analyze trace evidence, 42 percent have forensic biology/DNA sections, and 51 percent have latent print sections.

ASCLD (2004) states that a "classical" crime laboratory is a single laboratory or system composed mainly of scientists analyzing evidence in at least two of the following disciplines: controlled substances, trace, biology, toxicology, latent prints, questioned documents, firearms/tool marks, or crime scene. A "non-classical" crime laboratory is a site or laboratory providing analysis in one or more of the disciplines of digital evidence, latent prints, questioned documents, and crime scene, with the workforce composed mainly of sworn personnel who may not have scientific training. These sites are often referred to as identification units. ASCLD (2004) notes, "If the definition of a crime laboratory is expanded to include identification units operating in the 14,000 police departments and law enforcement agencies in the U.S., there could be at least 1,000 crime laboratories. The actual total is unknown. The average size of classical laboratories is 30 personnel (25 of whom would be considered analysts). The average size of the non-classical crime laboratory is estimated to be three (all three would be considered examiners)."

St. Clair (2003) states, "There is no average crime laboratory." While there are a number of private laboratories, the majority of facilities are supported by public funding, with authority vested at the local, state, or federal level. Forensic laboratories can be large or small, and housed in a variety of environments, including a law enforcement agency, such as a police or sheriff's department, or a medical examiner's office or they may be freestanding and independently operated.

Some private laboratories specialize in the analysis of biological samples from certain types of offenders, such as in sexual assault cases that require analysis of rape kit contents. A word about these kinds of facilities: St. Clair (2003) notes, "Often the individuals in public laboratories are skeptical of the training and abilities of those employed by private forensic laboratories. This usually stems from the fact that these examiners are testifying against their findings or provide criticism or arguments to defense attorneys to muddy the waters. Private examiners operating for the defense bar have an image of unethical individuals willing to accept cases for which they possess minimal expertise only to derive income. However, with available certification and accreditation, these laboratories and examiners can demonstrate that they only perform within their expertise and produce an ethical product."

Laboratories also vary in the kinds of forensic evidence they process. According to the American Academy of Forensic Sciences (2004) the majority of forensic laboratories in the United States engage in the following nine disciplines and face unique challenges:

- *Latent print examinations.* Although courts have for many years accepted the work performed in latent fingerprint examinations, current needs include improved recovery and visualization methods, interoperability and improvement of search and retrieval systems, and shared databases for use in training and harmonization efforts. According to the ASCLD (2004), latent prints are fingerprints that are not visible until some type of processing, often chemical, is performed; lasers are also often used in this visualization process. Comparisons are performed by analysts trained for up to two years. An Automated Fingerprint Identification System (AFIS) is used to conduct computer-assisted searches against a known database.

- *Questioned document examinations.* This discipline is said to be in a chaotic state, because courts have questioned the scientific basis of handwriting identification and because of ongoing changes in the ways in which documents are created and transmitted. Current needs include validation of the scientific basis for handwriting examination, harmonization of comparison criteria, improved nondestructive methods for determining characteristic features of documents, image-enhancement methods for linking documents to machines, and shared databases of writing and machine-document exemplars for use in training and harmonization efforts. According to the ASCLD (2004), the questioned documents section conducts handwriting analysis and examines documents and its components. It also includes obliterated writing. Work in this section is labor intensive and training time is three years.

- Firearms/tool marks and other impression-evidence examinations. Courts routinely accept identifications of firearms, tools, and other implements through comparison of microscopic impressions on questioned and authenticated specimens. Nevertheless, current needs include validation of the basis for impression-evidence identifications, development of portable nondestructive analytical approaches for characterizing features of bullet impact areas, and statistical analysis of performance of algorithms used in automated pattern recognition. According to the ASCLD (2004), the firearms/tool marks section involves evidence associated with firearms. When a weapon is fired, marks are left on shell casings and projectiles by the weapon. The examination of these marks allows the examiner to associate weapons, casings, and projectiles. There is also a firearms database, the National Integrated Ballistic Identification Network (NIBIN), which can be used to facilitate the association of casings, hopefully to a weapon and ultimately to a person. Training time for firearms examiners is in excess of two years in many cases.

- *Crime scene response and related examinations.* The quality of analyses depends heavily on the quality of evidence recognition, documentation, collection, and preservation. Current needs in this area include sample location, identification, capture, and stabilization technology in a kit suitable for recovery of trace evidence, portable and remote hazardous materials detectors, and computerized crime scene mapping supported by the Global Positioning System (GPS) and multimedia capture technologies.

- *Explosives and fire debris examinations.* Very few laboratories routinely analyze post-blast debris. Needs include improved methods for assessing the size, construction, and composition of improvised explosive devices from macro-effects at post-blast scenes, enhanced cleanup techniques for post-blast debris, method development for recovery of explosive and ignitable liquid residues from a variety of matrices, enhanced field-detection capabilities and mapping technologies for bomb scene investigation assistance, and continued validation of the current methods by intra-laboratory studies.

- *Postmortem toxicology and human-performance testing.* Although courts routinely accept these laboratory determinations, interpretive controversies still exist in several areas of toxicology. Current needs include nondestructive analytical techniques, well-controlled studies of the effects of drugs on the operation of motor vehicles and complex equipment, more accurate methods for determining time of death, and a central database of postmortem "incidental" drug findings in deaths unrelated to drugs. According to the ASCLD (2004), the toxicology section analyzes biological specimens (primarily blood and urine) for the presence of alcohol and/or drugs in cases involving driving under the influence (DUI). Coroner's cases may also be analyzed in the laboratory to assist with the determination of cause of death. Much of the same type of instrumentation used in the controlled substances section is used in the toxicology section. Unfortunately, the analytical parameters for the analysis of drugs from body fluids are different from those analyzed in the controlled substances section, which prevents the use of the same equipment for both types of analyses. Training for this section often requires one year.

- *Forensic biology and molecular biochemistry.* Forensic DNA analysis allows for comparisons to be made between an individual's genetic makeup and biological evidence found at a crime scene. Current needs include robotic methods to replace the time-consuming process of extracting biological fluids and tissues, including differentials for semen strains; access to microchip technology to enhance and advance DNA testing methods; and sampling devices for stabilizing evidence during in-field collection. According to the ASCLD (2004), the tasks of the forensic biology or pre-DNA biology section include locating stains and identifying body fluids (e.g., blood, semen, or saliva). Chemical and microscopic methods are used. Training for the forensic biology section can require up to six months and when combined with DNA testing can require up to two years.

- *Trace evidence evaluation.* Trace evidence materials include transfer evidence of all types except biological fluids. These commonly include paints, hairs, fibers, glass, and building materials. Current needs include standardization of trace analysis methodologies, enhancements of non-destructive techniques for analysis of materials, and development and coordination of databases. According to the ASCLD (2004), the trace evidence section examines a wide variety of evidence not elsewhere analyzed. It may include microscopic examinations of aforementioned evidence such as hairs and fibers or glass, or it may involve analyzing accelerants from a suspected arson scene. This section uses a wide range of expensive equipment. Training for individuals working in this section may be in excess of two years due to the wide range of materials encountered.

- *Controlled substance examinations.* The determination of controlled substances is the most common service delivered by forensic laboratories all over the world. Current needs include standardization of methods, automation of sampling and analysis, remote sensing equipment, and non-disruptive sampling. According to the ASCLD (2004), the chemist analyzes materials for the presence of controlled substances such as cocaine, heroin, and marijuana, as well as a wide range of prescription drugs. Products from clandestine laboratories, such as methamphetamine, are also analyzed by the controlled substances section. Many laboratories use sophisticated instrumentation for the analysis of drugs. These instruments are expensive to purchase and have an effective lifetime of approximately five years. Training for this position can take up to one year.

It is important to note that not all laboratories have units in all nine of these disciplines; frequently a laboratory will be able to process and analyze trace evidence such as fingerprints, but for sophisticated (and expensive) DNA analysis and interpretation of results, a smaller facility may have to contract with a larger facility that specializes in DNA testing. Moreover, not all cases involve DNA evidence; hence, many laboratories do not possess in-house DNA analysis capabilities. This distinction is important when considering the issue of evidence analysis backlogs and case processing backlogs, a challenge that will be explored fully in subsequent chapters.

Because they receive public funding, public laboratories function much like other bureaucracies. They are located within the executive branch of government, and operate at local, state, and federal levels. As such, they are expected to deliver a high level of fiscal accountability and operational efficiency, comply with appropriate legislation, and strive to produce a work product that is accurate, efficiently performed, and fair and objective to the end user and the final disposition of an adjudicated criminal case.

St. Clair (2003) states, "The level of government at which a public laboratory operates, as well as its dependency status, has a great deal to do with how easily funding is made available, how efficiently it operates, and the opportunities to which it has access." For example, although smaller local laboratories frequently operate more efficiently, larger state labs often can tap into a larger pool of funding and resources. Local laboratories can be mated with police departments, while larger state laboratories are partnered with a state police agency or an attorney general's office. Federal forensic laboratories, such as the laboratory of the Federal Bureau of Investigation, it would seem, capture the lion's share of anything: funding, resources, manpower—and high-profile cases. However, these kinds of laboratories face their own unique challenges while basking in the criminal justice limelight. There are many trade-offs in the overall operation of forensic laboratories, and as we shall see through the upcoming chapters, there is a wide variance in the way different laboratories function.

To the uninitiated (including those among the few who don't watch the television show *CSI*), the forensic laboratory can seem like a labyrinth of complex scientific endeavor. While television portrayals of forensic laboratories are quite different than real life (see Chapter 18 for a discussion of the so-called "*CSI* effect"), they do depict in some small way the general purpose of a forensic laboratory—to process, analyze, and interpret forensic evidence. But before the inner workings of a forensic laboratory can be appreciated, one must depart from the crime lab and head out into the field, to the crime scene, for an understanding of how forensic evidence is first handled.

The initial process of crime scene investigation greatly affects the quality of what bench analysts in forensic laboratories have to work with; crime scenes are not controlled environments, and crime lab analysts have no control over the condition in which the evidence arrives at their facility. This is why careful, deliberate, and meticulous processing of a crime scene is critical to the overall viability of forensic evidence.

On arrival, the crime scene investigator (CSI) conducts a scene "walk-through," which provides an overview of the entire scene and also allows the investigator the first opportunity to locate and view the body, identify valuable and/or fragile evidence, and determine initial investigative procedures providing for a systematic examination and documentation of the scene and the body. To ensure the integrity of the evidence, the CSI then establishes and maintains a chain of custody to safeguard against subsequent allegations of tampering, theft, planting, and contamination of evidence. The CSI employs photographic documentation of the scene to create a permanent historical record of it; the photographs provide detailed corroborating evidence that constructs a system of redundancy should questions arise concerning the report, witness statements, or position of evidence at the scene. In the same manner, the CSI undertakes written documentation of the scene to provide a permanent record that may be used to correlate with and enhance photographic documentation, refresh recollections, and record observations about the scene and the location of pertinent evidence.

If there is a body at the scene of the crime, the CSI will check it, the clothing, and the scene itself for consistency or inconsistency of trace evidence and indicate location where evidence is found. The photographic and written documentation of evidence on the body allows the investigator to obtain a permanent historical record of that evidence. To maintain chain of custody, forensic evidence must be collected, preserved, and transported properly. In addition to all of the physical evidence visible on the body, blood and other body fluids present must be photographed and documented prior to collection and transport. Fragile evidence (that which can be easily contaminated, lost, or altered) must also be collected and/or preserved to maintain chain of custody and to assist in determination of cause, manner, and circumstances of death. Finally, the CSI conducts a post-investigative walk-through to bring closure to the scene investigation and to ensure that important evidence has been collected and the scene has been processed.

THE EVIDENCE: GARBAGE IN, GARBAGE OUT

CSIs are taught to observe Locard's exchange principle, which states that whenever two objects come into contact, a transfer of material will occur; trace evidence that is transferred can be used to associate objects, individuals, or locations (Locard, 1930). The integrity and significance of trace material as associative evidence relies on proper detection, collection, and preservation, and an understanding of the transfer and persistence of trace evidence will assist the examiner in interpreting the significance of the analytical results. Because trace evidence is a building block of a criminal case, proper collection and preservation of this evidence will ensure its integrity when it arrives at the forensic laboratory for analysis. To provide proper protocol, the U.S. Department of Justice (DOJ, 1999) created its *Trace Evidence Recovery Guidelines,* which describe procedures and techniques for the documentation, detection, collection, and preservation of trace evidence from crime scenes, individuals, and items submitted to the laboratory for examination.

Proper documentation is one of the most important aspects of trace evidence collection. When a case is initiated, a file specific for that case must be created to contain the case documentation for the length of time required by prevailing laws. Documentation of questioned and known trace evidence collection, whether done in a laboratory or at a scene, must include permanent notes about date (and time, when appropriate) of the collection, name of person or persons collecting the evidence, a descriptive listing of item or items collected, a unique identifier for each item collected such as an item number and case number, and location of each item (documented by notes, sketches, measurements, photographs, or a combination of these). Importantly, the chain of custody for each item must be initiated upon collection and maintained until final disposition.

Guarding against contamination and/or loss of trace evidence is an imperative. General principles and practices to avoid evidence contamination and loss include the following:

- Contact between items and personnel before the appropriate trace evidence has been secured should be restricted.
- Appropriate protective apparel, such as laboratory coats and disposable gloves, must be worn to prevent contamination from the clothing of the examiner. The apparel must be changed as necessary to avoid contamination or transfer between evidentiary items, locations, and personnel.
- Items being collected for trace evidence examination must be handled as little as possible to minimize loss of the trace evidence and to limit exposure of the items to contaminants.
- Collect, package, and seal items individually in appropriate packaging. Keep items in a secure, sealed package until the item is processed in a controlled environment.
- Equipment and work surfaces used during collection and examination must be cleaned in an appropriate manner before processing begins and as often as necessary during processing to prevent contamination.
- Adhesive lift materials (used for collection, storage, or both) must be maintained in a manner to avoid contamination. Caution should be used to prevent tape edges from contacting any potentially contaminated surfaces.
- Evidence examination areas should have adequate lighting, easily cleaned surfaces, and a physical environment designed to restrict excessive air currents, static electricity, and general foot traffic.
- The examination of questioned and known items for trace evidence must be conducted separately in different locations, at different times, or both, to prevent contamination. It is recommended that questioned items with the most probative value be examined first.
- Any contact, condition, or situation that could cause contamination or otherwise compromise the trace evidence examination must be documented and communicated between the laboratory analyst or analysts and the submitter.

CSIs are instructed in the proper detection, collection, and preservation techniques related to evidence at a crime scene:

- When selecting detection, collection, and preservation methods and the processing sequence, consider the circumstances of the case, ambient conditions, the discriminatory power of the different techniques, and the need to preserve or collect other types of evidence.
- Record the techniques used for detection, collection, and preservation of the evidentiary items and the location from which they are removed.
- Methods used for detecting trace evidence include but are not limited to general visual searches; visual searches assisted by different types of illumination, such as oblique lighting and alternate light sources (UV, laser, high intensity); and visual searches assisted by magnification.
- The trace evidence recovery or collection techniques used should be the most direct and least intrusive technique or techniques practical. Collection techniques include picking, lifting, scraping, vacuum sweeping, combing, and clipping.
- Appropriate preservation and packaging of trace evidence and items to be examined for trace evidence will vary. Appropriate packaging must prevent loss or contamination of the trace evidence.

- All evidence packages must be properly sealed in a manner to prevent tampering and eliminate loss or contamination of the trace evidence through open edges.
- Small or loose trace evidence must be secured in clean, unused primary containers such as paper packets or petri dishes. The primary container should then be appropriately secured in an envelope or paper bag.
- Large items, such as whole garments, should preferably be sealed individually in clean, unused packaging.
- Clothing and other items that are wet must be air dried as soon as possible, without exposure to heat or sunlight, in a secured area in a manner that will prevent loss or contamination of trace evidence. An arrangement to collect any trace evidence that may fall from the item during drying should be used.
- Small or manageable items at a crime scene that bear visible, firmly attached trace evidence should be documented, packaged intact, and transported to the laboratory for examination.
- Items at a crime scene that bear visible but easily lost trace evidence or items that are impractical to transport should be documented and the trace evidence collected by an appropriate technique.

Security of the evidence, employed through the proper chain of custody, is essential:

- Trace evidence shall remain in secure, controlled-access areas, protected from loss, damage, or contamination. It must have a documented and continuous chain of custody from the time of evidence collection until the time the evidence is admitted into court or the case has been disposed and the evidence is no longer needed.
- The security and integrity of evidence is the responsibility of all persons who may identify, collect, package, store, transport, or examine evidentiary items.

Properly collected, documented, and preserved forensic evidence is delivered to the forensic laboratory, with the proper chain of custody intact. The *chain of custody* is a process used to maintain and document the chronological history of the forensic evidence as it circulates from crime scene to laboratory and throughout the crime lab's various analysis units. Chain-of-custody information includes the name or initials of the individual collecting the evidence, each person or entity subsequently having custody of it, dates the items were collected or transferred, agency and case number, victim's or suspect's name, and a brief description of the item. Most forensic evidence is not processed immediately, and must be stored properly in secure lockers or other storage devices at the law enforcement agency or at the forensic laboratory to prevent further degradation and optimize the analysis process.

When it is ready to be analyzed, the evidence is taken by the analyst to a clean, contamination-free work area and unpackaged carefully. The evidence is visually inspected and documented (including being photographed) before any analysis is conducted. The analyst then determines which tests need to be performed, and whether or not there is a sufficient amount of evidence to test. The portion of the evidence to be tested is prepared and the process documented before it is subjected to the various steps in the chemical or mass spectrometer analysis, for example. Some tests require a number of steps in the process, and each step is documented by the analyst before continuing. When finished, the analyst properly repackages and relabels the evidence, again, to maintain the chain of custody, and the evidence is returned to storage. The results of the tests must then be interpreted, and a comprehensive report prepared. This process may be repeated if the evidence is retested.

This process is an intricate one, with numerous opportunities for technical or human error to be introduced. Kruglick points out, "No other type of evidence is exposed to anywhere near as many opportunities for destruction, mishandling, contamination, and any other conceivable catastrophe that can be brought on by human or natural error, than is forensic evidence."

The goal of a laboratory's trace evidence analysis program is to provide quality trace evidence assessment, identification, comparison, and reconstruction associated with forensic investigations. Guidelines from the DOJ (2000) indicate that a quality assurance program should be established and maintained in forensic laboratories. The DOJ adds that personnel responsible for the program must have that responsibility clearly stated in their position descriptions and should have direct authoritative access to the highest level of management concerning laboratory policy. The quality assurance program must ensure that all procedures, examinations, and reports associated with trace evidence are within the established guidelines. Thus, the forensic laboratory must maintain documentation on significant aspects of trace evidence analysis procedures, including any related documents or laboratory records pertinent to the analysis or interpretation of results, to create a documented audit trail. According to the DOJ (2000), documentation should also exist for the areas discussed in the following subsections.

Test Methods and Procedures

The documents must describe in detail the protocols currently used for the analytical testing of trace evidence. The protocols must identify the reference standards and required controls. Revisions must be clearly documented and appropriately authorized.

1. Authenticated reference samples (list the source and include the data document or the manufacturers' letter of authenticity)
2. Reagents documentation (date of receipt, opening, and preparation)
3. Evidence-handling protocols
4. Equipment calibration and maintenance records
5. Equipment inventory (manufacturer, model, serial number, and acquisition date)
6. Proficiency testing data
7. Personnel training and qualification records
8. Quality assurance and audit records
9. Quality assurance manual
10. Safety manuals
11. Material safety data sheets.

Equipment and Materials

Only suitable and properly operating equipment should be employed. Monitoring of equipment parameters should be conducted and documented. The manufacturer's operational manual for each instrument should be available at the workplace.

Materials and chemicals must be of suitable quality and demonstrated to be compatible with the methods employed. Documentation must be maintained for chemicals and must include the date received and the date of opening or preparation. Written formulas must be available for all chemical reagents produced in the laboratory. Labels for reagents prepared within the laboratory must include the identity, concentration (when appropriate), and date of preparation; the identity of the personnel preparing the chemicals; and the storage requirements, if applicable, according to laboratory policies and/or appropriate regulations. Commercial and laboratory-prepared reagents must be tested against a reference sample prior to use in casework. The results of the test must be documented. Supplies must be inspected for cleanliness appropriate for the analysis performed.

Analytical Procedures

The analysis of unknown trace evidence can be accomplished by a variety of methods. Non-destructive tests should be performed first. Limited sample size, the possibility of future analyses, and other limitations should be considered before destructive tests are performed. Appropriate reference samples or collections must be authenticated. Refer to established published procedures. The laboratory's quality control guidelines should contain specific protocols to assess critical parameters in normal operations. Instruments must be routinely monitored to ensure that performance is maintained and documented. Instrumentation used in the analysis of trace evidence must be tested with reference standards, when appropriate, to ensure that the instruments are performing adequately. Documentation must be maintained to create an audit trail that can be reviewed. Documentation must contain sufficient information to allow a technical peer to evaluate case notes and interpret the data. Documentation should include data obtained through the analytical process. It should also include information regarding the packaging of the evidence on receipt and the condition of the evidence. All documentation of procedures, standards, controls, observations, results of the tests, charts, graphics, photographs, printouts (hard copy and disk), spectra, and communications generated during an examination must be preserved according to written laboratory policy.

Reports should contain the following: name and address of the laboratory; case identifier; name, address, and identifier of the contributor; date of receipt; date of report; descriptive list of submitted evidence; identification of the methodology; and identity and signature of examiner.

Results and Conclusions

A case review should be conducted by a minimum of two personnel. The review should consist of a technical review and an administrative review. A technical review should be conducted on each report and the notes and data supporting the report must be reviewed independently by a technical peer. Once a report has been reviewed, initials or other appropriate markings must be maintained in the case file by the personnel conducting the review. An administrative review should be conducted on each report to ensure adherence to laboratory policy and editorial correctness. Laboratory administration will determine the course of action if an examiner and the reviewer fail to concur.

The quality assurance coordinator or other designated personnel will review all test documentation and compare the results with the information received from the manufacturer of the test. The quality assurance coordinator will provide a written summary report for each proficiency test to the participating examiner or other appropriate personnel as established by the laboratory policy. This review should be conducted in a timely manner. All original notes, records, and other data pertaining to the open proficiency test results must be retained according to laboratory policy. Prior to a proficiency test, all participating laboratory personnel should be provided with the specific policies, procedures, and criteria for any corrective action that may be taken as a result of a discrepancy in a proficiency test. It is the responsibility of the quality assurance coordinator or designated personnel to ensure that discrepancies are acknowledged, the reasons for any discrepancies are determined, and any subsequent corrective action is documented.

Any discrepancy in a proficiency test determined to be administrative (clerical, sample confusion, improper storage, or documentation) will be corrected according to established laboratory policy. Any discrepancy in a proficiency test determined to be the result of a systematic error may require a review of all relevant casework since the trace evidence section's last successfully completed proficiency test using that equipment. Once the cause of the discrepancy has been identified and corrective action has been taken, examiners in the relevant area should be made aware of the appropriate corrective action. Any difference in a proficiency test result proven to be the consequence of an analytical or interpretative discrepancy may prohibit the personnel who produced the discrepant result from further examination of case evidence until the cause of the discrepancy is identified and corrected. The quality assurance coordinator or designated personnel will determine the need to audit prior cases according to established laboratory policy. Before resuming analysis or interpretation of casework, one additional proficiency test should be successfully completed by the personnel responsible for the discrepancy. The results of all proficiency tests should be maintained by the laboratory according to established policy.

Proficiency Testing

Proficiency testing pertains to examiners, support analysts, technical managers, and technical consultants engaged in the field of trace evidence. At least one proficiency test must be completed annually by each of the personnel. Test samples must be of sufficient quality so that a conclusion can be drawn from the results of the analysis. All test samples must be handled and stored appropriately to maintain their integrity and condition.

Validation

The laboratory must use validated techniques and procedures, and techniques and procedures currently accepted by the scientific community should be considered valid. New techniques developed for the characterization, identification, and comparison of trace evidence should be based on accepted scientific principles. Validation studies should be performed as soon as practicable to establish the technique's reliability. It is important that the results of validation studies be shared as soon as possible with the scientific community through presentations at scientific and professional meetings and through timely publication in peer-reviewed, scientific journals.

Laboratory Audits

Audits should be conducted at least once a year by the technical manager in conjunction with the personnel responsible for the quality assurance program. Records of each audit should be maintained and should include the date of the audit, name of the person conducting the audit, findings, and corrective actions, if necessary. The laboratory must establish an audit schedule. Case files to be reviewed should be chosen randomly.

REFERENCES

American Academy of Forensic Sciences. Status and Needs of Forensic Science Service Providers: A Report to Congress. Available at http://www.aafs.org/pdf/180%20day%20study.pdf#search=%22 the%20majority%20of%20forensic%20laboratories%20in%20the%20United%20States%20engage %20in%20the%20following%20nine%20disciplines%20%22.

American Society of Crime Laboratory Directors/Laboratory Accreditation Board. *Accreditation Manual.* Garner, N.C.: ASCLD, 1994.

American Society of Crime Lab Directors. *180-Day Study.* Garner, N.C.: ASCLD, 2004.

Locard E. The analysis of dust traces, part I. *American Journal of Police Science,* 1:276–298, 1930.

St. Clair JJ. *Crime Laboratory Management.* Boston: Elsevier Science/Academic Press, 2003.

Technical Working Group on DNA Analysis Methods. *Guidelines for a Quality Assurance Program for DNA Analysis. Crime Laboratory Digest,* 22:21–43, 1995.

U.S. Department of Justice. Trace evidence recovery guidelines. *Forensic Science Communications,* 1(3), October 1999.

U.S. Department of Justice. Trace evidence quality assurance guidelines. *Forensic Science Communications,* 2(1), January 2000.

RECOMMENDED READING

Kruglick K. *A Beginner's Primer on the Investigation of Forensic Evidence.* Accessed at http://www.kruglaw. com.

CHAPTER 4

THE U.S. FORENSIC LABORATORY SYSTEM UNDER SIEGE

As we have seen in Chapters 1 and 2, a number of stakeholders in the criminal justice system hold high expectations of the ability of the forensic laboratory community to deliver timely, accurate forensic analyses and examinations for the adjudication of cases within the U.S. legal system. There has been no shortage of detractors of forensic science, with the bulk of the criticism, echoed by the media, coming from legal scholars and social scientists. This criticism, some of it rife with hyperbole, has been unrelenting of late. Possley (2004) observes, "Revelations of shoddy work and poorly run facilities have shaken the criminal justice system like never before, raising doubts about the reputation of labs as unbiased advocates for scientific truth. The far-reaching crime lab scandals roiling the courts are unlike other flaws in the criminal justice system—the rogue prosecutor, the incompetent defense attorney, the unscrupulous cop—because for years the reputation of the labs had been unquestioned. But the consequence of lab errors, whether due to incompetence, imprecision or fraud, is frequently the same—an innocent person behind bars."

While it has been faulted for examples of malfeasance and misconduct, forensic science takes a hit most often for its implicated role in wrongful convictions. *The Chicago Tribune* examined a number of the approximately 200 DNA and death row exoneration cases since 1986 and reported that more than 25 percent of these cases involved "faulty crime lab work or testimony." Possley (2004) states, "In recent years, evidence of problems ranging from negligence to outright deception has been uncovered at crime labs in at least 17 states. Among the failures were faulty blood analysis, fingerprinting errors, flawed hair comparisons, and the contamination of evidence used in DNA testing."

Scandal related to missteps in the laboratory hasn't been limited to small, underfunded forensic facilities; the Federal Bureau of Investigation (FBI) Laboratory, long considered the nation's top forensic powerhouse, has been rocked by allegations of exaggerated claims in pattern identification science, as well as lack of adherence to protocol. In the mid-1990s, a whistle-blower in the FBI Laboratory touched off a broad inquiry over allegations of improper handling of evidence. It led to the firing of several lab officials and the overhaul of the facility's protocols and procedures. It also set a precedent for the continued scrutiny of crime laboratories across the country by various stakeholders in the U.S. criminal justice system.

Possley (2004) notes, "In most cases, however, lab problems have come to light only after defendants have challenged their convictions. Given the sheer volume of cases that labs handle, the discovery of even a single flawed analysis raises the prospect of re-examining hundreds, if not thousands, of cases." Possley adds, "In many jurisdictions, the task of re-evaluating that many cases is so daunting that authorities have declined to conduct broad audits, despite evidence that analysts have committed errors or engaged in fraudulent practices. One of their well-placed fears: that uncovering additional problems in a lab would spawn lawsuits or unravel an untold number of convictions."

The problems with flawed forensic science—whether alleged or real or somewhere in between—are coming to be widely recognized in the profession. Barry A. J. Fisher (2002), in his well-regarded and popular textbook *Techniques of Crime Scene Investigation*, notes in his introduction the following scenarios, which are based in fact, not fiction:

- Planting evidence at a crime scene to point to a defendant
- Collecting evidence without a warrant by claiming exigent circumstances
- Falsifying laboratory examinations to enhance the prosecution's case
- Ignoring evidence at a crime scene that might exonerate a suspect or be a mitigating factor
- Reporting on forensic tests not actually done out of a misguided belief that the tests are unnecessary
- Fabricating scientific opinions based on invalid interpretations of tests or evidence to assist the prosecution
- Examining physical evidence when not qualified to do so
- Extending expertise beyond one's knowledge
- Using unproved methodologies
- Overstating an expert opinion by using "terms of art" unfamiliar to juries
- Failing to report a colleague, superior, or subordinate who engages in any of these activities to the proper authorities.

Fisher is director of the Los Angeles County Sheriff's Department's forensic laboratory, past president of the American Academy of Forensic Science, past chairman of the American Society of Crime Laboratory Directors, and past president of the International Association of Forensic Sciences. That he acknowledges some problems in the forensic science community is indicative of the field's willingness to explore its hindrances, its missteps, and its challenges, and establish a course of self-reflection and self-correction.

Fisher (2002) asserts, "Criminal justice practitioners should know how to behave and what actions are right and honorable. For whatever reasons, notions of ethics, duty, and honor are ideals that have been forgotten by some. . . . As humans, we are subject to mistakes. It is impossible to handle every investigation without making some mistakes. At best, we can try to make as few errors as possible and to learn from past errors."

Fisher (2002) emphasizes that discernment must be utilized when attempting to separate fact from fiction in the great debate over the quality and accuracy of forensic science. "Generally speaking, people have been rooted out who have been shown to be doing terrible things. There are a few instances where there are some really bad apples that need to be dealt with," Fisher says. "I think it is disingenuous to claim faulty lab work was done in cases where the laboratory work was conducted 15 or 20 years ago, and older technology was used. It's not right to state in cases where a conviction resulted, and new technology clearly shows that DNA could not have come from the defendant, that this was an error. In such instances, a suggestion of inappropriate conduct on the part of forensic scientists is wrong, yet some commentators use those situations to blame crime labs and analysts for misconduct."

"However," Fisher says, "when analysts and forensic scientists are doing wrong, blatantly or flagrantly, that is not acceptable. We are working in a fishbowl environment, and that should mean total transparency in what we do in the lab. So when you have instances of malfeasance or ethical lapses, those are readily apparent, as they should be, and they should be addressed. But to look at a few cases where there have been errors, without comparing that to the hundreds of thousands of cases labs handle, is, again, inappropriate."

Fisher says he believes these unfair comparisons spring from ulterior motives designed to undermine the forensic laboratories' role in the criminal justice system. "I have come to believe that people are using us to further their political agendas," Fisher asserts. "For example, that individuals who are against the death penalty who are using alleged lab errors to make a claim that the death penalty should be done away with. My personal opinions aside on this issue, I don't believe there is a clear connection between the two in all cases. I think that Innocence Project groups have helped create a cottage industry of lawyers and defense experts who are looking at these cases much more closely. This is not a bad thing, because it is important to take a critical look at what's going on in these capital cases. If there have been problems, they need to be brought to the forefront and dealt with. But what oftentimes happens is they use these cases in subsequent litigation to point fingers and raise doubts about what is going on in the field of forensic science instead of litigating the specific case. And I have some problems with that."

Going to the heart of the situation, beyond the misconduct of a few individual scientists and analysts, is the posturing by prosecutors and defense attorneys in the courtroom, Fisher says, adding, "Frequently, the defense bar makes a claim of some sort involving alleged wrong-doing, and the prosecutor looks at that and wonders if it's sour grapes or just the typical pos-turing that goes on in trials." Fisher adds, "One of the things I agree with that Barry Scheck and Peter Neufeld have been calling for, is the need for some sort of review process when a serious problem related to a forensic examination is uncovered. Some problems are systemic, like the problems experienced at the Houston crime lab. It is a fair question to ask how could these mistakes have gone undetected for so long."

Fisher says he suspects part of the difficulty can be traced to the field's status as being largely unregulated. "There are very few states that require crime labs to be accredited or individuals to be certified, and I think that's an issue that must be attended to. Would you knowingly go to a hospital that wasn't accredited or deal with a doctor who wasn't licensed? Why should it be any different with forensic laboratories and their analysts? It's something to think about."

Author and forensic science media consultant Lawrence Kobilinsky, Ph.D., a professor and science adviser to the president of John Jay College of Criminal Justice, says that the criticisms from commentators, while occasionally warranted, detract from the first order of business—improving forensic science. "There are some people who have made reputations based upon their criticisms of forensic science," Kobilinsky says. "The bottom line is that solutions need to be found, instead of standing around and finding fault and pointing fingers. If eyewitness identification is not working, for example, we need to address the issue and look at the way line-ups are done, or the way confessions are handled. There are ways we can improve the system, and that's where we should focus our energies. I do not think forensic science is broken, but I think it can be improved; however, I don't think the field needs drastic changes just because there are some isolated problems that can be fixed. Nothing in life is perfect or absolute. It's an old cliché that to err is human, and where there are people involved in testing, there are going to be errors. These things happen but there are also safeguards to help catch them. Things do fall between the cracks, but the truth of the matter is that it is possible to get a handle on how often these problems come up, and figure out how to prevent them."

The days when forensic evidence and the methods used to test it were accepted on blind faith appear to be over, according to Arvizu (2000) who states, "All too often, forensic evi-dence is accepted at face value. Yet even where the test method meets *Daubert* criteria, the method as performed by the laboratory may be flawed. Perhaps attorneys are unaware that forensic laboratories can—and do—make serious errors during the testing process. Perhaps they are unaware that laboratory test results can be subject to valid and compelling technical challenges. Or perhaps attorneys simply don't have the necessary scientific or financial resources. For whatever reasons, counsel is often unprepared, unwilling, or unable to investigate and assess the scientific validity and technical pedigree of forensic evidence. In almost any industry, it would be a serious lapse of due diligence to simply accept and use test laboratory results without question. In the case of forensic laboratories, it can result in a miscarriage of justice."

The critics assert that there is a widening gap between principle and practice. Arvizu (2000) launches this grenade: "In principle, forensic laboratories operate in an objective and scientifically sound manner to consistently generate unbiased data that are accurate, technically defensible, and thoroughly documented. Would that it were so. Although this theoretical world is a reasonable goal, and although many laboratories strive to achieve it, it does not represent today's reality."

"I think there was a time when everything was gee-whiz and people were saying, 'Wow, isn't DNA and forensic science wonderful?'" says Paul Ferrara, Ph.D., director of the Virginia Department of Forensic Science and board member of the Virginia Institute of Forensic Science and Medicine. "And now it's viewed with suspicion. There are people who have a fundamental distrust of government no matter what, and those individuals who have a conspiracy theory to advance will believe what the detractors say. There's not much you can do to change that, except continue to deliver the same high level of quality your lab always has."

Arvizu (2000) enumerates what she calls the common threads running through criticisms of forensic laboratories' performance: First, the existence of serious problems "not recognized, acknowledged, and acted upon" until they were identified by observers from outside of the laboratory; laboratories were "unable to prevent serious problems from occurring" because they did not effectively monitor their own performance; and finally, "the systemic problems that were identified in these forensic laboratories are the predictable outcome of laboratories that perform production-scale testing without benefit of a strong and effective quality assurance program." Arvizu adds, "Practicing good science on a day-in and day-out basis requires more than simply disciplinary knowledge and individual initiative. For decades, the scientific community has recognized that a production laboratory needs formal systems, controls, and processes to institutionalize the practice and documentation of good science."

"In the last five years or so in particular, the scrutiny has increased considerably and unfortunately, when a mistake is made in forensic science, it impacts people's lives, either through incarceration or a death sentence," acknowledges W. Earl Wells, president of the American Society of Crime Lab Directors (ASCLD) and laboratory director of the South Carolina Law Enforcement Division. "That's the weight we, in the crime lab, carry on our shoulders, and that is why we take our profession very seriously. We don't have the luxury of going back and correcting the mistakes we did make, unlike some other professions. I think one of the things about to occur in the near future, necessitated by a Congressional mandate, is the convening of an independent committee by the National Academy of Sciences to evaluate forensic science. If they will conduct an unbiased examination and evaluation of forensic science, I think we will have a valuable product that comes out of the process. It is my understanding that there will be great pains taken to keep people off of the committee who have an agenda to promote, and that safeguard will lend quite a bit of credibility to their findings."

Wells says he is aggravated by those who exaggerate and capitalize on what he calls isolated incidents of mistakes by forensic practitioners. "When you consider the thousands and thousands of cases that are handled daily by crime labs all over the country, and yet you only hear about the problem cases, it is frustrating. You rarely, if ever, hear about the successes that crime labs experience daily. If you compare the problem cases that have made the news and which are put forth by the defense community to the number of cases that have no problems—that is a miniscule number. Of course, it's the cases that make headlines that are held up as criticism of the profession, and other cases are invisible. I suspect we are dealing with people who have personal agendas and they are putting the good of community and the good of the justice system and the judicial process to promote their own personal gain, whatever that may be."

Houde (2006) observes, "If only it were a perfect world. All of our tests would be specific, all criminalists would be well trained, well spoken and proceed with all due caution before announcing test results. Of course we are human and make mistakes, but knowing this we design our procedures to catch mistakes before they escape from the lab, resulting in an erroneous report. . . . It's how a person handles a mistake that really counts. Do they hide it, fabricating a lab report? Or do they come clean, and issue an amended lab report acknowledging the error and correcting it?" Houde comments further, "Of the thousands of dedicated professionals working in the forensic sciences, a few bad apples have been discovered. A few have been caught 'dry-labbing,' where evidence isn't really examined but results are written anyway. A few others have been found to be incompetent, incorrectly performing tests that they don't understand, even after having received training. One or two have been exposed as outright frauds, testifying to practically anything the prosecutor or detectives wanted to hear. When they are caught, they are marked forever. . . . Credibility is the only thing a criminalist really has and once lost, it cannot be easily recovered."

Don Wyckoff, director of the Idaho State Police Laboratory, chair of the American Society of Crime Laboratory Directors/Laboratory Accreditation Board (ASCLD/LAB), and a member of the board of directors of the National Forensic Science Technology Center, concurs: "No matter what, if humans are involved, unfortunately, there may be some kind of error. You must also consider how science has progressed; what we were doing 20 or 30 years ago, which is when a lot of these cases originated, is not what is being done today, and many old cases are being judged against the newest technology. There may have been some questionable people, like Fred Zain, involved in what are now high-profile cases who may have lacked training or used inferior procedures to arrive at their conclusions. There have been analysts who attempted to make results appear better or worse than they were, or they have testified to things they truly believed in at the time, and many did not have the training to critically review what they were testifying to. These are isolated incidents, and I don't think they are indicative of a system that is broken."

THE DIRTY DOZEN: COMMON CHARGES LEVIED AGAINST LABS

Without formal, rigorous quality assurance programs, Arvizu (2000) asserts that forensic laboratories will be plagued by poor control of contamination and environmental conditions, ineffective internal technical reviews, inadequate documentation of laboratory work, inappropriately trained or unqualified analysts, and a complete lack of independent oversight and monitoring. We now explore the various charges that critics have made regarding the performance of forensic science in general and crime laboratories in particular.

Charge No. 1: Lack of Transparency

Whitehurst (2004) states, "Reported failures within forensic crime labs lead us to question why. The U.S. justice system's addressing questions of guilt and innocence through discovery in an adversarial process should theoretically act as the quality assurance (QA) mechanism for forensic crime laboratories. However that process has been found to have failed across the nation."

"Transparency" of an organization is a favorite term used by QA experts to describe a process of optimal functioning for the benefit of all stakeholders. It is a word that is being used increasingly by those describing a desired reform of forensic laboratories' daily operations. To this end, proper documentation is essential for the QA process; health-care practitioners have long recognized the adage that if it wasn't documented, it didn't happen. Kelly and Wearne (1998) state, "Examiners have proved remarkably loath to write up their bench notes in any adequate scientific manner. No names, no chain of custody history, no testing chronology, no details of supervisory oversight, no confirmatory tests, no signatures . . . what they do contain is obfuscation and overstated conclusions written in an often-incomprehensible style that some experts have termed 'forensonics.' Terms like 'match' or 'consistent with' are common; chronicled scientific procedures and protocols to justify them are not. The motive seems to be to say as little as possible as unintelligibly as possible with what passes for scientific jargon and process."

For example, in their analysis of the FBI crime laboratory scandal, Kelly and Wearne (1998) note, "Since lab reports are discoverable and have to be provided to the defense, the FBI lab believes that as little as possible should be given away. The approach to research is no different. The publication of findings or methodologies might be used to undermine the prosecution of cases, so no dissemination has been the rule. In short, the FBI's interpretation of the adversarial approach on which the U.S. judicial system is based works to serve neither science nor truth."

As part of a federal monolith, it may come as no surprise that the FBI Laboratory is perceived as an impenetrable fortress; however, critics believe the same ideology exists at other forensic laboratories operating at all levels of government. Jonakait (1991) asserts that "Since forensic labs have never allowed a detailed look at the caliber of their work, only fragmentary information is available. Those fragments, however, reveal a consistent pattern of unacceptable errors and inaccuracies." This charge was levied in the 1990s, when the only study of forensic laboratories was a 1978 report undertaken and funded by the Law Enforcement Assistance Administration (LEAA), which many believed painted the most complete picture of the quality of these laboratories at the time. Jonakait (1991) says that initially, labs were "somewhat reluctant" to participate in the survey based on concerns about their independence, that standardized methods might be required, and that the confidentiality and anonymity of results might be compromised. The LEAA assured the labs that they would remain anonymous and that all research and statistical data would be considered confidential, because anonymity and the confidentiality of the data would ensure a high rate of participation in a voluntary program.

Jonakait (1991) reports that this three-year investigation was the first broad, nationwide proficiency examination in which known samples in a wide range of forensic specialties were sent to labs for analysis. In the study, "unacceptable responses" included wrong outcomes as well as any correct answers given for the wrong reasons, unnecessarily equivocal results, and inconclusive results unsupported by the analytical work or based on improper or inadequate methods. All such results, the report stated, could pose dangers to criminal justice. For example, an inconclusive response could appear to be inculpatory although it should have provided exculpatory evidence.

One illustration of this point is a paint comparison. The LEAA report stated that in one test, one-fifth of the labs reported that two different paint samples could have shared a common origin. Although these analyses were not erroneous, the report stated that if the labs had conducted a more complete round of testing, they would have concluded that the paint samples did not come from the same source; thus, instead of presenting what should have been exculpatory information, these facilities would have presented an inculpatory report. Jonakait (1991) calls this error "inexcusable." Although the study's committee stated that it does not criticize the reporting of inconclusive results, when appropriate, since laboratories may be dealing with an inadequate amount of evidence or a contaminated sample, Jonakait emphasizes, "This is not the case in this test sample. The state of the art in criminalistics is certainly advanced to the point that these samples of paint should be easily distinguished by techniques available to any laboratory attempting to conduct paint examinations."

In another test, laboratories were asked whether two bloodstains could have shared a common origin; the LEAA study revealed that 52 out of 132 labs correctly reported that the stains were different, but 14 labs made typing errors. Jonakait reports that just about 29 percent of labs performed the analysis correctly. The LEAA study said these results were "unacceptable." Jonakait (1991) states somewhat obviously, "Incorrect analyses can lead to miscarriage of justice not only by condemning the innocent, but also by helping to free the guilty." He adds, ". . . the most thorough study of crime labs ever done proves crime lab performance is dangerously poor."

Forensic practitioners' documentation habits, as a way to uphold transparency, have continued to come under fire. Bashinski (1984) writes, "Many forensic scientists regard their written reports merely as a means of recording their analytical results, rather than as vehicles for conveying their conclusions, in the belief that the courtroom, not the report, is the appropriate place for interpretation. However, critical decisions about the case may be made by others in advance of trial on the basis of the written report and without consultation with the criminalist." Bashinski believes that the true purpose of any laboratory report should be "to communicate to its reader both the analytical results and the conclusions of the analyst, conveying the essence of what the expert would say if asked for his opinion in court."

Bashinski (1984) states, "Most criminalists acknowledge that one of their fundamental professional responsibilities is to provide interpretation of their laboratory results. They accept the premise that their obligation as forensic scientists goes beyond conducting analyses and generating data to include the formulation of conclusions based on their analytical results and the presentation of those conclusions in the form of an expert opinion in court." Although criminalists are aware of the importance of their role as witnesses, Bashinski observes that ". . . other than the general exhortation to be accurate, honest, and impartial in testimony, there has been relatively little attention paid in the literature to the substantive content of the interpretations offered in court by forensic scientists. There has been even less consideration given to another very significant aspect of their work, that of communicating laboratory findings in the form of written reports."

Bashinski (1984) explains further, ". . . Ignoring the impact of the written report can have serious consequences which should not be discounted. First, significant decisions about a case may be made in advance of trial by police officers and attorneys, based on their limited understanding of a laboratory report and without any contact with the criminalist . . . a report may be accepted at face value in court by stipulation with no opportunity for the analyst to explain the results. Since criminalists themselves often agonize over the interpretation of their own data, it should be anticipated that there is a significant risk that non-scientists will misinterpret a technical result, unless that result is very carefully explained in simple and unambiguous terms."

A forensic practitioner's report is the vehicle through which the defense may discover what physical evidence has been examined and what its potential significance may be. Bashinski (1984) cautions, "If the analytical data in a report are incomplete or if the criminalist has failed to provide a summary of his substantive conclusions derived from the data, a possibility exists that he will have omitted information which will prove critical at time of trial. Thus, the criminalist may have unwittingly obstructed the ability of the opposition to prepare its case."

"You have to write down your conclusions, you have to cite your sources, you have to source your data—no phantom data and no phantom databases, no making stuff up," asserts forensic scientist and author Brent Turvey, senior partner of Forensic Solutions LLC. "That's the big problem with many of the forensic science reports that exist; they cite nonsense databases or nonexistent databases, or phantom numbers, but they don't show where they get their data from. And they get angry when you ask."

In addition to facilitating transparency of a forensic laboratory's operations, proper documentation helps to "reduce a mass of analytical data to a concise, unambiguous conclusion (that) can be of immense benefit in the performance of the laboratory work itself and in preparation for any subsequent testimony," according to Bashinski (1984).

Documentation further serves to verify that all of the analyst's conclusions are fully supported by the analytical data. Bashinski (1984) notes that "Reflecting on the data allows the analyst to discover and rectify possible flaws or omissions in his work which he might otherwise discover, to his dismay, only the day before trial or worse yet while on the witness stand. Further, if the analyst takes the trouble at the outset to consider possible alternative interpretations of his data, and if he deliberates carefully over his conclusions while the facts are fresh in his mind, there is little chance of his being pressured to produce hasty, ill-considered opinions in the stress of the courtroom situation."

Thus, a forensic analyst's report should include both data and conclusive statements interpreting the data and should address in detail the substance of the opinions that are put forth in this critical communication vehicle. However, as Bashinski (1984) points out, there is a fine line between what constitutes sufficient and insufficient data or expertise when a case reaches the courtroom. "The fact that there may be a degree of uncertainty in his conclusions should not deter the forensic scientist from rendering expert opinions or from articulating those opinions in his written reports. It should, instead, inspire him to work very hard to define the limitations and uncertainty in his work. Awareness of his own limitations should motivate him to find ways to communicate to the ultimate users of his work, the jury, his best judgment as to what the degree of uncertainty in his analysis really is. Only in this way can he help the jury weigh his opinions appropriately, along with all the other information before them, to make the ultimate decision about the truth of the matter in the case at hand" (Bashinski, 1984).

"Honest people who just want to work cases and figure out what happened, those who don't have an agenda, are open to transparency," says Turvey. "People who have an agenda don't want their work looked at, and they want to be able to prove their theories without anyone checking it out or second-guessing their work. They get defensive about their work, and that's a red flag. Science demands constant review. If you are any good at your job, you want other people to look at your work; you also document what you did, how you did it, and how you support your findings, because you are proud of them. Forensic science is the only scientific community that does the exact opposite of that. Many forensic scientists do not want anyone looking at their data, and they get extremely defensive if you question them about it. That's not science, that's something else; it's science in the image of law enforcement, and that's a problem."

Charge No. 2: Tainted Science and the White-Coat Phenomenon

One of the most prominent critics of forensic laboratories is Paul Giannelli, a law professor at Case Western Reserve University in Cleveland, Ohio. Giannelli (2003) says the most egregious wrongdoing centers on poor science that leads to wrongful convictions of the innocent. Like many critics, Giannelli points to the analysis conducted by Innocence Project founders Barry Scheck and Peter Neufeld of 62 convictions that were later overturned due to what they called "tainted or fraudulent science." Giannelli claims that forensic science lacks a "truly scientific culture," or one with "an empirical basis for the most basic procedures." He says, "This results in an environment in which misconduct can too easily thrive. Stated another way, forensic science needs more science."

Terrence Kiely, J.D., L.L.M., professor of law, and director of the Center for Law and Science at DePaul University in Chicago, points to a case in Connecticut in which an African-American man was accused of raping a Caucasian woman. "A pubic comb of the woman was performed and some foreign hairs were found," Kiely says. "One of the top forensic hair analysts in the state decided it was male Negro pubic hair consistent with the defendant's. So he is convicted. On appeal, the smart public defender consulted with another forensic analyst, Dr. Terry Melton, of Mitotyping Technologies, an expert in mitochondrial DNA testing, who ran the mtDNA testing. She said that not only was it not the defendant who did the crime, but that the hair was not that of a black man, but that in fact it was the victim's hair. So on one side, you have one of the top hair analysts in the country who says, 'Well, using microscopy comparing this to that, the hair is consistent in all respects,' and on the other side, you have a top mtDNA expert who says, 'No way.' So you have a questionable discipline, hair analysis, pitted against DNA."

Many commentators have remarked on the white-coat phenomenon that can obscure tainted science. McRoberts et al. (2004) state, "One facet of the problem is that while those involved in forensic disciplines wear the white coat of science and portray themselves as scientists, they often do not operate under the same rules as those in other scientific pursuits." Kiely comments, "I tell my students this, and it is absolutely true . . . if you're involved in defending a case and forensic evidence is being used, you may face a serious problem. I call it the white coat-and-resume problem. That's where someone in court gets up and says, 'I wrote the book on the subject and I've been doing this for 25 years,' why *wouldn't* an ordinary person give them some credence? I remind my students that jurors are ordinary people, and they will listen to what this expert has to say very carefully."

Kiely says attorneys depend upon what has now become a basic strategy for defusing or poking holes in cases containing questionable forensic evidence or expert testimony. "The first thing you do as a defense attorney is you try to make the science go away. That's tough to do these days in some cases. Then you try to make the expert go away. With more and more ammunition in the literature, you have the opportunity of bouncing an expert who has been around forever. The third thing is you try to make what they say go away based upon their own premises. That's what's happening now in challenges to cases built on what could appear to be faulty forensic evidence."

Kiely says that going after an expert's credentials is one way to deconstruct a house of cards built on a shoddy or tainted scientific foundation. "I conducted a significant amount of research on experts' credentials, looking into how these professionals become a hair analysis expert or a footprint impression expert. The standards from the various forensic associations are quite high, but in many states, with a high school diploma and six weeks of training you can get into a lab and start working. So there needs to be a higher standard for training and hiring forensic professionals, coupled with better uniformity in laboratory procedures and oversight, which I think would address the issue of tainted science and mistakes made by analysts. And I mean accidental mistakes; intentional fraud, on the other hand, is another matter. The push for better training of analysts and better documentation is absolutely essential. There is never an excuse for shoddy science."

"When forensic scientists point to lack of funding and infrastructure, these are totally legitimate reasons not to be able to practice good science," says Turvey. "But the next thing out of their mouths needs to be, 'And because of that, I am not able to give complete, competent, or insightful results.' It's better to give no results than to give uninformed or erroneous results. The other thing is, they need to stop going into court and pretending to be psychic with their evidence interpretation. It would be a reasonable response if they didn't go into court and pretend they knew everything and pretend as if there were no problems. That's the biggest issue I have—the active, pathological, belligerent ignorance of the forensic science community to the problem of fraud and error. If they really believe in what their lab is doing, let's see their proficiencies. Put them on the table for all to see. How often are you right, and how often are you wrong? That's what we want to know. And if you can't answer that question, then you are being dishonest, in my view."

The theory of "garbage in, garbage out" is a fundamental axiom that can apply to almost any construct involving the intake of raw material and the output of processed data. It certainly has valid application to criminalistics some experts say, particularly when forensic laboratories have no control over the quality of the evidence they are analyzing, hence a situation where some evidence is tainted before it ever reaches the crime lab.

"Forensic science is the application of hard sciences to soft situations," emphasizes Ferrara, "a point which detractors conveniently forget when they talk about tainted science." Ferrara continues, "They just don't understand that we do not function like clinical labs, where pristine science occurs in a pristine lab environment under pristine conditions. In crime labs, we simply delve into the detritus of man's inhumanity to man, and you get what you get. No two cases are alike, and there aren't the controls present that there are in clinical laboratories. Samples aren't pristine, and the evidence is already contaminated, by its very definition, because it came from a crime scene—an uncontrolled, variable, unpredictable, unstable environment. And that's what we have to work with."

"There is an expectation that you are going to go into any crime scene and be able to recover physical evidence that will lend itself to proper forensic analysis," says Joseph Polski, chief operations officer of the International Association for Identification and chairman of the Consortium of Forensic Science Organizations. "Having been there and done that, I know too well that it doesn't always happen. Frequently, there is evidence left behind by the perpetrator of the crime, but not always, or it's not always left behind in such a fashion that it can be recovered, or it is not recovered in a timely enough fashion before it becomes contaminated or lost. In cold climates, for example, if a crime happens outside during the winter, and it's snowing, the evidence is covered with snow, shoe prints are lost, and things like that. From what we hear from the courts, from prosecutors, from forensic scientists, and from investigators, the public is being led to believe that forensic science can solve any case, and if you don't have the forensic evidence, then you must not be doing your job. It's an unfair portrayal."

Inman and Rudin (2001) state, "A forensic examination is not a controlled experiment. In fact, it is not an experiment at all. By definition, a scientific experiment requires not only known conditions, but also controlled conditions. Ideally, one variable at a time is altered while the others are held constant. This allows the scientist to determine specifically what is causing the change, if any, in the final results." Inman and Rudin add further, "Case samples have a whole history of which we are unaware. They are the element in the analysis over which we have no control. . . . We accept this as a limitation of the testing and interpret our results accordingly."[1]

Turvey says that the issue of tainted science is rife with red herrings that deflect from the issue of inadequate training of forensic scientists. "I think the biggest problem we face is that the majority of the people doing forensic science are technicians, they are not actual scientists. We have a community calling itself scientific which has no idea what the scientific method is or what science is all about, and the majority of practitioners have no scientific background. It's a systemic issue. Most of the people who get hired to work in the crime lab come to work for or with the police department. Too many crime labs are under the direction of a district attorney's office, and they want people who they can control, and opinions that they can control."

Turvey asserts that there are two breeds of forensic scientists who work for the state. "People can disagree with me if they want to, but it's my opinion that there's the brand new forensic scientist who comes in all bright-eyed and optimistic, thinking, 'I am going to change the world, I'm going to fix everything,' and they believe solemnly that there is special knowledge they are going to gain that is going to help them interpret evidence in a way that is different from anybody else. They believe they are going to learn special, secret things about the evidence and how to interpret it, and they promote this belief throughout the first 10 or 15 years of their career. Then they get to a certain point and they realize that this kind of evidentiary magic doesn't exist. Actually, it's an egocentric exercise in projection; a lot of their interpretations are nonsense, they have no basis in actual science, and they haven't received the training they need. So therefore the research they are claiming to base a lot of their findings on is very weak or non-existent. They then become the second kind of forensic scientist, the disenfranchised scientist whose entire career is based on a history of findings that are questionable, and of interpretations that are influenced by righteousness or politics. Then they have to spend the next half of their career protecting and defending everything. Because if they don't, the doors will swing wide open on them."

Charge No. 3: Fraud Perpetrated by Forensic Scientists

Both the members of the forensic community and its detractors agree that while human errors made in the pursuit of scientific truth can be justified by the human condition, deliberate fraud is unacceptable for any reason.

"The community doesn't police itself well enough. Crime lab analysts who have been caught being fraudulent can resign and move on to another lab or get shuffled around," says Turvey. "Melnikoff resigned from Montana, went to Oregon, then to Washington; each lab he was at suffered. Chuck Vaughn moved from Oregon to Washington. And the FBI has its own solution—they transfer fraudulent examiners out of the lab to some other duty. You can name dozens of cases like that. The reason I know is that I have done the research on it. When someone tells me it it's an isolated problem, I say I don't think it is. It's not isolated, it's everywhere you take the time to look. Agencies whose employees lie in their CVs, in their work, or on the stand should not have to be told by the court to bar their people from testimony. The current habit is to retire them out, force them to resign, move them around and in any way, hide them—or at least hope that nobody brings it up."

Moriarty and Saks (2005) state, "In addition to honest errors, DNA exoneration cases revealed that false or misleading testimony was more likely to be offered by forensic science expert witnesses than by any other kind of dissembling witness." They assert that as a group, forensic scientists "offer considerably more than their share of false testimony." They point to forensic scientist-turned-law professor Andre Moenssens, who once stated, "All (forensic science) experts are tempted, many times during their careers, to report positive results when their inquiries came up inconclusive, or indeed to report a negative result as positive." Moriarty and Saks also observe that fraudulent expert testimony has been a "terrible problem" for the criminal justice system, referring to "numerous" forensic science experts who have testified fraudulently in cases. They explain, "Not only are innocent people wrongly convicted on such evidence, but the state must then review those convictions involving the fraudulent testimony to determine which cases must be retried. This process is an expensive and time consuming endeavor for the government. More importantly, it is a nightmare both for crime victims and those innocent people sent to prison or to death row."

The causative agent of this kind of fraud, Moriarty and Saks (2005) say, is inherent subjectivity of the examination and the structure of the examination process. They state, "Often the forensic science expert is the only person to have looked through the microscope at the evidence, and the judgment of similarity or not, and inference of common source or not, takes place entirely in the head of that person. If other examiners serve as verifiers, they typically know what the first examiner concluded and . . . find it difficult to see and conclude other than what the first examiner claims to have seen and concluded. If an examiner claims to have drawn an inference of common source between indistinguishably similar questioned and known evidence, with what can one test the candor of such an opinion?"

Polski takes issue with these kinds of statements, he says, and comments, "If you talk to 20 examiners who do fingerprint identification and get their view of what they do, there isn't going to be one of them who thinks they are manufacturing anything," Polski says. "They very strongly believe that what they are doing is right and correct, and that they are contributing very greatly to the criminal justice system. In the pattern evidence disciplines in particular, you do hear the allegation that they are the 'police sciences' because there is supposed bias or because the work is done by members of law enforcement. There is condemnation of analysts who do not have the same mind-set as those who work for the National Science Foundation, for example. I've seen this prejudice at work in crime labs where different kinds of people do different kinds of work and oftentimes in the pattern evidence, firearms, tool marks, fingerprints, questioned documents, footwear, or tire tread units, the people who do that are very much looked down upon by the people who do toxicology, DNA, drug analysis, or other bench sciences."

Charge No. 4: Rogue Experts Gone Wild

Undermining forensic science, Giannelli (2003) says, are the "rogue experts" who should be blamed for promulgating a brand of science not fit for the adjudication of criminal cases. One of the most notorious and commonly cited examples of a scientist gone bad is that of now-deceased scientist Fred Zain, who was the chief serologist of the West Virginia State Police Crime Laboratory. Giannelli writes, "A judicial report found that Zain committed many acts of misconduct over 10 years, including overstating the strength of results, reporting inconclusive results as conclusive, repeatedly altering laboratory records, grouping results to create the erroneous impression that genetic markers had been obtained from all samples tested, and failing to report conflicting results." He points to the fact that the West Virginia Supreme Court considered the case to hold "shocking and egregious violations" and was a "corruption of our legal system."

At the time, more than 1,000 convictions were in question because Zain, who worked in West Virginia and Texas, was accused by courts and colleagues of faking evidence for 18 years. Zain had denied any wrongdoing. In the late 1970s, Zain was hired as a chemist at the West Virginia police crime lab, even though allegedly he had failed a college-level chemistry course.

While testifying as an expert in dozens of rape and murder cases, he reported results of tests that he had not performed, Zain's coworkers told the court. They had complained to Zain's superiors as early as 1985, but nothing had been done to address the situation. In 1989, Zain was named head of serology at the Bexar County Medical Examiner's office in San Antonio. At that time, the San Antonio medical examiner requested a forensic specialist to review a few of Zain's cases; the consultant found something amiss in each of the 14 cases that were picked at random and examined closely. Zain reportedly testified about blood on evidence when lab notes showed no blood had been found, and also reportedly conducted tests his lab was incapable of. In 1993, the West Virginia Supreme Court discredited Zain's work, finding that "any testimonial or documentary evidence offered by Zain at any time in any criminal prosecution should be deemed invalid, unreliable and inadmissible." According to various reports, Zain's deceitful laboratory work led to the erroneous incarceration of at least six individuals in several states. He was indicted for false testimony, but died before he could be brought to trial.

"I don't think we can take a stand that says, 'Forensic science has no bad apples,'" says Wells. "I think people like Fred Zain are definitely bad apples. However, I don't think we are different than any other profession that has its share of bad apples, so to speak. That doesn't excuse anything or anyone. We are human beings and we're going to have those experiences due to the fallibility of human nature. It doesn't excuse what they have done. We do have in place, as a general rule, provisions that hopefully will catch these occurrences before they become problems. Most forensic scientists do good work, but nothing and no one is perfect."

Zain represents what many commentators consider to be one of the more serious problems facing forensic laboratories—undue influence of law enforcement and biased forensic testing. Even as an increasing number of critics are pushing for autonomy, the state Supreme Court of Appeals in West Virginia in June 2006 unanimously petitioned for the removal of the crime lab from oversight by the West Virginia State Police, the same organization which employed Zain as a serologist. Instead, the court is asking for the lab to be placed under an independent agency. Korris (2006) reports, "The justices enacted a special habeas corpus procedure so that any prisoner convicted on serology evidence from 1979 to 1999 may petition for a new trial. . . . The justices ruled that a prisoner may file a petition even if a court previously rejected a challenge to the evidence. Normally a prisoner can challenge evidence only once. Justice Spike Maynard wrote for the Court that the special procedure would guarantee 'searching and painstaking scrutiny' of serology evidence. . . . In a final footnote Maynard wrote that while removing the crime lab from state police supervision and creating an independent supervisory board were beyond the Court's purview, the proposals 'deserve further consideration by the appropriate authorities.'"

The BBC (1998) reports that forensic scientist Zakaria Erzinclioglu, former director of the Forensic Science Research Centre at Durham University in the United Kingdom, warns that the criminal justice system could be undermined by "cowboy" practitioners unless it is more tightly regulated. Erzinclioglu says "quack practitioners" are infesting the courts; he says despite attempts to correct the mistakes of the past, forensic science in the United Kingdom is now in a "very poor and disordered state." He adds, "Forensic science is totally unregulated and sharks and cowboys abound. Apart from the specialist field of forensic medicine (or pathology), there is nothing to prevent anyone—qualified or not—from advertising themselves as a forensic scientist, whether purporting to be a specialist in toxicology, ballistics, DNA, document forgery, blood analysis or whatever."

"Unfortunately, these cowboy types probably have a sense that what they are doing, whether it is stretching the evidence or what have you, is right," says Fisher. "In their minds they don't think they are doing anything inappropriate. There is a danger when one becomes a forensic scientist/expert witness. Testifying in court when jurors hang on your every word can become an ego trip, as is knowing that you may be influencing the outcome of a case. Sometimes people get caught up in that, and you need to be constantly checking yourself and be wary of what you are saying."

Fisher says it can be a slippery slope for the ego-driven person working in forensic science. "Sometimes you may be going only so far in your testimony and the prosecution is trying to get you to go out on a limb. You may not have the good sense to say, 'Well, I'm going to go this far and no farther.' And you just continue to go crawling out a little farther and a little farther and then the limb breaks off and you are in trouble."

"It would be very easy to assume a siege mentality, where you begin to circle the wagons in anticipation of battle," Fisher adds. "I have read some of the stories about the Houston Police Department crime lab where the morale at the facility is pretty bad because not only are they looking at the possibility of disciplining employees, but there may be the possibility of criminal charges. The investigating attorney wanted subpoena powers to compel people to talk to him because some former lab employees did not want to speak with him. There is a certain amount of fear out there, but I think it's limited to specific jurisdictions and isn't necessarily infiltrating the entire forensic community. There is concern, however, that the defense bar is using this situation in Houston to take pot shots at everybody, and paint everyone with the same brush."

Many commentators believe that rogue experts are cultivated by the influence of law enforcement that permeates some forensic laboratories. "You constantly hear charges about cops in lab coats running the labs, but I don't think most forensic scientists work in a coercive environment," says Wyckoff. "If you are an egotist and you want to get your name known, you may get away with that for awhile, but you will be found out eventually and reckoned with. But I don't think most of us have experienced that kind of pressure. By and large, lab analysts are hard-working, honest people who like their jobs and the profession in which they work. I think they would do whatever was right, no matter where they were or what kind of pressures they faced. There have been a couple times over the years when attorneys have asked me to testify in a particular way, and I have replied, 'First, it's not right, and second, you cannot not answer a question to the best of your ability and state the facts if you spin something.' "

Jonakait (1991) asserts that analysis of evidence must be separated from the interpretation of evidence, and conducted by two separate people for the best possible results free from potential bias. Wyckoff notes, "I think this would be very challenging because that's what the scientific method is—you do the tests, you consider the results, and you write the conclusion. The laboratory accreditation process addresses the importance of peer review; most labs now require all cases to be peer reviewed. I find it hard to believe there are cases in labs that are not being reviewed carefully. Someone ignorant about the accreditation process is making that charge, and my guess is they don't understand what's going on in laboratories today."

Besides Zain, a number of other analysts in recent history have come under fire for malfeasance or mistakes. Arnold Melnikoff, who managed Montana's state crime lab, has had his work questioned in a number of cases, especially those in which new DNA testing reversed earlier convictions based in part on his expert testimony. Joyce Gilchrist, a long-time analyst for the Oklahoma City Police Department, had her expert testimony criticized by a judge, which ultimately led to FBI and internal police reviews that revealed numerous problems with her work, including a misidentification of trace evidence that sent a man to prison, but whose conviction was overturned. FBI lab employee Jacqueline Blake was investigated by the Department of Justice for failing to complete a negative control test for contamination in about 90 cases, and for falsifying documentation to conceal her faulty work. These cases of alleged and actual malfeasance and others can be recited by heart by every journalist covering forensic science, by every defense attorney and prosecutor, and certainly by members of the forensic science community who roll their eyes at yet another retelling of these medico-legal misadventures that continue to reverberate in the headlines.

"I think there is some merit to the statement that there are a few bad apples in the barrel," says forensic pathologist and law professor Cyril Wecht, M.D., J.D., former coroner of Allegheny County, Pennsylvania. "We've had some horrible examples of practitioners gone wrong in the likes of Fred Zain, Joyce Gilchrist, and Ralph Erdman. I think another generation coming up with different ethics will probably get rid of the problem, but we still have many places in the U.S. where people who have little or no training are practicing forensic science. It may be someone on the police force who, instead of being assigned to traffic duty, was assigned to the crime lab and told, 'You are going to be a lab technician,' regardless of whether he or she even took high school chemistry, let alone had any other forensic training." Wecht continues, "Even worse than that is the prosecutorial bias and the failure to have adequate oversight in forensic facilities. There is no doubt that this issue is moving in the right direction with accreditation due to exposure by the media and in the courts. There is no reason why any of this should exist, however."

Wecht charges that much of what people assume is poor behavior on the part of forensic analysts is covered up by what he asserts to be prosecutorial bias. "A lot of people don't like to hear this, but there is tremendous prosecutorial bias in courtrooms today," Wecht adds. "They say they are only interested in justice, but that's naïve. In my opinion, the overwhelming majority of prosecutors are in fact prosecutors because they have a mind-set about looking ahead to future elections or re-elections to a higher office or other political aspirations. It's not that they are evil people who conspiratorially plot against others, it's just the nature of the beast, and it's simply who they are."

Wecht adds, "Being in a position to wield political power to effectuate one's own philosophy and political ambitions is a dangerous thing in the courtroom. You have to be an incredible saint to resist the spin. In many places, ambitious prosecutors want to control the forensic labs and that's not a good system. These crime labs must have total autonomy, with proper oversight and monitoring with ongoing quality controls to ensure that these kinds of terrible things do not occur. I am not one for the utilization of excessive procedural controls that don't accomplish much substantively and just create a lot more paperwork and administrative bureaucracy. However, in terms of true quality control, training and education as well as testing work, as does objective inspection by a body akin to the Joint Commission on the Accreditation of Healthcare Organizations (JCAHO). I think an intellectual, honest, objective approach to quality control is needed."

Kelly and Wearne (1998) state, "Of course, every profession has its rotten apples. Forensic science is no different from the law, medicine, academia, law enforcement or anything else. The issue is not the Zains per se, but the questions their conduct raises. How did they get into the profession? How did they get away with it so long? Why are they not stopped and punished? Why do juries, judges, prosecutors and even defense attorneys believe them? Take a close look at forensic science and answers are not hard to come by." Kelly and Wearne point to several issues that will be discussed in greater detail elsewhere in this chapter and in Chapter 5. The first reason for rogue experts, they say, is that "most forensic scientists are not in fact independent experts." They add, "About 80 percent of forensic scientists in North America are affiliated with police or prosecution agencies. Most of these work in police laboratories; many are themselves law enforcement officers, as are most of their superiors . . . the potential conflict of loyalties and interests is obvious. Scientists are expected to retain a critical sense, to follow nothing but reason, to maintain an open mind. We expect the results, the science, to bear witness in court unencumbered by any other considerations. Complete impartiality may be an inspirational ideal but what chance is there of coming anywhere near this ideal if the police or FBI pay your wages?"

That the forensic laboratory is an extension of the already long arm of the law enforcement community is a common complaint. Kelly and Wearne (1998) quote James Starrs, a professor of law and forensic science at George Washington University and vocal critic of forensic science, as opining, "It is quite common to find laboratory facilities and personnel who are, for all intents and purposes, an arm of the prosecution. They analyze material submitted, on all but rare occasions, solely by the prosecution. They testify almost exclusively on behalf of the prosecution. As a result, their impartiality is replaced by a viewpoint colored brightly with prosecutorial bias."

Kelly and Wearne (1998) explain that Starrs, who has been publicly calling for the adoption of a standard code of ethics for forensic scientists for more than three decades, has viable suggestions, including the following tenets:

- No consideration or person should dissuade the forensic scientist from a full and fair investigation of the facts on which opinion is formulated.
- The forensic scientist should maintain an attitude of independence, impartiality, and calm objectivity to avoid personal or professional involvement in the proceedings.
- A forensic scientist should not tender testimony that is not within his or her competence as an expert, or conclusions or opinions within the competence of the jury, acting as laymen.
- Utmost care should be given to the treatment of any samples or item of potential evidentiary value to avoid tampering, adulteration, loss, or other change of original state.
- The forensic scientist should provide full and complete disclosure of the entire case in a comprehensive and well-documented report, to include facts or opinions indicative of the accused's innocence and the shortcomings of his or her opinion that might invalidate it.
- Forensic scientists should testify to the procedures undertaken and the results disclosed only when opinions can be stated in terms of reasonable scientific certainty.
- Unless there are special circumstances of possible intimidation or falsification of evidence, a forensic scientist for the prosecution should permit the defense to interview him or her before the trial, an obligation that should not be contingent on the approval of the prosecutor.

Jami St. Clair, manager of the Columbus Police Crime Laboratory in Ohio and past president of the ASCLD, says she does not see a broken, biased system to the extent others may claim exists. "I'm sure that in the past, there was probably a stronger belief in the existence of the cops-in-lab-coats situations," St. Clair says. "I won't lie, however; there are still crime labs that have police officers do the testing, or labs that require their analysts to go through police academy training. So to that extent, I guess there still are some cops in lab coats, but that also doesn't necessarily mean that they are going to be biased toward putting someone in jail no matter what. It's not about wanting justice, although I suspect everyone wants justice to be served in the end, but if you can identify somebody's DNA and that solves a case, then justice is done, but done in the right way."

St. Clair acknowledges that it is only human to "want the victim to feel someone has done all they can in order to put the bad guy away. But I think the big issue isn't putting the bad guy away, it's putting the *wrong* guy away. Then, the defense attorneys and advocates say, 'Well, because these analysts are employed by a police department, automatically have this bias toward putting everyone away.' I just don't see that happening, for a number of reasons, and accreditation is one of them. There are so many controls in doing our analyses, and so many quality assurance checks that we go through; it's the way to demonstrate to others that your analysis is upfront and that you're not going to be able to skew your analysis to show what the police or the prosecutor want it to show."

St. Clair says that technology itself can serve as a safeguard against bias. "The technology has advanced so much, especially in the biological sciences and with DNA; it's not like it was 25 years ago when I started out, when you're putting people away on ABO typing, where someone belonged to a group that was 40 percent of the population. So analysts have a completely different technology base now than what was used in the past. Because of this technology, and because of accreditation and certification standards that exist now, I don't think you are seeing in reality what some people may think still exists. Frequently you see in the news many reports about bad analysts, but there are bad people within every profession. There are bad police officers, bad journalists, bad attorneys, bad doctors, so it's going to happen everywhere and not just in forensic science, but with the accreditation standards in the community now, the chance of bias and other problems is minimized. There are other checks and balances too, to minimize the bad things that can happen."

Polski says that the total separation of law enforcement from the forensic laboratories is "too much of a change in how the whole system operates." Polski adds, "I don't see that happening in two lifetimes. I understand the argument that you can't be objective in your analysis of evidence if you are part of a law enforcement agency that has an agenda to catch bad guys. Commentators cite cases where they assert there was undue pressure to alter the test results, but you can't legislate ethics. If someone wants to cut corners or wants to fabricate evidence or slant things in a way that lacks objectivity, to me it's not going to make any difference if you're independent or affiliated with a law enforcement agency—they are still going to do it. Having independent verification of results is a very good thing, but I think you can take it to a point where it just isn't practical due to manpower issues. There have been some news stories where an identification was made by a senior person and then a member of the prosecution team takes the result to a junior person in the organization and says, 'Well, we've identified the bad guy, what do you think from a peer review standpoint?' Bear in mind that the senior person may have just hired the junior person. That's not a good situation, because of course, if the boss says, 'This is a match and this is the perpetrator,' even if you think it's not, is the junior person going to disagree? Probably not, if he or she wants to keep his or her job. I think independent peer review is highly desirable, but translating that into the real world requires thinking about these kinds of scenarios. I don't think you could do double-blind verification, as you would see things grind to a halt in the crime lab, but there has to be a plausible compromise somewhere in the middle."

"We do serve law enforcement of course," says Ferrara, "but I have never seen them try to influence us in our work. Sometimes when we eliminate suspects, and even though we are using DNA technology, they might sometimes question us, 'Are you sure?' We call it like it is, and it falls like it is, period. We try to figure out what happened, not sit around the crime lab and contemplate, 'Gee, how do we prosecute somebody?' or 'How can we implicate this guy?' That's ridiculous. There are such a high percentage of cases where suspect samples come in and we eliminate that suspect and then are able to identify who the real suspect is; 25 or 30 percent of the time, we're eliminating suspects. That's a good thing. And we're doing it as early as when we get to the case. It's no skin off our noses; on the contrary, we are delighted actually to eliminate a suspect. And regarding the separation of analysis from interpretation, it can be done, but is it efficient? No. On the contrary, it is very inefficient. There is so much review that goes on anyway. We have to be fighting backlogs, not creating new ones, or hunting witches."

The behavior of rogue experts or biased practitioners is revealed most notably in the courtroom, of course. Legal scholars have argued that the rules for admitting the testimony of experts have been softened by the transition from a general acceptance rule for the admissibility of novel scientific evidence (the Frye test) to a standard upheld by the *Federal Rules of Evidence* that supplanted Frye and declared that a scientist only had to satisfy a judge that he or she could provide technical assistance to the jury beyond its perceived competence. With this change in admissibility standards, critics say, has come a flood of pseudo-science, a topic that will be discussed in greater detail in Chapter 10.

Kelly and Wearne (1998) state, "The inability of courts to tell the difference between real and junk science was partially responsible for what seems like downright laxity when faced with the shortcomings of forensic examiners." They explain, "Ralph Erdmann, the medical examiner from Lubbock County, Texas, pleaded no contest to seven specimen felonies involving faked autopsies, falsifying evidence, and brokering body parts, yet got only a 10-year probation order and community service. Fred Zain, the West Virginia and Texas serologist, was not even punished being acquitted of a variety of criminal charges brought against him in West Virginia."

Kelly and Wearne (1998) question whether forensic practitioners even consider bad behavior to be illegal or even unethical, and claim that much of this malfeasance is not regularly caught in the first place. They explain that defense attorneys lack the training needed to spot questionable forensic findings that would indicate errors committed by the forensic examiner or analyst, and the clients they represent often do not possess the financial wherewithal needed to adequately question scientific findings through hired experts. Regarding defense attorneys, Kelly and Wearne state, "Few are prepared to orchestrate a defense around a scientific subject or technology they know little about; even fewer are prepared to spend the hours or weeks it may take to prepare. The vast majority of law schools still offer no specific courses devoted to scientific opinion or expert-witness testimony." They add, "Financing is another obstacle. Experts cost money, the vast majority of defendants do not have it, and the courts are often reluctant to spend it by authorizing the funds to pay for a defense expert. The result has been what some experts have termed an economic presumption of guilt. Many courts have required defendants to cross near impossible thresholds of proof of need in order to secure the help of court-ordered experts. Ironically, proving an expert would make a material difference to the defense case or that doing without one would result in an unfair trial, as many courts demand, often in itself requires an expert." A lackluster performance on the part of defense attorneys is not always the case; as we shall see in Chapter 15, the defense camp is getting smarter about challenging scientific evidence and filling their war chests to pay for hired guns. Another example of bad behavior on the part of forensic scientists is connected to the phenomenon of observer effect, or inherent bias.

In quoting Lucas et al. (1985), Koppl and Kobilinsky (2005) assert that as many as 80 percent of U.S. forensic laboratories "are within law enforcement agencies." Mills and McRoberts (2004) estimate that about 90 percent of accredited labs are organized under police agencies. Koppl and Kobilinsky (2005) comment, "The forensic worker depends on the police (or other law enforcement agency) for his salary and performance evaluation. This frequently creates a demand for the services of forensic workers who deliver results consistent with the police theory. . . . This situation is beginning to change, however. In recent years there has been a move toward "civilianization" of forensics in the U.S. . . . Forensic workers tend to identify with the police. They tend, therefore, to seek out evidence supporting the police theory."

While the accuracy of testing, analysis, and data interpretation by forensic scientists, especially those who work in police-housed laboratories, has been questioned by critics, so has the objectivity of these activities. There have been many allegations of subconscious and even intentional bias on the part of the examiner in the forensic laboratory. The more elaborate theory of bias is called the "observer effect," which in essence asserts that "the desires and expectations people possess influence their perceptions and interpretations of what they observe" (Risinger et al., 2002). In other words, experts say, the results of observation depend on the state of the observer as well as the thing observed.

"For starters, most people don't know what examiner bias and observer effects are," comments Turvey. "The most common response is, 'Well, I am a scientist and I use the scientific method, which helps prevent me from having any bias.' What that does is tell me that they actually don't know what examiner bias or observer effects are. These influences are subconscious—you don't know they are happening. An analyst in a crime lab associated with the state police is down the hall from the cops. Even though the analyst is not a cop himself, they basically make him feel like he is one of them. He can hang out with them, and he wants to identify with those cops; the camaraderie that develops is a huge factor in the development of unconscious bias. When you hang around the badge, you bask in its warm glow. I worked a case with the cops for about a year and a half and they gave me a badge and a gun, and I worked as a detective. It's like being in the presence of God when you are around police officers with their badges and guns and all of the power that comes with those symbols of authority. There is great allure in how the brotherhood can make you feel. The forensic analyst will lose that brotherhood if he comes up with findings from the data that don't help the police's case. That's examiner bias at work."

Inman and Rudin (2001) state, "Because we are all human, we cannot help but have our own personal and professional prejudices. With or without knowledge about a case, we must constantly be on guard both to identify and to put aside any inclination to prejudge the evidence. Understanding one's own limitations and biases, and taking them into consideration in one's work, is key to a competent professional life."[1]

Koppl and Kobilinsky (2005) state, "Group-serving bias is a probable source of bias in forensic work. Group-serving bias is created when a person considers himself a member of a 'coalitional alliance' (Kurzban et al. 2001). A coalitional alliance is characterized by coordinated action toward a common goal." Koppl and Kobilinsky (2005) add, "Police and forensic workers are engaged in coordinated action toward a common goal and thus seem to be in a coalitional alliance in the evolutionary sense. The forensic worker and the police are on the same team. They are 'us' and suspects are 'them.' This deep-seated bias in forensic analysis is inconsistent with objective scientific analysis."

Moriarty and Saks (2005) seem to affirm this kind of experience: "The problem of unintended bias can be organizational as well as psychological. When examiners produce results that are disappointing to investigators, they sometimes are asked to reexamine only those displeasing results. Rarely, if ever, are they asked to reexamine the results that investigators liked. This ensures that only findings inconsistent with an investigator's theory of a case get reversed. All of this can occur though only the best and most honest of intentions are operating, and yet it can produce conclusions that undermine true facts."

St. Clair (2003) states, "A common point of discussion and often disagreement among supporters and critics of crime laboratories is how close a relationship a forensic scientist should have with the police. While communication is important, it is equally important that a forensic scientist remain objective. Many people outside the criminal justice system infer that crime laboratories that reside in police departments owe their primary allegiance to their employer. While it is important that a crime laboratory assists the police, it is equally important that forensic scientists do not view themselves as 'cops in lab coats.'"

Moriarty and Saks (2005) explain that the biggest danger lies in the areas of expectation and suggestion: "Many fields recognize the risk that people tend to see what they expect to see." They add, "The work of forensic scientists subjects them to many opportunities to be affected by expectation and suggestion. Before conducting their examinations, they sometimes learn facts or theories about the case from police investigators or from transmittal letters or forms accompanying the evidence and making the request for examination. (These often tell the examiner what the investigators expect or hope will result from the examination.) Examiners sometimes learn what fellow examiners testing different items of evidence found, which they then are likely to expect will be consistent with their own examinations. One of the few published audits of crime laboratories found that examinations resulted in conclusions excluding submitted evidence only 10 percent of the time on average—a finding consistent with expectation and suggestion effects."

Moriarty and Saks (2005) assert, "Despite occasional recognition of the problem, forensic science in the United States has refused to develop procedures to prevent the problem from being able to occur in the first place. In contrast to many other fields of endeavor, forensic scientists have generally insisted that they can avoid falling prey to such influences merely by telling themselves to be immune." Jonakait (1991) observes, "Failure to follow established protocols is not the only inferior analytical technique. Another is the failure of forensic scientists to shield themselves from possible bias."

Commentators suggest that evidentiary material frequently is presented to the forensic scientist in a "needlessly suggestive manner" according to Jonakait (1991) who explains, "The analyst is given crime scene evidence (hair, fingerprints, blood) and one other sample, labeled as the defendant's (or victim's). This is frequently accompanied by a synopsis of the investigation indicating the reasons why the investigators believe the suspect is guilty. Such a presentation, of course, suggests to the analyst what the 'right' answer should be. This suggestiveness coupled with the understandable prosecutorial orientation of many forensic scientists will naturally, even if unconsciously, skew subjective judgments."

The problems created by observer effects date back to the times of the creation of the scientific method. Risinger et al. (2002) point to Sir Francis Bacon, who in 1620, recognized the problem and commented, "It is the peculiar and perpetual error of the human understanding to be more moved and excited by affirmatives than negatives, whereas it ought duly to be impartial; nay, in establishing any true axiom, the negative instance is the most powerful."

Bacon realized that the attributes of an observer could influence the accuracy of an observation, leading to confirmation bias, or, as Risinger et al. (2002) explain, "The tendency to test a hypothesis by looking for instances that confirm it rather than by searching for potentially falsifying instances, even though most scientists and philosophers of science today agree with Bacon that the best scientific method is to proceed by doing the latter." Bacon had once observed, "The human understanding resembles not a dry light, but admits a tincture of the will and passions, which generate their own system accordingly, for man always believes more readily that which he prefers."

Risinger et al. (2002) state that since the 1700s, scientists have learned that observer factors "can distort findings and produce misleading conclusions in myriad ways not so easily corrected for." For instance, individuals may not read dials correctly, and their errors are nonrandom, as particular numbers or patterns are more likely to be read than others, resulting in systematic errors in the data garnered from the measuring instruments. The bottom line is that scientists may "equate what they think they see, and sometimes what they want to see, with what actually happens. These realizations and attention to them have evolved into a 'science of science,' a careful study of the causes of the random and systematic errors induced by observer effects and the methods for their prevention," say Risinger et al. Critics have said that forensic science is one of a handful of fields that has not yet profited from this "science of science," and that "the most obvious danger in forensic science is that an examiner's observations and conclusions will be influenced by extraneous, potentially biasing information" (Risinger et al., 2002). However, other potentially error-producing sources of expectation beyond those induced by intentional or unintentional suggestion exist.

Commentators are quick to point out that the context effect does not encompass intentional distortion or deliberate falsification, such as in the cases where forensic scientists report inculpatory results when the findings were actually exculpatory or inconclusive, or incompetence through which erroneous conclusions are reached. Instead, at the heart of the issue, according to Risinger et al. (2002), are the "distorting effects that motivational bias and examination-irrelevant information can have on the conclusions of even those forensic scientists with the most sincere and honest intentions." They fear that if unaddressed in forensic science, observer effects "can lead competent and honest forensic scientists, using well-validated techniques, to offer sincere conclusions that are, nevertheless, distorted and inaccurate. Such results may occur in large numbers, completely without examiner awareness, much less with any wrongful intent. Indeed, such distortions will be more ubiquitous and more insidious precisely because they are not intended and their presence goes unnoticed."

The phenomenon of observer effect encompasses errors of apprehension, recording, recall, computation, or interpretation that result from some trait or state of the observer (Risinger et al., 2002). In essence, forensic scientists may have a preexisting expectation about a particular observation or, in other words, they may very well see exactly what they expect to see or have been asked to see, such as in the case of an overzealous prosecutor.

Selective attention to evidence, for example, is based in an individual's expectations of a situation or a hypothesis. Risinger et al. (2002) note, "Often there is too much information for a human to process or to give equal consideration to all of it. If one has expectations about an event, or hypotheses about its cause, one tends to draw selectively from the available evidence and focus on those items that confirm the working hypothesis." They point to Seymour Kety who suggested, "It is difficult to avoid the subconscious tendency to reject for good reason data which weaken a hypothesis while uncritically accepting those data which strengthen it."

Risinger et al. (2002) add, "Thus, expectations, among other factors, lead us to conclude more readily that we have perceived one thing rather than another, and having done so it becomes more difficult to perceive details that run contrary to the original perception. These effects can be reinforced as we establish the initial interpretation of what we have perceived, and further still when we later try to remember what we perceived. Indeed, there is evidence that the most powerful effects occur during the integration and retrieval phases, as the new percepts become part of the original schema and the schema is used to recall the perception." For example, Risinger et al. point to the forensic scientist who takes inadequate notes during an examination of evidence, prepares an incomplete report, and then shores up these notes right before trial. Risinger et al. state, "Even assuming the most honest of intentions, that examiner is inviting errors to infiltrate his conclusions and his testimony. The error potential of the original skimpy report, which leaves much to be supplied from memory, facilitates the creation of testimony more consistent with assumptions and later acquired expectations than would be the case with a more detailed and complete contemporaneous account. Reconstructive errors are given room to manifest themselves during the 'spruce-up' stage."

Also important to the concept of observer effect are the cognitive effects of role, which is when an individual adopts a certain function or perspective; this in turn affects the kind of data which the individual seeks and how effectively and in what vein the person processes that information. Risinger et al. (2002) assert, ". . . investigators whose role is to solve a problem may become convinced of the truth of a proposed solution more easily than investigators whose role is to describe a situation, or to describe the likelihood of various options. In this regard, the following observation about forensic laboratories by James Starrs, made many years ago, appears to remain true today: It is quite common to find . . . laboratory facilities and personnel who are, for all intents and purposes, an arm of the prosecution. They analyze material submitted, on all but rare occasions, solely by the prosecution. They testify almost exclusively on behalf of the prosecution. They inevitably become part of the effort to bring an offender to justice. And as a result, their impartiality is replaced by a viewpoint colored brightly with prosecutorial bias."

Experimenter effects have relevance for forensic science, Risinger et al. say: ". . . the larger organizational setting of a crime laboratory is analogous to an 'experiment,' where the police investigators, prosecutors, lab directors, and colleagues in the lab are the 'experimenters' and the individual forensic examiners are the 'subjects' of the experiment. From this perspective, the beliefs and expectancies of superiors, coworkers, and external personnel are manifest in their behavior toward the forensic scientist 'subject,' in turn affecting the behavior of those 'subjects,' their observations, recordings, computations, and interpretations, not to mention the additional impact role and conformity effects may have." They add, "Thus, the more complex experimenter effect findings indeed appear quite relevant to what happens in the forensic science laboratory."

Researchers have studied when in the observation process observer-effect errors occur: They can happen at any time in the scientific discovery process, including during the formation of the initial perception and its imprint in memory; at the time when correct observations are accurately remembered but transformed into incorrect results when calculations are performed on them; and when individuals draw incorrect conclusions from the data. There is margin for error, then, when individuals must interpret their observations, especially when the "true values of the underlying observations are often so vague, ephemeral, and submerged in the interpretation, that one often cannot discover the inaccuracy in the interpretative conclusion" (Risinger et al., 2002).

Things can get dicey when individuals accumulate increasing amounts of data and grow increasingly confident in their observations and interpretations, yet their accuracy of analysis remains unchanged during this escalation of thought processes. Risinger et al. (2002) note with concern that "the lack of relationship between substantial additions of information and accuracy of result under some conditions, the direct relationship between such information and confidence in one's conclusions, and the resultant lack of relationship between confidence in one's conclusion and actual accuracy, is especially troublesome in any field where subjective probability estimates are the primary conclusion. As previously noted, many traditional forensic science fields, most particularly identification disciplines such as toolmark, bite mark, or handwriting analysis, rely on such subjective probability estimates. Information can expand and subjective probability will go up, but the accuracy—the objective probability—may not. Indeed, if new information is sufficiently overvalued, confidence could go up while accuracy goes down."

Hence, the potential for observer effects to occur in forensic science is substantial, some experts say. Risinger et al. (2002) remark, "In their daily work, forensic scientists are observers of a wide variety of objects, shapes, colors, instrumentation, and test results. The observations that must be made present varying degrees of ambiguity. Subjective judgment and interpretation by the human observer remain the principal methods of reaching conclusions in most forensic disciplines, and the working environment of the forensic scientist is not lacking in sources of expectations or outcome preferences. Such circumstances facilitate the operation of observer effects, particularly when observers have armed themselves so lightly against the infiltration of distorting influences."

The fact that forensic science has grown up, to a large degree, in the construct of law enforcement, further complicates the discussion of observer effects. Members of the law enforcement community and forensic scientists have vastly different approaches to how they cultivate their information. A detective's job is to determine the material facts of a criminal case by gathering all pertinent information from a crime scene. Many are aided in this task by highly subjective forces, including following intuitive hunches or pursuing even the most undependable information as investigative leads that may not pan out.

Risinger et al. (2002) state, "Such exercises may precipitate a change in focus leading to the discovery of more dependable information that was previously overlooked, even if the exercise is itself without rational content. All this is true because, in the end, the detective's conclusions about the material issues of the case must be backed up by legally admissible evidence, and that evidence must convince prosecutors to prosecute, judges to send the case to a jury, and a jury to convict. Most importantly, however, the detective . . . is not allowed to testify concerning her conclusions. No doubt a detective's solution to a case is often subject to all sorts of observer effects, but the system has been built in such a way that the ultimate fact finders are insulated to a great degree from the results of those effects on the detective."

A forensic scientist must take a radically different path to reach a conclusion about a case. He or she is bound by the scientific method and the protocols dictated by the scientific disciplines in which they practice, and their work is dictated by the parameters of rigid scientific inquiry, which do not include conjecture. Risinger et al. (2002) observe, "The conclusions of the forensic scientists are put before the jury. The reason the products of the forensic scientist's efforts are admissible is not because forensic scientists are better at drawing conclusions about the meaning of normal relevant evidentiary information than detectives or jurors; it is because the law has accepted that, as to a defined area of specialized knowledge or skill, the products of their practice are better than the jury could do alone. When the forensic scientist is exposed to, relies on, or is influenced by any information outside of her own domain, she is abusing her warrant, even though she may honestly believe that such information makes her conclusion more reliable, and even, or especially, if she is right about this. Her role is not to give a conclusion based even partly on information outside her domain, which the jury can presumptively evaluate at least as well as she, but only to give the jury the reliable product of her discipline that is beyond what they could deduce on their own."

Risinger et al. (2002) use the example of a forensic odontologist who examines a human bite mark. If this forensic practitioner happens to know that (in addition to whatever incomplete tooth marks were left on the victim by the perpetrator) the victim says she was also raped by the man who bit her and that a positive DNA match was made from spermatozoa recovered from her vagina, there is a strong random match probability. The odontologist could be tempted to say that the bite mark evidence can be ascribed to the defendant with a high degree of probability—without necessarily conducting an extensive battery of forensic tests. Risinger et al. (2002) comment, "On one level, there is a certain apparent backwardness to his conclusion, since he is using information about the identity of the attacker to draw a conclusion about the source of the bite mark, instead of providing a conclusion about the source of the bite mark to be used as a basis for inferring the identity of the attacker."

Koppl (2005) expresses concern about the disparity in techniques used by forensic practitioners: "They may choose, for example, which of several serological tests to use in matching a suspect's blood to a sample. Jonakait (1991) reports that there are no protocols for most forensic procedures; (since then), accreditation has somewhat mitigated this problem. Accredited labs in the U.S. must have protocols, although protocols may vary from lab to lab. But as we have seen, not all labs are accredited. Without protocols, forensic workers have considerable freedom to choose their techniques of analysis."[2] Koppl (2005) cites Pearsall (1989) who notes, "The crime laboratories' diversity of procedure reflects . . . disunity. For example, individual laboratories, and even individual technicians, frequently set their own idiosyncratic standards concerning testing protocols for the same basic serological test. Variation of protocols ('Protocol drift') may cause inconsistent test results. Especially troublesome, the interpretation of test results may represent only one analyst's opinion." Feigenbaum and Levy (1996) indicate that choice of technique and selective reporting introduces bias to scientific analysis because, as Koppl (2005) explains it, "The scientist may apply several techniques to a problem and publicly report only those tending to support his preferred theory. . . . Freedom of choice increases the chances that the worker will be able to produce the result he wants by the use of techniques that are, considered in isolation, perfectly objective and legitimate. He has no need to engage in willful fraud; fraud is obsolete. He has only to apply several tests and report on those that point in the desired direction."[2]

Koppl (2005) adds further, "This problem would be serious if only dishonest workers used choice of technique and selective reporting to produce biased results. Unfortunately, however, even honest workers may do the same thing. Scrupulously honest workers may systematically reject unexpected or undesired results and accept expected and desired results. The honest, but unconsciously biased forensic worker will readily seize excuses to cast doubt on tests producing undesired results. He will search for reasons to dismiss doubts about tests producing desired results. The techniques of the sincere and conscientious worker can be almost as biased as those of the unscrupulous cheater."[2]

Risinger et al. (2002) address what they call the improper information contamination in forensic science, asserting that "forensic examiners should be insulated from all information about an inquiry except necessary, domain-specific information." They assert that much of forensic analysis is subjected to undue external influence and the availability of extra-domain information that could potentially sway an analyst's conclusions. They charge that the accreditation standards of the ASCLD do not address the problem of controlling domain-irrelevant information, and that no studies have been conducted on the actual practices in forensic science laboratories that would document the statistical incidence of the use of domain-extraneous information. Risinger et al. observe, "Responsibility for the absence of such studies can only be placed on the forensic science community itself, since no one else is in a position to conduct such studies." They also claim that "anecdotal evidence is extensive and uniform in indicating that extraneous information is rife in most, if not, all areas of forensic practice."

For example, they say that providing forensic examiners with extensive case histories may provide undue influence by way of external expectations for the forensic evidence being processed. Risinger et al. (2002) describe the efforts of a researcher who contacted managers of several ASCLD-certified laboratories to ask about the practice of passing along substantial case information to forensic examiners who were testing the evidence. The researcher reported that the lab managers "confirmed that, to the best of their knowledge, the practice was virtually universal."

Reaching into related domains for context information is common in forensic science; however, forensic practitioners must know where the line in the sand exists. Risinger et al. (2002) point to specific sources of observer error in forensic practice. One of the most common instances is when law enforcement investigators communicate directly with forensic examiners and may relay to them more information than is necessary to perform the forensic testing. Commentators say this information can include other inculpatory evidence that has been found in the case, and may include what the investigator making the submission expects or hopes the requested tests will conclude (Risinger et al., 2002).

Another source of observer-effect errors in forensic science is when examiners are influenced by word of new findings in other evidence or in the facts of the case that can be construed as being inconsistent with their conclusions. It would be very easy, critics say, for forensic examiners to revise their original conclusions to bring them in line with these new developments in the case. This, in turn, may lead to a third source of observer-effect error: selective reexamination of the evidence. Risinger et al. (2002) explain, "Sometimes police or prosecutors respond to test results that are negative or inconclusive by suggesting to forensic scientists what they should have found and asking them to test again in hopes of obtaining a 'better' result. The contamination here can be quite crude; the investigator or prosecutor might be signaling to the examiner that a more inculpatory result is desired and inviting the examiner to rethink the conclusions with that in mind."

Forensic laboratory managers bristle at the suggestion of impropriety on the part of analysts triggered by subtle or blatant bias. "I have been in this profession for 36 years and I work in a lab that is a part of a law enforcement agency; in those 36 years I have never been asked to sway my testimony or to change a report or to do anything that was short of reporting accurately what I found as a result of my examinations and analyses," Wells says emphatically. "I have 100 people who work in my laboratory and none of them has been asked to change his or her testimony or the results of their analyses to help anybody. We do our work down the middle and we testify for the defense community as well as for the prosecution. Needless to say, by the very nature of the work, most of our analysis and interpretation of evidence is done to prosecute suspects, but any time our work helps exonerate an individual, it goes out the same way. If it frees the innocent, that's great, and if convicts the guilty, that's good too, but we don't have an ax to grind on any side."

"There is this notion entertained by outsiders that forensic practitioners are interested in what the outcome of a result is," Fisher says. "In reality, we are simply conducting tests and reporting what we found. The prosecutors and the cops do the rest."

Some experts have opined that the incompetent may not know that they are incompetent, and this has ramifications for every profession, not just forensic science. Kruger and Dunning (1999) suggest that the incompetent are not in a position to judge their performances accurately. Ehrlinger and Dunning (2003) state, "Not only does their lack of skill prevent the incompetent from forming current responses to situational demands, but it also prevents them from recognizing when judgments will be accurate and when they will be erroneous." Kruger and Dunning demonstrated in studies that incompetent individuals (i.e., those performing poorly relative to their peers) were the least able to assess the quality of their performance as well as the performances of others.

Does this mean, then, that incompetence can somehow mask malfeasance? And how can this disguised malfeasance be rooted out? Some commentators argue that fraud and incompetence are both perpetuated and masked by external controlling factors, such as undue pressure upon forensic practitioners from authorities. "Forensic scientists don't control anything, instead it's the police and the district attorney that control everything," asserts Turvey.

"The forensic analyst only gets a very small picture of the entire case; they only get the picture that the DA wants to show them. The police go to the crime scene and they collect and document the evidence, and while they are doing so, they already have a theory in their head, a preconceived theory about what's going on with the case. So they collect only the evidence that might support that theory and pass on everything else. Then they select from that evidence what they want to have sent out for analysis. The crime lab is a mere service provider; it examines the evidence that it is told to examine, nothing more, nothing less. Law enforcement and DAs have cut labs out of the crime reconstruction process; they don't want them doing it because they want to be able to have the detective get up on the stand and be a witness without any expert qualifications, giving their observations about what they think happened. You have police crime scene analysts who say openly that 'reconstruction is based on my observations at the crime scene.' That's not only ignorant and biased, that's belligerently ignorant and biased. It's absolutely an affront to the scientific method and the practice of interpretation of evidence using science. They don't want the flow of information going directly to the labs because of the likelihood that the crime lab will disagree with them or their findings. The majority of criminal cases in this country are not prosecuted using physical evidence, most are still prosecuted using witness identification and confessions. And there's a lot of room to hide."

Inman and Rudin (2001) point out, however, "Interestingly, neither law enforcement nor the legal participants are under any injunction to display objectivity. In particular, the attorneys on both sides are not only allowed, but required to advocate strongly for one side of the other. This is not the arena from which objective interpretation is expected to emanate."[1]

Charge No. 5: Soft Science Has Replaced Hard Science

As we will see later in this chapter, there are aspects of forensic science that some experts acknowledge is more cognitive than applied, an issue that riles commentators who push for greater scientific rigor. "With AFIS, you put in the latent print and you get the top 10 matches, for example, but it still comes down to a human sitting there, looking at those print candidates and saying, 'This is or this is not the person we are looking for,'" says Polski. "You can use a mass spectrometer to analyze evidence, and because it's a machine it should be accurate, right? But it still takes a human being to ensure the machine is calibrated correctly and that standards are correct, and protocols are followed. So can the machine now be completely objective because you presumably take the human element out of the equation?"

Polski recalls a conversation with a pathologist that highlights the issue: "He said to me, 'You know, I am kind of worried about these criticisms and charges being leveled at the pattern evidence community, because what I do is very similar to what you do. I look through microscopes at cells and it is my job to determine whether those cells are normal or abnormal, and if they are abnormal, what kind of abnormality is it. Are they cancer, or precancerous, or something else?' He said, 'I can give a slide to a person right out of their internship in a pathology residency and they'll look at it and say, I think that looks fine and write it off. I can give it to a five-year pathologist and he will look at it and say well, I don't think something is right here. I am going to show it to someone else. And that third person says, I've been doing this for 25 years and yes, that's cancer. He said, I don't know how I know that but I have been looking at this stuff for a long, long time and I can tell you for sure that's cancer.' I thought that was a great analogy to latent prints. Latent prints don't look anything like the fingerprints you see on a 10-print card. A trained and experienced latent examiner can look at latent lift and discern similarities or dissimilarities required to make an individualization. Some day we'll likely have a machine that will be able to do that, but until technology improves, you're still going to have to have the human element involved in identification. And I suppose if you have a human element involved in making these judgment calls, it's going to be difficult for mistakes to be eliminated. Education, training, and experience levels factor into it, because people with different levels of ability gained through experience can make identifications where people without that training and experience couldn't."

Wyckoff has a bone to pick with those who assert that forensic science is not science. "This is science, for the simple reason that analysts are using techniques that are grounded in the traditional sciences, including biochemistry and microscopy," Wyckoff says. "Look at the theoretical and experimental physicists who can do whatever they want to come up with a hypothesis which they may or may not actually check out. They may or may not do a rigorous study, and you may disagree on who you define 'rigorous,' but some will take a very long time to check everything out, and some may do a very simple proof that asserts that something does or does not meet that hypothesis and the science goes on from there. Then there are the applied sciences. There are some disciplines of forensic science that may have been in those theoretical and experimental areas, but people are moving away from that direction now. There are many more peer-reviewed journals in forensic science now than there were years ago, and there is a slow increase in the amount of research being done, so there is a difference in the way forensic science is becoming more rigorous."

"Not all forensic science is the same," asserts Kobilinsky. "There are parts of forensic science that are art, and parts that are science. A simple example is pattern evidence. When you are dealing with pattern evidence, such as comparing latent prints to inked prints, or when you look at a bite mark on skin, I think there's a certain amount of artistic endeavor included in the scientific skill set. It's obviously not the same as something based on a solid scientific foundation like DNA. Obviously, a lot of money has been invested in DNA and that is why it has become the gold standard. We must ask ourselves, 'How can we make something that is subjective more objective and more scientific?' There have been a number of cases where the likes of pattern evidence has banged heads with DNA and the DNA wins, but it also tells you that the other stuff is not always right. It's a signal that we better be very careful when it comes to pattern evidence."

Much of the criticism levied against forensic science goes to the heart of what kind of "science" forensic science truly is. It's a distinction that has some forensic practitioners up in arms, and still other members of the legal community insisting it's about time that distinct scientific striations were noted. This issue will be explored in greater detail in Chapter 10. Kelly and Wearne (1998) say that former FBI supervisor special agent Dr. Frederic Whitehurst "turned whistleblower" from the pressures of reconciling "the culture clash between the needs of science and the needs of law enforcement that are accentuated by the dominance of a law enforcement ethos rather than that of science in the FBI lab." Kelly and Wearne state, "Many accused him of being unable to make the distinction between pure and practical science. Yet Whitehurst is actually quick to acknowledge the uniqueness of the forensic process within science. The forensic scientist seeks to link a sample to an individual, to a substance, to distinguish it from other specimens in a way no other scientist would even attempt. The forensic scientist's standard fare is the sort of degraded, soiled sample that research scientists would trash if it ever came near their laboratory. The forensic scientist's goal is not pure knowledge but practical supposition."

Kelly and Wearne (1998) explain further: "Whitehurst's contention was simply that such ends had to be underpinned by scientific method, proven protocols and validated procedures or they would yield no proven truth, the ultimate aim of both law and science. Forensic science had to use procedures and processes that had withstood traditional scientific scrutiny, or been subjected to publication and peer review, the sort of 'institutional skepticism' that is the cornerstone of the scientific process. Forensic science examinations should be full-documented, subject to cross-examination and the results and process available to the defense. The reality is somewhat different. The openness, democratic debate, public dissemination, and protracted research that are the hallmarks of proper science contrast sharply with the secrecy, haste and authoritarian hierarchy of the crime lab."

Numerous critics have asserted that forensic science is an oxymoron. Kennedy (2003) pondered, "One would have thought that the issues surrounding homeland security would have increased the government's desire to apply better science to the detection of criminal activity and the pursuit of perpetrators. And of course our society has a long-standing concern about protecting the rights of the accused. Both these public interests—security and justice— would be furthered by a more scientific and reliable technology for analyzing crimes. The mystery here is why the practitioners don't seem to want it!"

Kelly and Wearne (1998) add to the allegations: "For years, some lawyers and many scientists have argued that forensic science is hardly a branch of science at all in its refusal and institutional inability to accept or conform to scientific norms. With relatively little research done in forensic science itself, there has been a propensity to adopt or adapt half-baked research done elsewhere. The result: Time after time definitive research in the field of forensic science has only been done after questions have been raised about the accuracy and reliability of its procedures, usually in court."

Charge No. 6: Bad Science Equals Wrongful Convictions

One of the greatest attacks on forensic science has come from critics who point to prosecutorial bias and forensic practitioner ineptitude that has resulted in wrongful convictions. In addition, addressing wrongful convictions has been one of the cornerstones of the demand for reform of forensic science. While we address this topic briefly here, it will be explored in much greater detail in Chapter 11.

Casey (2005) reports that in an analysis of at least 85 criminal convictions that DNA evidence later found to be wrong, the following factors were to blame: incompetent defense lawyers, police misconduct, eyewitness errors, false testimony by forensic scientists, prosecutorial misconduct, false confessions, errors in scientific testing, false testimony by lay witnesses, and dishonest informants. Frank and Hanchette (1994) cite a Gannett News Service (GNS) analysis of legal and media databases which found that there had been at least 85 instances in the past 20 years in which prosecutors "relied on fabricated, mishandled or tampered evidence to convict the innocent or free the guilty." Frank and Hanchette write, "Often, the wrongful prosecutions hid behind science." They quote Ray Taylor, a San Antonio lawyer and forensic pathology expert, as remarking, "In the United States, we take science as gospel. The public perception is that (faking science) is rare. The truth is it happens all the time." Frank and Hanchette add, "If science is gospel, then the scientists are its preachers. And when the scientists work for the police, critics say, the gospel can take a certain slant."

"We must look at the issue with a balanced perspective, which the detractors do not have," asserts Kobilinsky. "When you look at how many cases are handled—and handled well—every day in this country, there is no comparison. The vast majority of cases are done appropriately and solved and there are no issues. I am not saying that people aren't wrongfully convicted, but that happens for a lot of other reasons than for faulty forensic science. There is a lot going on with eyewitness identification, with false confessions, a lot of stuff other than pure forensic science, although there are some issues in forensic science that must be addressed. A lab must be open to scrutiny, and there must be transparency. That's very important, especially relating to the issue of wrongful convictions. If a lab doesn't want to be transparent in the way it functions, that lab should be closed down."

Much of the criticism is directed at soft or questionable sciences used in laboratories; however, fingers are being pointed at the kind of forensic science previously assumed to be unassailable. Frank and Hanchette (1994) write, "The 'science' in the wrongful convictions studied by GNS ranges from the absurd—an evidence-sniffing dog that could solve decade-old crimes—to the advanced, such as DNA tests touted as fail-safe genetic fingerprints. . . . And in each case in the analysis, the jury or the judge believed the science, sometimes despite reams of evidence to the contrary." They quote George Washington University law professor James Starrs as saying, "Faking or lying about evidence is not out of the ordinary at all. There are so many things of this kind, I'm horrified."

Many critics say that forensic science is a mixed bag of tricks, heavy on the smoke and mirrors, and skimpy on the science. Scheck and Neufeld (2001) write, "For much of the 20th century, prosecutors served up the forensic scientist as a source of certainty amid fleeting glimpses, shaky memories, and disputed confessions. Or so it seemed. . . . Thousands of prisoners are serving time based on . . . bogus science, which often props up wobbly eyewitness testimony or dubious tales peddled by jailhouse snitches. . . . Unsound techniques survive because forensic science has been woven into the culture of prosecution and insulated from routine quality assurance standards we impose on medical testing labs. . . . Too often, forensic laboratories are run by law enforcement officers in lab coats. The laboratories cannot be allowed to operate as arms of police departments and prosecutors' offices. They need to be independent agencies, serving as fact finders for both the prosecution and the defense. . . . In forensic laboratories, by contrast, few are held accountable for a bad practice or botched results. Under this system, the innocent pay, not the criminals."

According to Neufeld (2005), forensic science can "fail" in two ways: "lacking reliability (i.e., the inability to reproduce valid results) and bias, incompetence, or a lack of adequate internal controls for the evidence introduced by the forensic scientists and their laboratories." Neufeld elaborates, "Bad forensic science is bad law enforcement. Each time unreliable science, incompetent scientists or crime lab misconduct is used to arrest, indict, or convict an innocent person, the real perpetrator remains free to commit more crime. Faulty forensic science may wrongly exclude suspects. Guilty defendants can be wrongfully exculpated. In criminal cases that use forensic science during the investigation and trial, meaningful precautions must exist to guard against junk science and unreliable results."

Charge No. 7: Lack of Forensic Laboratory Management

Vilified in the 1998 book, *Tainted Evidence,* by John F. Kelly and Phillip K. Wearne, the FBI Laboratory was established by detractors as the poster child for ineptitude. A 1997 report by the inspector general (IG) stated that it found scientifically flawed testimony, inaccurate testimony, testimony beyond the competence of examiners, improper preparation of laboratory reports, insufficient documentation of test results, scientifically flawed reports, inadequate record management and retention, and failures of management to resolve serious and credible allegations of incompetence.

Whitehurst (2004) states, "Lest the reader should suspect that media coverage is the only suggestion of failure in crime labs, we are referred to government and academic descriptions of these issues. Giannelli (2003) says these problems could have been prevented by proper management. Kelly and Wearne (1999) state, "The means of making physical evidence proof is forensic science, the application of science to legal processes, the application of science to crime-fighting. Together or apart, the words 'forensic' and 'scientific' are today commonly used as everyday adjectives that imply definitive, detailed, and comprehensively argued. It is an image burnished by popular television detective series like *Quincy* and the coverage of big cases by *Court TV,* an image epitomized by the source of the country's most famous forensic science, the FBI's crime lab."

Kelly and Wearne (1998) state, "Forensic science is now genetics and microbiology in DNA typing, nuclear physics in neutron activation analysis, analytical chemistry in infrared, ultra-violet or X-ray spectrometry and statistics in computerized number crunching. These new technologies have in many cases been grafted onto a profession that in many of its traditional sub-fields, like fingerprints, questioned documents, ballistics, hair and fibers, explosives, was not actually based on science at all but on subjective comparisons by individual examiners. Yet either way, whether the 'soft' science of the traditional visual comparisons of two hairs, bullets or fingerprints, or the 'hard' science of neutron activation analysis or DNA typing, forensic science cannot ultimately avoid the human factor. The examiners who do the tests, run the machines and make the comparisons are only human. At the FBI lab and the nearly 400 other crime labs in the United States, those people have turned out to be as flawed as the eye-witnesses, juries or lawyers who make up the rest of the judicial process."

Charge No. 8: Lack of Forensic Laboratory Oversight and Accreditation

A common chorus heard from detractors of forensic science is that it lacks adequate oversight. Jonakait (1991) states, "Forensic science . . . determines whether people are jailed as well as whether the guilty are mistakenly freed. Accurate forensic science is essential to justice, but abysmal quality remains widespread. The quality of forensic science must be improved. Since regulation can produce better performance, forensic laboratories should be regulated."

Giannelli (2003) notes, "More than a decade ago, molecular biologist Eric Lander, who served as an expert witness in one of the first court cases involving DNA evidence, noted: 'At present, forensic science is virtually unregulated, with the paradoxical result that clinical laboratories must meet higher standards to be allowed to diagnose strep throat than forensic labs must meet to put a defendant on death row.' Since that time, there have been a number of voluntary attempts to improve crime laboratories, such as the accreditation process of the ASCLD/LAB. Nevertheless, except for New York, Texas, and Oklahoma, there is no manda-tory accreditation. A similar situation exists with death investigation agencies accredited by the National Association of Medical Examiners (NAME). Although 40 medical systems have been accredited, they cover only 25 percent of the population. In addition, accreditation rates are low for practicing forensic scientists, even though forensic certification boards for all the major disciplines have been in existence for more than a decade."

While the ASCLD/LAB accreditation program has been in operation since 1989, critics continue to push for a better system of peer review and oversight of forensic laboratories. Jonakait (1991) states, "The effect of inadequate education, training, and research on reliable and accurate forensic results might be mitigated if these facilities had meaningful quality control programs—formally instituted procedures that, if followed carefully, assure the best possible results. Crime labs, however, are not required to follow quality control plans. Thus, quality control in American crime laboratories remains on the honor system. This system, however, has not produced widespread quality control programs. Instead, forensic science has often treated the topic of quality control with hostility."

Turvey says he sees "an epidemic of scientific ineptitude" in forensic laboratories today. "Why have we had crime lab scandals? We have them because of the accreditation process. To become accredited, you have to have an independent audit, and it's the independent audits that are causing all this introspection and it's exposing one by one all the problems in crime labs." But Turvey takes issue with ASCLD/LAB, the body that accredits forensic laboratories. "ASCLD has some good things going for it. But why do we as a forensic science community have to wait for ASCLD to tell us how to be scientists? That part always confuses the heck out of me. Why are forensic scientists in need of instruction or permission to do good science? That and its requirements have some fairly palpable weaknesses; ASCLD relies on formalistic review, not actual double-blind peer review, for example. In an environment where all the members are lab directors—part of the same group of friends with mutual interests to be served—formalistic peer review cannot be trusted."

Kobilinsky says he views accreditation as providing a mechanism for peer review. "If a lab only has one person determining results, the lab is probably not doing the right thing," he says. "You need to have someone verify that the tests were done correctly, the analysis was done correctly, and the interpretation was done correctly. You need at least another person who is separated from the case for the greatest objectivity. When a lab is accredited, there is assurance that people are scrutinizing protocols and procedures. There should never be an organization without some oversight because that's an excuse for abuse; people slack off, they take shortcuts, or they do things the wrong way. It's a minority of people, but a system like accreditation can catch things like that. The amount of oversight needed, and who will conduct the oversight, is still under discussion in the community. I think if a crime lab has a problem, there should always be an organization that is ready to go in and take a look at the problem and give some kind of evaluation and perspective on what went wrong and how it can be corrected in the future."

Jonakait (1991) comments, "Assuring quality, however, is crucial for forensic laboratories. Experience and data have shown that quality control programs are necessary for guaranteeing proper clinical lab performance. The absence of such plans from crime laboratories only assures unreliable testing by forensic facilities. . . . Instead of instituting and following good, formal quality control procedures, forensic laboratories too often cling to methods and routines that only decrease accuracy and reliability."

Critics maintain that forensic science, unlike other scientific disciplines, lacks clearly delineated, enforceable protocols. Jonakait (1991) remarks, "Protocols, the lists of instructions for performing scientific procedures, are the recipes of science. Like good recipes, good protocols are tested procedures that, if followed, assure that the desired results are most likely to occur. Scientific procedure and common sense dictate the use of such protocols. If the scientist and others are to have confidence in the results, tested procedures must be followed to get those results. Procedures that do not follow an established protocol can only produce experimental outcomes. Of course, a crime lab should not be reporting these experimental results as scientific fact."

Jonakait (1991) asserts, "Crime laboratories, however, frequently perform analyses without adhering to established procedures. In many crime laboratories in the United States, the analyst is not required to possess or to follow a printed protocol, nor is he required to heed any instructions or warnings. In some areas of forensic science, established protocols do not even exist. An absence of tested protocols means that crime lab analysts are left to determine for themselves what modifications in established procedures or what new procedures will best fit their abilities, their equipment, and the evidence. Forensic scientists, then, are often using procedures that have never been truly scientifically tested."

Critics say that forensic practitioners defend an absence of tested procedures "by asserting that such protocols cannot be used," because, as Jonakait (1991) states, "They maintain that standardized practices can only be used with standard samples and crime labs do not analyze such samples. This assertion is simply bad science. Although the forensic sample may be unknown, proper analysis will not be enhanced by introducing additional unknowns. Accurate analytical determinations require the elimination of variables, not the introduction of more. Adherence to protocols eliminates unnecessary unknowns. A distinguished scientist has asked, 'If there is a proper way to do it, why not do it that way every time?' If there is no proper way, how can anyone be confident of the results?"

Jonakait (1991) and others ask this rhetorical question: If DNA has established protocols that must be followed, why then do other forensic disciplines lack the appropriate protocols? Jonakait adds, "If protocols can be established for DNA identifications, they can be devised for any area of forensic science. That forensic scientists in fact do not institute and routinely follow tested analytical procedures is an indication that forensic labs cannot produce consistently accurate results."

Forensic laboratories are frequently compared to clinical laboratories, although many forensic professionals say it is a comparison of apples and oranges. Critics assert that forensic facilities are faced with a greater number of unknown variables than other laboratories. If errors are made, the critics charge, the very nature of the forensic laboratory lends itself to a more facile cover-up. Jonakait (1991) states, "Forensic tests may have fewer inherent controls than other kinds of testing. Also, errors in forensic labs will not be highlighted as are errors in research labs. Good researchers often recognize incorrectly performed procedures because the results will conflict with existing knowledge." Therefore, he summarizes, ". . . forensic procedures should be carried out even more meticulously than other kinds of tests. Forensic labs should require more stringent quality control programs than labs where errors will be fewer and more apparent."

Without proper oversight, critics assert, laboratory results are akin to crap shoots. Arvizu (2000) states, "Outside the scientific establishment, laboratory results are often believed to be 'answers.' In fact, laboratory measurements of unknowns are only estimates of the true values. Laboratory analysis of an unknown material always involves a degree of uncertainty. However, if a laboratory's measurement system is operated in a state of statistical control, and if all elements of a laboratory's system are carefully controlled, monitored, and documented, it is possible to evaluate the quality and reliability of the reported results."

Inman and Rudin (2001) state, "In the current climate of intense scrutiny, it is necessary to demonstrate that any test system is working as expected and providing reliable results. It is also good scientific practice to do so. Historically, this has nether been offered nor expected with any consistency."[1]

Detractors bemoan the lack of quality control in today's forensic laboratories, and while it isn't a blanket indictment of forensic science, these charges do make it appear that forensic science is the Wild West of old. Arvizu (2000) comments, "Make no mistake about it; many of the individuals who labor in private, state, local, and federal laboratories are talented, ethical, and capable forensic scientists. However, the quality of a laboratory's work product depends on more than the technical ability of individual scientists. Experience has shown that consistent production and reporting of high quality results depends on a carefully designed, comprehensive and technically rigorous quality assurance program. Yet, in our nation's forensic laboratories, scientists and laboratory managers can complete their careers without a practical understanding or formal experience with quality assurance."

Proper laboratory practice encompasses processes to ensure validity and reliability, including optimization, validation, standards, and controls. Inman and Rudin (2001) state, "Optimization establishes that the test system is working properly so that variation seen is due to the samples themselves. . . . In contrast to optimization, which concentrates on the test system, validation concentrates on the samples themselves. In performing validation studies, we ask what quantitative and qualitative properties of the samples themselves might confound our ability to get reliable results or to get no results at all."[1] They add, "For the science in forensic science to be taken seriously, each analytical test must be accompanied by the appropriate standards and controls."[1] Efforts at standardization for the forensic science community commenced in part thanks to the advent of DNA testing; they were strengthened by complementary programs established by the American Society for Testing and Materials (ASTM) and the National Institute of Standards and Technology (NIST). The ASTM Committee E-30 on Forensic Sciences was established in 1970 to standardize terminology and scientific methods particular to the field, while the NIST develops and distributes standard materials used in a variety of forensic disciplines to establish that instruments and methods are providing the expected results.

Forensic laboratories also conduct several levels of reviews of an analyst's work product, including internal review by a qualified peer or supervisor, as well as independent review, as is common within the accreditation process. The elements of these reviews frequently consist of evaluation of the hypothesis involved in the analysis, the documentation of the testing conducted, the veracity and the integrity of the results, the standards and controls used, the accuracy of the calculations, and the appropriateness of the interpretation and conclusions. In addition, the reviewer ensures that validation studies are in place for procedures performed on a daily basis. Inman and Rudin (2001) state, "Before evidence is examined or analyzed, the system must be optimized and validation studies performed. These efforts ensure, respectively, that the maximum information can be obtained from the evidence and that interpretation is performed within the limits established for the system."[1]

Arvizu (2000) observes, "The current situation, in which forensic laboratories operate without independent oversight, is intolerable. It represents a systematic failure by the criminal justice system to demand compliance with quality standards, and that the work of forensic laboratories be subject to independent quality assessment. In no other industry are laboratories shielded from independent oversight."

Wells says that the ASCLD/LAB program and the accreditation process are maturing and growing and moving into a more international mode that models the International Standards Organization, a program universally accepted by the private sector. "It's all in a move toward producing a standardized, quality product and to establish expectations for practitioners to live up to," Wells affirms. "The process of accreditation means that a lab is saying, 'Come into my lab, open the drawers, look behind the doors, kick the tires, tell me where I have shortfalls so I can correct them.' When a crime lab does that, it makes a powerful public statement that it is committed to providing a quality operation, and that there are safeguards in place to catch mistakes or intentional fabrications. One of the keystones of the accreditation process is peer review that requires more than one scientist to verify that conclusions are scientifically sound, that the work that led up to the conclusions is scientifically sound, and that the entire testing process meets the standards as we know them today. We have to go back to the FBI crime lab situation; they were accredited and had peer review in play, and yet it failed. Why did it fail? That's what the community is looking at now and trying to determine how to prevent other failures like that."

As we will see in Chapter 5, ASCLD was designed to provide training to managers operating forensic laboratories, and Wells says he stands behind the organization's ability to serve as a fail-safe haven for the crime lab community. "As part of our mission, we provide training opportunities to lab managers at our annual symposium. The training and education that ASCLD promotes is to help managers maintain quality forensic service in labs in order to support the judicial process. We take very seriously the responsibility of producing a quality product, knowing that our practitioners live up to certain standards and their educational expertise standards are sufficient to do the work."

There are charges by commentators that ASCLD/LAB is rife with cronyism; lab directors like Ferrara dispute the claim and say they simply are insisting on the important tenet of self-determination. "Detractors and critics want oversight of crime labs by someone other than the forensic laboratory profession itself," says Ferrara. "The American Medical Association would not want to be regulated by the American Bar Association and vice versa, so what they are proposing for labs is ridiculous. If we are going to be regulated, we should be regulated by a body that meets the standards recommended by the National Academy of Sciences' National Research Council. That is ASCLD/LAB. But again, the defense bar likes to suggest we are just a bunch of cops in lab coats, or a bunch of cronies and golfing buddies. I can't think they really believe that, but I guess they do, because the law schools seem to be full of them."

"I don't think we are any more of a good ol' boys club than the American Bar Association or the American Medical Association," Wells concurs. "ASCLD/LAB was a child of ASCLD; it sprang from the organization and since separated itself in an effort to get away from this fox-guarding-the-henhouse perception. In order to provide oversight to any profession, it takes people who are familiar with the work to evaluate that work product. I certainly could not judge whether an attorney lived up to proper representation of a client. But other attorneys can and do, so do judges, and that is only right. But an attorney cannot and should not be allowed to evaluate and pass judgment on a field in which he does not practice, meaning science."

"Usually the people who claim that ASCLD or ASCLD/LAB is only a guild probably are not very educated, for the simple reason that if you look at any profession, they oversee their own people," Wyckoff asserts. "Whether it's the AMA or the ABA, they oversee their own people; they don't bring in outsiders. Engineers don't bring in doctors, and attorneys don't bring in psychologists. They work within their own field. I don't think that's any different than what you should expect of oversight of forensic science. Lots of people assume that once a crime lab is accredited, from here on out it's a good ol' boy network, therefore problems can be swept under the rug when they arise, instead of being addressed and resolved. That's simply not true. I was on the ASCLD/LAB board for four years, and in that time we conducted a lot of internal reviews of labs that were in trouble, where they voluntarily asked us to come in and examine closely what they were doing. To me, that doesn't sound like a facility that is hiding behind anything."

Charge No. 9: Lack of Proficiency Testing and Certification

Numerous commentators have asserted that there is an abysmal lack of testing and certification of forensic analysts and examiners. Some have even gone so far as to suggest certification should be mandatory. Jonakait (1991) observes, "Forensic scientists have failed to rectify the lack of governmental oversight with a self-regulation system. A few voluntary certification programs do exist, but forensic science has not developed general, national standards to assure competency. Indeed, the largest segment of forensic science has fiercely resisted even a voluntary certification program. A proposal for national certification of criminalists was made in 1979 by the Criminalistics Certification Study Committee on the basis of a three-year study of the issues conducted under the auspices of the Law Enforcement Assistance Administration. This proposal did not receive support of the majority of the profession at the time, and the profession has yet to adopt a national certification program. That the proposal did not receive support is an understatement. It was resoundingly rejected by the criminalists. It was defeated by a 2-to-1 margin."

Jonakait (1991) emphasizes that voluntary certification would have only a limited effect on forensic science quality; he points to clinical laboratory studies that have established that non-mandatory regulatory systems are not as effective in producing quality control as are mandatory programs. Jonakait (1991) adds, "Moreover, certification can be meaningful only if it has important consequences. The value of certification is in the prestige and economic advantage afforded to those certified. For example, physicians certified as specialists benefit economically and are eligible for more hospital affiliations. However, no consequences flow from the lack of a forensic science certificate. Courts do not deny forensic scientists expert status because they lack certification. The forensic scientist continues to work with or without participation in one of the few existing certification programs."

Polski says he is in favor of accreditation because it not only puts into place solid quality assurance and improvement programs, it gets people thinking about the next logical step: the analysts themselves. "Accreditation applies to the organization, of course, but the natural extension of that is certification of the individual examiner or analyst," Polski says. "Over the next five or 10 years you will see increased emphasis on accrediting the organization and moving to ensure that the people who work in that organization have the right skills, knowledge, and ability to do the job. I'm not sure if in my lifetime we will ever see mandatory certification, but I think it's certainly a good thing to move toward."

"I know many forensic scientists don't like the idea of licensure or certification, especially if it is mandatory, but I do think in some respects, whether we like it or not, we are headed that way," Wyckoff says. "My state, Idaho, requires certification of our lab people, and as far as I know it's the only one that does. Many people don't feel certification is necessary because they have advanced degrees. If you hold a Ph.D. in biochemistry, you can go out and do things and not be certified, and that by and large doesn't detract from you. But I would tell you there are people right now who have Ph.D.s in biology or biochemistry who may decry the fact that forensic scientists aren't certified, but they themselves would not become certified even if they are practicing in the field themselves. A defense attorney may go to a doctorate-level chemist and say, 'I would like you to reanalyze this sample to see if it is really what this forensic scientist says,' even though that forensic scientist may be certified. Publicly, the defense attorney and that chemist say all forensic scientists should be certified. But if you ask that chemist if he is certified, he'll say, 'Well, I don't need that, I have a Ph.D.' That's more than a little ironic to me. If the ABA wants anyone who is going to be a witness in court to be certified, then you'd better make sure you require that of your defense experts as well."

"I used to think that people like Paul Giannelli and Barry Scheck were the enemy, but I've come to believe that nothing is ever going to change until there are some standards in place," Fisher says. "When I first started working 37 years ago, the conventional wisdom was that it will be sorted out in the courtroom, and that the courts will dictate how we run our operations and they will not permit shoddy, substandard work. The truth is, the people in the courtroom, whether it's the judges, the prosecutors, or the defense attorneys, are not scientists. They don't understand what is going on. Until there are requirements for practitioners and better training of lawyers and judges, the situation will continue."

Fisher remains cautious, however, about the level of regulation needed for forensic laboratories. "In the early 1970s, crime labs were being attacked by the defense bar on drunk-driving cases. The California Association of Criminalists spearheaded legislation to license labs that conduct blood-alcohol testing," Fisher recalls. "That was a big mistake because it became a case of bureaucracy gone berserk. People who had no idea about forensic science, or even science, were dictating to labs; the things they were requiring us to do were asinine. We would have to have our procedures approved by the state health department. In some cases, if they didn't like an abbreviation that was used, they would send it back for rewriting. For example, once we used an abbreviation for gram as 'gm' instead of 'g,' and they would disallow your procedure. After years of fighting with them and getting nowhere we retained the services of a lobbyist, got the law changed, and we got them partially out of the forensic science regulatory business. So yes, there is a very real possibility of regulation and oversight of crime labs going too far. I think that if the language is written carefully enough and there was enough oversight and the ability to make good course corrections, that these problems could be avoided."

Moriarty and Saks (2005) advocate for a stringent system of proficiency testing for forensic analysts and examiners because this mechanism can reveal the risks of error in a systematic and wide-ranging fashion. They state, "Before proficiency studies, forensic scientists could assert that their conclusions rarely, if ever, were in error and that what one examiner concluded about a given examination all examiners would agree with. As long as no evidence existed testing these claims, examiners could say almost anything without risk of contradiction. In most cases, an item of evidence would be examined, an opinion would be announced, no one could know whether the examiner was right or wrong, and no one could know whether or not other examiners would have reached other conclusions."

Proficiency testing essentially provides known materials to a number of forensic examiners who are then asked to perform their usual examination of the evidence. Their conclusions can then be compared not only to the correct answers but to other examiners' conclusions. According to Moriarty and Saks (2005), these tests have been known to reveal a number of things: that examiners sometimes reached erroneous conclusions; that some fields on average made more errors than others; that within specialties the level of incorrect conclusions varied depending on the nature of the evidence to be examined; and that for some forensic disciplines, accuracy was not significantly related to years of experience, certification, or other qualifications.

For commentators who criticize forensic scientists' statements of absolute certainty, proficiency testing can conveniently refute their assertions of near-perfect accuracy. Moriarty and Saks (2005) report that proficiency testing has revealed spectrographic voice identification error rates as high as 63 percent; handwriting error rates ranging from 40 to 100 percent; false-positive error rates for bite marks as high as 64 percent; tool mark identification errors as high as 35 percent; and the fact that one-fourth of fingerprint examiners fail to correctly identify all latent prints in a typical proficiency test.

Moriarty and Saks (2005) note, "Still, these tests probably understate the actual error rate in everyday casework. The tests often are relatively easy. The tests are non-blind, so that participants are aware that their accuracy is being evaluated, and they know to work harder to try to avoid the embarrassment of making discernible errors. Also, in contrast to everyday cases, proficiency tests provide no extrinsic cues to expected or desired answers, and change the examiners' base rate assumptions. And, of course, if some examiners are making errors and others are not, then examiners cannot all be in agreement with each other. Thus, claims such as that all qualified document examiners would reach the same conclusions in all cases, though once asserted confidently, can now be seen to be groundless exaggerations—hopes and assumptions offered as facts."

The forensic sciences are not without a history of studies on proficiency testing, although critics are swift to point out their less-than-stellar results. In 1974, the Forensic Science Foundation issued a series of 21 tests for a range of evidence types to some forensic laboratories. According to Peterson et al. (1978), the tests revealed unacceptable proficiency in identifying animal hair specimens as well as determining paint, soil, glass, blood, and handwriting samples that shared a common origin. Labs also lacked analysis techniques for discriminating bloodstains; according to Peterson and Markham (1995a), analysis of these findings identified the following causes of the inadequacies: misinterpretation of test results; examiners who were careless or lacked training or experience; mislabeled or contaminated standards; inadequate databases; and faulty testing procedures. Peterson and Markham (1995b) reviewed the ability of laboratories to determine if an unknown sample shared a common origin with a known sample. The evidence examined was firearms, tool marks, hair, footwear, physiological fluids, glass, paint, fibers, latent fingerprints, questioned documents, and metals. Error rates ranged from 0.5 percent for latent print cards to a high of 23 percent for automotive parts.

In 1995, Collaborative Testing Services tested 156 U.S. fingerprint examiners in a proficiency test sponsored by the International Association for Identification. Forty-four percent of examiners correctly identified all seven latent fingerprints provided 56 percent got at least one print wrong, and 4 percent of examiners failed to identify any prints correctly. The testing was conducted in a controlled, relatively pressure-free environment, where examiners could be more careful and exacting—the complete opposite of a normal workday environment, leading some to worry about rampant error rates.

Jonakait (1991) reports that researchers Risinger, Denbeaux, and Saks obtained the handwriting identification proficiency tests from 1984 to 1987 and that their summary of those tests discloses an "astonishing lack of proficiency on the part of crime labs." The data had indicated that 45 percent of the forensic document examiners reached the correct finding, in 36 percent they erred partially or completely, and in 19 percent they were unable to draw a conclusion. Jonakait (1991) states, "If we assume that inconclusive examinations do not wind up as testimony in court, and omit the inconclusive reports, and remain as generous as possible within the bounds of reason, then the most we can conclude is this: Document examiners were correct 57 percent of the time and incorrect 43 percent of the time." Risinger, Denbeaux, and Saks concluded that "the kindest statement we can make is that no available evidence demonstrates the existence of handwriting identification expertise."

Jonakait (1991) also points to a test conducted by the California Association of Crime Laboratory Directors which reported that two out of three private forensic laboratories made an error in analyzing samples. One organization was erroneous in one of the 44 matches it identified, while another organization was wrong in one of 50 matches, and only the third organization was correct in all of its matches. Jonakait (1991) states, "Information which surfaced later indicates that the results of that testing were more disturbing than first thought. Documents obtained through discovery in a criminal case indicated that one of the three tested labs had actually produced two reports. The first response 'contained an extraordinary number of misclassifications, including one false positive, at least three false negatives . . . and at least two incorrect reports of mixed stains.' A commentator, after reporting this further information, concluded that this study 'is the only meaningful blind trial of the proficiency of DNA laboratories' and it 'raises serious concerns' about the quality of the work being done."

Charge No. 10: Lack of Forensic Laboratory Funding

Even the most ardent detractor of forensic science admits that something must be done to shore up a crumbling infrastructure in a significant number of crime labs and medico-legal offices throughout the country, as well as address a striking polarity in terms of the so-called "haves" and "have-nots."

"Here I am in New York City, with the office of the chief medical examiner that is building a 13-story DNA structure, which makes it the biggest DNA lab in the country," remarks Kobilinsky. "So it's definitely not your typical medical examiner's office. In general, if you want the job done right, you need adequate personnel, facilities, and equipment, and you need a decent budget. And too many offices around the country are lacking in all three areas. I think the federal government is starting to realize this now, but we have a long way to go. We are also lacking in funding for critical forensic science research. Other countries, like Japan and England, spend so much more time and money on forensic research. Until the time comes that the U.S. can dig deeper into its pockets for this kind of funding, we're going to continue to have problems. In the same manner, the few people who are doing research, are not doing casework, and that's not the way to do it. You're only robbing Peter to pay Paul."

The current state of infrastructure for forensic laboratories and medico-legal offices will be explored in depth in Chapters 5 and 8. It's no surprise that around the country, lab managers have a growing wish list. "I want to see that every forensic laboratory is staffed and equipped equal to what we see on *CSI: Crime Scene Investigation*," Wells emphasizes. "If we could reach that level, then I think most of the problems forensic science faces today, including immense backlogs, would go away. We have so many issues that need to be addressed, including staffing shortfalls, inferior physical facilities, lack of equipment, low pay, and ever-shrinking budgets. Hopefully with more aggressive advocacy efforts, attention can be focused equally on all areas of forensic science, and we may see some improvement. DNA has received a tremendous amount of funding and it has borne fruit in the creation of an excellent database; but there are still problems relating to backlog, cold cases, no-suspect cases, completion of CODIS with all offenders accounted for, and evidence samples sitting in refrigerators around the country not being processed because of lack of funds."

As a result of being fettered by funding deficits, forensic laboratories are hampered in providing the highest level of service to meet the growing demand. "Much of our work consists of confirming what law enforcement suspects or has generated through their investigation," Wells says. "Because of the demand that is placed on us, and the lack of resources available to us, we can't provide the true service level that forensic science should be providing. That is, to be a better investigative tool; we don't have the resources to respond quickly enough to provide investigative services."

Wells also says that a lack of funding can jeopardize the quality of the work product produced by forensic laboratories. "I am convinced that a lack of funding is a major contributing factor to the forensic failures we read about in the newspapers," Wells emphasizes. "Meeting accreditation and certification standards costs money, and crime labs have been chronically shortchanged."

Wells and other forensic laboratory managers can tick off on their fingers the number of agencies that have noted this shortfall throughout the past several decades and presidential administrations. In 1967, President Lyndon Johnson's crime commission observed that a majority of police-affiliated crime labs had minimal equipment and lack skilled personnel able to use the current technology. In 1974, President Richard Nixon's crime commission commented that too many crime labs' budgets precluded the recruitment of qualified forensic professionals.

Charge No. 11: Lack of Scientific Rigor and Research in Forensic Science

Commentators have asserted there is a lack of empirical validation in forensic science disciplines. Jonakait (1991) states, "Forensic science is supported by almost no research. The laboratory practices are based on intuitions and deductions, not on empirical proof. For example, the forensic profession has not undertaken research to determine the optimal conditions in which to do their work and maximize their accuracy. One can only be astounded at the volume of research on eyewitness accuracy and the paucity of parallel work on forensic science accuracy."

Many claim that there is an abysmal lack of science in forensic science, an issue that is explored more fully in Chapter 10, particularly in the pattern evidence identification sciences involving fibers, hairs, and other trace evidence, bite marks, and footprints. Critics say that examiners in these disciplines overstep the boundaries of science. Jonakait (1991) observes, "Conclusions are frequently presented by people claiming to be scientists, but who have neither analyzed the basis of their own assertions nor undertaken experiments to test those hypotheses. When they do test their claims, they too often do it only after having already relied upon a new technique. Research patterns indicate that testing is frequently motivated not by the forensic scientists' scientific impulses but because of probing questions about the accuracy and reliability of forensic procedures raised by those outside of the field."

Jonakait (1991) adds, "These practices raise concerns about the quality of the forensic sciences. Certainly, the results of procedures and techniques supported only by the assertions or deductions of some forensic scientists, rather than by rigorous research, are suspect. But the research patterns raise a more fundamental concern. They indicate that substandard scientific thinking pervades these fields. Since the lack of scientific rigor is so widespread, even forensic science research which does occur may not be done adequately. Techniques and procedures based on inferior research should be as suspect as those based on no research. Even though inferior scientific techniques may not exist in all areas of the forensic sciences, enough substandard practices exist to suggest severe quality problems for crime laboratories."

Because they are unique in the scientific world, forensic disciplines require solid research more so than any other area of scientific inquiry, according to Jonakait (1991), who adds, "Since a cautious forensic scientist cannot readily use research techniques from other areas, forensic science has a greater need for research than other areas. This characteristic, however, is not the only one indicating that forensic science has exceptional needs for research. Special needs arise in forensic science because the use of a technique or test will not validate or expose the flaws in those procedures as it does in other scientific and technical areas."

"Unlike many other endeavors, forensic science is often unable to adopt scientific knowledge and techniques from related areas," Jonakait (1991) adds. "Frequently, there is no related discipline to draw upon. Only the forensic scientist is interested in studying for identification purposes such things as bullets, toolmarks, and fingerprints." The very nature of the research is singular as well; it is an entirely different scientific undertaking and would seem almost to run counter to traditional scientific inquiry. Jonakait explains that instead of identifying a sample, forensic scientists' goal is to distinguish the sample from other specimens. In addition, these samples are not the pristine samples found in clinical laboratories, for example, and whose potentially contaminated physical properties can skew the data.

Jonakait (1991) observes, "Crime scene samples are often unique, of unknown origin and unascertainable history. In contrast, most scientific researchers know what they are working with and its history. Whereas most scientists would not work with samples that have been dropped on the floor, the samples for a DNA identification quite literally may have been scraped off the linoleum. It cannot be assumed that research on pristine, known samples applies to the contaminated, degraded, aged samples of unknown history confronted by the forensic scientist. Validation studies must be done specifically on samples approximating forensic condition. This issue, which has been raised with respect to DNA profiling and blood tests, is relevant to many other areas of forensic science as well. It is only conjectural to conclude that the techniques and tools developed for related disciplines can be accurately applied to crime lab work without first validating those scientific procedures under forensic conditions. The assumption that a method proved valid in one area can be applied in crime laboratories has frequently led to faulty results."

Working against the forensic science community at times is a lack of university-level research. Jonakait (1991) asserts that while there is the expectation that universities are a major source of forensic science research, "they actually do very little of it." He explains: "As a matter of practice, academic institutions are heavily involved in basic scientific research, so it seems only logical that graduate programs in forensic science should be actively involved in such research. However, the fact remains that far less than what is expected is actually performed in the academic atmosphere." Jonakait points to a survey of forensic science institutions that revealed 95 percent spent less than 25 percent of their time on research, and none of the respondents reported that they devoted more than 50 percent of their time to research activities. In addition, the few institutions with any kind of research orientation experienced difficulty in securing funding to support these efforts. Jonakait states, "The absence of university research harms the quality of the forensic sciences and forces the research on to the crime laboratories. These facilities, however, cannot produce much significant research. Those who go into crime labs typically lack the training and skill required to be good research scientists . . . the academic programs that produce many forensic scientists often have low status and do not attract the best students. Research-inclined students are unlikely to enter such programs. Forensic science instructors, not themselves researchers, are unlikely and probably unable to teach their students the fundamentals of good research."

Several commentators, including Jonakait (1991), have observed that the forensic scientists who are most qualified to teach and to conduct research benefiting the field have little time and scant resources to do so. Jonakait states, "Surveys find that the mean amount of time spent in crime labs researching new laboratory techniques is 4.4 percent and that those laboratories not involved in research outnumber those that are. Commentators have concluded that American crime laboratories are not research laboratories, and many crime laboratory analysts have neither the education, training, time, nor resources to conduct extensive reliability experiments."

Michael Saks, Ph.D., M.S.L., a member of the faculties of the Sandra Day O'Connor College of Law and the Department of Psychology, as well as a faculty fellow of the Center for the Study of Law, Science & Technology at Arizona State University, says that he strongly encourages more and better forensic science research and practice, adding, "I think that choices have been made all along by practitioners and one choice is to refrain from doing research." Saks points to the many handwriting examiners who do not hold graduate or even undergraduate degrees, indicative of what he says is the 96 percent of forensic scientists working in crime labs who have bachelor degrees or less and who cannot perform research.

Saks recalls, "I was at a conference of handwriting experts where I was probably the only critic; in the audience were a few neutral people, and a dozen or so supporters of the faith. One person in the audience stood up and declared, 'I have learned more about science today than I ever wanted to know; I am not interested in keeping up with studies and research because I have a full caseload.' It makes sense, because for these people to take time out to conduct research is to take time out from earning money. I think we have created a culture in which the courts have apparently been content with what they have been getting from the forensic science field, therefore there is no need to do research. After all, this research would force these analysts to temper what they say; they could no longer go into court and make extreme statements without having any basis for it other than their own subjective confidence in it."

Saks continues, "The courts generally say, 'Terrific, glad to hear it,' so why do research if it takes time from making money or if you are in a government crime laboratory and it takes time from your caseload in which there is already a backlog? That's not going to make your supervisor happy, so why do it? Besides, you don't have the skills for research; you only have the skills to carry out whatever you have been taught to do in your forensic examinations. And to start doing research might require collaborating with people you don't know or like, or acquiring skills you don't have and that's painful. So these people don't do research."

"If someone suddenly came along with the money for research, it probably still wouldn't matter," Saks hazards. "I suppose the fact that the National Institute of Justice [NIJ] has put out requests for proposals in a number of areas for a number of years and gets very few takers is an indication that even if you offer the money, people aren't going to come get it. I suppose these practitioners say to themselves, 'I'd be glad to do it but I don't have the time.' The only people who do submit proposals for these funds turn out to be people in engineering departments doing artificial intelligence or computer-assisted pattern recognition, and it's not pure forensic science."

Lest Saks appear to be too harsh on forensic practitioners, he quickly adds that the same can be said about medicine. "Medical professionals also can say they're too busy, and not many practicing physicians are involved in research. I look to medicine, however, to be the shining example of trying to inform your practice by doing research and not infrequently, discovering that what you have been doing is all wrong, that you have been doing more harm than good, and it may take a while for those findings to become widely disseminated and acted upon, but the culture accepts that we need to constantly learn more and alter what we do in light of that. They don't have to be as precise as physicists. I think of medicine as a bit of a rough and tumble process in that its practitioners do the best they can with what they know, although there is this background of constantly increasing knowledge. And it's not as if medicine doesn't have huge problems of its own, the epidemic of medical errors, but at least there is a constant effort to recognize and improve. I think forensic science could say, 'Let's at least adopt that ethic and philosophy.'"

Saks continues, "There are some very intelligent, very thoughtful people in forensic science, and I am thinking of Keith Inman and Norah Rudin, who recognize the tension between asserting an absolute identification to the exclusion of all others in the world, the tension between giving an opinion like that in court, and the absence of a scientific foundation for being able to do so. Inman and Rudin sort of say, 'Well, here's the reality of science, and here's the reality of forensic science practice, and I guess we are going to have to live with things the way they are.' There is a real deference to the nonsense that is practiced and offered to courts, and in this kind of 'Gosh, I hope some day we can be more deferential to the limitations of science.' They are not railing against their colleagues, they are not saying, 'Stop making unsupportable statements of absolute certainty because it can't be done.' Or they could say, 'In light of lack of research, we need to temper what we say and we need to acknowledge it's only a probability, it's not a certainty. There is some wiggle room here and we might be wrong.' And they are wrong often enough that it wouldn't hurt to put a caveat on things."

Peer review is another safeguard some say is lacking in forensic science. "If you are not engaging in peer review in the lab, you are preventing your work from being subject to quality control before it leaves the door," Turvey asserts. "That's not acceptable, given what the results are going to be used for. If you don't write a report that shows your long division—what you found, how you found it, what it means and why—then you are essentially saying, 'My work is not competent to the point where it would withstand scrutiny if it were written down.' Too many lab analysts think that their findings will be unassailable if their premises and conclusions are not documented. And to a large extent they have been right, thanks to an uninformed defense bar."

Jonakait (1991) states, "The research picture indicates that good forensic studies are few, and that forensic scientists are generally outside of the peer review system. Science usually takes place in a setting where the scientific community judges the work of fellow scientists. As one commentator notes, 'Science is in some respects a self-governing republic, with scientists deciding what is good work and what is not.' This self-governance takes place through peer review. Peer review has been labeled 'institutional skepticism' and is best understood as a process that allows the scientific community to police itself."

There are two important vehicles for peer review; the first is the in-depth and critical review of a scientist's work when the individual seeks funding for research, while the second mechanism is the publication process. Industry experts who sit on the formal editorial boards of scientific publications scrutinize the content of the papers submitted for publication, as well as the author's background and professional credentials. Jonakait (1991) observes, "Since forensic scientists do not spend much effort on research, rarely publishing or seeking grants, they do not experience the forces of the peer review system that push science towards quality." Jonakait (1991) adds, "Forensic scientists are neither trained nor forced to think like scientists. Scientists seeking to advance knowledge about the empirical world do not rely on assertions, convictions, or mere logic. Instead, they analyze and test hypotheses. The process is always dependent on skepticism and doubt. Skepticism promotes inquiry, experimentation, and validation that may remove that doubt. The scientist looks at hypotheses and determines how they can be proved wrong by reproducible experiments. Only after the possible shortcomings of an assertion are tested and the experiments fail to discount the hypothesis does a new, accepted scientific thesis emerge."

Jonakait (1991) maintains that a capable researcher must have a probing, skeptical mind that can design experiments to test scientific assertions, and adds, "Most forensic scientists have not been placed into a crucible that is likely to forge that kind of analytical thinking. They are unlikely to have had the opportunity to learn how to design experiments which answer rigorous questions. Even if they have the abilities, most forensic scientists have not been educated to ask and answer probing questions; they have not been taught to develop skepticism and curiosity; they have not been trained to do experiments. As a consequence, the research that they do is frequently of low quality. Forensic scientists often lack the capability to do rigorous research validating their analytical techniques. And techniques without thorough validation can only produce suspect results.

Charge No. 12: Lack of Forensic Science Education and Training

Supporters and detractors of forensic science alike say that inadequate education and training of forensic scientists is one cause of substandard performance. There is no defined or organized preparation for the profession of forensic scientist in many disciplines, and it has only been recently that the National Institute of Justice has recognized the problem (see Chapter 16). And even if there were, a chronic lack of funding keeps many forensic practitioners from the pursuit of much-needed training.

"This is a problem we face every year," says Fisher. "We have virtually very limited funds available to send people to professional forensic science meetings and conferences. We have almost 100 scientists in our lab, and if they want to go to a meeting of the American Academy of Forensic Sciences (AAFS) and they want to pay their own way, we will generally grant them time to go. But if they aren't able to foot the bill, the chances of many of them going to conferences to network and to keep abreast are limited. I ask myself how this is possible because just about any other profession demands continuing education of its professionals. If there were some continuing education requirements, we wouldn't have such a tough time in trying to justify why it is important to send people to meetings. The other curious thing is, when you go to a salon or barber to have your hair cut, the person providing the haircut is licensed by the state. But if you are analyzing forensic evidence in a murder case, there is no licensure required. Does this make sense? I hope I am not proven wrong, but I would like to believe that it would be better if there is some kind of oversight and regulation. Some practitioners bristle when people question what they are doing. I would argue that it is in our best interests to work toward some form of oversight on our terms rather than allow others to do it for us."

Jonakait (1991) observes, "Forensic scientists are not required to establish competence by obtaining a license or certification. Although states require licenses for many occupations, no jurisdiction requires a forensic scientist to be licensed. Even when the forensic scientist performs the same analytical procedures that require a licensed professional outside the crime laboratory, he is not required to be licensed. For example, to determine whether a bloodstain at the crime scene came from the defendant, the forensic scientist must type the defendant's blood. This typing uses the same procedures used in a blood bank or a hospital. States that are concerned about the accuracy of clinical typing require clinical analysts to be licensed. However, they make no such demands on the forensic serologist."

Polski also recognizes a need for improved education and training for forensic practitioners of all disciplines, especially pattern evidence identification. "A few years ago I was part of a committee organized by the NIJ tasked with creating recommendations for a more standardized curriculum for those who want to work in forensic science," he recalls. "As the popularity of forensic science grows, some educational institutions that are in business to make money as well as educate people are uncertain as to which of the two priorities should come first. They saw an opportunity, so they began to offer degrees in forensic science. A criminology degree used to be for those who wanted to go into the criminal justice, corrections, or law enforcement fields. Some institutions are throwing in a few biology and chemistry classes on top of the criminology curriculum and calling it a forensic science degree."

Polski continues, "Young people would take these courses, would graduate with a degree in forensic science, and then would go to a crime lab or law enforcement agency and say, 'Look, I have this degree in forensic science,' and the lab director says, 'Show me your transcripts because I need to see what you can do.' At that point it became apparent those students didn't have the right skill sets. That became such a problem that NIJ assembled this technical working group to develop education and training recommendations. Young people need to know what their degree ought to consist of, and educational institutions need to know that if they want to offer a program that prepares their students to actually get a job in this field, then they better follow substantially the suggested curriculum from the NIJ or the bottom line is, no one is being serving very well."

While he thinks the education and training requirements for forensic science disciplines are now fairly well defined, Polski says he has not seen these recommendations resonate with the identification sciences world as much as it did in the forensic laboratory world. "If you look at people coming out of school today, and I think crime lab directors would tell you the same thing, there really is not much of a shortage of qualified people who apply for jobs as DNA analysts, toxicologists, or trace evidence technicians to some extent; however, when you look at the identification sciences particularly, because about two-thirds of these analyses are conducted in law enforcement agencies, oftentimes the people who are moved into those jobs are law enforcement officers who don't come out of that higher education stream. It wouldn't be surprising if as a result of the National Academies study, this issue is addressed more carefully. There may be some fairly strong recommendations that people who work in forensic science must meet a more stringent set of educational requirements than what exists now. That won't go down well with a lot of people who work in those fields because it would be a real paradigm shift. But I believe it will happen."

"Many problems can be resolved by improving the quality and accessibility of education and training opportunities for forensic scientists," Kobilinsky concurs. "But along with better education and training, for there to be real change in the field, I think there needs to be a restructuring of the location of crime labs. I don't believe they should be within police departments or other law enforcement agencies. I think they should be part of the state department of health so they would take on a more neutral position and have better access to participating in research and training opportunities. The current system is not too engrained to change. There were times when everybody in a crime lab had to be a sworn officer. That's changed. There can be gradual change in the way forensic professionals are trained, too, because some isolated problems do exist: A lab analyst takes a shortcut; a lab analyst leaves out controls from the experiment; a lab analyst makes a mistake in interpretation; a lab analyst isn't trained properly and makes mistakes. It can be addressed through better education and rethinking the current structure."

Jonakait (1991) states, "There is no uniform or core curriculum or internship that leads to the practice of criminalistics; there are no minimum course requirements in terms of a structured program; there is not even a consensus of what the educational requirements should be in the specialized forensic science subjects; and there are no codified standards of practice, either formal or informal, in the identification aspects of criminalistics toward which an educational program can be planned. While forensic science has gained importance in the criminal justice arena, it has not enjoyed a similar rise in stature in the academic community. Instead, the number of forensic science academic programs has been declining. The remaining group has done little to define educational requirements." Jonakait (1991) adds, "Furthermore, the few academic forensic science programs that do exist are not particularly strong. Since they have modest enrollments, university support is limited. Consequently, few if any of the programs can cost effectively support a full-time faculty and staff appropriately representative of the many subspecialties that make up forensic sciences. As a result, forensic science faculty have heavy teaching loads, are disproportionately composed of adjuncts, and are not highly regarded by academics in other areas. Students, often not the strongest in the institution, do not get the best possible education.

Because entry-level salaries in forensic science are low, the top graduates often pick other careers."

If colleges and universities do not properly prepare students for the rigors of the real world, Jonakait (1991) surmises that employers must pick up the slack. Many new analysts depend on post-education apprenticeships, workshops, and professional meetings as well as in-house training to advance and enhance their professional development. Jonakait states, "This on-the-job training is often insufficient. The quality of training will be dependent on continued budgetary support. Inasmuch as education is not the mission of a public service laboratory, it will necessarily take on secondary importance when funding becomes restricted or when services are in great demand. Reliance on on-the-job training is especially troublesome for the numerous small forensic labs and for many so-called full-service laboratories where forensic scientists are expected to be generalists with expertise in several diverse areas such as drug chemistry, arson and explosives, ballistics, toxicology, and trace evidence analysis. Although some labs continue a generalist approach, even when unnecessary, training anyone adequately for such positions seems impossible."

An issue separate but akin to tainted science and a lack of proper education and training and adherence to protocol is that of contamination of evidence. As we have seen earlier in this chapter, forensic evidence, by its very nature, is potentially contaminated before it even reaches the forensic laboratory for processing and analysis. However, a number of potential errors can occur in the evidence handling process in forensic laboratories; they are explored here.

Accidental mislabeling or mix-ups of samples in the forensic laboratory are a possibility. In a Philadelphia rape case, it was discovered that a crime laboratory had mixed up the reference samples of the defendant and the rape victim, a mishap that falsely incriminated the defendant because the lab discovered what it thought was the defendant's DNA profile in a vaginal swab from the victim. In reality, it was the victim's own profile, and was mistakenly matched to the defendant due to the mix-up. In another rape case in San Diego, a lab confused the victim's and defendant's samples, thereby mistakenly incriminating the defendant. Thompson et al. (2003b) observe, "In most instances the mix-ups readily come to light (and are caught by the lab) because they produce unexpected results: Samples that are supposed to be from a man show a female DNA profile, two samples known to be from the same person show different DNA profiles, and so on. The real danger arises when sample mix-ups produce plausible results. In these instances, forensic analysts may overlook subtle clues that something is amiss because they expected to find the very result produced by their error."

In a Las Vegas case, the reference samples of two men were mixed up, thus incarcerating a man for a rape committed by the other, with the innocent man spending more than a year in prison before the error was discovered by a defense expert who noticed inconsistencies in laboratory records. Thompson et al. (2003b) suggest, "It is not always possible to tell from the laboratory records whether samples actually were mixed up or cross-contaminated. However, careful review of the laboratory records will usually provide important information about whether such errors could have happened."

Cross-contamination is a likely culprit in tainted reference samples, such as when a reference sample from the defendant is processed in close proximity to samples from the crime scene. As an example, in one case cited by Thompson et al. (2003b), a defendant's pants, taken from his home, were transported to the laboratory in the same carton containing other items from the crime scene that were soaked with the victim's blood. This revelation was essential in helping to determine why blood from the victim was detected on the defendant's clothing. Thompson et al. write, "We suggest that defense lawyers obtain and review complete copies of all records related to evidentiary samples collected in the case. It should be possible to document the complete history of every sample from the time it was initially collected through its ultimate disposition."

Inadvertent transfer of DNA is another potential mishap. This is a significant pitfall due to the advances in technology that make it possible to detect and test increasingly minute biological samples. Thompson et al. (2003) point out, "Whereas the original DNA tests required a fairly large amount of biological materials to get a result (e.g., a blood stain the size of a dime), current DNA tests are so sensitive that they can type the DNA found in samples containing only a few cells."

With the sensitivity of DNA testing comes a new class of DNA evidence. Thompson et al. (2003a) explain: "Analysts talk of detecting 'trace DNA,' such as the minute quantities of DNA transferred through skin contact. DNA typing is currently being applied, with varying degrees of success, to samples such as doorbells pressed in home invasion cases, eyeglasses found at a crime scene, handles of knives and other weapons, soda straws, and even single fingerprints. These developments will bring more DNA evidence to court in a wider variety of cases and may well open new lines of defense. A key issue will be the potential for inadvertent transfer of small amounts of DNA from one item to another, a process that could easily incriminate an innocent person. Studies have documented the presence of typeable quantities of human DNA on doorknobs, coffee cups and other common items."

There is potential for the inadvertent transfer of human DNA from one item to another. As explained by Thompson et al. (2003a), "Primary transfer occurs when DNA is transferred from a person to an item. Secondary transfer is when the DNA deposited on one item is transferred to a second item. Tertiary transfer is when the DNA on the second item is, in turn, transferred to a third. There are published studies that document secondary transfer of DNA (in quantities that can be detected by STR tests) from items that people simply touched to other items."

One of the most high-profile examples of this kind of delicate transfer is the case of Dirk Greineder, M.D., who was accused of murdering his wife. The DNA profile of the couple was collected from gloves and a knife found near the crime scene, but Greineder stated he had never touched these items. To challenge how Greineder's DNA was discovered on these two items, the physician objected to the conclusion that his DNA matched that on the gloves, citing inconsistencies between his DNA and that found on the gloves. According to Thompson et al. (2003a), "The crime laboratory had shifted its threshold for scoring alleles in a manner that allowed it to count alleles that matched with Greineder, while ignoring some that did not. And the lab had to evoke the theory of 'allelic drop out' to explain why some of Greineder's alleles were not found."

Greineder also maintained that tertiary transfer was responsible for the presence of his DNA on the gloves. He explained that he and his wife had shared a towel the morning of the murder, and that his DNA could have been transferred from his face to the towel, and from the towel to his wife's face. According to Thompson et al. (2003a), Greineder reasoned that his wife was later attacked by a glove-wearing intruder who hit her face, strangled her, and stabbed her, thereby transferring Greineder's DNA from his wife's face to the gloves and the knife. According to Greineder, the alleles on the gloves and knife belonged to the perpetrator. Greineder commissioned a study that simulated his proposed sequence of events; the scientist who performed the reenactment was allowed to present his findings to the jury and although Greineder was convicted due to other incriminating evidence, Thompson et al. opine that this case "is a good example of how the amazing sensitivity of contemporary DNA profiling methods facilitate a plausible explanation for what might at first seem to be a damning DNA test result."

THE TALES OF TWO LABS UNDER THE MICROSCOPE

All Eyes on Virginia

Allegations of potential errors in evidence analyzed by the Virginia Department of Forensic Science (DFS) and used in a 1982 capital case involving a retarded man, Early Washington, Jr., who was accused of rape, triggered an investigation into DNA cases at Virginia's central forensic laboratory. In May 2005, an independent audit indicated that erroneous DNA testing may have been conducted, which prompted then-Governor Mark Warner to ask for a review of the lab's handling of testing in 150 other cases. Among the auditors' recommendations were that the governor restrict the work of the lab's leading DNA analyst, Jeffrey D. Ban; review 40 cases that Ban had analyzed in recent years; and develop procedures to protect the lab from external political pressure and influence. The audit triggered a reexamination of a number of past prosecutions, including those involving inmates on Virginia's death row, and threw into suspicion many current cases in which DFS analysts helped to identify or exclude suspects. DFS has four separate labs—the Eastern, Central, Northern, and Western divisions—and the department itself has been accredited by ASCLD/LAB since January 5, 1989.

In a statement responding to the April 9, 2005, audit report, lab director Paul Ferrara, PhD, wrote, "The audit report criticizes the work performed on one sub-sample five years ago based upon current technologies and standards. It also belies the major body of other work performed by this examiner in this case wherein he successfully eliminated Earl Washington and identified a new suspect, Kenneth Tinsley, on evidence found at the crime scene. Nonetheless, we accept the basic finding of the audit, i.e., that the examiner should have declared this sample as indeterminate or inconclusive instead of eliminating Earl Washington, Rebecca Williams, and Kenneth Tinsley."

Ferrara emphasized that DFS had already begun to implement all of ASCLD/LAB's recommendations, and added that the department was "gratified" that the audit report "did not suggest any evidence of a systemic deficiency," and that ASCLD/LAB had reinstated accreditation of the facility.

On April 9, 2005, the ASCLD/LAB issued a report detailing an interim audit of DFS' Central Laboratory Biology/DNA Unit. The report focused on certain deviations from protocol that had occurred during the retesting of DNA evidence in connection with an executive clemency petition in a capital murder case. After reviewing the case file, ASCLD/LAB determined that "there appear to have been deviations in protocol . . . that led to examination data that, in the ASCLD/LAB inspectors' opinion, should not have been relied upon by the DFS." The interim report recommended that the lab's quality manager determine "whether the deficiencies in the report are endemic" to the DNA operations throughout the Virginia lab system, and should be accomplished through examination of a minimum of 50 cases in the system dealing with low-level DNA to determine "whether process errors occurred and whether conclusions are scientifically supported." The quality manager should determine whether these cases had deficiencies that substantially affect the integrity of results in those cases, and conduct a review of analyst Ban's casework using internal and external reviewers.

In a May 6, 2005, letter from Ferrara to Ban, Ferrara terminated Ban's responsibility as technical leader pending completion of the investigation, and reinstatement once the review had been completed and disposition of the investigation accepted.

On May 31, 2005, Robert J. Humphreys, a judge in the Court of Appeals of Virginia, was appointed by the Virginia State Crime Commission as a "special master" to form a team of independent scientists to carry out the recommendations from ASCLD/LAB's interim report. Humphreys selected five members of the forensic sciences community to serve as investigators, and on June 13, 2005, the team began its work at DFS.

In a September 1, 2005, letter to Humphreys, the five investigators reported their findings. They had selected a random 63 cases for review in addition to those cases already selected by virtue of their association with Jeffrey Ban or the death penalty, for a total of 123 cases. DFS made available all reports, notes, scientific data, and department protocols, and also made available for interview analysts and supervisors. The investigators reviewed 28 capital cases, representing all of the capital cases that were analyzed by DFS since 1994, as well as 33 cases that were analyzed by Jeffrey Ban on or after January 1, 1999. They also selected at random 53 low-level DNA cases from all DFS examiners. Ten additional cases were selected for review, a selection not dependent on the concentration of DNA in the sample that had been analyzed. Each capital case was analyzed separately by at least two of the five investigators, and each of the other case files were reviewed by at least one investigator on the review team.

After reviewing all 123 cases; the review team found:

- Of the 28 capital cases reviewed, none of the cases contained a technical procedure error or deviation from accepted scientific protocol that substantially affected the integrity of the results in those cases.
- Of the 28 capital cases reviewed, one of the cases contained an interpretive conclusion with respect to one of the items analyzed believed to be inappropriate.
- Of the 33 cases analyzed by Ban, none of the cases contained a technical error or deviation from protocol.
- Of the 33 cases analyzed by Ban, none of the cases contained an interpretive conclusion that was not scientifically supported.
- Of the 53 randomly selected low-level DNA cases, none of the cases contained a technical error or deviation from protocol.
- Of the 53 low-level DNA cases, none contained an interpretive conclusion not scientifically supported.
- Of the 10 additional random DNA cases, none of the cases contained a technical error or deviation from protocol, and none contained an interpretive conclusion that was not scientifically supported.
- "It appeared to all of us that, over the time period covered by our review, DFS analysts have been consistently conservative in making allele calls, tending to disregard faint bands that arguably reported as alleles."
- "However, of the 123 cases reviewed, none of the cases contain an allele call that resulted in an individual being excluded from consideration who should have been included. Similarly, of the 123 cases reviewed, none of the cases contain an allele call that resulted in an individual being included for consideration who should have been excluded."

Based on these findings, the investigators concluded, "The testing methods employed by DFS contain no endemic deficiencies that may have substantially affected the results of low-level DNA cases analyzed by the laboratory in the past, or that may substantially affect the results of low-level DNA cases to be analyzed in the future. Over the time period covered by this review, DFS has consistently conducted its low-level DNA testing within the boundaries of established and scientifically accepted practices."

The reviewers did note one statistical inaccuracy in a capital case, explaining that the interpretive conclusion reached by the analyst was inappropriate with respect to one of the items analyzed. Of the 27 separate items analyzed for DNA, one item was found containing human DNA, isolated from a sample from the inside of a right glove and sample from the inside of a left glove. The samples were amplified and typed using the PowerPlex 16 Bio System. The DFS analyst identified five possible contributors to the DNA recovered from the gloves, the two victims and three suspects. The analyst concluded that the three suspects cannot be eliminated as possible cocontributors of the genetic material from the left glove; the victims were eliminated. To attach statistical weight to this conclusion, the analyst employed a likelihood ratio using the alleles reported at just 5 of the 15 tested loci, meaning that the analyst selected only those loci that fit her formulated hypothesis that the DNA mixture isolated from the left glove contained the DNA of all three suspects, and disregarded the loci that did not fit that hypothesis. The analyst also failed to document why the reference samples from the two victims and two of the suspects, each of which failed to yield interpretable results at one or more loci, were not rerun to obtain better results. The reviewers agreed that the three suspects could not be eliminated as possible contributors, but they said they believe that considering the complexity of the DNA mixture and the high probability of allelic dropout at one or more of the tested loci, rendering any statistical interpretation involving all three suspects, collectively, was inappropriate.

Based on the overall review, the investigators stated that certain improvements to the lab's protocols could be made, including:

- Implement written guidelines to improve analyst documentation of the rationale behind disregarding bands assigned as alleles by the PowerPlex typing instrument.
- Implement a written policy to provide improved guidance for selecting the appropriate statistical analysis in low-level DNA cases.
- Implement a written policy providing that if a probative reference standard fails to yield a complete profile, rerun the reference sample, if practical, until a complete profile is obtained.
- Implement a written policy providing that, when practical, separate technical and administrative reviewers be assigned for each individual case.

Humphreys, in a September 12, 2005, letter to then-Governor Mark Warner, stated, "Infallibility is too much to expect of any human endeavor, certainly including scientific analysis. No matter how educated, experienced, or well trained the scientist or technician, human frailty or equipment breakdown insure that mistakes can and eventually will occur. Given the increasing reliance by the commonwealth's criminal justice system on the DNA identification techniques used by DFS, those mistakes that inevitably do occur and which go undetected and uncorrected may result in the nightmare that all criminal justice professionals fear the most—an innocent person wrongfully convicted or a guilty person mistakenly exonerated. While ongoing training and state-of-the-art equipment can minimize them, we cannot completely prevent the occasional human error or equipment malfunction from ever occurring. Within our ability to anticipate such things, credibility of laboratories is achieved and maintained by the creation and periodic revision of a system of internal checks, audits, and peer review which are sufficiently comprehensive to detect such errors or malfunctions before a scientific report is tendered to the criminal justice system."

Humphreys alludes to DFS's "tradition of openness and a reputation for the unbiased reporting of scientific results" and mentions its "comprehensive system of internal review that has detected and corrected analytical anomalies in the past," but stated that in light of ASCLD/LAB's findings, "these internal review procedures clearly leave room for improvement." Humphreys did note that prior to the interim report and Humphreys' appointment, DFS had already begun a thorough reexamination of its internal review procedures.

In a letter dated October 12, 2005, from Donald A. Wyckoff, chair of ASCLD/LAB, to Paul Ferrara, Wyckoff stated that the scientific review team found "no technical procedural errors or deviations from accepted scientific protocol in the cases reviewed and found that conclusions in those cases were scientifically supported." Wyckoff's letter also stated that ASCLD/LAB was satisfied that all recommendations for corrective action regarding Ban have been followed.

Although DFS was eventually vindicated, the perception of a faulty facility lingers, thanks to highly publicized media reports that peaked at the onset of the investigation and then dwindled to nothing once the lab had been cleared of substantial wrongdoing. Partly to blame for the media frenzy is the emotional overtone inherent in any discussion of the adjudication of death penalty cases. At the time of writing, the Commonwealth of Virginia has executed more than 90 individuals since the U.S. Supreme Court allowed for the reinstatement of the death penalty more than three decades ago.

Earl Washington was initially sentenced to death for the 1982 rape and fatal stabbing of 19-year-old Virginian Rebecca Williams, but the sentence was commuted in 1994 by then-Governor Douglas Wilder. He was then pardoned in 2000 due to DNA evidence that raised doubts about his culpability. Washington's defense attorneys argued that due to errors in DNA testing conducted by DFS in 1993, he stayed on death row seven years longer than necessary; they also assert that additional erroneous testing in 2000 prevented a complete exoneration.

Dao (2005) quotes attorney Peter Neufeld, codirector of the Innocence Project, as saying, "This laboratory touts itself as the best state lab in the country, yet it generated these wrong test results in a capital case twice. This case raises very serious questions about the legitimacy of the capital justice system." Dao (2005) reports that Ban, "a nationally recognized forensic scientist who has helped other states develop DNA policies," had erroneously conducted and analyzed DNA tests in the Williams case, leading him to conclude incorrectly that a convicted serial rapist, Kenneth Tinsley, was not the contributor of semen found in Williams, even though he had been the source of DNA collected from a blanket found at the crime scene. A DNA test commissioned by Washington's defense attorneys in 2004 revealed that Tinsley was the most likely source of the DNA, and argued that if DFS had reached the same conclusion, Tinsley would have been prosecuted for the Williams murder.

Ferrara says defense experts are doing their best to shake public confidence in forensic laboratories. He points to a recent CNN report on whether or not crime labs' analyses can be trusted. "They mostly brought up old news, such as the FBI, Oklahoma, and West Virginia cases," he says. "It was terribly biased, one-sided reporting. I was disappointed by it because there was no opportunity for rebuttal, and it was full of misstatements in trying to suggest that forensic labs need more regulation and more oversight, and not by ASCLD but by some external force, probably attorneys. There is no way to refute that kind of stuff once it is put out there."

Ferrara says that the news media is selective in its choice of presenting the news about crime labs. He adds, "We had a case where a 13-year-old was raped and we made a DNA hit that identified the guy. It turns out we had hit him (in the database) once before in Richmond and in another jurisdiction where they didn't take any action on the hit, so the guy got off. Nobody did anything so he was free a year later to attack this girl. The fact that we are making an incredible number of DNA database hits is no longer newsworthy; what *is* newsworthy these days is what the lab screwed up. Even if the lab hasn't made an error, defense attorneys are practically making libelous statements about lab performance and getting away with them. It makes my blood boil and makes me want to throw in the towel. I have been at this for more than 35 years; you give your life's energy to it and then some unscrupulous defense attorney says whatever he wants and that's what the media wants to hear."

Ferrara says he takes issue with the defense camp and the media exploiting reports of old cases that were adjudicated by using evidence analyzed with old technology, or cases that involved as-yet accredited facilities. "Most of the egregious errors they talked about on CNN occurred in unaccredited labs years ago," he says, "so there was nothing very recent. The critics will then say that the forensic science community can't regulate itself, which is like saying the American Bar Association or the American Medical Association can't regulate itself, which is ridiculous. Let's put an attorney at the AMA to provide oversight and see what happens. It's ludicrous, but that's what they are pushing for and they use all this post-conviction stuff, ignoring the fact that in those cases where they allege the guy was convicted based on poor science, it was done years ago, when that was the best technology available. To me, it's an ill-disguised attempt at taking on the crime labs. They don't look at the totality of the work labs do, they just want to make it look like all the labs are lousy."

Ferrara continues, "When test results exclude a defendant, defense attorneys don't take issue with the results, but when the testing inculpates their client, then all of a sudden the technology or the lab is in question. They have spent years trying to attack the technology unsuccessfully, now they will try to attack the people conducting it. It's the only way for them to mount a defense. Peter Neufeld has been making the most outrageous statements and nobody stands up and says that's wrong. Fortunately they never contacted me for the CNN story because I never would have made it out of the cutting-room floor."

Even though his laboratory was cleared of wrongdoing, that fact didn't create splashy headlines like the accusations of impropriety did, and Ferrara says he does not feel vindicated. "The true facts never really came out," Ferrara says. "And if they do, we don't get a lot of coverage. You reach a point where you simply say to yourself, 'They have more time and ink than I've got,' and you can't challenge that. The problem is, the general public walks away with an impression that, 'Gee those labs are a mess,' which I guess is perhaps the intention some media outlets have when they publicize errors. In fact, when you get a clean bill of health, that's not news, and that doesn't sell newspapers. Unfortunately, a lack of ink in the newspapers about the positive stuff we do in crime labs everyday doesn't help to shape public confidence in forensic science."

Ferrara continues, "In the final analysis, I don't think the real truth will ever be known and understood except by those of us who lived the experience, and we're confident in our performance and the final outcome. We have strengthened even further the safeguards we already had in place, including establishing a scientific committee and an advisory board that oversees investigations and can investigate allegations. Sadly, as things typically go, it's the allegations that people remember, not the resolution."

Ferrara feels strongly that much of the attention that was focused on the Virginia lab stemmed from the advancement of political agendas relating to the death penalty. "I definitely think we get caught up in death penalty politics," Ferrara comments. "In this particular case, what people shouldn't lose sight of is we are the ones who eliminated Earl Washington based on the evidence, and we're the ones who identified foreign material and then identified it as coming from Tinsley. There's another problem. That case has not yet been adjudicated. The special prosecutor in that case has not yet made a decision, to my knowledge as to whether they are going to prosecute Tinsley or not. What was of primary importance, of course, was that Earl Washington was eliminated. But when we couldn't identify Tinsley in 2000, using

2000 technology, that was when we came under fire. Even when we exonerate people like this, often people still have lingering thoughts and questions in their minds. But when you can identify someone who did commit the crime and prosecute him sufficiently, then that tends to convince any skeptics as to this guy's innocence in the original case. We get stuck in the middle. I personally had no concerns; we had investigated this thoroughly, and we are a top-notch laboratory."

Ferrara bristles at critics' suggestion that analyst error contributes to a significant number of lab errors. "There may be individuals in any profession who are bad apples, but in forensic science, you're not going to get away with illicit, irresponsible behavior for very long; ours is a unique profession insofar as all of our results are subject to scrutiny in the courts by world-renowned experts. It's not like we bury our errors, as many critics suggest. On the contrary, this work is subject to immense scrutiny." Ferrara continues, "The travesty of it all is that the net result of all of this, like in the Earl Washington case, is when my analysts qualify and testify as experts for court, the first thing the defense says is, 'Well, isn't it true that you had some problems in your lab?' It has made me lose some respect for that profession. We know we're objective, and we know we never made a false positive in that case, and we've been doing this a long time. But you have the defense bar trying to take you down at every turn. I have examiners going to court to testify how and why they did not get any results in a case, and why that doesn't mean the defendant wasn't there. Or to explain why we didn't we test certain evidence in a particular case. It may be completely unrelated to the case at hand, but the defense will again drag us through the mill about the Earl Washington case, and blow the whole thing out of proportion. I was in a situation where I did not feel it was appropriate to admit to anything, and to stand by my analysts' results, which I still do and always will. You call an auditing team, and sure, they are going to find something. Does it have any bearing on the results in that case, or inability to include a suspect? You can't make something happen just for wishing it. Although they think we must do that when the shoe is on the other foot."

The Virginia lab is a frequent target, Ferrara says, because it has a high profile among forensic laboratories in the country and has demonstrated leadership in a number of areas. "When one lab has a bad day, it's very convenient for the defense community and for the death penalty opponents to want to condemn all the laboratories. The same is true of the FBI crime lab; they are high profile and elite, and equally subject to this badmouthing. When you are at the top of the game, you are an easy target."

The Virginia Department of Forensic Science has excelled in the areas of DNA data banking, as it was the first state-level forensic laboratory to build a database linking evidence from unsolved crimes to suspects through their genetic profiles. As of March 31, 2006, Virginia has had 3,281 total hits among the 245,566 total number of samples.

"I remember when people used to think this databank will be great for sex offenses, which of course it was, but it has played an important role in identifying suspects in so many other cases and for equally horrendous crimes," Ferrara says. "Just this morning, we had four inter-state DNA databank hits: three rapes and one homicide, some in three different states, going back to the 1980s—and that was just this morning's report. It's simply amazing what we are able to do. But you don't hear anything about these successes, or about Virginia in general because the hits are in other states, where again, by virtue of our databank, we're helping make these hits even when we are not doing the crime scene evidence. It underscores the media's lack of understanding of the importance of forensic science, how it works, and what it does. It's one thing to do textbook science and lab science, but it is quite another thing to see it work in the real world, where it matters the most."

Houston, We Have a Problem

Coming under immense scrutiny is the Houston Police Department (HPD) Crime Laboratory and Property Room, with an independent investigation being spearheaded by Michael R. Bromwich of the Washington, D.C., law firm of Fried, Frank, Harris, Shriver, & Jacobson LLP. Phase I of the inquiry (summarized in a June 30, 2005, report) examined the historical operations, practices, and management of the HPD Crime Lab and Property Room and assessed the scope of the work to be performed during the second phase of the investigation. Phase II, which began with the Houston City Council's approval on August 24, 2005, focuses on the review of approximately 2,700 cases originally analyzed by the lab's forensic scientists in each of the six forensic science disciplines in which the lab performed work: DNA/serology, trace evidence, controlled substances, firearms, toxicology, and questioned documents. Through early December 2005, the investigative team reviewed more than 1,100 cases across all of the sections of the lab and conducted interviews of lab personnel to gather additional information.

In the third and fourth reports in a series, Bromwich's team identified several key issues:

- *Lack of support for the crime lab within the HPD and by the city of Houston.* The report stated, "During at least the 15 years preceding the closure of the DNA Section in December 2002, HPD and the city failed to provide the Crime Lab with adequate resources . . . One of the most glaring examples of how HPD and the city failed the crime lab was that there was no criminalist III line supervisor over the DNA/Serology Section from August 1996 through December 2002."
- *Ineffective management within the crime lab.* The report stated, "The crime lab also suffered from a lack of strong and effective leadership within the lab. Senior managers in the crime lab, including in particular former director Donald Krueger and the former head of the DNA/Serology Section James Bolding, failed to make a strong case within the HPD chain of command for more resources, better training, and improvements in the lab's facilities."
- *Lack of adequate quality control and quality assurance.* The report stated, "HPD closed the DNA Section in December 2002 almost immediately after an outside audit—the first ever performed of the crime lab—found that the DNA Section fell woefully short of the standards established by the Federal Bureau of Investigation's Quality Assurance Standards for Forensic DNA Testing Laboratories. Again, for a period of over six years, there was no line supervisor in the DNA Section to oversee and provide quality assurance for the DNA work performed by the crime lab."
- *Isolation of the DNA/Serology Section.* The report stated, "The DNA/Serology Section was never audited by anyone outside of the Crime Lab until December 2002, and the results of that review were, ultimately, closure of the section, a large-scale post-conviction re-testing program, and this investigation. The complete lack of outside scrutiny of the crime lab's operations, procedures, and reporting of results allowed serious deficiencies, particularly in the DNA/Serology Section, to become so egregious that analysts in the lab simply had no perspective on how bad their practices were. The isolation of the crime lab also allowed deficient practices and poor scientific work to continue, as our case reviews are beginning to show, since at least the mid-1980s."

In the fourth report (issued January 4, 2006), Bromwich's team made the observation that "Our case reviews have demonstrated that problems with the crime lab's forensic scientific work and the reliability of the results reported by lab in the areas of serology and DNA analysis are even more severe and pervasive than we anticipated when we began Phase II of this investigation." There was a small bright spot, however; when the team added, "However, it is important to note that the problems we have seen are not spread uniformly throughout the crime lab; in fact, we have seen some very competent and high quality work, especially in the Firearms, Toxicology, and Questioned Documents Sections."

As of December 2005, the investigators reviewed 80 serology cases worked by the HPD lab and identified major issues in 18 of those cases, with several deemed as "pervasive and serious problems with the quality of scientific work performed by the serologists, as well as with the presentation of the results obtained." The investigators found that the deficiencies were not the result of analytical or interpretive errors made by individual serologists, but rather, they were the product of inadequate procedures employed in the Serology Section from around 1987 through the early 1990s, according to the report. The most significant problems relating to serology were:

- The absence in the serologists' reports of genetic profile frequency statistics or any discussion of the significance of the statement that a suspect could not be excluded as a potential donor of an evidence sample
- The failure to use substrate, positive, and negative controls in connection with ABO typing, which directly affects the reliability of reported results
- The routine and common failure to report the results of testing and probative findings
- The lack of any documentation of administrative or technical reviews of the serologists' work
- The absence of generally accepted documentation and evidence control procedures—such as assignment of unique identification numbers to items of evidence, descriptions of evidence, and preparation of complete tables of testing results—as well as numerous errors by analysts in transferring their test results to worksheets (Bromwich, 2005).

By December 2005, the investigators also completed reviews of 67 DNA cases analyzed by the PHD lab, including all 18 of the death penalty cases in which DNA work performed by the lab was involved. Bromwich's team identified major issues in 27 of these cases (including 3 death penalty cases). The team identified parallel, pervasive problems with both the quality of the lab's forensic DNA profiling work as well as with the lab's practices relating to interpretation of its DNA results. The report stated, "Many of the problems we have seen in the crime lab's serology work—including failure to report probative results, poor technical work, lack of controls, absence of technical reviews, and poor documentation—carried over into the lab's DNA work after the DNA Section became operational in the early 1990s. Many of the personnel who were involved with serology testing became the crime lab's DNA analysts." According to the report, the most substantial problems relating to DNA were:

- Failure to report typing results, including potentially exculpatory results
- Prevalence of poor quality results, particularly with respect to polymerase chain reaction (PCR)-based DQ Alpha, Polymarker, and D1S80 testing, likely attributable to some combination of poor technique on the part of the lab's DNA analysts and contamination
- Misleading reporting of the statistical significance of the DNA profiling results, particularly in cases involving samples containing mixtures of bodily fluids from more than one person
- Failure to use and to show proper regard for scientific controls, particularly negative controls in PCR testing and failure to compare typing results in STR testing
- Failure to perform and document meaningful technical and administrative reviews of the work performed by DNA analysts
- Failure to assign a unique identifier to evidence items so that evidence and specimens generated from evidence could be tracked from submission through analysis (Bromwich, 2005).

In its evaluation of the lab's Trace Evidence section, the team stated that much of the division's work "appears to have been done in a manner consistent with generally accepted forensic standards. However, we found that there were significant delays in the overall examination and reporting process as well as cases in which little or no effort was made to identify evidence that could have generated potentially significant investigative leads. Some cases involved an inexplicable lack of follow-up and communication between the crime lab and investigators." The report explained that due to these deficiencies, "the potential investigative value of trace evidence was not being used to its full advantage by the HPD during 1998–2003, the period of our review."

The bulk of cases worked by the HPD lab belonged to its Controlled Substances Section, accounting for more than 97,000 cases between 1998 and 2004. As of December 2005, the investigative team looked at more than 400 cases, and opined that "analytical work performed on commonly encountered substances, such as cocaine and marijuana, was generally quite good and was performed in a manner consistent with generally accepted standards of forensic science applicable to the analysis of controlled substances during the period of our review, 1998–2004. However, when analysts encountered more complex and less common substances, we found more deficiencies in their analytic work." The main problems relating to controlled substances were the reporting of definitive identifications based on inconclusive findings, and the issuance of reports containing quantitative findings when no quantitative analysis was actually performed.

Regarding the lab's Firearms Section, following the team's review of 109 cases, the report stated that most cases had been "properly examined, reported in a timely manner, and generally reflect work performed consistent with generally accepted forensic science standards. The issues identified have all been minor, involving primarily documentation issues and deviations from crime lab policies." The team did identify "a tendency to avoid reporting results as inconclusive, even when this would be the most appropriate conclusion." The report continued, "This occurred in cases where general rifling characteristics—which are patterns of impressions that a firearms examiner can use to identify the possible make and model of the gun from which a bullet was fired—suggested that a weapon or class of weapons could have created the characteristics observed on a bullet. We have not, however, found any cases in which the crime lab made an incorrect weapons identification or elimination."

In the fourth Bromwich report, the team indicated notable improvement in the lab's Toxicology Section, following earlier stumbles by the section leader. In October 2003, the supervisor failed a competency test, which triggered the suspension of toxicology analysis by the HPD lab that same month. In May 2005, the lab was accredited by the ASCLD/LAB to perform blood alcohol testing, and its toxicology casework is still limited to this arena.

Regarding the performance of the Questioned Documents Section, the investigative team's examination of 91 cases revealed overall competency and analysis that was consistent with generally accepted forensic science standards. However, the team noted that the section's sole examiner "sometimes does not issue reports, even when he performs work on cases and enters case numbers in the crime lab's logs. At times, these cases simply involve inquiries from investigators or from the District Attorney's Office, but, when technical advice has been given, the document examiner should track the evidence, take notes, and prepare a report on the case."

At the time of this writing, Bromwich's investigation of the PHD crime lab is ongoing.

REFERENCES

Arvizu J. Forensic labs: shattering the myth. *The Champion,* May 2000.

Bashinski JS. The criminalistics laboratory report: An editorial view. *CAC News,* Fourth Quarter, 2003.

BBC News. Warning over forensic cowboys. April 30, 1998.

Cable News Network (CNN) special report. Reasonable doubt: can crime labs be trusted? Accessed at http://www.cnn.com

Casey R. It's a crime when science gets it wrong. *Houston Chronicle,* September 18, 2005.

Dao J. Lab's errors in '82 killing force review of Virginia DNA cases. *The New York Times,* May 7, 2005.

Ehrlinger J and Dunning D. How chronic self-views influence (and potentially mislead) estimates of performance. *Journal of Personality and Social Psychology,* 84(1):5–17, 2003.

Fisher BAJ. *Techniques of Crime Scene Investigation,* 6th ed. Boca Raton, Fla.: CRC Press, 2002.

Frank L and Hanchette J. Convicted on false evidence? False science often sways juries, judges. *USA Today,* July 19, 1994.

Giannelli PC. Crime labs need improvement. *Issues in Science and Technology* online, Fall 2003.

Houde J. *Crime Lab: A Guide for Nonscientists,* 2nd ed. Rollingbay, Wash.: Calico Press, 2006.

Inman K and Rudin N. *Principles and Practice of Criminalistics: The Profession of Forensic Science.* Boca Raton, Fla.: CRC Press, 2001.

Jonakait R. How to improve forensic science. European Journal of Law and Economics. 2005. Available at: http://129.3.20.41/eps/le/papers/0503/0503001.pdf#search=%22Jonakait%2C%201991%22

Kennedy D. Forensic science: Oxymoron? *Science,* 302(5651):1625, December 5, 2003.

Koppl R. How to improve forensic science. European Journal of Law and Economics. 2005. Available at: http://129.3.20.41/eps/le/papers/0503/0503001.pdf#search=%22Koppl%20%20(2005)%20–%20Pearsall%20(1989)%22

Koppl R and Kobilinsky L. Forensic Science Administration: Toward a New Discipline. 2005. Available at: http://alpha.fdu.edu/~koppl/fsa.doc

Korris S. Court asks officials to consider taking crime lab from state police. *The West Virginia Record,* June 28, 2006. Accessed at http://www.wvrecord.com/news/newsview.asp?c=180999.

McRoberts F, Mills S, and Possley M. Unproven techniques sway courts, erode justice. *The Chicago Tribune,* October 17, 2004.

Mills S and McRoberts F. Critics tell experts: Show us the science. *The Chicago Tribune,* October 17, 2004.

Moriarty JC and Saks MJ. Forensic science: Grand goals, tragic flaws, and judicial gatekeeping. *Judges Journal.* 2005.

Neufeld PJ. The (near) irrelevance of Daubert to criminal justice and some suggestions for reform. *American Journal of Public Health,* 95(Suppl 1), 2005.

Peterson JL, Fabricant EL, Field KS, and Thornton JI. *Crime Laboratory Proficiency Testing Research Program.* Washington, D.C.: U.S. Government Printing Office, 1978.

Peterson JL and Markham PN. Crime laboratory proficiency testing results, 1978–1991, I: identification and classification of physical evidence. *Journal of Forensic Sciences,* 40(6), 1995a.

Peterson JL and Markham PN. Crime laboratory proficiency testing results, 1978–1991, II: resolving questions of common origin. *Journal of Forensic Sciences,* 40(6), 1995b.

Possley M et al. Scandal touches even elite labs; flawed work, resistance to scrutiny seen across U.S. *The Chicago Tribune,* October 21, 2004.

Pronin E, Gilovich T, and Ross L. Objectivity in the eye of the beholder: divergent perceptions of bias in self vs. others. *Psychological Review,* 111(3):781–799, 2004.

Risinger MD, Saks MJ, Thompson WC, and Rosenthal R. The Daubert/Kumho implications of observer effects in forensic science: hidden problems of expectation and suggestion. *California Law Review,* 90(1), January 2002.

Scheck B and Neufeld P. Junk science, junk evidence. *The New York Times,* May 11, 2001.

Scheck B, Neufeld P, and Dwyer J. *Actual Innocence: Five Days to Execution and Other Dispatches from the Wrongly Convicted.* New York: Doubleday, 2000.

St. Clair JJ. Crime Laboratory Management. Boston: Elsevier Science/Academic Press, 2003.

Thompson WC, Ford S, Doom TE, Raymer ML, and Krane DE. Evaluating forensic DNA evidence, part 2. *The Champion,* May 2003a.

Thompson WC, Taroni F, and Aitken CG. How the probability of a false positive affects the value of DNA evidence. *Journal of Forensic Science,* January 2003b.

Whitehurst F. Forensic crime labs: scrutinizing results, audits & accreditation, part I. *The Champion,* April 2004.

RECOMMENDED READING

Connors E, McEwen T, Lundregan T, and Miller N. *Convicted by Juries, Exonerated by Science: Case Studies in the Use of DNA Evidence to Establish Innocence after Trial.* Washington, D.C.: U.S. Department of Justice, 1996.

Office of Inspector General, U.S. Department of Justice. *The FBI Laboratory: An Investigation into Laboratory Practices and Alleged Misconduct in Explosives-Related and Other Cases.* Washington, D.C.: U.S. Department of Justice, April 1997.

President's editorial: the changing practice of forensic science. *Journal of Forensic Science,* 47:437–438, 2002.

ENDNOTES

1. *Principles and Practice of Criminalistics: The Profession of Forensic Science* by Inman and Rudin. Copyright 2007 by Taylor & Francis Group LLC—Books. Reproduced with permission of Taylor & Francis Group LLC—Books in the format Other Book via Copyright Clearance Center.
2. Koppl, Roger. "How to improve forensic science." Springer/Kluwer Academic Publishers *European Journal of Law and Economics,* Volume 20, Number 3, pgs. 255–286, 2005. With kind permission of Springer Science and Business Media.

CHAPTER 5

THE REALITY OF THE U.S. FORENSIC LABORATORY SYSTEM

In Chapter 13 we explore the inner working of what has come to be known as the "*CSI* effect," the impact of jurors' unrealistic expectations of forensic evidence in criminal cases. The slick images of sophisticated crime labs on television shows are in stark contrast with the harsh realities of many U.S. forensic laboratories, which lack essential infrastructure as well as adequate budgets with which to secure much-needed equipment and supplies and to pay the salaries of its criminalists, examiners, analysts, and scientists.

DiFonzo (2005) comments, "In our gritty criminal justice system, forensic testing is not conducted in the impeccable, prototypical laboratory of a major research institution. Nor does the analyst operate on the crystalline set of *CSI*. More typical is the Detroit Crime Lab. Here is a description: Housed in a former elementary school, the lab suffers from power surges and brownouts stemming from its irregular power source. The freezers to preserve DNA evidence and rape kits are completely full, but the building lacks the electrical capacity to add appliances. Bright yellow police tape cordons off a quarter of the chemistry lab because water leaks have lifted the linoleum tiles and made the floor unsafe. There is no vault to store evidence that has been processed for fingerprints. Shotguns and automatic rifles are stuffed into shopping carts for storage; inside the walk-in freezer for the DNA samples and rape kits, evidence bags are stacked on the floor. Plastic milk crates and cardboard boxes hold hundreds of manila envelopes marked with fluorescent tags. Materials used for the bomb disposal unit must be stored outside because the crime lab does not have an indoor storage area."

The Houston Police Department crime lab, which has been in the media spotlight, has its own troubles. A photograph of the interior of the lab that was published in *The Houston Chronicle* revealed the facility's deficits by depicting a trash can positioned to catch water from a leak presumably caused by missing ceiling tiles, the slippery area cordoned off by a yellow barricade. That these conditions could cause problems related to compromise of incoming forensic evidence was not lost on lay newspaper readers and lab personnel alike. DiFonzo (2005) cites an audit that noted analysts stored evidence in a room where the ceiling leaked so badly that, one stormy night, 34 DNA samples were destroyed, and quotes Houston City Councilwoman Carol Alvarado as describing the conditions she observed while touring the lab in 2002: "These were not just leaks; these were holes. . . . There were trash buckets and water buckets throughout the lab. They were having to move tables around, because some of the leaks were near and sometimes above where the analysis was occurring."

Quality assurance is a crucial issue for both members of the forensic laboratory community as well as for critics who assert that something more must be done to address unacceptable conditions in some crime labs. One of the ways in which forensic laboratories police themselves on quality control issues is through accreditation. With approximately 400 diverse forensic laboratories located in all 50 states, crime laboratories have a critical need for a mechanism to collectively communicate training, quality, and policy issues. The American Society of Crime Laboratory Directors (ASCLD) is the primary organization representing the management of state and local crime laboratories in the United States. It was organized in 1974, around the time when a national voluntary proficiency testing program was initiated and carried out by the Forensic Science Foundation with funding from the Law Enforcement Assistance Administration (LEAA). According to ASCLD, "The reported results of this voluntary proficiency testing soon made front-page headlines in most newspapers around the country. The results reported from the voluntary testing implied that there were serious concerns about the quality of work performed in some of the nation's crime laboratories. The newly formed ASCLD recognized that action must be taken to establish standards of operation for crime laboratories and to take appropriate steps to restore public confidence in the work performed by the nation's crime laboratories. As a result, one of the early committees appointed by ASCLD was the Committee on Laboratory Evaluation and Standards. For approximately four years, the committee considered and worked on various programs that could be used to evaluate and improve the quality of laboratory operations. The committee considered individual certification, a self-assessment program, and an accreditation program based on external peer review as a possible means of achieving the goal."

Each year the committee presented its work and proposals to the ASCLD membership at its annual meeting for input and approval. The committee eventually became the ASCLD Committee on Laboratory Accreditation and a program of laboratory accreditation was approved in concept by the ASCLD membership in the fall of 1980. In June 1981, the first board of directors of the American Society of Crime Laboratory Directors/Laboratory Accreditation Board (ASCLD/LAB) met and elected its first chairman and first executive secretary. In May 1982, the inspection reports for eight laboratories were considered by the board and the eight laboratories from the Illinois State Police became the first facilities accredited by ASCLD/LAB.

According to the ASCLD/LAB manual (1994), the objectives of the accreditation program are to improve the quality of laboratory services provided to the criminal justice system; to develop and maintain criteria that can be used by a laboratory to assess its level of performance and to improve its operations; to provide an independent, impartial, and objective system whereby laboratories can benefit for a comprehensive operational review; and to offer a means of identifying those laboratories that have demonstrated they have met established standards.

The program has three sections—management and operations, personnel standards, and physical plant standards—each containing a number of standards that describe acceptable levels of performance, excellence, and attainment for each specified criterion. An inspection team, comprised of volunteer inspectors who are laboratory managers themselves, reviews and observes the laboratory's operations, and then grades the facility based on the criteria. According to ASCLD/LAB, for a facility to achieve accreditation, it must meet 100 percent of the "essential" criteria (standards that directly impact the quality of the work performed or the integrity of the evidence), at least 75 percent of the "important" criteria (standards that indicate the quality of the laboratory but may not directly impact the work product), and at least 50 percent of the "desirable" criteria (standards that enhance the professionalism of the laboratory but have little impact on the work product).

While critics assert there is a deplorable lack of oversight of forensic laboratories, ASCLD/LAB is trying to make strides toward greater participation in the accreditation process. Note that there are many highly functional laboratories without accreditation, just as there are a number of accredited facilities that have been plagued with problems. So while accreditation is not the silver bullet critics wish it to be, in a more perfect world, greater oversight does encourage a higher level of quality and accountability in general.

ASCLD (2004) states, "Maintaining and increasing professionalism within the forensic science community requires attention to a wide range of issues. Many are related, either directly or indirectly, to quality and guides of best practice. Professionalism includes quality assurance measures such as accreditation and certification. It also includes the activities of professional organizations that provide quality services and work to establish scientific guides of best practice upon which the quality assurance measures are based. Research, innovation and technology transfer are also elements of professionalism in forensic practices."

While crime laboratory accreditation is not a guarantee against errors, it is a program that requires laboratories to have and follow written policies to monitor quality. ASCLD (2004) states, "Accreditation requires a laboratory to evaluate its operations and if problems are identified, they must be addressed. . . . ASCLD has established a formal mentoring program to assist its members in achieving accreditation by pairing a laboratory director from a non-accredited laboratory with one from an accredited laboratory. Participants in this program report the greatest impediments to accreditation are related to resources; both the personnel needed to work on the accreditation standards and the cost of the program itself."

Personnel resources are needed for participation in accreditation programs, of course. For example, according to ASCLD (2004), it is estimated that approximately 1.5 full-time employees (FTEs) are devoted to preparing for accreditation for at least one year prior to a first-time inspection. Quality assurance personnel are tasked with writing and implementing standard operating procedures, auditing existing practices, and compiling necessary documentation and background related to personnel, management operations, and the physical facility. To properly prepare a laboratory for an accreditation inspection and ensure a high likelihood for success, quality assurance (QA) personnel need training in the auditing process. An existing mentoring process, supported in part by the ASCLD and the FBI, allows QA and management personnel to participate in hands-on study with a laboratory that is already accredited, but this requires travel and resource expenditures that most non-accredited laboratories do not have. Increasing emphasis is being placed on accreditation and meeting QA standards for crime laboratory operations, but for many laboratories, the needed funds are not available to carry the process to completion. Many laboratories now face stagnant budgets and rising caseloads. Increasingly, accreditation is viewed as a required credential for crime laboratories. External funding to meet this need may be required, as well.

There is also a time commitment for individual scientists at accredited forensic laboratories. They must meet proficiency testing and record-keeping requirements in all disciplines in which they analyze evidence. Satisfactory completion of at least one proficiency test per discipline annually is the accreditation standard. Laboratories seeking accreditation must show one year of satisfactorily completed proficiency tests prior to the time of the initial inspection. Once accreditation is achieved, analysts must continue to maintain proficiency throughout the multiyear accreditation cycle.

One obstacle to accreditation is the substantial fees and inspection expenses associated with a forensic laboratory's participation in an accreditation program, because all expenditures associated with the assessment process are borne by the laboratory. The average cost per accreditation inspection for the ASCLD/LAB program is approximately $6,500; according to ASCLD (2004), the fees for the accreditation program of the National Forensic Science Technology Center (NFSTC) include an application fee of about $1,000, an assessment fee ranging from $2,900 to $3,900, and an additional fee of approximately $1,000 per discipline. The NFSTC fees do not include travel, lodging, or per diem.

As of late March 2006, 310 crime laboratories were accredited by ASCLD/LAB; they consist of 176 state laboratories, 85 local agency laboratories, 23 federal laboratories, 10 international laboratories, and 15 private laboratories. Thirteen of the facilities are non-U.S. laboratories.

To ferret out problems relating to quality, internal assessments and proficiency testing is essential, commentators insist. Arvizu (2000) charges, "If a laboratory has an effective quality assurance program, their internal systems are likely to find most of their technical problems. But in general, our nation's crime laboratories have immature and ineffective quality assurance programs. Don't depend on them to find their own problems." As for proficiency testing, Arvizu adds that although these programs provide an objective means to monitor laboratory performance, "because proficiency programs are conducted on an intermittent basis, and because laboratories generally know that they will be judged on their performance, they are not reliable indicators of routine performance."

Jami St. Clair, manager of the Columbus Police Crime Laboratory in Ohio and past president of the ASCLD, notes, "I don't think that anyone in the forensic community has ever denied that mistakes and errors occur, just as they occur in journalism or law. I do not believe that there is widespread misconduct in crime labs. Nor do I believe that there are cover-ups occurring. I believe that when errors, mistakes, and misconduct occur, there is action taken on a laboratory level. This is especially true for ASCLD/LAB-accredited labs that are required to take action per accreditation. The response at the laboratory level usually is comprehensive and scientific and may include the review of training, methods, and case files. I think that widespread reform began voluntarily through accreditation. As I said there will always be errors that occur and misconduct in a limited number of individuals, just as in every field. How the individual laboratory responds to these incidents is the real test of integrity."

St. Clair adds, "There are a couple of states, such as New York and Texas, which have mandated that all crime labs be accredited. Of course, Texas requires it as a result of the problems experienced at the Houston Police Department lab. Besides mandatory accreditation, I'm not sure how to address errors in a comprehensive, scientific manner. I'm undecided regarding national mandatory accreditation. Because of accreditation requirements for DNA labs and labs receiving funding from Coverdell grants, there are probably more labs that are accredited than aren't. The gentle shove toward accreditation seems to be working."

Don Wyckoff, director of the Idaho State Police Laboratory, chair of ASCLD/LAB, and a member of the board of directors of the NFSTC, says accreditation should not be construed as a way to eradicate errors, since nothing is completely foolproof. "Once you become accredited, it does not mean that you aren't going to make mistakes," Wyckoff says. "What ASCLD/LAB is trying to do through accreditation is to have in place safeguards for those times when there is an error, a process that the lab can use to go back and evaluate what happened, and to remedy the situation so it doesn't happen again. Too many people view accreditation as an endpoint, and that is not what it is. Even when defense attorneys view it that way; they'll think, 'Well, you got accredited, therefore you won't make any more mistakes.' That is hardly the case. But it is a safety net."

St. Clair emphasizes, "I definitely believe that accreditation by ASCLD/LAB improves lab performance. I'm not saying that a lab that is not accredited does inaccurate work, but third-party audits certainly help a laboratory find its weaknesses. There may be a belief that the ASCLD/LAB accreditation process is a 'good ol' boy' network, but I assure you that no deficiency goes undiscovered and it certainly isn't swept under the rug during an inspection. I'm sure that this can be confirmed by any laboratory that has undergone an inspection process. Knowledgeable, professional inspectors perform an in-depth audit of all aspects of the lab's operation."

Wyckoff notes, "Crime lab managers definitely have taken a hard look at accreditation and certification programs and the various things we and the attorneys want to improve; whether or not we are successful, only time will tell. Everyone thinks we can do these things quickly, but we can't. We must change people's perceptions and expectations and implement programs for improvement, and that takes a long time. When you look at the 300 or so accredited labs in the United States, these labs are by and large what you consider to be classic crime labs, or labs that are multidisciplinary, handling things like DNA testing, ballistics, and finger-prints. Those labs become accredited because there has been pressure brought to bear on them in some cases, or they just felt they should do it because accreditation is the right thing to do. But there are lots of single-discipline labs doing forensic work that we don't even know about, meaning that they are not necessarily in the public eye. A good example of this is the numerous police departments across the country where someone is doing fingerprint analysis. That is forensic science, yet I would venture to say very few of those kinds of labs are accred-ited. So you have the big labs doing the high-profile cases and then there are the tiny labs, and some more than others are working toward accreditation. There are only four states left in the country that don't have an accredited lab somewhere within their border. And those states tend to be states that are small or have low populations; we know that at least two or three of those labs are working toward accreditation. My goal is that by the end of 2006 all states will have accredited crime labs."

Accreditation is one important way in which forensic laboratories are trying to address quality issues, but in the midst of this course of self-improvement are a number of treacherous pitfalls that threaten to undermine the performance of these forensic service providers.

One of the many reasons why forensic science has come under siege is the ongoing reports of tremendous backlogs in case sample analysis. Harried forensic laboratory managers are forced to triage their workloads, establishing priorities based on any number of factors appro-priate to their facility's capacity, the forensic units that have the most number of cases, and their jurisdiction's demands.

Paul Ferrara, Ph.D., director of the Virginia Department of Forensic Science and board member of the Virginia Institute of Forensic Science and Medicine, reports that his facility is keeping its head above water, but only because it has worked hard to lobby for additional resources needed to keep up with the workload. "We are fortunate in that we have the money we need to train new scientists, and that we also have positions in which to put them when they are trained," Ferrara says. "We're lucky to have a queue of scientists going from under-graduate studies to graduate studies through our Institute of Forensic Science and Medicine and then into our laboratories. This has increased my capacity but the workload has increased as well. So we're holding our own but we are doing so at an unacceptably high level. For the greater crime lab community, buildings, people, and training and education are the top needs. Crime lab infrastructure must be expanded to accommodate the demand."

"The funding situation is better than it's ever been," Ferrara continues, "and I was glad to see that the Coverdell money increased because it is a challenge to pay for everything we still need. The bigger issue is that it's going to take time for that money to translate into reduced backlogs. That being the case, the situation may not get better for a while. Labs everywhere have to come up with novel ways in which to approach workloads and backlogs, including establishing triage systems.

In any major case, we require the law enforcement agency and prosecutor to sit down with us to go over the evidence before we do anything, but realistically, you can't do that in every case, of course. The same or worse is happening at other labs. I doubt too many of my coun-terparts get the funding that my lab does, so I am probably much better off than they are. One of the reasons why Virginia is where it is, is because of the support that we have received for years from the Virginia government. Other labs, especially those that are buried in the basement of a police department and are funded only after the new cruisers and taser guns are purchased, don't fare nearly as well, and that's a problem."

The conflicting priorities are everywhere in crime labs. St. Clair explains, "Crime labs have many different units, so the scientists doing the drug analysis are not the people doing DNA analysis or firearms examination. So, in most labs, each unit's backlog must be approached separately. In a drug analysis unit, for example, which for most labs is the bulk of the work, it's pretty much all court-driven. In fact, sometimes going to court is the only priority system that labs use. Because their backlogs are so large, they use a court date to prioritize cases; those cases without a suspect may sit longer than those cases with a suspect and an upcoming court date."

St. Clair admits that even this commonsense priority system can take a back seat to the squeaky-wheel approach: "Whichever police officer yells the loudest might get our attention," she says. "Investigators will tell us they're going to make a bust or a sweep next week and they need our analyses. Violent crimes often get pushed to the top of the list, too. And there are always the cases in which a pretty, young, blonde woman disappears and Fox News is sitting on your doorstep and you have 20 broadcasting trucks parked outside; that's when you feel the pressure to do those cases first, especially when the chief of detectives is saying, 'We need this (analysis result) now, because CNN might call at any minute.' In ordinary circumstances, the court date or the severity of a crime, or the possibility of a string of serial crimes can impact how cases are prioritized. Sometimes investigators will tell us that a great number of resources are being pulled into an investigation and they ask us to perform a test in a week as opposed to three months, to help them out."

SIDEBAR 5.1 THROUGH THE EYES OF THE CRIME LAB MANAGER

While no on could ever truly walk a mile in the average crime lab manager's shoes, it is possible to try to understand the numerous challenges they face and how they must respond to the many stressors out of their control. Sewell (2000) enumerates the many ways in which change has affected the field and forced these crime lab managers to rethink how they do their jobs: "Change in the forensic services has been explosive. The educational expectations for new forensic scientists, especially in the more technical fields, have expanded, and training time for beginning analysts has increased. Technological advancements and legal mandates have led to new, more exact, and often more complicated and complex procedures that require even greater skills on the part of practicing forensic scientists. The courts and the public in general, especially as a result of high-profile crimes and trials, have a greater, though not necessarily more realistic or valid, expectation of what forensic scientists can do and how they should perform their duties. Defense challenges to courtroom testimony by laboratory personnel and a wider use of defense experts demand the highest level of technical competency and courtroom presentation skills. The ethical requirements of the forensic sciences mandate the constant review and assurance of both organizational and individual integrity."

Sewell (2000) explains that these stressors represent two distinct categories: those created by the nature of forensic sciences, such as zero tolerance for mistakes, the quality of incoming samples for testing, and conflict with investigators and prosecutors; as well as those created by the nature of the job, including evolving managerial responsibilities, lack of managerial preparation, and the failure of upper management to fully understand complicated forensic laboratory issues.

One of the issues that keep crime lab managers tossing and turning at night is that related to errors—whether unintentional or otherwise—committed by lab analysts and examiners. Sewell (2000) observes, "The integrity of forensic evidence analysis and its implications with regard to the guilt or innocence of suspects demand the highest quality work by forensic scientists. . . . The importance of proper and accurate examination of forensic evidence leaves no room for error on the part of its examiners. The forensic manager is the first line of defense in a forensic agency's quality assurance effort. It is the manager whose supervision of technical and administrative reviews can identify professional and technical deficiencies. Like other law enforcement managers, it is this manager who must take firm and consistent steps, whether of a training or disciplinary nature, to ensure accuracy, quality, and system integrity. Like other individuals in managerial roles or supervisory positions, the forensic manager must deal with the consequences of necessary actions that may conflict with a desire to be liked by and get along with professional colleagues."

Another issue is managing conflict with law enforcement investigators and prosecutors. Sewell (2000) explains, "Less experienced investigators and prosecutors may fail to value the expertise and experience of the forensic scientist and may have expectations based only on textbooks or technical publications; their colleagues' lore; or movies, television, and news reports. As a result, investigators and prosecutors may find themselves at odds with the scientists so critical to their success. This becomes especially true when scientists find themselves in ethical dilemmas caused by pressure from investigators or prosecutors who expect the results of an examination to support a specific investigative theory." Sewell rightly describes a crime lab manager as serving the "dual role of gatekeeper and referee."

Finally, the stress accompanied with having to do more with less is a constant companion to forensic laboratory supervisors. Sewell (2000) notes, "The skills required for successful personnel management in a contemporary organization are particularly demanding and, if lacking, generate significant stress. As is the case with other managerial positions, the laboratory manager must cope with limited budgets, balance personnel and staff workloads, identify and coordinate training needs and personnel problems, handle a variety of routine administrative duties, and be fully prepared for and attend myriad meetings—accomplished, of course, within a 40-hour week." Sewell continues, "A forensic manager must be able to lead and motivate his or her scientific colleagues in a work environment characterized by continuing racial and ethnic diversity; differing levels of technological skills and comfort; and a younger generation of workers with different expectations of their job, its demands, and their responsibilities." Concurrent with tending their underlings, crime lab managers must appease their bosses. Sewell (2000) acknowledges, "It is difficult, at times, for non-scientific upper management to fully understand complex laboratory issues. At the highest levels of an agency, especially when the laboratory is a subordinate institution within a law enforcement organization, the

Continues on next page

chief executive must balance a variety of policy, personnel, fiscal, and budgeting issues. The activities and requirements of a forensic laboratory are scientifically demanding, technologically complicated, and expensive. For chief executives without a scientific or forensic background, the decisions relating to a laboratory are critical and complex and require reliance on and trust in the expertise of forensic managers. Managers, however, may feel that their advice and counsel are neither sought nor heeded."

Regardless of the type of priority system used in forensic laboratories, backlogs exist, St. Clair says. "Different labs have different backlogs," she explains. "For example, we don't have a backlog in DNA, but other labs have a horrendous backlog. Our backlog is in firearms, while other people are caught up in firearms. The drug cases keep on coming. The acceptance policies and the priority policies for each lab probably affect backlog levels; for example, if you're not accepting low-level marijuana cases, then you're not going to have a backlog in them. What happened with DNA is that when police officers around the country realized what this kind of typing could mean to their cases, they started pulling evidence out of their property rooms, and bringing it in to their labs, and that caused quite a backlog in labs where perhaps no backlog existed previously. So, many backlogs were created when crime labs started doing DNA analysis. I certainly wouldn't have it any other way because that means we're going to help solve crimes."

St. Clair says that further backlogs are created when legislators and other decision makers discover the power and potential of DNA and begin requiring the collection of DNA samples from arrestees and convicted offenders. "In my state, Ohio, we started out with 10 crimes requiring DNA samples, and now it's progressed to all felons, so if you were arrested for drugs, for example, you are required to give your DNA. And in other states it's all arrestees, so that in itself is creating a large backlog. As police officers discover that DNA can help with both old and new cases, they are going to start submitting samples like crazy."

Although there is no average workload, there are some parameters that the field tries to respect for the sake of its employees' general welfare. "Over the years there have been workload surveys that have been done by ASCLD to give lab managers some idea about what a normal workload in a given discipline for a person is," says Wyckoff. "In my lab, we are not under water, but there are labs elsewhere that are. Some labs resort to outsourcing, and that is cost effective for them; in other labs, outsourcing may not be the answer. It's highly individual to each crime lab."

Some labs look to tactics such as outsourcing, privatization, or partnerships with private labs to help ease workloads. St. Clair cautions, "I'm not sure that privatization would improve accuracy. Quality assurance (QA) costs money. Unless there is a profit at the end, I'm skeptical that a private company would institute the amount of QA that crime labs currently do. I've had vendors tell me that they have no plans on becoming ISO accredited because there's no profit in it. Private DNA labs have to be accredited because federal law requires it, but there are a lot of one- or two-person private labs that do questionable work or perform work beyond their expertise because they need the business. Now there are crime labs that operate on a cost-recovery basis. They charge for their services either through fee for service or contractual basis. Generally they are also supplemented by local taxes or have other funding mechanisms so they are not so concerned about finding the money to operate on a day-to-day basis." St. Clair continues, "Increased partnerships with some private labs may ease workloads. This is especially true with DNA labs that are accredited. But there have been stories recently concerning poor quality coming from private laboratories. So, in order to feel comfortable with subcontracting casework to labs, there are a lot of quality checks that have to be done by the contracting lab. This is also required as a part of accreditation."

Robotics may be too far ahead of the curve for most forensic laboratories currently, but it might be a way to stem the backlog tide. "I don't know that much about robotics but I do agree in general that science is only as good as the analyst running the instrumentation," St. Clair notes. "Automation has done a lot to improve accuracy in quantitative analysis. We know this because there have been a lot of quality assurance checks performed to show that the devices are accurate. There is no question that auto-samplers on instrumentation improve turnaround. But they also require quality checks. Analysts have to ensure that what the computer thinks is sample 1 really *is* sample 1. A lot of drug identifications are performed with the use of computer libraries. This is also true of electronic databases such as CODIS. There are also a lot of quality checks that go into ensuring that what gets entered as a standard is what it is supposed to be. As well, an analyst can't rely on a computer to call the match. A physical examination of the questioned to the known must still be done by the analyst. And computers can't testify."

It begs the question of the role technology plays in the advancement of the U.S. forensic laboratory system. Unprecedented advances in technology have intersected with an alarming lack of qualified individuals to work in forensic laboratories that are overwhelmed with case backlogs in many analysis units. Saferstein (2001) notes, "Crime laboratories have become the major benefactors of enormous advancements in scientific technology." Chromatography, mass spectrometry, spectrophotometry, DNA typing, capillary electrophoresis, liquid chromatography, scanning electron microscopes, and x-ray microanalyzers are among the most important tools in the modern laboratory. Many of these tools are run by cutting-edge technology driven by microprocessors that enhance the performance of analytical instrumentation.

Saferstein (2001) adds a caveat, however: "The unabated progress of analytical technology must not obscure the fact that the profession of forensic science has reached a critical junction in its history. The preoccupation with equipping a crime laboratory with elaborate and sophisticated hardware has left a wide gap between the skill of the scientist and the ability of the criminal investigator to recognize and preserve physical evidence at the crime scene. The crime scene is the critical first step in the process of using scientific services in a criminal investigation. All the expertise and instrumentation that any crime laboratory can muster will be rendered totally impotent if evidence has been inadvertently destroyed by careless investigators or curiosity seekers. Yet studies confirm that this is precisely what is happening at many crime scenes." Saferstein (2001) remarks that crime labs are "Overworked and understaffed. . . . The solution to the problem may seem obvious: more people, larger facilities, and of course, more money. In this respect, the crime laboratories must stand in line with the other components of the criminal justice system" due to challenges that have overburdened various agencies. "In light of public and political outcries, criminal justice administrators have sought programs geared to producing quick and dramatic reductions in crime rates. In this kind of atmosphere, hiring more scientists or buying a mass spectrometer or gas chromatograph may hardly seem to many to be the best solution to the problem."

Members of the forensic laboratory community say that technology cannot ameliorate manpower shortages in forensic laboratories. Saferstein (2001) concurs, noting, "It would be a mistake for forensic scientists to be lulled into a false sense of security by believing that the tremendous strides made in the development of analytical instruments and techniques are alone sufficient to meet the needs and goals of their profession. In truth, progress can be expected in the future only if crime laboratories are assured of staffs composed of trained and knowledgeable scientists. Unfortunately, because the rapid expansion of criminalistic services has created unprecedented demands for more forensic scientists, it has become exceedingly difficult to locate, train, and assimilate competent individuals into existing crime laboratory operations."

It is a tightrope that all forensic service providers must walk. Saferstein (2001) comments, "The present momentum of forensic research could very well falter unless individuals who possess relevant knowledge and skills are attracted to careers in forensic science. The recognition by a sufficient number of colleges and universities of the need for fostering undergraduate and graduate programs in this field is essential for assuring an ample supply of scientists to meet the anticipated personnel needs of the profession. Furthermore, the establishment of forensic education programs, especially at the graduate level, should be accompanied by the formulation of new academic research programs dedicated to investigating fertile areas of research that are pertinent to the expanding role of forensic science in criminal justice. In a university environment, these research programs can be pursued in an atmosphere unaffected by the pressures of everyday casework, a burden that presently weighs heavily on the shoulders of the working forensic scientist."

For now at least, workloads may have to be dealt with the old-fashioned way—through traditional case management instead of relying too heavily on expensive technological advancements many public labs cannot afford. Sewell (2000) observes, "Law enforcement officers and prosecutors recognize the need for and value of forensic evidence in successful criminal prosecution. With changing technology and the enhanced capabilities of forensic laboratories has come an increased submission of evidence. Corresponding to the increase in submissions are expectations that the evidence can be worked in a timely manner; the evidence will be of some value, that is, it can be related to some offender; and the number of outgoing or completed cases keeps pace with the number of incoming items. For the forensic analyst, this translates to a pressure to examine evidence in a timely and effective manner. For the laboratory manager, it requires an ability to manage increasing workloads in the most productive manner and, often, without a corresponding increase in human or technological resources."

"I think it's our job as managers to make sure the workload doesn't have an impact on our analysts," St. Clair notes. "There's a general lab testing standard which in part is designed to ensure that undue pressure doesn't exist, or that if it is reported, you do something about it. Some crime lab managers are concerned about backlogs and how their analysts are coping with their workloads; some of them are feeling pressured and are being asked to do too many cases. The reality is that we have a lot of cases, and we have to do them somehow. I'd say 90 percent of crime lab directors, managers, and supervisors have worked on the bench themselves, so they can empathize. We've all faced quotas; if you force people to do too many cases, will the quality of the work begin to suffer? I believe all crime lab managers are sensitive to this issue; they look at the average number of cases that are being worked at comparable labs throughout the country and try to come up with a number of cases that won't cause analysts to freak out about it."

St. Clair says that the definition of a manageable workload depends on the section within the crime lab and what type of analysis is being conducted. "It's not unusual for a drug analyst to see 100 or 200 cases if they are crack or marijuana cases. However, if you are working in a DEA lab doing huge drug cases, 100 could be way too much to handle. Workload definitions are lab-dependent and discipline-dependent. With DNA, you couldn't even conceive of asking an analyst to do 100 cases, but I have also heard of people only working five DNA cases a month."

Essential to any conversation about lab workload are workspace, resource, and manpower issues. "It all comes down to what kind of financial support labs have," St. Clair says. "I can't say that labs which are independent of law enforcement are better equipped and manned or vice versa, because it depends on your budget. I think that crime labs will be expected to have sufficient resources to perform competent analyses in all disciplines in which they offer services. So, for example, if they were offering drug analyses, they would have personnel educated in chemistry and trained in the identification of drugs, including knowledge (both theoretical and practical) of the instrumentation that is used. These individuals would have access to the instrumentation that they need to perform accurate, precise identification of controlled substances. So, for example, they wouldn't confuse cocaine base with cocaine hydrochloride or a non-controlled drug with a controlled one. DNA analysis, however, is federally regulated. The FBI requirements for DNA laboratories are very strict and go beyond this very basic premise. Accreditation also goes beyond this basic expectation. With accreditation, you are expected to document that the analysts performing the testing are competent by successfully completing testing prior to performing case analysis. Analysts are also required to prove proficiency by successfully completing ongoing testing throughout their careers. While the need for accreditation is growing as a minimum expectation in the criminal justice community I'm not sure that it has yet reached that status universally. There are still jurisdictions where the local laboratory is not accredited. It doesn't automatically mean that they are doing poor work. Their local police, courts, and even defense attorneys may have the utmost respect for their work."

Regarding infrastructure needs, St. Clair remarks, "Just anecdotally, I don't hear too many complaints concerning resources right now. There are a lot of new laboratories being built, for example. But there have been many laboratories that have discontinued a service because of costs and benefits considerations. The funds necessary to remain proficient in a discipline with little demand could be better spent in another area. For example, a lot of labs have discontinued trace evidence because the demand is no longer there (not as precise as DNA). If, however, you include timeliness as a demand, then I would have to say that there is a lack of resources in labs. I don't think that there is a crime lab in operation today that doesn't have a backlog in at least one discipline. I think that most labs and their users accept that they will always have a backlog. Just like you expect to wait in line at the grocery store or bank, unfortunately, our customers expect to wait in line to have their cases analyzed. On the positive side, I don't think that crime laboratories allow their backlog to affect the quality of their analysis."

While there is no empirical data that manpower shortages in forensic laboratories affect the quality of casework, it is an issue at the forefront of the minds of most lab managers. Ferrara bemoans the current state of manpower in many U.S. forensic laboratories because not only is it a challenge to secure the funding to pay salaries, it is a challenge to secure the services of qualified scientists with the proper education and credentials for the job. "I have noticed over the last few years that many people came out of college with a forensic science degree but they had no real depth of study in the traditional sciences," he says. "Most crime lab managers would tell you they probably don't want those kinds of people, even though they may have to hire them out of desperation. Most lab managers want people who have been rigorously schooled in biochemistry, chemistry, biology, or physics, but most graduates came out of institutions with only criminal justice coursework. They called it forensic science, but it was mostly law classes and lots of social science classes. I think we also can agree that we have very few scientists coming out of the university system compared to the time when I, and many of my peers, graduated. The other problem is, individuals who are bright people desire a well-paying job, and that conflicts with where many forensic scientists end up. If you are a top-notch biochemist and go on to graduate school, the likelihood that you are going to go into forensic science, especially in the public sector, is slim. Instead, you will invariably go into the private sector and make twice what you would in the public sector. That's a big draw for people right now. I am not saying that is bad, but that is the reality. If we are going to attract to our labs the upper echelon of forensic practitioners, we must start paying better salaries."

Ferrara continues, "In states with significant scientist turnover, legislatures and city managers will notice that I have to keep training people and sustaining these huge budgets; they will make me do something about that. They have to realize, however, that you can't train people quickly, neither can you offer increasing salaries and benefits to people instantly; you have to plan in your budget for contingencies and for an economy that has its ups and downs."

Once forensic laboratory managers find the warm bodies they need, the issue most often raised by critics of forensic science is the lack of competency testing of analysts. St. Clair notes, "All analysts should be competency tested prior to performing analysis on casework. This is an internal testing encompassing all analytical techniques, report writing, and even expert witness testimony, and certification or licensing is through external sources. I certainly encourage examiners to become certified. That being said, I am not certified nor are any of my employees. While I don't have exact numbers, I would guess that less than 20 percent of the nation's working forensic scientists have a certification. A major reason for this is that crime laboratories (especially ones that employ hundreds of employees) don't have the resources to pay for an individual to take the exam, or perhaps give them on-duty time to study for the exam, and ensure they keep it up by paying for them to attend continuing education—especially considering that after they've made the investment, the employee may leave. The certification remains with the employee, not the lab, therefore, the cost involved in maintaining individual certification usually falls to the forensic scientist. If they feel strong enough about their career to invest their own money, they will. In addition, certification is only part of the quality process. It does exhibit that an analyst has considerable knowledge regarding their discipline but a thorough laboratory-wide quality program includes considerably more than just examiner competence."

In addition to proficiency testing and certification of lab analysts, the state of education and training of forensic scientists is a contentious issue among both critics and members of the forensic science community, although each camp might readily agree there are not nearly enough opportunities for forensic analysts and examiners to enhance their skills.

St. Clair offers a slightly more optimistic perspective: "I think today's analysts are better trained and educated than ever before, as many of the students coming out of college have master's degrees. I suspect that it's partially due to the fact that jobs are scarce so they get a post-graduate degree when they either can't find a job or think it'll improve their prospects. Plus many agencies offer tuition reimbursement so employees are returning to school to get master's degree after becoming employed. There are several legitimate online programs available, so it's easier to attend college and work full time concurrently. In addition, for the past several years, the Coverdell funding has provided laboratories with training funds. If labs utilize funds in this way, they can send employees to specialized training courses."

W. Earl Wells, president of the ASCLD and laboratory director of the South Carolina Law Enforcement Division, states, "We have to train analysts before we turn them loose to work in a forensic setting and testify in court. Our lab, for example, is fairly representative of most labs, with the exception of several forensic disciplines. In the trace evidence unit in my lab, I can take a bachelor of science–degreed person or I can take a Ph.D. in analytical chemistry and before I can let him or her sign a report, they must go through anywhere from a year and a half to two years of training. The same is true for DNA and questioned documents, and there is absolutely no formal training that prepares you for that; but there's a two- to three-year training program they must successfully complete before they can work independently. The same is true for latent prints, firearms, etc. So we take very seriously that when we hire someone out of college with a degree, they are totally unprepared to perform the work they are being hired to perform without additional training and very, very close oversight. There is a period of time where all their work is co-signed regardless of the discipline. And we encourage them to become certified in their discipline."

CRIME LAB FUNDING

In Chapter 14, we will examine the current state of authorization and appropriation of funding for forensic laboratories and medico-legal offices; funding remains a grim reality for most crime labs, which must do more with less on a daily basis. One of the main lab funding vehicles, as we shall see, is the Paul Coverdell National Forensic Sciences Improvement Act of 2000, which is the lifeblood of most public forensic facilities.

"I had the honor of being the president of ASCLD when Coverdell was initially drafted and passed, so I'm pretty familiar with it," St. Clair recalls. "The interesting thing about Coverdell is that when we proposed the legislation to members of Congress, we had listened to what crime labs had to say about grant funding that existed at the time. Many of the local laboratories were receiving no grant funds; grants either came into the state and were gobbled up by state labs before the locals could get any funding, or they came directly from NIJ [National Institute of Justice] or another granting agency. Your ability to get one of these grants was dependent on your ability to write grants, so there were a lot of needy labs that weren't receiving any funding while other labs were getting lots of funding." St. Clair continues, "Coverdell grants have a block grant component so that all states get funding. The Coverdell funding includes a requirement that a statewide plan be adopted for improving forensic laboratories. The original language of the bill required that all labs in the state be provided the opportunity to contribute to the plan. I'm not sure if all states are following it, but Ohio is. It is up to the state to determine what their needs are and how much funding should go to each lab. So if they want to go strictly by number of analysts in the labs, they can do that or they can go by squeaky wheel. The other interesting thing with Coverdell funds is that laboratories are required to be accredited or going through accreditation in order to be eligible for the funding. It was meant as a gentle shove toward accreditation."

St. Clair explains further, "There is also a competitive component to Coverdell funding. So, if a lab has an especially pressing need, it can still write a grant and get funding through the NIJ. The Justice for All Act is primarily aimed at resolving the DNA backlog, as it authorizes the funding that NIJ uses for DNA grant programs. Some or all of these have block grant components. Since both Justice for All and Coverdell have block grant components, if crime labs meet the eligibility requirements, there is little reason why they couldn't at least get some funding from them. I do think that most labs do pursue grants and should be eligible to receive funding from the grants. Some feel that the reporting requirements are not worth the trouble but the majority of the labs accept that there is always an accountability that comes with the dispersal of federal tax dollars. After all, wouldn't you want to know if the programs that your taxes support are effective to correct a problem?"

Because most forensic laboratories depend on public funding for their survival, they must become ever vigilant about ways to not only make their budgets stretch farther, but be savvy about the inner workings of the state and federal governments, which clearly determine these facilities' fiscal destinies. Tax dollars are generally the largest source of laboratory funding, and legislators are in charge of determining how best to allocate scarce resources among increasing numbers of agencies with growing slates of needs. Competition for state and federal dollars is fierce, especially in an era of growing health-care and homeland security issues that tend to funnel the bulk of funding. Funding of forensic laboratories, within the context of various advocacy efforts within the forensic science community, will be discussed more fully in Chapter 14.

In short, many forensic laboratories are suffering from an abysmal shortage of funding. Koussiafes (2004) observes, "A budget crisis exists in many forensic services programs. Attracting and retaining competent employees are among the problems faced by forensic agencies. Although some states claim to offer competitive salaries, the reality is different."

Just how financially needy a forensic laboratory is greatly depends on its location in the criminal justice system's organizational structure, which, according to Koussiafes (2004) "can affect the budget, funding, and sometimes the objectives of public forensic laboratories. The three types of public forensic laboratories, local (city and county), state, and federal, have direct bearing on the budget picture."

Forensic laboratories that are housed with law enforcement agencies not only face budgetary competition from their host, they are often placed in a dicey political and ethical situation. Koussiafes (2004) explains, "The agency head may be a sheriff or police chief who may not be fully aware of the needs of the forensic laboratory. The administrator may funnel more of the limited budget to law enforcement services with which they are more familiar. Even when the administrator acknowledges the role of the forensic laboratory, public image is considered. A laboratory instrument is not as visible as a police cruiser. In addition, a close relationship with law enforcement may present an ethical dilemma for forensic scientists. The scientists may see themselves as working for law enforcement, and this could hinder scientific objectivity. However, forensic laboratories are sometimes able to work with law enforcement agencies to obtain grants and assistance that might not be otherwise available."

State forensic laboratories, when housed with state police or other similar agencies, experience many of the same budgetary and ethical dilemmas their smaller brethren do. There are some exceptions, however, like the Alabama Department of Forensic Sciences where the forensic laboratory reports to a civilian director. State law enforcement agencies submit samples to the laboratory, but the forensic scientists maintain a level of autonomy that may not be experienced by laboratories operating directly under law enforcement agencies. "With this structure however," Koussiafes (2004) observes, "the laboratory must compete with other state agencies for funding."

At the federal level, Koussiafes (2004) explains, "Laboratories are often in the same agency as the law enforcement officers with whom they serve, and their status in the organization is equal to the investigative divisions. The laboratories report to a civilian, who is often a political appointee. Federal forensic laboratories receive samples from local and state law enforcement agencies and maintain a level of autonomy from them. Other federal laboratories may provide services to law enforcement agencies but are not full-time forensic laboratories. They are often specialty laboratories performing routine regulatory analyses for environmental, health, and agriculture departments. Samples submitted to these laboratories usually come from the divisions in the laboratory's agency but may also come from other law enforcement agencies."

While demands for services increase and budget sources decrease, forensic laboratories and their directors are under tremendous pressure to examine their operations for ways to boost efficiencies and cut costs. Common cost-saving strategies include outsourcing, privatization, and consolidation. Koussiafes (2004) describes a survey of crime lab directors conducted in 2002 at the Federal Bureau of Investigation's (FBI's) annual symposium for crime laboratory directors. Of the 75 surveys distributed, 24 completed surveys were received, for a rate of return of 32 percent. Koussiafes reports that managers with budgetary responsibilities tended to be in charge of more than 20 employees at state facilities that frequently served a population of more than 1 million. For these aforementioned directors, the overwhelming choice for spending a one-time lump sum of $250,000 was the purchase of new instruments, followed by training for employees. According to Koussiafes, some directors indicated that although they would like to allocate bonuses for employees, there was no mechanism in place to do this or they were not authorized to do so, while other directors indicated a desire for overtime funds for employees to help with the work backlog. One respondent indicated a desire for a new building rather than improving the existing structure.

In addition, Koussiafes (2004) reports that if a laboratory were given an annual 10 percent budget increase, hiring additional employees would be the first choice for the lab directors. Koussiafes notes, "Laboratories are under increasing workloads and need more employees to do the work. Salary increases and conferences and training, means of rewarding hard-working employees, closely follow the request for additional employees. However, salary issues are often handled by the legislature, leaving little room for discretion by the supervisor. Supervisors often have discretion in how cuts should be made, whereas increases in funding are earmarked by the state legislature for specific objectives. Canceling conferences and training led the cutbacks because they are often seen as an employee reward. Canceling new equipment orders followed. Many respondents indicated that in an austerity program, the goal was to avoid personnel layoffs."

As we have seen, the federal government is the repository of funding for the vast majority of U.S. forensic laboratories. To foster greater forensic science research efforts, the NIJ makes funding available through directed solicitations, with its forensics portfolio separated into two categories: general forensic sciences and DNA research and development. The goal of the General Forensic Sciences Research Program is to increase the availability and improve the reliability and admissibility of non-DNA forensic evidence in the criminal justice system, with an emphasis on cultivating projects in the forensic disciplines of controlled substances, toxicology, trace evidence, and impression evidence. The goal of the Forensic DNA Research and Development Program is to identify and develop methods and technologies that will permit DNA to be used in all areas of criminal investigation.

The Paul Coverdell Forensic Sciences Improvement Grant Program provides funding to state and local governments to improve the quality and timeliness of forensic science and medical examiner services and/or to eliminate backlogs in the analysis of forensic evidence, including controlled substances, firearms examination, forensic pathology, latent prints, questioned documents, toxicology, and trace evidence. Coverdell funds are to be used to improve the quality and timeliness of forensic science and medical examiner services and/or to eliminate backlogs in the analysis of forensic evidence, including controlled substances, firearms examination, forensic pathology, latent prints, questioned documents, toxicology, and trace evidence. Both states and units of local government apply to the NIJ for funding. All applicants for Coverdell grants—whether states or units of local government—must have developed a program for improving the quality and timeliness of forensic science or medical examiner services and must specifically describe how grant funds will be used to carry out all or a substantial part of that program. States are expected to consider the needs of laboratories operated by units of local government as well as those operated by the state. Any forensic laboratory, forensic laboratory system, medical examiner's office, or coroner's office that will receive any portion of a Coverdell grant must use generally accepted laboratory practices and procedures as established by accrediting organizations or appropriate certifying bodies.

The holy grail of forensic laboratory funding has been and continues to be the Paul Coverdell National Forensic Sciences Improvement Act of 2000, which was enacted on December 21, 2000. The legislation's purpose was to "improve the quality, timeliness, and credibility of forensic science services for criminal justice purposes, and for other purposes." Any forensic laboratory can seek grants from this funding vehicle if it meets certain criteria, including the employment of at least one or more full-time scientists whose principal duties are the examination of physical evidence for law enforcement agencies in criminal matters, who provides testimony with respect to such physical evidence to the criminal justice system, who employs generally accepted practices and procedures, as established by appropriate accrediting organizations, and whose facility is accredited by ASCLD/LAB. The U.S. attorney general is the administrator of the funding mechanism for the Coverdell act, and grantees must provide evidence that these standards are met.

The Coverdell act distributes funds based on a sliding scale relative to a jurisdiction's population and crime rates. Grants received through the Coverdell act are used to support the essence of the spirit of the legislation, that is, to cover program expenses relating to facilities, personnel, computerization, equipment, supplies, accreditation and certification, education, and training; use of funds for any general law enforcement or non-forensic investigatory functions is prohibited. As a means of checks and balances, laboratories receiving grant assistance are required by the act to submit to the attorney general a report that includes a summary and assessment of the program carried out with the grant, and the average number of days between the submission of a sample to a forensic laboratory and the delivery of test results to the requesting agency.

In addition, the attorney general is required to make an annual report to Congress that outlines the aggregate amount of grants awarded for the fiscal year. The Coverdell act was appropriated in stages, with $35 million for fiscal year 2001; $85.4 million for fiscal year 2002; $134.7 million for fiscal year 2003; $128 million for fiscal year 2004; $56.7 million for fiscal year 2005; and $42 million for fiscal year 2006. With Coverdell funding coming to an end in 2006, efforts have been aimed at ensuring that Congress makes adequate provisions for the funding of the forensic science community. These efforts are discussed further in Chapter 14.

HUMAN RESOURCE ISSUES

Human resource issues are tied tightly to the funding needs of forensic laboratories, which must recruit and retain qualified forensic practitioners to meet the ever-growing demand for services. Becker and Dale (2003) assert that forensic laboratories must implement high-level human resource management methods to improve the retention of laboratory personnel, knowing that high rates of staff turnover impede the reduction of case backlogs.

Becker and Dale (2003) state, "Higher salaries for new and existing personnel, new and better facilities, and the increased use of technology should be implemented. However, these changes cost considerable taxpayer's dollars and take time and resources to put into practice. Although government leaders recognize the value of expanding forensic resources, additional funds are difficult to come by when national, state, and local budgets are already stretched."

Becker and Dale (2003) suggest that laboratory managers must develop savvy planning strategies to counter significant human resource challenges, including developing estimates of staffing requirements and determining the value of forensic services: "To optimize human resource planning, it is important to understand the labor market in the forensic science community. Forecasting involves reconciling the gap between today's labor supply and future labor demands. The demand for services includes performing analyses on all cases submitted to the laboratory."

Dillon (1999) says that because there is no general consensus on the extent of the supply of forensic scientists in the United States, determining the extent of the pool of potential applicants is challenging. Becker and Dale (2003) suggest that agencies estimate staffing needs based on a ratio of one forensic scientist to approximately 30,000 people in the population served by the laboratory. The next step, they say, is to estimate the value and/or costs of forensic science services to the community. While private laboratories charge law enforcement agencies up to $3,000 for forensic tests, state laboratories charge as little as $100 per test, Becker and Dale state, with an average value of a completed DNA profile at $500 per sample. They add, "Laboratories should determine the value of the costs and services that they provide to the community and then use these values as a common benchmark in resource planning and discussions with legislators."

Once laboratory managers know what they are up against, they can implement effective recruiting strategies that include techniques such as realistic job previews, internships, and shadow programs. Becker and Dale (2003) state, "The recruiting process in forensic science laboratories can take advantage of realistic job previews that present the characteristics of the job to the applicants. Realistic job previews provide details about the job to help applicants understand the work and venue before they are hired. These previews should include all aspects of the job. . . . Realistic job previews help ensure that time is not wasted with applicants who are not qualified, who will not succeed in all the selection hurdles, and who are unlikely to remain on the job." Cascio (2003) suggests that job satisfaction is elevated when a realistic job preview has been part of the selection process, and that the employee-retention rate is increased by an average of 9 percent.

Becker and Dale (2003) acknowledge that the costs of recruiting, selecting, training, and replacing forensic scientists can be extensive. In a recent survey of forensic laboratory directors, two of the major reasons cited for employee turnover were salary and personal reasons. This means that the early departure of scientists, some of which may have been prevented, was not identified in the laboratory's recruiting and selection program. Once the right people are in place, Becker and Dale (2003) encourage forensic laboratory managers to empower their people to prepare for the arduous road ahead of their employees. Becker and Dale comment, "An unskilled manager can have a ripple effect throughout the organization, creating lower motivation and the loss of good employees." They advise laboratory managers to retain valued analysts by helping them develop their skills, and then be certain to assess their job satisfaction regularly. They also emphasize the importance of ensuring that employees attend professional conferences so that they can update their skills and network with colleagues, an opportunity that passes by many forensic scientists due to budgetary constraints. They add, "Flexible work hours, good training, and a supportive work environment should be provided when other work incentives are limited by organizational constraints."

Dale and Becker (2004) report that many in the forensic laboratory community have hazarded guesses about the current number of forensic professionals, as well as the number of new forensic scientists needed to meet the demand for laboratory services. Fisher (2003) and Long (2001) estimate that at least 10,000 new forensic scientists are needed over the next decade. The ability to accurately forecast staffing needs within forensic laboratories will be a challenge faced by numerous managers, and it is a problem compounded by the need to estimate caseloads. Dale and Becker note, "There is a general lack of consensus on the definition of caseload, which can be configured as cases, items in a case, and other units of work. Variations from laboratory to laboratory in the use of batch processing and team analyses make it difficult to accurately predict the personnel needed to process cases in scientific laboratories. Yet the importance of accurate and precise measurement is widely acknowledged in order to build effective human resource systems."

Just as in any other industry, turnover within forensic laboratories is a costly proposition. Becker and Dale (2004) state, "Turnover costs also include additional costs to the organization, such as the cost of attracting and interviewing replacements, administration, severance pay, unemployment compensation, testing, travel and moving expenses, medical examinations, and acquiring and disseminating information. Turnover costs for an experienced scientist in biotechnology may exceed $250,000." Cappelli (2000) states that a number of factors can be associated with decreased voluntary turnover, adding, "Salaries and compensation, job design, social ties, and location have been linked to employee retention." Dale and Becker add, "Additional identification of innovative methods to improve retention rates is needed for technical employees in short supply, such as forensic scientists. Although turnover is a well-developed and active topic of empirical research, traditional human resource management theory does not offer specific guidance on retention of knowledge workers."

Becker and Dale (2003) comment, "In the forensic laboratory, it is essential that the best scientists are hired and retained so that the best science is available for processing probative evidence." To that end, Dale and Becker (2005) encourage laboratory managers to perceive human resources as intellectual capital: "Demonstrating that investments in human resources lead to improved laboratory performance is critical to laboratory directors. Originating from economics, the resource-based view considers human resources as assets as opposed to variable costs. The resource-based view is the philosophy behind initiatives to consider human resources as intellectual capital. In this model, human resource practices support the intellectual capital of the forensic laboratory by making the most of the job-related behaviors of the talent pool." Dale and Becker argue that intellectual capital adds value to the forensic laboratory, and Cascio (2000) suggests that through use of a measurement system laboratories may demonstrate further that skilled employees add this value. Methods include costing out employee turnover and determining the value of forensic services to customers and the community (Becker et al., 2005; Dale and Becker, 2004).

The bottom line is that forensic scientists are a precious commodity that should not be squandered. A number of experts suggest that forensic laboratories must encourage those analysts, examiners, and scientists who possess much-needed skill profiles to join and stay with the organization, as well as reinforce and motivate the necessary job behaviors. Creating an environment in which to practice good science is essential for the recruiting and retention of quality forensic practitioners. Dale and Becker (2005) note, "Laboratory structure must be designed to provide the best forensic service for the geopolitical area that the laboratory serves. The trend in designing modern organizations is toward flat, autonomous structures with direct reporting relationships to management. However, most large organizations have hierarchical structures with specialized units reporting to upper management. In the forensic laboratory, hierarchical structures may appear to be the most efficient. However, in practice, they may hinder the sharing of knowledge and become dysfunctional, especially when processing multidiscipline cases. For example, a high-priority multidiscipline case may involve ballistic, hair, fiber, and DNA evidence analyses. The most accurate and timely analyses are needed across all of the disciplines. One lead scientist must be given responsibility for managing the entire case. The best of both hierarchical and flat structures can be leveraged by implementing an organizational structure that facilitates communication between technical forensic disciplines and management. These new structures are essential for large laboratory systems with multiple facilities and disciplines."

Regardless of the structure or hierarchy, a forensic laboratory must be aware of its reason for existence: to provide timely, accurate forensic testing and analysis. Dale and Becker (2005) emphasize, "Forensic services must be identified and measured to meet the supply and demand of the laboratory's geopolitical area. For example, the laboratory must address such questions as, how many controlled-substance analysis cases need to be analyzed in a timely manner, for example, in less than 30 days? How many scientists and support staff are required to support this demand? The right amount of forensic intellectual capital in both the management and technical expertise of the laboratory will make a significant difference between mediocre and excellent performance."

NEEDS ASSESSMENTS OF FORENSIC LABORATORIES

It is only very recently that attention has turned to the needs of forensic science in a more meaningful way, and these efforts will also be explored in Chapters 15 and 16. From time to time, the U.S. Department of Justice has conducted studies to assess the status and needs of forensic laboratories. One of the latest studies, *Forensic Sciences: Review of Status and Needs*, issued in February 1999, was the first update in more than 20 years. The report was the work product of a two-day meeting held in March 1997, which assembled more than 40 scientists and administrators representing state, local, and federal forensic science organizations. The NIJ, the National Institute of Standards and Technology's (NIST's) Office of Law Enforcement Standards, and the ASCLD held a joint workshop, Forensic Science Summit: Road Map to the Year 2000, March 5–6, 1997, at NIST in Gaithersburg, Maryland. The purpose of the workshop was to determine the current status and needs of forensic laboratories on training; technology transfer; methods research, development, testing, and evaluation; and analytical services. The workshop also provided a forum to explore the use of national and federal laboratory resources and how best to take advantage of this external support.

The report acknowledged a few deficits in the current operations of the laboratory system. It stated in the executive summary, "For technology transfer to be successful, there must be a true partnership between local or state forensic laboratories and national laboratories. Existing strengths that are fragmented and dispersed need to be consolidated. Over the years, a large amount of development work has been done at the national laboratories that some forensic laboratories may be aware of because of their geographic location, but the work may not be known to the entire forensic community. No formal process exists for technology transfer to forensic laboratories. The key is to identify technology currently in use or under development at national facilities that can be quickly transferred for use in the forensic field. Areas of technology at national laboratories that could be applied to the forensic community include robotics, remote sensors, supercomputers for computational power, and satellite communications.

"In forensic science, as in other disciplines, cost-effectiveness and budgetary constraints are constant concerns. The technology must be affordable, reliable, and in some cases portable. The forensic community needs to be aggressive and creative in securing sources of funding to ensure that quality work is performed. It is important to examine not only the needs of the forensic community, but also the consequences of not meeting those needs—how does it affect the criminal justice system and the public that the forensic laboratories serve. When police are not able to work cases efficiently, when court dates are postponed, then taxpayer money is not well spent, efficiency is reduced, and justice may not be served."

The report also addressed what it called the "immense" training needs of the forensic community. It stated, "Training of newcomers to the field, as well as providing continuing education for seasoned professionals, are vital to ensuring that crime laboratories deliver the best possible service to the criminal justice system. Forensic scientists must stay up-to-date as new technology, equipment, methods, and techniques are developed. While training programs exist in a variety of forms, there is a need to broaden their scope and build on existing resources. Casework, the support crime laboratories provide to those in the field, is the essence of forensic laboratory work. Casework support includes routine and traditional analyses common to all forensic laboratory settings, methods development particular to the requirements of specific cases, and the identification of analytical sources to perform work that is considered non-routine."

As discussed in Chapter 5, nine common forensic disciplines are provided by the majority of local, state, and federal forensic laboratories in the United States. In its report, the NIJ noted that common needs of all laboratories included standardization, validation, and the creation of information databases. However, each discipline has specific concerns such as sensitivity, efficiency, precision, portability, and effectiveness of sampling methods. The NIJ stated, "If forensic scientists are to continue to provide valuable information and evidence efficiently, it is crucial for their needs to be addressed and resolved."

The report offered few concrete solutions, however. "There have been some surveys which I think have been pretty ineffectual," observes Barry A. J. Fisher, director of the Los Angeles County Sheriff's Department's forensic laboratory, past president of the American Academy of Forensic Science, and past chairman of the ASCLD. "The challenge for crime lab managers is defining what you need, which is very, very difficult. There used to be an annual workload survey that was sent out but there was no careful review of what people were saying; there was simply an assumption that if people put down a number, any number, it was valid. I don't give a great deal of weight to those particular things. These numbers were probably suggestive of something but they weren't a reliable indication of what was truly going on in the lab community. If someone really wants to figure out what's happening, he or she would have to pay researchers to conduct a solid study to determine exactly what they are trying to figure out. Therein lies the problem; we're not even sure how to define what the problem is."

Fisher continues, "Yes, there are backlogs but is having backlogs really such a terrible thing? Is it detrimental for the criminal justice system or is it just the cost of doing business? Nobody really knows what the scope of the issues really is. So, as a consequence, you have a number of studies out there, most of which I think are more anecdotal than anything else. There was a story in the newspapers that the Illinois governor wanted a 30-day turnaround on all DNA cases, and that sounds really good; it's a nice, concise soundbite. But did anyone investigate the current turnaround rate and what it needs to be? What is the level of evidence to be analyzed in one of these cases and what kind of testing is truly necessary for the case to move forward in a timely manner? None of this is crystal clear to me or to most other people. When I am in Washington, D.C., and advocating for our field, I may say that we ought to have a 30-day or 60-day turnaround on cases, but I am just trying to get people's attention. But nobody has a clear understanding of what's really going on in the system because it is so complicated and hasn't been adequately studied."

Fisher adds that studies are flawed because challenges mean different things to different stakeholders. "The results of these studies depend on who you are asking and what you are asking," he says. "When you are discussing crime labs you say, 'OK, who are the stakeholders?' Well, they are the investigators who invest the shoe leather and who work the case; the police administrators who have to answer to the public; the prosecutors who answer to the district attorney who is an elected official; the crime victims; and the courts, to name a few. When you ask each stakeholder what the nature of the problem with forensic science is, I believe you will get different answers. You must be very critical as to how you are framing these questions and that's problematic because you don't know what the question needs to be, you don't have a clear definition of all of the issues, and you're grasping at straws."

Fisher says that not much has changed since the earliest attempts at quantifying forensic laboratories' needs: "When the LEAA studies were done in the 1970s, a lot of the problems then are the same problems we have now. These difficulties are still in play and it's unclear to me at least how much progress we have made since then. You have the so-called '*CSI* effect' and you have new technologies, and together, these two factors foster a public perception that crime labs are able to do stuff a lot better, quicker, and cheaper, and that we are able to meet more demands, than we really can do in real life."

Because the old issues linger, Fisher says he is guarded about new initiatives to place forensic science under the microscope. "All of a sudden it's fashionable to talk about forensic science," he notes, "And everybody is out there trying to help. But they are not talking to one another, they are simply scurrying around trying to beat each other to the punch to come up with a way to 'fix' forensic science, and it's almost laughable."

On a more serious note, Fisher says he is concerned about the politics inherent in any attempt to study and shape a scientific discipline, especially when the efforts are made by a government entity. "There is just so much politics out there clouding the issues," Fisher says. "A year ago there was language passed in an authorization bill that said that the NIJ was to create a national forensic science commission to study the issues; the problem with that piece of legislation was that it was never funded. My understanding is that there are some issues between the NIJ and the Senate Appropriations Committee that is causing that to not move forward. A similar study was proposed in Senate appropriations language; this time it was authorized and appropriated under the National Academies. The NIJ is livid that this has happened because they feel this stuff is a birthright, and that they are the agency to handle forensic science matters. This is very much a moving target, however; it's likely to change with the weather."

Politics come into play particularly because the NIJ is in the executive branch of U.S. government; Fisher explains that any commission or study conducted by the NIJ would have to go to Congress for funding, with a partisan power play ensuing. "There is no clear sign that the Republicans are going to hang onto the White House in the next presidential election, and by the time this study gets out the door and published, we may be either close to or already in a new presidential administration," Fisher says. "If that happens, and this study is seen as a report coming from a Republican administration into a Democratic White House, that report is going to be boxed up and put into a warehouse, never to see the light of day again. Now if the study is produced under the auspices of the National Academies, it may fare much better. After all, the Academies are not politicized, and they are seen as a bunch of propeller-head scientists with few to no political ties. It's a neutral agency and it won't make a difference who is in power in Congress. Having said that, it is possible the NIJ would probably be savvier about the issues and might very well do a good job, but the politics would be a challenge."

Carol Henderson, J.D., director of the National Clearinghouse for Science, Technology, and the Law at Stetson University, and a visiting professor at George Washington University, also notes the inherent political challenges of two entities battling for control of a major study of forensic science issues. "I am concerned that everyone would be fighting over their turf and ignoring the real reason the study is being conducted," Henderson says. "But if we would all work together we would actually get somewhere. Everyone is clamoring to be on this national forensic science commission, but what are they actually going to do when they get there? People must educate themselves on the issues first. I am watching with great interest to see how this all plays out."

A much more recent attempt to enumerate and document the needs of forensic laboratories came in the summer of 2004, when a number of forensic science organizations examined their needs and contributed to the *180-Day Study Report: Status and Needs of United States Crime Laboratories* for the NIJ as part of a larger report of the status and needs of crime laboratories in the United States. While the forensic science community was glad to have yet another vehicle through which the field could be studied and its issues validated, some practitioners were concerned about the ultimate disposition of the information they shared with the NIJ.

"Members of the Consortium of Forensic Science Organizations (CFSO) were brought in for a couple of days to be subject-matter experts and make presentations and give our spin on what we needed from this project," Fisher explains. "What I was especially concerned about was that some of the issues we put forward as key were not included in this document, as they were either severely edited or edited out completely. For example, one of the issues we put forward was that there's not enough continuing education and training provided, and one entity that was doing a phenomenal job was the FBI. For years, the FBI lab offered high-quality training, but that was cut back. I found out third-hand that the FBI was very concerned about this critique we made, which I feel was done in a very positive way—we basically said we like this training and we wish there was more of it. The FBI claimed that the level of training is still out there; what they are doing is sending their scientists to professional meetings to give presentations, and so they are able to say that the number of contact hours provided is the same. Having people in a classroom setting and working on lab experiments is very different from hearing a 30-minute speech by a scientist at a professional meeting. So they have taken out the flavor of that issue."

Fisher continues, "So the bottom line is, here we have a study or a forensic science commission, and they say everything that we hope they will say but someone else in the Department of Justice edits it out or changes it—if they have some really serious public relations issues, how then can they truly speak for forensic science providers? It will be a challenge to articulate the issues, first and foremost, and then once you finally reach a consensus, how do you develop a strategy to address those issues?" Fisher says it is essential for forensic service providers to first define the problems, and then pin down constructive solutions. It is a process that Fisher recognizes as being complicated, time consuming, and not easily accomplished without proper research, commitment to reform, and the appropriate funding for implementation.

The recommendations that ASCLD made for the NIJ's 180-day report focused on the issue that while state and local crime laboratories are an integral part of the criminal justice system, demands for facilities' services have increased but funding has not kept pace. The 2004 report pointed to the already established fact that crime laboratory backlogs cause significant delays in evidence being analyzed, resulting in delays in the courts as well as in the investigation of crimes. It also alluded to the Bureau of Justice Statistics (BJS) survey (Hickman and Peterson, 2004) of the 50 largest laboratories in the United States, which revealed that in 2002, laboratories faced a 134 percent increase in their backlogs. Overall, for every four requests completed by a laboratory, one request remained unworked by the end of the year.

The 2004 ASCLD report covered a wide variety of laboratory infrastructure-related needs. The primary need identified by crime laboratory managers was personnel, with additional manpower needed in all sections. The need is so urgent that in order for laboratories to achieve a 30-day turnaround time for all requests, extra personnel would cost in excess of $36 million. Other needs included equipment (estimated in excess of $18 million), supplies, laboratory space, overtime, travel, and training.

The 2004 ASCLD study noted that another urgent need was in the area of training and education. Prior to conducting analyses of evidence, forensic scientists must have both basic scientific education and discipline-specific advanced and continuing training and education. Although minimum curricula guidelines for both undergraduate and graduate forensic science programs have been established by the NIJ (see Chapter 15) and an accreditation program has been established to accredit them, continued support is required to ensure that would-be and veteran scientists receive the training they need to become proficient and to remain competent in their fields of expertise.

Training needs for forensic laboratories are significant, driven by the increased demand for trained staff and succession planning. Initial training of laboratory analysts is largely done on the job and is labor intensive, and the ASCLD report (2004) called for collaborations, innovative approaches, and alternative delivery systems for forensic analyst and manager training. The report stated that maintaining and increasing professionalism within the forensic science community requires attention to a wide range of issues, many of which are related to quality and guidelines of good practice.

The report agreed that quality improvement measures such as accreditation and certification brought to bear increased expenditures for laboratories, and these costs can become problematic for some facilities. Although ASCLD acknowledges that laboratory accreditation "is not a guarantee against error," it is a program that requires a laboratory to evaluate its operations and address issues, and it requires a time commitment and substantial fees. Adding to this financial burden is an average cost per analyst for proficiency testing at approximately $500 per year, on top of the average fee per accreditation inspection at $6,500, exclusive of travel costs.

The report also acknowledged the lack of active research being conducted inside forensic laboratories due to constricted resources and manpower issues. The report indicated that practitioner partnerships are needed for these research programs, but at the same time, research takes a back seat to the primary work of the laboratory. The ASCLD report (2004) stated, "In addition to research into new techniques and the implementation of these techniques in the laboratory, crime labs must also identify innovative ways to work more efficiently and rapidly to reduce case backlogs and to bring forensic science to the crime scene. Crime laboratories barely have the resources to attend to core business and must direct resources to casework. Any innovation that does take place is largely uncoordinated."

We now explore each of these issues more fully. The demand for forensic services is escalating. In many jurisdictions around the country, the demand for testing has increased for crime laboratory analyses, but funding has not kept pace with this increasing demand. For example, between 1990 and 2000, the average forensic laboratory experienced an increase in caseload of 23 percent, but during this same time period, budgets grew by only 10 percent and staff size by only 9 percent.

The 2004 ASCLD study does not mince words when it describes the state of the average U.S. crime laboratory: "For all this rapid growth in forensic technology, crime laboratories are still the 'B' team of the criminal justice system. While investigators are seen as essential to the criminal justice system, the crime laboratory is often thought of as second-line support with limited and uncertain funding."

The 2004 ASCLD study pointed to the data contained in the 2002 census data from the BJS but made some of its own conclusions, including addressing the urgent need for improved and expanded laboratory space. The ASCLD study referred to the document *Forensic Laboratories: Handbook for Facility Planning, Design, Construction, and Moving* (U.S. Department of Justice [DOJ], 1998), which indicated that forensic personnel needs and functional processes are the driving factors for laboratory design. However, the report stated, "Many current crime laboratories were not built as laboratories but were converted from existing buildings. They were built or remodeled before many of the new technologies used by the laboratory were implemented. Staffing levels have also increased without a commensurate increase in laboratory space." According to the DOJ, "The measure of a forensic laboratory's success is how well it meets the current and future needs of the occupants. Designing and building a forensic laboratory is a complicated undertaking. Design issues include those considerations present when designing any building, with enhanced concern and special requirements involving environmental health and safety, hazardous materials, management, operational efficiency, adaptability, security of evidence, preservation of evidence in an uncontaminated state, as well as budgetary concerns." During the last decade, the numerous forensic laboratories that have been designed and constructed seem to point to a space ratio based on area per staff member. This ratio for most new facilities tends to fall within the range of 700 to 1,000 square feet per staff member. This ratio represents only a very loose rule of thumb that can be drastically affected by a number of variables. For example, laboratories with large amounts of low occupant space, such as evidence storage or vehicle examination bays, will unrealistically skew the ratio.

Education and training continues to be at the top of the priority list for many forensic service providers. The 2004 ASCLD study stated, "To be in compliance with widely-accepted accreditation standards, scientists in each of the disciplines must have, at a minimum, a baccalaureate degree in a natural science, forensic science, or a closely-related field. Each examiner must also have successfully completed a competency test (usually after a training period) prior to assuming independent casework. Education and training are also needed to maintain expertise and to keep up with advances and changes in technology."

ASCLD (2004) observes further, "The forensic community must work with our nation's educational institutions to ensure that scientists employed by crime laboratories have the education necessary to understand their scientific responsibilities, to provide a high-quality work product and are able to communicate their findings effectively. The Council on Forensic Science Education (COFSE) recognized a recent marked increase in the number of forensic science programs at colleges and universities. They note that many forensic educational programs have been established with very limited resources, insufficient personnel, laboratory space, and support. Students completing these programs expect to find employment in crime laboratories but are often surprised to learn that laboratory managers are not satisfied with their educational credentials. Crime laboratory directors generally expect applicants to have degrees in a natural science with a preference for degrees in chemistry or molecular biology. This is particularly important for work in the forensic disciplines of controlled substance identification, arson analysis, trace analysis and DNA (and pre-DNA) testing."

Research and innovation needs are another significant area of concern for the forensic laboratory community. ASCLD (2004) notes, "Traditionally, basic scientific research is performed at universities. Forensic science, however, is a very specialized applied science. Academic and forensic practitioner partnerships can bring the skills and strengths of both basic and applied science to a research program. Such partnerships exist within the forensic community where a strong forensic laboratory works closely with a well-established, graduate-level university forensic program. This model has been found to be effective both within and outside the United States. Few forensic laboratories (20 percent) have resources dedicated to research. Research in forensic science is focused primarily on how technology can be applied to forensic evidence. As applied research, work in the forensic sciences does not receive the type or level of funding that basic research receives. In addition to implementing new techniques in the laboratory, forensic science laboratories must identify innovative ways of working more efficiently and rapidly to reduce case backlogs and to bring forensic science to the crime scene."

Besides the 2004 ASCLD study, just a few surveys of the forensic laboratory community, conducted by the BJS, are available, and these studies are aging and limited in their ability to convey crucial information to stakeholders in the criminal justice system. However, these do attempt to paint a picture of the needs of forensic service providers.

In the BJS census report, *50 Largest Crime Labs, 2002,* Hickman and Peterson (2004) conclude that the 50 largest publicly funded forensic crime laboratories in the United States employed more than 4,300 full-time equivalent (FTE) personnel and had total budgets exceeding $266.6 million. The following subsections provide snapshots of the critical issues from the 2002 data.

Cases Received

In 2002, labs received more than 994,000 new cases, including more than 1.2 million requests for forensic services.

Backlogged Cases

In 2002, labs ended the year with more than 93,000 backlogged cases, including about 270,000 requests for forensic services—more than twice the backlog at the beginning of the year. The backlog increased in all categories of forensic services. The large labs estimated that about 930 additional FTEs would have been needed to achieve a 30-day turnaround for all 2002 requests for forensic services. Based on starting salaries for analysts or examiners in the large labs, the estimated cost of the additional FTEs exceeds $36.2 million. Most of the large labs indicated that resources beyond personnel increases would also have been needed to achieve a 30-day turnaround on all 2002 requests. These included equipment, supplies, and space requirements, as well as funds for overtime, travel, and training. Among those labs providing detailed cost estimates, additional equipment accounted for about $18.3 million.

Backlogged Requests

The 50 largest labs began 2002 with about 117,000 backlogged requests for forensic services. These labs received an additional 1.2 million requests during 2002 and completed nearly 1.1

million requests. The total estimated backlog at year end, about 270,000 requests, represents an increase of nearly 154,000 requests, or 132 percent, from the beginning of the year. Overall, for every four requests completed by these large laboratories, there was one outstanding request at year end. Eighty percent of the estimated 270,000 backlogged requests for forensic services in these large labs was attributable to requests for controlled substances (50 percent), latent prints (19 percent), and DNA analysis (11 percent).

- *Controlled substances:* Half of the total backlog—about 136,000 requests—was attributable to requests for analysis of controlled substances. For every three such requests completed in 2002, approximately one request was outstanding at year end.
- *Latent prints:* The backlog included about 51,000 requests for latent print services, or about one-fifth of the total. For every two latent print requests completed in 2002, approximately one request was outstanding at year end.
- *DNA analysis:* The backlog included about 31,000 requests for DNA analysis. Although these requests comprised about one-tenth of the total backlog, they had the greatest backlog relative to labs' current capacity to process requests; for every one DNA analysis request completed in 2002, an estimated 1.7 requests were outstanding at year end.

Expected and Actual Performance

Forensic laboratory directors were asked to report their performance expectations for one FTE examiner per year in each category of forensic services. Overall, examiners in the largest labs processed requests at or above 90 percent of the expected average in all but two categories: biology screening (82 percent) and DNA analysis (78 percent). Examiners performing biology screening were expected to process an average (median) of 166 requests per year. Examiners actually processed an average of 136 requests per year, or about 82 percent of the expected average. Examiners performing DNA analysis were expected to process an average of 69 requests per year. Examiners actually processed an average of 54 requests per year, or about 78 percent of the expected average.

Human Resource Needs

Overall, the largest laboratories estimated that an additional 931 FTEs would be needed to achieve a 30-day turnaround on all requests for forensic services received in 2002. The estimated total cost of the additional FTEs exceeds $36.2 million. Just over half of the needed FTEs were in the areas of controlled substances (10 percent), latent prints (17 percent), and DNA analysis (25 percent).

- *Controlled substances:* Labs performing analysis of controlled substances estimated that nearly 100 additional FTEs would have been needed to achieve a 30-day turnaround on all such requests received during 2002. These additional FTEs represent a 7 percent increase in FTEs currently performing controlled substance analysis. The estimated cost of additional FTEs needed for analysis of controlled substances exceeds $3.6 million.
- *Latent prints:* Labs performing latent print analysis estimated that about 160 additional FTEs would have been needed to achieve a 30-day turnaround on all such requests received during 2002. These additional FTEs represent a 55 percent increase in FTEs currently performing latent print services. The estimated cost of these additional FTEs exceeds $6.7 million.
- *DNA analysis:* Labs performing DNA analysis estimated that about 230 additional FTEs would have been needed to achieve a 30-day turnaround on all DNA analysis requests received during

2002, given current laboratory conditions and analysis tools. These additional FTEs represent a 90 percent increase in FTEs currently performing DNA analysis. The estimated cost of these additional FTEs exceeds $9.3 million.

Other Surveys

A separate survey, the *Census of Publicly Funded Forensic Crime Laboratories, 2002* (Peterson and Hickman, 2005), revealed that federal, state, and local forensic crime laboratories employed more than 9,300 FTE personnel in 2002 and had total budgets exceeding $750 million. These publicly funded labs received nearly 2.7 million new cases, including a much larger number of separate requests for forensic services during calendar year 2002. These labs ended the year with more than 500,000 backlogged requests for forensic services—a 70 percent-plus increase in the backlog of requests compared to the beginning of the year. The backlog increased in most categories of forensic services.

Publicly funded crime labs estimated that about 1,900 additional FTEs would have been needed to achieve a 30-day turnaround for all 2002 requests for forensic services.

Based on starting salaries for analysts or examiners in these labs, the estimated cost of the additional FTEs exceeds $70.2 million. More than three-quarters of the labs indicated that resources beyond personnel increases would also have been needed to achieve a 30-day turnaround on all 2002 requests. These resource needs included capital expenditures for new and renovated laboratory space and facilities; additional and updated equipment; instrumentation, robotics, and computers; basic and advanced training opportunities; and improved laboratory information management systems. The total estimated cost of these needs exceeds $500 million.

REFERENCES

American Academy of Forensic Sciences, Technical Working Group on Forensic Science Education and Training. *Education and Training in Forensic Science: A Guide for Forensic Science Laboratories. Educational Institutions and the Interested Student,* Draft Final Report. Colorado Springs, Colo.: American Academy of Forensic Sciences, 2003.

American Society of Crime Laboratory Directors. *Guidelines for Forensic Laboratory Management Practices.* Garner, N.C.: ASCLD, 1994.

Arvizu J. Forensic labs: shattering the myth. *The Champion,* May 2000.

Becker WS and Dale WM. Strategic human resource management in the forensic science laboratory. *Forensic Science Communications,* October 2003.

Becker WS, Dale WM, Lambert A, and Magnus D. Forensic lab directors' perceptions of staffing issues. *Journal of Forensic Science,* 50:1–3, 2005.

Cappelli P. A market-driven approach to retaining talent. *Harvard Business Review.* 78(1):103–111, 2000.

Cascio WF. Costing Human Resources: The Financial Impact of Behavior in Organizations, Fourth edition. Cincinnati, Ohio: South-Western College. 2000.

Cascio WF. *Managing Human Resources: Productivity, Quality of Work Life, Profits.* Boston: McGraw-Hill, 2003.

Dale WM and Becker WS. Managing intellectual capital, *Forensic Science Communications,* Vol. 7, No. 4, October 2005.

Dale WM and Becker WS. A case study of forensic scientist turnover. *Forensic Science Communications,* July 2004.

Dale WM and Becker WS. Strategy for staffing forensic scientists. *Journal of Forensic Science,* 48:465–466, 2003.

DiFonzo JH. The crimes of crime labs. *Hofstra Law Review,* 34(1), Fall 2005.

Dillon H. Forensic scientists: A career in the crime lab. *Occupational Outlook Quarterly,* 43(3):2–7, 1999.

Fisher BAJ. Field needs adequate funding, national forensic science commission. Forensic Focus. 2003. Available at: http://forensicfocusmag.com/articles/3b1persp1.html

Hickman MJ and Peterson JL. *50 Largest Crime Labs, 2002: Census of Publicly Funded Forensic Crime Laboratories.* Washington, D.C.: U.S. Department of Justice, Office of Justice Programs, Bureau of Justice Statistics, September 2004.

Josar D. Space crunch hampers lab work: Evidence is stacked in boxes, freezer is full as Detroit's technicians attempt to analyze data. *The Detroit News,* April 21, 2005.

Koussiafes PM. Public forensic laboratory budget issues. *Forensic Science Communications,* 6(3), July 2004.

Long J. Employment outlook 2002, *Chemical and Engineering News,* 79(46):38–39, 2001.

Peterson J. *Survey Data Presented at 180-Day Study Planning Meeting.* Washington, D.C.: National Institute of Justice, December 2003.

Peterson JL and Hickman MJ. Census of publicly funded forensic crime laboratories 2002. *Bureau of Justice Statistics Bulletin,* February 2005. Accessed at http://www.ojp.usdoj.gov/bjs/pub/pdf/cpffcl02.pdf.

Peterson J et al. 2002. Forensic crime laboratory survey results. *Proceedings of the AAFS,* p. 41, 2004.

Saferstein R. Introduction. In: *Criminalistics: An Introduction to Forensic Science,* 7th ed. Upper Saddle River, N.J.: Prentice Hall, 2001.

Sewell JD. Identifying and mitigating workplace stress among forensic laboratory managers. *Forensic Science Communications,* 2(2), April 2000.

U.S. Department of Justice. *Forensic Laboratories: Handbook for Facility Planning, Design, Construction, and Moving.* Washington, D.C.: U.S. Department of Justice, April 1998.

U.S. Department of Justice, Office of Justice Programs, National Institute of Justice. *Forensic Sciences: Review of Status and Needs: Issues and Practices,* NCJ 173412. Washington, D.C.: U.S. Department of Justice, February 1999.

RECOMMENDED READING

2002 Census of publicly funded forensic crime laboratories. *Federal Register,* 66(250), December 31, 2001.

Forensic Science Education Programs Accreditation Commission. *Accreditation Standards.* Colorado Springs, Colo.: American Academy of Forensic Sciences, May 16, 2004. Accessed at http://www.aafs.org/pdf/FEPAC-Standards-2004.pdf

International Laboratory Accreditation Cooperation. *ILAC G 19:2002 Guidelines for Forensic Science Laboratories.* Accessed at http://www.ilac.org/

Under the Microscope: California Attorney General Bill Lockyer's Task Force Report on Forensic Services, 2003. Accessed at http://caag.state.ca

U.S. Department of Justice, Office of Justice Programs, National Institute of Justice. Certification of DNA and other forensic specialists. *National Institute of Justice Update,* NCJ 154571. Washington, D.C.: U.S. Department of Justice, July 1995

Washington State University Division of Governmental Studies and Services, and Smith Alling Lane PS. *National Forensic DNA Study,* Final Report, December 2003. Accessed at http://www.ojp.usdoj.gov/nij/pdf/dna study report final.pdf

CHAPTER 6

AN INTRODUCTION TO THE U.S. MEDICO-LEGAL DEATH INVESTIGATION SYSTEM

To the uninitiated, the medico-legal death investigation system in the United States is a jumbled, random patchwork of jurisdictions, each with its unique parameters for the investigation of sudden, suspicious, or unexpected deaths. About 20 percent of deaths in the country are investigated by medical examiners or coroners, with the percentage varying from state to state. Although the guidelines for which deaths to investigate also vary widely from jurisdiction to jurisdiction, most require that the following types of deaths be investigated:

- Deaths due to homicide, suicide, or accidental causes such as motor vehicle crashes, falls, burns, or the ingestion of drugs or other chemical agents
- Sudden or suspicious deaths, deaths from sudden infant death syndrome (SIDS), and unattended deaths
- Deaths caused by an agent or disease constituting a threat to public health
- Deaths that occur while the decedents were at work
- Deaths of people who were in custody or confinement
- Deaths of other people institutionalized for reasons other than organic disease
- Deaths of people to be cremated.

According to National Association of Medical Examiners (NAME), the medico-legal death investigation system in this country is a conglomeration of medical examiner, coroner, and hybrid systems that loosely covers the landscape: Approximately 21 states have medical examiner systems, 11 have coroner systems, and 18 have mixed systems.

Because of the variability of the U.S. medico-legal death investigation system, the level of quality also fluctuates. A needs-assessment report by NAME (2004) observed, "It is readily apparent that quality of service varies greatly from one area to another. Unfortunately, with any particular person's death, the quality of the medico-legal death investigation is predicated on where that death occurs. While there are many high-quality medico-legal offices, in order to ensure excellent death investigation throughout the entire nation, we must improve those offices that are lacking in funding, competent staff, and facilities. Medico-legal death investigation requires a high level of competence, professionalism, and ethics. The work itself is critical and has widespread impact on not only the criminal and civil justice systems, but on the families of the deceased, the community, and issues of public health. The basis for a quality death investigation system is through the integrated practice of various highly trained and certified professionals."

The thoroughness of death investigations (and as a result the completeness of death investigation records) also varies from case to case. Sometimes a postmortem examination may consist of only an external examination of the body. The record of a complete death investigation, however, would include the following:

- The initial report of the death made to the medical examiner or coroner office by a family member, police officer, or attending physician

- A determination of circumstances surrounding the death
- Findings of a scene investigation
- Findings of a postmortem exam or autopsy
- Results of laboratory tests to determine the presence of drugs, toxins, or infectious agents
- Certification of the cause and manner of death.

The NAME report (2004) states, "Medico-legal death investigation systems operate at the interface between law and medicine. In every system, specific individuals are charged with officially investigating deaths falling under medico-legal jurisdiction, determining and certifying the cause and manner of death and fulfilling other jurisprudential and public health functions." Medico-legal death investigations are performed by both medical examiners and coroners, depending on the laws of each jurisdiction—be it county or state—that determine the scope of a death investigation and its eventual course of action and final disposition. This mixed system contains a striation of coroner-only systems, medical examiner systems (most of which are statewide and are administered by state agencies), and even more complex systems in which some counties are served by coroners, others by medical examiners, and still others by a hybrid known as a referral system, in which a coroner refers cases to a medical examiner for autopsy (Hanzlick and Combs, 1998). In addition, approximately 2,185 death investigation jurisdictions are spread across the nation's 3,137 counties (Hanzlick, 2003).

Elected county officials, or coroners, are responsible for medico-legal duties in most coroner systems. In some states the coroner must be a physician; in many other coroner systems, this requirement does not exist. NAME (2004) comments, "In many coroner systems, important decisions such as whether or not to perform an autopsy are made by persons without the appropriate medical education, training and experience." Medical examiners most commonly are licensed physicians appointed to perform official medico-legal death investigations and conduct postmortem examinations. Because most medical examiners are not pathologists and are therefore not trained to perform autopsies, they must rely on pathologists (ideally, qualified forensic pathologists) to perform autopsies. Although many pathologists are currently performing medico-legal autopsies, relatively few of them are trained and credentialed in the subspecialty of forensic pathology. Pathologist medical examiners are most often government employees but may be private practice or academic pathologists engaged to work for a particular medico-legal jurisdiction. The most highly educated and trained group in the death investigation field is the forensic pathologists. Forensic pathology is the distinct subspecialty within the medical field of pathology that deals specifically with the investigation of cause and manner of death and the performance of medico-legal autopsies and ancillary studies.

In some jurisdictions, the title of medical examiner is bestowed on non-pathologist physicians who respond to the initial notification of death and are responsible for screening and referring appropriate cases for further evaluation by a forensic pathologist. The term *medico-legal death investigator* or *death investigator* is commonly used for frontline lay investigators. An increasing number of jurisdictions opt to use "lay" (non-physician) investigators to perform scene and background investigations in support of physician medical examiners and forensic pathologists. The American Board of Medico-Legal Death Investigators registers and certifies such practitioners in accordance with the 1998 National Institute of Justice's *National Guidelines for Death Investigation*, which in 1999 were renamed *Death Investigation: A Guide for the Scene Investigator*. This, however, is a voluntary program, and in some jurisdictions, investigators are not required to have any formal education in basic death investigation procedures. According to the NAME (2004) report, "It is perhaps axiomatic that the accuracy of the forensic pathologist's determinations is contingent upon important decisions and procedures initiated by the individual who receives the first notification of death and performs the initial investigation. Working closely with the criminal justice system and law enforcement agencies, medical examiners/coroners must remain independent and objective watchdogs for the public they serve. Lack of qualified investigators and forensic pathologists, insufficient and outdated facilities, shortfalls in equipment and supportive manpower, insufficient funding, and disparate availability of needed consultative services can result in miscarriages of justice or unacceptable risks to the public's health: Homicides may be missed, the innocent may be wrongly accused and/or incarcerated, the guilty may be wrongly exonerated, civil actions and outcomes may be flawed, or infectious disease epidemics can spread."

In Chapter 8, we will delve into the erratic, occasionally controversial history of the development of the medico-legal death investigation system. In brief, Hanzlick (2003) states that because the system functions mostly at the county level, "The origin of death investigations as a local responsibility has led to wide variation in the scope, extent, and quality of investigations. The variability is manifest in the responsible office's organizational placement in the government; statutory requirements, including credentials and training of personnel performing the investigations; and funding levels."

Hanzlick (2003) adds that the most common placement for a medical examiner (ME) or coroner office is as a separate office of city, county, or state government, with approximately 43 percent of the U.S. population served by this type of system placement. The second most common placement is under a public safety or law enforcement office, while the least common placement (serving about 14 percent of the U.S. population) is under a forensic laboratory or health department. In 2003, there were 3,137 counties and 2,185 death investigation jurisdictions in the United States. There are approximately 258 ME jurisdictions and 1,927 coroner jurisdictions, but the ME system serves 48 percent of the population, and the coroner system serves 52 percent of the population. (Hanzlick, 2003). More than 75 percent of the U.S. population is served by a non-accredited office.

Hanzlick (2003) points to a "big chill" in the development of ME systems in the United States. A spike was seen in the 1960s, shortly after the Model Act of 1954; however, in every decade since, the emergence of state medical examiner systems has declined. This trend will be explored further in Chapter 8. These demographics may have shifted, with more current figures available from a new survey of medical examiner offices being conducted by the Bureau of Justice Statistics of the U.S. Department of Justice. These results will be discussed in Chapter 8.

ROLE CALL: THE CAST OF CHARACTERS IN MEDICO-LEGAL DEATH INVESTIGATION

As we saw at the beginning of this chapter, there are three key players in the medico-legal death investigation system; we explore each of these professional's roles and responsibilities next.

The Forensic Pathologist

Wetli (2005) observes, "Forensic pathology is perhaps the smallest of medical specialties, yet it is the one that is often in the forefront of intense public interest. Indeed, the forensic pathologist is the community pathologist who relates to the next of kin and allied professionals including law enforcement personnel, public health officials, attorneys in civil and criminal cases, physicians, insurance companies, and many others."

Leadership of the modern medico-legal office is provided by the medical examiner, who is usually, but not always, a forensic pathologist. At its essence, pathology is the study of disease, and the discipline of forensic pathology applies what is known about disease, along with all of medical science, to legal problems. Therefore, a forensic pathologist is especially prepared to conduct medico-legal death investigations. The primary responsibility of the forensic pathologist is to determine the cause and manner of death. In most jurisdictions, the manner of death is limited to one of five categories: homicide, suicide, accident, natural, and undetermined. Another equally important duty of the forensic pathologist is to ensure that the deceased is correctly identified.

The forensic pathologist is specially trained to perform autopsies to determine the presence or absence of disease, injury, or poisoning; to evaluate historical and law enforcement investigative information relating to manner of death; and to collect medical evidence in order to document injuries and to determine how a person received these injuries. A medico-legal autopsy is ordered by the coroner or medical examiner, as authorized by law, with the statutory purpose of establishing the cause of death and to answer other medico-legal questions.

Wetli (2005) acknowledges the subtleties that the forensic pathologist can detect relating to the position's expected responsibilities: "Traditionally, the forensic pathologist has been charged with determining the cause and manner of death of those decedents falling within the medical examiner's or coroner's jurisdiction. In reality, the cause and manner of death are already known in a great many, if not the majority, of cases. . . . Hence, the real, but often unstated, focus of the forensic pathologist is to identify, document, and preserve everything of a potentially evidentiary nature. Indeed, the 'art of forensic pathology' is to anticipate the questions that will be asked in the future: today, tomorrow, and several years from today."

Forensic pathologists are trained in traditional medicine as well as non-medical disciplines relating to toxicology, trace evidence, forensic serology, and DNA technology. The forensic pathologist acts as the case coordinator for the medical and forensic scientific assessment of a given death, making sure that the appropriate procedures and evidence collection techniques are applied to the body. And when forensic pathologists are employed as death investigators, they bring their expertise to bear on the interpretation of the scene of death, in the assessment of the consistency of witnesses' statements with injuries, and the interpretation of injury patterns or patterned injuries. In jurisdictions where there are medical examiner systems, forensic pathologists are usually employed to perform autopsies to determine cause of death.

What particularly empowers the forensic pathologist is a slate of advanced education and training. The future forensic pathologist earns an undergraduate degree, then another four years in medical school to earn an M.D. or D.O. degree. According to NAME, following medical school there are several routes by which one may become a forensic pathologist: One may spend four years training in anatomic and clinical pathology followed by a one-year residency or fellowship in forensic pathology; or one may train for several years in anatomic pathology and train for an additional year in forensic pathology. The residency training in forensic pathology involves practical experience supervised by a trained forensic pathologist. The forensic pathology resident performs autopsies and participates in death investigations.

In the United States, forensic pathology is a recognized subspecialty of the larger specialty of anatomic pathology. As such, this field has its own board certification exams offered by the American Board of Pathology, which can only be taken by physicians who have already passed the anatomic pathology boards. In the past, any board-certified anatomic pathologist with two years of experience in the field could sit for the forensic exam; however, today, only pathologists who have successfully completed an accredited forensic pathology fellowship may take the exam. According to a survey conducted in 2000, the number of active board-certified forensic pathologists at that time was around 700. Two-thirds were employed in or under contract to ME or coroner systems, while about a fourth were in private practice or consultation.

The Coroner

A coroner is a public official, appointed or elected, in a particular geographic jurisdiction, whose official duty is to make inquiry into deaths in certain categories. The office of the coroner (or "crowner") dates back to medieval times in England when the crowner was responsible for looking into deaths to be sure death duties were paid to the king. The coroner's primary duty in contemporary times is to make inquiry into the death and complete the certificate of death. The coroner assigns a cause and manner of death and lists them on the certificate of death. The cause of death refers to the disease, injury, or poison that caused the death. The coroner also decides if a death occurred under natural circumstances or was due to accident, homicide, suicide, or undetermined means or circumstances.

Although coroners are frequently called on to determine if a death was due to foul play, depending on the jurisdiction and the law defining the coroner's duties, the coroner may or may not be trained in medicine, law enforcement, or forensic science. Thus, the lay coroner may consult physicians, pathologists, or forensic pathologists to perform autopsies when there appears to be a question or manner of death that autopsy can elucidate. In some jurisdictions, the coroner is a physician, but in many more jurisdictions, the coroner is not required to be a physician nor be trained in medicine. A common criticism is that in the absence of medical expertise, the non-physician coroner may have difficulty sorting out subtle non-violent and violent causes of death.

The role of a medical examiner differs from that of the non-physician coroner in that the medical examiner is expected to bring medical expertise to the evaluation of the medical history and physical examination of the deceased. The physician medical examiner usually is not required to be a specialist in death investigation or pathology and may practice any branch of medicine. Most systems employing physicians as part-time medical examiners encourage them to take advantage of medical training for medical examiners to increase their level of medical expertise as applied to death investigation.

In many ways it has been said, medical examiners and coroners practice in the tradition of preventive medicine and public health by making their study of the dead benefit the living. This concept, as relating to public health needs, will be discussed in Chapter 8.

The Medico-Legal Death Investigator

A medico-legal death investigator is an individual who is employed by a medico-legal death investigation system to conduct investigations into the circumstances of deaths in a jurisdiction. According to the College of American Pathologists, "The medico-legal death investigation is structured to determine the cause, manner, and mechanisms of injury and death. This determination is made through the use of accepted scientific methods and procedures as well as through review of all available investigative information, including the examination of bodies, other medical or evidentiary material, and scene investigations."

That Hollywood has its own view of the process of death investigation and the practice of forensic pathology, may be a gross understatement. As we will see in Chapter 13, which examines the so-called "*CSI* effect," no corner of forensic science escapes dramatic interpretation for the small screen, with mixed results. While some forensic practitioners say television and other vehicles of popular culture have vaunted forensic science, others say it creates unrealistic expectations of the field.

Take forensic pathology, for instance. Johnson (2003) remarks, "Not since (the television show) 'Quincy, M.D.' has there been such interest in forensic science and the medico-legal system. A proliferation of television programs and movies, both documentary and fiction, claim to show viewers the behind-the-scenes activities of forensic pathologists and scientists."

Johnson (2003) points to one of the most egregious deceptions, the accelerated time frame in which crimes are solved: "These 'miracle workers' supposedly can find that crucial bit of evidence that ties the perpetrator to the crime, allowing for the perp's discovery, arrest and conviction—all in 60 minutes. Those of us who work in this field, therefore, find that when we are called to court to testify, we must overcome many misconceptions about what can and cannot be attested to. We often disappoint jurors—not to mention the attorneys who subpoena us—who wonder if doctors or criminalists are behind the times; otherwise, we would speak with more decisiveness about the time of death, the time of injury, or even the cause and manner of death, as do those famous fictional pathologists and scientists."

Also at issue is the erroneous perception that forensic practitioners are generalists and can step in and out of their professional boundaries as dictated by their office. Johnson (2003) writes, "Television depictions of forensic disciplines—whether it is one of the criminalists in 'CSI' or Dr. Jordan Cavanaugh in 'Crossing Jordan'—give the impression that the main character alone does the work that 10 or 20 other people together do in the real world. In reality, many experts are summoned to help on each case. Most forensic pathologists and criminalists do not go around chasing after and interviewing suspects for the simple reasons that, first, they lack the time, but more importantly, they lack the training. Evidence gained through an improper interview, for example, can later be dismissed outright in court if it was not obtained properly. Conducting a proper interview is as much a skill as conducting a proper autopsy, and the specialists, the homicide detectives, do those interviews. Toxicologists examine bodily specimens for drugs. Microbiologists work up blood and tissue cultures. Chemists analyze the vitreous humor for electrolytes and glucose. Blood may be sent to the nearest serology laboratory to rule out hepatitis or HIV. Fire debris analysts identify fuels used to start an arson fire. Trace analysts look at hair and fibers. Firearms and tool-mark examiners scrutinize guns, bullets, footprints, tire tracks and the tiniest scratches made to force a door. No one person is going to have all these skills. These are all specialty areas that take a great deal of training. In the real world, the body is under the jurisdiction of the coroner or medical examiner from the moment of death until he chooses to release jurisdiction to somebody else."

Johnson (2003) continues, "In the real world, the victim's hands would not be cut off at the crime scene and taken back to the lab for a fingerprint identification, as did Angelina Jolie's beat-cop character depicted in the film 'The Bone Collector.' This might happen in the real world after the autopsy, if the decomposed or mummified fingers need to be soaked or somehow manipulated to get a decent set of prints—but not until the pathologist has examined them first. The detective also would not be found rifling the pockets of the deceased for a driver's license and other possessions, as do TV detectives on 'Law and Order,' unless the coroner or medical examiner gives permission. The general rule is that whatever is on the body is the coroner's, and whatever is lying around the crime scene—even if it once was on the body—belongs to the police."

PLAYING BY THE (REAL) RULES OF MEDICO-LEGAL DEATH INVESTIGATION

As we have seen, Hollywood has created the medico-legal death investigation system in its own image, but in real life, the parameters of the medical examiner office were set by a piece of legislation from the 1950s that suggested a more refined way of conducting medico-legal death investigations. In 1954, the National Conference of Commissioners on Uniform State Laws (NCCUSL) drafted the Model Post-Mortem Examinations Act (MPMEA) which provided a model law for establishment of medical examiner death investigation systems. The act was drafted by the NCCUSL and was approved at the group's 63rd annual conference. The MPMEA provided a means whereby greater competence could be assured in determining causes of death where criminal liability may be involved. Its authors realized the need for greater expertise in forensic pathology than some coroners could furnish, and the act proposed that each state have an office headed by a trained pathologist, with jurisdiction over postmortem examinations for criminal purposes. The act was drafted as a Model Act rather than a Uniform Act, since the problem will be different in different states, particularly with respect to the constitutional status of the coroner's office. The MPMEA was the impetus for the conversion of some coroner jurisdictions to medical examiner jurisdictions, although a blanket transformation of a mixed system to an all-ME system was not achieved. The act also laid the foundation for many of the modern principles upheld in the medico-legal death investigation system.

The MPMEA dictated that the chief medical examiner should be a citizen of the United States and a physician licensed in the state in which he will practice, and who has a minimum of two years of postgraduate training in pathology. The act recognized the need for high personal standards and continued professional development and advised, "It is basic to any properly organized medico-legal investigative system that the head of the office be a person of the highest mental and moral caliber, with the best obtainable professional training in medicine and pathology, devoting full time to his duties and dedicated to the discreet and wholly impartial acquisition of post-mortem evidence. Whenever possible he and his principal assistants should keep abreast of medical advances by affiliation with a medical school and should to the extent of their abilities aid in the development of their professional field by contributions to medical literature and by teaching medical and law students in their special medico-legal field. They should also assist in the more immediately practical task of training police investigators in related techniques of their work."

The MPMEA laid out the kinds of deaths to be investigated by the medical examiner, including violent deaths, whether apparently homicidal, suicidal, or accidental, including but not limited to deaths due to thermal, chemical, electrical, or radiational injury, and deaths due to criminal abortion, whether apparently self-induced or not; sudden deaths not caused by readily recognizable disease; deaths under suspicious circumstances; deaths of persons whose bodies are to be cremated, dissected, buried at sea, or otherwise disposed of so as to be thereafter unavailable for examination; deaths of inmates of public institutions not hospitalized therein for organic disease; deaths related to disease resulting from employment or to accident while employed; and deaths related to disease which might constitute a threat to public health.

The MPMEA specified that autopsies were to be conducted by the medical examiner in cases in which "the public interest requires an autopsy." Investigations in which the facts call for further inquiry include those in which the cause or manner of death may not be readily recognizable, or the manner of disposal of the body may be an effort to conceal the true cause and manner of death.

The act empowered the medical examiner to perform the duties of the office with confidence, noting that "All law enforcement officers, [prosecuting attorneys,] [coroners] and other officials shall cooperate fully with the office . . . making the investigations and conducting the autopsies." The act also directs all physicians, undertakers, embalmers, and other persons to promptly notify the ME in the occurrence of all deaths coming to their attention, and making the dead bodies and related evidence available to the ME's office for investigations and autopsies. The act also gave instruction to police that in cases of apparent homicide, suicide, or accidental death the cause of which is obscure, the scene of the event should not be disturbed until authorization by the medical examiner is given.

One provision of the MPMEA, the creation of a lab for use by the medical examiner and maintained with law enforcement, could be construed as controversial in today's light; however, it was in keeping with the 1932 vision of the National Research Council, which desired easy access to labs for its medico-legal practitioners. The act states, "The medico-legal laboratory should be a flexible organization ready and able to handle investigations with all the tools of modern science including chemistry, microscopy, photography, X-ray, bacteriology and pathology. The laboratory should be able to help direct the course of an investigation by indicating the weapon, vehicle or material to be sought, or to halt a fruitless search for the assailant when it is shown that a death is suicidal or accidental. The most efficient and economical method for the creation of such a laboratory is to combine the personnel and equipment of an adequate police laboratory with those of the medico-legal investigator, not necessarily by consolidation in the same building but by making talent and equipment mutually available. An affiliation with a medical school is desirable in order that the medical personnel of the laboratory be acquainted with modern advances in medicine and so that the specialized knowledge of injury and disease acquired through the work of the laboratory will be made available for the common good. Where such laboratories now exist the state is spared the expense of experts to bolster the testimony of its own officials, and in criminal prosecutions the defense can rely on unbiased medical evidence. In states with extensive territory and large populations two or more laboratories, partially duplicating each other, may be necessary to give adequate service."

The MPMEA established the medical examiner's office as a repository of key records relating to death investigation, as well as death certificates, and noted that the records in the medical examiner's office are admissible as evidence in any court in the state in which the office resides. In addition, the personnel of the office are subject to subpoena as a witness, in any civil or criminal case, by any party to the cause.

While the MPMEA established many parameters for the medical examiner system in any given jurisdiction, it also officially abolished the coroner's office, with all medico-legal responsibilities transferred to the medical examiner's office. The act recognized the inherent difficulties of abolition due to constitutional protection of some coroners' offices, and suggested that a constitutional amendment may be in order.

Fast forward several decades since the MPMEA. Another set of rules that helps govern medico-legal death investigation and the actions of forensic pathologists is the *Forensic Autopsy Performance Standards,* prepared by Garry F. Peterson, M.D., and Steven C. Clark, Ph.D., and approved on August 17, 2005, by NAME. Efforts by this organization to promulgate practice standards began in the 1970s, and these early efforts focused on the operational aspects of medical examiner offices in relation to accreditation. Recently, NAME members advocated for standards that addressed the professional aspects of individual death investigations.

According to NAME, the primary objective of these new standards is to provide "a constructive framework that defines the fundamental services rendered by a professional forensic pathologist practicing his or her art."

Several pertinent points emerge from these new NAME autopsy standards, in light of criticisms that will be discussed in Chapter 8. According to the standards, to promote competent and objective death investigations, officers should operate without any undue influence from law enforcement agencies and prosecutors.

These standards nestle with the *Practice Guideline for Forensic Pathology*, authored by Brad B. Randall, M.D., Marcella Fierro, M.D., and Richard C. Froede, M.D. (1998), members of the forensic pathology committee of the College of American Pathologists. According to this guideline, the pathologist, as the chief investigator, should ensure that the essential components of the medico-legal death investigation are undertaken in coordination with law enforcement officials. These components may include:

- Taking charge of the body in accordance with statutory and regulatory jurisdiction
- Personally or by means of a duly authorized representative permitting removal of the body from the scene of death
- Investigating the circumstances surrounding the death, such as performing a scene investigation when appropriate and reviewing case records
- Conducting all necessary examinations of the body, including an autopsy if deemed necessary (retaining necessary tissues, biological and trace materials, and other evidence
- Collecting, securing, and maintaining the chain of custody for all evidence, including any object, article, record, or note that may be useful to the court, to law enforcement, or for the public good in coordination with law enforcement
- When requested or required, confirming or determining the identity of the deceased if not otherwise identified
- Summarizing and recording the results of the investigation and examination, and preserving the record for the legitimate use of persons and agencies (without bias) as determined by statute regulation and public policy
- Obtaining records, documents, and witnesses by subpoena as needed and authorized
- When appropriate in accordance with applicable statutes and regulations, allowing or assisting in the procurement of organs and tissues for transplantation. In addition, the guideline states, the pathologist "should be capable and proficient in presenting the findings of the medico-legal death investigation (including the autopsy results) before the applicable legal forum(s)."

REFERENCES

Hanzlick R and Combs D. Medical examiner and coroner systems: History and trends. *JAMA,* 279:870–874, 1998.

Johnson DG. Forensic pathology: separating fact from fiction. *Medical Laboratory Observer,* August 2003.

National Association of Medical Examiners. *180-Day Study.* Atlanta, Ga.: NAME, 2004.

National Institute of Justice. Death Investigation: A Guide for the Scene Investigator. November 1999. Available at: http://www.ncjrs.gov/pdffiles/167568.pdf#search=%22National%20Guidelines%20for%20Death%20Investigation%22

Randall BB, Fierro M, and Froede, RC. Practice guideline for forensic pathology. *Archives of Pathology and Laboratory Medicine,* 122:1056–1064, 1998.

Wetli CV. Foreword. In: *Forensic Pathology, Principles and Practice,* Dolinak D, Matshes E, and Lew E, Eds. Boston: Elsevier/Academic Press, 2005.

RECOMMENDED READING

Burns AC and Froede RC. The forensic autopsy. In: *Autopsy Performance and Reporting*, Hutchins GM, Ed. Northfield, Ill.: College of American Pathologists, 1990, pp. 33–38.

Combs DL, Parrish RG, and Ing R. *Death Investigation in the United States and Canada, 1995*. Atlanta, Ga.: Centers for Disease Control and Prevention, 1995.

Fierro M, Ed. *Handbook for Postmortem Examination of Unidentified Remains*. Skokie, Ill.: College of American Pathologists, 1986.

Froede RC and Goode R. Medico-legal investigation and forensic procedures: A problem oriented approach. In: *Handbook of Forensic Pathology*, Froede RC, Ed. Northfield, Ill.: College of American Pathologists, 1991, pp. 1–10.

Jentzen IM, Ernst MF, Haglund WD, and Clark SC. *Medico-Legal Death Investigator: A Systematic Training Program for the Professional Death Investigator*. Big Rapids, Mich.: Occupational Research and Assessment Inc., 1996.

Spitz WU, Ed. *Spitz and Fisher's Medico-legal Investigation of Death*, 3rd ed. Springfield, Ill.: Charles C Thomas Publishers, 1993.

CHAPTER 7

THE U.S. MEDICO-LEGAL DEATH INVESTIGATION SYSTEM UNDER SIEGE

According to the National Center for Health Statistics, which is under the auspices of the Centers for Disease Control and Prevention (CDC), in 2003, there were 2,448,288 deaths in the United States, the latest figure released in April 2006. The preliminary estimated number of deaths in the United States for 2004 is 2,398,343 (CDC, 2006). As we saw in Chapter 6, approximately 20 percent of all deaths involve a medico-legal investigation and autopsy, so about 489,645 of those annual deaths came under the scrutiny of a coroner of medical examiner.

A medico-legal professional would be quick to point to these statistics and state that given the number of deaths in the United States, taking into account that the majority of the cases are handled well and without incident, compared to the relatively small number of cases that are called into question, there is no national ethics crisis or job performance crisis within the medico-legal investigation system. Still, the handful of cases that have been splashed across newspaper headlines and been litigated in court are cause for a closer look into the functionality of medico-legal offices. Several Web sites have devoted prime virtual real estate to the tracking of cases involving medical examiners and coroners who have been accused or convicted of incompetence, malfeasance, and criminal intent. Some cases have been resolved, while others are still in protracted litigation; like their colleagues in forensic laboratories, these medico-legal professionals are facing criticism and condemnation from commentators, journalists, and legal scholars calling for greater attention to a system tasked with the critical role of tending to the deceased.

A "HUMAN" SCIENCE?

As we saw in Chapter 6, the U.S. medico-legal death investigation system is a complex entity charged with the heavy responsibility of determining the facts surrounding suspicious, unexpected, sudden, or violent deaths. One of the criticisms put forth by commentators is that the process of death investigation is infused with subjectivity on the part of its practitioners, and that there is a significant margin for error because of it. Death investigation has been around for centuries, but it is only within the age of television that any awareness about the discipline—erroneous or not—has been cultivated.

"Any time you get put into the spotlight, for a few moments you are on this wonderful pedestal, but then people start looking behind the curtain, like in the Wizard of Oz, and start finding things that aren't perfect," says Mary Fran Ernst, a medico-legal death investigator for the St. Louis County Medical Examiner's Office, director of medico-legal education at the St. Louis University School of Medicine, and past president of the American Academy of Forensic Sciences. "I think the forensic sciences and death investigation have not been appreciated for a long time, and the media is now so invasive to the point that it tries to find any dirt that it can."

One such criticism is that forensic science, and to some extent medico-legal death investigation, is a "soft" science, lacking in the scientific rigor demonstrated by biology, physics, and chemistry—even though forensic science draws from all of these fields for its determinations.

"There are hard sciences like chemistry that are reproducible, but I do believe there are some soft sciences," Ernst says. "I think sometimes forensic science is both a soft science and a hard science in some areas. To me, death investigation is a softer science, in that when I look at what kind of technology we use in actually performing death investigations at a scene, do we use a lot of machinery or technology? Well, no we don't, but a lot of the investigation process is based on tenets of science, blended with what we can draw from our education, training, and experience. We can anticipate results because we have seen this through experience, and I think that's what has happened in fingerprinting when people say it is a soft science. By contrast, DNA was born of hard science, and it is statistically valid and reliable."

Ernst says that, in many ways, forensic science is a "human" science. "Physics, chemistry, and biology have numerical values, but when these hard sciences are applied by humans, you naturally have the human aspect that influences the ultimate disposition of the science," Ernst says. "When this human factor enters the equation, the science is regarded with suspicion—are you, as the analyst or the investigator, a little bit biased because of something in your background? Medical examiners, for example, tend to become frustrated too, because when they must establish a manner and cause of death, some of their determinations are related to the process of a human being working as a scientist, weighing the different factors that determine if a death is a suicide or an accident or a homicide. The human factor is always there with the science."

The importance of standards and guidelines for the field of medico-legal death investigation is not lost on Ernst, who is a staunch advocate for establishing better parameters for practitioners to ensure they walk on the right side of science. It has only been since 1997 that standards for death investigators were promulgated by the National Institute of Justice, a fact that leaves the field open to charges of a haphazard operation without clear standards or expectations. Ernst says the politically charged nature of the system in general can be a deterrent to further development of the field. "Part of the reason death investigation didn't get standards was because it was so politicized," Ernst explains. "You're talking about 3,100 different counties, each with a medical examiner or coroner who has different priorities and different results they extract from the system. Some are in it for personal gain, while others want the very best for their communities; some jurisdictions have the resources they need while others don't, so there are many variables that dictate the quality of the system."

Ernst points to these variables as one reason why national guidelines have been slow in implementation. "The reason we didn't have guidelines until 1997 was because no one ever wanted to get all of these jurisdictions together, and because it looked like there was no way these groups could ever reach a consensus on what should be the standards for the field. In 1997, when those death investigation standards came out, they were called standards, and everyone agreed to them; but in 1999, the federal government called for changing the standards to 'guidelines' instead, to defuse a politically charged situation and to ensure that in court, the rigidity of standards didn't create a problem. For most of us in the field, we thought half a cup is better than an empty cup, which is where we came from, so the standards were changed to guidelines, and they were much better than nothing. Is the word 'guidelines' as good and as authoritative as the word 'standards'? No. But that was the political situation back then. And that is what is challenging for all of forensic science—it's political, since jurisdictions are controlled by some form of governmental constraint, be it county or state or federal, and these agencies are the ones who determine what kind of system you are going to have because they are the ones who determine funding you are going to get."

THE PROBLEM OF THE "COWBOY" EXAMINER

Although there is much that goes well within the U.S. medico-legal death investigation system, it is the headlines in a newspaper or on the 24/7 cable news outlet that create an indelible impression about the functionality of this system in the general public's mind. In 1992, coroner Ralph Erdman pleaded no contest to falsifying autopsies in three Texas counties; he also has been accused and convicted of falsifying results regarding examinations and tests that were never performed and has been sentenced to several prison terms. Charles Harlan, a Tennessee pathologist and former state chief medical examiner, has been accused of botched autopsies, sloppy record keeping, wrong diagnoses, and callous behavior toward families, actions that were in the process of being validated in late 2005 by a panel from the state Board of Medical Examiners, which has verified at least 18 violations stemming from a lengthy inquiry into his medico-legal practice. The state Department of Health has filed charges in 20 autopsy-related incidents.

"We don't have as many cowboys in the field as we once had," says Victor Weedn, M.D., J.D., professor at Duquesne University. "This is true whether it's in criminalistics or in forensic pathology. I believe that part of the history of forensic science has been the high-profile guy who has the bravado to come into court and assert his opinion, despite little foundational support. However, the forensic science community has been in the process of enhancing its level of professionalism, and getting beyond the cowboy mentality. Back then, you could get away with it and weren't always criticized; today, the level of scrutiny has increased, the professionalism has increased, and we work more as a community. You can trace this development within the creation of the professional associations that serve our field; at first they were networking groups but then they developed into sources of education, training, and standards. There is a lot to say about the need for continued professionalism of the forensic sciences, and I think it is a work in progress."

"It all comes down to the personal fortitude and ethics of the individual," suggests forensic pathologist Michael Dobersen, M.D., Ph.D., coroner for Arapahoe County in Colorado and president of the Colorado Coroner Association. "We have had that very discussion within the College of American Pathologists because we as pathologists spend so much time in court. We see people take the stand and run into trouble."

Dobersen recalls a case in which he was involved where a woman presented herself in court as a forensic pathologist when she was not. "She didn't have the training or experience required of a forensic pathologist, and I had to report her to her medical board. Testifying in court is like the practice of medicine; you can't testify to anything in court that you are not qualified to do on a daily basis. I felt I had to report her, but even in doing so, I am attacked by some attorneys who say that I am some sort of avenger and they blow it out of proportion. I think I did the right thing because I think we must always try to police ourselves. Sometimes it is difficult to do with all of this junk science flying around and some of the rogue experts who are out there; some of them are very high-profile types, forensic pathologists who don't have the best of reputations and in court they can get wild and wooly with their opinions."

Paul C. H. Brouardel, a French medico-legalist, advised physicians, "If the law has made you a witness, remain a man of science; you have no victim to avenge, no guilty person to convict, and no innocent person to save. You must bear testimony within the limits of science."

"All we can do, as forensic pathologists, is testify as to what we know regarding our findings and our opinions," says forensic pathologist Michael Baden, M.D., codirector of the New

York State Police Medicolegal Investigation Unit and former chief medical examiner of New York City. "We explain to the court what the science shows us, and we are not beholden to anyone. We have no interest in the outcome of the case, as what the prosecutor and the defense attorney are going to do is beyond our powers. All we can do is to explain what the autopsy findings mean or what the toxicology report means; we don't know if the defendant is guilty or innocent. We give our opinions; sometimes they are correct and sometimes they are incorrect, because experts don't have a market on truth. All we can do is give the best opinions we can; 10 years from now some of our opinions, in retrospect, may not be right, because thought is evolving in disciplines such as bite mark evidence, fingerprints, bullet lead analysis, and microscopic hair analysis. People testify to as much as they know, and sometimes they are wrong. The more we learn, the more we try to minimize mistakes. A few years ago, microscopic hair comparison was wonderful, now it turns out to be considered junk science. We have to take it one step at a time. The most important thing is that we, as forensic scientists, do our jobs as carefully and as accurately as possible, regardless of the outcome of the case.

"There are two sides to every case, and the opposite side isn't going to like you; however, that shouldn't affect the integrity of the forensic scientist. We are not there to make friends, we are there to tell the truth as best we can. In my experience, people who make unpopular decisions are probably doing the right thing."

"Certainly everybody makes errors," says Kurt Nolte, M.D., professor in the Department of Pathology at the University of New Mexico Health Sciences Center and assistant chief medical investigator for the state of New Mexico, "but the important thing about making errors is immediately recognizing you have made an error, and rectifying it. But there's a difference between making unintentional errors and deliberately falsifying data, of course, and ethics come into play." Yes, people make mistakes, and people fabricate data far less than they make mistakes, but it has happened and certainly doesn't help the reputation of the field."

Nolte continues, "You have surgeons who have been crackpots, for example, so they surface in all fields. Forensic pathology has had its share of crackpots, no doubt about it, but I wouldn't say there is a rampant or persistent problem with the falsification of data or other malfeasance. I think there have been problems, though, that have been triggered by poorly trained individuals engaging in the practice of forensic pathology, making errors that have had a significant impact on public safety; I am referring to individuals not trained in forensic pathology who are performing autopsies with minimal experience and a willingness to express opinions in court which, frankly, are ridiculous. Then you have coroners who have no training who also offer up opinions that can be just bizarre. That's what the field has to address."

As we will see in subsequent chapters, the level of education and training of medico-legal professionals is crucial to the quality performance of the job. Experts such as Nolte and Weedn say that individuals who practice in the field must be subjected to the right kind of occupational scrutiny, and certain safeguards must be in place to prevent errant individuals from slipping through the cracks in the system. "For starters, as physicians, pathologists must be licensed within their state to practice medicine," Nolte says. "Forensic pathologists also have the opportunity to sit for the examinations offered by the American Board of Pathology. To do that they must have completed training in pathology, with subspecialty training in forensic pathology, then sit for a board exam which is very rigorous. Another safeguard are medico-legal offices that are accredited by the National Association of Medical Examiners (NAME), but out of some 3,000 medico-legal jurisdictions, only a small number of offices are accredited. So, if you are not coming under the scrutiny of outside evaluation either as an individual or as an office, it's hard to tell what type of standards these medico-legal entities are achieving."

Nolte says he believes the board certification of forensic pathologists goes a long way toward ensuring appropriate behavior from medico-legal professionals. "Board certification is the cornerstone to evaluating forensic pathologists," Nolte emphasizes. "It's setting the crossbar at a certain height that says, 'We think these individuals have to have this particular knowledge base and be able to apply that knowledge base in a standardized manner in working cases, and this is how we're going to be able to ascertain those standards.' I think it's essential to ensure that forensic pathologists achieve this level of training; the board certifying exam takes three to four days and includes anatomical clinical boards and forensic pathology subspecialty boards, and if they can pass those examinations after the completion of their training, only then do I think they can be considered qualified in forensic pathology."

Nolte continues, "Requiring board certification is essential to ensuring quality, but you can't require board certification in all jurisdictions if there is a shortage of forensic pathologists. So, you have people who have trained but can't pass their boards, and they get jobs anyway because frequently they are viewed as better than someone who hasn't been trained at all. The question is, would you rather hire someone who has done a hospital pathology residency but has no fellowship training to do your forensic autopsies, or do you want to hire the guy who did the forensic pathology fellowship but he can't pass his boards no matter how hard he tries? So, faced with this dilemma, a lot of jurisdictions are put into a difficult position. Here at the University of New Mexico you can't be a faculty member if you don't pass your boards, but not every institution can apply that rigorous of a standard. Consequently, there are people out there who have not been properly trained, and that's kind of frightening. Up until a few years ago you even had lay individuals performing autopsies in some jurisdictions. For example there were crime lab personnel in Georgia (who were not physicians) doing medico-legal autopsies. Do you think they could properly recognize trauma and natural disease if they have never been trained in this kind of medicine? That kind of stuff boggles the mind. And why the medical boards never jumped on that, is beyond me."

Nolte says there are a number of pseudo medical boards in existence that concern him because they are cranking out a number of poorly trained and illicitly credentialed individuals. "If you are some kind of a crackpot medico-legal expert who can't get standard board certification, you need some sort of credential so you turn to a business providing a board credential with a little take-home exam on ethics," Nolte remarks. "You pay a couple thousand dollars and all of a sudden you are a credentialed member of the forensic community. It's alarming! It's become a real problem because a number of these sham boards have arisen in recent years, and the inability of attorneys, judges, and jurors to sort between these different boards is of great concern." Nolte continues, "So a guy like me, a forensic pathologist who is board certified by the American Board of Pathology, jumps up onto the witness stand in court and gives a long recitation of his training and his experience and his employment. Then witness B gets up and gives an equally long recitation and his sham board certification, and the jurors don't know a thing because they can't tell the difference between somebody who did a true forensic pathology fellowship and completed a rigorous program followed by legitimate board certification, vs. somebody who has had marginal training, failed his board exams, and then purchased a board certificate."

"There are a lot of people who went into this field because they are interested in it and they are good at it, but there are also a lot of people who fell into it years ago who may not have been board-certified or quite frankly, couldn't get other jobs," says forensic pathologist Randy Hanzlick, M.D., chief medical examiner for Fulton County in Georgia, and professor of pathology and laboratory medicine at Emory University School of Medicine. "The system accepted those people and that almost became the norm. The attitude of some was that if you couldn't pass your boards you can always be a medical examiner or you can be a forensic pathologist because you can do it without having to be board-certified. By not having stringent requirements, we have hurt ourselves; it has been self-defeating to allow that to happen because it's gotten to the point in some jurisdictions now where they say, 'Why do we even need a pathologist? We can get any old doctor to fill that position and do the job.' There are certainly people out there who make a fair amount of money going around testifying in court; some are highly reputable and some are less reputable. It's a problem but the professional organizations are trying to deal with that through their ethics committees. I think that with time, these efforts will become stronger and more aggressive because they realize that if they don't control the profession and demand quality from it, someone else is going to come in and do the job. I think the best way to handle it is through the boards and the professional organizations, and maybe even convince the judges to be a little more willing to recognize when they have a witness whose qualifications or motives may be a little questionable." Hanzlick says that the facts will sometimes reveal problems with an expert witness. "Many times we as medical examiners are barely going beyond serving as a fact witness; we talk about doing the autopsy: we took out the bullet, we examined the bullet wound, etc.," Hanzlick says. "If we are allowed to offer opinion beyond those kinds of facts, then we are testifying as an expert. As an expert in forensic pathology, other scientific disciplines impact our work and there is the possibility that we testify—knowingly or unknowingly—beyond the real scope of our expertise in forensic pathology. When an expert witness seems to be doing that, it's a tip-off that the court should notice and act accordingly."

Hanzlick says the problem of setting a high enough bar is evident in both the medico-legal world and the forensic laboratory world. "From a quality standpoint, even in the worst death investigation systems, you at least have physicians involved at some point, whether they are the local doc that the coroner goes to in order to ask questions, or the local pathologist who may not be a forensic pathologist but they know how to do an autopsy; at least those people got an education, they went to medical school, and they secured some kind of advanced training," Hanzlick explains. "But in the forensic laboratories in many jurisdictions today, there are a lot of people doing analyses who don't have a degree; it may be some guy who likes guns, and all of a sudden he's the lab's firearms expert, for example. That's precisely where that system got into trouble because their criteria to work in forensic science disciplines weren't stringent enough. Now, we have a situation where a lot of those people are grandfathered in, but most of the newer, incoming professionals are now required to have a minimum of a bachelor's degree, and maybe a master's or doctorate degree depending on what they are doing in the lab. I think the bar was set too low before, but it almost had to be that way in order to attract people to the field to get the job done."

THE EVERYDAY CHALLENGES

Sometime, however, it's the mundane situation, and not the high-profile mass disaster such as the attack on the World Trade Center and the Pentagon on September 11, 2001, that creates headlines. Autopsy backlogs are a major issue plaguing the medico-legal death investigation system in the United States. One of the most beleaguered medical examiner's offices in this regard has been the Washington, D.C., office, which, as of December 2005, according to newspaper reports, had a backlog of more than 1,000 unfinished autopsy reports, including some cases dating back more than 10 years. Thompson (2005) reports, "The agency's slow turnaround has delayed police work and criminal prosecutions, and forced some families to sue the office to obtain the paperwork about their loved ones." Thompson adds, "The District's incomplete autopsies include 765 that are at least a year old. Maryland and Virginia, by comparison, have no cases a year old. Among the unfinished D.C. cases are 84 homicides."

The D.C. office's troubles are compounded by the fact that four of its six chief medical examiners have departed amid controversy. Thompson reports, "Last year, the D.C. Council approved a chief after waiving the minimum qualifications. Several pathologists have left recently. And documents detail several questionable rulings by the chief and deputy medical examiners." Thompson adds, "The National Association of Medical Examiners, which inspects and accredits the offices, recommends that medical examiners complete 95 percent of the reports for homicide victims within 60 days and other deaths within 90 days. Last year, the D.C. office completed 47 percent of homicide cases and 34 percent of other deaths within those periods, far below the performance in Maryland and Virginia, according to records."

The D.C. office was not always a mess; the district's first chief medical examiner, James L. Luke, has stated that backlogs were nonexistent during his tenure from 1971 to 1983, but in the mid-1980s, Thompson (2005) reports, "The office was plagued by complaints about low productivity and mismanagement. Cockroaches and other pests congregated on autopsy tables in rooms with insufficient ventilation. Bodies in the morgue piled up beyond capacity."

Thompson (2005) describes how in 1998, district officials hired Jonathan L. Arden away from the Brooklyn medical examiner's office and tasked him with rejuvenating the office amid numerous challenges, including personnel shortages, a stack of incomplete autopsy reports, and an environment of disarray. Thompson reports that Arden convinced D.C. officials to increase the office budget to almost $6 million, launched an investigative unit, reopened the toxicology lab, and improved relations with the U.S. attorney's office. In the reorganization, however, Arden was accused of inappropriate behavior in his interactions with staff and was forced out.

Autopsy backlogs also plagued the Connecticut medical examiner's office, delaying investigations. The backlogs have been blamed on budget cutbacks that reduced the number of pathologists on staff as well as prevented personnel from conducting autopsies on weekends and holidays. Not having a death certificate can pose significant problems for the families of the deceased, in terms of insurance companies needing proof of the death; not having an autopsy report can hold up death certificates if there is a suspicious cause of death.

"I don't think there is a backlog in most areas in terms of processing the autopsies," says Hanzlick. "They get them done, or they do partial autopsies; they do whatever they think is necessary to get the work done and adapt to that workload. I would say only a few offices truly take several days or more to get an autopsy done. But what happens is instead of getting more staff and doing complete autopsies, you start doing partial autopsies just to get the work out faster. People seem to accept that over time and sometimes even rationalize it. In many public medico-legal offices the medical examiners have reasonable caseloads or maybe they are moderately overworked; then again, there is a segment of the profession that works in a privatized setting and they work on a per-case basis and they would rather do more cases. After all, the more cases they do, the more money they make."

"Yes, there are offices that have a backlog, not in doing the cases, but in writing the reports," says Weedn. "There are some offices with significant backlogs, but I believe most offices are up to date. Their turnaround time could be improved, however. It comes down to needing more forensic pathologists and medico-legal death investigators."

Another criticism leveled at the forensic sciences and medico-legal death investigation is the professional fallibility of its practitioners, a situation that can be remedied through certification, education, and training, as explored in Chapter 15. Ernst says she is concerned not only about the lack of opportunities for training, but about the bigger issue of a shortage of forensic science, pathology, and medico-legal experts who have the time and the skills to serve as educators for the future generation of practitioners.

"I think it's a huge problem that we don't have very many educators teaching forensic science," Ernst says. "Many of the brilliant experts we have in forensic science, such as Jay Siegel, Peter DeForest, and others, are reaching retirement age and we aren't seeing an influx of super-phenomenal educators coming in to take their places. That's one of the biggest challenges that forensic science is going to have in the future, and it's a problem that may not be that well recognized and appreciated right now. We need more people who are pursuing doctorate degrees in forensic science and related sciences, so that they are prepared to teach in the universities. Many of them prefer to work as consultants instead, where they are paid exceedingly well. That's fine, but if we don't have brilliant minds entering the university system to teach others, I'm wondering where the next Henry Lee is going to come from?"

Ernst says she is a big believer in the power of mentorship programs, especially for the forensic disciplines. "I have been mentoring someone (to take over) the St. Louis University medico-legal death investigation course for years; while it will be some years before I quit, at least I know she has the love and devotion to carry on the program after me. But not every agency or program is thinking ahead and making provisions for someone to carry the torch. We have a significant number of students who want to go into forensic science, and we have all these universities and colleges who want to start forensic science programs because everyone wants them, but there are few, if any, people to teach them. One time someone told me they were going to give a course in forensic science and I said, 'Well, who is going to teach it?' and they replied, 'Well, we'll just use our teachers,' and mind you, they don't have a single teacher in the forensic sciences—adding that they would just get a book on forensic science, read it, and regurgitate it back to the students. I was taken aback. I told this person, 'But what about things like testifying in court? Unless you have someone who has actually done that, there's no way you can prepare your students correctly. They said, 'Well, everyone does this stuff, and it's no big deal.' It really turned me off, and I think that kind of approach sells forensic science terribly short."

While the need for increased numbers of medico-legal professionals continues, so does the debate over where these practitioners should engage in their work. As we will see in several other chapters throughout this book, many commentators are calling for increased separation of medico-legal offices and forensic laboratories from law enforcement agencies to prevent examiner bias and subjective evidence-testing results. The criticism is that the medico-legal death investigation system is beholden to law enforcement, a complaint fired against the forensic laboratories, as we have seen in Chapter 4.

"I have been doing this for 30 years, and there are a few times when law enforcement wanted me to go farther than I was willing to go regarding what the details of the case were telling me," Ernst recalls. "But when you are well trained and experienced, you are able to apply the ethical brakes and ensure that you never overstep your boundaries or overstate what the evidence tells you. Medico-legal death investigation is not a good ol' boys club where it's 'you scratch my back and I'll scratch yours.' In forensic science, you report what you see and you don't exaggerate to make a better case for the prosecution. It's not that the prosecution or law enforcement has bad intentions, but sometimes they can be overzealous. They'll say, 'This guy had to have done it,' and they just want you to put a little extra icing on that cake."

"As members of the medico-legal system, we are in close contact with law enforcement, which is charged with bringing people to justice," says Dobersen. "We have a criminal justice system in this country in which the district attorneys advocate for the people of the state and the defense attorneys advocate for the accused, and certainly law enforcement is pushing for some kind of a conviction. However, as forensic scientists and forensic pathologists, we are only here to say what happened to the decedent; we are not advocates for anyone except for the victim and the truth."

Dobersen adds, "We must be exceedingly careful not to mix the cops and the lab coats. There are many medico-legal offices that share space with law enforcement, such as states in which the coroner's office is under the sheriff's office, and that's very troublesome for every-one . . . you kind of wince every time you hear something like that. In my career I don't think I have been pressured by law enforcement in any way, but it is up to all of us to maintain our objectivity. We must remind ourselves, 'I am the person speaking for the one who died and that's my No. 1 responsibility.' As a forensic pathologist, I am not there for the prosecution or for the defense, I am there for the deceased."

Weedn suggests another partnership: "I believe medical examiner's offices are a natural home for the crime labs. Increasingly, crime labs are being built together with medical exam-iner offices, in the same complex, even if one reports to the department of public safety and the other reports to the department of health. That's setting the stage for the movement toward independent medico-legal offices, which is a good thing, because I do not believe these offices ought to be under the auspices of prosecutors or law enforcement agencies, but rather should be in an independent, neutral, and objective scientific environment, whether under a department of forensic science or a medical examiner office."

In addition, some medico-legal professionals are better than others at working the inher-ently political system. "Some medico-legal chiefs are better than others at surviving or thriv-ing in the political system; some have no clue," Weedn says. "Some don't want to be involved in fighting for the betterment of the system and don't recognize what it could do for them. Some people have been able to show value to their communities while others haven't. Those offices in which the staff merely do their work and go home rather than becoming involved in their communities tend to wither. Some are good administrators, others aren't. Many are so overwhelmed they are unable to attend to the administrative or larger community needs. So there are many reasons for the varying levels of success and competence of medico-legal offices."

As we will see in Chapter 8, a crumbling infrastructure can sometimes exacerbate prob-lems associated with the quality of the performance of medico-legal offices and their profes-sionals. "There are many medico-legal offices that are swamped by the volume or cases or by poor facilities in which they operate, and as a consequence, these offices surface in the head-lines all the time," observes Nolte. "And when they do show up in the headlines, it's a black eye for the entire field. For example, the Washington, D.C., medical examiner's office has suffered with poor infrastructure for a long time. Yes, the state came up with the money, but it's unfortunate that nothing is done unless there is some kind of high-profile disaster or crisis. Iowa had an abysmal infrastructure and their crisis also made the news all the time. They couldn't attract a chief medical examiner and it wasn't until they agreed to provide a new facility that Dr. Julia Goodin took that position; they just moved into their new building very recently. So it often takes a significant crisis to convince states and municipalities to provide what's needed in medico-legal offices. There is a tremendous lack of facilities of adequate size and organization to handle the case volume nationally. All you have to do is take a tour of the Los Angeles coroner's office to get an idea of what many medico-legal offices are up against; their cases have been stacked and waiting for days for autopsies, the buildings are old, and there is a certain degree of obsolescence to some of their technology."

Nolte adds that indeed, there are some state-of-the-art medico-legal offices to be found in the country, but the polarity between these offices and the majority of facilities is startling in the severity of the contrast. "There are a number of jurisdictions with impressive facilities, including Fulton County in Georgia and Maricopa County in Arizona, so I don't want to be completely negative," Nolte says. "However, there are also places where you have forensic pathologists doing autopsies in funeral homes. Until a few years ago, one city in Texas had been autopsying decomposed bodies on an old door put across two sawhorses. Before its new facility was built, Phoenix only had two autopsy tables being used in shifts that were running 24 hours a day because they couldn't handle their volume; now they have 16 autopsy tables. But they were burning out their staff, losing people left and right. Can you imagine being on the graveyard shift doing autopsies? They had no space, so they had a crisis. There are many offices that are substandard like that; New Mexico is right now, and we're viewed as an exemplary medical examiner's office!"

Nolte explains that the caseload in many offices is growing so quickly that even new buildings are considered to be inadequate when they open for business. "We, here in New Mexico, are in the process of designing a new facility; the appropriations have been made through our legislature; however, they are not enough to cover the escalating costs of construction, so the whole project has been temporarily put on hold," Nolte says. "Some architects came through looking at our needs, and one of them who has worked with many medical examiner offices said that when these offices reach the point of crisis, and when the government agrees to provide a new facility, by that time, the medical examiner's office needs three times the space it currently occupies. That's how bad the crisis gets in a very short amount of time. What happens is, the government gives medico-legal offices twice the space of what they occupy currently, but very shortly thereafter, they are in crisis again because they really need three times the current amount of space to secure the longevity and functionality of the building. The government feels good about giving them twice as much space, but there's no horizon to the building; they are already at the horizon. I watched that happen here in New Mexico; as we went through the design and budget process, we had enough for double our space, but not enough for what we truly needed. So, by the time the building is constructed four years later, we've surpassed capacity again."

Much of the budget issue is exacerbated by the low-profile work of the medico-legal offices. The National Association of Medical Examiners has called its field "invisible," and Ernst agrees with the statement. "Only one half of 1 percent of any community ever comes into contact with the coroner or the medical examiner system," Ernst emphasizes. "The people whose families are involved, they think it's an important issue. But it isn't until the other 99.9 percent of the community creates an uproar will anyone really care."

As we will see in Chapter 8, the reality of the average medico-legal death investigation office is a far cry from the kind of well-funded agency most expect they are.

"The American Academy of Forensic Sciences is working hard to raise the profile of the contributions to death investigation made by medico-legal offices, and encouraging the government to put its money where the need is," says Ernst. "We must force good death investigation that is adequately funded. Unfortunately, it's not until the senator's son is killed will you ever see an advocate of the death investigation system. We have had a few advocates in the government, but overall, if it doesn't personally affect you, people just don't put any emphasis on it. I don't want any legislator to have to go through a death to realize the critical importance of the medico-legal death investigation system, but we need to find a way to bring attention to our issues. I think the medico-legal offices and the forensic sciences have taken huge strides forward in the last 10 years. Although we're not perfect, we're certainly one of the best in the world; look at all the other places where there is no such thing as forensic science in criminal justice. So I think we are on the right path."

REFERENCES

Centers for Disease Control and Prevention (CDC). *National Vital Statistics Reports,* Vol. 54, No. 13, April 19, 2006.

Hansen M and Hengstler G. Should coroners get the final word? *Atlanta Journal-Constitution,* June 25, 1995.

Johnson R. State finds 18 instances of sloppy work by Harlan. *The Tennessean,* April 21, 2005.

National Forensic Science Technology Center (NFSTC). *Needs Assessment of Forensic Services in the Commonwealth of Massachusetts.* Largo, Fla.: NFSTC, 2002.

Thompson CW. D.C. plagued by backlog in autopsy reports. *The Washington Post,* December 31, 2005.

CHAPTER 8

THE REAL STORY OF THE U.S. MEDICO-LEGAL DEATH INVESTIGATION SYSTEM

Much of the sentiment toward the U.S. medico-legal death investigation system could be summed up in the words of three prominent members of the community:

> "Is (death investigation) an enlightened system? No, it's not. It's really no better than what they have in many Third World countries."
> —Dr. Werner Spitz, National Institute of Justice, *Death Investigation: A Guide for the Scene Investigator*, 1999

> "As we jump to the end of the 20th century . . . we find medico-legal autopsies being badly bungled because the officials in charge are negligent, incompetent or simply unqualified in dealing with important and sophisticated forensic scientific questions."
> —Dr. Cyril Wecht, *Legal Medicine and Forensic Science: Parameters of Utilization in Criminal Cases*, 1996

> "We're still living in the dark ages (when it comes to death investigations). . . . It's a national disgrace."
> —Dr. Michael Baden, *Atlanta Journal Constitution*, 1995

As we saw in Chapter 7, there is no shortage of problems facing medico-legal death investigation; this chapter endeavors to describe the current state of affairs in this field, with suggestions for reform to be explored in Chapter 15.

THE HISTORY OF ME AND CORONER SYSTEMS: THE SONG REMAINS THE SAME, OR SECOND VERSE, SAME AS THE FIRST

Detailing the system's shortcomings and making recommendations for change is not something borne of the last decade; these efforts date back to the beginning of the 21st century. Schultz (1932) describes how the U.S. medico-legal system lags behind a more advanced and sophisticated system in operation in Europe for hundreds of years. A suggested form of remediation is for the U.S. criminal justice system to more fully embrace what forensic science can offer. Schultz states: ". . . a better administration of criminal justice must utilize much of the information that scientific medicine is in the position to furnish to the forces of justice." Schultz points to the advanced system of medico-legal institutes in Europe, where "the utilization of medical and other science in the administration of justice is a matter of everyday application." These institutes are an integral part of the ministry of justice, and since the state also controls higher education, the medico-legal institutes are part of the university system. The institutes examine bodies for the purpose of determining the cause of death, as well as in lesser degrees, the cause of injury and the psychiatric examination of accused and of witnesses. The director of the medico-legal institute has the title of professor of legal medicine at the university and holds great stature in the community. The academic link provides access to assistance from other disciplines, "housed in quarters whose size and character bespeak the importance and dignity of legal medicine." As an agency of government, it "makes application of medical science to the needs of law and justice. It does this in an impartial manner, through the highly trained experts of its staff, and does it for the court rather than for wither party to a legal action." It imparts knowledge to undergraduate and graduate students at the university. Functioning either as part of the medico-legal institute or as a separate organization within the ministry of justice is the laboratory of police science, in which "scientific facts and methods are applied for the purpose of detecting crime, or evaluating and preserving evidence, and of identifying and apprehending suspects and important witnesses" (Schultz, 1932).

Schultz (1932) contrasts this system with that in the United States, "where very little use is made of the aid that medical science might render," thanks to the American method of criminal procedure as well as the elective system in the selection of various agencies concerned with the administration of justice. Schultz asserts, "The application of scientific knowledge to police methods is practically unknown. The result is not only a much less efficient administration of justice, but also a shamefully backward state of the important field of legal medicine. Legal medicine as a distinct subdivision of medicine cannot be said to exist in this country. The number of experts in medico-legal science is limited. Most of these will be found in the ranks of full-time medical examiners. Others who have become expert in this field have done so through the experience obtained as pathologists. From time to time their services are utilized by the coroner's office, but usually under such conditions that he who is truly expert is not actually anxious to render the service that he is capable of rendering."

From the turn of the century, there have been critics of the coroner's office, opining that it falls short of the high mark left by the medical examiner's office. Mincing no words, Schultz (1932) states, "That the work of the coroner's office is not well done has been established," based on results of studies in a handful of metropolitan areas, made by the committee on medico-legal problems of the National Research Council (NRC). "All of these studies have been unanimous in declaring the average functioning of the coroner's office to be quite inadequate. Since the office is an elective one, with no continuity of service, the highly important work of determining in scientific manner the cause of death when homicide is suspected is poorly done. The post-mortem examinations are, as a rule, not nearly so well done as similar examinations in nonmedico-legal cases in the average hospital. The records of such examinations are usually of such character as to have no value as scientific documents or as documents which might be introduced as evidence in a criminal trial." Schultz adds, "Because the duties of the coroner are not clearly defined in most states, the investigation of non-homicidal deaths is usually quite inadequate to determine the cause of death in such cases. . . . The coroner's inquest frequently retards and impedes justice, and does not aid it."

The commonwealth of Massachusetts was the first entity "to realize the inadequacy of the coroner's office" according to Schultz (1932), abolishing the office in 1877 and appointing a medical examiner. In 1915, New York followed suit, and the change became effective in 1918. In the survey of the coroner's office made by the NRC's committee on medico-legal problems, the medical examiner system as it was operating in Massachusetts and New York was studied. The report (Schultz, 1932) refers to the "superior functioning" of the medical examiner system as "startling" when compared with the "poor functioning" of the coroner system. The report added. "Criticism made against the medical examiner system results from the failure of the public to realize the importance of the work done." Schultz goes on to list the deficits that account for any perceived lackluster performance of the medical examiner system, including inadequate financial support of the office so that the utilization of medical science is incomplete; lack of facilities to access sufficient disciplines such as toxicology and chemistry; and so forth.

In a naïve yet noble vein, Schultz (1932) remarks, "In both criminal and accidental violence, reliance upon the testimony of private physicians introduces the element of partisan, and therefore biased, testimony. It would be greatly to the advantage of prosecutors, courts, and claimants if it were possible to obtain, in all cases of the kind under discussion, the expert opinion of physicians who have no bias." These many years later, the search is still on.

The more things change, the more they stay the same. Schultz (1932) seizes on the fact that the various stakeholders in the criminal justice system are not as invested in medico-legal matters as perhaps they should be. In his push for the establishment of institutes of legal medicine in the United States, Schultz states, "Our elective method of selecting the officials of the agencies responsible for the administration of criminal justice is not conducive to continuity of service based upon fair and intelligent performance of duty." While Schultz blames administrators, he is equally quick to wag a disapproving finger at the general public for its malaise toward a vital system of inquiry. Schultz adds, "The importance of scientific methods in the work now usually devolving upon the coroner's office should be self-evident. That it is not evident is apparent from the inadequacy and inefficiency that characterize the average coroner's office. For that fault, blame should rest, not so much upon the individual coroner, as upon the body politic which retains so antiquated an office, or which fails to make available to that office existing facts and methods. But the medical examiner system does not function as well as it should, because the same public indifference which retains the coroner system results in inadequate financial support that does not permit the well-trained medical examiner to use the scientific procedures which he knows to exist and which he knows how to employ."

In essence, Schultz (1932) chastises both offices for failing to inform the public about what role they serve, and bring upon themselves their own cascade of ignorance and inefficiency. Schultz adds, "Since the office of medical examiner is less influenced by political considerations than is the office of coroner, and since the tenure of service of the personnel of the medical examiner's office is usually longer, this office as a rule serves the people who maintain it more efficiently than does the coroner's office. . . . Dollar for dollar, the office of medical examiner does more work and better work for its community than does the office of coroner."

Schultz (1932) lobbies for the total reformation of the office of coroner "if this office is to perform in a satisfactory manner its important function as the first agency to make application of medical science in suspected violent deaths." Schultz continues, "If the office of coroner is ever to make such use of science as it should be required to use in the public interest, drastic reform of the office is necessary and the laws defining the duties and functions of the office must be modernized to make the office fit modern conditions. Sufficient information, based upon study of functioning of the office in different localities, is at hand to indicate that proper functioning of the office, in matters entirely scientific in character, is out of the question, so long as the coroner's office remains the obscure political office that it is, and so long as it is required to operate under the present statutes relating to it."

Schultz (1932) takes the hard line when he states that proper reform of the office of coroner "would lead to its complete eradication and to the distribution of its duties among agencies better qualified to perform those duties. Such agencies would include the office of the medical examiner for the medical duties. A mere change in name from coroner to medical examiner, which has been proposed in some quarters as a reform, would be a useless gesture, if the official termed by legal fiat a medical examiner had to operate under the laws that at present apply to the coroner."

If abolition of the coroner's office is not feasible due to its constitutional nature or "because of veneration for the things of antiquity," Schultz (1932) states the office "could be modernized, first, by making the coroner simply an elective administrative official, and by creating for the office, as chief deputy coroner, a medical officer serving continuously under civil service, and by transferring the present inquisitional duties of the office to the prosecutor's office or to some other agency better qualified than in the coroner's office for the performance of technical legal procedures. And secondly, the laws relating to the duties and authority of the office would have to be revised in order that the duties and authority might be clearly and specifically defined. But neither such a reformed coroner's office nor the alterative office of medical examiner should be expected to perform its duties in scientific manner unless the financial support of the office is such as to enable it to use the necessary scientific procedures whenever required in the interest of the public."

Schultz (1932) advocates for the organization of an institute of legal medicine that encompasses a division of medical laboratory science that would act through the coroner or medical examiner and the public prosecutor, and would handle pathology, toxicology, chemistry, and so on; the division of clinical medical science would render unbiased expert opinion to the courts through medical opinion; and the division of police science, housing vehicles for police administration, identification, police school, and the police laboratory. Schultz (1932) further suggests the need for an affiliation between the institute and an institution of higher learning, stating, "Medico-legal practice has need of the aid that the medical school can render, and the medical school, if it is to do its proper share in the development of forensic medicine, needs the material and the problems that the proper practice of legal medicine would present."

More than 35 years after Schultz, Curran (1970) bemoans a less-than-optimal medico-legal system, observing, "The condition of forensic pathology has never been strong in the United States. It has been a specialty of virtually handfuls of dedicated people over the nearly 200 years of the American republic. By contrast, the field of legal medicine (a broader field than forensic pathology, but including this subspecialty) has been strong and vigorous in continental Europe for over 400 years." Curran adds, "There are many reasons for the lack of development in forensic pathology and legal medicine in this country. Among the most important deterrents is the lack of recognition and support in the legal system of this country for impartial, medical investigation, expert medical testimony and forensic science generally."

In his writings, Curran (1970) reflects on the lack of trained professionals that has only been exacerbated with the passage of time. Curran, describing the state of the system in the 1970s, reports that only about 164 specialists were certified by the American Board of Pathology at the time, although only 40 full-time forensic pathologists were in actual practice in the country, and these professionals were clustered in a few large metropolitan areas. Curran (1970) notes, "It is probably a conservative estimate to say that two-thirds of the American people live in jurisdictions without any kind of solid program in forensic pathology covering their communities. As these papers point out, the great tragedy for the American people in not having these services is felt not only in the criminal field, with the growing violence in the country, but also in all public health and community health areas. All these endeavors suffer greatly from inadequate and inaccurate death and cause-of-death investigation." Curran (1970) adds that more than 60 percent of the currently available positions for forensic pathologists in the country were unfilled; at the time, there were 15 approved residency programs in forensic pathology in the country. Curran comments, "Forensic pathology has waited, perhaps too long, and perhaps too patiently, for its time to come."

A few years later, Luke (1976) adds his voice to the chorus proclaiming the dire situation in which many forensic pathologists find themselves. He asserts, "Forensic pathology is the invisible profession," yet it holds the power to unravel the mysteries of death. Luke adds, "The responsibility of a forensic pathologist is not simply to determine the cause of sudden death, but to understand the particular circumstances of what happened. The daily challenge of unraveling the vagaries of fate, of discerning the truth by providing reasoned answers to the questions posed in all such case, and of anticipating well enough the ramifications of those interpretations, depends on one's experience and judgment to a degree not readily found in other fields of endeavor."

Luke (1976) testifies to the difficulty of grooming and growing new pathologists; he observes, "For the most part, forensic pathologists are created by chance. One of medicine's most interesting and rewarding disciplines is almost never offered as a legitimate career alternative. The extreme paucity of academically inclined forensic pathologists has served to restrict not only the scientific capabilities of the specialty but also its relevance to the medical and legal academic communities." He adds, "Recruitment into the discipline is largely a matter of proper exposure."

Although there has been improvement since the time of Schultz and even Curran, Luke (1976) says the field is lacking in structure. Luke notes, "Although modest gains in recruitment have recently been made, the majority of the population continues to be substantially unprotected by medico-legal systems unresponsive to the public interest staffed by persons untrained in their responsibilities. The illusion that the tenets of forensic pathology apply exclusively to homicide and to fatalities has served to justify and perpetuate its academic inconsequentiality. Unfortunately, the knowledge gained in this field is hardly ever used in the interpretation of nonfatal trauma because the precepts are not taught, except to a tiny fraction of physicians and attorneys."

Luke was ahead of his time in noting another significant deficit—that of research that could help advance forensic pathology in support of the entire medico-legal death investigation system. Luke states, "Because the numbers of practitioners required to sustain independent research are not at present available within the specialty, it seems that forensic pathology might best serve as a catalyst for other investigation of problem issues that cross disciplinary lines. . . . For the most part, research in forensic pathology has been either nonexistent, amateurish, or opportunistic, being used in the latter instance to further the interests of investigators from other disciplines. One of nature's best laboratories stands practically deserted."

Forensic pathology remained isolated from academia, Luke (1976) observes, further undermining any hopes of establishing solid research endeavors. Luke continues, "Concerning the criminal justice system, compartmentalization of professional responsibility has tended to insulate reality. Law schools teach attorneys all there is to know about the law but virtually nothing about how to find the truth through the use of objective scientific information. Physicians are taught to heal. The common ground of other forensic sciences is almost totally excluded from the academic process. Consequently, the potential for forensic scientific information to go unrecognized or to be misinterpreted, by both physicians and attorneys, poses a pervasive risk of the miscarriage of justice, The victim and what happened to him seem often to be relegated to secondary importance, by default—lost somewhere in the stampede through the courthouse door."

Luke (1976) comments, "To bring order from the chaos of violence, to separate fact from fancy, to provide impartiality to an adversary legal system, to search for the truth in terms of defining what happened to another human being, forces the forensic pathologist—uniquely—to examine death within the context of life, and the victim in terms of his community. Yet as a society we have abdicated this responsibility to reality. In denying death, we have compromised the sanctity of human life."

NEW ATTENTION TO OLD ISSUES

More than 70 years after the aforementioned NRC report (Schultz, 1932), in 2003, movement was afoot to readdress the critical needs of the U.S. medico-legal death investigation system. Many in the community were hopeful that issues could be addressed in 2001, when Kurt Nolte, M.D., Victor Weedn, M.D., J.D., and Randy Hanzlick, M.D., agitated for change, resulting in the National Association of Medical Examiners (NAME) proposing a status and needs study. That same year the Institute of Medicine (IOM) expressed interest in the study, and in July 2001, the IOM, NAME, the National Institute of Justice (NIJ), and the Centers for Disease Control and Prevention (CDC) met to discuss this issue. A second meeting was held later in July, and there was agreement that a conference could be held; the event took place March 24–25, 2003.

The original goals of the project were to determine the status of the criminal justice system overall and what was needed to improve it; to assess and improve the quality of medical care; to improve the U.S. public health system, including surveillance and epidemiological research; and to professionalize death investigation systems and operations. The IOM, NIJ, and CDC shared these interests, and the hope was that the conference proceedings, which were eventually compiled into a report from the symposium, would lead to a more formal study of the needs of the U.S. medico-legal death investigation system, and that the mechanisms for change would be identified and eventually effected.

In the report (Committee for the Workshop on the Medicolegal Death Investigation System [CWMDIS], 2003) of the Institute of Medicine's *Medico-legal Death Investigation System: Workshop Summary*, event chair Richard J. Bonnie, law professor and director of the Institute of Law, Psychiatry, and Public Policy at the University of Virginia, comments, "On first glance, official identification of human remains and certification of the cause of death appear to be mundane endeavors that serve mainly private needs of families, insurers, and litigants. In truth, however, valid and reliable data on the circumstances and causes of deaths serve a variety of important public needs, including fair and accurate adjudication in criminal and civil cases, maintenance of accurate vital statistics, effective public health surveillance and response, advances in health and safety research, and improvement in quality of healthcare."

Bonnie acknowledges that concerns about the adequacy of medico-legal death investigation in the United States have been raised for many decades, voiced by those who have a stake in the accuracy of data related to circumstances of death and in the official determinations based on them. Bonnie (2003) explains, "For the criminal justice system, concerns about the adequacy of data about deaths merge with general concerns about all aspects of forensic science."

Regarding the symposium, Bonnie (2003) says, "Presentations and opinions expressed at the workshop demonstrated clearly that the current practices of medico-legal death investigation in this country are in substantial need of improvement. The workshop discussions also showed that accurate data on the circumstances and causes of death (and the identification of human remains) are, in the language of economists, a valuable public good and that much of their value accrues to the benefit of the nation as a whole. To rectify the many deficiencies of the system, it will be necessary to solve many problems, including fundamental issues of financing. The workshop was a starting point for further study and, I hope, for eventual reform."

Many of the participants at the 2003 IOM symposium were hopeful that this meeting of the minds would lead to an in-depth study of the issues by the Institute of Medicine. According to Carolyn Fulco of the IOM, who oversaw the 2003 symposium, the Department of Justice and the NIJ were briefed on the proceedings of the meeting, but the government lacked the funding for a follow-up study, and the issue was dropped. In 2006, however, the National Academies launched a comprehensive study of the needs of the forensic science community (see Chapter 16, and some in the medico-legal death investigation system are hopeful that this community's issues will be examined as well.

"The three of us, Randy Hanzlick, Victor Weedn and myself, have the strongest interest in beating the drum for the support that forensic pathology needs in this country, and the Institute of Medicine workshop reflected those efforts, although all three of us are disappointed that that process has not gone farther," says Kurt Nolte, M.D., professor in the Department of Pathology at the University of New Mexico Health Sciences Center and assistant chief medical investigator for the state of New Mexico. "The workshop was a springboard to launch a preliminary evaluation of forensic pathology to determine if there were enough unresolved, important issues that the IOM could sink its teeth into with a full review. At the conclusion of that workshop, the IOM was overwhelmed at the number of issues that needed to be addressed in medico-legal death investigation, and advocated strongly for a full IOM evaluation and report. The impact those reports have on Congress is significant; they can actually change the course of medicine."

Nolte continues, "The initial workshop held in 2003 was funded by the National Institute of Justice, but following the workshop, nobody bellied up to the bar to fund a complete study. One would imagine that since forensic pathology is a platform that supports both public health and safety, and the criminal justice system, the two federal agencies that would be invested in the outcome would be the CDC and the NIJ. One would imagine further that these agencies would not hesitate to fund a full study. Shortly after the report from the workshop came out, the CDC disbanded its Medical Examiner/Coroner Information Sharing Program (MECISP), and it has not addressed the needs brought up in the 2003 IOM workshop to any degree. NIJ was pressed by IOM to consider funding a full study but they have not come up with money either. Now we're kind of betwixt and between, although there is hope that now, the National Academies will undertake a major study of forensic science. It is unclear to me as to how that will unfold and how that will involve forensic pathology. There is a great deal of frustration among forensic pathologists right now about the lack of federal interest in medico-legal death investigation, and the lack of interest in even examining what the issues are, what the shortcomings are, and what the needs are to remedy those shortcomings. I think we are at a crossroads. Forensic science gets a very high profile in the media and the expectations are very, very high, unreasonably high, and at the same time, the wheels are falling off the wagon. There's a lot for the IOM to sink its teeth into if it had the opportunity. All of this bears review and comment, and not only that, it requires a plan for surmounting it." (The National Academies study is discussed more fully in Chapter 16.)

"The Institute of Medicine went to the NIJ asking for money for the full panel, and NIJ wasn't interested in paying for it," says Victor Weedn, M.D., J.D., professor at Duquesne University. "Apparently they had other entities in which to invest their money. Neither could the IOM interest the CDC. Their goal was to secure funding for a full study, since those are the documents that are taken to Congress. So the issue died, but I still believe a full panel to investigate our issues further ought to be funded."

"I was hoping that what would come out of the 2003 symposium would be clear recommendation from the Institute of Medicine that states implement medical examiner systems to improve the quality of the medico-legal death investigation system overall," says Marcella Fierro, M.D., chief medical examiner of the commonwealth of Virginia, and a member of the board of the Virginia Institute of Forensic Science and Medicine. "I think the medical examiner office is the gold standard for the system. I think all of us fully recognize that there are tremendous political implications in death investigation systems where the person responsible for certification of cause and manner of death is an elected official, with or without training. I would like to see all death investigation systems in the U.S. evolve into medical examiner systems, and I would like to see them regionalize within a state."

Fierro explains the various existing models, including the regional model: "There is the model used, in New Mexico and Maryland, for example, where there is a single office to which all cases in the state are directed. Then there is the regionalized state system such as what we have in Virginia, where there is central administration and a chief pathologist for four regional offices that provide added convenience for funeral homes, for families, and for the courts—services are closer to the people who use them. The country has so much diversity in its medico-legal offices, however; the Florida model is a number of independent groups of forensic pathologists who are chiefs in their own regions, but they are subjected to policies which are set by a commission. Those are a couple of models that work, but if I had my druthers, I would like to see the current incumbent coroners become the investigators for the system and the forensic pathologists be appointed as the chiefs. In this way, the systems are run by forensic pathologists, not coroners, but we retain the expertise of the coroners and ensure they don't lose their positions."

A PATCHWORK OF JURISDICTIONS

In Chapter 6, we explored the breadth and depth of the medico-legal death investigation system in the United States. Hanzlick (2003) characterizes the so-called "system" as a misnomer, stating, "It is an umbrella term for a patchwork of highly varied state and local systems for investigating deaths." Bonnie (2003) concurs, noting, "There is little risk of dissent in pointing out that there is no such 'system' of death investigations, in the same sense that there is no healthcare system in this country. Instead, the processes and structure of death investigations vary widely according to the characteristics and practices of distinct jurisdictions. The source of variation is not only state law but also local authority. Responsibility for death investigations rests at the county level for over 2,000 counties. Remarkably, for well over a century, there has been continuous concern about the lack of standardization in death investigations and about high rates of errors, whether real or perceived."

"The oversight is patchy, and the whole infrastructure is patchy," asserts Nolte. "We have a patchwork quilt of medical examiner and coroner systems of varying scope and quality. We have jurisdictions where in order to be a death investigator you have to be 21, registered to vote, and never have fought a duel," Nolte says, laughing. "We actually have states with ridiculous statutes like that, and we have other states where I have heard the statute is where you are 21, registered to vote, and have never renounced the supreme deity. These are just some of the statutes that exist that underpin some of these systems, and we wonder why our system has issues. On the other hand, there are states like New Mexico, where I am, which has a statewide, centralized medical examiner office that is based out of the University of Mexico School of Medicine. So you have Cadillac systems and Pinto systems. At this point, there are no carrots or sticks offered by the federal government that would induce states to move to more exemplary models of death investigation. There are no unifying death investigation statutes or federal legislation that would help foster better systems. We have a mess on our hands currently."

In a 2004 report, NAME stated, "The level of expertise and the amount of training and continuing education of front-line death investigators (be they within medical examiner systems or coroner systems) vary widely from one jurisdiction to another, and sometimes within a given jurisdiction. A particularly striking weak link in the current national situation is the fact that in many jurisdictions, front-line death investigators who are not forensic pathologists are for all intents and purposes responsible for deciding whether or not autopsies will be performed in specific cases. Instead of having a well-organized system where the ultimate decisions regarding many important aspects of death investigation rest on a forensic pathologist, these systems allow important decisions to be made by persons with far less training and experience. Because of this, there are still many areas within the U.S. where various case types might not be autopsied. For this reason, it is imperative to establish nationwide, forensic pathologist-based death investigation systems."

As explained in Chapter 7, death investigations are conducted under the authority of state law and local ordinances by either a coroner or a medical examiner, at a minimum, in the case of unnatural or suspicious or unattended death, and when other deaths not clearly explained by natural causes are involved. Official death investigations are opened in approximately 20 percent of annual deaths in the United States. The scope of the investigations, although somewhat variable, generally includes investigation of the scene of the death, collection of evidence, external examination of the body, an autopsy, tests of body tissues or fluids, and the completion of a death certificate that certifies the cause of death.

As we will see in the next section, there is a growing nationwide debate about who excels in the medico-legal death investigation system, medical examiner or coroner. Referencing the 1928 NRC report, "The Coroner and the Medical Examiner," Bonnie (2003a) states, "The committee stated forcefully, in blunter terms than used today, that the coroner's office is an anachronistic institution, predating the Magna Carta. The office 'has conclusively demonstrated its incapacity to perform the functions customarily required of it.' The committee recommended that the office of coroner be abolished and be replaced by a well-staffed office of a medical examiner, headed by a pathologist. A key goal of the committee's recommendations was boosting the level of professionalism of death investigation, with medicine as its center. That vision relied heavily on the training and credentialing capacities of what was becoming modern medicine." That effort has continued over the ensuing decades when in 1959 the subspecialty of forensic pathology was recognized, and in 1966 when the National Association of Medical Examiners was established. The country witnessed a gradual conversion of many medico-legal offices from a coroner system to a medical examiner system, but the vision of federalized, all-medical examiner system has not yet been realized.

ALL INVESTIGATORS ARE NOT CREATED EQUAL: MAKING A CASE FOR AND AGAINST THE CORONER

The differences between medical examiners and coroners in training and skills are as broad and deep as the differences between the configuration of state and local organizations that support them. However, the coroner wins when it comes to longevity of the profession, with its origins dating back to medieval England, when the role of coroners was formalized into law in the 12th century under King Richard I. Coroners were dispatched to death scenes by the king, under order to protect the crown's interest and collect duties. Coroners were introduced to the colonies by way of the earliest settlers. The British Colony of Georgia followed British common law in 1733, the first state constitution mentioned coroners, and subsequent statutes continued to describe the duties of coroners.

The earliest break with convention and the move toward reliance on a medical examiner role came in 1860, when Maryland introduced legislation requiring the presence of a physician at the death inquest. Hanzlick (2003) observes that the role of the coroner and medical examiner evolved from a highly decentralized system rooted in local or county ordinances. With awareness of the need for expertise in death investigations, there has been a nationwide trend, since 1877, to replace coroners with medical examiners, but efforts have been stalled since the middle 1980s (Hanzlick and Combs, 1998).

Credentials for serving a medico-legal office vary for medical examiners as well as for coroners, and in general, the requirements for coroners are less stringent. Typically, coroners must be registered voters, at least 25 years old, with no felony convictions, having at least a high school education or equivalent, and must attest to the aforementioned by affidavit; they typically receive about a week's worth of training. Medical examiner definitions and qualifications vary, too, and range from a board-certified forensic pathologist, to a forensic pathologist, a pathologist, a physician, and even a non-physician. According to Hanzlick (2003), approximately one-third of the U.S. population lives in a jurisdiction where no or minimal training is required of the ME. Forty-four percent have their medical doctor degree and training; 25 percent have no training; 20 percent are MDs only; and 11 percent have coroner training. The result, Hanzlick says, is a TV crime show mentality, crash courses in medico-legal issues, and a lack of accredited education, professional certification, and evidence-based decision making. Hanzlick asks, "Do these serve justice, public health, or medicine?"

In some jurisdictions, the coroner is little more than a lay death investigator, and in some cases, the latter has more training than the former, says Mary Fran Ernst, a medico-legal death investigator for the St. Louis County Medical Examiner's Office, director of medico-legal education at St. Louis University School of Medicine, and past president of the American Academy of Forensic Sciences (AAFS). "A lay death investigator is an educated, trained, and experienced individual who evaluates decedents and the circumstances relating to their deaths, and relays that information to the forensic pathologist who then does the physical examination and testing and determines the cause and manner of death. The trouble is, when people speak of coroners, they are really talking about an elected official who doesn't have to have any specific background or training, unlike a death investigator. If you look at various state laws, you will find a wide range of requirements. In Indiana, deputy coroners must have 40 hours of training, but the coroners don't. In Missouri, coroners must receive 20 hours of training a year; if they don't, they can still be coroner, but they just don't receive a stipend each year. So the standards required of coroners may be lacking, but because this office is an elected one, the only way you can be remove a coroner is by the vote of the citizens. Until the office of coroner is no longer an elected position, we're going to have people who don't necessarily have the training needed to do the job properly. I think mandatory training is the answer, but again, unless we have standards and the states follow them, we are not going to be able to enforce the education requirements and it's a vicious circle."

Nolte concurs, adding, "When it is a politicized, elected office, it is viewed as a stepping stone from coroner to commissioner to state representative to whatever the next rung on the political ladder is, and the office takes on a quality that is not appropriate for death investigation."

Nolte advocates using coroners in a different role that is still essential to the death investigation system but it does not usurp the role of the forensic pathologist as medical examiner. "It is my belief that in any coroner system, the tail is wagging the dog. You have a guy who is a plumber, for example, making decisions about what needs to be done in a medico-legal case and interpreting the information that comes from these investigations. And you have pathologists, sometimes forensic pathologists, sometimes not, who are providing information to this tail that is wagging the dog, but they are not making the decisions, they are just saying, 'Well, this is what I found at autopsy, go off and sign the death certificate.' But if you reverse the system, and had individuals with the highest level of expertise and training leading the process, you could still use the individuals with lesser amounts of training in other capacities. For example, in New Mexico, which is a medical examiner system, we have trained lay investigators who work as our field investigators. You have to incorporate those individuals in the transition process; otherwise they'd be resistant to change because their political base would go away; so their investment in performing investigations and their identity can be maintained in a transition to a medical examiner system."

"It is true that some medical examiners are not perfect, and some coroners are pretty good," Weedn observes. "The question remains: Are coroners a hapless group of uneducated individuals or are they actually a decent sort but the target of a bad public relations campaign? The answer lies somewhere in the middle says forensic pathologist Michael Dobersen, M.D., Ph.D., coroner for Arapahoe County in Colorado and president of the Colorado Coroner Association. Dobersen is not your average coroner, however. He is a forensic pathologist who served as a researcher for the National Institutes of Health before completing his residency at the King County Medical Examiner's Office in Washington. He was appointed Arapahoe County coroner in 1993, and also serves as an associate professor in the department of pathology at the University of Colorado Medical School. During his tenure, he has investigated a number of high-profile cases, including the JonBenet Ramsey murder, the Columbine High School shootings, and was called to assist with the aftermath of the terrorist attack on the World Trade Center.

Dobersen acknowledges the bad press that the coroner system generates and agrees that, by and large, the coroner's reputation is much less sterling than that of the medical examiner. "I do see some of that attitude here in Colorado as well as nationally," Dobersen says. "For the most part we are a coroner state; we have 64 counties and I think we have forensic pathologists working as medical examiners in five or six counties, so it's the vast minority. We do have a lot of physicians in specialties other than forensic pathology; we have some ER physicians and some internists who are coroners and they do a very good job. We are also lucky enough to have some nurses and paramedics who also serve as coroners. There are probably 10 percent to 15 percent of coroners who have backgrounds outside of the medical field; one of them was a car mechanic. One of our biggest challenges is manpower. There are numerous counties here that you are lucky if you even have a coroner, even if he *is* a car mechanic. It's kind of a thankless job, it's usually fairly low-paying, and so the result is that the state has people in medico-legal offices that are not medically trained."

There are a number of factors at work, Dobersen says, including financial and political. "Medical examiner systems are more extensive and they are more expensive, but the biggest factor at work here is the political machine. We have found that probably the most politically active and well-connected coroners in the state are from the small counties; these people grew up in low-population areas and so they know everyone, including their legislators, and these policy-makers know them, too. So when the coroner in office says something to Uncle Bubba, the legislator, Uncle Bubba listens. It can be a very powerful relationship."

Regardless of whether a jurisdiction's medico-legal office has at its helm a medical examiner or a coroner system, Dobersen says the most important consideration is having a "dedicated person who wants to do the job, who is trained to do it, and who actually does it." Dobersen continues, "It's the character and competence of the person doing the death scene investigation that is most critical. What we have found here is that the coroners, no matter what their background is, if they are enthusiastic and can talk to their commissioners and understand what they do and how important it is to the system and to the public's welfare, then everything else, including funding and resources, will follow. And a lot of the coroners' offices really don't have a problem with adequate funding. It's the coroners who will only show up on the one day that they haggle for their budgets with the county managers being the ones who are going to have problems in their jurisdictions. They won't have enough money to do their jobs properly, and then one day they will get a case in which an autopsy should be done on and there is no money left to do so, so they don't do it. And that's when bad things can happen."

Those "bad things" Dobersen speaks of can range from erroneous determinations of cause and manner of death, to blatant malfeasance on the part of the investigator, coroner, or medical examiner. "One of the things I have always been struck by is as a coroner or as a forensic pathologist, for me, it's good if I am out of the media spotlight," Dobersen says. "If I am out of the headlines and things are going smoothly, that means things are working. Day to day, the system works pretty well, but on occasion you do hear about cases in which someone didn't do their job and it makes the news. I think these kinds of mistakes only represent a very, very small percentage of all of the cases that are handled. You don't hear about the routine cases where everything just clicks and everything goes right—the good things don't seem to grab the headlines."

Dobersen says that, in general, the medico-legal death investigation system and its medical examiners and coroners have a higher profile than ever before, thanks certainly to the television show *CSI: Crime Scene Investigation*, as well as shows that depict medical examiners, such as *Crossing Jordan*, where the star is a forensic pathologist with a flair for crime fighting. This glamorized persona does not sit well with some members of the medical examiner community; Dolinak et al. (2005) state, "Who are forensic pathologists? Contrary to popular belief, forensic pathologists are not socially isolated basement dwellers who perform autopsies in dimly lit morgues, nor are they flamboyant, volatile celebrities who drive to scenes in Hummers. First and foremost, forensic pathologists are physicians. As such, they are knowledgeable in human form and function, its derangements, and the interrelationship between health, trauma, toxin, and disease at both the individual and community levels. The understanding of medicine is fundamental to the practice of forensic pathology, and must never be subjugated or negated."

Dobersen says the so-called "*CSI* effect" manifests itself on occasion in the courtroom, and he sees it as an opportunity to tell the straight story about death investigation, not through the lens of a television camera. "Here in Colorado the courts are starting to let jurors ask questions, which is really interesting," Dobersen explains. "Most of the questions are very good but others are to the effect of 'So, did you test the gun for DNA so you could tell who fired it?' and questions like that. As coroners, we have to answer as best as we can and try to teach the jurors about forensic science and about death investigation, because on the witness stand, that's really what you are doing—teaching. I am concerned, of course, that people watch TV and they get a very superficial and misleading idea of what we do. It's usually the notion that we can do a lot more than we really can. I think we are still in the days of *Quincy, ME*, as to what we can do, not so much the whiz-bang of *Crossing Jordan*. When we testify, we must do so to a reasonable degree of medical certainty, which means we are 95 percent sure of everything we say, and if we can't do that, then sometimes the jury might see us as incompetent. They think, 'What do you mean you don't know for sure? You are supposed to know that.' Fingerprints have been on shaky ground in some cases, for example, but for the most part I think as forensic pathologists we have pretty much stayed in the area of medicine and science. I think we have been on pretty solid footing except when we are asked by attorneys to extrapolate on details, such as when they ask us, 'How would this person have acted under this level of cocaine?' If we are not careful to say, 'I don't know,' we can get into a lot of trouble."

Some concerns have been raised by commentators regarding the competence and training levels of coroners, not altogether different from some of the charges that have been levied against medical examiners. For example, are coroners able to discern complicated medicolegal issues relating to potentially suspicious deaths to warrant the call for an autopsy and further investigation? "For the most part, the coroner is not going to be the person to do the autopsy, but they are the ones who must know enough to order one," Dobersen says. "In Colorado we go to great pains to educate our coroners. We hold quarterly and annual meetings of the Colorado Coroners Association, and we also hold a course in which all new coroners receive a full week's education. They will be required to sit through a 40-hour weeklong program that will review the basics of the job, and I think that allows them to become fairly competent in performing death investigations. We also try to provide them with a good network of support; for example, everyone knows everyone else's phone number and if anyone has a question, they can call each other. They know they can always call me, and hardly a week goes by when I don't get a call from a coroner wondering about what to do if this or that happens, and so we really try to provide them with a safety net. That's not to say that bad things don't happen. We just had a situation where a coroner didn't autopsy two victims involved in an automobile accident. He didn't even take samples and then the bodies were cremated and now the families are asking questions: Who was the driver? Who was the passenger? I think he learned a big lesson but nevertheless, this could result in unfortunate consequences."

As we have seen, the ability of coroners to screen deaths for potential cases of foul play that deserve further investigation is of concern to others in the field. Dobersen notes, "Screening cases is a concern even in medical examiner jurisdictions because in even some of the medical examiner states, there have been examples of things missed in cases that led to devastating consequences. When it comes to death investigation in general, I think one of the things to keep in mind is, would you rather have a trained, interested car mechanic as coroner do the scene investigation, or the urologist who really couldn't give a damn about going out to a death scene even though he or she is a physician? It doesn't mean he or she is going to be a good investigator. I'd be willing to bet on the involved car mechanic in most cases."

Dobersen acknowledges a lack of uniform standards for coroners and other death investigators in some jurisdictions, noting, "Some states even have constitutional guidelines on what kinds of cases we must investigate, so the system is highly variable. I go to crime scenes, especially to scenes that are suspicious or whenever I am requested by the police, but other coroners don't do that. One of the problems is that there are not enough forensic pathologists to go around. Victor Weedn and others have emphasized that there are only about 400 practicing forensic pathologists in the country, and in Colorado there are only 14. So we tend to be spread pretty thinly. In some places investigators are in short supply; although an increasing number of people seem to want to go into this field, thanks to *CSI*, but it doesn't always translate into enough qualified people in the field."

COMPARING MEDICAL EXAMINER AND CORONER SYSTEMS

Fierro (2003) asserts that a statewide medical examiner system has numerous advantages, explaining that regardless of the degree of centralization, medical examiner systems are "highly desirable" in comparison with coroner systems and mixed systems. Fierro states, "The major advantages of a statewide medical examiner system are the quality of death investigations and forensic pathology services and their independence from population size, county budget variation, and politics. Certification of death is accomplished by highly trained medical professionals who can integrate autopsy findings with those from the crime scene and the laboratory. The professionals have core competency in assessing immediate and earlier medical history, interviewing witnesses, and physical examination. The recognized excellence of and confidence in a medical examiner system in Virginia have been vital for adjudicating the state's death penalty cases and for prompt payment of insurance claims."

Another major advantage of a statewide system is uniformity. Virginia's uniformity comes from its statute covering types of cases automatically in the jurisdiction of the medical examiner. . . . Uniformity also covers credentialing, training, and continuing education of medical examiners and death investigators; coding of deaths; access to case files through archive and retrieval policies; criteria for exhumation and disposition of unclaimed bodies; and appeals processes. Those features benefit not only death investigations but also public health epidemiology and surveillance.

A final set of advantages of a statewide system is related to central administration. A statewide system like that in Virginia can have statewide guidelines for case management and death scene investigation. It also can have 24-hour consultation with any site in the state, which is an especially important feature for isolated areas with little experience. Furthermore, a large cadre of forensic pathologists gives the state the flexibility to shift manpower in case of a mass disaster. Centralized administration can sustain the cost of central laboratories, and it can take advantage of economies of scale and purchasing power. Virginia's centralized administration devotes personnel to writing grants, which can be extremely time-consuming.

Fierro states, "A centralized medical examiner system also poses challenges. It requires strong leadership, attention to state budget priorities and competition with other public health and criminal justice programs, and human-resource management to ensure recruitment and retention of multiple types of professionals. An ideal statewide system ties a medical examiner system to a medical school and subspecialty pathologists, forensic science laboratories and scientists, and public health systems and laboratories. Such proximity facilitates sharing of knowledge, system refinement, and access to new technologies. In addition to grants for infrastructure, the most efficient expenditure of federal funds would be for uniform data elements collected in a way that allows easy comparability across jurisdictions and that could be used by all coroners and medical examiners nationwide."

Fierro advocates for a regionalized system so that no one county bears all of the costs, yet all jurisdictions could contribute to and receive medico-legal services. "You could have eight or so counties share a facility that has at least two pathologists, support people, and several autopsy techs; between these counties they could pool resources and build a several-million dollar facility without it being a strain on any individual county. Then they could do 1,000 cases a year, do the court work, and do the education and training. A regional model works well when everyone contributes."

Parrott (2003) states, "The major differences between coroners and medical examiners are embedded in the manner of their selection by electoral process versus appointment and their professional status. Coroners are elected lay people who often do not have professional training, whereas medical examiners are appointed and have board-certification in a medical specialty. The coroner system has advantages, but they are heavily outweighed by its disadvantages. The major advantages of the coroner system concern autonomy, access to power, and the ability to represent the will of the electorate. As an elected official, a coroner has the power to make decisions and has equal footing with other local elected officials. That places the coroner in a strong position to withstand political pressures imposed by other elected officials and to compete vigorously for the office's budget allocation. Furthermore, due to their English common-law origins, coroners also have subpoena and inquest powers. Finally, being an elected official resonates with American political culture, which views elected officials as the best representatives of a community's needs and values."

Parrott adds that two distinct disadvantages of coroner systems, as we have seen, are that coroner systems are "less likely to be medically proficient" and that "their structure often reflects piecemeal legislative reaction to inadequacies, rather than intelligent design. Parrott (2003) explains, "The coroner system is steeped in the vagaries of history rather than in a forward-looking, planned system that capitalizes on professional depth and knowledge. Coroner statutes are less specific about which types of cases are reported or investigated, and they tend to reflect the lowest common denominator in the qualifications of the office holder and the quality of investigations. The coroner may be deficient in knowledge and may have conflicts of interest; especially when funeral directors, prosecutors or sheriffs act as coroners. As elected officials, they cannot be dismissed for incompetence, except by the electorate after highly visible transgressions."

Parrott (2003) asserts further, "The county nature of the coroner system is a fundamental flaw as applied to the U.S. because the jurisdictional base is often too small to support a modern medico-legal office. The result is that coroner systems vary widely, with many counties having only a part-time elected coroner with few resources for operations or even training. The creation of medical examiner systems permits governments to consider regional or state systems that can provide more uniform coverage in an efficient manner. The key determinant is the resources of the county, as opposed to the circumstances of the cases. Cities have far greater resources than rural areas. The homicide rate is higher in cities, but homicides are less frequent than injury and suicide deaths, which vary less between urban and rural areas. Thus, the variability in circumstances of death between urban and rural counties cannot account for the enormous spending disparities. Other disadvantages are poorer quality of coroner investigations, poorer integration across jurisdictional boundaries, poorer information transfer, and poorer information-gathering."

THE VALUE OF FORENSIC PATHOLOGISTS AND THE CHALLENGES THEY FACE

That the living and the dead are both served by death investigation is not lost on practitioners. At the 2003 Institute of Medicine symposium mentioned earlier, Vincent Di Maio, chief medical examiner in the Bexar County Medical Examiner's Office in San Antonio, Texas, asserted the importance of medical expertise in death investigation, as the process begins with the examination of the body and collection of the evidence at the scene and progresses through the history, physical examination, laboratory tests, and diagnosis, which Di Maio (2003) emphasizes are "the broad ingredients of a doctor's treatment of a living patient." He adds, "The key goal is to provide objective evidence of cause, timing, and manner of death for adjudication by the criminal justice system."

Di Maio says that one of the most critical aspects of the inherent expertise of the medical examiner can be found in the screening process. He points to an example of one county in which 8,000 cases are reported to the medical examiner's office, but only 2,000 are accepted. Di Maio (2003) says, "Screening, which eliminates three-fourths of potential cases, must be handled in a scientifically defensible manner by people with medical training, knowledge, and objectivity. The medical examiner's office is especially important in subtler cases of criminal activity, where there is a possibility of a missed homicide. Such cases often are not aggressively pursued by either police or non-medical coroners. Confronted with the death of a 30-year-old woman, who dies apparently of a heart attack, a lay coroner would most likely not do an autopsy, but a medical examiner would, given its medical implausibility. Similarly, many lay coroners do not autopsy burned bodies, but a medical examiner would investigate the possibility of homicide masked as an accident. By interviewing, the medical examiner might uncover evidence of a crime. A medical examiner brings important skills to the interview of next of kin and others who provide a medical history."

Even among forensic pathologists, there is variation in the adequacy of screening for suspicious cases as well as the accuracy of the determination of cause and manner of death. "Sometimes it comes down to how well resourced you are, since that can affect the quality of investigations," says Weedn. "There also can be differences in the level of investigation of various medical examiners. While one medical examiner might say 'pneumonia,' and be done with it, others will be quick to ask themselves, 'Well, what kind of pneumonia? What's the microorganism causing it?' And that level of detail truly might make a difference in the investigation. There is also philosophical and nomenclature differences within the community. We can call something a homicide or maybe we don't call it a homicide. We are making a determination of the manner of death as a 'nosologic' classification system, but it is often fuzzy and subject to philosophic differences. There are a lot of medical examiners who wish we could just do away with manner of death, and I think that would be absolutely wrong. In my view, that would further undermine the value of the medical examiner. We are certainly not always in agreement in our community on how to call a death, but there is still value in us doing so; not doing it would detract from our value to society. Sometimes our determination is a problem for the prosecutors when they do not agree with a given call, but we are not making pronouncements of legal responsibility and thus just because we call it homicide doesn't mean that they have to prosecute, and because we don't call it homicide doesn't mean that they have to, and because we *don't* call it homicide doesn't mean they shouldn't proceed with prosecution. The same label, 'homicide,' is used for different purposes."

Weedn explains further: "A classic example might be the hunter who kills another person in the woods. Well, is that a homicide or an accident? There's a lot of philosophy involved. I think most medical examiners would call it a homicide even if accidental, as it is still one person killing another person; but not all medical examiners will see it that way. This is not an issue of criminal responsibility; this is an issue of classification. So, most medical examiners simply make a value judgment whether they are going to call these types of cases accidents or homicides. Another example is a motor vehicle accident where the driver is drunk; we tend to automatically call those homicides but that's convention. I don't mind that because it's consistent and we understand it, but we're not trying to tell the district attorney what to do. Meanwhile, some members of the general public also misunderstand and demand, 'Why didn't you call this or that case a homicide?' and make a great big deal about it."

Weedn says that when it comes to homicides, there is no question that forensic pathologists should take responsibility. "Homicides are the bread and butter for forensic pathologists. Homicides should have had an autopsy in every case. The prosecutor needs the testimony on the medical cause of death from the physician investigating the case."

One of the most important functions of a forensic pathologist is the determination of the cause and manner of death and the completion of the death certificate. In general, medical examiners or coroners are responsible for completing the death certificate in cases involving sudden unexpected or unnatural deaths such as those by homicide, suicide, or accident. Criteria for determining whether a case falls under a coroner's or medical examiner's jurisdiction vary somewhat by county. For most natural deaths with a physician in attendance, the coroner or medical examiner is not needed and will not have jurisdiction.

"There are two kinds of death certificates; one signed by the medico-legal officer; the other is signed by the attending physician," explains Weedn. "Unfortunately, most attending physicians have never had training on death certification. I have taught a class in it and I know a few medical examiners who teach house officers or medical school students, but I believe most physicians get no training whatsoever. It is not uncommon that the attending physician will merely sign a case as cardiopulmonary arrest. Well, thank you very much, but that doesn't help—that can be said of all individuals dying from whatever cause. I have more confidence in death certificates that come out of the medical examiner's office than from a coroner's office, but I have even less confidence in those signed by the general practitioners out there."

Roe and Thomas (2004) state, "Completing a death certificate is time-consuming and sometimes confusing, but it is a task that has important legal and public health ramifications. Death certificates are permanent legal documents that are needed in matters such as the settlement of an estate, transfer of property, and the receipt of insurance, pension, and worker's compensation benefits. They are also used in determining morbidity and mortality statistics, which are often the basis for evaluating public health trends and determining public health policies. For this reason, accuracy is very important on a death certificate. If the data is not correct, there may be delays in settling the estate, adding to the stress of surviving family members. Public health monies may not be spent in the most beneficial manner if the statistics gathered are inaccurate."

Although quality assurance programs for medical examiners are required for accreditation by NAME, programs specifically targeting death certificate completion have not been addressed. Hanzlick (2005) describes a pilot quality assurance program for death certificate information implemented by the Fulton County Medical Examiner's Office in Atlanta. Hanzlick explains that all death certificates are reviewed by the case medical examiner(s) and chief medical examiner prior to their release to funeral homes. Death certificates with errors are retained for quality assurance and review purposes, and needed corrections are made before death certificates are released. During a one-year period, death certificates with errors were collected and then reviewed and tabulated by type of error. Hanzlick reports that between May 26, 2003, and May 25, 2004, the Fulton County Medical Examiner certified 1,267 deaths. Of these, 47 (4 percent) were found to contain errors that were corrected and an additional 52 (4 percent) had been amended for various reasons. According to Hanzlick, the most common errors were misspellings in causes of death, or poor or incomplete wording in injury-related information; 47 percent of errors involved omitted, incomplete, or incorrect information that was potentially significant. The most common reason for amended certificates was unexpected detection of acute intoxications among people with significant cardiovascular disease. Hanzlick (2005) suggests that quality assurance review of death certificates can assist in preventing the release of death certificates with incomplete, erroneous, or omitted information and may also be useful as an educational forum regarding completion of the death certificate.

A forensic pathologist may find himself or herself on the receiving end of a subpoena related to improper completion of a death certificate. Hanzlick (1997) searched a database to determine the frequency in which a medical examiner was sued because of the cause or manner of death stated on the death certificate. Sixteen reported cases were found between 1948 and 1995, with 10 of the cases occurring since 1985. Hanzlick reports the frequency of cases is approximately 1 per 400,000 medical examiner/coroner-completed death certificates, but based on certain assumptions, the actual frequency may be estimated at 1 per 40,000 medical examiner/coroner-completed death certificates. Nine cases involved plaintiffs who contested when the manner of death was indicated as suicide, and in 15 of the 16 cases, the lower court decision favored the medical examiner/coroner viewpoint. Five of the 15 decisions were ultimately reversed by a higher court, but the ultimate outcomes of these cases were not available. According to Hanzlick, overall, it appears that most courts and decisions have recognized medical examiner and coroner actions as discretionary or immune and that these medico-legal professionals have been at low risk for such suits to date. Hanzlick states, "This seems especially true if the medical examiner/coroner position is defensible and the medical examiner/coroner has acted in accordance with statute and without evidence of corruption, incompetence, arbitrariness, capriciousness, abuse of discretion, or outrageous conduct."

Regarding the continued quality of death certificates Hanzlick adds, "I think that in the last 10 or 15 years, with NAME making available its manner of death guide, and with continued discussions in the medico-legal community, I think people are more aware these days than they used to be and they are doing things more consistently. There is still a problem, I think, with the quality of death certificates in terms of how complete the information is. I think medical examiners and coroners are coming around a little better on that because they do it so frequently, it's one of their main work responsibilities, so they are conscientious in how they do it. And they are becoming more aware of the potential outcomes if the death certificate is not done correctly."

The 2004 NAME report observes, "Medical examiners perform their duties for the sake of the living and play important roles in law enforcement, public health, and other public good, realizing a sense of satisfaction from helping society. Unfortunately, their value is not always recognized; medical examiners may be regarded by uninformed public officials as mere technicians that handle and dissect bodies."

In reality, of course, forensic pathologists provide a critical function in the criminal justice system through the application of medical science to death investigation. The 2004 NAME report explains, "Forensic pathologists provide expert consultation to, among others, investigators, courts, prosecutors and defense counsel. They provide unbiased, legally and scientifically defensible determinations of the cause and manner of death; interpret the nature and mechanism of injuries; determine the significance of particular injuries and natural diseases; collect evidence; rule out potential confounding conditions, including natural disease processes; and provide attorneys with essential information." The forensic pathologist is valued for his or her independent, objective, and scientific opinions, and so often plays a pivotal role as front-line public health officials committed to preserving health and identifying causes of preventable and unnecessary deaths.

Medico-legal offices are plagued by shortages of qualified personnel, including forensic pathologists. Because a medico-legal death investigation system is only as good as its practitioners, and if the optimum system is led by a board-certified forensic pathologist, the country is headed down a rocky road of manpower shortfalls. Since 1959, the American Board of Pathology (ABP) has defined the educational and training requirements of this field and has provided specialty certification to its professionals. As we saw in Chapter 6, most forensic pathologists undergo at least nine years of formal education after college, including a medical degree, postgraduate residency in pathology, and additional formal training in forensic pathology and medico-legal death investigation, after which they must pass examinations in anatomic and forensic pathology in order to become board certified by the ABP. It is a challenging and rigorous occupational pursuit, and is reflected in the relatively low numbers of professionals who enter and remain in the field.

In 2003, there were approximately 989 board-certified forensic pathologists in the United States; of these only about 600 appear to be active in the field, and fewer than 400 serve as full-time forensic pathologists working within and/or directing statutorily constituted medico-legal death investigation systems. According to the 2004 NAME report, the United States will need a minimum of 800 full-time, board-certified forensic pathologists to maintain medico-legal autopsy workloads at acceptable levels. The report suggests further that "The limited availability of forensic pathologists suggests that many current practitioners are exceeding recommended caseloads and/or many medico-legal autopsies are being conducted by non-forensic pathologist practitioners. The potential hazards of this practice include errors, autopsies being performed by unqualified personnel (or not being performed at all), and manpower burnout and attrition."

"I think we have been holding our own with the number of people coming in forensic pathology," says Nolte. "Are we generating enough forensic pathologists to meet the nation's *future* needs? No, we are not. If we had the ability to wave a magic wand and convert all the coroners to medical examiners, we'd have to wave that magic wand again and create a number of forensic pathologists because they just don't exist to fill all of those spots. It's a critical pipeline; you must engage the medical students who then go on to become residents of pathology and then specialize in forensic pathology. It's hard to engage these medical students if you are not well represented in academic medical centers; and so if there are no forensic pathologists who expose the specialty to medical students, how are students even going to know our specialty is available? And what medical student in their right mind would go into a field they never have been exposed to?"

Nolte emphasizes there is a second opportunity to entice would-be forensic pathologists: "So now you can reach people who are in a pathology residency," he says. "Many of them have gone into pathology because they have been exposed to general pathology, surgical pathology, neuropathology, and they have their minds made up, but some are undecided, and so you have a chance to expose them to forensic pathology as residents. You can catch some doctors this way, but the best way is to reach them while they are still medical students, so they can choose a pathology residency and continue into forensic pathology, as opposed to someone who goes into general pathology and is not entirely sure they want to be in forensics—not that it doesn't happen, of course. But I think it benefits the system if the path to forensic pathology is straight and short. It also helps that the perception of forensic pathology is changing. I have noticed that people consider my job with a lot less horror than they did when I got involved in it many years ago. And I guess popular culture has helped, too. A better image helps recruit physicians into the field."

Hanzlick (2003) observes that fewer than half of Americans benefit from adequate and proper death investigation practices in their jurisdictions. The 2004 NAME report states, "Death investigation needs to be conducted in a timely manner and performed correctly and professionally the first time, every time. A functional, high-quality death investigation system requires the development and promotion of accreditation and professionalism in the autopsy facility, the performance of the forensic autopsy, and the associated investigation of the circumstances pertinent to the death and of the death scene itself."

According to the 2004 NAME report, "These uniquely and highly skilled physicians provide the public with unbiased, legally and scientifically defensible determinations of cause and manner of death as well as expert answers to other issues that may arise in evaluating a particular death or series of deaths. By systematically investigating death, they are able to recognize previously unsuspected homicides as well as deaths caused by conditions that might constitute a threat to public health." The report adds, "The daily practice of forensic pathology extends far beyond questions related to medicine and forensic pathology and often involves dealing with political entities, the media, law enforcement, the judicial system, healthcare systems, families of the deceased and members of the general public. Forensic pathologists serve as expert consultants to investigators, courts, prosecutors, and defense counsel. Resources available to and salaries for these busy practitioners must be significantly updated in order to protect the sanctity and quality of the investigation of the deaths of our citizens that fall jurisdictionally under their auspices. Medical examiners and forensic pathologists are part of the fabric of homeland security and have been and will continue to be frontline participants in the event of terrorist acts. They are actively involved in surveillance for biological terrorism and newly emerging infectious diseases, and their testimony will be of critical importance in any trials that occur subsequent to any future terrorist events that the United States experiences."

"It's tough for medico-legal offices to choose how to spend their dollars when the needs are great on all fronts," Hanzlick says. "In my opinion, if you have to choose, it's more important to get trained people in the areas where they are needed, more so than building up facilities and increasing infrastructure. That said, however, appropriate facilities are needed in order to provide adequate levels of service, and make it a safer and much nicer work environment. It's a tough decision for small jurisdictions that can't afford to do both. Overall, we need more death investigators, more forensic pathologists and support people, better-trained people in all categories, and updated or new facilities in many areas."

Salaries are yet another challenge for medico-legal offices and for the highly skilled forensic pathologists who are looking for appropriate compensation. Very few can challenge the value of the forensic pathologist, but in many jurisdictions throughout the country, the pathologist's pay and benefits are not keeping pace. As the 2004 NAME report states, "It is difficult to recruit and retain these physicians with substandard salaries, especially when most physicians have significant debt as a result of the high cost of a medical education."

Dobersen comments, "Medicine is in such a state of flux right now that a lot of people aren't going into some of the primary-care specialties because they are coming out of medical school with huge debt and they can't afford it; they have to go into a specialty where they can make money. Forensic pathologists tend to make less than general pathologists who can make twice as much as we do, so lower salaries will be a problem in attracting new people to the field."

According to the 2004 NAME report, "As medical examiners, forensic pathologists are generally forced to accept lower salaries than those received by practicing hospital pathologists or other physicians in general."

Dobersen remarks, "Pay is not always an indication of career satisfaction, of course; there are days when I say I can't believe they pay me to do this, and I consider that to be a high watermark for being satisfied in what you are doing. On the other hand, the hours can be long and unpredictable, and the work can be sobering, and many people can't reconcile themselves with that."

For Fierro, it's a double-edged sword; even if enough professionals entered the field and received adequate training, would they be hired in the right jobs that pay them a livable wage? Fierro comments, "We have the capacity to produce more forensic pathologists, for example, because there is a greater awareness of the field now more than ever before because of the popularity of forensic science as portrayed by the media. I think if you were to pay decently and have a decent facility, you would have no trouble getting those doctors. However, death investigators are a much more homogenous group. There are adequate opportunities for them to be educated and trained in the proper procedures for investigating death scenes, but you always hope that when they leave, they can find a good position. When I say a good position, it doesn't have to make you rich, necessarily, it just has to be one where you have the resources you need to do your job, a decent facility so you can perform your job safely and well, and sufficient pay in a location where you can afford to live or raise a family. Unless you are a native son or daughter in California, for example, I don't know how anyone could go out there and buy a house and raise a family. The cost of living out there is a killer. In places like Virginia or Maryland, which have very good costs of living, we don't have problems recruiting people because they can afford to live and work here."

Nolte says that low salaries are driving would-be forensic pathologists to cushier, better paying medical specialties, thus robbing the death investigation system of well-qualified individuals. "In the past few years, applications to family practice residency programs by medical students fell by about 50 percent, and applications to dermatology programs have gone up by at least 1,000 percent," Nolte says. "It isn't hard to see why when you consider that the average salary for a family practitioner is $120,000 to $130,000 while the average salary for a dermatologist is $250,000 to $300,000. These people are not dumb; they have huge debts accrued by being in medical school, and they look at their options. Medical students also look for fields that offer them some lifestyle options; general surgery applications have been falling because being a general surgeon, you get hammered all the time, and dermatology becomes attractive for the gentler lifestyle it offers."

Nolte emphasizes that forensic pathology is challenging, yet satisfying in its own way. "You pretty much work during the day, although yes, there are some night calls, and in some offices you go to homicide scenes," Nolte adds. "However, it is nowhere near like being an obstetrician, for example, who can be on call day and night. People die at night, of course, but you autopsy them during the day, and the ability to sleep at night and be awake during the day is a good thing. Still, the salaries remain so poor. If forensic pathology paid dermatology salaries, we'd see a rush of medical students going into our field. There is a big discrepancy between the salaries of forensic pathologists and surgical pathologists; even though forensic pathology is a sub-specialty, the people who are performing in a base-level specialty make more than the sub-specialist. In medicine, the general internists don't make more than the cardiologists, generally. The more training you have and the more specialized you are, generally you make a higher salary. You have more skills and more experience, but in forensic pathology, that doesn't translate."

In addition to lower salaries, another challenge to the retention of forensic pathologists is the workload. Randall (2001) surveyed board-certified forensic pathologists to determine their current practice situations in order to provide information useful to the public and to the organizations that represent forensic pathologists to better understand and meet the needs of the forensic pathology community. Of the 773 surveys that were mailed, 337 forensic pathologists replied, a return rate of about 45 percent. For pathology practice status, Randall discovered that 72 percent worked more than 30 hours per week; 11 percent worked between five and 30 hours per week; 5 percent worked fewer than five hours per week; and 12 percent no longer practiced in the field of pathology. In terms of age, 7 percent of these respondents were in their 30s; 32 percent were in their 40s; 29 percent were in their 50s; 19 percent were in their 60s; and 13 percent were 70 years of age or older. In terms of gender, 79 percent were male and 21 percent were female. In terms of forensic pathology practice setting, Randall found that 54 percent were employed by medical examiner or coroner systems; 13 percent worked under contract to medical examiner or coroner systems; 27 percent worked in private practice or consultation; and 6 percent responded as "other."

On the surface, it would appear that the medico-legal death investigation system is working, but scratch that surface a little more aggressively, and you will see a system that is barely getting by. "I think the whole mindset is that things are bad, but we can make it," observes Hanzlick. "People just accept the status quo; yes, we do too many autopsies but we're making it, and we'll continue doing them; or yes, it's nice to say we should send a doc out to all death scenes, but we just can't do that, and we're not going to do that. There seems to be an acceptance of the status quo in many areas within our profession. In the forensic laboratories, our colleagues face huge backlogs and significant caseloads, which is analogous to a worker in the department of family and children's services where there is supposed to be one caseworker for every 12 or 14 kids, and instead they are working 40 cases at a time. But they do it because they love the work, they know it needs to be done, and they just accept it. We, as forensic pathologists, do the same thing."

NAME advises that forensic pathologists aim to perform no more than about 250 autopsies annually. "That figure is about right," says Dobersen, who adds, "Before I got a partner, I was doing about 400 to 500 autopsies a year, and that was a lot. Now that I am doing about 250, I am able to balance that with other responsibilities that all forensic pathologists have, whether it's administrative tasks, teaching or giving lectures, or going to court."

Weedn says that many medico-legal offices that are tight on manpower push the upper limits and beyond of the NAME-recommended workload: "NAME standards firmly indicated that a forensic pathologist shouldn't do more than 250 autopsies a year, however, they tolerate up to 350 autopsies per year after which accreditation is no longer possible." Weedn continues, "If you push those limits, there is an increased margin for error and a tendency to make mistakes. It becomes easier and more tempting to skimp on the investigation as a whole. Also, that leaves no time to do the other things that make you valuable, like talk to high schools, visit medical schools, talk with your colleagues, lobby your representatives, do research, and maybe throw in some clinical forensic medicine practice. A lot of forensic pathologists pride themselves on speed, proclaiming, 'I can do an autopsy in 30 minutes,' but I think this is a statement of not taking sufficient care and it also suggests that the actual dissection of the body is the job—further investigation, reviewing the microscopic slides, correlating the toxicology results, generating the report, and testimony collectively take far more time than the autopsy dissection."

INFECTIOUS DISEASE SURVEILLANCE, BIOTERRORISM, MASS DISASTERS, AND HOMELAND SECURITY ISSUES

Infectious disease surveillance, bioterrorism, mass disasters, and homeland security issues—they combine to make up a tall order, but to a forensic pathologist, it's all in a day's work. One of the most critical services a forensic pathologist can provide is expert epidemiologic and surveillance in the realms of public health. In an age of threats from anthrax, smallpox, or even an avian influenza outbreak, or more sinister bioterrorism attempts with infectious agents and chemicals being used globally, the role of medical examiners becomes all the more critical to the safety and well-being of the American public. Because they investigate so many deaths annually, medical examiners and coroners are an important source of surveillance data for infectious disease-related deaths.

Wolfe et al. (2004) observe, "Increasing infectious disease deaths, the emergence of new infections, and bioterrorism have made surveillance for infectious diseases a public health concern. Medical examiners and coroners certify approximately 20 percent of all deaths that occur within the United States and can be a key source of information regarding infectious disease deaths." Wolfe et al. add, "Infectious disease deaths in the United States substantially declined during the first eight decades of the 20th century as a result of public health interventions. However, the end of the century was marked by an increase in infectious disease deaths primarily due to AIDS and pneumonia and influenza. Increasing infectious disease deaths, the emergence of new infections, and the real or perceived threat of bioterrorist activities have made surveillance for infectious diseases a public health need."

While most laypersons think that the bulk of medico-legal death investigation cases consist of violent or unnatural deaths, sudden natural deaths, unexplained deaths, and deaths of public health importance are also investigated by these medico-legal offices.

Natural disease deaths investigated by medical examiners and coroners are often caused by infectious processes, and their investigation frequently includes an autopsy. In recent years, medical examiners and coroners have recognized outbreaks of Hantavirus pulmonary syndrome and invasive pneumococcal disease, identified cases of human plague, and participated in the investigation of West Nile encephalitis. For example, in the 2001 outbreak of bioterrorism-related anthrax, all the deaths were investigated by medical examiners, thus medical examiner/coroner databases can be a significant repository of data about infectious diseases. (Wolfe et al., 2004).

There are obstacles in the way of this kind of information gathering, however. Sosin (2003) states, "Medical examiner and coroner data hold great potential for public health surveillance and, ultimately, public health intervention. But barriers stand in the way of adopting a national surveillance system that uses common data elements from medical examiner/coroner offices. Medical examiner/coroner data have a proven ability to detect clusters and unusual deaths. They can be probed more deeply by using the detailed information collected during a death investigation. The data might be used to discern risk factors that are key to developing preventive interventions. If tissue is banked, it can be analyzed to characterize the natural history of a new and emerging illness, such as those caused by hantavirus or HIV. Finally, medical examiner/coroner data can yield timely and specific information about an unfolding epidemic. The data provide considerable potential in real time for addressing terrorism and bioterrorism." The impediments to the development of a national surveillance system using data from medico-legal offices, according to Sosin, include variability in data quality with respect to training and experience, investigation procedures and reporting requirements, variability in technology and standards, and the lack of policies for data interchange.

In addition to domestic infectious agents such as HIV or Hantavirus or other emerging pathogens, Nolte (2003) states, "We need to be concerned about the emergence of bioterrorism as a threat. Bioterrorism is the deliberate use of a biologic agent or toxin against a civilian population to induce fear or terror. Bioterrorism-related infections can be viewed as a subset of emerging infections because they have increased in incidence and threaten to increase in the near future. Together, emerging infections and bioterrorism constitute a strong rationale for improving our overall disease and death reporting system. If the nation builds the capacity to recognize fatalities from emerging infectious diseases and from other infections of public-health consequence, then it will have the capacity to recognize fatalities from bioterrorism."

Nolte (2003) points to two incidents that underscore the important of vigilance: "In 1993, an alert medical examiner in New Mexico was the first to report a cluster of fatal cases of respiratory disease. Three days later, an Indian Health Service physician reported similar cases to the New Mexico Health Department. A rapid multi-agency investigation followed, and it led to the identification by the [Centers for Disease Control and Prevention] (CDC) of an emerging infectious disease, Hantavirus pulmonary syndrome, within weeks of recognition of the index case. Also in New Mexico, a young woman who died of anticoagulant poisoning from the suicidal ingestion of rat poison had a presentation that mimicked a fatal infection. The two cases illustrate the importance of a high-quality death investigation system in recognizing fatal emerging infections and infections of public health importance and in sorting out conditions such as toxins which may mimic infections."

Since 1919, U.S. forensic pathologists, through autopsy-based surveillance, have detected several emerging diseases, including plague, malaria, and West Nile encephalitis. (Nolte, 2003) Overall, infectious disease mortality increased by 58 percent from 1980 and 1992 (Pinner et al., 1996). Pathologists were the first to identify an outbreak of anthrax in 1979 in the former Soviet Union, and they even identified the route of infection as inhalation (Walker et al., 1994). Nolte (2003) notes, "Today, autopsy-based surveillance not only has the capacity to determine pathogenesis, but it has broader reach and more rapid detection through diagnostic advances in immuno-histochemistry and nucleic acid probes."

As noted with national systems of surveillance, there are barriers to more effective recognition of emerging infectious diseases by medical examiners and coroners. Nolte (2003) explains, "The bias of most systems is toward violent death. Forensic pathologists are well equipped to make general pathologic diagnoses (such as pneumonia) rather than organism-specific diagnoses (such as pneumococcal pneumonia). Many systems do not have access to sensitive diagnostic tests. If an autopsy is performed on an infectious disease death, there is no guarantee that the causative organism will be identified. The interpretation of post-mortem microbiologic cultures is fraught with difficulties including issues of postmortem overgrowth and contamination. Serology has its limitations in that death may precede a detectable immune response. Investigators and pathologists may lack the training or the resources to recognize potential infections."

Despite these disadvantages, many believe that medical examiners and coroners are a cornerstone in the country's response to a known bioterrorist event, characterized as the use or threatened use of biological agents or toxins against civilians with the objective of causing fear, illness, or death. Nolte (2003) explains that because deaths occurring from a terrorist attack are considered to be homicides, these fatalities fall under the jurisdiction of medical examiners and coroners who must perform medico-legal death investigations in these cases. Nolte observes, "Bioterrorism has the potential for causing mass fatalities. Medical examiners are adept at responding to mass disasters; their skill sets having been honed through aviation accidents, heat wave deaths, and other large scale catastrophes. An unknown or covert terrorist attack is more difficult to detect. If sentinel cases die unexpectedly without a clear diagnosis, they would fall under medical examiner/coroner jurisdiction. The quick response to the hantavirus pulmonary syndrome offers a good frame of reference because its symptoms mimic how a bioterrorism agent might present itself. Another event to use as a reference is the medical examiner/coroner's quick response to 1985 fatalities from cyanide-contaminated acetaminophen."

Nolte says that forensic pathologists can aid the efforts of the National Institutes of Health (NIH) and the CDC, two federal agencies that focus on public health and mechanisms of disease, because there are a number of diseases for which autopsies can cast new light on pathogenesis. "For example, the autopsies on individuals who died of hantavirus pulmonary syndrome here in New Mexico in the early 1990s led to the understanding that it was capillary leak syndrome," Nolte explains. "There are a number of conditions that could use autopsy-derived information to help us understand them even more. Right now infectious diseases are at the forefront of everyone's attention; autopsies certainly can help identify infectious diseases and in the understanding of the pathogenesis of infectious diseases, especially those that are precipitous. SIDS is a huge area, and another huge area is another common natural cause of death—coronary heart disease. People who die precipitously, often die of coronary heart disease. They usually get medical examiner autopsies. There is evidence to suggest that these deaths are potentially infectious—the question is whether *Chlamydia pneumoniae* bacteria is involved in the pathogenesis of atherosclerosis. What better arena for evaluating the pathogenesis of disease than a disease that has the afflicted individuals come to autopsy. The tissue can be evaluated with new diagnostic methods. The problem is the individuals who have the diagnostic methods are not performing the autopsies; the individuals who perform the autopsies don't have the diagnostic method, so there needs to be some push to bring these sorts of groups together."

Mass disasters also test the mettle of the U.S. medico-legal death investigation system, as we saw briefly in Chapter 7. Fierro (2003) states, "Terrorism and mass disasters pose enormous challenges to medical examiner and coroner systems. The systems have dealt with plane crashes, train crashes, fires, and floods, but not with mass homicides. The magnitude of the deaths is a challenge, considering that terrorism brings the prospect of thousands of simultaneous deaths."

In most cases of mass disaster or terrorism, the federal government is the primary vehicle for investigation, whether it is through its National Transportation Safety Board (NTSB) or through the Federal Bureau of Investigation (FBI). Many medico-legal offices have rarely worked with the federal government in the management of local disasters, and so there are particular challenges related to jurisdictional issues such as access to the scene and to working cooperatively with federal agencies such as the FBI.

The 2001 anthrax experience in the commonwealth of Virginia revealed other problems of preparedness. Fierro (2003) explains, "It pointed to the likelihood that sentinel bioterrorism deaths would probably be declined by the medical examiner system because the event would not necessarily have been identified as resulting from bioterrorism, leaving the private physician with the responsibility for signing the (death) certificate. Virginia does not have a surveillance system that would allow the identification of bioterrorism deaths with any certainty. If cases are identified, one of the first decisions will be whether the bodies can be dealt with on site, at the medical examiner/coroner facility, which might risk site contamination."

Fierro (2003) explains further that debate arises about which types of cultures to take, or which first responders and other medical professionals should be exposed; surge capacity at local health-care facilities for survivors of a mass disaster is another troubling issue. Fierro notes, "Research has documented that mass disasters impose enormous strain; measures must be taken to help workers cope with the overwhelming stress of death and destruction." A highly sensitive issue is the final disposition of bodies. Fierro explains, "Bodies containing some infectious agents cannot safely be returned to families. In other cases, the medical examiner or coroner may not be able to identify human remains at all. This is a very difficult issue for a nation that has never resorted to mass graves."

One of the greatest tests for the United States was the destruction of the World Trade Center (WTC) in New York City on September 11, 2001. Altman (2001) calls the WTC "the largest effort in the annals of forensic medicine." Medico-legal professionals were responsible for providing evidence for those investigating the attacks and to providing answers to family members and friends.

"You don't really know how good the system is until you stress it," says Dobersen, a forensic pathologist and coroner who assisted in the investigation alongside hundreds of others from the field of death investigation. "I don't think there can be any greater stress than a mass fatality incident, a plane crash, or a force of nature like Hurricane Katrina, and that's when you see where the deficiencies are in the system. There probably isn't a jurisdiction in the country that wouldn't be deficient in some way under those kinds of circumstances. I think now, more and more, ever since 9/11, you see what a great job they did in Manhattan, and the extent of the work required of medico-legal professionals. There was no expense spared in trying to identify those victims, the effort was massive, and it was really something to see. You can't say enough about what they did and what it meant to the families."

One of the primary responses to a mass disaster in the United States is through the Disaster Mortuary Operational Response Team (DMORT), a federal-level response team designed to provide assistance in the case of a mass fatality incident and mandated to work under local jurisdictional authorities such as medical examiners and coroners, law enforcement officers, and municipal emergency managers. In the early 1980s, a committee was formed within the National Funeral Directors Association to address disaster situations and, specifically, mass fatality incidents. This group found that no standardization existed, and worked toward creating a national protocol for the formation of a proper response. Initially, the group focused on the role of funeral directors, but it was soon discovered that no single profession could handle all of the aspects of a catastrophic event. A multifaceted nonprofit organization open to all forensic practitioners was formed by the committee to support the idea of a national-level response protocol for all related professions. This group formed and purchased the first portable morgue unit in the country to support DMORT missions. Soon after this non-profit group of volunteers had formed, government interest in this topic came to the forefront. Families who had lost loved ones in airline crashes felt that the treatment that they had received was inadequate and demanded a response from Congress. As a result, Congress passed the Family Assistance Act in October 1996 and required all U.S.-based airlines to have a plan that would assist families in a mass-disaster scenario.

In 2003, DMORT was placed under the U.S. Department of Homeland Security as part of the National Disaster Medical System (NDMS). On activation for a natural disaster, terrorism event, or aviation or technologic disaster, its approximate 1,200 trained volunteers forensic, morgue, family-assistance, and management personnel become temporary government employees who supply portable morgue units, computerized morgue management, and specialized protocols for victim identification and family assistance. DMORT personnel are private citizens, each with mortuary or forensic expertise and with licensure and certification recognized by all states. Teams can be activated in any region of the United States when the capabilities of local resources are exceeded. Sledzick (2003) emphasizes DMORT's value, noting the system's work during the terrorist attacks of 2001 when DMORT teams were summoned by the coroner of Somerset, Pennsylvania, to the site of the crash of United Airlines Flight 93.

FEDERAL SUPPORT OF MEDICO-LEGAL OFFICES AND AGENCIES

As we have seen, medico-legal offices play a critical role in response to bioterrorism, mass disaster, and homeland security–related events, and work frequently with federal agencies to manage these high-profile death scenes. However, there is a chasm between the federal government and these medico-legal offices and forensic laboratories when it comes to the financial and organizational support these agencies need to fulfill their responsibilities to public health and security and to the criminal justice system.

"Forensic science is heavily woven into homeland security and disaster response," says W. Earl Wells, president of the American Society of Crime Lab Directors (ASCLD) and laboratory director of the South Carolina Law Enforcement Division. "If a catastrophic event occurs, it's going to be the forensic science community that responds, through medical examiners and coroners, DMORT teams, and lab personnel. It's the criminalist who collects the evidence and the forensic scientist and forensic pathologist who is going to tell us what happened. Forensic science is going to be right in the middle of it all, and yet our needs, relating to our ability to provide services, are not being recognized as they should."

The 2004 NAME report comments, "To date, the federal government has focused limited attention on medico-legal death investigation. Although traditionally a state or local function, medico-legal death investigation also serves the federal interests, since assuring citizen safety is a basic function of government. The federal government should thus recognize the value of medico-legal death investigation for criminal justice, public health, and homeland security and should actively support it via the National Institute of Justice (NIJ) for law enforcement issues, the Centers for Disease Control and Prevention (CDC) for public health issues, and the Department of Homeland Security (DHS) for homeland security and mass fatality issues. These agencies should take the lead in developing programs to assist medico-legal death investigation systems in the United States."

According to the 2004 NAME report, the only current federal medical examiner system is the Armed Forces Medical Examiner System, a specialty operation that primarily serves military combat and training casualties. NAME suggests that the federal government could begin to establish the infrastructure of a national support system by consolidating the DMORT division of the NDMS. The 2004 NAME report states, "The proper way to improve America's death investigation system is to ensure competent coverage for all citizens, no matter where they die—or live. Perpetrators of crimes should understand that no matter where in the United States a crime is committed, an expert investigation will be conducted. Furthermore, families of victims as well as the general public should be confident that a thorough and proficient death investigation will be conducted regardless of the jurisdiction in which a death, criminal or otherwise, occurs. Several groups are vitally important in addressing the weak links in the current system. NAME is willing to take the lead on many of these issues, but needs the support of local, state, and federal government officials and agencies that are responsible for public health and safety concerns."

In its 2004 report, NAME states, "To date, there has been limited interest in or support for medico-legal death investigation from the federal government, despite the fact that protection of citizen safety is a fundamental government function. By systematically investigating deaths, medical examiners recognize unsuspected homicides and other deaths from wrong-doing, as well as those deaths caused by diseases or other means constituting a threat to the public. The independent, objective, and scientific opinions of forensic pathologists educate society and help appropriately illuminate suspicious deaths. The federal government should recognize and actively support competent professional medico-legal death investigation as a critical component of criminal justice, public health, and homeland security, with value that transcends state and local interests."

As we have seen, medico-legal personnel and offices support several important pillars of society. In the criminal justice system, medico-legal professionals apply medical science to death investigation. For example, it is the forensic pathologist or medical examiner, and not a member of law enforcement, who possesses the expertise to address the medical issues that arise in homicides. It is also the forensic pathologist or the medical examiner, and not the detective or police investigator, who will testify in court as to the cause of death and address the medical issues pertinent to the case. As the 2004 NAME report states, "Perhaps most important is the ability to distinguish when facts and accounts fit the mechanism of death or injury and when they do not. Sometimes, the forensic pathologist will recognize an apparent natural death to be a homicide, and at other times examination may reveal a death to be a suicide, natural disease or other process rather than from a homicidal act."

There is no denying that medico-legal professionals fulfill their responsibilities to the criminal justice system, but the federal government, tasked with the care and feeding of the medico-legal system, some say, is not doing all it can to support this essential system. While it has demonstrated support for the forensic laboratory system, it has been only recently that the NIJ, of the Department of Justice, has expressed interest in the medical examiner and coroner community. In 2003 it participated in the aforementioned Institute of Medicine workshop on medico-legal death investigation in the United States, and several years earlier, had supported the creation of the national standards for medico-legal death investigators. However, as the 2004 NAME study points out, "The only NIJ funds that have been expended for medical examiner infrastructure have been from the recent and poorly funded Coverdell Act."

As we have seen earlier, medical examiners support public health by identifying the causes of preventable and unnecessary deaths, and through a system of standardized death report-ing, they furnish epidemiological data that provide information on population-based disease and injury patterns. Also, because they conduct medico-legal autopsies, forensic pathologists provide the best source of information on causes of death, especially those that are sudden and unexpected and those due to violence. According to the 2004 NAME report, "Medical examiners provide valuable information on deaths from drugs and alcohol, domestic violence, child abuse, and other patterns of injury and disease that affect the community at large. They provide surveillance for emerging infectious diseases, dangerous work environments, environmental conditions, adverse drug reactions, defective products and medical therapy-related deaths."

We have also seen the significant contribution medico-legal offices and personnel make in homeland security-related events. The 2004 NAME report states, "Forensic pathologists are part of the fabric of homeland security and should be recognized as first responders." In a mass fatality situation such as in the World Trade Center attacks, forensic pathologists led the efforts to not only determine the causes of deaths but to identify the victims. In addition, medical examiners are critical to effective national surveillance of emerging infections, ter-rorist threats, and infectious disease outbreaks. The 2004 NAME report asserts, "The threats to the public from emerging infections, bioterrorism and other attacks do not respect political boundaries. As state and local jurisdictions discover and grapple with them separately, precious time is lost until a coordinated response can be mounted. Clearly, this is of prime federal interest."

A logical relationship between medico-legal offices and a federal agency would be with the CDC; however, the 2004 NAME report observes, "The support of the CDC has waxed and waned over the years and has neither garnered significant consistent high-level CDC support nor substantially systemically impacted medical examiner office infrastructure."

In 1986, triggered in part by the lack of uniformity in death investigation policies and practices, the frequent lack of communication between jurisdictions, and the need for more widespread distribution of death investigation data, the CDC established the Medical Examiner and Coroner Information Sharing Program (MECISP) program, with the goals of improving the quality of death investigations in the United States and to promote the use of more standardized policies for when and how to conduct these investigations; facilitating communication among death investigators, the public health community, federal agencies, and other interested groups; improving the quality, completeness, management, and dissemination of information on investigated deaths; and promoting the sharing and use of medical examiner and coroner death investigation data.

Because medical examiners and coroners are responsible for investigating sudden or violent deaths and for providing accurate, legally defensible determinations of the causes of these deaths, the data provided by these professionals play a critical role in the judicial system and in decisions made by public safety and public health agencies. The records of medical examiners and coroners, which provide vital information about patterns and trends of mortality in the United States, are also a viable source of data for public health studies and surveillance. Through financial and technical support, the MECISP program was designed to assist medical examiners and coroners in the collection, management, and dissemination of data. Other benefits of the program included MECISP's ability to develop model death investigation forms and file structures as well as model formats for annual and statistical death investigation reports; collaborate with medical examiners, coroners, public health researchers, and others in epidemiologic studies of deaths routinely investigated by medico-legal professionals; and consult with medical examiner and coroner offices to help them establish computerized data systems. To the detriment of medical examiners and coroners everywhere, the lifeblood of the MECISP program, the Epidemiology Program Office, ceased to exist after September 30, 2004, due to a CDC reorganization process, with funding for the program ending approximately a month later.

"The medical examiner program started out in the National Center for Environmental Health and the folks there, over time, came to view the medical examiner program as a burden because they couldn't see how it fit into their narrow environmental health perspective," says Nolte. "So about four or five years ago they passed it off to the Epidemiology Program Office (EPO), viewing that office as the cross-cutting program at the CDC because it intersects with all of the other programs; they figured that would be a good place for the medical examiner/coroner program since MEs and coroners themselves intersect with so many different programs. When it got to the EPO, nobody watered the plant, so to speak. And it started dropping leaves, started losing epidemiologists and the funding for it, so they eventually cut the contracting medical examiners. Then the EPO was consumed in the CDC's re-organization process and the ME program was dropped; it was never picked up, never given a home, never re-vitalized. So it's gone, and that's a shame because the program was actually the only interface between the medical examiner community and the public health community. Through this program was how the CDC distributed to the medical examiner's public health information, support for information systems, and case evaluation, and it also was how the medical examiner system communicated with the CDC. So now, there's a chasm between our principal public health agency and the medico-legal death investigation institutions, which is unbelievable."

NAME advocates a more structured, cohesive, and supportive federal stance on medico-legal needs and issues. The 2004 NAME report states, "Medical examiners fall between the cracks in an orphaned community, not truly claimed by law enforcement, public health, or traditional medicine. Law enforcement sees us as public health, public health sees us as law enforcement, and traditional medicine scarcely acknowledges our existence. There is currently no lead agency or proponent for forensic pathology and medico-legal death investigation issues within the federal government."

To address this deficit, NAME states that the NIJ should operate as the lead agent for law enforcement, the CDC should be the lead agent for public health issues, and the DHS should be the lead agent for homeland security and mass fatality issues. The 2004 NAME report suggests further, "These agencies should develop programs to assist medico-legal death investigation systems in the United States." As NAME envisions it, Congress must fully appropriate funding as designated in the Coverdell authorization language, seeing that it is the only existing mechanism to directly assist state and local medical examiner and coroner offices with infrastructure-related needs. The NAME adds that the CDC and NIJ should foster an effort to computerize and connect offices to permit information sharing between medical examiner offices and agencies of the local, state, and federal governments as an expansion of the current National Violent Death Reporting System. NAME further advises the resurrection of the National Office of Death Investigation Affairs, to include the CDC, NIJ, and other appropriate federal agencies that would pay a small fee for use of the data extracted from this network.

The 2004 NAME report states that despite a significant budget, the NIH has not been a substantial source of research funding for the medical examiner community, even though medical examiners handle numerous high-priority, public health–related issues and "are the last stronghold of autopsy pathology." The report adds, "Nonetheless, most forensic pathology research is not considered basic research, but rather applied (or translational) research, and is otherwise not a favored area of research for funding by NIH. The NIH should develop a program of research on causes and mechanisms of deaths that is accessible to forensic pathologists in medical examiner offices; topics should include child abuse, gun violence, drug overdoses, transportation safety, autopsy surveillance for medical errors, etc. Investigators involved in projects dealing with such topics should be encouraged to include forensic pathologists in their studies. The NIJ should convene technical working groups of forensic pathologists and others to deal with related law enforcement issues."

Nolte (2003) issues a critique of federal support of the medico-legal community. He observes, "To be fair, NIJ has had substantial funding for the forensic sciences only recently. It also is probably true that the medical examiner community has not aggressively pursued NIJ projects. Regardless, NIJ could and should play a greater role in the support of the law-enforcement aspects of medico-legal death investigations. Substantial funding of the Paul Coverdell National Forensic Sciences Act and the National Forensic Science Improvement Act would help. However, NIJ most recently announced a DNA initiative to the exclusion of all other segments of forensic-science funding."

As for the CDC, Nolte (2003) alludes to this agency's support by way of "a small but important subsidy for the NAME annual meeting over many years," as well as the funding of several projects such as the investigation of unrecognized sudden deaths due to infectious diseases. Regarding the NIH, Nolte observes that the agency has "not been an important source of research funding, even for the medical examiner community, because forensic pathology research is not considered basic research. Seen as translational or applied, it is not a favored field of NIH research. Medical examiners have occasionally been asked to serve as consultant reviewers for investigations on drowning, SIDS, and the like. As forensic pathologists become the major experts in autopsy examinations, as medical examiners conduct more hospital autopsies, and as autopsies become more important sources of human tissue, NIH interest may increase."

Nolte (2003) points to what he characterizes as "virtually no funding" for medical examiner offices or its projects, adding, "Perhaps most important, the federal government seemingly has no interest in forensic pathology or medical examiners. Other than the small office in the military, there are no medical examiner offices in the federal government. It might seem logical that the CDC, FBI, or National Transportation Safety Board . . . would have forensic-pathology staff but they do not. They might, however, maintain contracts with experts to provide forensic pathology consultation."

Regarding this seeming lack of federal commitment, Nolte (2003) observes, "The message seems to be that the federal government has no interest in forensic pathologists or medical examiners. One might conclude that crimes resulting in death are not given a high priority in federal investigations. Certainly, dead victims will not bring lawsuits, complain to newspapers, or testify before Congress. As states look to the federal government as a role model, they see a medical examiner office in the military. That is not very relevant to the states. A medical examiner office could be situated in public health, but experience shows that it will always lose out in priority to live patients. A medical examiner office could be situated in law enforcement, which has a substantially better political lobby, but then it would not be seen as objective, would be misunderstood, and would lose out to the cop on the street. A medical examiner office is probably too small an endeavor to stand on its own as an agency in the federal government. It would stand a far better chance if combined with the federal crime laboratory as a department of forensic-science services, as is done in England. Indeed, it has often been argued that the forensic sciences should conceptually be on neutral turf and not in a prosecutorial or investigative agency. Theoretically, DHS is a possible home for a medical examiner office."

Nolte (2003) joins other commentators who have wondered aloud about the lack of a truly comprehensive regulatory system of oversight for medico-legal offices in the United States. Nolte acknowledges, "Theoretically, state medical licensure boards could oversee the medical practices, but in reality they fail to do so. In fact, some forensic pathologists continue to practice without medical licenses. Judicial scrutiny seems ineffective to weed out poor practices. Voluntary NAME accreditation standards have yet to be adopted by a majority of medical examiner jurisdictions. Medical examiners often lose their jobs over scandals when longstanding poor practices or misunderstood practices are publicized. Investigations of deaths from child abuse, elderly abuse, and domestic violence are important to many federal agencies but do not support the offices that form the basis of the investigations." Nolte adds, "One might consider medical examiner work to be essentially an unfunded federal mandate. Unless NIJ and CDC truly adopt the medical examiner community or a new lead federal agency is created, possibly in DHS, the medical examiner/coroner community will continue as an orphan without to a parent to care for and feed it."

THE QUALITY OF MEDICO-LEGAL DEATH INVESTIGATION IN THE UNITED STATES

As we have seen, a highly variable entity such as the current U.S. medico-legal death investigation system faces a number of factors that conspire against it. In its 2004 report, NAME articulates an ideal system: "The federal government should specifically develop a goal of quality medico-legal death investigation available to all U.S. citizens. Such a system should be based upon professional death investigation systems employing fully trained and qualified forensic pathologists with competent investigative and support staffs. Specifically, coroner systems should be eventually replaced by medical examiner systems wherein forensic pathologists oversee death investigations and certify the cause, manner, and circumstances of investigated deaths. The first important step is to enable appropriate distribution of forensic pathologists throughout the United States so they are readily available to all systems. Death investigation systems should be regionally based where needed to create a sufficient population to support the system. The federal government should develop incentives and programs to help states attain this goal. Since there is an insufficient number of board-certified forensic pathologists currently, the Department of Health and Human Services (DHHS) should establish policies to help attract physicians into the practice of forensic pathology. The federal government should help promote coverage of all Americans by board-certified forensic pathologists by fully funding the Coverdell Act and providing such additional federal monies as are necessary to build a national infrastructure and attract and train additional forensic pathologists, create additional full-time forensic pathologist positions, and help retain practicing forensic pathologists with competitive salaries and reasonable workloads."

As it stands now, much of the legwork conducted in medico-legal offices is done by death investigators. While the skill level of the forensic pathologist is critical to the quality of medico-legal death investigations, so is the competency of these lay death investigators who have become invaluable members of the medico-legal team. In most death investigations, the parameters for the examination of the body at a death scene are established by the jurisdiction's policies and procedures for medical examiners and coroners. In general, the body is held in the custody of the medical examiner or coroner while the scene itself is held in the custody of law enforcement. Jurisdictions dictate the level of involvement of medical examiners and coroners at the death scene; while some medical examiners attend the death scene, others delegate the work to investigators with varying levels of training and experience.

Up until about a decade ago, these individuals received on-the-job training but had no specified educational background or curriculum. The essential skills required of a death investigator now have been defined and have become the basis for professional certification by the American Board of Medico-Legal Death Investigators (ABMDI), which has about 800 registered death investigators. Around the same time, NIJ cultivated the development of national guidelines for death scene investigation, which promulgate more than 25 investigative tasks to be performed at every death scene, to further enhance standardization of scene processing.

Although the NIJ guidelines are voluntary, many medical examiner and coroner offices have adopted them as part of their standard operating practices, and a number of states have created statutory requirements for death scene investigators relating to a minimum number of hours of training and education, supplemented with standardized testing. However, according to a 2004 NAME report, "The largest challenges underlying inadequate scene investigations are the shortage of adequate personnel and the funds to train them. Death investigators at every level should have adequate training and perform their duties in accord with professionally accepted standards. The federal government can help by providing funding for training and professional certification of death investigators."

As we have seen, serving to further enhance the professionalism of medico-legal death investigation was the establishment and publication by the NIJ of the first cohesive standards for death scene investigations. Clark (2003) states, "The publication was the culmination of a five-year process that had been triggered by a national needs-assessment survey: in 1994, 60 percent of medical examiners and coroners had reported their dissatisfaction or extreme dissatisfaction with the level of investigative service that they received, either externally or internally."

The guidelines were welcomed by members of the forensic pathology community who long had detected inadequacies in the way some investigations were being conducted, as well as a lack of standards to guide the investigation process. Case (1999) comments on the "tremendous importance of medico-legal death investigation in the proper administration of justice and criminal proceedings, adjudicating estates, and handling of death certification," while Davis (1999) observes, "Sudden death investigation is multidisciplinary, with involvement of scientists representing . . . pathology, odontology, criminalistics, toxicology, psychiatry, questioned documents, jurisprudence, and even engineering. None of these scientists can be truly effective if the death investigation is faulted by errors of omission or commission during the initial scene investigation. Eventually, states . . . will see the wisdom of uniform quality of standards and training for medico-legal death investigators."

According to Hanley (1999), the guidelines "promote consistency, accuracy, predictability, and reliability in death scene investigations." They also can "eliminate unanswered questions, confusion, sloppiness, and lack of attention to detail" while assisting investigators in "following the proper protocol and consistently obtaining all available evidence to show that the death was the result of either unlawful or lawful activity. Proper adherence to the guidelines, coupled with proper training to implement the guidelines, will serve to satisfy finders of fact in criminal cases that the state has presented accurate, reliable, and trustworthy evidence. Additionally, it will serve to defuse attacks by defense counsel on the investigative methods and techniques, chain of custody, and the reliability of any testing that may have been conducted during the course of the investigation. It may also serve to prevent innocent people from being accused of criminal activity when, in fact, a crime was not committed, or the person suspected was not involved. The truth is the outcome sought, and the guidelines will assist the system in obtaining the truth. In a criminal investigation, when the government follows the rules and properly conducts its investigation, it will win most of the time. When it does not follow the rules or properly conduct its investigation, it should lose."

Most importantly, the guidelines can help level the playing field. Hanzlick (1999) observes, "Variations in statutes, levels of funding, geography and population density, and death investigator education, training, and experience result in variations in the quality and extent of medico-legal death investigations. Front-line, on-scene death investigations are performed by people whose jobs range from part-time to full-time, and whose education, training, and experience vary substantially and range from minimal to extensive. The outcome of death investigations may impact personal liberty and well-being, adjudication of cases, public health and safety, mortality statistics, research capabilities, and governmental approaches to legislation and programs. Therefore, high-quality death investigation throughout the United States is a desirable goal for many reasons. The creation of guidelines for medico-legal death investigations is one method of promoting uniformity in the approach to death investigations and improving or assuring their quality at the same time. Guidelines may also be used as a basis for developing educational programs, to evaluate work performance, and as a basis for credentialing or certification of death investigators."

Hanzlick (1999) cautions, however, that the guidelines, in and of themselves, are not enough: "The best intended and designed guidelines will have little effect if death investigators are not provided with funds adequate to meet the provisions of the guidelines. Funding for the education and training of death investigation practices and for the implementation of the guidelines will be necessary, and funding needs pose a significant obstacle to the long-term goal of nationwide improvement in death investigation practices. Governments at every level of organization will need to explore methods for acquiring or providing funds and providing the education, training, and manpower to effectively implement these and any subsequent guidelines."

The guidelines also serve as much-needed guidance for lay coroners without a comprehensive medico-legal background from which to draw. Kearns (1999) explains, "Historically, the office of coroner has been charged with the responsibilities and duties of answering pertinent questions related to death investigation: who, what, when, where, how, and why. Only when these questions have been answered correctly can all the proper legal issues that arise at death be handled expertly and completely for the administration of justice." Kearns adds, "These guidelines provide the necessary policies and procedures for universal and professional death-scene investigations, as well as the criteria for when to be suspicious. And by having properly coordinated death-scene investigative procedures, the community, the legal system, and family members will be well served. Coroners who are well trained in their jobs make fewer mistakes. The more training and confidence coroners have, the better our offices will run. An ideal coroner's office is well prepared to investigate and evaluate a scene, to examine a body, to write quality reports, and to interact with the family, all in a professional manner." Kuhler (1999) concurs, commenting, "With no official training required for elected coroners, it is difficult for the elected coroner to know what should be done in investigations. Most elected coroners have begun their jobs with little or no knowledge as to how and what they need to do. Having a set of national guidelines for medico-legal death investigation would ensure that at least the elected coroner would have a 'cookbook' to follow and would have some idea of what is expected of him/her in every case."

It may come as a surprise to the layperson that the country's medico-legal death investigation system is served by a relatively small number of forensic professionals who are specially trained and credentialed in their specialties. As we have seen, a medico-legal death investigator is an agent of the medical examiner and is generally the first point of contact for law enforcement; responsible for determining the details of the death and for assisting in the scientific identification of the deceased and in locating and notifying next of kin. The ABMDI offers two levels of credentials for death investigators.

Toxicologists are certified by the American Board of Forensic Toxicology, which offers two levels of certification: board-certified toxicologist and forensic-toxicology specialist, with about 185 people certified at one of those levels. Forensic odontologists apply dental science to the identification of human remains and make bite-mark comparisons by using both physical and biologic evidence. They are required to have a doctorate in dental science and specialized forensic training. About 90 people are certified by the American Board of Forensic Odontology. Forensic anthropologists are physical anthropologists who assist in the identification of skeletal remains. They can determine whether the remains are of human or animal origin; the deceased person's sex, age, and race; marks of trauma and occupational stress; and health status. Many are also trained in archaeological procedures. They are often used in facial reproduction when only the skull of the deceased person remains. There are about 64 people certified by the American Board of Forensic Anthropology. Only a handful of forensic entomologists are certified by the American Board of Forensic Entomology; these professionals study insects and other arthropods to identify the time of death, and, to help to determine the location of death, they can analyze whether fauna are indigenous or foreign to the site where the body was found (Ernst, 2003).

Akin to the death investigation guidelines, practice standards for forensic pathologists were also a somewhat political endeavor. "The forensic pathology practice standards weren't promulgated by NAME until 2005, and they almost didn't pass," Weedn says. "It was very close. I'm an ardent proponent of the standards, but I suspect many in the forensic pathology community were really naïve and frightened. Cynicism and fear can paralyze people. When you look at the standards, you think, 'So what's in here that anyone could possibly disagree with?' The various elements of the standards were put out for a vote. Now, in fact, there are a few things with which I disagree in the standards, but by and large they put into place what most people do already."

The *Forensic Autopsy Performance Standards*, approved on August 17, 2005, by NAME, state: "Medico-legal death investigation officers, be they appointed or elected, are charged by statute to investigate deaths deemed to be in the public interest—serving both the criminal justice and public health systems. These officials must investigate cooperatively with, but independent from, law enforcement and prosecutors. The parallel investigation promotes neutral and objective medical assessment of the cause and manner of death. To promote competent and objective death investigations: Medico-legal death investigation officers should operate without any undue influence from law enforcement agencies and prosecutors; and a forensic pathologist or representative shall evaluate the circumstances surrounding all reported deaths."

"The creation of these practice standards was about a two-year project involving huge discussions among members of the profession about whether we should even do it or not do it," recalls Randy Hanzlick, M.D., chief medical examiner for Fulton County in Georgia, and professor of pathology and laboratory medicine at Emory University. "There was also a lot of discussion as to whether they should be called guidelines or standards; people were afraid that if they worked in an office that couldn't meet 'standards,' they'd be sued for not accomplishing these best practices. The organization decided to go ahead and pursue them as standards and then at our annual meeting, they were voted on and there was a slim margin, but they were approved. There were arguments about whether they should just be voted on at the meeting which is typically how the group passes things, or whether they should be put out in a mailed ballot and have people who were not at the meeting represented. We went around and around on that. They were adopted in the fall of 2005 finally. So now we have these forensic autopsy performance standards, and there are disclaimers in there that not all offices are going to be able to meet these and that they are recommended guidelines, with the hope that some day everybody will at least be able to meet these basic tenets in every medico-legal office."

Hanzlick shares the detailed process of hammering out the guidelines: "A committee was formed to identify the most critical aspects of what we as forensic pathologists do. It was important to separate these elements from NAME's office-related standards within its accreditation program, which has to do with office policy and procedure rather than personal professional performance. The new standards were meant to deal with personal performance. For example, if you are a forensic pathologist and you are asked to work in an office that lacks access to an X-ray machine, should you even take that job? Can you do your job without an X-ray machine? There was a long list of basics, and we put that list out to the NAME membership and had them vote on whether they thought these items were important and whether they should be routinely performed by everyone. We whittled that list down and only considered elements, with very few exceptions, that had greater than a 90 percent approval rate. Over the ensuing year there were arguments about those, and the list got whittled down further. I think that the final product is pretty good."

The 20-page NAME standards address a wide range of issues, including medico-legal death investigation responsibilities, forensic autopsy protocols, procedures for identification, examination, and issues related to support services and documentation.

One issue raised by the standard development process is that of variability in the way individual medico-legal offices handle different investigations. "It is important to know what is going on in various jurisdictions, and this became apparent when we started working on the new standards," Hanzlick says. "People train somewhere, they get used to doing things how they are done in that jurisdiction, and they may not realize how things are done in other areas. A good example might be that one office may autopsy everybody who is burned up in a fire. Another office may just X-ray the body to ensure there are no bullets in it. They have been doing it that way forever and they feel they haven't had any problems but then they start thinking, 'Well gee, if that other office is autopsying all those bodies, there must be a reason for it, and maybe we should, too.' When you go out into the rural areas, it's probably even worse because perhaps there are people not fully aware of the issues and trends in metropolitan areas. That's when standards become valuable."

QUALITY OF SERVICE AND ACCREDITATION OF MEDICO-LEGAL OFFICES

According to the 2004 NAME report, of the 460-plus facilities performing forensic autopsies in the United States, only about 40 are accredited. The report states, "The majority of offices have not attempted to become accredited or cannot meet accreditation standards because they have inadequate staff, facilities, equipment, funding, or a combination of these factors. Many offices do not have such basic equipment as an X-ray machine and at least one-third do not meet the federal government's minimum safety guidelines. Some do not have available necessary laboratory services such as histology, microbiology, clinical testing, and genetic/metabolic services that are essential to competent and timely death investigation services."

Within forensic science, there are several opportunities for accreditation. As discussed in Chapters 4 and 5, ASCLD/LAB inspects and accredits crime laboratories in the areas of drug identification, toxicology, trace evidence, firearms examination, questioned documents, forensic serology, DNA testing, and latent print examination. For medical examiner offices and systems, accreditation is achieved through NAME. In addition, the Accreditation Council on Graduate Medical Education (ACGME) has an inspections and accreditation program related to training programs for physicians in various aspects of medicine, including pathology and forensic pathology.

Hanzlick (2003) states that the quality of a death investigation system can be difficult to assess but it can be measured by several indicators, including accreditation of medico-legal offices by NAME. If this is the case, it may be shocking to learn that in 2003, only 42 of the nation's medical examiner offices—serving approximately 23 percent of the population—have been accredited by NAME in recent years, and that most of the U.S. population (77 percent) is served by offices lacking accreditation (Hanzlick, 2003). As of August 2005, there were approximately 45 NAME-accredited facilities in the United States.

NAME offers an accreditation program consisting of peer review based on standards developed to improve the quality of medico-legal death investigation. Inspections are conducted by board-certified forensic pathologists associated with an accredited facility; their inspection is based on a series of inquiries that determine essential (Phase I) and nonessential (Phase II) elements; accreditation is conferred for a duration of five years, after which the office must undergo re-inspection. If an office or system fails to achieve sufficiently few deficiencies for full accreditation but is found to have fewer than 25 Phase I and fewer than 5 Phase II deficiencies, then provisional accreditation status can be conferred for 12 months. An office can extend its provisional accreditation for up to four subsequent sequential 12-month periods through written application and proof to NAME's Inspection and Accreditation Committee that there have been and are ongoing efforts to address deficiencies that continue to foreclose full accreditation. If the office has more than 25 Phase I deficiencies or more than five Phase II deficiencies, NAME will not accredit it. Coroner's offices may apply for inspection and accreditation, but must meet the same standards as medical examiner offices; coroners or coroner's pathologists, as office chiefs, must meet the personnel requirements of chief medical examiners.

The NAME accreditation manual explains that its standards were designed to improve the quality of the medico-legal death investigation. Accreditation applies to offices and systems, not individual practitioners, and the standards emphasize policies and procedures, not professional work product. The standards represent minimum standards for an adequate medico-legal system, not guidelines. The manual states, "NAME accreditation is an endorsement by NAME that the office or system provides an adequate environment for a medical examiner in which to practice his or her profession and provides reasonable assurances that the office or system well serves its jurisdiction. It is the objective of NAME that the application of these standards will aid materially in developing and maintaining a high caliber of medico-legal investigation of death for the communities and jurisdictions in which they operate."

According to NAME, "Accreditation is the desired outcome of a process in which the policies, procedures, and practices of laboratories, programs, or offices are reviewed, usually including on-site inspection, to determine compliance with accreditation standards. An accredited lab or office has successfully completed such a review and has demonstrated compliance with the requirements of the accrediting agency or organization."

"In general I think NAME's office accreditation program has been very good," says Hanzlick. "There aren't that many offices that are accredited but it is because the criteria are stringent; many offices have benefited from that because they have been able to use their accreditation status to secure additional funding."

Accreditation is one in a series of steps that can help ensure the professionalism of medico-legal offices and agencies. The 2004 NAME report explains, "Professionalism is defined as the basis of medicine's contract with society. It demands placing the interests of the patient above those of the physician, setting and maintaining standards of competence and integrity and providing expert advice to society on matters of health." NAME says it believes appropriate death investigation rests on an integrated system, a three-legged stool with the legs representing the forensic facilities/resources, forensic autopsies, and investigations. To achieve such a competent system, accreditation and professionalism in each of these areas must be developed and supported. NAME acknowledges that the majority of medico-legal offices have not attained accreditation, in many cases because of inadequate staffing, inadequate facilities, inadequate equipment, or a combination of these factors. This is particularly problematic, NAME points out, in light of the fact that the Paul Coverdell Act mandates that facilities be accredited or in the accreditation process to qualify for federal funding.

The reasons for the low number of accredited offices are varied, but NAME suggests that they relate mainly to the lack of resources and the absence of compelling incentives, both positive and negative. The 2004 NAME report states, "The accreditation process is difficult, time-consuming and potentially costly. Some offices obtain increased political and financial support as a result of the accreditation process, but otherwise realize few tangible incentives other than assuring the community that the office is functioning under the best practice the profession can enforce. Moreover, there are currently no negative repercussions for a non-accredited office, either professional or financial. An office that attempts to obtain accreditation but fails may motivate local authorities to increase support for the office, but may also open itself up to public ridicule, embarrassment, or courtroom criticism." NAME maintains that the only way to systemically upgrade medical examiner offices nationwide is to require accreditation. This could be accomplished, NAME suggests, by requiring any medico-legal office receiving federal grants to be accredited, or by requiring any district attorney's office or court receiving federal grants to require the medico-legal agency they deal with to be accredited.

Zumwalt (2003) says that outside of accreditation, formal programs in quality assurance for medical examiner practice are in their infancy, as most states do not require quality assurance in statute or regulation. Zumwalt explains, "NAME accreditation requires a quality-assurance program, but it does not specify the type of program. It merely requires a written policy or standard operating procedure that is scheduled and implemented regularly, with documentation of corrective action for identified deficiencies." Zumwalt adds that although the American College of Pathology and the American Society of Clinical Pathology offer various programs for individual pathologists, these are voluntary and infrequently used, and that a more systematic effort is needed for in-house evaluation.

The two most common methods are conference reviews and random case reviews. Zumwalt (2003) says that conference reviews consist of regularly scheduled conferences held to discuss difficult cases, while random case reviews (which are endorsed by NAME) provide greater independent oversight and evaluation. Zumwalt explains, "A pathologist other than the one who worked on the case reviews the entire case file the autopsy report, the microscopic slides, X-rays, police reports, and medical records. Then he or she fills out a checklist and gives the form to the pathologist who performed the original autopsy. However, there is no method for assessing the effectiveness of this program, that is, whether the reviews improve the quality of investigations." A suggested mechanism for improved quality assessment, according to Zumwalt, is case-type reviews, in which similar cases are grouped according to cause of death to determine how consistently they are handled. A second mechanism is an undetermined-cause-of-death review, in which an office takes every case of an undetermined cause of death and assigns it for review.

Fierro says she is fairly happy with the present system of accreditation for medico-legal offices, but adds, "My struggle with accreditation is, should you dumb it down so you can be more inclusive or should you maintain a standard and do what you can to help others rise to it? I have always held the latter position. If you don't meet the standard, what can we do to help you? I don't believe in dumbing-down the accreditation process so that more offices are accredited. I believe that accreditation is important; if the criminal justice system had any sense, it would realize the need for greater levels of accreditation. And if most prosecutors or police had any idea what they are not getting from non-accredited offices, I think they would come around, too."

Fierro believes accreditation serves as a critical safeguard against error, whether intentional or unintentional. She comments, "It's unacceptable for any medico-legal office or any forensic laboratory to have someone who dumps the sample into the sink and makes up a number for the report. The accreditation process can and does provide a way to keep these things from happening. The laboratory here in Virginia, for example, has very good quality-assurance programs in place, and so I think prosecutors can rely on them. We're also a capital crime state, which means that defense attorneys in these cases are given great latitude when looking into the quality of the evidence. They have outside experts review our work, and that's a wonderful way to keep people honest."

Fierro says she anticipates the same level of scrutiny for her office, and adds, "We expect our forensic pathology services to be reviewed by forensic pathologists engaged by the defense, and as far as I am concerned, that's fine with me, bring it on! If I make a mistake, I want someone to find it; if it's a mistake in the system and they find it, I need to know that, too, so I have no problem with outside auditors. Every office should have some form of internal and external review; we try to carry out internal peer review, but if you have a systemic error, it would require an outsider to recognize that. Audits are worthwhile and important components of the entire quality assurance process."

THE INFRASTRUCTURE NEEDS OF MEDICO-LEGAL OFFICES

The forensic pathology community generally believes that for the most part, its needs remain largely invisible because it is an underappreciated group. "If the government sees medico-legal offices as merely handling bodies, they won't be adequately resourced," Weedn asserts. "It's just that simple."

"In general, the government doesn't like to pay for dead people, because dead people don't vote," Nolte says. "So if you are a politician, and your constituents say they need a new soccer field, you're going to give it to them because they will vote for you in return. But if the medical examiner's office says it needs something, it's not seen as a constituency that is going to reward you for your efforts. So the political process does not serve forensic pathology well."

That an essential system like medico-legal death investigation can be denied so much in terms of infrastructure can be startling to the casual observer; however, to forensic practitioners a grave situation is all in a day's work. Fierro comments, "I think our needs have been there all along, it's just only recently that some small attention has been paid to them; however, it's still very difficult to get the big dollars we need to improve things. It's difficult to get the money for X-ray machines, or to hire new pathologists; neither comes all that cheaply these days. Death investigation can be an expensive endeavor; you need at least two forensic pathologists at a minimum of $130,000 in salary each, so by the time you get the two pathologists and supporting staff, you're talking about a half a million dollars, and then you need a facility that has certain specifications to function properly, so you are talking about a couple of million dollars just for the basics."

"A lot of people don't understand what we do, and I think we have done a poor job of telling people what we do," Weedn says. "Most forensic pathologists are overwhelmed, underfunded, and under-resourced. So what they do is, they go to work, and they keep their heads down and continue working. The upshot of this is that the forensic pathologist doesn't have time to interact with the public or administrators or policy-makers. They are not visible and they are not in a position to tell people what a good job they do, or how what they do is exceedingly relevant to society. I believe that our profession may wither unless we improve our relevance to society. So the forensic pathologist who just comes in, does the autopsies, writes the report, and goes home does us a disservice, but that is the overwhelming majority of forensic pathologists because there is no time, and they are exhausted. So you find a few individuals who have a little more time or who have the personal fortitude to say, 'This is important, I need to fight for my system.' While some give up in resignation to bean counters who see us as only body handlers, I would prefer to actively assert our value and our potential and make ourselves relevant enough that they see value in spending another dollar on us."

One of the great challenges is determining the status of needs and current infrastructure in medical examiner and coroner offices across the country. In 2001, NAME conducted an infrastructure survey; offices in approximately 125 jurisdictions covering 39 states replied, accounting for about 175,000 deaths and 90,000 autopsies per year. Weedn (2003) reports that the survey, which targeted funding, workload, staffing, services, and facilities, revealed that overall, systems were "small, poorly funded, and housed in outdated facilities."

Great discrepancies were reported in nearly every category of infrastructure addressed by the 2001 NAME survey:

- *Funding:* Program funding ranged from $30,000 to $16 million per office, with an average expenditure of $1 million to $2 million (or $1 to $2 per capita). The survey also revealed that NAME-accredited offices spent more per capita than did non-accredited offices.
- *Workload:* The number of autopsies performed annually on a per capita basis varied by a factor of about 40. The average office performed 707 autopsies annually, and more than half the offices conducted more autopsies than the NAME-recommended standard of 250 autopsies per pathologist. (NAME denies accreditation to offices if a pathologist performs more than 350 autopsies annually.)
- *Personnel:* The number of pathologists per office varied from 1 to 24, with 10 percent of the medical examiner slots being vacant. Of the 379 pathologists who responded to the survey, 80 percent were board certified, but the questionnaire neglected to ask whether they were board certified in anatomic pathology or in forensic pathology. Offices averaged 6.4 death investigators, with a range of 1 to 44.
- *Services:* Most offices had body transport and radiology, while 37 percent had in-house toxicology laboratories, and 14 percent had in-house crime laboratories or DNA testing. Regarding toxicology spending, the survey revealed an annual average expenditure of $50,000, including salaries.
- *Buildings:* Many medical examiner facilities were at least 50 years old, with an average age of 20 years; many offices reported having inadequate space.
- *Quality indicators:* Although 83 percent of offices had mass fatality plans in place, just 38 percent had bioterrorism plans. Slightly less than half of jurisdictions had both in-house toxicology facilities and death investigators; non-accredited offices were far less likely than accredited offices to meet this quality measure. Medical examiner and coroner systems said they needed more funding to enhance quality with greater staffing, lower workloads, and modernized facilities.

The report indicated that in many jurisdictions there exist polar opposites in the quality of infrastructure of medico-legal offices in the U.S. "Here in Fulton County, Georgia, we are reasonably well funded, we have a great staff, we do strong death investigations, and we conduct a lot of training of pathologists," says Hanzlick. "We also do a lot that is considered at the forefront of the field. But I look three or four counties away from here and then I have to ask myself, 'Are they in as good of a place as we are? Can they do what we do? What are the specific needs in their jurisdictions, and do they have the resources with which to meet those needs?' They may be operating in a totally different way than we are, and that may not be conducive to good medico-legal death investigation. But then again, how that office is functioning may be exactly what the jurisdiction needs. So the idea is not to make all medico-legal offices the same, but to identify the various local needs and then try to address them."

Another critical assessment of U.S. medico-legal offices was conducted by NAME in 2004; the report indicated that there is substantial need for additional staffing, infrastructure, and equipment, as well as for an overall strategy that addresses ways to improve the supply and availability of forensic pathologists, the capabilities of medico-legal offices, the safety of facilities, and the integrity of the forensic death investigation system.

Staffing issues are closely tied to workloads, of course, and many medico-legal offices across the country report shortfalls in manpower to be able to handle current workloads. For the past quarter century, NAME has studied staffing requirements and workload capabilities for medico-legal offices and forensic pathologists, and based on these studies, the organization recommends that a forensic pathologist who has no administrative duties should perform no more than 250 autopsies per year. The 2004 NAME report explains, "When the number of autopsies performed exceeds this threshold, there is a tendency for a forensic pathologist, no matter how skilled, to engage in shortcuts (e.g., performing partial autopsies when a full autopsy is warranted) or make mistakes (most commonly errors of omission such as failing to examine an injury or organ or to record complete relevant findings). By the time the workload exceeds 350 autopsies per year, mistakes are more likely to be flagrant and involve errors in judgment (e.g., a case may not be autopsied that should have been, or a diagnosis may be hastily made without sufficient basis, thought, or circumspection). Further, high caseloads may result in burnout and manpower attrition."

The 2004 NAME report recognizes the accountability and tremendous responsibility resting on medico-legal offices and states, "Each death case potentially involves issues of personal liberty, financial responsibility, culpability, criminal justice, public health, and/or public safety. Shoddy work can result in wrongful prosecutions, faulty attributions of blame, wrongful exonerations, missed homicides and other non-natural deaths, and threats to public health and safety. It is imperative that each death investigation be conducted correctly and professionally the first time, every time, by those who have proper skills and time to conduct the investigation."

The workload is staggering to consider; according to the 2004 NAME report, there are approximately 2.8 million deaths per year in the United States, up to 20 percent of which fall under the jurisdiction of medical examiner and coroner offices. Estimates are that approximately 90 percent of all traumatic or suspicious deaths should be autopsied; in addition, as much as 50 percent of cases handled by most medico-legal offices are sudden, unexpected natural deaths, about 33 percent of which require autopsy to identify the specific causes of death.

On the basis of these observations, approximately 195,000 forensic autopsies were estimated to have been performed in 2002, and based on the need for forensic autopsies and the NAME-recommended maximum workload, at least 780 board-certified forensic pathologists are needed to perform these autopsies. A serious shortfall becomes evident when one considers that currently there are only about 400 board-certified forensic pathologists practicing full time in the United States (NAME, 2004).

In a NAME survey of 128 medico-legal facilities, 40 percent of forensic pathologists reported doing more than the maximum recommended 250 autopsies per year, while 9 percent indicated they performed more than 350. In reality, according to NAME (2004), more than 780 forensic pathologists are needed because a ratio of one forensic pathologist to 250 autopsies assumes uniform distribution of cases and forensic pathologists. Further, forensic pathologists with administrative duties and those in areas in which there are high homicide rates require more time for court and related preparation should perform less than 250 autopsies annually. According to NAME, there is the contention that one forensic pathologist to 200 autopsies is a more desirable ratio, which would require 975 forensic pathologists to manage the current approximate caseload.

In addition to an insufficient number of forensic pathologists, they are also unevenly distributed in larger metropolitan areas, with access to their expertise somewhat limited in smaller regions or more rural areas. The 2004 NAME report comments, "The insufficient number and unavailability of forensic pathologists means that forensic autopsies are either not being performed as needed, being performed by unqualified individuals, or being performed by overburdened forensic pathologists. Consequently, in addition to increasing the number of forensic pathologists, a plan for more even geographical distribution also needs to be undertaken. Many political entities and the criminal justice community, including the courts, do not grasp the concept of board certification or the distinct differences in the training of forensic pathologists. As a result, in a number of jurisdictions throughout the U.S., physicians who are not qualified are performing forensic autopsies."

A wide range is seen in the education, training, and experience levels among the individuals who work in the U.S. medico-legal death investigation system, and it may be eye opening for laypersons to realize that many are not board-certified forensic pathologists, individuals with the highest level of expertise one can reach in the medical examiner's office. In fact, many individuals have little to no medico-legal training or experience at all. There are three other groups of professionals who operate in the system, as the 2004 NAME study explains: There are board-certified hospital pathologists who are not forensic pathologists and have not been trained in this subspecialty; physicians who have gained experience in forensic pathology but have not been able to qualify for or pass the board examination in basic or forensic pathology; and physicians who have not even trained in pathology. NAME maintains that these three groups of physicians must be "supplanted by fully trained and qualified, board-certified forensic pathologists."

The bulk of any death investigation office's budget is comprised of the medical examiner's compensation. According to the 2004 NAME report, the average salary of a hospital pathologist in the United States is about $270,000, whereas in many areas, chief medical examiners are earning less than $150,000, with other medical examiners making approximately $120,000 or less. The study comments, "With such a depressed salary range, a significant increase in the number of medical examiners is not very likely." About 30 forensic pathologists are trained annually, but approximately one-third practice hospital pathology only or forensic pathology only part time, and another one-third drop out within 10 years. The NAME study adds, "Low salaries contribute to medical examiner offices traditionally drawing a small core of highly qualified dedicated individuals and a host of people with marginal qualifications. In order to attract and retain qualified, competent, board-certified forensic pathologists, starting salaries should approximate $150,000 a year, plus benefits, with cost of living increases and adjustments based on experience and time in the position. Chief medical examiner salaries should begin at $200,000. Although the federal government cannot force local governments to raise salaries, it can fund new grant positions at the proposed higher salaries. If coupled with mandatory accreditation of medical examiner offices, the marketplace will cause all salaries to be raised and help draw talented individuals into forensic pathology." In its study, NAME advocated for federal funds to create 100 new forensic pathology positions nationwide at a salary of $150,000 per year (plus overhead and benefits) and 20 chief medical examiner positions at a base salary of $200,000. The report notes, "Additional monies are needed to provide equipment, create in-house toxicology laboratories, and otherwise enable medical examiner offices to become and remain accredited. A variety of other methods might also be employed to attract high-caliber individuals into the field of forensic pathology. Currently, ACGME does not require pathology residents to receive forensic pathologist training during anatomic pathology training. Ensuring such training would cause increased forensic pathology exposure to those persons most likely to consider entering the field, which may in turn ultimately boost the number of forensic pathologists. In addition, requiring forensic pathology training during general pathology residency would help equip non-forensic pathologists who must perform medico-legal autopsies until there are sufficient numbers of forensic pathologists. Another method by which persons might be attracted into the field would involve federal student loan forgiveness programs for medical, and perhaps even undergraduate, education for persons entering the field of FP and working as government (local, state, or federal) employed forensic pathologists, particularly in underserved areas. Finally, increased funding for forensic pathology fellowship programs would likely result in more forensic pathologists."

When it comes to equipment and facilities, many U.S. medico-legal offices are poorly equipped and inadequately housed. NAME (2004) reports that a recent survey of 128 medical examiner and autopsy-performing coroner offices reveals 8 percent of them did not have the X-ray equipment necessary to make basic diagnoses or locate radio-opaque objects such as bullets. Significant numbers of forensic autopsies are done in funeral homes, where not only is X-ray equipment lacking, but so is other necessary equipment such as adequate lighting and scales to weigh the body and organs. Thirty-eight percent of the offices surveyed did not have in-house toxicology laboratories and some were thus dependent on state or police crime labs that could take several months to a year to report results, posing difficulties for families and all parties involved in case disposition. Moreover, crime labs often perform limited toxicological analyses, using methods not sanctioned by the American Board of Forensic Toxicology, resulting in incomplete toxicological information and fodder for challenges in the courts. Other offices must rely on private toxicology laboratories or clinical laboratories.

The 2004 NAME report states, "It is highly desirable that all medical examiner offices have dedicated support laboratories and appropriate toxicology professionals in-house. The basic equipment cost to set up an in-house toxicology lab to handle 400 autopsies per year is over $300,000; thus, many jurisdictions cannot afford to equip, much less staff an in-house toxicology laboratories."

Funding and availability of basic services for case management such as histology, microbiology, clinical laboratory testing, and genetic/metabolic lab services must be assured to provide competent and timely death investigation services. The 2004 NAME report observes, "Even these basic, requisite services are unavailable or underutilized in some areas due to lack of funding or access to services. In many areas, bodies must be transported long distances for autopsy, which results in delays, hampers communication, endangers evidence preservation and integrity, and can complicate the interpretation of post-mortem findings. Death investigation services with fully qualified forensic pathologists and support staff need to be readily available in all areas of the United States, not just in metropolitan areas."

The 2004 NAME report acknowledges that the U.S. medico-legal death investigation system "has many holes" and addresses the pertinent issues succinctly: "There are approximately 2,200 medico-legal offices in the U.S., more than half of which are coroner systems in which a non-physician has the ultimate authority to make medico-legal rulings as to cause and manner of death—even if their rulings conflict with the findings of the doctors they employ. Less than half of the nation's citizens are covered by a medical examiner system with a board-certified forensic pathologist in charge. There are commonly deaths occurring and autopsies being performed in areas remote from accredited medico-legal facilities. Further problems arise in jurisdictions that cannot afford to pay for autopsies. Many medico-legal offices are under a sheriff or police agency, a clear conflict of interest for an entity that must be objective and impartial. For example, how can a death investigation office under the administrative and financial control of the police impartially evaluate a police shooting or an allegation that death resulted from police malfeasance? Such incestuous systems are more likely to foster public mistrust and claims of conspiracy or cover-up, whether perceived or real. Although some medical examiner/coroner offices are within law enforcement agencies, typically this set-up has occurred because the funding of law enforcement agencies has been given preference in recent years compared with that for other governmental agencies. In a model system, however, medico-legal systems should be independent of law enforcement in order to remain impartial and to avoid the appearance of impropriety and conflicts of interest."

OCCUPATIONAL HEALTH ISSUES

While infrastructure needs encompass many aspects of the duties of medico-legal personnel, none are more critical than the tools necessary to keep them safe in what can be a hazardous environment. Grist (1994) says that forensic pathologists and autopsy technicians have the highest rates of laboratory-acquired infections because of their daily exposure to aerosolization of blood and other potentially infectious body fluids and tissue. Nolte et al. (2000) say that a few high-profile cases of the transmission of disease among autopsy workers has focused attention on problems relating to inadequate ventilation and insufficient respiratory precautions in autopsy suites, especially those housed in aging facilities that are not in compliance with existing standards.

The 2004 NAME report concurs, stating, "Workplace quality and safety are important considerations in any environment, but particularly so in forensic facilities. In many areas, adequate facilities needed to perform forensic autopsies are simply non-existent; in others, they are quite old and do not meet CDC or OSHA specifications for workplace safety."

As the NAME report explains, the CDC and the Occupational Safety and Health Administration (OSHA), protecting workers from airborne and bloodborne pathogens requires autopsy suites to have separate air intake and ventilation systems that provide at least 12 air exchanges per hour and a negative air pressure system that creates air flow from relevant to surrounding areas from clean to less-clean areas, as well as HEPA-filtered exhausts to prevent release of pathogens into the environment. The 2004 NAME report adds, "Poor facility design and HVAC problems have resulted in the spread of tuberculosis in more than one medical examiner office. Facilities still exist that lack drains; consequently, blood and other body fluids must be collected in buckets and dumped down a sink or toilet. At least one-third of facilities lack appropriate design and airflow systems to facilitate control of airborne and other pathogens. Finally, even though deaths involving intentional use of bioterrorism or chemical agents are homicides and fall under the jurisdiction of the medical examiner/coroner, many autopsy facilities cannot function at the biosafety level 3 required for handling some agents likely to be used in bioterrorism or occasionally seen in the general community."

Nolte asserts, "I think the state of many offices is abysmal. One concern of mine is autopsy biosafety. Occupational career risks for forensic pathologists for getting hepatitis B virus and HIV infection from occupational exposure exist. A significant number of medico-legal offices occupy aging buildings that do not meet ventilation requirements or other requirements designed to protect the building's occupants, and not just the forensic pathologist, from the risk of airborne infections such as tuberculosis. There have been a number of tuberculosis (TB) outbreaks that have occurred in medical examiner's offices as a consequence, which is not surprising since many of these offices are operating with technology that existed in the early 1900s."

Nolte explains further: "There was a time when autopsy was the most common way for TB to be transmitted to health-care workers and medical students; large numbers of medical personnel got TB, and some died. The rates at which TB was being contracted fell, thanks to public health initiatives, so it became transmitted less frequently at autopsy because fewer individuals had it. But that is not to say that the risk of transmitting it in any given medico-legal case had changed. As a consequence, the efforts to change ventilation in ME offices never happened. So despite the development of HEPA filtration and particulate filters and other ventilation engineering changes, the application of that technology to medical examiner offices didn't happen. The outbreak of AIDS in the early 1980s coincided with the increased incidence of TB because it is associated with immuno-compromised individuals who have a higher chance of getting this disease. As a consequence, there was another spike of this infection being transmitted to forensic pathologists. Now we have technology that can prevent this, but the presence of biosafety standards in medical examiner offices has been poor. There is even the report of a fatality associated with occupational transmission of multi-drug-resistant TB in a medical examiner's office. I think it's critical to address this issue because if you can't protect the forensic pathologists and other personnel in these offices, how can you attract them to the field?"

EDUCATION AND TRAINING

The 2004 NAME report states, "The very nature of the death investigation process demands more than mundane competence, and this level of quality is the direct result of superior training and education of medico-legal practitioners."

One of the most essential needs voiced by members of the medico-legal community is greater opportunity for education and training on all levels for forensic practitioners. With a structured plan to address the education needs of its community, Hanzlick says the medico-legal workforce could be stabilized. "There are probably enough fellowship positions or close to enough that if they are all funded and filled, and everybody stayed in the field, within a relatively short number of years we could probably increase the workforce significantly," Hanzlick says. "But that doesn't happen because medico-legal programs are not adequately funded or people go into the field but they don't stay in it because of the low pay. The thing I see with students right now is that most of them seem to be people who see forensic science on television and they are fascinated by the field, but they have no understanding what the individuals who work in the field actually do. We receive inquiries all the time from high school students or freshman college students who want to enroll in our forensic pathology program, but they don't understand you have to complete college, go to medical school, you have to become a pathologist and then you must do a residency, etc. And they are shocked by the rigor of the course of study required of them."

Hanzlick fears that although television's portrayal of the field raises its profile among the lay public, it fosters unrealistic expectations about curriculum and encourages institutions of higher learning to take undue advantage of the swell in interest on the part of potential students. "In some ways, forensic pathology or forensic science in general has turned into a cottage industry," Hanzlick says. "There are an increasing number of universities that are developing forensic courses, and I guess that's good, but the question is, what are the students being trained to do, what is the quality of the education provided, and will there be jobs waiting for them when they get out of school?"

One area in medico-legal death investigation that lags significantly behind its peers in the academic world is forensic pathology fellowships. There are approximately 41 forensic pathology training programs with full accreditation, sponsoring about 76 positions. Most programs are based in the coroner's office or in the medical examiner's office rather than under the institutional umbrella of a medical school. Among the core competencies required of trainees for accreditation is performance of at least 200 but not more than 300 autopsies per year. Those figures are lower than the former requirement of at least 250 but not more than 350 because of the increased complexity of cases and the greater number of tests to interpret. Training programs in forensic pathology are monitored by the Accreditation Council for Graduate Medical Education, which confers accreditation on the residency program (Zumwalt, 2003).

So, the key to a forensic pathologist's success frequently is a stellar fellowship opportunity, and many members of the community are concerned about the dwindling number of opportunities for this advanced training. "The number of fellowships being provided has gone down over the years and part of that is due to a lack of funding," says Dobersen. "I think there are still 20 or 30 good places around the country to get training, but that's not enough. If we do want to increase our ability to respond to workload demands, we must increase the field's manpower levels."

Zumwalt (2003) puts it simply and directly: "Manpower is a major concern." Since 1959, about 1,150 certificates have been awarded; by 2002, that figure had dwindled to 34 forensic pathologists who were newly certified. Zumwalt explains, "The failure rate on the American Board of Pathology examination in forensic pathology has been about 38 percent but this rate represents a disproportionate number of failures of candidates qualifying for the exam by experience rather than by formal fellowship training. Recent changes requiring all candidates for examination to have formal accredited training are expected to increase the pass rate while ensuring quality. A greater pass rate, however, cannot fulfill the demand for sufficient board certified forensic pathologists for all medico-legal autopsies in the United States. More training programs and more trainees are needed."

Hanzlick (2003) concurs that the shortage of skilled personnel is problematic for the field: "Given that there are 2,000 death investigation jurisdictions in the United States, it is clear that there are not enough board-certified forensic pathologists to meet the nation's public health and criminal justice needs. The shortage of skilled personnel contributes to the overall problem of inadequate death investigations in many jurisdictions. The problem is perpetuated by insufficient funding by local governments for operations and personnel."

Recruiting is essential, Dobersen adds, explaining, "We must show physicians that this is a viable way to make a living and to practice medicine. It's a less usual way to practice medicine, granted. I like to quote a former coroner in Cleveland who said we're the family physician to the bereaved. That's probably what makes me feel most like a physician—talking to decedents' family members and somehow explaining things and seeing that their needs are met throughout the process. I think many people don't see this side to the occupation; they look at forensic pathology as only doing autopsies and for me, doing autopsies is only 20 percent of what I do. The rest is scene work, dealing with families and other things like teaching and lecturing. The job is so much more than autopsies."

CONTINUING EDUCATION

According to NAME, ongoing education of forensic pathologists is of great importance to their continued viability in the field. Staying current with rapidly evolving technology can be one of the forensic pathologist's greatest challenges and can be an area of continuing education of value to practitioners. At the very least, NAME says, forensic pathologists must be aware of the full spectrum of forensic science disciplines and their applications to the medico-legal process. The 2004 NAME report states, "Forensic pathologists not only require the services of the crime lab, but also are themselves forensic scientists who conduct their own forensic investigations. At the least, forensic pathologists need to be aware of the forensic laboratory analytic capabilities that can be applied to evidentiary material found on bodies and should know how to conduct a thorough examination and how to collect, preserve, and document evidentiary material. This requires knowledge of current forensic science principles and capabilities. The forensic sciences have been greatly expanding and maturing in recent years and it has been difficult for forensic pathologists to keep current with this burgeoning field."

Having said that, however, the NAME report (2004) is quick to add that funding for educational activities and national meetings are solid methods of fostering continuing education for forensic pathologists, but they come at a price. NAME adds that in addition to its educational program, those of the AAFS and the College of American Pathologists (CAP) offer quality conferences and continuing education programs, but they are "cash-strapped." The report adds further, "Continuing education costs run approximately $1,500 per year for each forensic pathologist, investigator, toxicologist, and administrator. Many offices cannot afford to defray or reimburse these costs, thus shifting the burden to individuals who can ill-afford them. Therefore, federal grant money is needed to support continuing education and encourage participation in professional meetings and conferences."

Because many practitioners are not afforded opportunities to pursue continuing education, the 2004 NAME report asserts that nationally, "many pathologists without adequate forensic training elect and are permitted to perform medico-legal autopsies. This practice leads to errors in both the performance and interpretation of the results of forensic autopsies."

The unsatisfying result is that because there are too few well trained and experienced forensic pathologists available to perform all of the forensic autopsies that are required, many jurisdictions rely on non-forensic, hospital-based general pathologists to perform these medico-legal autopsies. Non-forensic pathologists typically receive training in hospital autopsy performance, which is considered by the field to be insufficient preparation to perform a medico-legal autopsy. The 2004 NAME report states, "There are many issues of forensic interest that are typically not at issue or routinely addressed during hospital autopsies. Although some of these pathologists may do an adequate job in routine, uncomplicated cases, others do not. Moreover, even non-forensic pathologists who are capable of handling simple, straightforward cases will inevitably encounter cases that initially appear straightforward but subsequently become complex. In some cases, overt or subtle indications that a medico-legal autopsy is necessary may not be recognized by practitioners unskilled in forensic pathology resulting in failure to perform the appropriate examination. Unfortunately, there is no way to know how many homicides or other complex cases have been missed or improperly evaluated for these reasons."

NAME (2004) asserts that, from a medical standpoint, "allowing general pathologists to perform medico-legal autopsies is similar to having general surgeons attempt to perform open-heart surgery. It is doubtful that any patient would consent to an operation under those circumstances—if indeed any hospital would allow it." Therefore, NAME recommends a national standard requiring that all medico-legal autopsies be performed only by board-certified forensic pathologists. In 1998, CAP's forensic pathology committee created its *Practice Guideline for Forensic Pathology* in an attempt to codify the practice of forensic pathology. Implementation of the guidelines was voluntary and lacked incentive for pathologists to attain long-lasting change. Accordingly, NAME is currently working to articulate performance parameters for forensic autopsies.

TRAINING FOR MEDICO-LEGAL DEATH INVESTIGATORS

Saferstein (2001) calls for a staff of dedicated individuals trained and experienced in evidence collection: "The education of evidence collectors and investigators is a very critical factor in improving the quality of crime scene investigation. Although continued in-depth training of the investigators by forensic scientists is an essential ingredient for the success of such a program, many agencies, for lack of space, time or desire, have not implemented this training." Saferstein adds, "Of course, education alone will not guarantee the success of the criminal investigator or evidence collector. Experience, perceptive skill, persistence, and precise judgment are all ingredients essential to the make-up of the successful investigator and evidence collector. Combine all these with a careful selection process designed for choosing only those who qualify for this role, and the end result will be a substantial enhancement of the quality of criminal investigative services."

Ernst (2003) states, "The origin of lay examiners who work for medical examiners traces back to the 1950s. In the last half-century, greater training opportunities have emerged, but they remain jeopardized by scant funding. The first formal one-week training course was offered in 1974 by St. Louis University. Seven states now mandate minimal training requirements for death investigators. The basic week-long course for death investigators includes death-scene investigation, examination of the decedent at the scene, estimation of time of death, evidence recognition, notification of next of kin, legal issues, mass-casualty instant response, organ and tissue donation, and testifying in court. There are lectures on the ancillary forensic sciences, such as anthropology, odontology, toxicology, archeology, and forensic psychiatry.

Credentialing of individual death investigators has improved over time. Death investigators can now be recognized as affiliate members of NAME or members of the American Academy of Forensic Sciences, a society of diverse professionals dedicated to the application of science to the law. In 1995, NIJ organized the first technical working group to develop national guidelines for scene investigation by death investigators. The guidelines, which were released in 1998, specify 29 essential components of a thorough death scene investigation. Also in 1998, the American Board of Medico-legal Death Investigators was created to certify death investigators. It confers two levels of certification registry and board certification and recertifies people every five years. The goals of certification are to identify professionally qualified death investigators and to assist the courts and public in assessing their competence.

ASSESSING FORENSIC PATHOLOGY PROGRAMS REVEALS VITAL DEMOGRAPHIC DATA

Weedn advocates for the forensic pathologist to be well versed in all aspects of forensic science. "I worked with Keith Pinckard on a study published in *the Journal of Forensic Science* focusing on the forensic science training of forensic pathologists. By that I mean, does the forensic pathologist know something about ballistics, toxicology, DNA, etc." Weedn says. "The study shows that most forensic pathologists don't receive much, if any, forensic science training. I realize that the forensic pathologist is not a criminalist, and in fact, during the survey we conducted, one very prominent forensic pathologist, the chief of a very large medical examiner office, essentially said, 'Look, this isn't our job.' Well, I do believe that it is part of our job as forensic pathologists to be aware of what goes on in criminalistics, at the crime scene, and in the crime lab. We ought to be people who make particular use of the crime lab. We ought to be aware of what samples might be collected for the testing of gunshot residue or toxicology. We ought to look at the bodies for trace evidence, and we need to know the lab's capabilities. Many forensic pathologists aren't tremendously aware of these things. I am always struck by when medical examiners and crime lab analysts get together in one facility that they both realize, 'Wow, this was more useful than I thought,' because they don't even recognize what they don't know. That's why I would like to see more interaction between forensic pathologists and forensic science, and to have that interaction formalized. It's not my intent to turn them into criminalists, but because these are people they should be working with, there should be more knowledge-sharing between them." Weedn also says that forensic pathologists need additional training in administration: "The vast majority of chief medical examiners are not fired because of technical ability, but they are fired because of their lack of administrative skills and know-how about financial aspects of running the medico-legal office. And then there's the ability to interface with technology. In this computer-savvy world, there are few forensic pathologists who regularly use computer imaging technology; the rest of us could benefit by having some skills in this area. Forensic pathologists have a lot to learn, and we must be careful not to overdo it, but the demands of the profession require us to be more conversant about more issues and proficient in more areas than ever before."

In an analysis of the nation's 40-plus forensic pathology programs accredited by the ACGME, Pinckard et al. (2003) acknowledge the growing complexities in forensic science, believe it is essential for forensic pathologists-in-training to appreciate these complexities, and advocate for a solid educational grounding that will be "increasingly important for the future of forensic pathology."[1] Of interest to Pinckard et al. was to determine to what extent forensic pathologists received instruction in forensic science-related, non-pathology disciplines. The researchers sent a survey regarding the nature and quantity of forensic science training to the directors of all 43 active, ACGME-accredited forensic pathology fellowship programs. Of the 43 surveys sent, 31 (72.1 percent), representing 22 states were returned; the completed surveys accounted for 59 of 84 fellowship positions available annually (or about 70 percent of all fellowship positions).

The survey revealed interesting nuggets of demographic insight. Pinckard et al. (2003) reported that the majority of the medical examiner/coroner offices employed an average of four full-time pathologists performing about 1,200 autopsies annually. Interestingly, several offices reported performing as many as 2,000 autopsies each year. All programs were affiliated with a university, medical school, and/or teaching hospital, and were located within a relatively short distance from the medical examiner/coroner office.

The survey also revealed an intriguing association between medical examiner/coroner offices and forensic laboratories. According to Pinckard et al. (2003) four programs indicated that the entire crime lab is under the supervision of the medical examiner/coroner office; 11 programs responded that they had a "close" working relationship with the crime lab; five stated that they interacted primarily to turn over evidence obtained from the body; four indicated that they consulted with the crime lab in unusual cases; four stated that technologists from the crime lab attended the autopsy; two stated that they did not have a close relationship with the crime lab; and one indicated that most consulting with the crime lab was by telephone due to the large distance between them.

Medical examiner/coroner offices responding to the survey indicated—for each of the crime lab disciplines included in the study—who performs each of the types of casework, where that facility is located, and how far away from the medical examiner/coroner office that laboratory is located. Pinckard et al. (2003) revealed that most of the specialized analyses were performed by a governmental or police laboratory; however, some degree of integration was reported. According to the researchers, 67 percent of programs reported that toxicology casework was performed at the medical examiner/coroner office. Some of the other surveyed disciplines, such as toxicology and serology, are also performed there, ranging from 13 percent for fingerprint examinations and arson analysis to 29 percent for DNA-based identification. The remainder of the analyses was performed by governmental laboratories, police laboratories, or private laboratories.

Regarding training in the forensic sciences, 25 percent of survey respondents stated that fellows attend the Armed Forces Institute of Pathology forensic pathology course; 46 percent take a forensic anthropology course; 64 percent attend the annual meeting of the AAFS; 43 percent attend the annual meeting of NAME; and 14 percent take a death investigation course. One program also listed courses in forensic entomology, evidence collection, and bite-mark analysis. According to the survey, the total time spent training in the crime lab varied from 1 to 10 weeks, with an average of just slightly more than 4 weeks.

The researchers also asked respondents about the number of papers written or presentations made on research into the criminalistic aspects of forensic investigation by forensic pathology fellows in their program. One program cited two, and two programs cited one or more papers in toxicology. The remainder of the programs replied "zero."

Notable, according to the researchers, were some of the comments included on the survey forms, which, according to the researchers, "indicated that the opportunity for the forensic science training is often pre-empted by autopsy casework or otherwise, or that such training is not needed if their graduates would not be engaged in such practices" (Pinckard et al., 2003).[1]

The researchers categorize the extent of pathologists' training in a variety of forensic science disciplines as "widely variable" and "generally deficient." The same could be said for pathologists' exposure to crime laboratories, because 41 percent of the programs responding to the survey do not meet the 4-week minimum established by the ACGME. According to Pinckard et al. (2003) NAME's Subcommittee on Forensic Pathology Fellowship Training has finalized its own set of recommendations for what the ACGME should require of forensic pathology fellowship programs. NAME recommends 80 hours of toxicology training and 40 hours in aggregate for other forensic disciplines. Using these NAME standards as a measuring stick, the researchers concluded that 44 percent of programs that participated in the survey do not meet NAME's recommendation for toxicology training. The researchers noted, "This result was somewhat surprising, given that 67.7 percent of medical examiner/coroner offices reported having an integrated laboratory for toxicology, more than any of the other surveyed forensic disciplines. Toxicology is probably the most important of the non-pathology forensic sciences for the forensic pathologist. Toxicology is performed in the majority of autopsy cases; the results can often be the deciding factor that dictates how the pathologist signs out the cause and manner of death. This being the case, it seems that half of programs not meeting the NAME recommendations for toxicology represent a substantial deficit in training."[1] The researchers suggested that besides practical instruction in the toxicology laboratory, training could also be supplemented by weekly case review of toxicology analyses from medical examiner/coroner offices in order to integrate toxicology results with their interpretation in the context of the autopsy.

The bright spot of the survey was that all respondents either met or exceeded NAME's recommendation for all of the surveyed disciplines of forensic science other than toxicology; however, almost half of respondents who itemized training times cited no training in at least one of the surveyed areas. Additionally, up to 28 percent of responding programs do not train their fellows in the various areas of forensic sciences in the crime laboratories that normally perform the casework in the area served by the medical examiner/coroner offices.

The researchers noted, "Supplemental training in both toxicology as well as the other disciplines, by means of conferences, individual case follow-up, or independent study throughout the year of fellowship training is also advocated (and expected) by the NAME recommendations but is intended to extend above and beyond the recommended amounts of formalized training in the laboratory. While we were not able to identify any predictors of training times from the information we collected, it is possible that the number of autopsies performed by fellows . . . in some programs precluded much time spent training in the other forensic sciences. While we asked about the autopsy caseload for the entire office, we did not inquire specifically about the number of cases each fellow completes. There was, however, no correlation between training times and the calculated ratios of the number of cases to the number of fellows or to the number of full-time pathologists" (Pinckard et al., 2003).[1]

Still troubling to the researchers, however is the trend that some program directors believed that the opportunity for the forensic science training was frequently "pre-empted by autopsy casework such that the non-pathology forensic science training is actually less than the survey results suggest. Some program directors felt that such training is not needed if their graduates would not be engaged in such practices" (Pinckard et al., 2003).[1] The researchers expressed dismay at this deficit in exposure to real-world experience, stating, "First, even though forensic pathologists will likely never actually perform most of these analyses themselves, we believe that they must be able to effectively communicate with other forensic scientists. Medico-legal death investigation is a multifaceted approach combining the forensic pathologist determining the cause and manner of death and the crime lab obtaining as much information as possible from the evidence, which together, will assist law enforcement in their investigation. No one discipline can work effectively without communicating with the others. Forensic pathologists must at least know the language of the other forensic scientists (and vice versa) in order to work effectively together."[1]

Pinckard et al. (2003) advocate for forensic pathologists' greater understanding of common terms and concepts of forensic science, such as "friction ridge" and "short tandem repeat" so that they are able to communicate effectively with fingerprint examiners or DNA experts, for example. Pinckard et al. (2003) state, "Ideally, these interactions should consist of more than simply the turning over of evidence to another department."[1] The researchers also state that forensic pathologists must possess a solid working knowledge of both the capabilities as well as the limitations of the non-pathology forensic sciences. They emphasize, "How can a forensic pathologist know what type of specimens or evidence is important if he/she does not know what the toxicologist or trace evidence expert is capable of doing with that material? The forensic pathologist does not need to know how to repair or operate a gas chromatograph/mass spectrometer, but he/she does need to be able to understand the difference between a drug screen and a confirmatory test, and have a concept of how each is performed."[1]

Pinckard et al. (2003) add that forensic pathologists must comprehend how the forensic laboratory operates, and what it can and cannot do in the name of forensic science. They observe, "Pathologists must have a firm grasp on how specimens or evidence is handled once it leaves the medical examiner/coroner office; they must know how the various types of testing are performed in order to properly collect and handle the material. The best way to obtain this sort of realistic understanding of how the crime lab works is to have some actual hands-on, or at least eyes-on, experience-based training at the bench."[1]

Importantly, the researchers suggested, "Training in the non-pathology forensic sciences would also expose the forensic pathology fellow to the legal and political issues common to the forensic sciences. Forensic pathology has, in general, not faced the same magnitude of legal scrutiny experienced by the other forensic sciences, but it may evolve in that direction. Forensic pathologists and non-pathology forensic scientists have also worked together in the political arena, for example, lobbying for the passage and appropriation of the National Forensic Sciences Improvement Act, which will provide financial backing for both groups of forensic scientists. Moreover, exposure to the broader law enforcement community is bound to be of import to the trainee."

RESEARCH ISSUES

The aforementioned survey hinted at a lack of research being conducted by forensic pathologists. Nolte (2003) states, "The field of medico-legal death investigations is strikingly limited in its research capacity. Only 11 percent of the nation's 125 medical schools have full-time faculty members who are forensic pathologists—39 total faculty members. Only two are principal investigators on research grants, one other forensic pathologist has some degree of research funding (co-investigator), and the field's research potential is curtailed by a shortage of future researchers. Only 38 percent of forensic pathology training programs offer any research opportunities to trainees."

Nolte says he has been involved in research for most of his career, and was delighted when asked to address the topic at the 2003 Institute of Medicine's symposium on medico-legal death investigation. "When I was asked to speak, I knew I wanted to conduct new research so that I would be able to give the symposium attendees something quantitative," Nolte explains. "Because the IOM is a high-visibility place, I wanted to present something substantial into which they could sink their teeth. After I gave the talk, I thought I might as well organize the material for publication, which is what I did. What I discovered is that forensic pathologists are poorly represented in academic medicine; essentially we have only about 14 out of the 125 U.S. medical schools that employ forensic pathologists—that's abysmal. If you only had 14 U.S. medical centers that employed neurosurgeons, people would be up in arms. So, essentially, forensic pathologists do not occupy positions in medical schools. The question is, where does medico-legal and forensic research take place?"

Nolte says there are a few important factors that come into play when examining the paltry number of opportunities for forensic pathology research: "You know the phrase 'time is money,' well, in academic medicine, money is time, meaning if you have funding for research, you get time for research; individuals who practice forensic pathology in a municipal setting have their salaries paid to handle casework, and that's what they are focused on; to be able to do anything other than small pilot projects is really not plausible. The only place that any project of significant size will really be carried out is in academic institutions, but the only way they get under way there is if the researcher has funding that supports the time investment necessary to conduct the research. So in addition to being poorly represented in academic medical centers, I think the number of research dollars available to forensic pathology is virtually nil. So you have a group of physicians who are not represented in academic medicine, and who have no access to research funding."

While conducting his study, Nolte says he found a total of six fellowship programs in those 14 academic institutions. "My initial reaction was 'Gee, this is terrible,'" Nolte recalls. "I looked at the program books for forensic pathology residency programs to determine what is represented for research, and two-thirds of the six forensic pathology programs at academic medical centers offer research training; these institutions are a minority of the 44 forensic pathology training programs in the U.S. Then I looked at 22 other fellowship programs and found only 10 that offered a research opportunity. So, you have hardly anyone in the research pipeline. The bigger issue is that nobody would really *want* to get into the pipeline because the number of jobs in the field of academic forensic pathology is so few and then on top of everything, there's so little training available. It's a convoluted loop."

Nolte says he also looked at the forensic pathology journals to back up his observations and conclusions from his study. Specifically, in 2002, there were 113 scientific reports in the field's two forensic pathology journals. "What that revealed is that the majority of the papers in these journals were not hypothesis-driven research studies, but were descriptive studies in the form of case reports or case series; I think I found five funded by U.S. sources and none of those funded studies had a forensic pathologist as the principal investigator," Nolte says. "So within the field of forensic pathology, there's no funding, there's no training of fellows in research methods, and no representation in academic medical centers."

In his study, Nolte states, "The most frequently cited reasons for lack of research commitment were time constraints, lack of academic institutional support for research in forensic pathology, and isolation from academic institutions. Other reasons were regulations covering confidentiality, poorly standardized data acquisition and information technology, and lack of federal research support." Nolte explains that he sent a questionnaire to determine the perceived limitations on the performance of forensic pathology research, and reports that the top reason was being overwhelmed by service work and the lack of protected time, and the second reason was funding, followed by minimal training for forensic pathology fellows in research. As for the top perceived opportunities for research by forensic pathologists, Nolte says, "It was far and away public health surveillance."

Nolte says there is a sad footnote to the study, in that since the time his study was published, one of the institutions, Indiana University, dropped its forensic pathology unit. "And now we have 13," Nolte says, "I hope that it won't dwindle to none." He adds, "How can we have an evidence-based field of knowledge for these practitioners if there's no significant research, and if it's just related to episodic case reports. How can we have evidence-based research that is used in the courtroom? How can we have public health data that is of the highest quality if it's not informed by a robust research agenda?"

Nolte says he thinks the present research scenario is "pretty sad," adding, "I think I used the word 'lackluster' at one point in my paper. To me, 'lackluster' certainly defines the situation. It's horrific. But to be fair, there *is* a small ray of sunshine. In November 2005, the NIJ issued a program funding announcement which targeted the forensic pathology community as a group from whom they were soliciting research proposals. In the past, NIJ's solicitations for research projects to fund were for general forensic science, and there were no forensic pathology applicants. We will see what this portends for the field."

Nolte says he is in the process of submitting a full research proposal, but adds, "It doesn't help if I keep getting funded. What really needs to happen is other people need to get funded so that there is a cadre of funded forensic pathologists engaged in research, who then can be role models for other individuals." Other sources of funding include the CDC, he says, however, "its funding is almost always tied to health departments and medical examiners are usually not members of health departments; very few offices are. And so in order to access those funds, they have to work through their health department and there is a lot of competition within the health department for hanging onto that money. It's difficult to convince the health department that you want to put together a proposal with them that will pass through some of the money to your medical examiner office."

Another source is the NIH, which Nolte says has "a huge research budget" but whose funded projects typically are not undertaken by forensic pathologists. "For example, there have been about 59 NIH-funded SIDS projects, but none of these had a forensic pathologist as a principal investigator despite the fact that forensic pathologists investigate and autopsy all of these deaths," Nolte says. "It's not completely NIH's fault. Yes, they could be better about soliciting research from forensic pathologists, but the flip side is, very few, if any, forensic pathologists have come to the table either. It's going to take an organized effort by federal agencies to create targeted programs for which forensic pathologists can be solicited. NIH must think about what they want from a health standpoint, NIJ from the public safety standpoint, the CDC from the public health standpoint, and they have to make funding available. And forensic pathologists have to be able to step forward and say, 'OK, we are going to do this because research is important; we might need mentors from outside the field, and we might need to set aside some time apart from casework to make it happen.' But until both sides acknowledge that it needs to happen, it's not going to happen."

When asked which areas lack research conducted by forensic pathologists, Nolte says, "I'd like to see research that addresses autopsy-based mortality surveillance in a comprehensive way, and that involves research into what sort of questions need to be asked of these databases, how these databases should be formulated, and how they should all pull together. For example we have local, regional, and state data, so how can we assemble this data to achieve comprehensive mortality statistics? That has been done largely through death certificates, but the information on a death certificate is very minimal. I think we must ask ourselves what kind of information goes into those death certificates, because it's a matter of garbage in, garbage out. We have to ask ourselves, what are the important surveillance questions that need to be addressed on a national scale, and how do we evaluate that data and pull it together from a public health standpoint? Our national mortality data, which is used for the allocation of health dollars, needs to be looked at very closely; what comes out of medico-legal death investigation is a significant component of that—all of the unnatural deaths and a significant fraction of the natural deaths, and it's largely autopsy-based data, and we have to have comprehensive programs to make the data work. A significant amount of money must be thrown into developing comprehensive surveillance, as well as the kind of training that needs to take place in order to be able to institute that surveillance. That's a big endeavor, sort of like the human genome project; do we look at this gene or that gene and do a little research, or do we look at all the genes? All is better than some; the same is true for mortality surveillance data."

Another item on Nolte's research wish list is steeped in public safety: "I think we need more research that evaluates the accuracy and consistency of the characterization of injuries that forensic pathologists accomplish," he says. "We must be able to know what error rates are, and what our level of accuracy is; this information frequently is used in a courtroom, and it's never really been validated. Instead, much of it has been developed anecdotally; no one has truly evaluated how forensic pathologists evaluate injuries. With new standards in admissibility in courts, it's only a matter of time until forensic pathology gets creamed about the information it proffers in court. Unless we start looking at how we make our determinations, the same way the forensic science community has done with DNA, it's going to be excluded at some point in the future."

Several years earlier than Nolte's undertaking, Hanzlick and Parrish (1998) found that over a three-year period from 1993 to 1996, the CDC's *Morbidity and Mortality Weekly Report* (MMWR) included 48 articles to which a medical examiner or coroner contributed. Nolte says that a small amount of research funding is available from several agencies, including the CDC, NIJ, AAFS, and the NIH. Nolte says, "The latter has the largest commitment, totaling six studies, but none has a forensic pathologist as principal investigator. Despite the low level of research support, there is an abundance of research opportunities in forensic pathology, largely through collaborations with other fields: epidemiology and surveillance of violent deaths, substance abuse, unintentional injuries, environmental hazards, and infectious diseases."

Forensic pathology researchers can play a key role in research on public health interventions, trauma care, pharmacogenomics, and pathogenesis. Forensic pathology has a treasure trove of research assets including population-based epidemiologic data, a window on unnatural deaths, and the only remaining significant source of autopsy tissues. None of the field's research opportunities can be realized, nor can the evidence base of the field grow, without greater funding from federal research institutions.

As educators, forensic pathologists play a critical role in shaping the future of U.S. medico-legal death investigation offices. With their special training and experience, forensic pathologists are best equipped to direct death investigation systems and to educate the general public and professional and allied personnel who should have a basic understanding of forensic pathology, including death investigators, pathology residents, forensic pathology fellows, physicians, nurses, hospital and clinic personnel, emergency medical workers, nursing home/long-term care facility staffs, law enforcement personnel, and funeral home workers.

According to the 2004 NAME report, "It is extremely important that local, state, and national government officials understand the importance of forensic pathology and death investigation. It is imperative that all of the foregoing groups have appropriate knowledge of forensic pathology and related forensic issues if we are to attain nationwide, high quality, consistent, professional, and comprehensive death investigations. In particular, medical and funeral home personnel must be aware of which cases are to be referred to the death investigation agency, and to know appropriate ways to deal with bodies, evidence, etc. Local, state, and federal government personnel and elected officials should understand the profession of forensic pathology, its role in society, and what it requires to provide the best possible service to society. Death investigators must have adequate training and perform their duties at or above minimally acceptable standards. While many jurisdictions have attained such high-quality operation, many more have not. Even within certain statewide systems, there can be wide variation in death investigation practices between locales. When judging the state of death investigation, it is important to remember that a system is only as strong as its weakest link. Therefore, we must not be satisfied with the nation's death investigation system until every jurisdiction has attained high-quality death investigation practices. Better forensic pathology education is a vital component of this process. The federal government can help by providing funds to: develop curricula for various groups; enable NAME liaisons to travel to meet with various governmental agencies that impact FP practice; and establish federal loan forgiveness programs for persons who become employed as government-paid MEs in areas of critical need. Further, the federal government could encourage the adoption of uniform adequate standards for competent death investigation by providing federal subsidies to states that require and provide certified medico-legal death investigator training in accordance with the NIJ's National Guidelines for Death Investigation and ensure forensic pathology education and experience for all anatomic pathology residents via grants for positions and courses to be included in ACGME-approved training. Finally, forensic pathology fellowship training and research would benefit greatly from additional federal funding."

FUNDING OF THE U.S. MEDICO-LEGAL DEATH INVESTIGATION SYSTEM

Participants in the 2003 IOM symposium discussed earlier in this chapter determined that funding of medico-legal offices varies greatly. County systems range from $0.62 to $5.54 per capita, with a mean of $2.6 per capita. Statewide systems are generally funded at lower levels of $0.32 to $3.20 per capita, with a mean of $1.41 per capita. Third-party payors generally do not support the costs of operations, nor are there medical billing systems. Funding is almost exclusively from tax revenues.

Current funding mechanisms leave little room for the fiscal support of an ambitious research agenda for the medico-legal community. "If you look at what has been made available within the forensic pathology community for scholarly inquiry, it is appalling," says Nolte. "It is abysmal, and it is embarrassing. If that sort of mediocre funding was made available for pediatrics, for example, you'd have people screaming, but there's nobody raising their voices about the abysmal level of funding that has been made available for forensic pathology research. There are problems within forensic pathology, including the way it is structured, the lack of education and training, the lack of academic ties; the issues are multi-factorial, so it's not just the funding, but the funding *is* abysmal."

Nolte is concerned because while the forensic pathology community makes significant contributions to society, it is frequently not rewarded and supported for its services. "All of our national mortality data on violent deaths and a large fraction of natural deaths comes from our community; this mortality data determines how we spend our health-care dollars, so our role and our contributions are incredibly important from a public health and surveillance standpoint," Nolte explains. "Additionally, all of the information that flows into the criminal justice system in homicide cases comes out of our medico-legal community, too. The outcomes from the criminal justice system are based on conclusions reached by forensic pathologists and forensic scientists, and we need those conclusions to be as evidence-based as possible. Therefore, it is essential we receive adequate funding for research, yet the amount of money that is going into making those conclusions is appallingly small. You would assume that we want to create a well-funded system with a cadre of reasonably trained and educated people who investigate these issues, come up with evidence-based conclusions, and then apply them to real-life problems. We have done everything but that."

"When you look at the amount of money from the Forensic Science Improvement Act that is actually plugged into the death investigation system, it's trivial," Hanzlick says. "It's almost not even worth applying for those funds. To me, it's going to take a combined effort of more federal dollars and more state dollars being specifically dedicated to improve the system overall, rather than making practitioners repetitively apply for grants to convince somebody about why they need the money. There must be a commitment to the medico-legal system recognizing that it takes a certain amount of money to run it and we need to fund it. What's not working is a system in which every year a medico-legal office must apply for money that by the time you get it, you can hardly buy anything with it. It's almost as if it's a token gesture rather than a significant form of assistance."

"Policy-makers are confronted by an array of funding priorities, with each special interest group demanding that their issues take top priority, and we just don't have the resources to do everything that everybody wants," Weedn explains. "Most of the time, these demands are made by groups acting out of self-interest only. Politicians recognize this, and have to make difficult choices. So when a policy-maker, a legislator, or an administrative funding agent are faced with making these choices, they come to the medical examiner office and think, 'Well, since everyone wants something, and because these people only deal with dead bodies, I prefer to spend the money on someone who's alive.' They think it's a waste to spend money on the dead. I don't agree with that, of course, because I think that what we do as forensic pathologists is also very much for the living. There are times when we speak for the dead, clearly, but I think we do good things for both the living and the dead, and that we represent an important financial investment in the country."

MEDICO-LEGAL OFFICES AND FORENSIC LABORATORIES: A SYMBIOTIC RELATIONSHIP

Some members of the forensic science community lament that it is all too easy to overlook the need to champion the relationship between medico-legal offices and forensic laboratories. Not only do medico-legal offices and forensic laboratories share a similar abysmal lack of resources, they are two interlocking components of the U.S. criminal justice system. Narveson (2003) explains that forensic laboratories assist medico-legal practitioners with death investigation in two important ways: first, these laboratories provide information used to help determine the identification of victims, and help determine the cause and manner of death. Through DNA testing and fingerprints, forensic laboratories can help establish who the victim was, while forensic analysis of firearms, tool marks, controlled substances, and toxic substances can help establish the circumstances leading to the death event and potentially the weapons used in the crime and the perpetrator at the scene.

Dobersen notes, "There is a lot we can share and all too often we work in a parallel manner but not together. I think it would be best if there was more communication and I think that would come about with a greater number of integrated facilities. A crime lab attached to the medical examiner's office as a regional justice center or regional forensic center would be a terrific solution to many issues."

Narveson (2003) comments, "Factors that affect whether a medical examiner or coroner office takes full advantage of a crime laboratory include its proximity and working relationships, knowledge of which laboratory services are available, the workload of the crime laboratory, and knowledge of the laboratory's requirements for sample collection, packaging, and preservation. The utility of the crime laboratory in death investigations can be improved by promoting effective partnerships with medical examiner and coroner offices; by encouraging discussion of the range, value, availability, and use of crime laboratory capabilities; and by supporting the development of procedures that maximize the contribution of the crime laboratory's expertise."

REFERENCES

Altman LK. How doctors identify the dead among the Trade Center rubble. *The New York Times,* September 25, 2001.

Bonnie RJ. Opening remarks. Chapter 2 in: *Medicolegal Death Investigation System: Workshop Summary.* Washington, D.C.: National Academies Press, 2003a.

Bonnie RJ. Closing remarks. Chapter 10 in: *Medicolegal Death Investigation System: Workshop Summary.* Washington, D.C.: National Academies Press, 2003b.

Case MES. Commentary. In: *Death Investigation: A Guide for the Scene Investigator.* Washington, D.C.: National Institute of Justice, November 1999.

Clark SC. NIJ guide for death scene investigations. Institute of Medicine. Medico-legal Death Investigation System: Workshop Summary. National Academies Press, 2003.

Committee for the Workshop on the Medicolegal Death Investigation System. *Medicolegal Death Investigation System: Workshop Summary.* Washington, D.C.: National Academies Press, 2003.

Curran WJ. The status of forensic pathology in the United States. *New England Journal of Medicine,* November 5, 1970.

Davis JH. Commentary. In: *Death Investigation: A Guide for the Scene Investigator.* Washington, D.C.: National Institute of Justice, November 1999.

Di Maio V. Medicolegal death investigation and the criminal justice system: The value of medical expertise in death investigation. Chapter 7 in: *Medicolegal Death Investigation System: Workshop Summary.* Washington, D.C.: National Academies Press, 2003.

Dolinak D, Matshes E, and Lew E. *Forensic Pathology, Principles and Practice.* Boston: Elsevier Academic Press, 2005.

Ernst MF. Adequacy of expertise and services available to death investigations. Institute of Medicine. Medico-legal Death Investigation System: Workshop Summary. National Academies Press, 2003a.

Ernst MF. Training, registry, and certification of death investigators. Institute of Medicine. Medico-legal Death Investigation System: Workshop Summary. National Academies Press, 2003b.

Fierro M. Comparing medical examiner systems: advantages and disadvantages of the medical examiner system. Chapter 6 in: *Medicolegal Death Investigation System: Workshop Summary.* Washington, D.C.: National Academies Press, 2003a.

Fierro M. The challenge of terrorism and mass disaster. Institute of Medicine. Medico-legal Death Investigation System: Workshop Summary. National Academies Press, 2003b.

Grist N. Association of Clinical Pathologist's surveys of infection in British clinical laboratories. *Clinical Pathology,* 47(5):391–4, 1994.

Hanley BH. Commentary. In: *Death Investigation: A Guide for the Scene Investigator.* Washington, D.C.: National Institute of Justice, November 1999.

Hanzlick R. The impact of homicide trials on the forensic pathologist's time—The Fulton County experience. *Journal of Forensic Science,* 42(3):533–534, May 1997.

Hanzlick R. Commentary. In: *Death Investigation: A Guide for the Scene Investigator.* Washington, D.C.: National Institute of Justice, November 1999.

Hanzlick R. Public health and homeland security issues. Chapter 3. In: *Medicolegal Death Investigation System: Workshop Summary.* Washington, D.C.: National Academies Press, 2003.

Hanzlick R. Quality assurance review of death certificates: A pilot study. *American Journal of Forensic Medicine and Pathology,* 26(1):63–65, March 2005.

Hanzlick R, Combs D. Medical examiner and coroner systems: History and trends. *Journal of the American Medical Association,* 279(11):870–874, 1998.

Hanzlick R, Combs D, Parrish RG, and Ing RT. Death investigation in the United States, 1990: A survey of statutes, systems, and educational requirements. *Journal of Forensic Science,* 38(3):628–632, 1993.

Hanzlick RL and Parrish RG. Epidemiologic aspects of forensic pathology. *Clinics in Laboratory Medicine,* Mar;18(1):23–37, 1998.

Hanzlick R, Smith GP. Identification of the unidentified deceased: Turnaround times, methods, and demographics in Fulton County, Georgia. *American Journal of Forensic Medicine and Pathology,* 27(1):79–84, March 2006.

Kearns ML. Commentary. In: *Death Investigation: A Guide for the Scene Investigator.* Washington, D.C.: National Institute of Justice, November 1999.

Kuhler GH. Commentary. In: *Death Investigation: A Guide for the Scene Investigator.* Washington, D.C.: National Institute of Justice, November 1999.

Luke JL. Forensic pathology. *New England Journal of Medicine,* July 1, 1976.

Narveson S. The role of the crime laboratory in medico-legal death investigations. Institute of Medicine. Medico-legal Death Investigation System: Workshop Summary. National Academies Press, 2003.

National Association of Medical Examiners (NAME). *Preliminary Report on America's Medico-legal Offices.* Report prepared for the National Institute of Justice Forensic Summit, May 18–19, 2004.

National Research Council. *The Coroner and the Medical Examiner,* Bulletin of the National Research Council No. 64. Washington, D.C.: National Research Council, 1928.

National Research Council. *Possibilities and Need for Development of Legal Medicine in the United States,* Bulletin of the National Research Council No. 87. Washington, D.C.: National Research Council, 1932.

Nolte K. Research issues. Institute of Medicine. Medico-legal Death Investigation System: Workshop Summary. National Academies Press, 2003a.

Nolte K. Homeland security and emergency preparedness: the potential role of medical examiners and coroners in responding to and planning for bioterrorism and emerging infectious diseases. Chapter 9 in: *Medicolegal Death Investigation System: Workshop Summary.* Washington, D.C.: National Academies Press, 2003b.

Nolte KB, Yoon SS, and Pertowski C. Medical examiners, coroners, and bioterrorism. *Emerging Infectious Diseases,* 6(5):559–560, 2000.

Parrott C. Advantages and disadvantages of the coroner system. Institute of Medicine. Medico-legal Death Investigation System: Workshop Summary. National Academies Press, 2003.

Pinckard K, Hunsaker D, and Weedn VW. A comprehensive analysis of forensic science training in forensic pathology fellowship programs. *Journal of Forensic Science,* February 2003.

Randall B. Survey of forensic pathologists. *American Journal of Forensic Medicine and Pathology,* 22(2):123–127, June 2001.

Roe SJ and Thomas LC. Completing a death certificate properly. *Minnesota Medicine,* 87, January 2004.

Saferstein R. Introduction. In: *Criminalistics: An Introduction to Forensic Science,* 7th ed. Upper Saddle River, N.J.: Prentice Hall, 2001.

Schultz OT. *Possibilities and Need for Development of Legal Medicine in the United States,* Bulletin of the National Research Council. Washington, D.C.: National Research Council, October 1932.

Sledzick P. Disaster mortuary operational response team. Institute of Medicine. Medico-legal Death Investigation System: Workshop Summary. National Academies Press, 2003.

Sosin D. Medico-legal death investigation, public health, and health care: The use of medical examiner and coroner data for public health surveillance. Chapter 8 in: *Medicolegal Death Investigation System: Workshop Summary.* Washington, D.C.: National Academies Press, 2003.

Weedn V. Infrastructure and training infrastructure of the medical examiner system. Chapter 4. In: *Medicolegal Death Investigation System: Workshop Summary.* Washington, D.C.: National Academies Press, 2003.

Zumwalt RE. Training and certification in forensic pathology. Institute of Medicine. Medico-legal Death Investigation System: Workshop Summary. National Academies Press, 2003.

Zumwalt RE. Quality assurance in medical examiner practice. Institute of Medicine. Medico-legal Death Investigation System: Workshop Summary. National Academies Press, 2003.

Wolfe M, Nolte KB, and Yoon SS. Fatal infectious disease surveillance and the medical examiner database. *Emerging Infectious Diseases,* 10(1), January 2004.

RECOMMENDED READING

Adelson L. *The Pathology of Homicide.* Springfield, Ill.: Charles C Thomas Publisher, 1974.

Agency for Healthcare Research and Quality. *The Autopsy as an Outcome and Performance Measure,* Evidence Report/Technology Assessment No. 58. Rockville, MD: Author, October 2002.

Bell JS, Ed. *Standards for Inspection and Accreditation of a Modern Medico-Legal Investigative System.* St. Louis, MO: National Association of Medical Examiners, 1980.

Centers for Disease Control and Prevention. Biosafety in microbiological and biomedical laboratories. *BMBL,* January 2, 1997.

Centers for Disease Control and Prevention. Update: Investigation of bioterrorism-related inhalational anthrax: Connecticut, 2001. *Morbidity and Mortality Weekly Report,* 50:1049–1051, 2001.

College of American Pathologists. *Death Statements and Certification of Natural and Unnatural Deaths Manual.* Northfield, Ill.: Author, 1997.

Combs DL, Parrish RG, and Ing R. *Death investigation in the United States and Canada, 1992.* Atlanta, Ga.: Centers for Disease Control and Prevention, 1992.

Dijkhuis H, Zwerling C, Parrish G, Bennett, and Kemper HCG. Medical examiner data in injury surveillance: a comparison with death certificates. *American Journal of Epidemiology,* 139(6):637–643, 1994.

Froede RC, Ed. *Handbook of Forensic Pathology,* 2nd ed. Northfield, Ill.: College of American Pathologists, 2003.

Graitcer PL, Williams WW, Finton RJ, Goodman RA, Thacker SB, and Hanzlick R. An evaluation of the use of medical examiner data for epidemiologic surveillance. *American Journal of Public Health,* 77(9):1212–1214, 1987.

Hansen M. Body of evidence: When coroners and medical examiners fail to distinguish accidents from murders from suicides, a botched autopsy can be the death of a fair trial, an insurance settlement or a civil suit. *ABA Journal,* pp. 60–67, June 1995.

Hanzlick RL. Automation of medical examiner offices. *American Journal of Forensic Medicine and Pathology,* 14(1):34–38, 1993.

Hanzlick R. Coroner training needs. A numeric and geographic analysis. *Journal of the American Medical Association,* 276(21):1775–1778, 1996.

Hanzlick R. Principles for including or excluding mechanisms of death when writing cause-of-death statements. *Archives of Pathology and Laboratory Medicine,* 121:377–380, 1997.

Hanzlick R and Parrish RG. The failure of death certificates to record the performance of autopsies. *Journal of the American Medical Association,* 269(1):47, 1993.

Hanzlick RL and Parrish RG. Death investigation report forms (DIRFs): Generic forms for investigators (IDIRFs) and certifiers (CDIRFs). *Journal of Forensic Science,* 39(3):629–636, 1994.

Hanzlick RL and Parrish RG. Epidemiologic aspects of forensic pathology. *Clinics in Laboratory Medicine,* 18(1):23–37, 1998.

Hanzlick RL and Parrish RG. Epidemiologic aspects of forensic pathology. In: *Clinics in Laboratory Medicine: Forensic Pathology, Part 1.* Froede RC, Ed. Philadelphia: W. B. Saunders, 1998, pp. 23–37.

Jobes DA, Berman AL, and Josselson AR. The impact of psychological autopsies on medical examiners' determination of manner of death. *Journal of Forensic Science,* 31(1):177–189, 1986.

Jones AM, Mann J, and Braziel R. Human plague in New Mexico: Report of three autopsied cases. *Journal of Forensic Science,* 24:26–38, 1979.

Kircher T and Anderson RE. Cause of death. Proper completion of the death certificate. *Journal of the American Medical Association,* 258:349–352, 1987.

Kircher T, Nelson J, and Burdo H. The autopsy as a measure of accuracy of the death certificate. *New England Journal of Medicine,* 313:1263–1269, 1985.

Lipskin BA and Field KS, Eds. *Death Investigation and Examination: Medico-Legal Guidelines and Checklists.* Colorado Springs, Colo.: Forensic Sciences Foundation Press, 1984.

Milroy CM and Whitwell HL. Reforming the coroner's service: Major necessary reforms would mean an integrated service and more medical input. *British Medical Journal,* 327:175–176, 2003.

Nolte KB. Safety precautions to limit exposure from plague-infected patients. *Journal of the American Medical Association,* 284(13):1648; author reply, 1649, 2000.

Nolte KB, Simpson GL, and Parrish RG. Emerging infectious agents and the forensic pathologist: the New Mexico model. *Archives of Pathology and Laboratory Medicine,* 120:125–128, 1996.

Nolte KB and Wolfe MI. Medical examiner and coroner surveillance for emerging infections. In: *Emerging Infections 3,* Scheld WM, Craig WA, and Hughes JM, Eds. Washington, D.C.: American Society of Microbiology Press, 1999, pp. 201–217.

Parrish RG, Maes EF, and Ing RT. Computerization of medical examiner and coroner offices: a national survey. In: *American Academy of Forensic Sciences 1992 Annual Meeting.* Colorado Springs, Colo.: American Academy of Forensic Sciences, 1992, p. 152.

Prahlow J and Lantz PE. Medical examiner/death investigator training requirements in state medical examiner systems. *Journal of Forensic Science,* 40:55–58, 1995.

Randall BB, Fierro M F, Froede, RC. Practice guideline for forensic pathology. *Archives of Pathology & Laboratory Medicine,* 122:1056–1064, December 1998.

Silverberg SG. Surgical pathology fellowship training in the United States and Canada. Results of a survey by the Arthur Purdy Stout Society of Surgical Pathologists. *American Journal of Surgical Pathology,* 11(3):231–233, March 1987.

Spitz WU, Ed. *Spitz and Fisher's Medico-Legal Investigation of Death: Guidelines for the Application of Pathology to Crime Investigation.* Springfield, Ill.: Charles C Thomas Publisher, 1993.

ENDNOTE

1. Extracted, from "A Comprehensive Analysis of Forensic Science Training in Forensic Pathology Fellowship Programs," *Journal of Forensic Sciences,* Volume 48, Issue 2, copyright ASTM International, 100 Barr Harbor Drive, West Conshohocken, PA 19428.

CHAPTER 9

THE COURTS: BATTLEFIELD FOR THE TRUTH AND A CHANGING PARADIGM

As we have seen previously, both the medico-legal death investigation system and the forensic laboratory system are faced with enormous pressure to meet workload demands under less than ideal conditions; in a time when the criticism has reached a crescendo, it is not surprising that the criticisms have been played out in the courts. It is the place where forensic science is most celebrated and most vilified. However, some commentators maintain that the courts are not well suited to ferreting out the truth as it relates to the veracity of forensic science and how it is used to adjudicate criminal cases.

Jonakait (1991) observes, "The courts seem to provide an external mechanism to enforce higher quality in forensic science. However, they can not adequately accomplish this task. Courts only deal with the evidence in the cases before them. This prevents them from confronting the full range of issues concerning forensic laboratories. Courts only see a fraction of a forensic scientist's analyses. They almost never examine the inaccurate work that produces inconclusive findings or leads to a false exclusion. Indeed, despite widespread inaccuracies in forensic lab reports, courts are unlikely to discover such problems, and are therefore unable to remedy the widespread consequences of poor forensic work."

Kiely (2003) observes, "The scientific nature of information generated by one or more forensic sciences, such as hair or fiber evidence, may require a preliminary determination of whether the scientific methodology on which a forensic expert's testimony is based, is either generally accepted in the scientific community or, under federal *Daubert* standard, is relevant and reliable. If information produced and testified to by expert witnesses successfully survives the evidence rules and foundational processes, it and other items of inference-based information become available for jury consumption."

As we will see more fully in Chapter 12, U.S. courts are charged with the responsibility of determining the admissibility of forensic evidence based on a number of factors relating to accuracy, reliability, and acceptance by the scientific community. Current standards for admissibility of scientific evidence, some commentators argue, inhibit courts' inquiry into the level of quality of the forensic testing, analysis, and interpretation of results. Critics say further that the courts do not assess how an analysis has been performed, the protocols and standard operating procedures followed, and the quality controls that were in place to monitor the quality assurance process.

While some commentators expect the courts to aid in the transformation of the quality of forensic science, others say the courts lack sufficient know-how and resources. Jonakait (1991) asserts, "Courts are essentially restricted to excluding evidence. If the courts regularly refused to admit analyses when laboratories had not followed programs assuring high quality work, improvements could follow. Judges, however, are unlikely to adopt such a procedure. Furthermore, such court action would not be an efficient way to produce the needed systemic reforms. For example, until the highest court in a jurisdiction had ruled on an issue, laboratories would have to guess what quality control efforts each court might demand of them. Labs might be subject to as many regulators as there are courts in a state. Such multiple regulation would lead to inefficiencies."

Jonakait (1991) argues that the adversary nature of the courtroom hampers courts in their ability to properly assess science, and adds, "An adversary process that performs properly requires lawyers who can effectively expose weaknesses in scientific evidence and a judiciary not overawed by science. These qualities are often absent because lawyers and judges usually lack high levels of scientific training and are thus unable to challenge or evaluate science. Both prosecutors and defense attorneys seem unwilling to challenge the accuracy of test results. Even though shoddy forensic science may help free the guilty more often than inculpate the innocent, prosecutors are unlikely to verify whether the exculpatory finding is warranted. Similarly, defense attorneys often seem to trust the reliability of forensic test results. . . . Furthermore, meaningfully challenging the evidence may not be possible because of discovery limitations, the inability to retest the evidence, and the lack of adequate expert assistance. Courts, therefore, are unlikely to bring about better forensic science practices because those practices are seldom fully analyzed and challenged in our adversary system."

One of the criticisms leveled at forensic science is that is has not been subjected to proper scrutiny of its validity and its reliability. "It's a significant problem that most forensic sciences that are used in the courts to adjudicate cases have never been tested," asserts Terrence Kiely, J.D., L.L.M., professor of law and director of the Center for Law and Science at DePaul University in Chicago. "They may have been tested years ago, and what happens in our system is that in one case, the court will give it a quick look and say 'OK,' and then in the second case the court will give it a lesser look and say 'OK,' and the third one will cite the first two, and there you go. So these forensic disciplines really have not been tested as they should have been. This is changing, because the defense attorneys and the public defenders who handle most of the appeals from these trials, are becoming much more educated about the process. *Daubert*'s standards of admissibility of evidence are very much alive and well in criminal cases, but most evidence is found to be admissible. It's just a matter of getting the right case to make a significant challenge to forensic evidence that could change everything. Fingerprints are being challenged all the time, as is hair analysis and document examination, but again, much of it is still being admitted into court. And sometimes it's a matter of what is considered questionable science—all forensic disciplines are up for grabs. Sometimes you don't want to waste your time on admissibility issues because the courts have said, 'We've recognized this for X number of years,' but in some cases, courts are starting to revisit issues."

Forensic science's performance in court seems to be the new measuring stick for this field. Following the issuance throughout the 1990s by the U.S. Supreme Court of the so-called *evidence trilogy* (which will be discussed in great detail throughout the next several chapters), which essentially hands down stricter parameters for the evaluation of expert testimony in civil trials (to a greater degree) and criminal trials (to a lesser degree, although this, too, is debatable) and thus the presentation of forensic evidence used to adjudicate cases, forensic science found itself under siege as never before.

THE PARADIGM SHIFT

In an attempt to characterize the changes wrought by the so-called evidence trilogy of *Daubert, Kumho,* and *Joiner,* Michael Saks, of the College of Law, Arizona State University, and Jonathan Koehler, of the McCombs School of Business at the University of Texas in Austin, lobbed the shot heard round the forensic science community in the form of an August 2005 *Science* paper called "The Coming Paradigm Shift in Forensic Identification Science."

Saks and Koehler (2005) say the term *paradigm shift* rightly characterizes the "converging legal and scientific forces" that are "pushing the traditional forensic identification sciences toward fundamental change." They say they use the notion of paradigm shift not as a literal application of Thomas Kuhn's concept (see Chapter 10) but "as a metaphor highlighting the transformation involved in moving from a prescience to an empirically grounded science." They note, "Legal and scientific forces are converging to drive an emerging skepticism about the claims of the traditional forensic individualization sciences. As a result, these sciences are moving toward a new scientific paradigm."

They cite four forces, to be discussed throughout this section, as driving this paradigm shift. Two forces, they say, are outgrowths of DNA typing—the discovery of erroneous convictions and a model for a scientifically sound identification science; the third force is the momentous change in the legal admissibility standards for expert testimony; the fourth force stems from studies of error rates across the forensic sciences.

Saks and Koehler (2005) observe, "Changes in the law pertaining to the admissibility of expert evidence in court, together with the emergence of DNA typing as a model for a scientifically defensible approach to questions of shared identity, are driving the older forensic sciences toward a new scientific paradigm." They explain that as little as 10 years ago, practitioners in the field of forensic individualization "compared pairs of marks (handwriting, fingerprints, tool marks, hair, tire marks, bite marks, etc.), intuited whether the marks matched, and testified in court that whoever or whatever made one made the other. Courts almost never excluded the testimony. Cross-examination rarely questioned the foundations of the asserted expertise or the basis of the analyst's certainty. Today, that once-complacent corner of the law and science interface has begun to unravel—or at least to regroup."

Saks and Koehler (2005) point to the headlines that tell of supposed erroneous identifications by forensic examiners that have in part helped to trigger a greater questioning of forensic science in general, and the identification sciences in particular. Their fear is that undiscerning judges and jurors believe unsubstantiated claims by forensic practitioners, and note with pleasure that courts have begun to question this asserted forensic science expertise. They observe, "A dispassionate scientist or judge reviewing the current state of the traditional forensic sciences would likely regard their claims as plausible, under-researched, and oversold."

In their paradigm shift paper, Saks and Koehler take aim at the concept of "discernible uniqueness" that is the foundation of the forensic identification sciences, and assert that this foundation has been weakened by errors not only in proficiency testing, but in actual cases as well. A tenet of forensic science is to link the crime scene to an individual perpetrator through the discovery of evidence. Edmond Locard's Principle of Exchange states that when any two objects come into contact, there is always transfer of material from each object onto the other. This principle was postulated by 20th-century forensic scientist Edmond Locard, the director of the very first crime laboratory in existence at the time in Lyon, France. Essentially, Locard's principle is applied to crime scenes in which the perpetrator(s) of a crime comes into contact with the scene; in doing so, the perpetrator will both bring something to the scene and leave behind something, and that every contact leaves a trace.

What Saks and Koehler (2005) object to is the examiner's insistence that two indistinguishable marks must have been produced by a single object, to the exclusion of all others in the world, thus relying on the assumption of discernible uniqueness. Saks and Koehler observe, "According to this assumption, markings produced by different people or objects are observably different. Thus, when a pair of markings is not observably different, criminalists conclude that the marks were made by the same person or object. Although lacking theoretical or empirical foundations, the assumption of discernible uniqueness offers important practical benefits to the traditional forensic sciences. It enables forensic scientists to draw bold, definitive conclusions that can make or break cases. It excuses the forensic sciences from developing measures of object attributes, collecting population data on the frequencies of variations in those attributes, testing attribute independence, or calculating and explaining the probability that different objects share a common set of observable attributes."

One of the underpinnings of this paradigm shift is undeniably triggered by post-conviction exonerations, made possible by the retesting, or sometimes testing in the first place, of evidence through cutting-edge DNA technology. Saks and Koehler (2005) state, "It was not surprising to learn that erroneous convictions sometimes occur, and that new science and technology can help detect and correct those mistakes. Nor was it surprising to learn, from an analysis of 86 such cases, that erroneous eyewitness identifications are the most common contributing factor to wrongful convictions. What was unexpected is that erroneous forensic science expert testimony is the second most common contributing factor to wrongful convictions, found in 63 percent of those cases. These data likely understate the relative contribution of forensic science expert testimony to erroneous convictions. Whereas lawyers, police, and lay witnesses participate in virtually every criminal case, forensic science experts participate in a smaller subset of cases—about 10 percent to 20 percent of criminal cases during the era when these DNA exonerations were originally tried."

Saks and Koehler (2005) assert that forensic scientists "are the witnesses most likely to present misleading or fraudulent testimony." They add, "Deceitful forensic scientists are a minor sidelight to this paper, but a sidelight that underscores cultural differences between normal science and forensic science. In normal science, academically gifted students receive four or more years of doctoral training where much of the socialization into the culture of science takes place. This culture emphasizes methodological rigor, openness, and cautious interpretation of data. In forensic science, 96 percent of positions are held by persons with bachelor's degrees (or less), 3 percent master's degrees, and 1 percent PhDs. When individuals who are not steeped in the culture of science work in an adversarial, crime-fighting culture, there is a substantial risk that a different set of norms will prevail."

Part of the so-called paradigm shift has to do with the general acceptance of DNA testing as the gold standard for all other disciplines of forensic identification disciplines. Saks and Koehler, like many commentators on forensic science, show respect for DNA typing, something they laud as the one aspect of forensic science actually steeped in traditional science and biochemistry. They say DNA typing serves as a model for the traditional forensic sciences in three important respects:

- DNA typing technology was an application of knowledge derived from core scientific disciplines. This provided a stable structure for future empirical work on the technology.
- The courts and scientists scrutinized applications of the technology in individual cases. As a result, early, unscientific practices were rooted out.
- DNA typing offered data-based, probabilistic assessments of the meaning of evidentiary "matches." This practice represented an advance over potentially misleading match/no-match claims associated with other forensic identification sciences.

Saks and Koehler (2005) describe the great debate that ensued shortly after DNA's first appearance in the courtroom in the 1980s: "Blue-ribbon panels were convened, conferences were held, unscientific practices were identified, data were collected, critical papers were written, and standards were developed and implemented. The scientific debates focused on the adequacy of DNA databases, the computation of DNA match probabilities, the training of DNA analysts, the presentation of DNA matches in the courtroom, and the role of error rates. In some cases, disputants worked together to find common ground. These matters were not resolved by the forensic scientists themselves, by fiat, or by neglect. Most exaggerated claims and counterclaims about DNA evidence have been replaced by scientifically defensible propositions. Although some disagreement remains, the scientific process worked."

According to Saks and Koehler (2005), the strength of DNA testing is that it is steeped in population genetics theory and empirical testing, a foundation they say should be emulated by traditional forensic sciences. They explain: "Each subfield must construct databases of sample characteristics and use these databases to support a probabilistic approach to identification. Fingerprinting could be one of the first areas to make the transition to this approach because large fingerprint databases already exist. The greatest challenge in this effort would be to develop measures of the complex images presented by fingerprints, tool marks, bite marks, handwriting, etc. Forensic scientists will need to work with experts in differential geometry, topology, or other fields to develop workable measures."

Another factor in the paradigm shift, as Saks and Koehler see it, is evolution of the law. As we will see in Chapter 12, trial courts have received instruction from the U.S. Supreme Court to step up its efforts in the scrutiny of scientific evidence proffered, using the scientific method as a measuring stick of sorts, and applying new evaluative standards. To determine admissibility, judges were advised to consider whether the proffered science had been tested, the level of methodological soundness of that testing, and the results of that testing. According to Saks and Koehler (2005), this new order "lowers the threshold for admission of sound cutting-edge science and raises the threshold for long-asserted expertise that lacks a scientific foundation." When applied, they say, these standards "subject the forensic sciences to a first-principles scientific scrutiny that poses a profound challenge to fields that lack rigorous supporting data."

This paradigm shift also has helped focus increasing attention on error rates of various forensic identification disciplines, as we will see further in Chapter 10. One of the most common assertions made by critics of forensic science is the paucity of research relating to the accuracy of disciplines such as latent fingerprint or bite mark identification. Saks and Koehler (2005) state, "Proficiency tests in some fields offer a step in the right direction, even though simple tasks and infrequent peer review limit their value. Nonetheless, the available data hint that some forensic sciences are best interpreted in tandem with error rates estimated from sound studies. Unfortunately, forensic scientists often reject error rate estimates in favor of arguments that theirs is an error-free science."

Many critics point to fingerprint examiners who say all fingerprint experts would reach the same conclusions about every print. Saks and Koehler (2005) observe, "Such hubris was on display in spring 2004 when the FBI declared that a fingerprint recovered from a suspicious plastic bag near the scene of a terrorist bombing in Madrid provided a '100 percent match' to an Oregon attorney. The FBI eventually conceded error when Spanish fingerprint experts linked the print to someone else. The FBI and other agencies often seek to preserve the illusion of perfection after disclosure of such errors by distinguishing between human errors and errors of method." Saks and Koehler argue that claiming the infallibility of a forensic analysis method is disingenuous: "It is impossible to disentangle 'method' errors from 'practitioner' errors in fields where the method is primarily the judgment of the examiner. Second, even if such disentanglement were possible, it is a red herring. When fact-finders hear evidence of a forensic match, a proper assessment of the probative value of that match requires awareness of the chance that a mistake was made."

Saks and Koehler (2005) also assert that it is unreasonable to claim that error rates do not exist because they evolve over time: "In this fallacy of reasoning, people underuse (or willfully ignore) general background data in judgment tasks because they believe the data are irrelevant to the instant case. However, general background data (or base rates) are relevant for specific predictions." Saks and Koehler explain that a base-rate risk of error in any forensic discipline can indicate that a certain conclusion is erroneous. They point to data extracted from proficiency tests that have shown error rates as high as 40 percent to 60 percent, and comment, "Forensic science proficiency tests and examinations are obviously imperfect indicators of the rate at which errors occur in practice. This fact does not justify ignoring the worrisome data these tests have yielded. Indeed, these data are probably best regarded as lower-bound estimates of error rates. Because the tests are relatively easy, and because participants know that mistakes will be identified and punished, test error rates (particularly the false-positive error rate) probably are lower than those in everyday casework."

Saks and Koehler (2005) assert that one of the easiest ways to take a corrective course of action is to study the model provided by DNA typing and use it to inject science back into forensic identification science. They state, "This effort should begin with adoption of the basic-research model. Just as DNA scientists tested the genetic assumptions that undergirded DNA typing theory, traditional forensic scientists should design experiments that test the core assumptions of their fields. As basic research knowledge grows, experts will be able to inform courts about the relative strengths and weaknesses of their theories and methods, and suggest how that knowledge applies to individual cases."

Whether or not there is a true paradigm shift taking place at the intersection where forensic science and the law meet, Saks and Koehler (2005) have, at the very least, established a vision in which "untested assumptions and semi-informed guesswork are replaced by a sound scientific foundation and justifiable protocols." They add, "Although obstacles exist both inside and outside forensic science, the time is ripe for the traditional forensic sciences to replace antiquated assumptions of uniqueness and perfection with a more defensible empirical and probabilistic foundation."

THE SHIFTY PARADIGM

The Saks/Koehler paper created quite a stir in the forensic and legal communities. One of the more comprehensive rebuttals to this paper was one called "The Shifty Paradigm," in which forensic and legal experts Norah Rudin and Keith Inman penned a two-part response to Saks and Koehler published by the California Association of Criminalists in its association publication in late 2005 and early 2006. The articles are both a defense against the social scientists' barbs, and an impassioned plea for the reader of all three papers to engage in some serious critical thinking about tenets of criminalistics and forensic science, as well.

Perhaps sensing the inherent battle that serves as an underpinning of the war waged between forensic science and the law, Rudin and Inman (2005) ask themselves, "Who gets to define the practice of forensic science?" They rightly observe, "Being nestled (or perhaps more often wedged) between science and the law, each profession claims a piece of ours. It is all too easy to allow ourselves to become fractured and unfocused by the forces pulling in different directions. Only when criminalists take responsibility for, and control over defining and directing the profession of forensic science will we achieve a degree of earned and respected autonomy."

Pointing out that Saks is a law professor and Koehler is a behavioral sciences professor and are thus "observers rather than practitioners," Rudin and Inman (2000) pick up on what they feel to be errors in content and the subtle nuances that further muddy the waters in any discussion of forensic science and its impact on medico-legal matters. They comment, "Interestingly, 'forensic identification science' is used interchangeably with 'forensic individualization science' throughout the paper. An understanding of these terms as fundamental concepts in forensic science is key to a clear discussion of the issues outlined in the article. Although both identification and individualization are used in the forensic community to describe a conclusion of common unique source, the term 'identification' has historically been used by fingerprint examiners (and some other pattern comparison disciplines), while 'individualization' is used by most other disciplines, as well as the forensic academic community. We have previously suggested that, for the purpose of clarity, 'identification' should be used to describe the categorization of items, while 'individualization' should be reserved for the process that attempts to determine if two items share a unique common source."

Rudin and Inman (2005) continue, "Even more important than a misuse of terms is the failure of the authors to recognize that determination of source (whether described by identification or individualization) is only one element of a complete forensic analysis. . . . This seemingly subtle shift in naming our profession has far-reaching consequences. It limits scientists to addressing only the question of source, excluding us from commenting on the very relevant forensic questions of contact and event ordering. . . . Whether intentional or not, this artificial constraint on the role of forensic science and forensic scientists allows others, most often attorneys, to control discussions regarding the significance of physical evidence in the context of the case. While this may provide an attorney the chance to arrange the facts to suit a particular theory in some instant case, it does not serve justice well in the long run. This is exemplified no more clearly than their circumscription of forensic science as a single-use tool, to answer only questions of source, limits their thinking about the issues they present and leads them to overly simplistic and poorly conceived solutions."

In recognizing the importance of nuance, Rudin and Inman prefer to use "identification" to describe the process of categorization (the physical nature of the evidence) and "individualization" to describe the process of source determination (the origin of the evidence).

One of Saks and Koehler's major criticisms in the *Science* paper (2005) is that forensic examiners "intuit" pattern matches. While Rudin and Inman (2005) acknowledge the need for "fundamental change" in the forensic discipline of pattern matching, they maintain that criteria do exist for the comparison of dermal ridge prints, tool marks, shoe prints, and other visual comparisons.

A second major criticism by Saks and Koehler (2005) is that the core assumptions of numerous forensic sciences are being questioned by other scientists, including the fact that "traditional forensic sciences rest on a central assumption: that two indistinguishable marks must have been produced by a single object." Saks and Koehler call it the "assumption of discernible uniqueness."

Rudin and Inman (2005) say that by referring to "uniqueness," Saks and Koehler created a "blatant mischaracterization of the nature of physical objects." Rudin and Inman explain that by its very definition, every object is unique in space and time, so that any discussion of uniqueness is irrelevant to answering the question of whether evidence and reference ever shared a common source. In other words, they explain, a forensic examination typically compares two items: a trace or mark recovered as evidence, and a trace or mark derived from a suspected reference object. They say the critical question to ask is if they originated from a common source. They say, "Precisely because each object is unique, even two items that in fact do share a common source will exhibit differences at some level of analysis. Thus Saks and Koehler's 'assumption of discernible uniqueness' is actually a given, even for objects that share the same source; in fact it complicates every forensic comparison in a way that the authors apparently do not appreciate. The forensic examiner not only compares characteristics that look the same, but must actively search for differences. A critical aspect of the examination is to determine if the differences are explainable or not."

Rudin and Inman (2005) hold that "explainable differences" direct the forensic examiner toward a conclusion of common source, while "unexplainable differences" suggest different sources. They state, "The determination of whether a difference is explainable is anything but trivial; it leads to a long and complex discussion of the origin of evidence and the very nature of physical matter itself."

Rudin and Inman (2005) bristle at Saks and Koehler's suggestion that, "Although lacking theoretical or empirical foundations, the assumption of discernible uniqueness offers important practical benefits to the traditional forensic sciences. It enables forensic scientists to draw bold, definitive conclusions that can make or break cases. It excuses the forensic sciences from developing measures of object attributes, collecting population data on the frequencies of variations in those attributes, testing attribute independence, or calculating and explaining the probability that different objects share a common set of observable attributes. Without the discernible uniqueness assumption, far more scientific work would be needed and criminalists would need to offer more tempered opinions in court."

Rudin and Inman (2005) emphasize that Saks and Koehler wrongly dismiss the measurement of object attributes, because, they say, all matter changes continuously over time. They write, "A source object continually loses and acquires traits as do any fragments separated from it that might become evidence after being recognized as relevant to a crime event. After separation, the two objects experience different environments and forces, so that individualizing traits inevitably begin to diverge in random fashion. Our ability to determine that items once shared or were derived from a common source necessarily weakens over time. This unrecognized ambiguity most often results in a false exclusion or an inability to perform a comparison. Again, this is not bad or wrong; it is simply inherent in the nature of the material and the question being posed. In the case of pattern transfer, the method of transfer, the transfer medium, and the substrate upon which the pattern is deposited each introduce another element of potential ambiguity. These are difficult problems, both conceptually and practically, as they involve exploring and understanding the very nature of matter."

Where Rudin and Inman, as well as Saks and Koehler do agree, however, is that forensic science would benefit greatly from partnering with researchers rooted in academia who could help define the controversial limitations involved in comparing physical objects and the patterns made by them. Rudin and Inman (2005) assert that, however, "While much work remains to be done on the theoretical foundation of pattern comparison, the authors' claim that no empirical foundation exists is patently untrue. Estimating the strength of an evidence-to-source connection is critical to a responsible communication of the results of any forensic examination. Saks and Koehler make the implicit assumption that this must necessarily be a quantitative estimate. While we agree that every attempt should be made to collect data to support quantitative estimates of the frequency of sets of traits, we must also recognize the possibility that, in the end, this may be neither realistic nor practical; in some cases it could be possibly more misleading than providing no estimate."

The two sets of researchers also part ways on the topic of DNA as setting the pace for all other forensic disciplines to follow. Rudin and Inman (2005) comment, "Saks and Koehler rather cavalierly suggest that the model for forensic DNA typing can and should be applied wholesale to non-biological evidence. To put it simply, this is naïve." They explain that because non-biological evidence requires compositional and microscopic analyses of trace evidence, there exist fundamental differences in the nature of the evidence and the mechanisms of source populations making it impossible to directly apply the DNA typing model. Rudin and Inman explain: "The fundamental challenge in comparison of non-biological print and impression evidence is to determine which traits are relevant, and whether they are class traits, potentially individualizing traits, or even artifacts. This challenge is rarely encountered in DNA testing and even for dermal ridge prints, the traits, although complex, are all of a similar nature. In neither case are traits typically acquired or changed, only lost until there is nothing to compare. For non-biological prints and impressions especially, the divergence of traits between evidence samples and their true source in the time period between division and comparison may result in the addition or change of traits, as well as their disappearance. This complicates the interpretation of any comparison."

Rudin and Inman (2005) take issue with Saks and Koehler's assumptions about error rates in forensic identification disciplines, claiming that they were made based on case data provided by the Innocence Project that "have been propagated through the media as fact." Rudin and Inman observe, "The overwhelming in-your-face assumption here is that both the total and relative proportion of 'factors' associated with DNA exoneration cases are factual and unassailable and representative of all criminal cases." Rudin and Inman claim that the cases reviewed by the Innocence Project and used by Saks and Koehler to make their point "have already undergone a highly selective screening process." Rudin and Inman observe, "The most obvious point is that this case set does not even include cases for which biological evidence was never collected or is not relevant. That excludes all cases where non-biological evidence was at issue and also all cases where physical evidence played no part in the case. Second, cases for which conclusive DNA testing has already been performed are not included. We don't attempt to determine here exactly how the selection criteria might skew the data, but at the very least, an entire class of data is missing in which physical evidence played no part. Therefore all errors in that set of data are also not represented." At the heart of the matter, Rudin and Inman say, is that the information is pejorative in the sense that the data set does not adequately represent all cases involving forensic science. They comment, "The problem is that the reader is left to implicitly assume that it does."

Rudin and Inman (2005) also take exception to Saks and Koehler's (2005) assertion that "forensic science testing errors" and "false/misleading testimony by forensic scientists" constitute the majority of wrongful convictions, and state, "We must ask ourselves how many forensic science 'errors' . . . have been exposed precisely because definitive tests can be performed to expose the errors. The remaining causes of wrongful convictions all relate to human frailties that are much less amenable to formal and definitive testing. How can we quantify prosecutorial misconduct, defense counsel incompetence, or police misconduct? What test reliably distinguishes dishonest informants, false confessions, and false testimony by lay witnesses from truthful ones?" Rudin and Inman add, "The determination of human 'errors' depends on the believability and credibility of other humans. While an overwhelming amount of contrary information might convince most of us that an informant lied, no definitive test exists. So, even defining an 'error' as an apparently wrongful conviction, the proportion estimates for causes that do not relate to physical evidence must have wider confidence limits, however difficult they may be to measure. Saks and Koehler treat all the data as if it had equal reliability."

One of the more contentious issues in the forensic community is that of error rates, of course, and Rudin and Inman (2005) go so far as to state, "We continue to argue that there is no such animal as an error 'rate.' Inclusion of this wording in a controlling legal decision by a federal judge does not automatically legitimize it as a relevant quantifier of forensic science. A rate implies a constant for a defined procedure or process, both of which are totally inapplicable to forensic work taken as a whole. And, at the risk of beating a hole in the drum, we feel compelled to note that, like other observers who like to harp on error rates, Saks and Koehler completely sidestep the issue of actually defining an error."

Rudin and Inman (2005) continue, "While we can deduce an implicit legal definition of a wrongful conviction, this is ultimately not helpful on a scientific level. The disconnect seems to be that the legal profession has attempted to commandeer a perfectly reasonable quantifier of error for a single controlled scientific process, for example fidelity in PCR amplification, and apply it wholesale to a complex human endeavor that includes many different scientific as well as human processes. Even if the oft-suggested solution of blind proficiency testing could be implemented wholesale, trying to predict the rate of undetected errors (however those might be defined) from analysis of such data seems to us tenuous at best."

Instead, Rudin and Inman (2005) say focus should be directed at undetected errors: "This is actually a much thornier problem and one to which no easy answer exists. It forces all of us, the forensic profession, the legal profession, the judicial system, and the public, to acknowledge that undetected errors can, do, and will exist. Such errors are likely sporadic, unpredictable, and sometimes undetectable as well as undetected. What society must understand is that, with or without forensic analyses, the risk of convicting an innocent person will never be zero. Most people appreciate, at some basic level, that human endeavors are fallible. But they have the unrealistic expectation that scientific endeavors carried out by human beings are infallible; the label of science confers the patina of certainty. In reality, what science does is measure uncertainty. Any answer we provide must, by definition, be probabilistic in nature, and be conditioned on various assumptions. If science is involved, the possibility of error always exists. Because our judicial system is predicated on the presumption of innocence, this realization appropriately makes people uncomfortable. But what is the alternative? Clearly, the non-scientific evidence is also at risk for error, the difference being that it is much more difficult to both detect and quantify."

SCIENCE AND THE LAW: CLASH OF THE TITANS

As Jonakait (1991) observed earlier in this chapter, the adversarial nature of the courtroom does not lend itself to a smooth scientific inquiry regarding issues of admissibility of evidence.

Some members of the forensic science community say that certain disciplines are dismissed by judges without recognition of the value they bring to the adjudication of cases, but add that research must be done to further solidify these disciplines' scientific integrity. "Fingerprints are far more important than DNA simply because fingerprint evidence solves far more cases," asserts Barry A.J. Fisher, director of the crime lab of the Los Angeles County Sheriff's Department. "When you look at the number of cases that fingerprints have solved in a given day or year, it's probably hundreds and hundreds more cases than DNA evidence. What might happen if an appellate court decided that we can't testify that fingerprints can be linked to a single person? We would have to lessen the conclusions that we make should courts question the reliability of fingerprint or other pattern-recognition evidence. If this happened, experts might have to testify that 'I personally believe that fingerprints are reliable. We don't know the statistical likelihood of one print matching up to an individual, but I'm confident the print in question came from the defendant.'" Fisher continues, "Just like with DNA evidence, if through solid research we can develop statistics and further scientific proof for pattern evidence such as fingerprints or handwriting, etc., that will effectively eliminate some of the arguments voiced by critics. But until we do some credible research, it's not going to happen.

Of course the problem is not that there are people out there that are capable of doing the research, it's just that someone has to pay for it. The research must be funded at the federal level by organizations such as the NIJ or the National Science Foundation. We need to not lose sight of the real problem; there is insufficient funding at the federal level in the area of forensic science research and development. We run the risk of our science being questioned in the courts because there is so little research. Everything we do in forensic science is going to be played out, or has an expectation of being played out in the courts."

And so, science and the law meet, with varying degrees of success and failure in these disciplines' attempts to see eye to eye. It is an uneasy meeting in some cases. Jasanoff (2005) observes, "Law often completes the work of politics and public affairs, and science as frequently underwrites the rationality of public decisions."

Perhaps with an unknowing irony, Jasanoff (2005) comments, "As relatively apolitical institutions, law and science are powerful generators of trust. The findings of both are expected to be impartial, disinterested, valid without regard to the immediate context of production, and true insofar as participants in either institution are able to gauge the truth. Social order in democratic nations depends on both institutions living up to this ethos, or at least strenuously attempting to do so. Together, law and science have underwritten a time-honored approach to securing legitimacy in public decisions. If their interactions are governed by flawed principles, then the capacity of either to control the arbitrariness of power is greatly weakened. Complicating the picture is the fact that the interests of law and science—though often congruent—are neither entirely nor inevitably so. Nowhere in the western world have the conflicts between these institutions been so dramatically exposed nor so hotly debated as in the United States."

Since the 1990s, law has had new sources of ammunition to use against science, thanks to the evidence trilogy alluded to at the beginning of this chapter and discussed in greater detail in subsequent chapters. Jasanoff (2005) refers to this evidence trilogy of *Daubert v Merrell Dow Pharmaceuticals*, *Kumho Tire Co. v Carmichael*, and *General Electric v Joiner*, which she characterizes as "immensely relevant to the workings of American democracy." Jasanoff asserts that "addressing the relationship between law and science and finding workable means of coping with their frictions emerge as essential components of any good-faith attempt to create an international order."

Jasanoff (2005) argues that *Daubert* rests on serious misconceptions about the nature of science, the goals of legal fact-finding, and the role of the judiciary. She states, "A sociologically grounded approach to science and technology calls for a different kind of jurisprudence that is better attuned to the law's primary function of doing justice." Jasanoff says that from a doctrine point of view, *Daubert* was the first case in which the U.S. Supreme Court addressed the admissibility of scientific evidence in federal proceedings. She explains that not only did *Daubert* effectively set aside the so-called "*Frye* test" in many states, but that the landmark decision also "formally ended disagreements that had arisen since then among the federal circuit courts."

Most importantly, according to Jasanoff (2005), *Daubert* represented "a change in long-standing habits of judicial tolerance toward party experts, coupled with habitual judicial deference to the jury's fact-finding function." She explains, "Procedurally, the case changed the rules of the game for pretrial hearings in which judges consider motions by a party . . . to exclude the opposite party's . . . offer of scientific or technical evidence. *Daubert* instructed judges to be more proactive in their response to such motions. Judicial discrimination, the Court indicated, should act as a filter to screen away from juries any evidence that did not pass threshold tests of relevance and reliability. Judges, in short, were to act as gatekeepers, guarding the courtroom door against what some saw as an uncontrolled onslaught of 'junk science.'"

Jasanoff (2005) observes that *Daubert* essentially required judges to think like scientists: "The judge's role, according to this reading, was to bring the legal assessment of science into closer alignment with assessment of science by scientists. The Court apparently concluded that conforming judicial criteria of admissibility to scientific ones would serve the interests of reason and of justice."

Jasanoff (2005) believes that *Daubert*'s attempt to make the adjudicature of cases more scientific is part of a "tectonic shift in U.S. legal and political thought that aims to modernize legal decision-making by making it more efficient, standardized, and predictable." Jasanoff points to *Daubert*'s "progeny," the *Joiner* and *Kumho* decisions, which "opened up a wider debate on the principles and procedures by which law and science should regulate their interactions with each other and thereby with parties seeking legal redress for the failures of science and technology."

Jasanoff (2005) boldly asserts that the more important question for the legal field is "not how judges can best do justice to science; the more critical concern is how courts can better render justice under conditions of endemic uncertainty and ignorance." She clarifies, "It becomes clear that the law should not see itself as a simple transcription device for science, automatically writing into legal decisions whatever facts science has—or has not—generated in relation to specific controversies. Rather, the legal process should develop a more searching, self-critical awareness of its own pivotal role in producing new knowledge (and potentially hindering its production). Only by admitting its agency, and its limitations, in this regard will the legal system position itself to use science as it should be used in legal environments: for doing justice."

Many legal scholars have declared that *Daubert* created a no-spin zone in the courtroom, where science and law could pursue the truth, but Jasanoff (2005) pokes a sizable hole in this noble idea: "Law, so conventional wisdom holds, is at fault when it subjugates science and the scientific process to its own unbridled, ends-driven, win-at-any-cost ethic. This diagnosis carries an implicit prescription: to preserve the integrity of science, one must carve out for it an essentially de-legalized space—a space in which science can be true to itself, free from the distorting influence of the adversarial process and its pressure for closure." This, Jasanoff asserts, is "shaky ground." Jasanoff asserts further that the standards to which law and science are subjected have varying conceptions of what is considered to be reliable and how reliability should be demonstrated.

Despite the similar quest for truth, law and science part ways in several respects. While the law exists to reach a conclusion, the adjudicature of a case, science can afford to be open-ended in its inquiry. Jasanoff (2005) adds that while lawsuits require a choice between competing claims, science is allowed latitude in its ability to be less unproved with regard to a given hypothesis or question. Regarding deference to the process, Jasanoff says, "the relationship between law and science is asymmetric." She adds, "The law has historically carved out a quasi-autonomous place for scientific knowledge and expertise, for example, by creating exemptions for expert testimony from 'ordinary' rules of witnessing. Science has borrowed procedural devices from the law, but scientific processes are not formally accountable to the law except on those aspects of practice that are explicitly regulated. Among the many instruments used by the law to produce credible approximations to scientific fact-finding are scientific advice and regulatory peer review, the use of special masters and expert panels, and the hearings enabled by *Daubert*. The law, in short, claims to do justice by partially preserving the independent authority of science—by, in effect, writing science into the law. This notion of science's special status dominated the Supreme Court's evidence decisions, but neither *Daubert* nor succeeding cases took note of the law's considerable role in motivating (or hampering) the production, testing, and validation of scientific knowledge."

Various commentators have remarked upon what they refer to as the myth of the scientific method, explaining that the U.S. Supreme Court assumed that trial judges could, through the use of criteria, ably recognize science for what it is and evaluate its quality and validity. Two of these criteria, testability and error rate, suggest that the majority of the Supreme Court justices viewed experimental science as the controlling model of scientific inquiry, according to Jasanoff (2005), who adds, "These assumptions greatly oversimplify the complexity of approaches and methods that characterize contemporary scientific practice. They rest on an idealized conception of the scientific method that pays little attention to the diverse contexts in which scientific research is conducted, assessed, and interpreted."

But what is considered to be truly scientific? Commentators assert that a theory can be universally accepted yet lack an empirical foundation, such as theories relating to the origin of the universe that cannot be tested through controlled (read: "scientific") experiments. Jasanoff (2005) suggests, "Scientific validity cannot be assessed in terms of a single, universally applicable criterion of good scientific method. Scientific inquiry conforms most basically to historically and culturally situated standards of valid reasoning, persuasion, and proof. These standards can and do change over time."

Science and the law need each other; however, some may take issue with how the law extracts the information it needs. In Chapter 10 we explore the phenomenon of *litigation science,* a concept some commentators have condemned as a mechanism for the further cultivation of faulty forensic science. Jasanoff (2005) observes, "The scientific knowledge that the law needs for its purposes is frequently unavailable until the legal process itself creates the incentives for generating it; nor are methods that technical communities regard as valid necessarily at hand until interested litigants seek out the expertise to help them win their case. When negotiations over method are successfully concluded, the resulting science looks secure not because it necessarily presents a better picture of reality but because most or all conflicts among relevant investigators have been resolved. But cessation of conflict does not in itself guarantee the validity or objectivity (in the sense of lack of identifiable bias) of the methods underlying the prevailing consensus."

REFERENCES

Jasanoff S. Law's knowledge: science for justice in legal settings. *American Journal of Public Health,* 95(S1), 2005.

Jonakait R. Forensic science: The need for regulation. *Harvard Journal of Law Technology,* 4:109–191, 1991.

Kiely T. Forensic science and the law. In: *Forensic Science: An Introduction to Scientific and Investigative Techniques,* 4th ed., James SH and Nordby JJ, Eds. Boca Raton, Fla.: CRC Press, 2003.

Rudin N and Inman K. *Principles and Practice of Criminalistics.* Boca Raton, Fla.: CRC Press, 2000.

Rudin N and Inman K. The shifty paradigm, part II: errors and lies and fraud, oh my! *CAC News.* Fourth Quarter 2005.

Saks MJ and Koehler JJ. The coming paradigm shift in forensic identification science. *Science,* 309, August 2005.

RECOMMENDED READING

DeForest P, Lee H, and Gaensslen R. *Forensic Science: An Introduction to Criminalistics.* New York: McGraw Hill, 1983.

Faigman DL, Kaye D, Saks MJ, and Sanders J. *Modern Scientific Evidence: The Law and Science of Expert Testimony,* 2nd ed. St. Paul, Minn.: Thomson-West, 2002.

Houck M. Statistics and trace evidence: The tyranny of numbers. *Forensic Science Communications,* 1(3), 1999.

Inman, K and Rudin, N. The origin of evidence. *Forensic Science International,* 126:11–16, 2002.

CHAPTER 10

NOT ALL SCIENCE IS CREATED EQUAL

As we have seen, many critics assert that forensic science is somehow lacking in scientific rigor. It is prudent, then, to come to an understanding of what science is and what it is not, and how one makes this determination.

DO WE UNDERSTAND SCIENCE?

If science is a method of seeking the truth, it follows that scientific reasoning and comprehension should be the pursuit of every human being who seeks knowledge. If we hold our scientists to a high level of expertise, isn't it fair to expect the American public to take an interest in these scientific undertakings? And at the very least, shouldn't Americans have a rudimentary understanding of important scientific concepts? And can the argument that there is a lack of science in forensic science be made if, in general, science itself is not well understood?

"I don't think forensic science is different from any other science, and I'm not sure there are a lot of people in the general population who have been rigorously schooled in science," says Don Wyckoff, manager of the forensic laboratory of the Idaho State Police, and chairman of ASCLD/LAB, the laboratory accreditation program of the American Society of Crime Laboratory Directors. "There are more science classes than ever, but it would appear that knowledge of science is lower than ever."

Miller (2004) asserts that a scientifically literate citizen must have a basic vocabulary of scientific terms and constructs and a general understanding of the nature of scientific inquiry. The National Academy of Engineering and the National Research Council have specified indicators of technological literacy (Committee on Technological Literacy, 2002) including the recognition of the pervasiveness of technology in everyday life and the understanding of some of the ways in which technology shapes human history and people shape technology. Miller (2004) observes further, "The proportion of U.S. adults qualifying as being scientifically literate has doubled over the last two decades, but the current level is still problematic for a democratic society that values citizen understanding of major national policies and participation in the resolution of important policy disputes."

To what degree should the layperson be able to understand scientific concepts? Many commentators assert that the process of comprehension ranges from "an elementary idea of what something means (or how it works) to a deep professional understanding of a concept or construct in the full context of its field" (Miller, 2004). While some say that the level of understanding necessary for proper participation in dialogue about scientific matters is not attainable and unnecessary for the average person, Miller says that the level of understanding needed for scientific literacy is akin to being able to read and comprehend the science news presented in *The New York Times*. However, Miller points out, "No pride can be taken in a finding that 4 out of 5 Americans cannot read and understand the science section of *The New York Times*."

Scientific literacy, defined here as knowing basic facts and concepts about science and having an understanding of how science works, is fairly low in the United States, according to the National Academies (2002), with the majority of the general public knowing "a little but not a lot" about science and being especially unfamiliar with the scientific method. Maienschein (1999) suggested that comprehending how ideas are investigated and analyzed is a sure sign of scientific literacy and the ability to keep up with important science-related issues. Miller (2004) notes, ". . . the truth is that no major industrial nation in the world today has a sufficient number of scientifically literate adults."

A small bright spot is Americans' increasing familiarity with genetics. In a 2001 National Science Foundation (NSF) survey, 45 percent of respondents were able to define DNA. The percentage of correct responses to this survey question increased in the late 1990s, a trend that most likely reflected the heavy media coverage of DNA use in forensic science and in medical research. More recently, a 2003 Harris poll revealed that 60 percent of adults in the United States selected the correct answer when asked "What is DNA?" (the genetic code for living cells), and two-thirds chose the right answer when asked "What does DNA stand for?" (deoxyribonucleic acid) (KSERO Corporation, 2003).

Concurrently, however, pseudo-science continues to thrive, to the disdain of scientists and scientific educators everywhere. *Pseudo-science* (or *junk science*) has been defined by Shermer (1997) as "claims presented so that they appear to be scientific even though they lack supporting evidence and plausibility." Conversely, Shermer defines *science* as "a set of methods designed to describe and interpret observed and inferred phenomena, past or present, and aimed at building a testable body of knowledge open to rejection or confirmation." During the last two decades, a number of studies sponsored by the NSF have provided baseline measures of the public understanding of science and technology. Miller (2004), citing these surveys, reports that the percentage of U.S. adults who understand the basic idea of a scientific experiment has increased from approximately 22 percent in 1993 to 35 percent in 1999. This uptick in comprehension is attributable both to the increases in the proportion of the adult population that has attained some college-level education, including science courses, and to the growing emphasis on science, medicine, and technology reporting by print and broadcast news outlets.

The NSF's latest report, "Science and Engineering Indicators 2006," is an interesting look at Americans' relationship with science and technology:

- *How Americans receive information about science:* The report indicates that television is still the main source of information about science and technology, but the Internet is a strong competitor. In the U.S., most adults pick up information about science and technology primarily from watching television, including educational and nonfiction programs, newscasts and newsmagazines, and even entertainment programs. While the media can positively affect the public's view of scientific issues, the NSF 2006 report states, "Television and other media sometimes miscommunicate science to the public by failing to distinguish between fantasy and reality and by failing to cite scientific evidence when it is needed."

- *How Americans view scientists:* The NSF 2006 report seems to indicate that most people have confidence in the scientific community and maintain a high opinion of science as an occupation. The report also alludes to a recent Harris poll of occupations that hold the most prestige; scientists share (with doctors) the top spot. Most Americans also say they would be happy if their son or daughter chose a career in science.

In another NSF report, "America's Pressing Challenge: Building a Stronger Foundation," the state of science education in the country is explored. Nearly 25 years ago, the National Science Board's Commission on Pre-college Education in Mathematics, Science and Technology assessed the state of U.S. pre-college education in the subject fields and found it wanting. In the intervening years, experts say institutions of learning have failed to raise the achievement of U.S. students commensurate with the goal articulated by that Commission: that U.S. pre-college achievement should be "best in the world by 1995." The report notes, "Not only are (U.S. students) not first, but by the time they reach their senior year, even the most advanced U.S. students perform at or near the bottom on international assessments."

This aforementioned report stated, "If the U.S. is to maintain its economic leadership and compete in the new global economy, the nation must prepare today's K-12 students better to be tomorrow's productive workers and citizens. Changing workforce requirements mean that new workers will need ever more sophisticated skills in science, mathematics, engineering and technology."

According to both NSF reports, there remains growing inequality of K-12 students' access to solid science and mathematics education, as well as the necessary science and mathematical courses and prerequisites for entering colleges and universities. The number of certified science and math teachers at the middle and high school levels is down, science education for pre-service teachers at U.S. education schools appears to be less rigorous compared to other subjects, and elementary teachers have expressed that they do not feel qualified to teach science. College graduates entering the teaching profession tended to have somewhat lower than average academic skills as evidenced by their lower rates of participation in rigorous academic courses in high school, lower achievement tests, and lower entrance exams scores than students in other majors.

Another need, according to the NSF, is to equip teachers for the rigors of teaching science. The NSF report states, "With the advances in science and technology, it cannot be expected that teachers will understand—and then teach students—about the advances in DNA sequencing, or cloning, or a myriad of other scientific breakthroughs if they have not themselves had a solid scientific foundation. Obviously this lack of professional development has a direct bearing on the content knowledge of our teachers and on their classroom practices."

Experts agree that introducing science to young people is one of the most important ways to ensure that there will be enough scientists to meet future demands and needs, as well as simply provide a citizenry that is educated about science in general. In 2001, the American Academy of Forensic Sciences (AAFS) launched a program to help equip elementary and high school science teachers to introduce forensic science in their general science curriculums. The AAFS offers its Forensic Science Educational Conferences program to increase science teachers' knowledge of the forensic sciences and to assist them as they enrich and/or develop challenging, innovative curricula. The two-day conference offers an indoor, mock crime scene, as well as lectures from AAFS forensic practitioners who discuss the technical aspects of their forensic fields and provide concrete examples on how the specific forensic science components under examination may be incorporated into middle and high school physical and biological science curricula. Teachers are also allowed to break into smaller groups wherein they participate in laboratory-based forensic science exercises presented by the AAFS specialists. In addition, hands-on exercises demonstrate the analysis of particular types of evidence that have been removed from the simulated crime scene. The teachers are exposed to such forensic disciplines as forensic anthropology and odontology, forensic pathology, toxicology, DNA analysis forensic botany, forensic entomology, and the collection and analysis of trace evidence. The conference concludes with a demonstration of courtroom testimony where experts in several of these areas not only testify on the analytical data obtained during the workshops but also suggest how middle and high school teachers may engage their students in their own moot court presentations with students acting as forensic experts, attorneys, jurors, and judges.

"We're doing the right things at the right time, especially with the academy's outreach to science teachers," says Mary Fran Ernst, a medico-legal death investigator for the St. Louis County Medical Examiner's Office and director of medico-legal education at St. Louis University School of Medicine. "We knew that our country will need more people with solid scientific backgrounds, and if they have that, then they might be interested in getting into forensic science. And we also knew that U.S. school systems need better instruction in the sciences and teachers who knew how to inject more science into the curriculum. So that's when the AAFS started hosting conferences for high school and middle school science teachers, using forensic science disciplines. Our speakers show these teachers how they can create different lab experiments that use forensic science as its foundation. For example, they can teach their students about blood spatter, which is nothing but physics and geometry. The kids love it because they absorb important scientific principles, but they are doing it in a fun and creative way. And it might just encourage them to pursue a career in forensic science."

According to a 2004 survey by the National Science Teachers Association (NSTA), which represents 55,000 science teachers, science supervisors, administrators, scientists, business and industry representatives, and others involved in science education, forensic science investigations have become the hottest new trend in science teaching. Of the 450 middle and high school science educators who responded to an informal survey, 77 percent indicated that their school or school district is using forensic investigations to teach science. When asked if the popularity of forensic-based TV shows had ignited students' interest in science, 78 percent of the respondents said yes. "It is unmistakable that popular new forensic science shows like 'CSI: Crime Scene Investigation' and 'Forensic Files' are resonating with students, especially those at the middle and high school level," says NSTA past-president Anne Tweed. "Science teachers are capitalizing on this interest and using it to immerse students in science learning. It's helping students discover how science is related to the real world how science can be used to solve problems."

Many teachers agree. When asked by the NSTA survey to comment on the popularity of forensic science lessons, hundreds of teachers responded; one teacher remarked, "My kids are enthralled when we do forensics in class . . . they love the scientific testing, the thinking, and the conclusions they reach. They love being 'real' scientists." Another teacher observed, "The students are able to see the power of science, as well as how it is done," while one educator commented, "Our forensic chemistry courses are the most popular science elective in the school."

The NSTA asked if teachers actually incorporated particular forensic TV shows into their lessons; 46 percent said yes, while 36 percent said they did not. The availability of solid forensic science lessons has been a stumbling block for many teachers, however. When asked if forensic lesson plans and activities were secured from an outside source or developed in-house, 24 percent of teachers indicated they obtained lessons from an outside source, 13 percent credited their district for developing the lessons, and 42 percent said that their district used both approaches. To provide teachers with opportunities to use forensics in the classroom, NSTA partnered with Court TV in 2003 to develop curriculum units on forensic science for middle and high school students. The collaboration resulted in two new forensic units now available as part of Court TV's award-winning Forensics in the Classroom (FIC) educational science initiative, developed in partnership with the AAFS. FIC was launched on Court TV's Web site in 2002 as the first-ever, free standards-based forensic science curriculum for high school science teachers. Since its debut, more than 20,000 teachers have downloaded the materials. Teachers can download the new forensics curricula free at www.nsta.org/resources or www.courttv.com/forensics_curriculum.

So what, then, is the bottom line on American's appreciation of science? Miller (2004) observes: "The evidence suggests that the salience of science to Americans is deeply held. Since 1988, national samples of U.S. adults have been asked periodically to agree or disagree with the statement, 'It is not important for me to know about science in my daily life.' Throughout the last decade, approximately 15 percent of U.S. adults have agreed with this statement, but more than 80 percent of Americans have disagreed with the idea that science is not important in their daily lives."

DO WE UNDERSTAND SCIENTISTS?

In the previous section we explored the question of whether the general public understands science in general, but do they understand the practitioners as well? And does this play even the smallest of roles in the bigger picture of how forensic science is being shaped by the mass media and being perceived by the consumers of this media? (For a related discussion of the "*CSI* effect," see Chapter 13.)

Crichton (1999) comments, "Scientists dislike negative portrayals of scientists and scientific research in the media. However, a closer examination reveals that these media images are inevitable and probably cannot be changed. Science should turn instead to practical steps to improve its image with the public." Crichton says of greater importance and relevance to the scientific community is how the scientific method is portrayed.

A second complaint about dramatized portrayals of science is the inaccuracy and fictional plot devices. Crichton (1999) remarks, ". . . our society is now dependent on technology, and dependent on science. With so much power, science will inevitably receive strong criticism. It comes with success. It's entirely appropriate. Take it as a compliment. And get over it." But some scientists, including forensic scientists who bristle at the portrayal of their field's victories and defeats, can't. After all, they think, why not demonstrate the real scientific method? Crichton (1999) quotes television producer David Milch, who stated, "The scientific method is antithetical to storytelling."

Crichton (1999) adds further, ". . . the scientific method presents genuine problems in film storytelling. I believe the problems are insoluble. The best you will ever get is a kind of caricature of the scientific process. Nor will the problems be solved by finding a more intelligent, dedicated or caring filmmaker. The problems lie with the limitations of film as a visual storytelling medium. You aren't going to beat it."

WHAT IS SCIENCE?

Central to any examination of how forensic science is coming under siege is the determination of what constitutes science and what does not. It is in this effort that much of the controversy lies within the forensic science and legal communities. In Chapter 2, we explored the fundamental structural components of forensic science and medico-legal death investigation; here, we examine the contentious argument that not all science is created equal. Some sciences, to borrow liberally from George Orwell's politically charged novel, *Animal Farm*, are more equal than others.

Goodstein (2000) observes that one of the most prominent early clashes between science and the law occurred in the case of Galileo, who promulgated the idea that careful experiments in a laboratory could reveal universal truths and reveal the kinds of discoveries that shaped scientific thought. In 1633, Galileo was put on trial for his scientific teachings, and although this was a conflict between science and the established church, it had all the trappings of a formal legal procedure and set the stage for many more to come. Goodstein (2000) makes a salient point when he observes, "Today, in contrast to the 17th century, few would deny the central importance of science to our lives, but not many would be able to give a good account of what science is. To most, the word probably brings to mind not science itself, but the fruits of science, the pervasive complex of technology that has transformed all of our lives. However, science might also be thought to include the vast body of knowledge we have accumulated about the natural world. There are still mysteries, and there always will be mysteries, but the fact is that, by and large, we understand how nature works."

The same may not always be said about forensic science, and the understanding may differ among the practitioners themselves. Goodstein (2000) notes, "If one asks a scientist the question, what is science, the answer will almost surely be that science is a process, a way of examining the natural world and discovering important truths about it. In short, the essence of science is the scientific method."

The *Academic Press Dictionary of Science & Technology* defines *science* as "the systematic observation of natural events and conditions in order to discover facts about them and to formulate laws and principles based on these facts; the organized body of knowledge that is derived from such observations and that can be verified or tested by further investigation; any specific branch of this general body of knowledge, such as biology, physics, geology, or psychology."

In the landmark case *Daubert v Merrell Dow Pharmaceuticals,* the U.S. Supreme Court acknowledged the importance of defining science. The court opined, "Science is not an encyclopedic body of knowledge about the universe. Instead, it represents a process for proposing and refining theoretical explanations about the world that are subject to further testing and refinement." This opinion indicates the assumption that the reasonable person knows what the scientific method is; however, Woodward and Goodstein (1996) are quick to point out, "We don't really know what the scientific method is."

With critics calling for increased scientific rigor in forensic science, it is imperative that the forensic science and legal communities agree on just what constitutes scientific endeavor. Many would say that the cornerstone of science itself is the much-lauded scientific method, which has generally been characterized as the process through which scientists—with minimal prejudice—construct an objective representation of the facts when testing a theory or hypothesis. Wolf (2002) states, "The scientific method is intricately associated with science, the process of human inquiry that pervades the modern era on many levels. While the method appears simple and logical in description, there is perhaps no more complex question than that of knowing how we come to know things."

The four steps of the scientific method are as follows:

1. Observation and description of a phenomenon.
2. Formulation of a hypothesis to explain the phenomena.
3. Use of the hypothesis to predict the existence of other phenomena, or to predict quantitatively the results of new observations.
4. Performance of experimental tests of the predictions by several independent experimenters and properly performed experiments.

Wolf (2002) states, "For scientists, the goal is to confirm or reject a hypothesis; under the precepts of the scientific method, a hypothesis must be discarded if its predictions are indisputably and consistently incompatible with experimental tests. Most scientists agree that a theory's predictions must match seamlessly with these experiments if it is to be accepted as a valid description of nature. Experiments may test the theory as well as any associated consequences derived from the theory using mathematics and logic; it is assumed at the onset that the theory in question is capable of being tested; otherwise they cannot be considered scientific theories.

EXPECTATIONS OF SCIENCE

What science means is often shaped by the worldview of those who perceive science and who try to make sense of it within their particular frame of reference. These expectations include several tenets, one of which is that scientists are supposed to be unbiased observers who employ the scientific methods to prove or disprove various theories, and who entertain no preconceived notions about the data they are testing so that they can come to purely objective, verifiable conclusions. Commentators on science have suggested that the field is self-correcting, since everyone knows scientists automatically reject theories when they are shown to lack validity through rigorous testing. In reality, data can be subjective, scientists can harbor bias, and pet theories are clung to long past the point of rationality. Another tenet about science to which the layperson subscribes is the idea that science leads to an understanding of the natural world. Quite often, it is the immense complexities of the natural world that teaches science about its own assets and liabilities, its limitations and its potential.

The building blocks of science are data, theories, and shaping principles. Data are the collections of information about physical processes. Such information is malleable, and in the wrong hands, it can be interpreted to fit any particular theory, flawed or otherwise, or else be overgeneralized so that it fits better with a given theory. Theories can be technically scientific and correct yet be rejected because the larger body of scientific knowledge or evidence is strongly against them. Shaping principles, based on logic, are to help guide scientists to their conclusions. Therein lies some conflict, especially when the aforementioned scientific method comes into play. There is the expectation that science was the systematic, rational, objective method of acquiring empirical evidence about the natural world. The scientific method was created to establish a rigid protocol and to safeguard against human frailties of bias or conjecture. It is impossible for scientists not to be influenced to some degree by cultural, social, and personal beliefs that may color the way scientists conduct their work. The very process of creating a theory is a creative enterprise that taps into the wellspring of an individual's collective being, drawing upon knowledge and experiences in addition to scientific principles. Science is still a human endeavor, and whatever impacts humans will eventually impact science. Individual shaping principles, then, can influence how one scientist interprets data differently from another scientist. It can be argued that the scientific method cannot insulate science from the human factor after all. And if humans are fallible, science therefore is fallible.

Thus we come to the margin for error inherent in any scientific undertaking. In some cases, a scientist commits fraud when he or she hastens the conclusion-reaching portion of an experiment because the scientist "knows" the answer. In other cases, because scientific disciplines vary in their protocols and procedures, some research experiments do not subscribe to a standard set of rules; what appears to be fraud or misconduct is actually scientifically valid in that particular discipline. Historically, however, errors are attributed to faulty systems, not the people who employ them.

Wolf (2002) explains, "Error in experiments has several sources. First, there is error intrinsic to instruments of measurement. Because this type of error has equal probability of producing a measurement higher or lower numerically than the 'true' value, it is called random error. Second, there is non-random or systematic error, due to factors which bias the result in one direction. No measurement, and therefore no experiment, can be perfectly precise. At the same time, in science we have standard ways of estimating and in some cases reducing errors. Thus it is important to determine the accuracy of a particular measurement and, when stating quantitative results, to quote the measurement error. A measurement without a quoted error is meaningless. The comparison between experiment and theory is made within the context of experimental errors. Scientists ask, how many standard deviations are the results from the theoretical prediction? Have all sources of systematic and random errors been properly estimated?"

Wolf (2002) states that erroneous applications of the scientific method are common; they include the following:

■ Mistaking the hypothesis for an explanation of a phenomenon, substituting logic and reason for the performance of performing experiments.
■ Rejecting data that do not support the hypothesis or theory; in other words, questioning data that may contradict the researcher's expectations, or not examining closely data that appear to substantiate the expectations; at its simplest, all data must be treated identically.
■ Failure to estimate quantitatively all errors, and possibly rejecting new phenomena.

Perhaps the myth that hits closest to home for forensic science is the debate over "real" science versus pseudo-science. Goodstein (2002) points to philosopher Popper's standard of falsifiability as a means to provide a means of demarcation between real science and impostors. But Goodstein warns, ". . . real scientists don't do as Popper says they should. But quite aside from that, there is another problem with Popper's criterion for demarcation: Would-be scientists read books too. If it becomes widely accepted (and to some extent it has) that falsifiable predictions are the signature of real science, then pretenders to the throne of science will make falsifiable predictions, too. There is no simple, mechanical criterion for distinguishing real science from something that is not real science. That certainly doesn't mean, however, that the job can't be done . . . the Supreme Court, in the Daubert decision, has made a respectable stab at showing how to do it."

If there is good science and bad science, where does forensic science fall? It depends on whom you ask. The answer may be that the bad can be changed, and the good can get even better as forensic science matures. The key to improvement, many say, is increased scientific rigor, particularly in the disciplines some say rest on a weak science to begin with.

Risinger and Saks (2003) put it bluntly: "Forensic science needs to build a base of rigorous research to establish its reliability." They join the ranks of many other social scientists and legal commentators who say fingerprints, microscopic hair analysis, and ballistics, to name a few, are rooted in very little research leading to validation. They add, "This forensic 'science' differs significantly from what most of us consider science to be."

Ronald Singer, supervisor of the Forensic Criminalists Laboratory of the Tarrant County (Texas) Medical Examiner's Office, takes exception to this charge, and addressed the topic as one of the few representatives of the forensic science community participating in the November 2005 symposium Forensic Science: The Nexus of Science and the Law, presented by the National Academy of Sciences. Singer remarked, "Forensic science is in a transition period right now. We are moving away from the investigator-based approach, in that we are moving away from operating on personal experience to operating from a more highly technical arena over the last 10 to 15 years. I am aggravated by the general consensus of there being no science in forensic science. There is a tendency to indict the entire profession of forensic science for the deeds of a few; they do not constitute real forensic scientists nor do they represent forensic science."

Roger Kahn, Ph.D., forensic biology director at the Harris County (Texas) Medical Examiner's Office, also speaking at the symposium, referenced the now-infamous 2003 editorial, "Forensic Science: Oxymoron?" in the journal *Science* by Donald Kennedy and remarked that the piece had some "pretty tough statements" in it. Kennedy had alluded to the battle over the reliability of pattern evidence analysis, specifically fingerprinting, noting, "It's not that fingerprint analysis is unreliable. The problem, rather, is that its reliability is unverified either by statistical models of fingerprint variation or by consistent data on error rates." Kennedy claimed, "Criminal justice agencies have been slow to adopt new scientific procedures and defensive about evaluation of their present ones," and also charged, "... Despite repeated calls for accreditation and oversight, many government crime labs continue to lack either one." Finally, Kennedy noted, "One would have thought that the issues surrounding homeland security would have increased the government's desire to apply better science to the detection of criminal activity and the pursuit of perpetrators. And of course our society has a long-standing concern about protecting the rights of the accused. Both these public interests—security and justice—would be furthered by a more scientific and reliable technology for analyzing crimes. The mystery here is why the practitioners don't seem to want it!"

Kahn described the response crafted by members of the forensic science community, which also was published in *Science* a few months later: "Forensic science professionals heartily support research into the scientific underpinnings of forensic science. ... Research conducted by impartial scientists working in research institutes coupled with input from the forensics community is needed by the forensic community." Kahn remarked, "We can banter and talk about whether there should be a calculation of error rates, and whether there should be statements of certainty we all like, but this group needs to identify areas needing research and resources. We need a top-to-bottom assessment to prioritize issues."

Also responding to the Kennedy editorial that questioned the scientific basis of forensic evidence examination is Palenik and Palenik (2003), who state, "To some extent, the field of forensic science must acknowledge these criticisms. Overshadowing this scolding, however, is the more troubling divide between academic and forensic science that is prevalent throughout and, unfortunately, encouraged by Kennedy's editorial. A glaring illustration of this division was the unsuccessful National Academies' project on Science, Technology and Law 'to examine science and its uses in forensic examinations.' A review of the members of this program reveals that not a single forensic scientist was included. Would such a project examine science and its uses in chemistry without a chemist? This attitude ignores the fact that, although forensic science has developed through the integration of principles from every scientific field, it has evolved into its own scientific discipline. The fact is that there is a great deal of science that cannot be packaged into standardized and verifiable techniques developed to be run by technicians." Palenik and Palenik add further, "The mystery in forensic science is not why practitioners do not want a more scientific technology for analyzing crimes, as Kennedy asks, but rather, why traditional sciences will not work with forensic science, rather than above it. Forensic science may be a redundant phrase, but it is not an oxymoron."

The aforementioned 2005 National Academy of Sciences symposium also generated debate over the corresponding issue of the law, academic science, and forensic science being at odds. David Faigman, M.A., J.D., a law professor at the Hastings College of Law at the University of California, and a panelist at the symposium, noted, "We have glossed over how deep a problem this really is. There is tension between the science and forensic science community. Forensic science has not, except for DNA, been a part of mainstream academic science. ... We have failed to look at the academic question about the validity of general principles of forensic science, or the pattern sciences." Faigman explained that there are three levels of investigation that must be considered in the examination of forensic science, including a look at the general principles underlying a forensic technique, the error rates associated with technologies used with these techniques, and the reliability of the application of otherwise accepted and reliable science. Faigman also asked symposium participants to consider how the U.S. Supreme Court, in its *Daubert* decision, gave credence to the move from the adversarial approach of the law to a more inquisitorial approach, again, to challenge and contest the admissibility of scientific evidence. "If we stand with the traditional advertorial process, are the tools available to have transparent forensic science?" Faigman asked. "There must be full discovery of the processes used in forensic science. And how can we adopt a more inquisitorial process with criminal cases? We must keep an eye on the inherent political perspective, the politics involved in not applying Daubert to criminal cases. Daubert changed the position from general acceptance and deference to forensic guilds to an independent cultural perspective—judges have to ask: where are the data? If a judge doesn't ask, he or she is not doing his or her job."

Faigman added, "There is a most notable divide between forensic science and mainstream science—I think it's startling. We have to bring science to forensic science. I'm not sure what the cause of (this void) is. . . . When science was still a gentlemanly activity in the 20th century, scientists moved into the academy but forensic science moved into the laboratory. The greatest challenge before us is figuring out a way to bring science to forensic science. Most forensic scientists are technicians. . . . Saks and Kaye and I have asked scientists to start collecting data and do the research. It's not that difficult. The reality is that they are not trained, don't have the inclination, or don't have the time or resources to do it. Give them money and make the questions academically interesting to get scientists in academia involved in forensic science."

Some of the representatives of the forensic science community took issue with these remarks, and explained why they felt forensic science has been unduly criticized for lack of participation in academic pursuits. Kahn pointed to the symposium audience when he remarked, "I see a lack of practicing forensic scientists in this audience. Based on their numbers, they could have filled this hall many times over and they have chosen not to do so. This sort of conference frightens the profession to some extent. They don't feel it is appropriate to be making grand-scale futuristic predictions; maybe this is a boycott—I can't explain it any better than that. But it seems there is a lot of hope here and good ideas and they should have been here. DNA was held up as an example for modeling the rest of the forensic disciplines. I didn't feel that statement was correct based on all of the criticisms at the time; in fact it felt as though we—and DNA—were under siege. In hindsight it's as if we slid into home without being touched. I ask those who have revised their memories about all of this to remember that we work in an adversarial justice system. As far as we can say this is the correct model because it seems to do the best job. For those of us who toil as expert witnesses, it's quite odd to (engage in) science with a professional opponent. It causes you to say things like 'go team' and you come here and for a brief interlude, it hardens your positions; you think as a team, not as a scientist. It's only natural that people react that way. You say you want people looking at pattern evidence to reconsider the basis for reliability; that's hard to do in a crime lab because we expect the things we do to be valid or we should just go home."

Kahn continues, "It's not just about a lack of funding to get these things done; it's a lack of academic scientists interested in fingerprinting, for example, as very few consider it a worthwhile academic endeavor. There is criticism of people who do so; one of the grantees of a National Institute of Justice (NIJ) award has never conducted fingerprint research before. This is a call to those in academia to open your mind a little, look at our problems, and jump in. A lot of research is done in the lab that no one sees; labs know they must validate their findings but they don't always have the resources and there is no meeting of the minds of people outside the forensic science community." Kahn added, "There must be an understanding of the pressures that the forensic scientists feel; it is a cinch to be here (at the symposium) and think lofty thoughts, but life in a crime lab is quite hectic. Forensic scientists frequently don't have time to think about the validity of their work. What they hope they have are reliable systems in place, and then they crank out the results. A crime lab is very different from a clinical lab. If you have a homicide, how much (evidence) do you test? You find yourself in arguments over the technology used, which tests are to be done, what gets tested first; in that environment you find yourself challenged and under pressure to get this done. Thanks to *CSI*, we have even more to do, and we must do it right and make sure it is reliable."

COMPARING SCIENCE AND THE LAW

In Chapter 9, we examined the courtroom as a quasi-battlefield upon which law and science seemingly wage war. Goodstein (2000) holds that semantics may have much to do with the opposing viewpoints to which attorneys and scientists ascribe. Shirley Abrahamson, chief justice of the Wisconsin Supreme Court, in remarks made during the opening session of the November 2005 symposium Forensic Science: The Nexus of Science and the Law, sponsored by the National Academy of Sciences, commented that the relationship between law and forensic science is not an easy one to foster. "Each discipline has its own language and culture; we may use the same words, but it means different things to us," she said.

It may be beneficial for both camps to review the suppositions being made in light of the words being used to make an argument. For example, Goodstein (2000) asserts that the concept of evidence "is used much more loosely in science than in the law." He explains, "The law has precise rules of evidence that govern what is admissible and what isn't. In science the word merely seems to mean something less than 'proof.' A certain number of the papers in any issue of a scientific journal will have titles that begin with 'Evidence for (or against).' What that means is, the authors weren't able to prove their point, but here are their results anyway."

A second example is that to the attorney, the word *theory* suggests "a proposal that fits the known facts and legal precedents and that favors the attorney's client." Goodstein (2000) adds, "The requisite of a theory in science is that it makes new predictions that can be tested by new experiments or observations and falsified or verified . . . but in any case, put to the test."

A third example of Goodstein's may pique the interest of the forensic community. Goodstein (2000) says that to an attorney, the word *error* is more or less synonymous with the word *mistake,* in that a legal decision may be overturned if it is found to be contaminated by judicial error. "In science," Goodstein observes, "error and mistake have different meanings. Anyone can make a mistake, and scientists have no obligation to report theirs in the scientific literature. They just clean up the mess and go on to the next attempt. Error, on the other hand, is intrinsic to any measurement, and far from ignoring it or covering it up or even attempting to eliminate it, authors of every paper about a scientific experiment will include a careful analysis of the errors to put limits on the uncertainty in the measured result. To make mistakes is human, one might say, but error is intrinsic to our interaction with nature, and is therefore part of science."

In Chapter 9, Jasanoff (2005) alludes to the occasionally opposing yet complementary nature of law and science; Goodstein (2000) observes that "science and the law differ fundamentally in their objectives." He adds, "The objective of the law is justice; that of science is truth," citing D. Allen Bromley in an address to the 1998 annual meeting of the American Bar Association. Goodstein clarifies, "These are not at all the same thing. Justice, of course, also seeks truth, but it requires that a clear decision be made in a reasonable and limited amount of time. In the scientific search for truth there are no time limits and no point at which a final decision must be made. And yet, in spite of all these differences, science and the law share, at the deepest possible level, the same aspirations and many of the same methods. Both disciplines seek, in structured debate, using empirical evidence, to arrive at rational conclusions that transcend the prejudices and self-interest of individuals."

In Chapter 12, we will examine the evidence trilogy comprised of U.S. Supreme Court decisions *Daubert, Kumho,* and *Joiner,* and its impacts on expert testimony and forensic evidence, but a brief word about how a scientist views the law is in order. Goodstein (2000) states, "In the 1993 Daubert decision, the U.S. Supreme Court took it upon itself to solve, once and for all, the knotty problem of the demarcation of science from pseudoscience. Better yet, it undertook to enable every federal judge to solve that problem in deciding the admissibility of each scientific expert witness in every case that arises." Goodstein adds, "The presentation of scientific evidence in a court of law is a kind of shotgun marriage between the two disciplines." He explains, "Both are forced to some extent to yield to the central imperatives of the other's way of doing business, and it is likely that neither will be shown in its best light. The Daubert decision is an attempt . . . to regulate that encounter. Judges are asked to decide the "evidential reliability" of the intended testimony, based not on the conclusions to be offered, but on the methods used to reach those conclusions." Goodstein instructs that these methods should be evaluated through use of the following four criteria:

1. The theoretical underpinnings of the methods must yield testable predictions by means of which the theory could be falsified.
2. The methods should preferably be published in a peer-reviewed journal.
3. There should be a known rate of error that can be used in evaluating the results.
4. The methods should be generally accepted within the relevant scientific community.

It is through this filter that judges scrutinize forensic evidence, determining its soundness and separating it from pseudo-science, or what is commonly known as junk science.

THE AGE OF JUNK SCIENCE

Huber (1991b) does not mince words when he asks, "What accounts for the proliferation of pseudoscientific shantytowns all around the modern American courthouse?" He points to the codification in 1975 of the federal rules of evidence as the impetus for the federal and state courts becoming more permissive about scientific testimony. He says many judges abandoned the *Frye* rule, which had previously required an expert witness to report views "generally accepted" in the wider scientific community, after a 1923 ruling on the use of lie-detector evidence in a criminal case.

Huber (1991b) notes further, "The upshot has been what federal court of appeals Judge Patrick Higginbotham has criticized as the 'let it all in' approach to evidence." He points to the comments of Donald Elliott, general counsel of the Environmental Protection Agency, that the law today "extends equal dignity to the opinions of charlatans and Nobel Prize winners, with only a lay jury to distinguish between the two." He also points to Edward Imwinkelried, co-author of the treatise *Scientific Evidence,* who says that today's courts "accept a wide range of scientific testimony that would have been patently inadmissible 10 years ago."

But because science and the law clash, Huber (1991b) calls the result "scientific anarchy in court." He says, "In court, scientific facts remain perpetually in play. . . . Tentative outlooks are often suppressed, views are quickly polarized, and a 'great confidence game' replaces serious science."

Huber (1991b) is confident that "Modern science, unlike modern law, has an excellent track record in sifting out the wheat from the chaff, in working out the differences between high-temperature superconductivity, an astonishing discovery that proved real, and low-temperature fusion, astonishing and unreal. Any single scientist may err, and most do sooner or later, but the modern scientific process, a process of replication, verification and the development of consensus, has proved exceptionally powerful and reliable."

Huber (1991b) adds, "Once one understands that the core of science is consensus, the need for strong enforcement of something much like the *Frye* rule becomes apparent. An expert who appears in court to present nothing but his own idiosyncratic opinions . . . is, for all practical purposes, just a lawyer in scientific drag. Science, by definition, is never a matter of individual opinion; it is always a matter of consensus in a much larger community."

Huber (1991b) says the courts have the power to discover where consensus lies, "if judges ever rediscover the will." He says answers can be found in the reputable, authoritative institutions, be it the National Institutes of Health or the Centers for Disease Control and Prevention (CDC) and their various guidelines and recommendations. He says, "Such institutions, established and funded to make difficult scientific calls, draw on the best and broadest scientific resources. This is not to suggest that they are infallible; of course they aren't. They are just less fallible—much less fallible—than a thousand juries scattered across the country grappling with the complexities of immune system impairment after being educated by a pliable clinical ecologist who believes in chemical AIDS."

Huber (1991b) asserts that absent definitive pronouncements of these institutions, "the next best place to look for the consensus views of mainstream science is in the peer-reviewed scientific literature. A witness whose views have survived peer review in a professional journal will already have been forced into a candid disclosure of cautions and qualifications; good journals won't publish without them. If the published claim is of any importance, publication will also mobilize other scientists to repeat, verify, contradict or confirm. By requiring professional publication as a basis for expert opinion, judges will help line up the larger community of scientists to shadow the necessarily smaller community of expert witnesses."

Huber (1991b) notes, "Some will always insist that all truth is relative and subjective, that anyone should therefore be allowed to testify to anything, that science must be viewed as a chaotic heap of unconnected and contradictory assertions, and that the best we can do is invite juries to decide scientific truth by majority vote. But anyone who believes in the possibility of neutral law, as many fortunately still do, must at the same time believe in the existence of objective fact, which ultimately means positive science. The only real alternative is nihilism."

One possible solution being bandied about cautiously is the concept of professional experts and their counterparts, professional juries.

Huber (1991b) observes, "The strongest antidote to bad science in court remains one that most American judges are still regrettably reluctant to use. European judges routinely summon their own experts. Our judges have similar powers, but few choose to exercise them. Most trial lawyers vehemently oppose court-appointed experts, perceiving (correctly, no doubt) that consensus cannot be good for a conflict-centered livelihood. Lawyers will therefore assure you that there is no such thing as a neutral expert. But it is obviously possible to find knowledgeable scientists of high principle, and having a nonpartisan judge do the finding, considerably improves the prospect of locating a less partisan expert."

PSEUDO-SCIENCE: WILL WE KNOW IT WHEN WE SEE IT?

A group of judges recently asked physics professor Robert L. Park for guidance on how to recognize questionable scientific claims; Park (2003) enumerated seven "warning signs" that a scientific claim is probably suspect:

- The discoverer pitches the claim directly to the media (thus bypassing the peer-review process by denying other scientists the opportunity to determine the validity of the claim).
- The discoverer claims that a powerful establishment is trying to suppress his or her work. (The mainstream science community may be deemed part of a larger conspiracy that includes industry and government.)
- The scientific effect involved is always at the very limit of detection.
- The evidence for a discovery is anecdotal.
- The discoverer says a belief is credible because it has endured for centuries.
- The discoverer has worked in isolation.
- The discoverer must propose new laws of nature to explain an observation.

"There is massive ignorance about what forensic science is, what it is capable of, and what its limitations are," says author and forensic science consultant Brent Turvey. "Most people believe we have the same abilities as the forensic scientists on television, where you can just look at something and know the answer without actually using the scientific method—reading the scene, some call it. They think that forensic science and physical evidence are intuitive processes that don't involve any sort of methodology, any sort of rigor, or any sort of peer review or independent validation. That's a contradiction to what we say it is. We keep saying we're scientists and we practice science, but most of us can't even define what science is. If you really want to mess with a forensic scientist on the stand, ask him or her to define the scientific method, ask him or her to define science. Ask him or her to explain how he or she tried to falsify their theories. Most won't even know why that would be important, even though it's the cornerstone of the scientific method."

Turvey continues, "If you look at the history of forensic science, and how we even got here, most of it comes out of law enforcement. The reason why the AAFS cannot require forensic scientists to have a degree in anything, let alone a science degree, is that too many of the people who practice forensic science in labs around the country have no degree at all—because they're cops. The AAFS would exclude that group and that's the problem. Every person you talk to quietly off the record will say, 'Look, we are trying to make it better. We know there's no science, we know there are no practice standards, we know that people who are unqualified are giving opinions in court.' But the cops have the ball and they are running with it. The problem with casework is that forensic scientists do not have the ball; they are employees of the police department rather than independent scientists. They don't get to call the shots, and so we have bad science."

"Sir Arthur Conan Doyle came to forensic science just like everybody else, thinking that there were these scientific detectives who were using the scientific method," Turvey adds. "The same thing with Locard. He thought, 'Ah, science applied to crime solving, this is it!' He went around the world looking for examples, but he couldn't find anyone who was doing it. That's what happened with Conan Doyle. What he found was a political organization of law enforcement officers trying very hard to prove their theories based on their experience, without any consideration for the physical evidence. When it matched, they used it, and when it didn't match, they ignored it and set it aside, and worse, either concealed it, or even fabricated it. Conan Doyle became thoroughly disgusted with law enforcement and how police investigations worked, and because of his work and his celebrity, he became friends with the prime minister and they worked together to create the appellate court to help look into science. For so long, forensic science has been the province of law enforcement that its scientists don't even know what science is. So when you hear them talking about what science is and what science is not, you have to laugh because only in this hall of justice where they control the evidence and they control the cases, would they be allowed to get away with saying nonsense like that. There is no new definition of science, it's just that finally, because the documentation is so overwhelming and the evidence is irrefutable and it's so widespread, that you can no longer deny there are problems. Forensic science should be owned by the scientific community, but the spine of that community has been intentionally fractured by the changing paradigm of science, and by challenges from the defense."

"I think everyone has to assume responsibility for the quality of forensic science that is proffered in the courts," says David Faigman, law professor at the University of California Hastings College of the Law. "Forensic scientists have a responsibility to give opinions in court that are based only on good science, or else they are operating in an unethical, reckless capacity. Forensic scientists should have their own code of ethics, but I also think defense attorneys and prosecutors have responsibility to the criminal justice system to ensure that the evidence has, at the very least, passed the standards of reliability and validity. Judges also have a great responsibility to ensure that their courtroom is not being used to peddle bad science or what people refer to as junk science. Judges are the gatekeepers and must establish a fundamental threshold of rigorous testing over which all science and all expert testimony is expected to pass."

Faigman adds, "I think many forensic scientists are simply not being held to traditional standards of scientific inquiry." He says he participated in a panel on handwriting identification and forensic document examination that was sponsored by the AAFS some years ago. "There was a very large group of document examiners in the room and what occurred to me as I listened to the discussion, was that they don't think that they are committing fraud," Faigman says. "They have no intention of committing fraud, and they really believe in what they do—I don't have any doubt about that. They don't think they are practicing, at least as I understand it, junk science in any way. They really believe in what they do; the problem is, they don't have the tools to do the research required to make their discipline scientific. These scientists are not scientists; what they are, really, are technicians. They are given a set of tools and they use these tools very rigorously and they take their jobs extremely seriously, but they don't research the validity or the reliability of their tools, they simply apply whatever technology has been handed to them."

Faigman says he equates poor science with a lack of education and training and the proper research skills that must be used to test hypotheses correctly. *Science* published a survey of those who call themselves forensic scientists, and less than 1 percent of those individuals held doctorate-level, research-focused degrees. When I saw that, I realized that the majority of these individuals don't know how to conduct hypothesis testing, and they certainly are not trained in statistics. If you gave them a million dollars and said, 'Go out and test the validity of fingerprints or bite marks, they wouldn't know where to begin or what to do. I don't blame them for their lack of education, training and research skills; however, I blame the field and

I blame the law to some extent for failing to demand that forensic science be more of an academic-based science."

For forensic science to make the leap from pseudo science to real science, in the minds of some critics, Faigman says, the field must involve itself into mainstream academic science. "For example, there's no one at Johns Hopkins conducting research on bite mark analysis or fingerprints; it would be a career-ending decision for a mainstream academic scientist to start doing research on any of these subjects. In some ways, forensic science has a schizoid reputation among mainstream scientists; it is looked down upon because it is considered to be too applied, too practical. The lay public and forensic specialists are very proud of their 'science.' I think they really believe that what they do is impressive, but academic-based scientists do not. Donald Kennedy wrote an editorial in *Science* questioning whether forensic science is an oxymoron. That's a blow to one's ego."

"The way to redemption is testing forensic scientists' underlying assumptions," Faigman suggests. "I was on the National Research Council panel on the scientific validity of polygraphs, and one of the things all polygraph operators cited as support for the value of what they did was the reliability of their craft, with, of course, reliability referring to consistency of results. It turns out that polygraphs actually have a great deal of reliability; the results of one examiner's tests are going to pretty much agree with another examiner's test. The problem is that scientists separate reliability from validity; validity refers to the accuracy of the test while reliability refers to the consistency of the test."

Faigman explains further, "It's like if you have a thermometer that's always 10 degrees too high; you have 100 percent reliability in scientific terms because it always gives you the same reading, but it's always wrong, with zero percent validity. Polygraph operators are able to demonstrate very high reliability but they were unable to demonstrate validity. The same is true of latent print examination, bite marks, and handwriting identification; the reason they have high reliability is that they are all trained in the same methods and technology, and so if you apply the same bad technology consistently, it will give you the same result, which is wrong, all the time. If you go back to the 19th century, almost all science was conducted by wealthy amateurs, the Charles Darwins of the world, but in the 20th century you see a movement of scientists into the academic world, with biologists, physicists and the chemists entering the university setting, Similarly, the statistician who came up with fingerprints and who came up with the basic hypothesis about them, was one of these amateur scientists, plying his trade largely outside of the university community. In the 20th century, rigorous scientists moved into the academy. Forensic science didn't do that; forensic science went into the police laboratory and did not go into the university. Throughout the 20th century there has been this divide between forensic science, which is serving the police community, and academic science, which is serving the general community and private industry. We have inherited that system, where mainstream academic scientists have no history and no interest in studying these subjects and therefore forensic science has not been studied adequately."

In a panel, "Junk Science, Pre-Science, and Developing Science," held in April 1999 during the National Conference on Science and the Law and sponsored by the National Institute of Justice, the American Academy of Forensic Sciences, the American Bar Association, and the National Center for State Courts, law professor Michael Saks, of Arizona State University, who acknowledged that part of the problem of distinguishing real science from pseudo-science was that attorneys and scientists "live their lives in two different intellectual universes." Saks said that muddying the waters is the proliferation of studies that produce little verifiable data. He commented, "The only way anyone can know whether any technique . . . will produce valid results or not . . . is going to be if we can test them with well-designed, systematic empirical studies."

Saks pointed to the U.S. Supreme Court as arbiters in the science/pseudo-science debate. "For an expertise based on testable empirical claims to be admitted under *Daubert* and *Kumho*, it (must) survive . . . reasonably convincing empirical testing to show that it is or can do what is claimed for it," he explained, adding, "What is one to do with fields that do not have traditions of systematic self-testing? Are their claims to be taken on faith? Are the courts to merely accept the sincere and heartfelt self-assertions offered by members of those fields? What can a court do with fields that purport to be talking about the empirical world, but have done little empirical research to evaluate themselves?"

In answer, Saks proposed three models with which to approach the debate: The applied science model, the DNA model, and the black box model. Saks explained, "In the applied science model, it could be that a field of forensic science is borrowing well-established methods from what I'll call 'normal science.' Take chemistry as an example. If you become a forensic chemist, and you apply the principles and the techniques being used in . . . nonforensic chemistry, then there would be a very good basis for a court to conclude that if it works in industry and it works in academic chemistry labs, then it will work when applied properly to forensic science problems. Handwriting identification, by contrast, cannot point to any basic science discipline from which it is borrowing its concepts or methods."

Saks explained that the DNA model is an empirically based probability analysis. He stated, "DNA typing has shown, largely through the work of population geneticists, how to calculate the probability of a coincidental (erroneous) match. Since all forensic identification fields operate by the same basic notions of probability as DNA—that there is an enormous amount of variability with respect to the features being examined, whether those are handwriting or DNA, fingerprints or striations on bullets. What the DNA model suggests is that what needs to be done is to measure . . . how much variability exists among the relevant population. Then take the case at bar and, by measuring the observed elements using the background probabilities found in the larger database, one can calculate the likelihood that the crime scene evidence and a defendant's evidence share a common source. In the case of handwriting identification, experts would report to the fact finder the probability of a coincidental match associated with a conclusion that a ransom note and the defendant's writing came from the same hand."

Saks then characterized his black box model as a last-resort approach that can be used with any claimed special skill. He explained, "What one would do is to present problems with known answers to experts for examination. For example, one could test handwriting samples, markings created by toolmarks, two bullets that may or may not have been fired from the same gun, etc. People giving the test know whether they had a common origin or not, while the people taking the test don't know. And the answer given is compared to the answers known to be correct. Now, this has certainly been done in the realm of what is referred to as proficiency testing. I would just take it one step further and use it as a technique to try to map the extent of special skill of various kinds of experts. How fuzzy can the latent print and the known inked print get and still produce valid conclusion? Or how partial can it be? In the instance of handwriting experts, by testing different kinds of FDEs, with various different kinds of stimulus writings, under different types of testing conditions, using different methods of examination, eventually one could map the extent of special abilities and limitations of different types of FDEs, examining different types of writing, using different comparison methods, under different types of conditions. By doing this, we can discover in what domain experts really bring some expertise that is over and above that which a jury could accomplish on its own."

Saks said he believed that these strategies could provide trial courts with an improved ability to evaluate claimed expertise. "Courts play a large role in how good the data are that they receive from experts about the claimed expertise," Saks remarked. "When courts set a very low threshold they will receive little data about the expertise, and probably a low quality of expertise. When courts raise the bar, experts will work harder to get over more demanding standards and ultimately offer the courts better evidence."

Terrence Kiely, J.D., L.L.M., professor of law and director of the Center for Law and Science at DePaul University in Chicago, urges courts, as well as other stakeholders in the criminal justice system, to exercise care when using the word *science*. "I call some of these forensic disciplines 'observational' disciplines. Disciplines such as fingerprint examination or footprint examination are not science; these are observational disciplines. They are, however, sometimes of a very high order if the person doing them is accurate, but nonetheless, it's *not* science. People think it's science, so it must be right."

Kiely says there is a distinct disconnection between science and these disciplines, explaining, "These disciplines are not considered to be science by scientists. You're not going to get instruction on fingerprints as an academic subject because it is not an academic subject, and neither are footprints. What must be done is to push legislators for more and better funding to train people in the sciences, and defense attorneys must read the literature and stay on top of these sciences and continue to challenge them in court. It's a question of who is selling the information and what is their purpose for doing so. The prosecutor who has a ballistics problem can pitch that stuff in a way different from someone who is a defense attorney. I think lawyers are getting much better at understanding and explaining the science and discerning that in much of the forensic evidence presented in court, very little real science is used."

Kiely continues, "People think that when they have someone's fingerprints, well there's the guy who did the crime, case closed. The AFIS databank spits out the 10 closest prints in the system and then a man or woman with a looking glass sits down and makes a judgment about a match. They may say, 'Well, I think it's this guy.' It's the same with footprint impressions and the rest of it; much of it is visual comparison of features of an item from the crime scene. The whole purpose of all of this stuff, DNA included, of course, is to associate the defendant with the crime scene, and trying to compare the items found at the scene to the defendant. That's what forensic evidence is. It's all about location, location, location, like they say in the real estate industry."

THE DEFINITION OF PSEUDO-SCIENCE

The debate over admissibility of scientific evidence in the courtroom has brought the issue of pseudo-science to the forefront. As we will see in Chapter 12, a number of U.S. Supreme Court decisions created new measuring sticks by which to evaluate technical evidence and expert testimony. Prior to this trilogy of cases in the 1990s, courts employed what was called a "marketplace" test with which to scrutinize proffered opinions from experts. According to Saks (2004), ". . . courts asked themselves whether, in the commercial marketplace, consumers of that expertise found its opinions and advice worth purchasing with their hard-earned money. If the expertise were valued in the marketplace, then courts also were willing to value it and allow it as expert testimony. Thus, consumers of an asserted expertise were the principal judges of its validity." However, courts were stumped when faced with expertise relating to novel technology or disciplines that were outside of the commercial marketplace. Saks says courts adopted a new test of general acceptance, and "employed an analog to the commercial marketplace: the intellectual marketplace. The court asked not whether an expertise enjoyed general acceptance among consumers, but whether the expertise had gained general acceptance 'in the particular field in which it belongs.' Thus, the *Frye* test replaced consumers with producers as the principal judges of validity." According to Saks, the evidence trilogy in the 1990s empowered judges to become the deciders of the validity of expert testimony, essentially requiring them to think like scientists to help determine whether empirical evidence exists to support various claims, and if tests have been conducted using sound research methodology. While a torrent of scientific evidence streamed through U.S. courts, suddenly judges were closing the floodgates. What may have passed muster two decades ago is now suspect in the greater scrutiny of evidence by courts under a court decision in *Daubert v Merrill Dow Pharmaceuticals*. Saks (2004) reports, "As one federal court later observed: [*Daubert*] may mean, in a very real sense, that 'everything old is new again' with respect to some scientific and technical evidentiary matters long considered settled."

What is new again to the courts may be what some consider as pseudo science, but the debate rages on as to which forensic disciplines land in the junk heap. Saks (2004) comments, " A field that has the right stuff, and has done its scientific homework, would have no trouble demonstrating that what it is selling is worth buying. If its claims are true, its adherents should have no trouble showing that to be so. But a field that has been engaged in a parody of science, dressing up in lab coats but never doing the research needed to test the extent and limits of its claims, and making claims that exaggerate what is known about its subject matter and its own skills, such a field would have the gates closed to it—unless and until it can demonstrate the validity of its claims."

And that, as we shall see in the next section, goes to the very heart of those forensic sciences that are under siege.

THE SCIENCES MOST UNDER SIEGE: THE PATTERN IDENTIFICATION SCIENCES

The areas of litigation that attract scientific controversy in civil and sometimes criminal courts include brain mapping and brain fingerprinting, environmental hypersensitivity, chronic fatigue, repetitive strain injury, repressed or recovered memory syndrome, false memory syndrome, facilitated communication (among autistic children), premenstrual syndrome defense, hypnosis as an aid to memory, and various other forms of stress disorders, such as Gulf War syndrome, rape trauma syndrome, battered woman syndrome, and shaken-baby syndrome. To the horror of some in the forensic science community, some commentators are asserting that these concepts are akin to the disciplines of fingerprinting and other pattern evidence analysis and interpretation. The intent of this book is not to be instructive on the various disciplines of forensic science, but rather to explore how these disciplines and others commonly used by prosecutors to adjudicate cases have come under fire in the courtroom.

"The sciences must be treated uniformly, in that all science demands certain critical methods and paradigms of research," states Faigman. "Whether you are a physicist, biologist, chemist, or psychologist, the basic question that you are confronted with is how you rigorously study this phenomenon to determine the cause of the fact, and the relationships between different variables. It is my view that there is no fundamental difference between how a biologist approaches a subject and how a physicist approaches a subject; the problem is, what methods are demanded? A physicist might use one method to talk about how electrons operate and another method to determine how hurricanes advance into a category 5 classification, and that's applied physics. I had that sensibility when I came to the law; I looked around, and whether it was rape trauma syndrome, hypnosis, or repressed memories, or whether it was fingerprints or bite marks, what I was really asking myself is, 'Are these fields using the critical scientific methods available to test their hypotheses?' That's the bottom line for me. Are they using the tools available to test their hypotheses, and the clear answer in a lot of areas, is no. If you look at handwriting, ballistics, or bite marks, they have found their way into the courts, yet they have not really benefited from systematic, rigorous, scientific testing using whatever methods might be available, almost to the point of embarrassment."

Faigman continues, "And so when one asks, 'Why don't the law and science get along better?' I actually think that the law and science could get along very well, but forensic practitioners must be scientists first and not advocates. The law is basically using science as a tool for its own objectives for fairness, justice, and truth. Lawyers must understand enough of science to make good decisions about validity, given the state of the art of the science in question."

In its 100-plus-year history, fingerprint identification has been lauded and criticized. We next explore how this identification science has become and remains controversial in the courtroom. Of all the forensic disciplines, fingerprints may be the identification science best known for triggering the ire of commentators. Fingerprints, of course, are impressions of the ridged skin surface of the fingers, and these small whorls and loops are at the center of a very big controversy.

At issue are latent fingerprints collected from crime scenes, whose very nature can be comprised of partials and fragments. Critics say these fragments may have an insufficient number of identifying points with which to make a match, and that examiners employ methods to restore and enhance prints. Epstein (2002) writes, "The Department of Justice has recently suggested that the average size of a latent fingerprint fragment is only one-fifth the size of a full fingerprint."

A latent print found at and recovered from a crime scene is compared by a fingerprint examiner with inked or digitally scanned fingerprints taken directly from a suspect's fingers. An examiner makes a positive identification if he or she believes there is an adequate number of common ridge characteristics, in terms of both type and location, between the latent and inked print under comparison. The ridge characteristics are points along the ridge path where something dramatic occurs, and an average human fingerprint contains between 75 and 175 ridge characteristics of different types, such as islands, spurs, enclosures, and bifurcations.

Going to the heart of fingerprint identification, of course, is source attribution; the poor quality of many latent prints from crime scenes is what makes latent print identification problematic. Cole (2005) states, "The most valuable aspect of the latent print testimony in criminal justice proceedings is the attribution of the latent print to the defendant. Although latent print testimony is often phrased as claiming that the latent print and the known print of the defendant are 'identical,' this is not strictly true; all fingerprint impressions, including those taken from the same finger, are in some way unique. The true import of latent print testimony is not that the unknown print and the known print are 'identical' but rather that they derive from a common source. Since the source of the known print is known to be the defendant (because someone in the chain of custody took them from the defendant), the unknown print is then attributed to the defendant. The defendant is said to be the source of the latent print."

"Latent print identification is actually supported by virtually no research at all," Faigman asserts. "It is almost impossible to find a well-done proficiency study or any kind of study that looks at base rates of fingerprint identification criteria; there are no standards that are scientifically validated that determine at what point you have a match. I am not talking about individualization, I am talking about the ability to match an unknown latent print found at the crime scene, where you have very little information and fewer than 10 points to match to a known, rolled print. It's actually easy to testify on that subject because there are no studies on latent print examination; it's like shooting fish in a barrel."

Faigman points to a study conducted in the United Kingdom in which fingerprint examiners were given samples of prints that they had analyzed in a criminal investigation and found to be a match. In the study, however, they were given contextual information that suggested that no match should be found. "Three out of the five examiners said there was no match even though earlier they had said that there was," Faigman says. "Only one of the five examiners said 'I think this is a match,' and the fifth examiner said it was inconclusive. So, four out of five examiners facing their own identification from the past stated there were no matches. That's profound. It goes back to how science deals with hypothesis testing; good science will tell you that you don't give information to the examiners under these circumstances because of the presence of experimenter expectancies. When you tell someone what to expect, they are much more likely to see the world in the way they expect to see the world. I could not design a system where the main characteristics were more salient than what occurs day to day in crime labs. For example, I just testified against a woman who had only a community college degree but was working for a county crime lab as a forensic scientist. The prosecutor was saying, 'Well, we have very little evidence but we know this guy did it; see, we have this partial print that is pretty smudged but it's a match because our 26-year-old technician says it's a match.'"

"Fingerprints have come under a good deal of fire lately," acknowledges Joseph Polski, chief operations officer of the International Association for Identification and chairman of the Consortium of Forensic Sciences (CFSO). "The last number I've heard is that there have been approximately 55 *Daubert* hearings on fingerprints, none of them sustained. So the courts are starting to reject those challenges out of hand; they are saying it is just a waste of time. If you are a trial judge and the defense wants to have a Daubert hearing, you may say, 'Well, 55 courts in practically every state have upheld this, don't waste my time.' The more current tactic is to take some of the *Daubert*-related questions and criteria and apply those to the examiners themselves in an attempt to disqualify the examiner based on *Daubert*-related questioning. That may be a little more successful because you find scientists who may be less familiar with how to answer those challenges. Notwithstanding these challenges, however, physical evidence is far better and carries more objective weight than eyewitness identification, for example, which can be unreliable."

Why the courts considered the admissibility of fingerprints so easily has been the subject of much contemplation by commentators and legal scholars. Mnookin (2001) hazards a guess that "fingerprinting and its claims that individual distinctiveness was marked on the tips of the fingers had inherent cultural plausibility," stemming from the popular notion of nature's infinite variety. Many held that just as every snowflake was unique, so too were people's fingerprints unique when examined in a meticulous fashion. Mnookin suggests, "Individual distinctiveness was taken for granted, and it was further believed that this distinctiveness was inevitably marked upon the human body if one only knew where to look. The idea that upon the tips of fingers were minute patterns, fixed from birth and unique to the carrier made cultural sense; it fit with the order of things. One could argue, from the vantage point of one hundred years' experience, that the reason fingerprinting seemed so plausible at the time was because its claims were true, rather than because it fit within a particular cultural paradigm or ideology."

"Judges generally do the best job that they can," says Polski. "However, I think there is a lot of room for judicial education, especially in the technical areas of fingerprinting. Judges are there because of their knowledge of the law, not for their understanding of the finer technical points of a forensic discipline." Mnookin (2001) suggests further that fingerprints "worked" in part because courts did not subject the discipline to enough scrutiny, again in keeping with this pervasive cultural plausibility. It also didn't hurt that fingerprint evidence was, as previously discussed, a visually oriented discipline, where courts could see the science in action, so to speak. Mnookin comments, ". . . fingerprints turned jurors into virtual witnesses who could peer upon the prints and see the swirls and whorls for themselves. They could even peer down at their own fingertips for comparison. Just as this visibility of the evidence offered a way of persuading juries of the identity of two prints, it also offered a way of persuading judges of the legitimacy of the technique. All jurors and judges had to do was believe the evidence of their own eyes. Although learning to see a match required skill and judgment, experts used enlarged images with the similarities between prints carefully numbered, to help the jurors see the identification firsthand. Given that matches were so visible, that they could be brought into focus before the court and jury, it is not surprising that judges failed to take the step from noticing a match to asking difficult interpretive questions about the meaning of a match. In fact, for non-scientific evidence of identity, judges did not (and still do not) require evidence about base rates as a prerequisite to admissibility."

Most importantly, commentators assert, fingerprints were the kind of forensic evidence that satisfied the courts' expectations about what forensic science could accomplish in the detection of a crime's perpetrator. Fingerprints were an appealing form of science, incontestable in its unwavering claim of authoritative certainty; who could question something they could see with their own eyes? It was everything anyone—judges, prosecutors, and jurors—could want from science.

Mnookin (2001) observes, "Courtroom observers and judges aspired to have the light of scientific truth shine directly into the courtroom. Legal writers hoped that science, with its privileged access to the natural world, could provide certainty and objectivity . . . judges and legal commentators were in search of methods for making authoritative judgments, trustworthy and credible mechanisms by which the jury could determine facts. The Holy Grail was evidence that could simultaneously be definite and dispositive, a way to find the truth beneath the contradictions of witnesses. Expert evidence held out the promise of offering such a superior method of proof, rigorous, disinterested, and objective. But in practice, scientific evidence almost never lived up to these hopes."

Expert testimony had become problematic and contentious, and the evidence appeared contradictory and inconsistent, shaking courts' faith in the harmony of one united search for truth under science. Stakeholders became disillusioned, and jurors found themselves having to choose sides as these experts failed to inspire awe and win trust. But fingerprints continued to offer the courts a safe harbor from the bickering. Mnookin (2001) notes, "Unlike so much other expert evidence, which could be and generally was disputed by other qualified experts, fingerprint examiners seemed always to agree. Generally, the defendants in fingerprinting cases did not offer fingerprint experts of their own. Because no one challenged in court either fingerprinting's theoretical foundations or, for the most part, its actual operation in any particular instance, the technique came to seem especially powerful. Fingerprinting therefore offered precisely the kind of scientific certainty that judges and commentators, weary of the perpetual battles of the experts, yearned for. Fingerprinting gained tremendous authority from the claim that a match could not be made erroneously. Initial challenges to this claim only resulted in increasing fingerprinting's clout." Furthermore, Mnookin says, "Fingerprinting somehow avoided the spectacle of clashing, competing experts whose contradictory testimony befuddled jurors and frustrated judges. Instead, the evidence that a defendant's fingerprints matched those found at the scene of a crime was typically uncontested. And because it was uncontested, fingerprint evidence came to be seen as uncontestable. Fingerprinting grew to have cultural authority that far surpassed that of any other forensic science. It came to be seen as an especially powerful, especially compelling form of evidence, one that simply could not be challenged as erroneous. Because the reliability of fingerprinting was not challenged in court, it came to have a great deal of epistemological authority—both within the courtroom and outside it. That fingerprinting is generally viewed as a tremendously reliable technique hardly needs to be established—it is common knowledge, almost beyond dispute."

Getting judges and jurors to look beyond the impressive visuals has been the mission of commentators who charge that the pattern identification sciences are steeped in inherent subjectivity, particularly when it comes to determining a match. Moriarty and Saks (2005) acknowledge, ". . . one might conclude that determining whether something is a match or not is relatively straightforward, and that the difficulty lies only in interpreting the meaning of that match. But even this initial step is fraught with more problems than even many forensic scientists are aware of. When two examiners look at the same visualization of evidence, they see different things more often than we might expect."

Critics say there are no standards to guide whether two images are judged to be indistinguishably alike or not, and that in the United States, there is no minimum number of points of comparison required to conclude that two fingerprints are indistinguishably alike. As Mnookin (2001) states, "Some leading examiners reject the point-counting method altogether, arguing that it oversimplifies the complex information provided by a fingerprint by focusing exclusively on the location of particular characteristics. The lack of objective standards means that determining a match is necessarily subjective; it is based on the personal judgment of the examiner rather than inter-subjective criteria that remain the same from print to print and from examiner to examiner."

Epstein (2002) charges that latent fingerprint examiners in the United States currently operate in the absence of any uniform objective standards, adding, "The absence of standards is most glaring with respect to the ultimate question of all fingerprint comparisons: What constitutes a sufficient basis for making a positive identification? The position of the FBI, as well as the IAI, is that no minimum number of corresponding points of identification is necessary for an identification. Instead, the determination of whether there is a sufficient basis for an identification is left to the subjective judgment of the particular examiner."

Epstein (2002) points to the remarks of David Ashbaugh, a staff sergeant with the Royal Canadian Mounted Police with more than 25 years of experience as a fingerprint examiner, in the 2000 case of *United States v Mitchell,* in which he stated that a fingerprint examiner's opinion of identification is "very subjective." Ashbaugh had been called by the government as an expert witness in connection with the *Daubert* challenge at issue in the case. Epstein notes, "While the official position of the FBI is that there is no basis for a minimum point requirement, many fingerprint examiners in the United States continue to employ either their own informal point standards or standards that have been set by the agencies for which they work. In addition, while there is no uniform identification standard in the United States, many other countries have set such standards." Australia has a minimum standard of 12 matching ridge characteristics, while France and Italy each have 16. Epstein continues, "As commentators have recognized, the question of whether there should be a minimum point standard for latent print identifications has bitterly divided the fingerprint community. While latent print examiners have somehow managed to maintain a united front in the courtroom, they have been at odds in the technical literature. Ashbaugh, for example, has written that 'it is unacceptable to use the simplistic point philosophy in modern day forensic science.' "

Commentators have charged that the selection of any particular point standard is based not on scientifically conducted probability studies, but, as Ashbaugh noted in the case of *United States v Mitchell*, "through what can best be described as an educated conjecture." Epstein (2002) adds further, "The lack of uniform standards for latent print comparisons extends well beyond the question of what ultimate standard should apply for a positive iden-tification. Objective standards are lacking throughout the entire comparison process . . . fingerprint examiners are not even in agreement as to what it is that they are looking for when comparing fingerprints. Examiners hold widely varying beliefs as to the number, nomenclature, and frequency of the standard ridge characteristics."

Ashbaugh remarked on examiners' reliance on "third-level detail" such as sweat pores and ridge edges for their analyses, while others have questioned the reliability of identifications that are made on the basis of such detail. In a 2000 presentation at the 84th annual training conference of the California State Division of International Association for Identification, John Thornton stated that identifications based on level-three detail have yet to be rigorously tested either in a scientific venue or in court, and that he had not seen a level-three detail comparison of a latent fingerprint that did not require some level of rationalization.

Some commentators charge that fingerprint examiners establish their own standards, or abide by the standards of the agency for which they work, or some combination of the two options. Moriarty and Saks (2005) say, "When a fingerprint examiner determines that there is enough corresponding detail to warrant the conclusion of absolute identification, then the criteria have been met. In other words, there are no criteria." They point to a study conducted in Great Britain in which 130 fingerprint experts were presented with 10 pairs of fingerprints. Researchers discovered that the examiners frequently disagreed on how many points of simi-larity a pair of prints shared; for one of the pairs, the reported number of matching points ranged from 10 to 40, while for another, it ranged from 14 to 56. Moriarty and Saks comment, "This is not science; it is one person's perception and judgment."

At issue then, is the way source attributions are phrased by experts in the courtroom. In cases in which DNA evidence is crucial, an analyst will typically say that the defendant may be the source of the DNA sample, and then give a random-match probability to indicate the frequency with which randomly chosen individuals with the same racial or ethnic background would also be consistent with the unknown DNA sample. It is a different story with assertions about fingerprints, critics charge. Cole (2005) explains, "When latent print examiners make a 'match,' they always testify that the defendant is the source of the latent print to the exclu-sion of all other possible sources in the universe. Latent print examiners are, in fact, ethically bound to only testify to source attributions; they are banned from offering probabilistic opinions in court." Cole explains further that latent print examiners are the only forensic expert witnesses who are restricted in their testimony; they can offer only three possible con-clusions from any comparison of a known and unknown set of prints: individualization, inconclusive, and exclusion.

But semantics remains a convincing form of leverage in the courtroom. Mnookin (2001) observes, "From its earliest uses as legal evidence, fingerprint identification was generally presented in the language of certainty, rather than in the language of opinion. The typical, though not exclusive, practice in the late 19th century was for experts to testify as to their opinion. But from the very beginning, fingerprint examiners resisted this norm. Speaking in the language of certainty—rather than the language of possibility or probability—became the standard operating procedure for fingerprint identification evidence. One of the hallmarks of fingerprint identification evidence is the now-institutionalized reluctance of fingerprint examiners to testify in the language of probability. According to the norms of the professional community, identifications must be certain and absolute, or they must not be made at all."

Inman and Rudin (2001) observe, "Because the law works in absolutes, while science provides anything but, the never-ending struggle is for scientists to render their opinion in a way that is useful to the lay person in making a decision about guilt or innocence. In medical testimony, the phrase 'to a reasonable medical certainty' is often used to convey the idea that, although we can never positively prove that the victim was killed by the third bullet, the pathologist's expert opinion carries enough weight that the trier of fact may accept it as true. From the medical model has come the phrase 'to a reasonable scientific certainty.' Both the judicial system and some experts have latched onto this phrase as a convenient way to render an opinion as fact. As convenient as it might be, it is a nonsequitor . . . the notion of scientific certainty does not exist."[1]

Paul Ferrara, Ph.D., director of the Virginia Department of Forensic Science and board member of the Virginia Institute of Forensic Science and Medicine, notes, "It is nothing but semantics when you use terms like 'absolute.' When you think about DNA identification and the stats we use and what we have been doing, we still simply say that it could be this one person in the world's population; we don't even say it's absolutely this person to the exclusion of all others, because, for example, there are identical twins. There aren't any real absolutes, so again, it's a matter of trying to compare knowns and unknowns and trying to provide leads for investigative purposes. Just because you put the word 'forensic' in front of it hardly means it is an exact science, it just means you are applying that science in some way, shape, or form. Consider fingerprints and think about how many millions and millions of accurate identifications are affected. I read an article years ago where two scientists had, in fact, isolated two identical snowflakes. So here's the strategy by the critics: jump on something like that as typifying the science. Or they attack fingerprinting by attacking the process of quantifying a latent fingerprint comparison and our process for looking at the frequency of bifurcations, trifurcations, ridge endings, all of those characteristics."

Many commentators say that the problem, in part, is a lack of empirical statistical evidence supporting the claims made by fingerprint examiners. Mnookin (2001) states, "[They] have no statistical basis for determining the probability that a match really indicates that both prints come from the same human being. This is viewed as especially problematic when they examine partial, smudged prints that provide less information from which to draw a conclusion. How likely is it that two people could have four points of resemblance, or five or six or eight or 10? Is the chance of two partial prints from different people matching one in 100, one in 100,000, or one in 1 billion? No fingerprint examiner can honestly answer that question, even though the answer is of course critical to evaluating the probative value of the evidence of a 'match.'" Critics assert that numerous fingerprint examiners are philosophically opposed to probabilistic models, Mnookin adds, "taking it as a principle that fingerprinting should provide certain and absolute, rather than probabilistic, identification."

Mnookin (2001) says that fingerprint examiners violate the "one dissimilarity doctrine," which holds that if there is even one genuine dissimilarity between two fingerprints, the prints cannot be said to have come from the same finger. Mnookin explains, "The problem, of course, is in the word 'genuine.' What counts as a genuine dissimilarity and how can an examiner recognize it? In practice, as some examiners acknowledge, an examiner who is convinced that two prints come from the same finger will be tempted to explain away any seeming dissimilarity as an artifact, the result of distortion in the print, or dirt, or a scar. Without clearly articulated standards for determining when a characteristic can be said to 'match,' separating distortions from genuine differences becomes both subjective and subject to manipulation. Both of these arguments also go generally to the 'existence and maintenance of standards controlling the technique's operation,' one of the factors mentioned in Daubert as an appropriate criterion for evaluating the reliability of scientific evidence."

To this end, in 1979, the IAI passed a resolution making it professional misconduct for any fingerprint examiner to provide courtroom testimony that labeled a match "possible, probable or likely" rather than "certain." Polski says, "Today there is a great amount in the literature about fingerprint identification because that is where the current controversy seems to be. Many of the principles involving fingerprint identification came out of the IAI, by means of various resolutions that were passed and studies that were conducted. Because of the controversy, the IAI is undertaking a review of issues such as error rates, absolute identification, standards for identification, and the issues related to the Daubert decision on admissibility of scientific evidence. We must ask ourselves, is this the way it was 30 years ago? Not that we have been wrong for 30 years, but the world has changed and we need to know where we go from here. Our knowledge of the discipline has expanded greatly over the past 30 years and I believe certain ways of testifying can be improved."

Critics have long asserted that fingerprint identification is not a science. Epstein (2002) asserts, "From the very outset, law enforcement has claimed that latent fingerprint identification is a science. Over the years, this claim has achieved almost universal acceptance." Interestingly, he believes that forensic practitioners are the source of the unrest, saying, "Recently, however, some of the leading voices in the forensic science community have begun to question the scientific foundation of the fingerprint field and suggest that latent fingerprint identifications may not be nearly as reliable as people have long assumed. Indeed, some commentators have even gone so far as to suggest that fingerprint experts are vulnerable to challenge pursuant to the Supreme Court's seminal decision in *Daubert v Merrell Dow* Pharmaceuticals Inc. Defense attorneys have started to pick up on these suggestions."

There is unison among members of the legal community in the charges being levied against the identification sciences. One challenge is that fingerprint characteristics are not verifiable. Epstein (2002) writes, "While some occasional research has been conducted with respect to the relative frequencies with which these and other characteristics occur, no weighted measures of the characteristics have ever been adopted by fingerprint examiners on the basis of these studies. Research, moreover, has shown that different fingerprint examiners hold widely varying opinions regarding which characteristics appear most commonly. All prints, both inked and latent, are subject to various types of distortions and artifacts." Epstein explains that these distortions can include pressure distortion, which occur when the print is being deposited, as well as other distortions created by the characteristics of the surface upon which the print is laid. Epstein comments, "No study has been conducted to determine the frequency with which such distortions occur. Latent fingerprint fragments found at crime scenes are often very distorted."

Haber and Haber (2003) point out that a latent print can differ from the finger itself, and from the fingerprint image taken by technicians under controlled conditions. They state, "Each one of these differences serves to diminish, obscure, distort, or eliminate information necessary to the comparison process." Haber and Haber explain that latent prints can be affected by the following factors:

- *Size:* A latent print can be a partial; the average latent print is only about one-fifth of the finger surface contained in an inked print.
- *Location:* Some areas of a finger's surface contain more information than others, so a partial print may yield less helpful detail.
- *Surface quality:* For example, the print may be impacted by surface dirt or contaminants; it may also be deposited on a surface such as wood, which has ridged properties that can complicate imagery.
- *Quality of the print:* It may be smudged, smeared or otherwise compromised, or it may be overlaid or underlaid by other prints.
- *Medium:* The substance in which the print was deposited, such as blood or sweat, may interfere with its definition.
- *Lift procedure:* This may interfere with loss of detail.

Haber and Haber (2003) emphasize, "The result of all these factors is that latent prints almost always contain less clarity, less content, and less undistorted information than a fingerprint taken under controlled conditions, and much, much less detail compared to the actual patterns of ridges and grooves of a finger. These transformations between inked or scanned fingerprints and latent prints must be understood, described, and addressed in the methodology for making comparisons. Further, the impoverished quality of latent prints must be recognized as an inevitable source of error in making comparisons." Haber and Haber charge further, that when fingerprint examiners do not recognize this loss of information inherent in the latent print, it makes the comparison process problematic. They observe, "The profession persists in the non-responsive claims that fingers are unique and fingerprint examiners do not make errors. This gap between the professional's claims and the problems inherent in the fingerprint comparison task has led researchers, the press, and the legal system to challenge the assertions of an exact science and of a zero error rate."

The concept of individualization in pattern identification sciences such as fingerprinting also is a frequent target of criticism. The goal of individualization is an inference of singular common source, according to Inman and Rudin (2001), who explain that two objects are considered to share a common origin if they were at one time contiguous or if they both originate from the same unique source. Cole (2005) says that latent print examiners reach conclusions of "individualization" by finding corresponding ridge characteristics between the unknown and known prints. Any unexplainable dissimilarity triggers a conclusion of "exclusion." Insufficient correspondences result in a conclusion of "inconclusive." "Sufficient" correspondences result in a conclusion of "individualization," or source attribution. Cole asks, "A crucial question is, of course, where the boundary lies between insufficient and sufficient correspondences. The latent print community has been unable to answer this question with any precision or consistency other than to posit a circular answer, which simply rests upon the analyst's subjective measure of 'sufficiency.'"

Inman and Rudin (2001) state, "Most laypersons, and perhaps even a majority of scientists, accept the concept of uniqueness at face value. It is imperative to appreciate that this view, while eminently reasonable, constitutes a leap of faith. Our belief that uniqueness is both attainable and existent is central to our work as forensic scientists. But we must be clear that it is a belief, not a fact. Not only has it not been proved, it is unprovable. In the language of science, the theory of uniqueness is not falsifiable."[1]

Saks (1998) says that the identification sciences base their claims of variation and "unique identifiability" on the multiplication rule of probability applied to populations: "The essential idea of this concept is that if objects vary on a number of independent (i.e., uncorrelated) dimensions, the probability of occurrence of any one combination of characteristics is found by multiplying together the probabilities associated with each dimension. Such calculations typically produce probabilities that are vanishingly small. Having made this general point, the next step in the argument—and it is offered by the forebears of each forensic identification science subfield—is to appeal to the audience's intuition to make the leap into concluding that no two handwritings, toolmarks, fingerprints, gun barrels, or whatever, could be alike."

Saks (1998) says further that these probabilistic models cannot prove absolutes, such as that no two are alike, adding, "This is not physics, where two objects cannot occupy the same place at the same time. This is micro-taxonomy, where no law of nature prevents two or many objects from falling into the same category." Saks argues that in forensic science, "there has been a leap from notions of probability to belief in a doctrine of unique individuality. Even if unique individuality did rule the universe, establishing the validity of a forensic technique would require testing the system of measurement and classification as well, even (or especially) if its principal tool is human perception and judgment." Saks adds that "the steps from observation of similarity to the conclusions that are offered to courts must traverse a minefield of potential errors of probabilistic inference that few forensic scientists, and even fewer lawyers or judges, are equipped to navigate."

Saks and other commentators say they would like to see forensic science in general, and pattern identification sciences in particular, base their observations on a foundation of real data and formal probability models. One is that it is the main road from subjective impressions to science. Another is that for several identification techniques, the assumption of no-two-alike has already been empirically disconfirmed. As a result, the need to make more accurate estimations of the reduction in uncertainty afforded by these techniques has become patent.

Challenges to the identification sciences focus on this concept of individualization, or the idea of unique identification distinct from all others. Criminalistics has been called the science of individualization, something Saks (1998) ponders, "The question posed is whether a bullet can be traced back to the one and only one barrel through which it was fired, a signature to the hand that wrote it, a bite mark to the mouth of the biter, cut bolts to the instrument that cut them, and so on. Affirmative answers are offered daily in courtrooms across the country as firearms examiners, document examiners, forensic odontologists, tool mark experts, and numerous other forensic identification scientists purport to identify the gun, hand, mouth, tool, and so on, that left its traces at a crime scene, 'to the exclusion of all others in the world.'"

Inman and Rudin (2001) cite Charles Sanders Peirce, who defined truth as "whatever scientists say it is when they come to the end of their labors," and add, "This is a particularly appealing bit of philosophy for those of us working in the applied sciences, particularly one such as forensic science where an entirely unrelated discipline depends on us to provide it with 'facts.' Although we govern ourselves by the rules of science, we also embrace the practical nature of our endeavor."[1] They assert that to be convinced of an individualization, one must be convinced that a possibility exists: "This conviction grows from an understanding of the nature of the evidence, including its inherent possibilities and limitations. This is rarely accomplished by a single person. A communal effort is needed to produce a body of empirical work that can support that pragmatic leap of faith to a conclusion of a single common source. In addition, each practitioner must rely on an individual body of education, training, and most of all experience, to justify his conclusion of individuality. The greater the common wisdom and the more extensive the individual experience, the more confidence we have that the leap of faith is both appropriate and justified. Equally important are the checks and balances that a working community provides in helping the individual analyst determine when the limitations of the evidence or the tests prevent the individualization as a reasonable conclusion in any specific case."[1]

Saks (1998) says that forensic practitioners have characterized individualization as "absolute specificity and absolute identification," which he says is unique to forensic science yet "contrasts with conventional science of virtually every kind." The difference, he explains, is that while science groups objects and events into meaningful classes, reveals systematic relationships among these classes, and develops and tests theoretical explanations for those shared attributes and relationships, forensic identification science purposefully looks beyond class characteristics and looks within classes.

Saks (1998) says that while normal science is concerned with establishing regularities, forensic science is concerned with exploiting irregularities among objects within classes. Its central assumption is that objects possess enough differences that on adequate inspection one object cannot be mistaken for another. Detractors have charged that forensic scientists are "content to assert that no two of various types of objects can be alike, and leave it at that," a behavior rooted in the probability theory.

Saks (1998) says astute individuals soon realize that "probability theory simply cannot get there from here, and next they look in vain for another route." Saks also says that forensic scientists "retreat to anecdotes, assumptions, and appeals to intuition. A small but perhaps growing number of forensic identification scientists accept the unavoidable: such identifications are in reality estimates of probability."

A crucial step in criminalistics is providing an assessment of the strength of the inferences made about the evidence. Inman and Rudin (2001) state, "Without some expression of the strength of the source determination, the results of an examination are virtually worthless and potentially misleading. . . . Some practitioners argue that a mere description of the tests performed and the results obtained fulfills the responsibility of the forensic scientist. . . . Results of an evidence examination presented without a statement about the strength of the relationship of the evidence to the punitive source is an abdication of the responsibilities of the competent examiner."[1]

One of the tools used by forensic scientists is the concept of probability, or the degree of belief in a proposition about the test results. Statistics are employed to provide information about the strength of evidence. Frequency estimates are the number of times the evidence is found in some defined population and used to relate the probability of finding the evidence as a random occurrence. Likelihood ratios compare the probability of competing hypotheses, and the results are expressed as how much more likely the evidence would be under one scenario compared with another (Inman and Rudin, 2001).

Saks (1998) says that the probabilities employed by traditional forensic identification science are "subjective and intuitive," and that only DNA typing "takes the burdens of the probabilistic nature of forensic identification science seriously. Only DNA typing collects data and calculates the objective probability of a coincidental match. All other forensic identification fields content themselves with intuitive estimates of subjective probability."

Michael Saks, Ph.D., M.S.L., a member of the faculties of the Sandra Day O'Connor College of Law and the Department of Psychology, as well as a faculty fellow of the Center for the Study of Law, Science & Technology at Arizona State University observes, "I would simply like to see forensic examiners provide the accuracy rate right along with the judgment or opinion they provide in court. Instead of saying, 'I think these two footprints or finger-prints came from the same person,' they'll say, 'Let me tell you the probability associated with this statement I just made to you.' A friend of mine is a forensic psychologist who is called upon from time to time to predict the dangerousness of individuals. He says that he is careful to explain why he is making the prediction, and then he provides data on how accurate the predictions are. So he says, 'This is my best prediction, but you need to know the limits of the prediction.' And he gives the jury probability data. That's all that I am asking forensic science to do. I think if forensic science had grown up entirely in an academic setting, it would routinely behave in that fashion. My hunch is that the reason forensic scientists make these unsupportable, extreme statements of probability or certainty, is that it represents the distortion created by the litigation process. Over the decades, prosecutors, not scientists, have applied as much pressure or persuasion to make cases as airtight as they can be. But if there was more science to these cases, perhaps they wouldn't feel compelled to do this. It has every-thing to do with the need to persuade a jury that they should vote a certain way. The irony is, at the end of the day, that most of the forensic identification sciences, and perhaps even all of them, are going to have something useful to contribute. It's just going to be standing on a more solid foundation, and it's going to be offered with appropriate measured limita-tions, and the result is it will be more tempered. The science may win fewer cases, but I think all of us, including juries, are mature enough to know that it's not perfect. I once said to a colleague, Michael Risinger, 'It's possible, isn't it, that a fingerprint could match, DNA could match, handwriting could match, all in the same case, and it could be an innocent person who is erroneously identified by these various different things, and the probability that it's not him is miniscule, but it's not him.' And Risinger said, 'Well, that's all true, but for some-thing like that to happen, God must really have it in for this person, and that's just the way it's going to have to be.' Sometimes this is hard for people to accept, and it's even harder to say, but sometimes errors will be made, and there's nothing we can do about it. I think we need to face those realities. We don't want to make errors, and if we do, we don't want to know about it; we want forensic scientists to reassure us that everything is fine and we have the right guy, and let's send him away or let's execute him and then society, and those who operate the criminal justice system, can feel good about what we're doing. I think we use forensic scientists and their overstatements as much to help drive out this horrible demon of incomplete certainty; if one were on a jury and the judge said, 'You don't have to banish all doubt, you just have to banish any reasonable doubt,' and if I do I'm going to send someone to prison, and I am not absolutely certain that's the person who did it . . . well, that's a trou-bling feeling. So we suggest part of the process is to reassure the judge and the jury, perhaps falsely, that there is no doubt, but there is always some doubt."

Many forensic scientists who conceded the inherently probabilistic nature of their enter-prise nevertheless refrained from undertaking data collection and the calculation of empiri-cally based probabilities. Others, however, have been distressed by the "almost complete lack of factual and statistical data pertaining to the problem of establishing identity" in their areas, and have started the belated work of building a rigorous foundation for forensic identification science. In contemporary practice, reliance on objective data and computations based on the data are found only in DNA typing (Saks, 1998).

Claims of "absolute certainty" springing from the concept of individualization set up exam-iners for a fall in court, many critics say. Epstein (2002) comments, ". . . examiners opine that the latent print at issue was made by a particular finger to the exclusion of all other fingers in the world. But, fingerprint examiners themselves have recognized that such assertions of abso-lute certainty are inherently unscientific." Epstein points to a law enforcement fingerprint examiner who noted, "Imposing deductive conclusions of absolute certainty upon the results of an essentially inductive process is a futile attempt to force the square peg into the round hole . . . this categorical requirement of absolute certainty has no particular scientific principle but has evolved from a practice shaped more from allegiance to dogma than a foundation in science. Once begun, the assumption of absolute certainty as the only possible conclusion has been maintained by a system of societal indoctrination, not reason, and has achieved such a ritualistic sanctity that even mild suggestions that its premise should be re-examined are instantly regarded as acts of blasphemy. Whatever this may be, it is not science."

While examiners may hold onto the theory that a latent fingerprint fragment can be identified to the exclusion of all other fingers in the world (stemming from the field's basic premise that no two people in the world have the same fingerprints), it is a theory that has not been scientifically established, commentators say. Epstein (2002) observes, "Even assuming that it is true that no two people in the world have the same fingerprint, this premise is logically flawed when it comes to the identification of latent fingerprint fragments. It simply does not follow from that premise that a fingerprint examiner can reliably make an identification from a small, distorted fingerprint fragment that might reveal only a small number of ridge characteristics . . . fingerprints from different people can have a limited number of characteristics that appear to match. Furthermore, fingerprint examiners in making their comparisons must rely on the naked eye, along with their judgment to decide when two things are alike or different. Thus, even if all fingerprints are in some sense unique, the undisputable reality remains that fingerprint examiners sometimes make false identifications."

So, the bottom line for many critics is that fingerprint analysis is one of reliability, not uniqueness. These critics claim that unique identifiability is not the order of the universe, and they trace forensic scientists' ideas that no-two-are-alike to the 19th-century statistician Adolph Quetelet, who hypothesized that nature never creates biological duplicates. Saks (1998) comments, "Of course, the best way to avoid finding duplicates is not to look for them. As long as one refrains from looking for black swans, one's belief that all swans are white is insulated from falsification."

Haber and Haber (2003) assert that every forensic science requires five components in order to achieve individuation:

- A description of the patterns of the objects being used to individuate
- Evidence that those descriptions of the patterns can be used to individuate
- Descriptions of how the patterns are transformed when deposited in a crime scene, and how each change can be related back to the original pattern
- Evidence that the descriptions of the trace crime scene patterns are also unique to every individual, so that two different people would never leave patterns that could be confused
- Descriptions of a tested methodology to carry out comparisons between pattern traces associated with a crime and the object itself

Haber and Haber (2003) thus conclude that, "When this forensic science of fingerprint comparison is well described, tested, and verified, then the sources of errors in making fingerprint comparisons can be understood, error rates can be determined for different kinds of latent prints and different procedures for making comparisons, and improvements in technology, training, and comparison procedures can be made to reduce the rate of errors. However, at present, a forensic science of fingerprint comparison is neither well described, nor well tested. For these reasons as well, researchers, the press, and the legal system are questioning the magnitude of error rates in fingerprint comparisons."

Detractors to the pattern identification sciences say they want proof provided through rigorous research leading to empirical evidence that backs their claims of absolute certainty and individualization. Epstein (2002) represents many commentators when he states, "While fingerprint examiners have long claimed the mantle of science so as to bolster the credibility of their profession, the reality is that the fingerprint community has never conducted any scientific testing to validate the premises upon which the field is based."

Essentially, critics are calling for scientific proof that examiners can make reliable identifications from challenging kinds of evidence such as latent prints, as well as testing to determine the probability of two different people having a number of fingerprint ridge characteristics in common.

The Department of Justice (DOJ) may have admitted that the field is lacking in research when in March 2000 it issued, through its research arm, the National Institute of Justice, a formal solicitation for forensic friction ridge (fingerprint) examination validation. The solicitation was drafted by a panel comprised of fingerprint examiners from the FBI, the U.S. Secret Service, and the U.S. Army. The call for research was designed to help determine the scientific validity of individuality in friction ridge examination based on measurement of features, quantification, and statistical analysis, with the DOJ explaining its actions, "the theoretical basis for (fingerprint) individuality has had limited study and needs additional work to demonstrate the statistical basis for identifications."

The critics descended, using this solicitation as proof that the fingerprint field did indeed have its weaknesses that needed shoring up. Epstein (2002) comments, "This is quite an admission. For the past 90 years, fingerprint examiners have been testifying in court that the basic premise of fingerprint identification evidence is the individuality of all fingerprints. Indeed, the notion of fingerprint individuality . . . is deeply ingrained in our popular culture. Yet we now discover from the DOJ's solicitation that fingerprint individuality has never in fact been scientifically established and that basic research in this area needs to be conducted. . . . DOJ's admission that fingerprint individuality has not been scientifically validated is nothing short of remarkable."

Of note is that the solicitation came on the heels of the *Daubert* decision, which established a higher standard for the admission of scientific evidence into courts. Critics say that this opens the door to further discussion of the need for validity of fingerprinting examination and a closer look at error rates.

Any conversation about errors demands a discussion of the distinctions between false positives and false negatives. In the context of fingerprint identification, Cole (2005) explains that a false positive would consist of reporting that an individual is the source of an impression when in fact he is not, while a false negative would consist of reporting that an individual is not the source of an impression when in fact he is.

Cole (2005) advises, "These errors can be of differing importance depending on the context. For example, in criminal law the classic formulation of this is Blackstone's maxim which states that it is better to let 10 guilty people go free than to falsely convict one innocent person. This would suggest that false positives are 10 times more catastrophic than false negatives."

It should be noted that many false positives are caught and corrected by forensic examiners within the forensic laboratory. However, another examiner may disagree with the original conclusion in the process of validation, and this dispute would be resolved by reporting the finding as inconclusive or as an exclusion. Cole (2005) notes, "No one outside the laboratory would know that there had been an 'error.' We know very little about these types of errors. They are unlikely to generate media attention, officially published reports, or legal records, our primary sources for learning about fingerprint errors. In all likelihood the disagreement is resolved quietly within the laboratory. There is legitimate reason to distinguish between errors that are detected in the laboratory and errors that are not detected until after a laboratory has in some way input its conclusions into the criminal justice system, leading to arrest, indictment, trial, or conviction."

Cole admits that forensic practitioners would argue that the system worked, ultimately, because the error was detected and it prevented erroneous information from being introduced into court. However, Cole (2005) states, ". . . whether the error is ultimately detected before conviction or after conviction, the error is nonetheless far more serious. Once the laboratory inputs a conclusion into the criminal justice, it has effectively terminated whatever processes it has in place to detect errors. At this point, responsibility for exposure of the error rests with other actors, such as the prosecutor, judge, jury, or, most important, the defense expert, if there is one."

This would indicate that a closer look at the definition of error is in order. Cole (2005) suggests, "Are we interested in errors exposed within the laboratory, errors exposed after they leave the laboratory, or are we interested in estimating the prevalence of all actual errors, whether or not they are exposed?"

"I think it's illogical to say there are no error rates," says Polski, "whether you are talking about fingerprints or anything else, including all disciplines of forensic science. However, current discussions about error rates seems to be most closely associated with fingerprint identification. Whether it is practitioner error or scientific error, it's still an error. A statement frequently heard is that 'the science is infallible but the practitioners are not, so therefore there could be some error rate.' My feeling is if a defendant is sitting in court and looking at 20 years in prison, and there's an error in the fingerprint testimony, regardless of whether it is scientific or human, it's still an error and it's critical that errors be recognized and addressed."

Polski continues, "I know there is movement on this topic at the national level; during a recent meeting at the NIJ, I talked at length to people who are interested in doing a study of error rates and fingerprint identification in particular. I think it's important that a baseline be established, and I believe there is research needed to establish a quantification of these rates. To the extent that you move in that scientific direction, it moves the fingerprint discipline and some of the other pattern evidence disciplines increasingly into the scientific world. The scientific world agrees that even DNA has an error rate that can be identified. Is it significant? Well, probably not, but on the other hand, to say it doesn't exist is burying your head in the sand."

"Scientific principles note that there is nothing absolute in science," Polski emphasizes. "Scientific principles are built on the fact that something exists or established as a given is because nothing has been shown to prove differently. Scientific hypotheses are accepted because no one has ever proved them wrong. Even in the world of pure science, nothing is 100 percent certain. From a commonsense observation, if human beings are involved, there will likely be some error involved, and in forensic science as an example, it is very small; the point is that errors or mistakes do not confine themselves exclusively to forensic science but apply to any scientific endeavor in which human beings are involved."

Polski says the intensity of the focus on error rates in forensic science is heightened because the stakes are much higher. "The court process changes everything," Polski explains, "because we are dealing with evidence that can condemn someone. If a scientist in a laboratory analyzing some brand-new aluminum compound makes a mistake in a hypothesis, it's no big deal because he can try again tomorrow and try to do it right. But if a forensic scientist is wrong, the consequence could be that someone goes to prison. That's why forensic science and the pattern-identification sciences attract much more scrutiny that other scientific disciplines."

Polski says much of this scrutiny—and criticism—comes from what he calls the pure-science community. "They argue to the point of 100-percent certainty, an infallible statement. If you look at the newest thing to hit forensic science, which is DNA, it was validated in a way that was very different than a lot of other scientific methods in forensic science. It was validated through studies by the National Research Council, an arm of the National Academy of Sciences, which issued several reports. Those reports are what I call the "thud" factor; when one of those reports goes 'thud!' onto the witness stand and someone asks, 'Why does this work,' the reply is, 'It works because the National Academy of Sciences said so; you follow these protocols and they work.' Who is going to argue with that?"

Polski continues, "Fingerprint identification has been around for a long time, and for years has been seen as the gold standard of identification. If you look at the way DNA testimony is presented, it's a probability. It's stated as 1 in 10 million, or whatever it might be. I do think that we would get rid of a lot of detractors of fingerprint and other pattern evidence if it was said, 'I can't say that I am infallible when I make this identification but I can say that based on what we know through research, there is a 1 in 10 billion chance that this print would be someone else.' I don't think it would affect the weight of the identification one bit, but I do think it would make it much more difficult for those people who want to attack that absolute identification to attack that kind of statement; after all, that is the scientific way of looking at things because in science, nothing is absolute. The scientist will never say, 'There is not another cell like this on the face of the earth,' unless he or she has looked at every cell on the face of the earth. Ultimately the science of fingerprint identification works well. On the other hand, the way testimony is presented by examiners may need to be looked at differently than what has been the status quo for the past 100 years."

Haber and Haber (2003) observe, "For almost 100 years, fingerprint evidence has been accepted as fact in court in the United States and other countries. Until very recently, when the fingerprint expert declared an identification—a match between the defendant's prints and trace prints associated with the crime—this assertion went unquestioned by judge, jury, and defense attorney."

Haber and Haber (2003) point to the persistent claim by the fingerprint community that they do not make mistakes and that fingerprint examination is an exacting science. Hazen and Phillips (2001) state, "The fingerprint expert is unique among forensic specialists. Because fingerprint science is objective and exact, conclusions reached by fingerprint experts are absolute and final." On the other end of the argument is Stoney (1997), who states, "In fingerprint comparison, judgments of correspondence and the assessment of differences are wholly subjective: there are no objective criteria for determining when a difference may be explainable or not."

Error rates are frequent fodder due to the aforementioned court decisions on the scientific requirements for the presentation of expert opinion in court, including *Daubert v Merrell Dow Pharmaceuticals* (1993) and *Kumho Tire v Carmichael* (1999). These oft-cited cases require experts to demonstrate that their opinions are derived from a scientific base and a science documented in a research literature and accepted by peers; they also require experts to demonstrate knowledge of the error rate associated with the methodology on which their opinions are based. Haber and Haber (2003) state, "At present, the fingerprint profession insists that fingerprint comparisons are based on an exact science and that competent fingerprint examiners have a zero percent error rate."

Haber and Haber (2003) outline the major complaints about fingerprint examinations: the fingerprint profession's focus on the details on actual fingers in ascribing a science to the comparison of prints; the potential poor quality of latent prints found at crime scenes; and the field's "failure to develop an explicit forensic science of fingerprint comparisons that defines the transformations that occur in fingerprint patterns when fingers touch surfaces, and defines methodologies for making comparisons."

Proficiency testing is a significant issue among commentators who believe this process reveals what they allege are the many chinks in fingerprint examiners' armor.

Haber and Haber (2003) describe the proficiency testing efforts contained within the accreditation process of laboratories by the American Society of Crime Laboratory Directors (ASCLD). Beginning in 1983, ASCLD administered by mail an annual proficiency test wherein each laboratory requesting accreditation was sent a dozen latent prints with a number of 10-print cards. The latent prints either were selected from actual cases or were constructed to represent the range of quality found in typical latent prints. The 10-print cards were also selected to be of typical quality. The examiners in the laboratory had to judge whether each latent print was scorable, and if scorable, whether it matched a fingerprint on one of the 10-print cards, or could be eliminated as matching none of them. Haber and Haber report that on average, 2 percent of the scorable latent prints were erroneously judged to be unscorable, and so were not examined further when they should have been; while 8 percent of the unscorable latent prints were erroneously judged to be scorable and were examined further when they should not have been. With respect to eliminations and identifications, 8 percent of the identifiable latent prints were eliminated, and 2 percent of the elimination prints were scored as identifications. Haber and Haber comment, "These 2 percent findings are extremely troublesome. While an individual 2 percent erroneous identification rate or an individual 2 percent erroneous unscorable rate may seem negligible, they assume serious proportions in these tests, because the errors result from consensus and not individual, independent judgments."

Haber and Haber (2003) argue that the meaning of proficiency tests offer no real value to the courts when attempting to evaluate erroneous identification rates, explaining that since the tests are administered by mail, there is no control on how the test is conducted or timed, nor any determination of whether the responses came from a consensus or an individual examiner, or the years of experience or amount of training of those who took the test. They add that the test assesses only a small portion of the examiner's typical job duties and "if these tests are to measure proficiency in a way that generalizes to performance accuracy in court, they must include an assessment of handling AFIS search outputs, of eliminations as well as identifications, of prints that cannot be scored at all, and of 10-prints that do not match the latent prints."

Haber and Haber (2003) also point to the lack of information about a forensic laboratory's verification procedures; they note, "Verifying the accuracy of a result produced by an examiner in a crime laboratory is comparable to auditing the quality-control procedures of a water testing laboratory, or to an experimental test of the efficacy of a new drug compared to a placebo. In general, accurate results are obtained if the person being verified, audited, or tested does not know that a verification, audit, or test is being performed, does not know the specific purposes of the test, and does not know the expected or desired outcome by whoever is administering the procedure. In addition, the persons administering the verification, audit, or test should have no stake in its success or outcome, and should not know the correct, expected, or required answers. Finally, the verification, audit, or test results should be scored and interpreted by an external and neutral body. When any of these procedures is violated, biased outcomes and inflated scores result."

The issue then turns from the competency of the forensic laboratory overall, to the competency of individual examiners, revealed through additional proficiency and certification testing. Haber and Haber (2003) report that since 1995, the FBI has mandated annual proficiency testing of its latent fingerprint examiners and uses its own system of examination, whose results have not been published. However, seven years of results from 1995 to 2001 were under scrutiny in the landmark case of *United States of America v Plaza et al.* (2002). Meagher (2002) reports that in this case, the FBI contended that the results of the annual proficiency tests showed its examiners did not make errors in court. Meagher describes the FBI's testing method, in which approximately 60 fingerprint examiners took the test annually: The test included between five and 10 latent fingerprints to be compared to several 10-print cards. The results showed that none of the examiners taking the tests each year over the seven-year period made an erroneous identification; three examiners each missed an identification once in the seven years, a miss rate of less than 1 percent. Haber and Haber note, however, ". . . these results should not be interpreted as indicating virtually perfect accuracy by FBI examiners when they testify in court. The FBI proficiency test procedures are so fraught with problems that the results are uninterpretable. These problems include difficulty level, unrealistic tasks, and lack of peer review."

Attorney William Webster, former director of the FBI and the CIA, says commentators have been cavalier in their assumptions about the FBI's examiners. "The FBI must always demand a level of standards that will survive intensive cross-examination because the evidence and expert witnesses are certainly going to encounter scrutiny in the courtroom," Webster says. "Like every other organization in the world, in terms of its internal culture, the FBI has its good people and its not so good people. I have known many FBI special agents through the years, including my nine years as the bureau's director, and I believe that the culture of the FBI is to not overstate the evidence. While I was a federal judge for eight years, many a criminal case that depended on FBI testimony came to my attention, and bureau personnel were uniformly cautious about the statements they would make. They say what's there, and in some cases they have to qualify what they are saying because it may be second-hand or other than what that agent knows, but they don't pretend to know what they don't know. I really believe they have received a bad rap. One of the things that impressed me most is, from my perspective as a lawyer, a prosecutor, and as a judge, was their consistent desire to tell it as it was, not as they thought it could be, because they are trained to be that way. Their supervisors track their performance and they take corrective action if they feel someone is trying too hard to get a conviction. The expression I often heard was, 'Tell the truth, warts and all,' when they testify; they weren't hiding the bad stuff from the defense, and if there were holes in the case, they would acknowledge them. Their job is to protect the innocent as well as bring the guilty to justice. That's a high calling and it requires them to be as accurate as they can be. I have to say there was a period after I left the agency when the laboratories came under fire, and I think that was probably not because they were either corrupt or incompetent, but because they counted too much on the scientific backgrounds and capabilities of their own special agents. There has been a tendency among special agents in the past to think there wasn't anything they couldn't do better than the next guy. There was a confidence in their team that they could do it better, so special agents ought to be doing the lab examinations. But most special agents did not join the FBI to be scientists, they joined to catch criminals. So when you put them in that work, they do the best they know how but it is not necessarily as good as people who are trained from the beginning to do scientific work. They have finally begun to come around to that way of thinking."

Mnookin (2001) states the FBI argues that the error rate for fingerprint identification is zero because fingerprints are unique and permanent and can be accurately distinguished from one another, but says, "Fingerprint examiners make this same argument that, although practitioners may on rare occasions misapply the science of fingerprinting and make errors, the error rate of the science of fingerprinting is zero. Of course, what Daubert must mean when it refers to an error rate is the error rate in practice; to speak of the idealized error rate that would exist if all examiners were perfect all the time is irrelevant, indeed practically meaningless. The same argument could be made of eyewitness testimony, a notoriously unreliable form of evidence. People are all distinct from one another in observable ways; therefore the theoretical error rate of eyewitness identification is zero, though in practice observers may frequently make errors."

Critics (Haber and Haber, 2003; Bayle, 2002; Arvizu, 2002) argue that the latent prints used in the testing were clear, distinct, and rich in information content—a complete opposite of what real-world examiners see on a daily basis. Haber and Haber comment, "In the absence of an independent measure of difficulty, a result that nearly everyone gets a high score is vacuous in meaning. There is no way to establish any measure of validity for these results, because the results have no variation. These scores have a zero correlation with supervisory ratings, number of prints examined in the past, years of training, or years of experience. The tests sampled only a narrow portion of a typical FBI print examiner's workload: None of the latent prints was unscorable; virtually all comparisons were identifications; there were very, very few eliminations; and there were no comparisons made to AFIS search outputs." They add, "The results of the FBI proficiency tests do not generalize either to an FBI fingerprint examiner's performance on his job, or to the accuracy of the identifications to which attests in court. Their test results, like those of the ASCLD crime laboratory certification test results, are useless to the profession and useless to the courts as an index of erroneous identification error rates."

Adding to the dialogue on examiner certification is the IAI, which, in 1993, through its Latent Print Certification Board, began offering certification to individual latent print examiners. The IAI mandates that in order to sit for the examination, examiners must meet a stringent set of criteria, including possessing a minimum of 40 hours of formal training in inked fingerprints, as well as a minimum of 40 hours of formal training in latent prints. The certification test is comprised of practical-knowledge sections and 15 latent prints that must be compared to a number of 10-prints. To pass the fingerprint comparison portion, the test taker must identify 12 or more of the 15 latent prints correctly, without making a single false identification. Haber and Haber (2003) report that in 1993, 48 percent of the 762 applicants passed the test, and that according to the IAI, the pass rate hovers around 50 percent through 2001. Haber and Haber note, "According to the IAI, the section on latent to 10-print comparisons accounted for nearly all of the failures. No data are available as to what percent of the failures resulted from false identifications."

Commentators maintain that proficiency and certification tests should fulfill two objectives: allow quantitative assessment of the individual examiner's skill and accuracy on the particular tasks examiners perform in their job setting, and scrutinize examiner skill on the tasks required for their accuracy when they testify in court. Haber and Haber (2003) state, "To fulfill the first function, test results must be demonstrably valid: They correlate with years on the job, with supervisory ratings, etc. To fulfill the second, the proficiency test must include the range of tasks the examiners typically perform in the course of their work, including elimination prints, unscorable prints, and AFIS outputs. Like the FBI internal proficiency test, the IAI certification test fails to meet either criterion."

Another common allegation is that the identification sciences are biased, in part, because they are beholden to law enforcement. Saks says he is concerned about a science constructed in the image of the criminal law. He comments, "Forensic science plainly has something of value to offer criminal investigators and the courts. Why, then, does so much of it cling, instead, to an untenable absolutism and committed subjectivity? By contrast, conventional science would have proceeded along a different course, one guided by the necessity of collecting and analyzing data to test assumptions. In court, conventional scientists might be expected to share with the fact-finder the analytic basis of their opinions, their data, and their data-based assessments of the risk of error. In short, conventional scientists would collect better data and offer them to the courts with far less exaggeration. Why doesn't forensic science proceed along that more recognizably scientific path? The answer likely is that forensic science grew up in the criminal law. The exigencies imposed on it by police and prosecutors molded it into its contemporary shape. A particularly dramatic demonstration of this is the lengths to which some forensic scientists have been willing to go to provide courts with the testimony prosecutors wanted courts to hear, regardless of the truth."

Giannelli (2003) has summarized an array of fraudulent science, faked tests, and perjured testimony. But one need not look to such scandalous examples to find the influence of the adversary process at work. Consider the following demands under which forensic science has been required to operate.

To win a conviction, of course, the prosecution must prove its case beyond a reasonable doubt. But one commentator recognizes the bind that the witness for the prosecution is in. Saks (1998) notes, "If the forensic scientist testifies: 'I cannot tell these questioned and known evidence items apart, so they probably share a common origin, but of course this is only a subjective estimation based on intuition, because we've never mapped the distribution of what is out there,' or 'based on our sampling of the population we calculate the probability of a coincidental match to be at the following level of probability,' room is left for some doubt. But doubt vanishes if the forensic scientist can say something along these lines: 'Because the questioned and the known look alike, and because each person's or object's marks are unique in all the world, I can state with certainty my opinion that the defendant left the markers found at the crime scene.'"

In other words, the witness for the prosecution is loath to leave any loopholes open for the defense, which could then argue to the jury, according to Saks, "If there is even one other match out there, that makes two people who might have done it, only one of whom is my client; that implies a 50-50 chance that someone other than my client is guilty. Surely you cannot regard that as guilt beyond a reasonable doubt. Courts have reversed convictions on the reasoning that a merely rare probability is not sufficient to prove guilt."

Saks (1998) explains that due to its "institutional position within the legal system," the forensic identification sciences have "taken on a shape that resembles no other science." It is a criticism that has been echoed by many commentators throughout this book: that forensic science, including and especially pattern identification disciplines, is beholden to law enforcement. Saks charges, "No other fields are as closely affiliated with a single side of litigation as forensic science is to criminal prosecution. Police crime laboratories were not begun in order to provide science for police and courts, but as a public relations device. Even today, few of the personnel of crime laboratories have scientific training beyond the undergraduate level, and some not even that. Crime laboratories generate very little research, which to a scientist means they are not doing science, and to a lawyer should say at least that little progress is being made. At best, they apply science, but even that often is not the case. Progress might come from their colleagues in industrial or academic departments. But there are no industrial uses of what forensic identification scientists do, and the number of university programs to train forensic scientists has long been surprisingly few."

Because the distribution of forensic scientists greatly favors the prosecution, Saks (1998) says that frequently, the defense has little access to them, which "prevents the adversary process from working as intended to expose error." Saks adds, "The institutional setting of forensic science promotes habits of thought that more closely resemble the thinking of litigators than of scientists. While science pursues knowledge through falsification, prosecutions are won by confirmatory proofs. This confirmatory bias dominates the thinking of most forensic scientists. Where science advances by open discussion and debate, forensic science has been infected by the litigator's preference for secrecy. Tests of the proficiency of crime laboratories are conducted anonymously, and for a long time were kept secret and not routinely published. It is ironic that while the effectiveness and accuracy of so many professional enterprises are available in published literature, the same is not true of a field whose sole purpose is to do some of the public's most public business."

"Many forensic scientists aren't sure if fingerprints should even be put in the same rubric as other forensic disciplines," says Victor Weedn, M.D., J.D., a professor at Duquesne University. "For example, fingerprint examiners are not part of the American Academy of Forensic Sciences. I, as a forensic scientist, believe that it is not correct to put me in the same basket as them. Michael Saks, in his *Science* paper, lumps us all together. Most of the forensic scientists in the labs have chemistry or biology degrees, but if you look at the fingerprint examiners who work in crime labs, they frequently are police officers who may have no degree and have parlayed an interest in fingerprints into a job in the lab. They are called examiners, like firearms examiners, or document examiners, because they are not analysts. What Saks and his colleagues primarily have a problem with is pattern evidence, and the claims being made by these examiners. I am sympathetic to Michael and to a lot of what he wants to do, but there are some words in that paper that distress me. I'm not like some who just dismiss him out of hand. I think there are a lot of good points Michael makes. I believe there should be a strong forensic science academic community in order to scrutinize forensic science issues. I have a problem with people coming into court, talking about the forensic sciences when they only know about general science."

Weedn continues, "Michael asks, why isn't the Academy dealing with these issues and I say, there's no money to do it. All of this requires research and it requires money to do research. There needs to be significant funding to support faculty and research in academia. That's where you have your neutral body to vet these issues that we're all talking about. I don't want money to simply go to a given government agency or lab to do the research, less because of the bias or appearance of bias, but rather because pluralism in research is important. A topic should be investigated by different people with different views in different ways. Over time, any given theory is proved or disproved, and that ought to happen in forensic science. The reformers usually call for a commission, but that is not the way you do science, either. If you really want forensic science to be credible, there must be dollars for research by independent bodies."

WHERE'S THE SCIENCE? THE IDENTIFICATION COMMUNITY ANSWERS BACK

Budowle et al. (2006) say that two approaches may be considered when assessing the scientific basis of identification using latent print evidence: treating the examiner as a black box and rigorously testing his or her performance in a controlled manner, or developing more objective minimum criteria to establish a threshold for rendering an identification. Regarding the so-called black-box approach, Budowle et al. assert, "Assume for the moment that it is not possible to define minimum criteria for rendering an identification and that the latent print community's position of no scientific basis for a minimum criterion is correct. Some detractors might suggest that the lack of a definable, scientifically derived minimum threshold means that identifications should not be made; the process is too subjective. (We) do not support such a position because vast experience demonstrates that latent print and reference print analyses and comparisons can be performed, and identifications and exclusions can be properly effected. One can embrace the subjective approach and accept that the examiner is a black box. The examiner(s) can be tested with various inputs of a range of defined categories of prints. This approach would demonstrate whether or not it is possible to obtain a degree of accuracy. Under the black-box approach, there is a subjective component to varying degrees in all phases of the ACE-V process. To reduce examiner bias, a blind technical review comprising the ACE portion of the ACE-V process should be carried out by another qualified examiner during routine casework. This review should include all aspects of the ACE portion but is particularly important for the Analysis step, during which quality is assessed and ultimately results in an 'of value' or 'no value' decision. To be truly blind, the second examiner should have no knowledge of the interpretation by the first examiner (to include not seeing notes or reports). Such a technical review is absolutely necessary under the black-box scenario. A blind verification process will have a significant impact on resources; therefore, a study should be carried out to determine the best and most cost-effective approach to accomplish the objective."

Budowle et al. (2006) acknowledge the current furor over the need to develop a quantifiable minimum threshold for identification, based on objective criteria, and report, "In discussions with examiners, (we) discovered that although there is no official minimum threshold, some examiners would not proceed with an analysis . . . unless the pattern contained seven detectable points. . . . The practice of using seven points may be pervasive because most examiners were taught by the same few people; the criteria were not derived independently. Thus there may be a bias in ascertainment for a seven-point guideline. Yet seven points may be a good first-level approximation. A minimum of seven points does not necessarily connote identity; it conveys only that the print should be photographed and then analyzed more intensely. It is possible that two prints may share seven or more points in common and not be from the same source. Relying solely on points for an identification would be improper. It is the entire arrangement and the ridges and features in sequence that should be analyzed and compared when rendering an identification."

A minimum threshold must both consider the clarity, quality, and quantity of features and include all levels of detail, according to Budowle et al. (2006), who add, "Variability is inherent in the production of any two prints from the same source, due to a number of factors (surface, environmental factors, size, etc.). Latent prints in particular are not produced in a controlled manner and are subjected to various development processes that may add to the variation between the latent print and the source fingerprint. One has to accept a certain amount of explainable variation in the representation of a print; otherwise, everything would be excluded and no effective print comparisons could be made. The human eye is quite good at correcting for distortion and degradation, much better than current computer systems. Although the human expert may be better at identifying and accounting for distortion, this process is somewhat subjective and dependent on the individual examiner." The researchers are quick to point out that guidelines describing quality metric features for prints should be established, and acknowledge the attempt by the FBI to invoke a minimum 12-point guideline for requiring a supervisor's approval for a rendered identification because quality may be low. The researchers add that this 12-point system should be tested to determine if a correlation exists between the number of points and clarity.

Making a conclusive identification, of course, is perhaps the most controversial aspect of latent fingerprint examination. Budowle et al. (2006) observe, "Simply because no latent print of sufficient quality and quantity was found with features similar to the suspect does not mean that the suspect did not handle the evidence. Someone can handle an object and leave no latent print(s); therefore, practitioners espouse that no one can ever be excluded as having touched the evidence. In keeping with this philosophy, a latent print examiner tends to approach the comparison to make an identification rather than to attempt to exclude. This concept is similar to any other forensic analysis in that a lack of evidence does not necessarily exclude a suspect. However, it contrasts slightly with the doctrine of other forensic science disciplines. In forensic science examinations, regardless of the discipline, a pattern or profile is generated from the evidence, and it is compared with that obtained from a reference sample(s) in an attempt to exclude the two samples as having originated from the same source. When an examiner fails to exclude, then some significance is placed on that observation or finding. The more powerful or resolving the analysis, the more likely it is that wrongly associated samples will be excluded. The tremendous variability observed in friction ridge skin makes analysis of latent prints one of the most powerful exculpatory tools available to the forensic scientist. In fairness, an examiner does look for discrepancies in ridge detail that would result in an interpretation of exclusion. However, this approach is implemented only for prints deemed suitable for comparison." The researchers emphasize further, "The issue of exculpatory power of evidence is complex but needs further investigation."

FINGERPRINTS AND CASE LAW

One of the first important cases that upheld the admissibility of fingerprint evidence was the 1911 Illinois case of *People v Jennings,* in which the court noted, "The courts of this country do not appear to have had occasion to pass on the question." At the time, Saks (1998) explains, "Little more than the passage of time was necessary for eventual universal acceptance. These cases, germinal not only for fingerprint identification but for the many other forensic individualization techniques soon to spawn in its path, invested little effort assessing the merits of the proffered scientific evidence. Rather, for the most part, these courts casually cited treatises on criminal investigation, or general approval of science, or, eventually, other cases admitting such evidence."

Saks (1998) adds, "Popular and judicial intuitions about fingerprints are so strong that not a case can be found that entertains any serious doubt about the scientific perfection that has been achieved by fingerprint examination. Modern courts in which fingerprint evidence has begun to be challenged—*United States v Mitchell* and *United States v Harvard*—find no help in the earlier cases."

Saks (1998) asserts, "Fingerprint evidence may present courts applying Daubert with their most extreme dilemma. By conventional scientific standards, any serious search for evidence of the validity of fingerprint identification is going to be disappointing . . . yet the intuitions that underlie fingerprint examination, and the subjective judgments on which specific case opinions are based, are powerful. When and if a court agrees to seriously reconsider the admissibility of fingerprint identification evidence under the Daubert and Kumho approach— that courts may admit scientific evidence only if it meets contemporary standards of what constitutes valid science—is likely to meet its most demanding test: A vote to admit fingerprints is a rejection of conventional science as the criterion for admission. A vote for science is a vote to exclude fingerprint expert opinions."

Neufeld and Scheck (2002) write, "In 1993, when the Supreme Court demanded real scientific standards for expert evidence in federal courts, some critics correctly anticipated that several criminal identification techniques would be attacked in the courts with some success: microscopic hair comparison, bite mark analysis, handwriting comparison. Few, if any, predicted what is happening now: The bedrock forensic identifier of the 20th century, fingerprinting, has started to wobble." They point to a pretrial hearing in a Philadelphia federal court when Judge Louis H. Pollak limited the use of fingerprint evidence in a murder case, finding that there was no persuasive proof that the methods employed by forensic examiners had been adequately tested in objective, controlled experiments. At issue is how much of a match is required to say that a particular fingerprint is from a particular person. Neufeld and Scheck add, "Fingerprint experts had conceded that the process they use—matching large, evenly pressured prints taken from suspects at the police station to smaller, unevenly pressured prints from crime scenes—is ultimately subjective and bedeviled by inconsistent standards. The French, for example, require that two fingerprints match at 16 points before they can be accepted as coming from the same person; the Australians, 12; and the Swedes, seven. The FBI refuses to state a number at all, relying instead on case-by-case judgments."

Pollak had taken notice of what he called "alarmingly high" error rates in proficiency tests taken by fingerprint examiners, so he ruled that experts would be permitted to testify only to the points they viewed as similar, and refrain from expressing an opinion about whether fingerprints match. Neufeld and Scheck (2002) write, "No one doubts that fingerprints can, and do, serve as a highly discriminating identifier, and digital photographic enhancement and computer databases now promise to make fingerprint identification more useful than ever before. But to what degree incomplete and imperfect fingerprints can be reliably used to identify individuals requires more scientific examination. And the criminal system needs forensic examiners who can pass rigorous proficiency tests. Forensic science has rarely been subjected to the kind of scrutiny and independent verification applied to other fields of applied and medical science. Instead, analysts testifying in courts about fingerprint analysis, bite marks, handwriting comparisons and the like have often argued that in their field the courtroom itself provided the test. . . . Independence and scientific rigor should be the norm for forensic science. Crime victims, the wrongly accused, and the public will all have more confidence in the system if forensic scientists and their laboratories are completely independent, not beholden to prosecutors or defense attorneys."

The call for the elimination of any verisimilitude of subjectivity or bias in the identification sciences may stem from the new development of DNA testing, coupled with the long-standing expectation of judicial gatekeeping of expert evidence. These two factors created a medico-legal climate in which challenges to evidence became less astonishing. With DNA quickly establishing itself as the gold standard, the continued validity and accuracy of certain forensic disciplines such as pattern evidence identification, were called into question. Mnookin (2001) observes, "The move toward focusing on reliability and validity of evidence rather than using a proxy criterion like general acceptance made fingerprinting a more plausible target. So long as the dominant standard for assessing expert evidence was the *Frye* test, which focused on whether a novel technique was generally accepted by the relevant scientific community, it would have been extremely difficult to dislodge a form of evidence that had such deep and longstanding institutional support. Of course fingerprinting was accepted by the relevant scientific community, especially if that community was defined as fingerprint examiners. Even if the community were defined more broadly—perhaps as forensic scientists in general—it would have been nearly impossible to argue that fingerprinting was not generally accepted. After all, fingerprinting was not just generally accepted; it was universally accepted, forensic science's gold standard. Even before Daubert, a number of judges were beginning to approach the question of the admissibility of expert evidence as a question of reliability and its assessment, rather than presuming that general acceptance was the central issue."

Mnookin (2001) suggests that *Daubert* offers two important doctrinal advantages for anyone attempting to challenge fingerprint evidence; she explains, "First, the views of the relevant community are no longer dispositive, but are just one factor among many. There is a good argument that, for a question like the reliability of fingerprinting, the views of fingerprint examiners should carry only limited weight . . . when there is challenge to the fundamental reliability of a technique through which the practitioners make their living, there is good reason to be especially dubious about general acceptance as a proxy for reliability. But when there is an argument that the field itself is inadequate, the participants' perspective should be a starting point, not the end of the discussion."

Critics like *Daubert* because it does not provide a "safe harbor" for scientific techniques with a long-standing history. Under the *Frye* test of general acceptance, if a form of evidence had been used and accepted as legal evidence for a long time, it provided prima facie evidence of general acceptance. Judges were not expected to keep re-inventing the wheel, or scrutinizing evidence that historically had been admitted into court. But if *Daubert*'s key factor was reliability, and if there are new arguments that a well-established form of evidence is unreliable, the U.S. Supreme Court made it clear that judges should not dismiss these arguments.

Mnookin (2001) comments, "Daubert, then, made it imaginable that courts would revisit a long-accepted technique that was clearly generally accepted by the community of practitioners. Even without the so-called DNA wars, challenges to fingerprinting might have emerged after Daubert. But DNA brought to light problems that had been lurking in the shadows around fingerprinting. They made the problems far easier to see and invited defense attorneys to recognize that fingerprinting might not fare so well if subjected to a particular kind of scientific scrutiny."

In the face of a form of evidence that appears unassailable, DNA, critics say some judges still do not use DNA as a beacon to light the way to scientific truth. Commentators have charged that judges still cling to the admissibility of fingerprint evidence because it is the last vestige of a simpler time in the adjudication of cases. Mnookin (2001) comments, "It is easy to see why judges are reluctant to exclude fingerprinting: it is a long-used technique, an extremely valuable form of evidence to prosecutors, and one in which the public has enormous faith. What is harder to understand is why judges are so reluctant to acknowledge that determining whether fingerprint evidence should survive scrutiny under Daubert is, at a minimum, a difficult question. Fingerprinting's claims and assumptions are clearly surprisingly unproven, and yet the trial court judge in Harvard ended up concluding that 'latent print identification is the very archetype of reliable expert testimony under (Daubert and Kumho Tire).'"

Mnookin (2001) voices an opinion about this predilection of judges that is shared by numerous other commentators: that if fingerprinting does not survive *Daubert* scrutiny, neither will a great deal of other evidence presently considered to be admissible in court. Mnookin asserts, "Rejecting fingerprinting would, judges fear, tear down the citadel. It would simply place too many forms of expert evidence in jeopardy. Even to allow that fingerprinting is a close case would put at risk too many other forms of evidence that strike judges as being noticeably less scientific, objective, or empirically grounded than fingerprinting. Judges prefer, instead, to uphold fingerprinting without careful scrutiny, perhaps telling themselves that Daubert was not intended to bring about massive transformations in the range of admissible evidence. Moreover, like almost everyone else, judges who are assessing fingerprinting most likely believe deeply in fingerprinting. Rightly or wrongly, the technique continues to have enormous cultural authority. Dislodging such a prior belief will require, at a minimum, a great deal of evidence, more than the quantity needed to generate doubt about a technique in which people have less faith. As these challenges continue, some judge some place may well decide that fingerprinting evidence, especially when it is only a partial, smudged latent print, simply does not pass muster under Daubert, at least not until fingerprint examiners can offer some valid statistical basis for declaring the probability that two prints match. This is, perhaps, the better view, if the Daubert criteria are taken seriously."

Mnookin (2001) suggests that these judges are akin to the proverbial ostriches burying their heads in the sand, instead of executing their duties under *Daubert*; however, she notes that reluctance to scrutinize the fingerprinting discipline reflects "a deeper and quite problematic issue that pervades assessments of expert evidence more generally." Mnookin suggests further that judges try to uphold tradition, and that a certain pervasive, long-standing "culture" related to the admissibility of fingerprint evidence "cannot be extricated from determinations of expertise and reliability. If a form of evidence conforms to cultural expectations and generally-shared conceptions, judges may not scrutinize it carefully."

Numerous observers have raised the issue of whether or not fingerprinting is a science. Imwinkelried (2002) points to the landmark 2002 case of *United States v Llera Plaza,* in which Senior Judge Louis H. Pollak ruled that fingerprint examination is not "science" under Federal Rule of Evidence 702, and that fingerprint examiners may not testify to the ultimate question of whether a particular fingerprint impression found at a crime scene was made by a certain person. Imwinkelried states that although Pollak later reversed himself, "the initial decision sent shock waves through the expert community," since, he adds, "at least prior to the advent of DNA, fingerprinting had been regarded as the gold standard of forensic science." In his initial decision, Pollak noted that fingerprint examiners do not directly examine fingerprints. Rather, they compare impressions left by the prints, and many of the impressions are incomplete as well as distorted. Moreover, he pointed out that even among examiners, there is no consensus on the number of points of similarity required to declare a match.

Imwinkelried (2002) notes that Pollak rejected the substantial body of literature on fingerprinting techniques, concluding that this literature did not constitute the type of scientific testing required by *Daubert,* and that neither the fingerprint community nor any other scientific discipline had subjected the underlying premises of fingerprint analysis to rigorous, systematic scientific investigation. Pollak ordered that both parties in the case should be able to present fingerprint testimony describing how any latent and rolled prints at issue in this case were obtained; identifying, and placing before the jury, such fingerprints and any necessary magnifications; and pointing out any observed similarities and differences between a particular latent print and a particular rolled print alleged by the government to be attributable to the same persons. Pollak prohibited the prosecution and the defense to present expert testimony expressing an opinion that a particular latent print matches, or does not match, the rolled print of a particular person and therefore is, or is not, the fingerprint of the individual in question.

The U.S. government asked Pollak to reconsider his ruling and conduct a hearing on testimony relating to internal proficiency tests of FBI fingerprint examiners; following this hearing, Pollak reversed his previous position. Imwinkelried (2002) suggests that the proficiency tests were not what changed Pollak's mind, but that he was persuaded by the defense testimony in which a fingerprint expert from Great Britain declared that the prints in the test were so clear that they were unrepresentative and if he gave those prints to his trainees as a test, they would laugh. Imwinkelried says that Pollak found the fingerprinting technique used by New Scotland Yard to be virtually indistinguishable from the FBI's method, and also might have been swayed by "several civil opinions admitting expert testimony despite the presence of a large element of subjectivity in the formation of the final opinion." He adds, "That survey convinced the judge that the subjectivity of the examiner's final opinion is not fatal to the admissibility of the opinion. The judge ruled that the opinion was admissible only as nonscientific expert testimony, but it was nonetheless admissible."

At issue in the two *Plaza* cases is that in the original case, there had been insufficient rigorous testing of the underlying assumptions of fingerprint analysis, and whether this lack of testing mandated the exclusion of the testimony as nonscientific expertise. Imwinkelried (2002) muses, "Given the lack of testing, should the judge altogether exclude the testimony, the outcome in Plaza I? Or should the judge admit the evidence as nonscientific expertise but perhaps give the jury a cautionary instruction that the testimony was not full-fledged science, the result in Plaza II." The answer lies partly in the language of *Daubert*, Imwinkelried says, which supported Karl Popper's statement that, "the criterion of the scientific status of a theory is its falsifiability, or refutability, or testability." Imwinkelried adds that when the testing is customary in that field, a failure to test is "arguably fatal" under the *Kumho* decision, and "that an expert who neglected to test would not be bringing to bear in the courtroom the same level of intellectual rigor that characterizes his or her practice." Imwinkelried (2002) acknowledges the possibility that as long as a solid inference of reliability exists, a lack of testing should cut to weight, not to admissibility. Imwinkelreid comments, "After all, in Daubert, Justice Blackmun mentioned the possibility that on occasion 'shaky . . . evidence' would be admissible under Federal Rule of Evidence 702. In his two Plaza decisions, Pollak struggled with this policy choice; and other courts are likely to grapple with the same question in the near future."

"It's a complex problem that has existed for more than 100 years, so there is not going to be a simple silver bullet that will solve all the issues related to fingerprinting," says Faigman. "I think the courts and judges need to have the backbone and the courage to stand up and exclude some of this material because it doesn't meet Daubert criteria for admissibility into evidence. There isn't a college sophomore in the country applying Daubert at any level who wouldn't see that handwriting and bite mark analysis and probably latent fingerprint analysis largely fail the Daubert test. When judges say incredibly dumb things like the testing requirement of Daubert is met by 100 peers in the adversarial system, it doesn't help matters very much. That is so profoundly dumb, that it's laughable, and it demonstrates those judges' ignorance about the scientific method and how testing is done. I think if Judge Pollack, in the Plaza case, had stuck to his guns in the first decision, or if any federal judge excluded fingerprints, or at least limited what they can testify to, I think you would have seen major research studies done. It would be instant if the federal courts started excluding testimony on fingerprinting. The reason why they don't feel this pressure, although the pressure is growing, is right now there is no upside to doing the research on fingerprints. Their objective is to get into court and testify, and as long as the courts are allowing them to do that, then why do research, because research then can only do one thing—it can demonstrate the weakness of what you are testifying to. So the courts really are not only the gatekeeper, they are the consumer; if you buy Ford Pintos, even though they are exploding on you, then why would Ford ever build anything more expensive or safer? In a sense, forensic science is the Ford

Pinto, and we're starting to see these explosions in certain cases, and it's going to take some consumer, a judge, at some point, to stand up and point out these issues."

While that has yet to happen in any real way, the forensic science community has endeavored to address the fingerprinting debate from more of a literature review–driven perspective. Budowle et al. (2006) report that the FBI Laboratory tasked a three-member review committee to evaluate the fundamental basis for the science of friction ridge skin impression pattern analysis and to recommend research to be considered to test, where necessary, the hypotheses that form the bases of this discipline: "The committee reviewed the scientific basis for comparing a latent print found at a crime scene with a reference print obtained by a more controlled process [inking method, live scan, etc.] and the ability to render an interpretation of whether or not the two originate from the same source. There is indisputable evidence supporting that such practices can be carried out reliably and that the general process should not be rejected."

Addressing the issue of subjectivity, Budowle et al. (2006) comment, "All forensic analyses have a subjective component, in which the analyst decides whether or not to interpret the evidence and the thresholds to institute during the evaluation. The latent print Analysis, Comparison, Evaluation-Verification [ACE-V] process has a greater component of subjectivity than, for example, chemical analyses or DNA typing. Yet this does not in itself call into question the reliability of the latent print analysis methodology. However, at some level, the examiner might be considered a 'black box.' The examiner makes an interpretation, and one may not know, understand, or appreciate the machinations that the examiner made to arrive at a conclusion. One also may not be able to codify the data used to make that interpretation. But reliable results have been obtained, and thus there can be confidence in the process. Alternatively, some suggest that more objective criteria would be useful to set minimum criteria across the field, provide greater confidence in the process, and provide better evaluation criteria to review cases critically. Both of these positions [i.e., the black box and objective criteria] have merit and should be considered to address the scientific underpinnings of friction ridge skin impression pattern analyses."

One point of contention about fingerprinting has been changeability. The use of friction ridge skin comparisons as a means of identification is based on the assumptions that the pattern of friction ridge skin is both unique and permanent. Budowle et al. (2006) assert, "The assumption of uniqueness is grounded in the belief that the stresses, strains, and tensions that occur during ridge formation are infinite, random, and independent and that these forces yield tremendous variation in the population of fingerprint ridge formations produced. However, it is well accepted that wide variations in the amount of detail transferred during any given contact from the three-dimensional world of a finger to the two-dimensional realm of a fingerprint may not permit individualization. Thus, although the ridge pattern arrangement on friction ridge skin is unique, one may not be able to render an identification or an exclusion of a source from the limited amount of detail in certain latent prints. The second assumption, that friction ridge skin detail is permanent, is supported by basic biology [i.e., the structure of friction ridge skin] and by empirical observation. The patterns on friction ridge skin do not change over time, except that they become larger during growth to adulthood or may change as a result of a serious injury (which may produce scarring, for example) or some disfiguring disease. These two assumptions, uniqueness and permanence, are based to a lesser or greater degree on empirical research, probabilistic models, anecdotal evidence, and extrapolation."

As we have seen, pattern evidence examiners and commentators are locked in a battle over the certainty of the uniqueness of fingerprints. While some critics insist on the development of empirical data to settle the issue once and for all, Budowle et al. (2006) remark, "Empirical studies can never prove absolutely the hypothesis of uniqueness. Doing so would require comparing the friction ridge arrangements on all fingers, palms, and soles of every person who has ever lived or, at a minimum, everyone who is currently alive. This is an impossible task and, in the committee's opinion, an unnecessary one." Instead, the researchers argue that fingerprinting should be accepted based on certain immutable concepts, much like the scientific theories and laws that are not proven absolutely but are well accepted. Budowle et al. explain, "Not all prints can be collected, and the technical power to carry out empirical comparisons on such a scale is beyond current capabilities. Instead, the assumption of uniqueness has been based on anecdotal evidence comparing prints for more than 100 years and never observing two fingerprints with the same friction ridge skin arrangement; controlled studies of genetically identical twins and never observing exactly the same pattern; and the belief that the stresses, strains, and tensions across an area of friction ridge skin are random, infinite, and independent."

Impatient with the assertions by critics that fingerprinting fails all *Daubert* criteria, Budowle et al. (2006) state, "Although one can always find a few detractors, overwhelming evidence supports that an individual fingerprint pattern is unique. Because some Daubert challenges have focused on the assumption of uniqueness of an entire print, several research studies within the last few years have attempted to test this hypothesis both empirically and through statistical modeling. Such effort is not a good use of resources because further testing of the hypothesis of uniqueness of a whole print does not provide any gain in the fundamentals of the science of friction ridge examinations. It shifts resources away from addressing more pertinent questions."

Budowle et al. (2006) conclude that latent print examinations can be carried out and that reliable identifications can be made; however, they add, "There are scientific areas where improvements in the practice can be made, particularly regarding validation, more objective criteria for certain aspects of the ACE-V process, and data collection. The main benefit would be to better ensure the consistency of interpretation practices across the field." Budowle et al. outline a list of research priorities for the fingerprint examination community; the high-priority projects are as follows:

1. *Quality:*
   - Develop guidelines for describing quality metric features.
   - Test whether 12-point system is correlated with total number of points and clarity.
2. *Quantity:*
   - Test hypothesis of independence of features.
   - Test hypothesis that there is no scientific basis for minimum-point threshold.
   - Establish a quantitative model for identification.
   - Survey latent print units (and community) to determine if unwritten minimum threshold of seven detectable points is applied routinely.
   - If seven-point minimum threshold (or whatever is used by majority) is generally accepted, test with statistical models and by black-box approach.
3. *Performance:*
   - Establish minimum number of features that can be evaluated pragmatically in friction skin ridge casework comparisons.
   - Test performance of examiner as a black box rigorously in a controlled manner.
   - If a minimum threshold for an identification can be developed, test a selected panel of latent print examiners.

4. *Exclusions:*
- Review value and reliability of exculpatory power of evidence.

Other priority projects are the following:

1. *Permanence Test:*
- Test hypothesis of permanence of Level III features.
- Test hypothesis of permanence of features on the lower joints, soles, and palms.
2. *Data Collection:*
- Test existing algorithms and collect existing data for review.
- Develop well-defined protocol(s) describing the process for recording, collating, evaluating, and editing research materials.
- Develop a sourcebook and collate existing data within the latent print units (and with members of the Scientific Working Group on Friction Ridge Analysis, Study and Technology).
3. *Cluster Impressions:*
- Develop more explicit definitions on cluster prints, and guidelines on when it is appropriate to assume that cluster prints are deposited simultaneously.
- Test hypothesis of independence of features across fingerprints and lower joints on the same hand (simultaneous impression interpretations).
4. *Additional Validation Studies:*
- For quality testing, develop method to artificially generate patterns and test degree of variation at which incorrect matches are made.
- Assess accuracy of representation of the friction ridge detail on the finger when using the image capture systems that record reference prints.

THE NEEDS OF THE IDENTIFICATION SCIENCES COMMUNITY

No discussion of the attacks on the identification sciences is complete without looking at the bigger picture of the world in which these pattern identification examiners work. They inhabit the same world as most other forensic practitioners, and work in environments that lack important infrastructure, as we have seen in Chapters 5 and 8. In 2004, the International Association for Identification (IAI) was named by the Senate Appropriations Committee as one of four forensic science organizations asked to evaluate and return recommendations regarding the state of forensic disciplines beyond DNA. The IAI was requested to address manpower and equipment needs, continuing education policies, professionalism and accreditation standards, and the level of collaboration needed between federal forensic laboratories and state/local forensic science facilities for the administration of justice. The IAI took upon itself to review and make recommendations for patterned evidence disciplines such as fingerprints, footwear/tire tracks examination, crime scene investigation, bloodstain pattern analysis, and digital evidence. The IAI sent a survey to approximately 180 individuals throughout the country, including the organization's officers, board members, committee chairs, certification board chairs, and IAI division secretaries; approximately 85 surveys were returned.

"In this joint effort, each member organization of the Consortium of Forensic Science Organizations (CFSO) took a piece of the pie that they were well suited to represent, made conclusions, and created a report for the committee," Polski says, adding that the primary need shown by the survey was the need for increased education and training of practitioners. "What was also discovered from that survey in part is that approximately two-thirds of the work in fingerprint identification in this country is done outside of traditional crime labs; it's performed in law enforcement agencies, such as police and sheriff's departments. The people who do this kind of work in those units don't see themselves necessarily as scientists. They see themselves as fingerprint examiners, and for the most part they are very good at what they do, but they are not living in the rarified academic or research atmosphere where they can challenge someone who has three PhDs and publishes articles in *Science* magazine. Those forensic practitioners are easy targets to attack because it's not a level playing field. Scandals and shenanigans have been exposed in every area of forensic science, including fingerprints and DNA, suggesting a need for continued education, training, and professional development within the entire forensics profession."

Through its survey, the IAI (2004) discovered that approximately 66 percent of fingerprint identification analysis is not performed in a forensic laboratory, and that many fingerprint examiners are sworn law enforcement officers. The survey found that the average staff size is 9.1, with the largest at 51 and the smallest at one examiner, and that any of the personnel in these units testify to latent fingerprint identifications. Common needs included additional personnel, computer equipment, and training. The survey also revealed a large backlog of latent fingerprint cases; in the largest 12 organizations, backlogs ranged from several hundred to 1,000 cases. The average backlog time in these large agencies is 166 days, with total backlogs in these agencies of 5,147. The IAI found that while these agencies do their best to prioritize serious crimes against person before property crimes, it is often not an effective strategy with which to combat backlogs. Many of the agencies that record no backlog process few cases; six of these large organizations are service centers for a number of law enforcement agencies, so their backlog reflects back on their customer agencies.

The IAI (2004) states, "It is very clear this latent print backlog allows offenders to remain at large while the unworked cases sit in evidence storage. Fingerprint identification is one of the few forensic sciences that can positively identify individuals, convicting criminals and exonerating the innocent. It is one of the most valuable and yet underutilized forensic disciplines and ranks at least equal in forensic importance with DNA. It should be noted that fingerprints are one of the most frequently found types of evidence at a wide variety of crime scenes ranging from homicide, assault, rape, and other crimes against persons as well as property crimes such as theft, robbery, drugs, auto theft and just about any other type of crime."

The survey uncovered a lack of IAI-certified fingerprint examiners to fill many vacant positions across the country. The organization states that although the need is increasing, the number of certified examiners remains flat, and to address this issue, the IAI is exploring the idea of recognizing latent fingerprint competency at an entry level, and then building on experience to reach the traditional certified examiner level.

The survey also identified the increasing need for better computer equipment with which to access the federal fingerprint databank AFIS, as well as improved networking and connectivity to state and regional systems. The survey found that about half of the fingerprint units have AFIS capability, although many of those that do not are very small agencies. Nonetheless, many agencies with a relatively large number of fingerprint cases do not have an AFIS capability. The IAI (2004) states, "It is clear that AFIS, the FBI's large capacity fingerprint computer is underutilized for latent fingerprint identifications, particularly at the local level. Only 17 of 85 agencies routinely search unknown latent fingerprints through IAFIS and most state agencies do not do that as a matter of routine. It is clear there is a great need for the FBI to provide more information and expand its program to install Universal Latent Workstations (ULW) in local agencies. The capacity of AFIS with respect to latent fingerprint searches is very, very underutilized. Survey returns indicate strong interest on the part of local agencies in obtaining this capability but a lack of support for such equipment and training at the state and federal levels."

Notably, the IAI (2004) indicates that basic research to establish the scientific underpinnings of fingerprint identification is needed: "While no one believes fingerprint identification does not work, there have been numerous troubling articles written by legal scholars as well as scientists who call into question the validity of fingerprint identification, particularly as it applies to partial latent fingerprints. The time has come for a carefully directed research program to put these issues to rest." Some years ago the IAI issued a position statement that indicated, "There is no scientific basis for requiring that a minimum number of corresponding friction ridge details be present in two impressions in order to effect individualization." According to the IAI, a suggested research project would entail an empirical examination of the data that supports or refutes that position statement; the group would take into account the existing body of literature along with input from IAI-affiliated latent print practitioners. According to the IAI (2004), this research project should not be limited to level-two detail but should be inclusive of all available friction ridge area detail information.

Another advisable research project, according to the IAI (2004), would be an analysis of current and historical empirical research projects addressing the biological uniqueness of friction ridge areas of the fingers, palms, and soles of the feet to analyze it in such a manner as to determine if there already exists sufficient corroboration to support the hypothesis of individuality using level-two friction ridge area information. The report states, "If indeed this research project were able to determine that sufficient corroboration already exists, then the IAI would request that the results of this research be made available to practitioners of the science in a manner deemed consistent with the position and reporting methods of the scientific community. If this research finds the general empirical data lacking, then develop recommendations for additional research to include the areas of concentration and methodology."

In its analysis of crime scene investigation needs, the IAI (2004) discovered that most of this kind of work is performed by sworn law enforcement officers rather than specialized crime scene investigation units or evidence technicians. The report states, "The overwhelming need in the area of crime scene processing is almost evenly divided between more personnel and better equipment and training with many agencies giving equal weight to both needs. Television shows such as 'CSI' provide a very high visibility to the technology involved in crime scene processing and evidence evaluation. Not surprisingly there is a high expectation from the judiciary as well as detectives or other investigators, that this type of equipment and analysis ought to be available everywhere. We all know that's not possible but equipment such as digital cameras are still beyond the reach of many agencies." In addition, alternate light sources, a very elementary tool, are another common item requested but not affordable by many agencies. Another notable area of need is university-based research grants, which the report calls "virtually non-existent." The report adds, "Yet court challenges to any evidence often cite the absence of research or independent (i.e., non-forensic) studies.

One common thread throughout the responses from identification sciences practitioners was the overwhelming need for accessible, affordable continuing education opportunities. The IAI (2004) states, "Technology has advanced all aspects of forensic science to a level unheard of only a few years ago but training has not kept pace with those advances." According to the report, most often cited was the lack of funding for training; exacerbating the problem is that most respondents to the questionnaire were not part of forensic laboratories, but rather a unit within a law enforcement agency. In that organizational model, the report explains, training dollars most often go to the law enforcement side, with support units left lacking. Importantly, the IAI noted that agencies lamented the FBI's decision to withdraw from the provision of training to the forensic science community. Several respondents to the IAI survey indicated that this training was one of the few places where education could be obtained at little cost to the agency. The FBI had once offered a program of training that was largely underwritten by the bureau, with virtually no out-of-pocket expenses to forensic science examiners.

The IAI (2004) acknowledged the great unrest surrounding competency and quality systems in the forensic science community, and the relatively low number of forensic laboratories accredited by ASCLD/LAB. The report states, "Many recent horror stories involving misidentifications or shoddy laboratory work stem from non-accredited laboratories. In a crime laboratory environment, quality systems such as proficiency testing, accreditation, etc. are a way of life. However, we are quite certain outside that laboratory environment there is less appreciation for quality systems and how best to apply those systems to the types of units that operate in a non-laboratory setting. Fertile ground exists for organizations like the IAI and the accrediting organizations to make these units aware of such quality systems. Individual competency accepted and understood within the individual forensic discipline is an area that must also be addressed. As one of the survey respondents noted, officers are required to have a certification to operate equipment to detect alcohol impaired drivers and to operate radar equipment. It seems incongruous that those who practice in the forensic disciplines are not required to have any certification or other evidence of competency." The study notes that, with the exception of DNA, there is no universal requirement to ensure examiner competency. The report states, "We recognize that some federal laboratories sponsor their own in-house certification programs available and applicable only to their personnel but that does not solve the larger problem. A movement toward mandatory certification over a period of time will go a long way to ensuring quality results from forensic examinations. An added benefit of certification is the mandatory training required to obtain and maintain certification. Typically forensic science certification programs require a minimum of 48 hours of continuing competency activities over a five-year period. We have seen a successful example of this in the area of DNA and believe this model will be beneficial to other forensic science disciplines as well."

REFERENCES

America's Pressing Challenge: Building a Stronger Foundation. 2006. Available at: http://www.nsf.gov/statistics/nsb0602/

Budowle B, Buscaglia J, and Perlman RS. Review of the scientific basis for friction ridge comparisons as a means of identification: Committee findings and recommendations. *Forensic Science Communications,* 8(1), January 2006.

Cole SA. More than zero: Accounting for error in latent fingerprint identification. *Journal of Criminal Law and Criminology,* 95(3), May 2005.

Committee on Technological Literacy, National Academy of Engineering and National Research Council. *Why All Americans Need to Know More About Technology.* Pearson G and Young AT, Eds. Washington, D.C.: National Academy Press, 2002.

Crichton M. Ritual abuse, hot air, and missed opportunities: Science views media. Presentation at the American Association for the Advancement of Science. Anaheim, Calif., January 25, 1999.

Department of Justice. An executive summary of the review of the FBI's handling of the Brandon Mayfield case. Washington, D.C.: Office of the Inspector General, January 2006.

Epstein R. Fingerprints meet Daubert: The myth of fingerprint science is revealed. 75 *Southern California Law Review,* 605, 2002.

Faigman D, Kaye D, Saks MJ. *Modern Scientific Evidence,* Vol. 1. West Publishing, 1997.

Federal Bureau of Investigation. Press release: Statement on Brandon Mayfield case. May 24, 2004.

Frieden T and Schuster H. "Sloppy FBI work led to wrong man." Report, CNN. Air date: January 6, 2006. Accessed at http://www.cnn.com/2006/LAW/01/06/mayfield.report/index.html.

Goodstein D. Scientific fraud. 60 *American Scholar,* 505, 1991.

Goodstein D. *How Science Works,* 2nd ed. Reference Manual on Scientific Evidence. Federal Judiciary Center, 2000.

Goodstein D. Scientific misconduct. *Academe,* online issue. Accessed at www.aaup.org/publications/Academe/2002/02JF/02jfgoo.htm.

Haber L and Haber RN. Error rates for human fingerprint examiners. In: *Advances in Automatic Fingerprint Recognition Systems,* Ratha and Bolle, Eds. New York: Springer-Verlag, 2003.

Hazen RJ and Phillips CE. The expert fingerprint witness. In: Lee HC and Gaensslen RE (Eds.), Advances in Fingerprint Technology (2nd ed.), pp. 389–418. Boca Raton: CRC Press, 2001.

Huber, P. *Galileo's Revenge.* New York: Harper Collins, 1991a.

Huber P. Junk science in the courtroom. *Forbes,* p. 68, July 8, 1991b.

Imwinkelried EJ. Fingerprint science. *National Law Journal,* 26(18–19), December 23–30, 2002.

Inman K and Rudin N. *Principles and Practice of Criminalistics: The Profession of Forensic Science.* Boca Raton, Fla.: CRC Press, 2001.

Institute of Medicine and National Research Council Committee on Assessing Integrity in Research Environments. *Integrity in Scientific Research: Creating an Environment that Promotes Responsible Conduct.* Washington, D.C.: National Academies, 2002.

International Association for Identification (IAI). *180-Day Study Final Report to the National Institute of Justice,* 2004.

Jonakait RN. The meaning of Daubert and what that mans for forensic science. 15 *Cardozo Law Review,* 2103, 1994.

Kennedy D. Forensic science: Oxymoron? *Science,* 302(5651):1625, 2003. Accessed at: http://www.sciencemag.org/cgi/content/short/302/5651/1625.

Kuhn T. *The Structure of Scientific Revolutions.* Chicago: University of Chicago Press, 1962.

Martin B. Scientific fraud and the power structure of science. *Prometheus,* 10(1):83–98, June 1992.

Martinson BC, Anderson MS, De Vries R, and Wadman M. One in three scientists confesses to having sinned. *Nature,* 435:718–719, June 9, 2005.

McCook A. Scientific fraud: Is prosecution the answer? *The Scientist,* February 10, 2006.

Miller JD. Public understanding of, and attitudes toward, scientific research: What we know and what we need to know. *Science,* 13:273–294, 2004.

Mnookin JL. Fingerprint evidence in an age of DNA profiling. *Brooklyn Law Review,* 67, December 2001.

National Academies Press. Can Scientists and Lawyers Get Along? The Age of Expert Testimony: Science in the Courtroom, Report of a Workshop, 2002.

National Science Foundation. Science and Engineering Indicators 2006. Available at: http://www.nsf.gov/statistics/seind06/

Neufeld P and Scheck B. Will fingerprinting stand up in court? *The New York Times,* March 9, 2002.

Oransky I. All Hwang human cloning work fraudulent. *The Scientist,* January 10, 2006, online issue. Accessed at http://www.the-scientist.com/news/display/22933/.

OSTP Federal Policy on Research Misconduct. Accessed at http://www.ostp.gov/html/001207_3.html/. 2005.

Palenik CS and Palenik SJ. Forensic science and academic science. *Science,* 302, December 2003.

Park RL. The seven warning signs of bogus science. *Chronicle of Higher Education*, 31, January 2003.

Payne D. Researcher's faked data leads to lifetime ban on U.S. grants. *The Scientist*, April 11, 2005, online issue. Accessed at http://www.the-scientist.com/article/display/15409/.

Peterson JL and Markham PN. Crime laboratory proficiency testing results, 1978–1991, II: Resolving questions of common origin. *Journal of Forensic Science*, 40:1009, 1995.

Pincock S. Lancet study faked. *The Scientist*, January 16, 2006, online issue. Accessed at http://www.the-scientist.com/news/display/22952/.

Risinger DM. Brave new post-Daubert world. *Seton Hall Law Review*, 29(405), 1998.

Risinger DM and Saks MJ. A house with no foundation. *Issues in Science and Technology*, Fall 2003.

Risinger DM, Saks MJ, Rosenthal R, and Thompson W. The Daubert/Kumho implications of observer effects in forensic science: Hidden problems of expectation and suggestion. 90 *California Law Review*, 1, 2002.

Saks M. Lessons from the law's formative encounters with forensic identification science. 49 *Hastings Law*, 1, 1069, 1998.

Saks M. (Comment on) Johnson v. Commonwealth: How dependable is identification by microscopic hair comparison? 26 *The Advocate*, 14, January 2004.

Saks MJ and Koehler D. What DNA fingerprinting can teach the law about the rest of forensic science. *Cardozo Law Review*, 13:361. 1991.

Saks MJ and Van Duizend R. *The Uses of Scientific Evidence in Litigation*. Williamsburg, Va.: National Center for State Courts, 1983.

Science and the Public. State University of New York at Buffalo. Accessed at http://www.scienceandthe-public.org/description.htm.

Starrs JE. More Saltimbancos on the loose? Fingerprint experts caught in a world of error. *Scientific Sleuthing Newsletter*, Spring 1988.

Stoney DA. Fingerprint identification. In: *Modern Scientific Evidence: The Law and Science of Expert Testimony*, Faigman DL et al., Eds. St. Paul: West Publishing, 1997.

Thompson WC and Cole SA. Forensics: Lessons from the Brandon Mayfield case. *The Advocate*, April 2005.

Thornton J and Peterson J. The general assumptions and rationale of forensic identification. In: *Modern Scientific Evidence*, Faigman D et al., Eds. West Group Publishing, 2002.

United States v Llera Plaza, 188 F. Supp. 2d 549, 566 (E.D. Pa. 2002).

Wadman M. One in three scientists confesses to having sinned. *Nature*, 435:718–719, June 9, 2005.

Weed DL. Preventing scientific misconduct. *American Journal of Public Health*, 88:125–129, 1998.

Wertheim PA. Scientific comparison and identification of fingerprint evidence. *The Print*, Vol. 16(5) September/October 2000.

Wilson EB. *An Introduction to Scientific Research*, McGraw-Hill, 1952.

Wolf S. *Introduction to the Scientific Method*. Physics Lab Manual. Rochester, N.Y.: University of Rochester, 2002. Accessed at http://teacher.pas.rochester.edu/phy_labs/AppendixE/AppendixE.html.

Woodward J and Goodstein D. Conduct, misconduct and the structure of science. 84 *American Scientist*, 479, 1996.

Woolf PK. *Projection on Science Fraud and Misconduct, Report on Workshop Number One*. American Association for the Advancement of Science, 1988, p. 37.

RECOMMENDED READING

Ashbaugh D. Ridgeology: Modern evaluation friction ridge identification. *Journal of Forensic Identification*, 41:16–64, 1991.

Ashbaugh D. Incipient ridges and the clarity spectrum. *Journal of Forensic Identification*, 42:106–114, 1992.

Ashbaugh D. Premises of friction ridge identification, clarity, and the identification process. *Journal of Forensic Identification*, 44:499–513, 1994.

Ashbaugh D. *Quantitative-Qualitative Friction Ridge Analysis*. Boca Raton, Fla.: CRC Press, 1999.

Barrow J. *Theories of Everything*. London: Oxford University Press, 1991.

Bridges BC. No duplicate fingerprints. *Finger Print Magazine*, pp. 5–6, March 1946.

Broad W and Wade N. *Betrayers of the Truth: Fraud and Deceit in the Halls of Science*. New York: Simon and Schuster, 1982.

Byrd JS. Confirmation bias, ethics, and mistakes in forensics. *Journal of Forensic Identification*, 56(4):511–525, 2006.

Cole S. *Suspect Identities: A History of Fingerprinting and Criminal Identification*. Harvard University Press, 2001.

Cole SA. Witnessing identification: Latent fingerprint evidence and expert knowledge. *Social Studies of Science*, 1998.

Cole SA. Grandfathering evidence: Fingerprint admissibility rulings from Jennings to Llera Plaza and back again. 41 *American Criminal Law Review*, 1189:1196–97, 2004.

Dror IE and Charlton D. Why experts make errors. *Journal of Forensic Identification*, 56(4):600–616, 2006.

Evett IW and Williams RL. A review of the 16 points fingerprint standard in England and Wales. *Journal of Forensic Identification*, 46:49–73, 1996.

Fienberg SE, Martin ME, and Straf ML, Eds. Report of the Committee on National Statistics. In: *Sharing Research Data*. Washington, D.C.: National Academy of Sciences, 1985.

Houck MM. Statistics and trace evidence: The tyranny of numbers. *Forensic Science Communications*, 1(3), October 1999.

Langenburg GM. Pilot study: A statistical analysis of the ACE-V methodology, analysis stage. *Journal of Forensic Identification*, 54:64–79, 2004.

Locard E. The analysis of dust traces, part I. *American Journal of Police Science*, 1:276–298, 1930.

Locard E. The analysis of dust traces, part II. *American Journal of Police Science*, 1:401–418, 1930.

Locard E. The analysis of dust traces, part III. *American Journal of Police Science*, 1:496–514, 1930.

Miller JD. Scientific literacy in the United States. In: *Communicating Science to the Public*, Evered D and O'Connor M, Eds. London: Wiley, 1987, pp. 19–40.

Miller JD. The scientifically illiterate. *American Demographics*, 9(6):26–31, 1987.

Miller JD. The acquisition and retention of scientific information by American adults. In: *Free-Choice Science Education: How We Learn Science Outside of School*, Falk JH, Ed. New York: Teachers College Press, 2001, pp. 93–114.

Osterburg J. An inquiry into the nature of proof: The identity of fingerprints. *Journal of Forensic Sciences*, 9:413–426, 1964.

Osterburg J, Parthasarathy T, Raghavan T, and Sclove S. Development of a mathematical formula for the calculation of fingerprint probabilities based on individual characteristics. *Journal of the American Statistical Association*, 72(360):772–778, 1977.

Pretty IA and Sweet D. The scientific basis for human bite mark analyses: A critical review, *Science and Justice*, 41:85–86, 2001.

Saks MJ. Merlin and Solomon: Lessons from the law's formative encounters with forensic identification science. *Hastings Law Journal*, 49:1069–1141, 1998.

Shamos M. *The Myth of Scientific Literacy*. New Brunswick, NJ: Rutgers University Press, 1995.

Stacey RB. A report on the erroneous fingerprint individualization in the Madrid train bombing case. *Journal of Forensic Identification*, 702, 2004.

Stacey RB. Forensic report on the erroneous fingerprint individualization in the Madrid train bombing case. *Science Communications,* 7(1), January 2005.

Stoney D. Distribution of epidermal ridge minutiae. *American Journal of Physical Anthropology,* 77:367–376, 1988.

Stoney DA. Measurement of fingerprint individuality. In: *Advances in Fingerprint Technology,* 2nd ed. Boca Raton, Fla.: CRC Press, 2001, pp. 327–387.

Stoney D and Thornton JA. Critical analysis of quantitative fingerprint individuality models. *Journal of Forensic Sciences,* 31:1187–1216, 1986.

Stoney D and Thornton J. A systematic study of epidermal ridge minutiae, *Journal of Forensic Sciences,* 32:1182–1203, 1987.

Wynne B and Jasanoff S, Eds. *Public Understanding of Science: Handbook of Science and Technology Studies,* revised ed. Thousand Oaks, Calif.: Sage Publications, 2002.

ENDNOTE

1. *Principles and Practice of Criminalistics: The Profession of Forensic Science* by Inman and Rudin. Copyright 2007 by Taylor & Francis Group LLC—Books. Reproduced with permission of Taylor & Francis Group LLC—Books in the format Other Book via Copyright Clearance Center.

CHAPTER 11

DNA: CONVICTING THE GUILTY, EXONERATING THE INNOCENT

Deoxyribonucleic acid (DNA) testing has exonerated the innocent and convicted the guilty, and it also provides a mechanism for the solving of numerous cold cases through the use of DNA databanks. However, DNA is a frequent flash point in the legal and forensic science communities because of the power that it wields, with each group seemingly desiring to be sole master and commander of this technological wonder.

In its position statement on DNA technology, adopted in 2003, the National District Attorneys Association (NDAA) states," America's prosecutors consistently have embraced DNA technology as a scientific breakthrough in the search for truth. Starting in the mid-1980s, with the introduction of DNA evidence in America's courtrooms, local prosecutors have fought for its admission in criminal trials. Prosecutors also have advocated vigorously for the expanded use of DNA technology as a highly effective method of solving crimes and identifying the criminals before they can commit further offenses." The NDAA position statement adds, "Forensic DNA typing has had a broad, positive impact on the criminal justice system. In recent years, convictions have been obtained that previously would have been impossible. Countless suspects have been eliminated prior to the filing of charges. Old, unsolved criminal cases, as well as new cases, have been solved. Mistakenly accused defendants have been freed both before trial and after incarceration. And increasingly, the unidentified remains of crime victims are being identified."

In a statement on its Web site the Innocence Project asserts, however, "The American criminal justice system fails sometimes. One price of these failures is the loss of life and livelihood for those unfortunate enough to be wrongfully convicted. The cases of those exonerated by DNA testing have revealed disturbing fissures and trends in our criminal justice system. Some claim that the eventual exoneration of innocents proves that the system works. If that were true, then justice is not being administered by our police, prosecutors, defense lawyers, or our courts. It is being dispensed by law students, journalism students, and a few concerned lawyers, organizations, and citizens. The pace of post-conviction DNA exonerations continues to grow. Not only has DNA testing proven that these individuals are innocent, it has also shown that our criminal justice system makes mistakes that leave true perpetrators on the streets while the innocent are incarcerated or face execution."

The Innocence Project adds, "DNA testing is a powerful tool for catching and correcting these mistakes, but it is not a panacea for the ails of the criminal justice system. Its scope is limited to the few individual cases in which biological evidence is available, can be tested, and is connected to the crime. Even in those cases, the biological evidence is often reported lost or destroyed, or is too degraded to get a conclusive result. For every DNA exoneration, there are countless where testing cannot help because no DNA was left at the scene or the evidence that was once there has been lost or destroyed. DNA exonerations do not solve the problem—they prove its existence and illuminate the need for reform. The lessons learned from these exonerations must be used to prevent all wrongful convictions—including those where DNA testing cannot provide answers."

As of May 2006, 175 individuals have been exonerated, according to the Innocence Project, and as we will see in a section on wrongful convictions later in this chapter, the technology is at the heart of a number of key issues impacting the entire criminal justice continuum.

DNA typing techniques first began to be used in criminal cases in the United States in 1988. The emergence of numerous scientific and legal issues led to the formation in 1989 of the National Research Council (NRC) Committee on DNA Technology in Forensic Science. That committee's report (1992) affirmed the value of DNA typing for forensic analysis and hailed it as a major advance in the field of criminal investigation. To improve the quality of DNA-typing information and its presentation in court, the report recommended various policies and practices, including the following:

- Completion of adequate research into the properties of typing methods to determine the circumstances under which they yield reliable and valid results
- Formulation and adherence to rigorous protocols
- Creation of a national committee on forensic DNA typing to evaluate scientific and technical issues arising in the development and refinement of DNA-typing technology
- Studies of the relative frequencies of distinct DNA alleles in 15 to 20 relatively homogeneous subpopulations
- A ceiling principle using, as a basis of calculation, the highest allele frequency in any subgroup or 5 percent, whichever is higher
- A more conservative "interim ceiling principle," with a 10 percent minimum until the ceiling principle can be implemented
- Proficiency testing to measure error rates and to help interpret test results
- Quality assurance and quality control programs
- Mechanisms for accreditation of laboratories
- Increased funding for research, education, and development
- Judicial notice of the scientific underpinnings of DNA typing
- Financial support for expert witnesses
- Databases and records freely available to all parties
- An end to occasional expert testimony that DNA typing is infallible and that the DNA genotypes detected by examining a small number of loci are unique

Many of the recommendations of the 1992 NRC report have been implemented, and some of the perceived difficulties at the time, such as insufficient information on the differences among various population subgroups, have been addressed for the most part. New techniques and improvements in old ones have increased the power and reliability of DNA data. Nonetheless, controversy over the forensic applications of DNA has continued, and the 1992 report was criticized. The most contentious issues have involved statistics, population genetics, and possible laboratory errors in DNA profiling. In 1994, the NRC established a committee to update the 1992 report, and a follow-up report was published in 1996. The major issues addressed were as follows:

- *The accuracy of laboratory determinations:* How reliable is genetic typing? What are the sources of error? How can errors be detected and corrected? Can their rates be determined? How can the incidence of errors be reduced? Should calculation of the probability that an uninvolved person has the same profile as the evidence DNA include an estimate of the laboratory error rate?
- *The accuracy of calculations based on population-genetics theory and the available databases:* How representative are the databases, which originate from convenience samples rather than random

samples? How is variability among the various groups in the U.S. population best taken into account in estimating the population frequency of a DNA profile?

■ *Statistical assessments of similarities in DNA profiles:* What quantities should be used to assess the forensic significance of a profile match between two samples? How accurate are these assessments? Are the calculations best presented as frequencies, probabilities, or likelihood ratios?

These issues will be explored throughout this chapter. To begin, however, a short primer on DNA is in order. DNA is a molecule that encodes the genetic information in all living organisms, with its chemical structure first described in 1954. More than 50 years later, DNA is being used to adjudicate criminal cases. For the last 15 to 20 years in particular, DNA has been the subject of intense scrutiny by the legal and scientific communities; although barriers to its admissibility in court have been broken in almost all jurisdictions, some issues still linger. Berger (2002) observes, "Only 15 years have passed since DNA evidence was first introduced in a criminal trial in the United States, but in that remarkably short period of time DNA has revolutionized the criminal justice system. This impact goes beyond DNA's effect on investigating crimes, convicting the guilty, and exonerating the innocent. DNA testing has also brought about changes in unrelated fields by forcing laboratories and courts to rethink how they treat forensic evidence."

Berger believes that DNA's impact was heightened by two factors: the nature of the DNA forensic technique and the historical moment at which DNA entered the courtroom. Berger (2002) states, "DNA profiling is an offshoot of science. It is a technique that exists beyond its forensic usefulness, such as ballistics, handwriting analysis, or fingerprinting. Forensic DNA is a fortuitous byproduct of some of the most highly regarded, cutting-edge research in the scientific community."

Berger (2002) suggests that DNA's origins in hard-core science imply that from the very beginning, "scientists whose work was far removed from the courtroom showed an interest in issues regarding the forensic application of DNA. I suspect this attention was due in part to scientists' fear that without adequate supervision, lawyers untrained in forensic techniques would misinterpret evidence. In addition, distinguished scientists from a variety of fields were happy to participate when, at the request of various government agencies, the National Academy of Sciences empaneled committees to make recommendations aimed at improving laboratory work and the presentation of DNA evidence in judicial proceedings."

It is significant that from the outset, DNA testing and analysis was viewed by all stakeholders as a legitimate offspring of scientific efforts, and that this very involvement of scientists lent professional credibility and new levels of validation to forensic science. The essence of DNA's significance to the process of identification lies within the molecular biology research, which revealed two premises: that among humans, 99.99 percent of DNA nucleotide sequences are identical, and that 100 percent of an individual's DNA is the same throughout the body. Kreeger and Weiss (2003) explain that this shared DNA creates characteristics that are similar to all humans, including two hands, 10 toes, blood that can be transfused, and organs that can be transplanted. The .01 percent of DNA that is not shared is different in every individual, with the exception of identical twins who share a complete DNA sequence. In addition, DNA sequencing is the same, whether the cells of an individual's blood, skin, semen, saliva, or hair is examined. Nuclear DNA is found in blood, sperm, vaginal secretions, mucus, sweat, saliva, hair roots, earwax, bone, and teeth. It is found in organs, muscles, and/or skin. Nuclear DNA is found in every cell and tissue of the body, except for red blood cells.

Kreeger and Weiss (2003) explain further, "Scientists have developed a methodology to identify the variations within an individual's sequencing, and these methods form the basis for DNA profiling. By determining which alleles are present at strategically chosen loci, the forensic scientist ascertains the genetic profile, or genotype, of an individual."

Three billion base pairs are grouped in 23 pairs of chromosomes: one set from the mother and one set from the father, for a total of 46 chromosomes. Specific sequences of bases that code for a characteristic are called *genes,* and a gene's position on a chromosome is called its *locus.* The possible sequences or variations of a gene are called *alleles,* and humans have two alleles at each locus. When a DNA sample is analyzed, the results are called *profiles.* In a criminal case, DNA samples can be collected from either a crime scene or an individual; when analyzed they produce either an evidence profile or a suspect (or known reference) profile.

DNA TYPING

The NRC (1992) declared, "The techniques of DNA typing are fully recognized by the scientific community." However, it did acknowledge the continued disagreements over the use of these techniques to produce evidence in court. Not to oversimplify, but the debate is most often triggered, of course, when the DNA profile of an evidence sample from a crime scene and that of a sample from a suspect appear to be a match. The NRC explains that when two profiles are virtually indistinguishable, there are three explanations: The samples came from the same person; the samples came from different persons who happen to have the same DNA profile; and the samples came from different persons but were handled or analyzed erroneously by the investigators or the laboratory.

DNA is durable and long lasting, and scientists are able to find DNA suitable for testing in smaller and more degraded samples than ever before. Historically, large samples were needed to enable scientists to extract DNA from evidence found at a crime scene. The earliest method of forensic DNA analysis, restriction fragment length polymorphism (RFLP), involved comparing lengths of specific DNA fragments. The disadvantages of this method included the need for a relatively non-degraded sample, and the fact that the analysis demanded a significant amount of manpower and time.

Scientists knew they had to find a way to handle biological samples from crime scenes that were less than ideal, knowing the uncontrollable conditions at crime scenes further served to degrade evidence possibly containing DNA. According to Kreeger and Weiss (2003), "Their underlying motivation was to produce more samples to enable more testing so that other scientists could find the same results obtained by the initial scientist. Because of the accuracy and the durability of the copies, scientists less frequently face the dilemma of exhausting all of the evidence during analysis. Once the crime scene evidence is copied, more than one scientist may test it and confirm accuracy."

The first useful marker system, the ABO blood groups, was discovered in 1900; the second, the MN groups, came 25 years later. By the 1960s, there were 17 blood group systems known, but not all were useful for forensics, and in the 1970s a few serum proteins and enzymes were added. By the 1980s, about 100 protein polymorphisms were known but most were not generally useful for forensic science. The year 1985 brought a major breakthrough, when variable number of tandem repeats (VNTRs) showed much greater variability among individuals than previous systems and immediately began to be used for forensic studies. They are still used, but are rapidly being replaced by short tandem repeats (STRs) (National Institute of Justice [NIJ], 2000).

The new method of DNA testing, consisting of an amplification/replication process, was polymerase chain reaction (PCR), which assists scientists in developing DNA profiles from extremely small samples of biological evidence. A second significant development in the science of DNA was proficiency in the testing of the aforementioned STRs, a PCR-based technology. Kreeger and Weiss (2003) explain, "In the most modern method of DNA profiling, scientists exploit interpersonal genetic variation found in STR sequences. While those repeats are constant in an individual person's DNA, the repeats vary by individual. Comparing the number of repeats is STR testing. Taking advantage of PCR technology, STR testing can be performed with smaller and even degraded samples and is the fastest testing technology presently available. Slab gel and capillary electrophoresis are the two separation methods used in the STR process to extract the DNA for visual analysis and comparison."

Kaye and Sensabaugh (2000) state, "Just as the scientific foundations of DNA extraction are clear, the procedures for amplifying DNA sequences within the extracted DNA are well established. The first National Academy of Sciences committee on forensic DNA typing described the amplification step as 'simple . . . analogous to the process by which cells replicate their DNA.'"

By using the 1/100 percent of person-specific DNA, Kreeger and Weiss (2003) state, scientists can make determinations with significant forensic value to the prosecution of a case. "First, they can determine the genetic profile drawn from biological evidence found at a crime scene and match it to the genetic profile from a defendant, which would tie this defendant to this charged crime. Then, a scientist can calculate the statistical probability that a random unrelated person within the human population would coincidentally have the same genetic profile as the one taken from the crime scene evidence. Such a determination helps the prosecutor to meet the burden of proving that this person committed this crime."

According to the National Institute of Justice (2000), "The great variability of DNA polymorphisms has made it possible to offer strong support for concluding that DNA from a suspect and from the crime scene is from the same person. Prior to this period, it was possible to exclude a suspect, but evidence for inclusion was weaker than it is now because the probability of a coincidental match was larger. DNA polymorphisms brought an enormous change. Evidence that two DNA samples are from the same person is still probabilistic rather than certain. But with today's battery of genetic markers, the likelihood that two matching profiles came from the same person approaches certainty. Although the evidence that two samples came from the same person is statistical, the conclusion that they came from different persons is certain (assuming no human or technical errors)."

When performing forensic DNA testing, analysts first compare the profile generated from the crime scene evidence sample to the profile generated from the offender's sample. The analyst examines 13 loci along the chromosome, a method that the scientific community has identified as suitable for comparison purposes. Each locus contains two alleles, one from each parent. When the STRs from a crime scene profile match an offender's profile, it means that there is a match at each and every one of the 26 alleles (genes) that comprise the 13 loci. The specificity of this forensic identification is one of the most significant powers of DNA.

VNTRs are DNA regions in which a short sequence, usually 8 to 35 bases in length, is repeated in tandem 100 or more times. The exact number of repeats differs considerably from one person to another, so this provides an enormous amount of variability. The number of length-types that can be reliably distinguished is typically 20 to 30 per chromosomal locus. With five or six loci, the number of combinations is enormous, and the probability of a random person's profile matching that of a suspect can be 1 in 100 billion or less (NIJ, 2000).

STRs have a number of advantages compared to VNTRs, with the most important being that because of their smaller size, their DNA can be amplified by PCR. Because PCR can amplify DNA just like the natural process that occurs when DNA copies itself in a cell, this method can produce almost any desired amount of DNA. This means that DNA from a trace sample, such as that from a cigarette or the saliva on a postage stamp, can be increased to an amount that can be readily analyzed. The interpretation of STRs is usually less ambiguous than that of VNTRs, and the process is more rapid—days instead of weeks. It also lends itself to automation, and kits are now available in which 16 loci can be analyzed simultaneously (NIJ, 2000).

The Federal Bureau of Investigation (FBI) has chosen 13 STR loci to serve as core loci for the Combined DNA Index System (CODIS), the intention being that all forensic laboratories be equipped to handle these 13. Laboratories may, and usually do, have the capability of dealing with other loci as well. In addition there are other systems. Single nucleotide polymorphisms (SNPs) detect changes in a single base of the DNA. There are millions of these per individual, so the opportunities for further exploitation are almost unlimited.

Kreeger and Weiss (2003) comment, "When scientists compare the crime scene evidence profile and the offender's profile, they look for a 100 percent match of the two profiles at the 13 loci. This comparison is not a statistical determination, but rather a scientific one. DNA analysts, however, do speak in terms of statistical probabilities when describing the rarity or frequency of finding a certain profile among human populations. There are approximately 6 billion people on the earth. Comparing DNA at 13 loci can generate a random-match probability greater than 6 billion. In other words, the analyst may testify that there is no likelihood that anyone else, other than the offender, will have the same genetic profile as the profile generated from both the crime scene evidence and the offender. By calculating the random match probability, scientists can conclude from whom the DNA originated, also called source attribution of the DNA. In other words, these statistical formulae allow the analyst to demonstrate, using 13 loci in STR testing, that an individual profile matching the profile generated from the crime evidence will not be found in any other unrelated person on earth."

The negative, or absence of the profile being found among others, is a very important distinction to make, Kreeger and Weiss (2003) emphasize. They state, "In the forensic identification of an offender, the analyst discusses probabilities. The analyst is not saying the offender's profile is the only one of its kind in existence, simply because not every person on earth has been DNA profiled, so a direct comparison to all human DNA is impossible. Instead, there can only be an estimate of the probability of finding the same profile among all possible arithmetic combinations."

Kaye and Sensabaugh (2000) explain that the primary determinants of whether DNA typing can be conducted on any particular sample are the quantity of DNA present in the sample and the extent to which it is degraded. Generally speaking, if a sufficient quantity of reasonable quality DNA can be extracted from a crime-scene sample, no matter what the nature of the sample, DNA typing can be done without problem. Thus, DNA typing has been performed successfully on old bloodstains, semen stains, vaginal swabs, hair, bone, bite marks, cigarette butts, urine, and fecal material. The amount of DNA in a cell varies; for example, the DNA in the chromosomes of a human cell is about 2,000 times greater than that in a typical bacterium. DNA is constant, however, from cell to cell in any organism, therefore, a human hair root cell contains the same amount of DNA as a white cell in blood, or a buccal cell in saliva. Kaye and Sensabaugh (2000) explain further that amounts of DNA present in samples vary from a trillionth of a gram for a hair shaft to several millionths of a gram for a post-coital vaginal swab. RFLP typing requires a much larger sample of DNA than PCR-based typing. As a practical matter, RFLP analysis requires a minimum of about 50 billionths of a gram of relatively non-degraded DNA, while most PCR test protocols recommend samples on the order of one to five billionths of a gram for optimum yields. Thus, PCR tests can be applied to samples containing 10- to 500-fold less nuclear DNA than that required for RFLP tests. These sample-size requirements help determine the approach to be taken for a DNA typing analysis. Samples that, from experience, are expected to contain at least 50 to 100 billionths of a gram of DNA typically are subjected to a formal DNA extraction followed by characterization of the DNA for quantity and quality. This characterization typically involves gel electrophoresis of a small portion of the extracted DNA. This test, however, does not distinguish human from non-human DNA. Since the success of DNA typing tests depends on the amount of human DNA present, it may be desirable to test for the amount of human DNA in the extract. For samples that typically contain small amounts of DNA, the risk of DNA loss during extraction may dictate the use of a different extraction procedure.

The primary determinant of DNA quality for forensic analysis is the extent to which the long DNA molecules are intact. Within the cell nucleus, each molecule of DNA extends for millions of base pairs. Outside the cell, DNA spontaneously degrades into smaller fragments at a rate that depends on temperature, exposure to oxygen, and, most importantly, the presence of water. In dry biological samples, protected from air and not exposed to temperature extremes, DNA degrades very slowly. In fact, the relative stability of DNA has made it possible to extract usable DNA from samples hundreds to thousands of years old.

RFLP analysis requires relatively non-degraded DNA, and testing DNA for degradation is a routine part of the protocol for VNTR analysis. In RFLP testing, a restriction enzyme cuts long sequences of DNA into smaller fragments. If the DNA is randomly fragmented into very short pieces to begin with, electrophoresis and Southern blotting will produce a smear of fragments rather than a set of well-separated bands. In contrast, PCR-based tests are relatively insensitive to degradation. Testing has proved effective with old and badly degraded material, such as the remains of the Czar Nicholas family (buried in 1918, recovered in 1991) and the Tyrolean Ice Man (frozen for 5,000 years). The extent to which degradation affects a PCR-based test depends on the size of the DNA segment to be amplified. For example, in a sample in which the bulk of the DNA has been degraded to fragments well under 1,000 base pairs in length, it may be possible to amplify a 100 base-pair sequence, but not a 1,000 base-pair target. Consequently, the shorter alleles may be detected in a highly degraded sample, but the larger ones may be missed. As with RFLP analysis, this possibility would have to be considered in the statistical interpretation of the result.

Kaye and Sensabaugh (2000) observe, "Surprising as it may seem, DNA can be exposed to a great variety of environmental insults without any effect on its capacity to be typed correctly. Exposure studies have shown that contact with a variety of surfaces, both clean and dirty, and with gasoline, motor oil, acids, and alkalis either have no effect on DNA typing or, at worst, render the DNA untypeable." Mixtures, however, are another story.

Kaye and Sensabaugh (2000) explain, "Finding three or more alleles at a locus indicates a mixture of DNA from more than one person. Some kinds of samples, such as post-coital vaginal swabs and blood stains from scenes where several persons are known to have bled, are expected to be mixtures. Sometimes, however, the first indication the sample has multiple contributors comes from the DNA testing. The chance of detecting a mixture by finding extra alleles depends on the proportion of DNA from each contributor as well as the chance that the contributors have different genotypes at one or more loci. As a rule, a minor contributor to a mixture must provide at least 5 percent of the DNA for the mixture to be recognized. In addition, the various contributors must have some different alleles. The chance that multiple contributors will differ at one or more locus increases with the number of loci tested and the genetic diversity at each locus. Unless many loci are examined, genetic markers with low to moderate diversities do not have much power to detect multiple contributors. Genetic markers that are highly polymorphic are much better at detecting mixtures. Thus, STRs and especially VNTRs are sensitive to mixtures."

DNA is a proved method of determining a person's identity, but it also can be used to determine several key issues at stake in criminal cases. Kreeger and Weiss (2003) explain, ". . . DNA evidence can prove and/or corroborate other elements of substantive crimes such as sexual battery, burglary, robbery, or homicide. Its constraints are only limited by a prosecutor's creativity. In proving all of the elements of a crime, all the questions of who, what, when, where, and sometimes, why, must be answered. Extrapolating meaning from the source, location and type of DNA evidence found during an investigation can help answer these questions." For example, the location of the DNA sample can help corroborate a victim's description of the crime or refute a defendant's claim, and it also can help investigators determine what happened during a crime, including the sequence of events and when a specific incident may have occurred.

Kreeger and Weiss (2003) observe, "DNA's evidentiary value can go far beyond proving the defendant's identity. DNA evidence should be used just as any other form or type of evidence—to corroborate, validate and/or impeach evidence or testimony." However effective the various methods of DNA typing are, at issue is the reliability of this evidence and the assurance that the samples have not been contaminated or further degraded in the collection, preservation, and analysis process.

Kreeger and Weiss (2003) state, "Prosecutors, defense attorneys, and judges frequently make mistakes in their translations or descriptions of the statistical frequencies. These errors can result in misstatements of fact, mistrials, or worse, miscarriages of justice. In answer to the question, 'What is the chance of a coincidental DNA match?' one common erroneous statement is, 'The numbers mean there is only a million to one chance the DNA came from someone else.' A correct statement would be, 'The statistical frequency that the evidence profile will be found in a population of unrelated individuals is one time in 'X' billion or quadrillion.' Another fallacy is, 'Anyone else with the same profile has an equal chance of having committed the crime.' Assuming the statement could be used in a situation involving identical twins, an evaluation of all of the evidence and its applicability to each twin would significantly alter the equality of chance. More importantly, the random match probability regarding the DNA evidence in no way projects odds or likelihood of guilt."

Of concern in the legal and forensic science communities are the issues of match probability. If a DNA sample from a crime scene and a DNA sample from a suspect are compared, and the two profiles match at every locus tested, one may assume that either the suspect left the DNA or someone else did, and it is exactly this "someone else" that prompts the need to determine the probability of finding this same profile. It is assumed that this individual is a random member of the population of possible suspects, therefore the frequency of the profile in the most relevant population(s). This frequency is the random match probability, regarded by most as an estimate of the answer to the query, what is the probability that a person other than the suspect, randomly selected from the population, will have this profile? According to the National Research Council (1996), the smaller that probability, the greater the likelihood that the two DNA samples came from the same person. Alternatively stated, if the probability is very small, it can be said that either the two samples came from the same person or a very unlikely coincidence has occurred.

The probability of any given match has been the subject of much scrutiny and debate among commentators. Berger (2001) comments, "As with many forensic sciences, the essence of DNA analysis is determining whether two samples match; most important, a sample from the crime scene and a sample from a suspect or victim. Sometimes matching is all that is needed when, for instance, the investigator is trying to exclude samples at the crime scene that may have been left by persons who are not under suspicion. But when DNA evidence is offered to prove that the defendant was at the crime scene, or that the victim's blood was found in defendant's car, the enormous probative value of the evidence stems not from the bare fact of the match but on the statistical frequency of the match. We can be almost certain that a match means that the DNA at the crime scene must have come from the person with whose DNA the crime scene sample is being compared."

"Anybody who will misstate what the statistics mean in DNA is doing himself or herself and the system in general a grave injustice," asserts Lawrence Kobilinsky, Ph.D., professor of criminal justice and biochemistry at the Graduate Center of the City University of New York (CUNY) and science adviser to the president of John Jay College of Criminal Justice in New York City, and a frequent consultant and expert witness on DNA issues. "Statistics used to describe DNA testing results are meant simply to illustrate the rarity of a matching profile in the relevant population. That's how it is generally stated, but if someone twists these statistics, there could be great misunderstanding of what it all means, so I think we must be very, very careful." Kobilinsky adds, "I have heard practitioners in court make statements that to a degree of scientific certainty that this particular defendant is the contributor of this biological evidence, when the evidence in question did not merit that comment. I have seen the evidence and the statistics overstated, and while it doesn't happen too often, when it does, it must be addressed. Statements not merited by the science should never be made."

The Research and Development Working Group of the DNA Commission on the Future of DNA Evidence concluded that, "Evidence that two DNA samples are from the same person is still probabilistic rather than certain. But with today's battery of genetic markers, the likelihood that two matching profiles came from the same person approaches certainty." Berger (2001) observes that, "With the help of scientists and tools such as the two reports from the National Academy of Sciences, judges became aware that they had to analyze two separate questions in determining the admissibility of DNA evidence: What is the scientific basis for concluding that accurate matches of DNA samples can be made and what is the scientific basis for providing reliable estimates of the frequency of a match? The first question raises a host of laboratory performance and biological issues; the second question requires consideration of population genetics."

The significance of a match depends upon the frequency with which each of the loci being matched could be found in particular populations. Berger (2001) explains, "For instance, in assessing the probative value of an expert's conclusion that shoe prints left at the crime scene match prints made by shoes found in defendant's closet, the value of the evidence will be much higher if the shoes were custom-made than if the shoes were mass-produced. And if the defendant's shoes had been repaired in a particular way, the prints may indeed have unique characteristics that serve to identify the defendant. Prior to the advent of DNA evidence, lawyers often failed to analyze the probative value of testimony about a match. This could lead to improper inferences by jurors, especially when the match was obtained through an impressive, seemingly infallible forensic technique, which was unaccompanied by any proof about the frequency of the match."

There exist, however, seemingly contradictory numbers. The NRC (1996) observed, "The uncertainties of assumptions about population structure and about population databases and a desire to be conservative have led some experts to produce widely different probability estimates for the same profile. In court one expert might give an estimate of one in many millions for the probability of a random DNA match, and another an estimate of one in a few thousand—larger by a factor of 1,000, or more. Such discrepancies have led some courts to conclude that the data and methods are unreliable. However, probability estimates, particularly the higher values, are intended to be conservative, sometimes extremely so."

Also causing concern are very small probabilities. The NRC (1996) cautioned, "If a testing laboratory uses genetic markers at four or five VNTR loci, the probability that two unrelated persons have identical DNA profiles might well be calculated to be one in millions, or billions, or even less. The smaller the probability, the stronger is the argument that the DNA samples came from the same person. Some have argued that such a small probability—much smaller than could ever be measured directly—lacks validity because it is outside the range of previous observations. Yet they might accept as meaningful the statement that the probability that two persons get the same bridge hand in two independent deals from a well-shuffled deck is about one in 600 billion, a number far outside anyone's bridge experience and 100 times the world population."

The right argument, then, is not whether the probability is large or small, but how accurate it is. It is important to emphasize, according to some experts, that probabilities are not dubious simply because they are small. In most cases, given comparable non-DNA evidence, a judge or jury may reach the same conclusion if the probability of a random match were one in 100,000 or one in 100 million. According to the NRC (1996), "Because of the scientific approach of statisticians and population geneticists, treatment of DNA evidence has become a question of probabilities. But some other kinds of evidence are traditionally treated in absolute terms. The probative value of DNA evidence is probably greater than that of most scientific evidence that does not rely on statistical presentations, such as firearms, poisoning, and handwriting analysis. We urge that the offering of statistical evidence with DNA profiles not be regarded as something unusual and mysterious. In fact, because much of science is quantitative, the DNA precedent might point the way to more scientific treatment of other kinds of evidence."

The next obvious question in the debate is, should match probabilities be excluded, and are small frequencies or probabilities inherently prejudicial? Kaye and Sensabaugh (2000) state, "The most common form of expert testimony about matching DNA takes the form of an explanation of how the laboratory ascertained that the defendant's DNA has the profile of the forensic sample plus an estimate of the profile frequency or random match probability. Many arguments have been offered against this entrenched practice. First, it has been suggested that jurors do not understand probabilities in general, and infinitesimal match probabilities will so bedazzle jurors that they will not appreciate the other evidence in the case or any innocent explanations for the match. Empirical research into this hypothesis has been limited and inconclusive, and remedies short of exclusion are available. Thus, no jurisdiction currently excludes all match probabilities on this basis. A more sophisticated variation on this theme is that the jury will misconstrue the random match probability—by thinking that it gives the probability that the match is random."

Many savvy defense attorneys encourage judges to exclude random match probabilities, while some prosecutors suggest it is desirable to avoid arguments about probabilities, and instead to present the statistic as a simple frequency—the indication of how rare the genotype is in the relevant population. The NRC (1996) explains that "few courts or commentators have recommended the exclusion of evidence merely because of the risk that jurors will transpose a conditional probability." In addition, some research indicates that jurors may be more likely to be "swayed by the defendant's fallacy than by the prosecutor's fallacy." The NRC (1996) adds, "When advocates present both fallacies to mock jurors, the defendant's fallacy dominates." Furthermore, it can be suggested that if the initial presentation of the probability figure, cross-examination, and opposing testimony all fail to clarify this point, the judge can counter both fallacies by appropriate instructions to the jurors that minimize the possibility of cognitive errors. According to Kaye and Sensabaugh (2000), to date, no federal court has excluded a random match probability or an estimate of the small frequency of a DNA profile in the general population as unfairly prejudicial simply because the jury might misinterpret it as a probability that the defendant is the source of the forensic DNA.

Another issue is whether or not an expert should be allowed to offer a non-numerical judgment about a DNA profile, seeing that some courts have held that a DNA match is inadmissible unless the expert attaches a scientifically valid number to the figure. The National Research Council voiced two opinions; in its 1992 report, the NRC stated, "to say that two patterns match, without providing any scientifically valid estimate of the frequency with which such matches might occur by chance, is meaningless," while the 1996 report stated that "before forensic experts can conclude that DNA testing has the power to help identify the source of an evidence sample, it must be shown that the DNA characteristics vary among people. Therefore, it would not be scientifically justifiable to speak of a match as proof of identity in the absence of underlying data that permit some reasonable estimate of how rare the matching characteristics actually are." Kaye and Sensabaugh (2000) add that determining whether quantitative estimates should be presented to a jury is a different issue. They state, "Once science has established that a methodology has some individualizing power, the legal system must determine whether and how best to import that technology into the trial process."

Kaye and Sensabaugh (2000) observe that since the loci normally used in forensic DNA identification have been shown to possess significant individualizing power, it is scientifically sound to introduce evidence of matching profiles. They add, "Nonetheless, even evidence that meets the scientific soundness standard of Daubert is not admissible if its prejudicial effect clearly outweighs its probative value. Unless some reasonable explanation accompanies testimony that two profiles match, it is surely arguable that the jury will have insufficient guidance to give the scientific evidence the weight that it deserves. Instead of presenting frequencies or match probabilities obtained with quantitative methods, however, a scientist would be justified in characterizing every four-locus VNTR profile, for instance, as rare, extremely rare, or the like."

Uniqueness, as shown elsewhere throughout this chapter, is an incendiary term in the legal and forensic science communities. In its 1992 report, the National Research Council said that an expert should avoid "assertions in court that a particular genotype is unique in the population." Kaye and Sensabaugh (2000) note, "Following this advice in the context of a profile derived from a handful of single-locus VNTR probes, several courts initially held that assertions of uniqueness are inadmissible, while others found such testimony less troublesome."

With the advent of more population data and loci, the NRC (1996) observed, "We are approaching the time when many scientists will wish to offer opinions about the source of incriminating DNA." Kaye and Sensabaugh (2000) state, "Of course, the uniqueness of any object, from a snowflake to a fingerprint, in a population that cannot be enumerated never can be proved directly." To this end, the NRC (1996) stated, "There is no bright-line standard in law or science that can pick out exactly how small the probability of the existence of a given profile in more than one member of a population must be before assertions of uniqueness are justified . . . There might already be cases in which it is defensible for an expert to assert that, assuming that there has been no sample mishandling or laboratory error, the profile's probable uniqueness means that the two DNA samples come from the same person."

Moriarty and Saks (2005) say that DNA typing has provided forensic science and the courts with the first scientifically grounded approach to forensic identification, and a benchmark for high-quality forensic evidence, as well as a device that "illuminates the weaknesses of the other forensic sciences and provides a guide to their future improvement." Because DNA is grounded in molecular biology and genetics, Moriarty and Saks say it "refrains from relying on unproven (and likely unprovable) assumptions of uniqueness to reach its conclusions." They add, "Thus, DNA typing only begins, but does not end, with a judgment that two samples appear indistinguishably alike. It recognizes that such an observation does not necessarily lead to the conclusion that the two samples came from the same person. This is because it is both practically and theoretically impossible to know whether all members of any large class are in fact unique. But, even if they were unique, crime scene evidence usually provides examiners only with samples, not full objects. A dozen alleles, not the entire genome, is what DNA typing looks at; latent fingerprints are usually only partial prints; handwriting is a tiny sample from a vast potential output from any given writer; bite marks are only partial; tools and weapons change with use; and so on. So it is necessary to use methods of analysis that are capable of making useful estimates about samples or a temporally changing target."

Koehler (2001) states that the early forensic DNA years were marked by controversy over the proper computation of DNA match statistics, adding, "Although disagreement has abated, little is known about how jurors think about and use DNA match statistics. It is widely assumed that DNA statistics are persuasive. That is, people assume that, after hearing that a suspect matches traces of DNA evidence from a violent crime scene, and the chance that a randomly selected person from the population would match is one in a million or billion, jurors will be convinced that in the matching the suspect and a genetic sample, the suspect is excluded as a possible donor of the sample and statistics are not provided."

Most persuasive, of course, are the DNA match statistics that target an individual suspect rather than the statistic that targets a broader population. However, Kaye and Koehler (1991) suggest that individuals, including jurors, have poor intuition when it comes to reasoning with statistics in general and forensic science statistics in particular. They say that research with mock jurors indicates that the impressions left by DNA statistics vary as a function of perceived and actual error rates, expectations, and the mathematical form of the DNA statistic.

Kaye and Koehler (1991) describe why some descriptions of DNA match statistics have a greater impact on jurors than others: "The perceived probative value of a statistical DNA match (and, by extension, other forensic match evidence) depends on the ease with which triers of fact can imagine examples of others who would also match the DNA profile. When triers of fact find it hard to imagine examples of others who might match by chance, the evidence will be treated as compelling proof that the matching suspect is the source of the recovered DNA evidence. But when such matches are easier to imagine, the evidence will seem less compelling." This theory, known as the "exemplar cueing theory," is so named because it is based on the assumption that people evaluate the probative value of a DNA match by the ease with which examples of others who might also match are cued in their minds. Kaye and Koehler explain: "When people find it hard to imagine such examples, it will seem reasonable to assume that the matching suspect is the source of the recovered DNA evidence. But when such examples are more easy to imagine (for whatever reason), the evidence will seem less compelling or, perhaps, insufficient." The exemplar cueing theory indicates, according to Kaye and Koehler, that triers of fact do not base their evaluations about the probative value of a DNA match on the magnitude of the DNA match probability, but instead, look at the perceived probativity of a DNA match inversely proportional to the ease with which coincidental match exemplars are cued. Therefore, when jurors can easily recall instances in which such coincidences have occurred, they will find the evidence relatively less impressive. Kaye and Koehler add, "If true, this could lead to the unusual situation in which objectively strong DNA evidence (as measured by its match probability) is accorded less value than objectively weaker DNA evidence when exemplars are cued for the strong evidence but not the weak evidence."

Koehler describes a study in which a researcher was able to conduct a test with four actual jurors in a Texas capital murder case several years after the jury convicted the defendant. The conviction was based on a PCR DNA blood match between the victim and a spot on the clothing owned by the defendant, with the test revealing that the blood matched the blood type of the victim. The test provided a DNA match statistic of 1 in 20, or 5 percent. The researcher asked the former jurors to consider a murder case in which an expert testified that DNA evidence recovered from clothing worn by a suspect matched the victim, and the frequency of this DNA profile in the general population is 1 in 100. The researcher then presented the former jurors with a series of statements related to the meaning of the 1-in-100 statistic and requested them to indicate whether each was true or false.

Koehler describes the results of this test as "abysmal." One juror accepted as true the misstatement that a 1-in-100 frequency indicates a 99 percent chance that the victim is the source of the evidence. Koehler notes that this source probability error consists of equating the frequency of the DNA profile with the probability that a person who matches the profile is not the source of that profile. Koehler remarks, "Thus, when judges, experts, and attorneys claim that a DNA match probability of, say, 1 in 1 million means that there is only one chance in a million that the suspect is not the source of the recovered sample, they have committed the source probability error."

The other jurors believed that the 1-in-100 statistic indicated that there was only a 1 percent chance that the blood belonged to the victim, an error by which, Koehler says, "these jurors turned the notion of probative value on its head." Koehler adds, "If the profile frequency actually did equal the source probability, then an extremely rare blood match (such as 1 in 1 million) would be less probative than an extremely common blood match (such as 4 in 5) because there would be an 80 percent chance that the blood belonged to the victim in the latter case, but less than a 1 percent chance in the former case. This is obviously wrong. Apparently, then, service on a jury in which DNA evidence plays an important role provides little reason to believe that people who reason badly about DNA statistics in a laboratory setting will improve in a courtroom setting."

TRIAL ISSUES RELATED TO DNA

As we will see in Chapter 12, the U.S. Supreme Court, in a trilogy of cases decided in the 1990s, established a set of standards by which judges could determine the admissibility of forensic evidence. Because DNA was so very new to the scene at the time the High Court was handing down these standards, legal scholars and commentators were busy trying to determine how this new technology could possibly establish new precedents in the courtroom. Walsh (1999) states, "Despite the increase in rulings at both the federal and state level that seek to map the standards and define the limits for admitting scientific evidence proffered through experts, the problem is far from being resolved. There are two factors that hinder the effort to formulate a consistent framework for testing the admissibility of scientific evidence. The first is the evolving nature of the scientific knowledge as it is brought to the courtroom; the second is the highly subjective judgment brought to bear under a gatekeeper construct."

Walsh (1999) acknowledges the ascent of DNA technology as part of an overall increasingly complex slate of technical evidence presenting itself in court, and notes, "The emergence of

DNA evidence as a forensic tool for identification purposes and as a prediction of physical and emotional abnormality is a good example of how knowledge outstrips the ability of courts to accommodate its implications. DNA matching evidence, once viewed as controversial, is now readily accepted for identification purposes. The scientific basis for this evidence is now so well established that its admissibility is sanctioned by statute in many jurisdictions with only the projection of a random match left to expert opinion. The current state of the law seems to sanction the general scientific basis for DNA identification by permitting only the challenge to individual results." Walsh adds that "whenever new legal relationships are created, advances in genetic science will bring to the courtroom an array of expert witnesses opining on the emerging science of genetics. The opinions they will give (and the counter views which will inevitably arise) will occur on the developing edge of science. Will testability, general acceptance, and peer review continue to be appropriate criteria for determining the admissibility of such testimony?"

Already, we have seen that some evolving science may demand greater flexibility than current admissibility constraints will allow. Walsh (1999) suggests, "It seems reasonable to insist that the current doctrinal framework spawned by Daubert be flexible enough to accommodate novel evidence. Yet, at the same time, the prospect of new scientific learning presents the risk that practitioners of junk science will seek to enter the courtroom to take advantage of the lack of a formalized body of knowledge. The real challenge for gatekeeper judges in the future will be to balance these competing considerations."

As we will explore in Chapter 13, trial judges face what Walsh (1999) calls a "highly subjective duty" to serve as the gatekeeper of expert testimony to ensure that it is relevant and reliable. Walsh comments, "Daubert's underlying rationale is a sound one: lay jurors should not be exposed to unfiltered scientific or technical testimony that may adversely influence their findings of fact. But this rationale is built on two underlying assumptions: that the trial judge is more knowledgeable in assessing complex scientific testimony than is the average lay juror and that each judge brings to the specific task of gate-keeping a general attitude or philosophy concerning the level of scrutiny appropriate for scientific gatekeepers. Experience, however, has demonstrated that judges are not fungible. Intelligence aside, judges vary considerably in how they view their role in the courtroom; active or passive, dominating or deferential to counsel, prone to independent inquiry or content to let the lawyers try the case."

That being said, the effectiveness of the gatekeeper role is determined, Walsh (1999) says, by the idiosyncrasies or predisposition of the trial judge. Thus, Walsh adds, "scientific evidence which would gain admissibility in one courtroom might be rejected in another. To make matters worse, an aggrieved litigant seeking to appeal a lower court ruling on scientific evidence will be required to overcome the highest standard of review—abuse of discretion. Moreover, it may plausibly be argued that, unlike the reliability prong of Daubert which is fact-intensive, the determination of relevancy is more akin to an issue of law and, thus, not requiring the same level of deference."

Walsh (1999) says that with *Daubert* and its progeny, the United States Supreme Court accomplished the task of repudiating the *Frye* rule and replacing it with a standard vesting significant discretion in the trial judge. Walsh adds, "The new standards, however, have not won acceptance in all state jurisdictions and pose significant problems in application. Courts following Daubert's lead will be required to deal with a fundamental shifting of the responsibility for dealing with suspect scientific evidence. The contest for admissibility will be less and less a competition between opposing experts and more and more the independent responsibility of the gate-keeping judge. It remains to be seen whether this expanded duty assigned to the trial judge will disturb the traditional role of the fact finder as determiners of the weight of testimony. Therein lies the challenge facing litigators and judges as DNA science evolves."

Forensic use of DNA technology in criminal cases debuted in 1986 when law enforcement requested Dr. Alec J. Jeffreys of Leicester University in England to verify a suspect's confession that he had committed two sexual homicides. Tests proved that the suspect had not committed the crimes, so police began collecting blood samples from several thousand males in the region to help identify a new suspect. In a 1987 case in England, Robert Melias became the first person convicted of rape on the basis of DNA evidence. In the United States, one of the earliest uses of DNA in a criminal case occurred in 1987 when the circuit court in Orange County, Florida, convicted Tommy Lee Andrews of rape after DNA tests matched his DNA from a blood sample with that of semen trace evidence collected from a rape victim. Another milestone case was that of *State v Woodall*, in which the West Virginia Supreme Court was the first state high court to rule on the admissibility of DNA evidence. The court accepted DNA testing by the defendant, but inconclusive results failed to exculpate Woodall. The court upheld the defendant's conviction for rape, kidnapping, and robbery of two women, but subsequent DNA testing determined that Woodall was innocent, and eventually he was released from prison. *Spencer v Commonwealth* was the first case in the United States where the admission of DNA evidence resulted in guilty verdicts that led to the death penalty. The Virginia Supreme Court upheld the murder and rape convictions of Timothy Spencer, who had been convicted on the basis of DNA testing that matched his DNA with that of semen evidence collected from several victims. In the case there was no testimony from expert witnesses that challenged the general acceptance of DNA testing among the scientific community.

Finally, the first case that posed a significant challenge to the admissibility of DNA evidence was *People v Castro,* in which the New York Supreme Court, in a 12-week pretrial hearing, examined numerous issues relating to the admissibility of DNA evidence. The defendant, Jose Castro, was accused of murdering his neighbor and her 2-year-old daughter. A bloodstain on Castro's watch was analyzed for a match to the victim. The court held that DNA is generally accepted among the scientific community, that DNA forensic identification techniques are generally accepted by the scientific community, and that pretrial hearings are required to determine whether the testing laboratory's methodology was substantially in accord with scientific standards and produced reliable results for jury consideration.

According to Connors et al. (1996), "The Castro ruling supports the proposition that DNA identification evidence of exclusion is more presumptively admissible than DNA identification evidence of inclusion. In Castro, the court ruled that DNA tests could be used to show that blood on Castro's watch was not his, but tests could not be used to show that the blood was that of his victims." In this case, the court recommended extensive discovery requirements for future proceedings, including copies of all laboratory results and reports; explanation of statistical probability calculations; explanations for any observed defects or laboratory errors, including observed contaminants; and chain of custody of documents. Adding to this list was the Minnesota Supreme Court, which, in *Schwartz v State,* noted, "ideally, a defendant should be provided with the actual DNA sample(s) in order to reproduce the results. As a practical matter, this may not be possible because forensic samples are often so small that the entire sample is used in testing. Consequently, access to the data, methodology, and actual results is crucial . . . for an independent expert review." According to Connors et al. (1996), the Supreme Court of Minnesota "refused to admit the DNA evidence analyzed by a private forensic laboratory; the court noted the laboratory did not comply with appropriate standards and controls. In particular, the court was troubled by failure of the laboratory to reveal its underlying population data and testing methods. Such secrecy precluded replication of the test."

The issues of greatest concern to prosecutors in criminal cases that include DNA are not all that different from cases involving other forensic evidence; they are: admissibility, discovery, case presentation, defense attacks, and proper closing argument. Bieber (2004) states, "The rigorous challenges to DNA evidence have in a meaningful way altered the landscape of admissibility of all types of forensic evidence and have increased the scrutiny placed on collection and transfer analysis and interpretation of all forensic evidence." Another perspective is voiced by Reinstein (1996): "What is frustrating to many who are excited about the possibilities of the use of DNA in the forensics area is the slow pace it is traveling on the road to admissibility. Many jurisdictions do not have sufficient funds to establish their own laboratories or to send to private laboratories items of evidence for typing. Laboratories that perform testing often have backlogs measured in months. Courts, prosecutors, and defense counsel impose a great burden on laboratories' time in the usual discovery battles that occur whenever a new technique arrives on the forensic scene. It is interesting to observe how quickly some DNA-evidence opponents embrace the science when it benefits certain defendants' interests but how defensive they become when the evidence points toward other defendants. But this is not unique to DNA evidence."

Not even DNA is ironclad against objections these days. DiFonzo (2005) expresses concern that even DNA is subject to the presumed capricious nature of forensic science: "DNA's reputation for scientific precision is in fact unwarranted. The record is littered with slapdash forensic analyses often performed by untrained, underpaid, overworked forensic technicians operating in crime labs whose workings reflect gross incompetence or rampant corruption. Why does this matter? It matters because the average jury is not exposed to the track record of forensic science in the courtroom . . . The scientific basis of DNA testing can mislead the unsuspecting into believing that the introduction of DNA evidence in court not only ensures procedural regularity, but also washes away the need to examine any corroborating or contradictory evidence. One prime example of the cultural sway of DNA is seen in the 'CSI effect,' popularly defined as the perception of the near-infallibility of forensic science in response to the TV show. 'CSI: Crime Scene Investigation' and its forensic cousins have led juries to worship forensic testimony. Prosecutors and defense attorneys have begun to *voir dire* potential jurors on their 'CSI' viewing habits. In the world portrayed on 'CSI,' forensic technicians are always above reproach."

What this does, DiFonzo (2005) asserts, is set up jurors for failure as they search for the truth: "DNA is only perfect in theory. In the real world, DNA analyses are subject to the same forces of incompetence and inveiglement as any other evidentiary process. We have become enraptured by DNA, and are thus blind to what we know is true in all other corners of our lives. Human folly can pervade even scientific evidence. In fact, because the algorithms of forensic analysis are so removed from our quotidian existence, we become credulous at the very moment when skepticism is most needed. We understand, on an abstract basis, that there is no dispute over the scientific validity of DNA testing. But we then give credence to an evidentiary conclusion in a specific case without reflecting on the potential for errors in the undertaking. If we were to concede that DNA always and unmistakably identifies the rapist, then there would indeed be no entries on the other side of the ledger: No concern for cloudy memories or cavalier proof; no acknowledgment of the need to bestir the human and technical apparatus of the State to act expeditiously in apprehending and prosecuting evildoers; and, finally, no sense that limitations periods help assure accuracy in the criminal justice system. But, as case after case has shown, forensic testing and testimony are as prone to error as is any human endeavor. The record is larded with instances of contaminated samples, mislabeled vials, rushed and inaccurate analyses, and outright perjury."

Reinstein (1996) adds, "It is the responsibility of the court to promote the search for truth. If that search can be assisted by science that can give reliable results, the whole system as well as society benefits. It is also the responsibility of the court to try to prevent juror confusion caused by lawyers and experts who sometimes seem unable to explain scientific evidence in language the jury understands."

DNA is just one of the many fronts upon which expert witnesses will do battle. Reinstein (1996) says, "The future should be brighter as the technology improves so that the process of DNA typing will likely become much quicker, less complex, and less expensive. The battle of the experts, it is hoped, will also subside eventually, especially in the confusing area of the statistical meaning of a match. The conflict between various forensic experts, population geneticists, and statisticians on the meaning of a match is a prime example of how science and the law sometimes do not mesh, especially in jurisdictions that follow the Frye test of general acceptance in the scientific community. The numbers being bandied about by various experts are almost beyond comprehension for trial jurors." Reinstein adds that it is only logical to admit into court relevant, reliable, qualitative expert opinion, but comments, "Restrictions currently imposed in some jurisdictions on the use of DNA evidence unreasonably divest such evidence of its compelling nature. If our justice system's goal is the continuing search for truth, as evidenced by the results of the study described in this report, then a similar argument can be made for the admissibility of relevant and reliable DNA-match testimony in our courts."

TRENDS IN THE ADMISSIBILITY OF DNA EVIDENCE

The NRC (1996) acknowledges that application of the standards for admitting scientific evidence to the admissibility of DNA evidence has produced "divergent" results. Kaye (1993) remarks that a number of more recent cases focused less on the laboratory methods for characterizing and matching DNA and more on the statistical methods for interpreting the significance of similarities in DNA samples. Many opinions in that period lagged behind the scientific publications, which responded forcefully to early speculations and questionable analyses of the importance of departures from the assumptions of statistical independence of alleles within and among VNTR loci. More recent cases, benefiting from PCR-based methods, involve legal assaults on the procedures for ensuring the accuracy of such analyses and questions about the quantitative interpretation of genetic typing. With greater frequency, the defense bar is questioning if the protocols and standard operating procedures used for forensic work are sufficient to prevent false-positive results, and challenging the procedures for estimating the frequencies of the genotypes that are detected after PCR amplification. In addition, according to Bieber (2004), additional challenges are being made on issues relating to the collection, transport, and preservation of evidentiary samples, chain-of-custody documentation, and other matters pertaining to state and federal rules of evidence. Berger (2001) explains, "DNA evidence made its debut at the same time that a very different kind of scientific evidence was coming under attack. Incensed by the huge damages awarded some plaintiffs in toxic tort and product liability cases, critics claimed that plaintiffs' successes were attributable to venal expert witnesses who relied on 'junk science' to prove causation. The allegations about junk science sparked considerable debate in the legal community about proper standards for scientific expert proof."

While it remains to be seen what lasting legacy DNA will ultimately leave, Berger (2001) says that courts' interest in the debate about science "undoubtedly led to a heightening of judicial attention accorded DNA profiling." It was a trend noted by the National Commission on the Future of DNA Evidence, which commented that DNA evidence received "an intensity of scrutiny far greater than the other methods of criminal investigation" had ever received. Berger (2001) notes, "In the beginning, DNA evidence was routinely admitted. But when defendants began to challenge the admissibility of DNA evidence, spurred by the growing insistence on the need for reliable scientific proof, some courts initially upheld these contentions. They found that insufficient scientific work had as yet been done to satisfy their jurisdiction's test for the admissibility of scientific evidence. The result was that DNA profiling was placed on a much more secure footing because of additional scientific input: The technical standards for DNA testing were strengthened, the databases used to generate probabilities of matching became larger and more representative, and laboratory performance was improved. The judicial demands for more stringent science, and the resulting response, provided a model of how scientists test a hypothesis, accumulate data, and seek to reduce error. All players in the legal system—judges, lawyers, law enforcement and laboratory personnel— observed and were educated by this process, which had not been used in evaluating other forensic techniques. Ultimately this development had a spillover effect into other forensic fields."

At the heart of proper discovery, especially in DNA cases, is the communication and coordination between the forensic laboratory analyst, the prosecutor, and law enforcement, according to Kreeger and Weiss (2003). To comply with criminal procedures relating to pretrial discovery, the prosecutor describes the state's efforts to make available scientific test reports and relevant raw data used in a given case, as well as the state's efforts to maintain and preserve the evidence. Kreeger and Weiss explain, "The prosecutor's ethical responsibilities pertaining to biological evidence are to preserve evidence that possesses both an apparent exculpatory value and that cannot be obtained by other reasonably available means, and to ensure that the defendant has access to the raw materials integral to the building of an effective defense." The possibility exists that evidentiary samples are exhausted through the testing processes in the course of an investigation, leaving no evidence available for testing by the defense; in this case, it is the prosecutor's ethical responsibility to disclose this fact in good faith.

Kreeger and Weiss (2004) add that one of the foremost aspects of prosecution is discovery demands involving DNA evidence and expert witnesses. They state, "Errors in handling discovery requests can result in the exclusion of evidence, reversal of convictions or the imposition of other sanctions." Related to this process is the question of sample consumption or remaining sample available for testing. Kreeger and Weiss state, "In some jurisdictions, defense attorneys have obtained pre-trial orders that prohibit testing by a crime laboratory that would alter or consume in any way biological material obtained from crime scene evidence. Such orders essentially prevent any DNA testing, since DNA profiles cannot be developed without consuming at least some of the sample evidence. This fact was not lost upon the United States Supreme Court when it found that, 'In general, the destruction or failure to preserve potentially useful evidence does not constitute a violation of the due process clause, unless it can be shown that the police, the prosecutor or the laboratory acted in bad faith.' Consequently, when appropriate, prosecutors should aggressively pursue denial of defense motions that prohibit testing." According to Kreeger and Weiss, in the majority of states, DNA testing can proceed legally without notice to defense counsel even though the testing will consume all of the sample material, while several states require that advance notice be provided to the defense before consumptive testing can be performed. In all states, upon consumption of a biological sample, it is the prosecutor's duty to inform the defense of such consumption. Whether or not required by state law, a policy of having the laboratory routinely indicate in its reports that the sample was consumed fulfills the prosecutor's discovery duty. Kreeger and Weiss state, "One issue raised repeatedly in appellate exculpatory evidence cases is a lack of biological evidence for the defense to test independently. A wrongly accused person's best insurance against the possibility of being falsely incriminated is the opportunity to have testing repeated . . . Clearly, the prosecutor must disclose evidence consumption as early as possible, ideally on the lab report."

Another potentially exculpatory issue is the inconclusive test result, according to Kreeger and Weiss (2004), who add, "Across the nation, crime laboratories generally indicate inconclusive results clearly in their reports. Such reports should be disclosed to the defense as a matter of course—regardless of whether the prosecutor intends to call the analyst as a witness or whether the prosecution believes the finding is relevant. Providing exculpatory evidence, regardless of whether it has been requested, goes to a prosecutor's ethical responsibility to ensure that the defendant receives effective assistance of counsel. Satisfying this requirement early in a prosecution is a preemptive action—to keep an eventual conviction secure. To accomplish that purpose, prosecutors can provide the defense every opportunity to retest the evidence, and insist that the trial record include a strategic, legitimate reason not to retest."

In Chapter 13, we discuss the ways the defense bar is educating itself about the forensic science community. In response, prosecutors are being coached about increasingly sophisticated ways to present DNA evidence. Kreeger and Weiss (2003) advise, "Less is more, generally speaking, in the courtroom presentation of DNA evidence. There are two important goals to achieve with the direct examination of the state's DNA expert witness, the analyst: to assure the jury they can rely upon DNA by educating them about its widespread use and accuracy, and to explain to the jury how the DNA evidence incriminates this defendant in this crime." According to Kreeger and Weiss (2004), jury persuasion can be accomplished by reviewing the many ways DNA can exonerate or exclude individuals based on evidence. They state, "To assure the jury they can rely upon this evidence, it is necessary to demonstrate the specific qualifications of your witness: his or her education, training, and experience examining DNA in school; training and experience with forensic DNA typing; ongoing education and professional development through scientific associations or conference participation; and a thorough description of the analyst's current employment as a forensic scientist in a forensic laboratory. An analyst employed in a forensic laboratory, whose job responsibility is to conduct forensic identification testing, is the best person to testify about forensic identification results."

Jury education about the incriminating meaning of DNA evidence, Kreeger and Weiss say, is accomplished through pretrial preparation of the DNA analyst. In the courtroom, they advise prosecutors to ask the analyst to explain the meaning of the 100 percent match between the crime scene profile and the offender profile on specific pieces of evidence. Kreeger and Weiss (2004) state, "How the analyst responds can be powerful. To say that 'the profile generated from testing the saliva swabbed from the bite mark on the victim's breast matches the profile generated from the offender sample at each and every one of the 26 spots examined' more powerfully explains the evidence than to say that 'no exclusion could be made between sample 1 and sample 3.'" Kreeger and Weiss emphasize that when both the forensic laboratory analyst and the prosecutor discuss evidence within the context of the crime, the value of the DNA evidence is enhanced.

A final recommendation from Kreeger and Weiss is for the prosecutor to discuss, before the trial, the laboratory analyst's willingness to attribute the source of the crime scene evidence to the defendant within a reasonable degree of scientific certainty. They state, "If testing excluded someone else as the source of the sample, the direct testimony of the analyst should say so. Finally, questions about the remaining sample, or lack thereof, should be addressed in the analyst's direct testimony to explain the reason for preserving the remaining sample (i.e., to provide for retesting or further testing as a quality control measure). That fact speaks to the certainty of results everyone can have. The analyst can then reinforce the value of re-testing and the consequent confidence in the test results when responding to cross-examination and re-direct questioning."

Tactical maneuvers come into play in every case, and DNA cases are no exception. Kreeger and Weiss (2003) advise prosecutors, "Learning as early as possible what a credible defense attack of the DNA evidence could be is important to effectively responding. When the DNA analyst provides a report, then is the time to ask if there are any foreseeable criticisms, attacks, concerns, or problems. When there have been no identifiable issues relating to the DNA (or lack thereof), prosecutors have been successful in limiting the defense expert's testimony or even excluding it from trial." Kreeger and Weiss suggest that it may be possible for prosecutors to attempt to exclude or limit the expert's testimony by questioning his or her credentials or the relevance of the testimony in the context of the case. Prosecutors are advised to consider whether the expert is a forensic DNA examiner, a non-forensic scientist, an academic, or a population geneticist, and whether the expert has ever worked in a forensic laboratory.

If the defense expert is allowed, Kreeger and Weiss (2003) say prosecutors should endeavor to limit the witness's testimony to a specific attack on the case evidence. They add, "A soft beginning to a cross-examination, however, can often induce the defense witness to agree with the reliability and accuracy of the science or the method of analysis. If the defense witness attacks the statistics but agrees that the science is accurate, the match between crime scene evidence and offender sample is not discredited. If he or she attacks the science, compare and contrast sharply the specific scientific, forensic, and non-forensic work experience of your analyst with that of the defense expert." Prosecutors are advised to inquire if the defense expert works solely on forensic science cases in a laboratory that is accredited or working toward accreditation, or who has examined the evidence in the case. Kreeger and Weiss (2003 observe, "DNA is an easily validated and trustworthy science. Statistics is not new or fuzzy math. Consequently, a defense expert cannot attack the fields of science and statistics credibly. To be relevant, experts should challenge facts in a case. Prepare your response strategically, bearing in mind that the DNA evidence is merely one piece of evidence in your entire case."

A well-argued DNA case can crumble if closing arguments are faulty or weak, Kreeger and Weiss say, resulting in a conviction reversal. They explain, "One potential problem occurs with the prosecutor's discussion or description of the statistics in the case. The random match probability pertains to the likelihood of reoccurrence of the crime scene profile in another unrelated person in the population. This probability, cannot be characterized as proof of the defendant's guilt at trial, but merely as evidence in the case—powerfully persuasive, but only evidence nonetheless. The second issue that has been raised successfully is argument pertaining to the defendant's actual testing or burden of re-testing the DNA evidence. It is permissible argument that remaining sample is a quality control of the lab. Approximately a dozen states have found the following argument permissible: that there is an absence of defense evidence that contradicts or conflicts with the DNA evidence presented."

The results of DNA testing can be presented in several ways, with profiles usually expressed in terms of a match or a non-match. There are hazards inherent to using this verbiage, as Kaye and Sensabaugh (2000) point out: "If the genetic profile obtained from the biological sample taken from the crime scene or the victim . . . matches that of a particular individual, then that individual is included as a possible source of the sample. But other individuals also might possess a matching DNA profile. Accordingly, the expert should be asked to provide some indication of how significant the match is. If, on the other hand, the genetic profiles are different, then the individual is excluded as the source of the trace evidence. Typically, proof tending to show that the defendant is the source incriminates the defendant, while proof that someone else is the source exculpates the defendant."

DNA testing is used for exclusion and inclusion, but it is a process fraught with contention. Kaye and Sensabaugh (2000) may have said it best: "The use of DNA techniques to exclude a suspect as the source of DNA has not been a subject of controversy. In a sense, exclusion and failure to exclude are two sides of the same coin, because the laboratory procedures are the same." However, there are two key differences. Exclusion, which is the process of declaring that two DNA samples do not match and therefore did not come from the same person, does not require any information about frequencies of DNA types in the population. Therefore, issues of population genetics are not of concern for exclusion. However, in a failure to exclude, these issues complicate the calculation of chance matches of DNA from different persons. The other issue is that errors—of both a technical and a human nature—will occur regardless of how reliable the procedures are and how careful the analysts are in their work. Kaye and Sensabaugh (2000) comment, "Although there are more ways of making errors that produce false exclusions than false matches, courts regard the latter, which could lead to a false conviction, as much more serious than the former, which could lead to a false acquittal."

Sometimes, the result of DNA testing is regarded as a slam-dunk. Kaye and Sensabaugh (2000) explain, "When the DNA from the trace evidence does not match the DNA sample from the suspect, the DNA analysis demonstrates that the suspect's DNA is not in the forensic sample. Indeed, if the samples have been collected, handled, and analyzed properly, then the suspect is excluded as a possible source of the DNA in the forensic sample. Even a single allele that cannot be explained as a laboratory artifact or other error can suffice to exclude a suspect. As a practical matter, such exclusionary results normally would keep charges from being filed against the excluded suspect."

However, some cases present a challenge; DNA testing may come up as inconclusive in whole or in part because the presence or absence of a discrete allele can be in doubt, or the existence or location of a VNTR band may be unclear. Kaye and Sensabaugh (2000) clarify, "When the trace evidence sample is extremely degraded, VNTR profiling might not show all the alleles that would be present in a sample with more intact DNA. If the quantity of DNA to be amplified for sequence-specific tests is too small, the amplification might not yield enough product to give a clear signal. Thus, experts sometimes disagree as to whether a particular band is visible on an autoradiograph or whether a dot is present on a reverse dot blot. Furthermore, even when RFLP bands are clearly visible, the entire pattern of bands can be displaced from its true location in a systematic way." In recognizing this phenomenon of band shifting, analysts may regard some seemingly matching patterns as inconclusive. Kaye and Sensabaugh (2000) point out that at the other extreme, "the genotypes at a large number of loci can be clearly identical, and the fact of a match not in doubt. In these cases, the DNA evidence is quite incriminating, and the challenge for the legal system lies in explaining just how probative it is. Naturally, as with exclusions, inclusions are most powerful when the samples have been collected, handled, and analyzed properly."

Kaye and Sensabaugh (2000) explain further the difference between exclusions and inclusions: "If it is accepted that the samples have different genotypes, then the conclusion that the DNA in them came from different individuals is essentially inescapable. In contrast, even if two samples have the same genotype, there is a chance that the forensic sample came—not from the defendant—but from another individual who has the same genotype. This complication has produced extensive arguments over the statistical procedures for assessing this chance or related quantities."

If scientific protocol is followed and results are in question, what is the logical conclusion? Kaye and Sensabaugh (2000) comment, "If the defendant is the source of DNA of sufficient quantity and quality found at a crime scene, then a DNA sample from the defendant and the forensic sample should have the same profile. The inference required in assessing the evidence, however, runs in the opposite direction. The forensic scientist reports that the sample of DNA from the crime scene and a sample from the defendant have the same genotype. To what extent does this tend to prove that the defendant is the source of the forensic sample? Conceivably, other hypotheses could account for the matching profiles. One possibility is laboratory error—the genotypes are not actually the same even though the laboratory thinks that they are. This situation could arise from mistakes in labeling or handling samples or from cross-contamination of the samples."

LABORATORY QUALITY-RELATED ISSUES AND DNA

As Kaye and Sensabaugh stated previously, it's a given that if DNA from an evidence sample and DNA from a suspect or victim share a profile that has a low frequency in the population, this suggests that the two DNA samples came from the same person, as the lower the frequency, the stronger the evidence. However, there is a possibility that an error has occurred and the true profile of one of the sources differs from that reported by the forensic laboratory. DNA's power is disarmed, of course, by errors in determination; mistakes can lead to the conviction of an innocent person, and an erroneously reported exclusion could also have serious consequences. Although there are more ways for an error to lead to a false exclusion than a false match, the U.S. criminal justice system is more concerned with the latter, since it regards false conviction as worse than false acquittal (National Research Council, 1996).

As the NRC (1992) cautioned, "Errors happen, even in the best laboratories, and even when the analyst is certain that every precaution against error was taken." Another possibility, however, is that the laboratory analysis is correct and that the genotypes are truly identical, but the forensic sample came from another individual. In general, the true source might be a close relative of the defendant (known as *kinship*) or an unrelated person who just happens to have the same profile as the defendant (known as *coincidence*). Kaye and Sensabaugh (2000) add that to infer that the defendant is the source of the crime scene DNA, one must reject these alternative hypotheses of laboratory error, kinship, and coincidence.

Kaye and Sensabaugh (2000) state, "Although many experts would concede that even with rigorous protocols, the chance of a laboratory error exceeds that of a coincidental match, quantifying the former probability is a formidable task. Some commentary proposes using the proportion of false positives that the particular laboratory has experienced in blind proficiency tests or the rate of false positives on proficiency tests averaged across all laboratories." The researchers point out that while the NRC (1992) says, "proficiency tests provide a measure of the false-positive and false-negative rates of a laboratory," the same report recognizes that "errors on proficiency tests do not necessarily reflect permanent probabilities of false-positive or false-negative results." The NRC (1996) suggests that a probability of a false-positive error that would apply to a specific case cannot be estimated objectively.

Kaye and Sensabaugh (2000) suggest that instead of pursuing a numerical estimate, each laboratory should document all the steps in its analyses and reserve portions of the DNA samples for independent testing whenever feasible. They state, "Scrutinizing the chain of custody, examining the laboratory's protocol, verifying that it adhered to that protocol, and conducting confirmatory tests if there are any suspicious circumstances can help to eliminate the hypothesis of laboratory error, whether or not a case-specific probability can be estimated. Furthermore, if the defendant has had a meaningful opportunity to retest a sample but has been unable or unwilling to obtain an inconsistent result, the relevance of a statistic based on past proficiency tests might be questionable." Kaye and Sensabaugh comment, "DNA profiling is valid and reliable, but confidence in a particular result depends on the quality control and quality assurance procedures in the laboratory."

The NRC (1996) stated, "We recognize that some risk of error is inevitable, as in any human endeavor, whatever efforts a laboratory takes to eliminate mistakes. Nonetheless, safeguards can be built into the system to prevent both types of errors and to identify and correct them. It is important that forensic laboratories use strict quality-control standards to minimize the risk of error." In an earlier report (1992), the NRC outlined several quality assurance steps that laboratories could take to safeguard against errors, including providing adequate training and education of all analysts so that they possess a thorough understanding of the principles, use, and limitations of methods and procedures applied to the tests they perform; that reagents and equipment are properly maintained and monitored; that appropriate controls are specified in procedures and are used; that new technical procedures are thoroughly tested to demonstrate their efficacy and reliability for examining evidence material before being implemented in casework; and that clearly written and well-understood procedures exist for handling and preserving the integrity of evidence, for laboratory safety, and for laboratory security.

The NRC also called for every forensic laboratory to participate in a program of external proficiency testing that periodically measures the capability of its analysts and the reliability of its analytic results. The crime laboratory accreditation program sponsored by the Laboratory Accreditation Board of the American Association of Crime Laboratory Directors (ASCLD/LAB) requires extensive documentation of all aspects of laboratory operations (including the education, training, and experience of personnel; the specification and calibration of equipment and reagents; the validation and description of analytic methods; the definition of appropriate standards and controls; the procedures for handling samples; and the guidelines for interpreting and reporting data), proficiency testing, internal and external audits of laboratory operations, and a plan to address deficiencies with corrective action and weigh their importance for laboratory competence. ASCLD has published general guidelines for forensic laboratories that address all aspects of forensic analysis and affirm the key element of quality assurance: the responsibility of laboratory managers for all aspects of laboratory operations and performance, including definition and documentation of standards for personnel training, procedures, equipment and facilities, and performance review.

Both the 1992 and the 1996 NRC reports support the key role that proficiency testing and audits play in the quality assurance process for forensic laboratories. Proficiency testing entails the testing of specimens submitted to the laboratory in the same form as evidence samples, while audits are independent reviews of laboratory operations conducted to determine whether the laboratory is performing according to a defined standard. An optimum program contains both internal and external assessment processes.

An "open" or "declared" type of proficiency testing presents the analyst with a set of samples in a mock-case scenario, and the analyst is asked to determine which samples could have a common source. The analyst is aware that the samples are being used in a proficiency test. Open proficiency testing evaluates analytical methods and interpretation of results; it identifies systematic problems due to equipment, materials, the laboratory environment (such as contamination), and analyst misjudgment. A benefit of open proficiency testing conducted by external entities is that many laboratories can test the same set of samples, thus allowing inter-laboratory comparison of performance and statistical evaluation of collective results.

In "full-blind" proficiency testing, the analyst does not know that a proficiency test is being conducted. It has been argued by commentators that full-blind testing provides a more accurate test of functional proficiency because the analyst will not take extra care in analyzing samples. Whether or not that is so, this form of proficiency testing evaluates a broader aspect of laboratory operation, from the receipt of the evidence at the front desk through analysis and interpretation to final reporting.

At the time of the NRC reports, the National Institute of Justice (NIJ) had reported that although several of the large laboratory systems conduct blind testing in-house, there is no blind, external, DNA proficiency testing program generally available to public or private laboratories. The NRC reports pointed to a few problematic issues with blind testing, including the cost of implementation, the risk that DNA data from an innocent donor to the test might end up in criminal DNA databanks, and the chance that the test would impose excessive costs and time demands on law enforcement agencies.

The NRC reports advised that regular audits of laboratory operations complement proficiency testing in the monitoring of general laboratory performance. The objective of any audit is to compare a facility's performance with its professed quality policies and objectives. Audits normally address all aspects of laboratory operations related to performance, including issues not covered by proficiency testing, such as equipment-calibration schedules and case-management records. The 1996 NRC report cautioned, however, "The objective of both proficiency testing and auditing is to improve laboratory performance by identifying problems that need to be corrected. Neither is designed to measure error rates."

ERRORS AND CONTAMINATION

The NRC (1996) declared, "Every human activity is associated with some risk of error. There are potential sources of error at every stage in the processing of physical evidence, from collection in the field through laboratory analysis to interpretation of results of analysis. Not all lapses have deleterious consequences; many have no consequences. Many are readily identified and can be corrected. The lapses of most concern, however, are the ones that might lead to a false match. False exclusions are important but are unlikely to lead to false convictions. There is no single solution to the problem of error. To achieve accurate results, care and attention to detail and independent checks must be used at all stages of the analytical process."

One issue of concern is sample mishandling and data-recording errors. The complexity of the evidence-handling process lends itself to mishap unless those individuals handling the evidence are meticulous. Mix-ups and mislabeling of biological samples, trace evidence, or results can occur at any point from the time of collection at the crime scene to the writing of the final report.

Undetected mishandling of evidence can lead to false matches; while the genetic types of the samples might have been determined correctly by the analyst, the inferred connections between the samples can be incorrect because of sample mix-up. The 1996 NRC report states, "Sample mishandling and incorrect recording of data can happen with any kind of physical evidence and are of great concern in all fields of forensic science. The concern regarding mishandling is compounded by the reality that most forensic laboratories have little or no control over the handling of evidence elsewhere. Accordingly, it is desirable to have safeguards not only to protect against mix-ups in the laboratory but also to detect mix-ups that might have occurred anywhere in the process."

Safeguards against sample mishandling in the field include proper training of crime scene investigators who collect evidence in the field, as well as analysts on the bench in the forensic laboratory who are trained to handle only one piece of evidence at a time to prevent mix-ups. The 1996 NRC report adds further, "Sample mix-up or mislabeling in the analysis stream (for example, transfer of a sample solution to the wrong tube, loading of a sample into the wrong lane on an electrophoresis gel, and misrecording of data) can be minimized by rigorous adherence to defined procedures for sample-handling and data entry."

Key to determining if an error has been made is multiple testing to ensure sample integrity and consistency of results, as inconsistencies among samples believed to be of common origin can indicate a mix-up. For example, gender testing in cases in which both males and females are involved can serve as a consistency check and has been used to verify suspected mislabeling. The 1996 NRC report states, "One benefit of the high discriminating power of DNA typing is the detection of sample-mishandling errors that might not have been recognized with classical blood-group and protein-marker testing. Because an analyst might fail to notice an inconsistent result or a recording error, it is important to have analytical results reviewed by a second person, preferably one not familiar with the origin of the samples or issues in question. An independent reviewer can also catch flaws in analytical reasoning and interpretation."

The NRC (1996) adds that retesting is the ultimate safeguard against sample mix-ups; in most cases, it is possible to retain portions of the original evidence items and portions of the samples from different stages of the testing. For example, sample retention is facilitated when PCR-based typing methods are used for testing. The NRC adds, "Allegations of sample mishandling lose credibility if those making the allegation have rejected the opportunity for a retest . . . whenever possible, a portion of the original sample should be retained or returned to the submitting agency, as established by laboratory policy."

Allegations of contamination in forensic laboratories around the country are an issue that has made headlines of late. Inadvertent contamination can occur during sample handling by crime scene investigators and law enforcement personnel out in the field, or by analysts on the bench in the forensic laboratory. The background environment from which the evidence is collected can also cause contamination, as can extraneous evidence such as items left behind by investigators such as hairs, cigarette butts, or footwear impressions. At issue is that this kind of cross-contamination can result in samples that appear to be mixtures of material from several persons and, in the worst case, that only the contaminating type might be detectable.

The NRC (1996) explains the dilemma: "The concern is greater with PCR-based typing methods than with VNTR analysis because PCR can amplify very small amounts of DNA. A false match could occur if the genetic type of the contaminating materials by chance matched the genetic type of a principal (such as a suspect) in the case or, worse, if the contaminant itself came from a suspect in the case."

"The issue with PCR is simply that it is a sensitive procedure and therefore you have the potential for contamination," says Kobilinsky. "What it boils down to is how you reach conclusions about your results. Is there any indication of contamination? That's why forensic laboratories include so many kinds of controls, both positive and negative controls, because we hope that if there is contamination, it will be revealed at that point. If it is not, it may be revealed in the analysis of the evidence itself. It's something that every defense attorney can talk about just as they did with the O.J. Simpson case, but that doesn't mean it happened in a particular case. PCR is an incredibly wondrous procedure."

"The Simpson case set a low watermark for DNA," adds Kobilinsky, who served as a consultant to the CBS network on this case. "It was a case where the defense attorneys took the evidence and they painted it in such a way as to make the jury simply not pay attention to it. At that stage in the DNA revolution, scientists did not know how to properly deliver testimony about DNA. The jury didn't pay attention to it. There was no contamination. The evidence pointed strongly in one direction; the stats were astronomical. The outcome of the case was compromised because the testimony was not delivered properly and there were flaws in the crime scene work. With all the flaws, the evidence still was not contaminated." Recommendations from the NRC for the safeguarding against inadvertent contamination include following rigorous procedures for sample handling from field to laboratory.

The NRC recommends keeping evidence samples separated from reference samples. Contamination from sample handling or from the background environment can be detected in several ways. Background control samples can be used to determine whether background contamination is present, and testing for multiple loci increases the chance of differentiating between contaminant and true sources of a sample. Finally, redundancy in testing provides a consistency check; the chance that multiple samples would all be contaminated the same way is small.

Mixed samples present an entirely different challenge, since they are contaminated by their very nature. The 1996 NRC report explains, "Post-coital vaginal swabs, for example, are expected to contain a mixture of semen and vaginal fluids, and shed blood from different persons might run together. Such samples are part of the territory of forensic science and must be dealt with whenever feasible. Sperm DNA can be separated from non-sperm DNA with differential DNA extraction. Detection of sample mixtures of other kinds is generally revealed with genetic typing. Mixtures show the composite of the individual types present; the proportions of the different types reflect the proportions of the contributors to the mixture. Testing samples collected from different areas of a mixed stain can sometimes allow the genetic types of the contributors to be more clearly distinguished."

A third type of contamination, known as *carryover contamination*, is not an issue with VNTR analysis, but it can be problematic for PCR testing. Carryover contamination can occur when a PCR amplification product finds its way into a reaction mix before the target template DNA is added. The carryover product can then be amplified along with the DNA from an evidence sample, and the result can be that an incorrect genetic type is assigned to the evidence sample. A false match can occur if the genetic type of the contaminant matches by chance the genetic type of a principal in the case; in the worst case, the contaminant originates from another party in the case. According to the 1996 NRC report, primary safeguards against carryover contamination include the use of different work areas for pre-PCR and post-PCR sample handling, the use of biological safety hoods, the use of dedicated equipment for the task, and maintenance of a one-way flow of material from pre-PCR to post-PCR work areas so that PCR product cannot come into contact with sample materials.

Sometimes, errors can be introduced into the DNA analysis process through the inadvertent use of faulty reagents, equipment, controls, or techniques, leading to failed tests without results, or ambiguous test results. For example, in the loading of an electrophoresis gel, a sample loaded in one lane might leak into an adjacent lane, which might then appear to contain a mixed sample. Confusion resulting from lane-leakage problems is typically avoided by leaving alternate lanes empty or by placing critical samples in nonadjacent lanes. In situations involving these kinds of lapses, a breakdown is usually readily apparent from the appearance of the results. Review of analytical results by a second analyst who is unfamiliar with the issues in the case can protect against lapses of judgment on the part of the primary analyst.

In addition, the NRC reports emphasize that adherence by laboratory personnel to the provisions of a rigorous quality assurance program can help detect and prevent these kinds of missteps. The NRC adds, "Moreover, regular monitoring of test outcomes with standards and controls allows recognition of gradually emerging problems with reagents, equipment, controls, standards, and overall procedure that might otherwise be overlooked."

DNA AND WRONGFUL CONVICTIONS

Nowhere are the stakes as high as they are in capital cases. According to the Capital Case Data Project of the American Judicature Society, in 2005, for example, 139 people were sentenced to death in the United States. Of these, 125 were first-time death sentences, and 14 were imposed through new sentencing proceedings after appellate reversals. Almost half of those sentenced to death were multiple murderers (66 of 139), based on the fact that they either were convicted for multiple murders, or were otherwise proven to have committed multiple other murders closely connected with those for which they were convicted.

Nearly nothing can polarize the legal and forensic science and law enforcement communities like the death penalty can. Capital punishment is an incendiary topic, and wrongful convictions are the powder keg that can set off heated dialogue about the role forensic science plays in exonerating the innocent and convicting the guilty. Taking the temperature of the general public about its thoughts on the issue, a nationwide Harris Poll of 1,015 adults surveyed in 1999 revealed a 71 percent to 21 percent majority in favor of capital punishment. This number is less than it was in 1997 (when 75 percent favored it), but more than it was in the 1980s, 1970s, or 1960s (in 1965 a 47 percent to 38 percent plurality opposed the death penalty). The poll also revealed a 43 percent plurality that actually favored an increase in the use of the death penalty, while 21 percent favored a decrease, and 28 percent favored no change. However, in 1997, 53 percent of those polled wanted to see more executions.

The 1999 Harris Poll found that 95 percent of those surveyed accepted that some innocent people were wrongly convicted of murder; on average they believed that 11 percent of all those convicted were innocent. Women (13 percent) thought that wrongful convictions occur more often than do men (8 percent), and Democrats (12 percent) more than the Republicans (7 percent). That many people favor the death penalty while being cognizant of wrongful convictions is not necessarily an oxymoron; another question showed that if everyone believed that many innocent people were convicted of murder, they might not support capital punishment. Ninety-five percent of all adults said they would not support capital punishment if they believed that a "substantial number of innocent people are convicted of murder." Pollsters cautioned, however, that responses to these kinds of questions as to what people might favor in hypothetical situations are notoriously faulty at predicting how people would react in real-world situations.

While some members of the legal and forensic science communities debate the fact that they are in pursuit of the concept of an absolute truth in the courtroom, others believe truth is the reason for the adjudication of cases. Former Attorney General Janet Reno has commented, "Our system of criminal justice is best described as a search for the truth. Increasingly, the forensic use of DNA technology is an important ally in that search. The development of DNA technology furthers the search for truth by helping police and prosecutors in the fight against violent crime. Through the use of DNA evidence, prosecutors are often able to conclusively establish the guilt of a defendant. Moreover, as some of the commentaries suggest, DNA evidence—like fingerprint evidence—offers prosecutors important new tools for the identification and apprehension of some of the most violent perpetrators, particularly in cases of sexual assault. At the same time, DNA aids the search for truth by exonerating the innocent" (Connors et al., 1996).

Reno acknowledges, however, that the U.S. criminal justice system is not infallible, and says that "the search for truth took a tortuous path" when the final disposition of a case is that of a wrongful conviction. Many blame the perception that DNA is unassailable (Connors et al., 1996). Thompson et al. (2003) assert, "Promoters of forensic DNA testing have done a good job selling the public, and even many criminal defense lawyers, on the idea that DNA tests provide a unique and infallible identification. DNA evidence has sent thousands of people to prison and, in recent years, has played a vital role in exonerating men who were falsely convicted. Even former critics of DNA testing, like Barry Scheck, are widely quoted attesting to the reliability of the DNA evidence in their cases. It is easy to assume that any past problems with DNA evidence have been worked out and that the tests are now unassailable. The problem with this assumption is that it ignores case-to-case variations in the nature and quality of DNA evidence. Although DNA technology has indeed improved since it was first used just 15 years ago, and the tests have the potential to produce powerful and convincing results, that potential is not realized in every case." Many critics of DNA say that even when the reliability and admissibility of the underlying test is well established and has been validated, there is no guarantee that a test will produce reliable results every time. As with any kind of scientific test, there can be case-specific issues that affect the quality and relevance of DNA test results, thus reducing the probative value of the DNA. Thompson et al. add, "The criminal justice system presently does a poor job of distinguishing unassailably powerful DNA evidence from weak, misleading DNA evidence. The fault for that serious lapse lies partly with those defense lawyers who fail to evaluate the DNA evidence adequately in their cases."

Wrongful convictions of the innocent are the U.S. criminal justice system's equivalent of a major catastrophe, such as an airplane crash, say attorneys Barry Scheck and Peter Neufeld, co-directors of the Innocence Project. They explain that the guilty are not punished, the innocent are imprisoned or sentenced to death, and the real perpetrators remain free to commit more crimes. And when an innocent person is exonerated by DNA testing or other evidence, our justice system has no institutional mechanism to evaluate and address the causes of that wrongful conviction. Unlike a wrongful conviction, Scheck and Neufeld say, in the case of an airplane crash, the crash is subjected to a thorough investigation into the cause of the event and determinations are made on how the problem can be corrected and a future event can be prevented.

Those involved in the work of the Innocence Project say that to effectively address the recurring, institutional problems that contribute to the conviction of the innocent, states should create innocence commissions to monitor, investigate, and address errors in the criminal justice system. When a wrongful conviction occurs, these commissions should be empowered to undertake a comprehensive review of the system's failures, and ask: What went wrong? Was it systemic error or an individual's mistake? Was there any official misconduct? What can be done to correct the problem and prevent it from happening in the future? Innocence commissions have been created in several states; in 2002, the Supreme Court of North Carolina, in response to highly publicized wrongful convictions, became the first state to announce the creation of an innocence commission. In 2003, Connecticut became the first state to use legislative action to create an innocence commission. Several other state legislatures have considered proposals for similar commissions.

In Chapter 15, we discuss the ways defense attorneys are educating themselves about challenging scientific and forensic evidence, including DNA testing results—and ways prosecutors are shoring up their cases. No matter where these respective legal and science practitioners fall on the adjudication continuum, they cannot deny that wrongful convictions are triggering a tremendous amount of scrutiny of the way the criminal justice systems conducts its business. The case of Glen Woodall, of Huntington, West Virginia, captured its share of headlines and helped expose an analyst's malfeasance that rocked the forensic science and legal universes. Two women, in separate incidents, were abducted at knifepoint in a shopping mall parking lot. Both times the perpetrator wore a ski mask and forced the victims to close their eyes throughout the attack. In the first instance, the attacker drove around in the woman's car, repeatedly raped her, and stole a gold watch and $5 in cash. The victim opened her eyes briefly to note that the assailant wore brown pants and was uncircumcised. In the second case, the man repeatedly raped the woman and stole a gold watch. This woman was able to note the man's boots, jacket, and hair color; she also noted that he was uncircumcised.

On July 8, 1987, a jury found Woodall guilty of first-degree sexual assault of one woman, first-degree sexual abuse of a second woman, kidnapping both women, and aggravated robbery of both women. He was sentenced by the circuit court to two life terms without parole and to 203 to 335 years in prison, to be served consecutively. The prosecution based its case on several points: A state police chemist testified that Woodall's blood secretions matched secretions in a semen sample from the evidence; a comparison of body and beard hair from the defendant was consistent with hair recovered from a victim's car; partial visual identification of the defendant was made by one of the victims; one victim identified clothing that matched clothing found in the defendant's house; both victims testified that the assailant was not circumcised, in common with the defendant; and a distinctive odor lingering on the defendant was noted by both victims and also was detected at the defendant's workplace.

During the pretrial hearing, the judge denied a defense request for an "experimental" DNA test of the defendant's blood and semen samples from the victims' clothing. Denial was based on defense inability to offer any expert testimony on the test's validity or reliability. After trial, the defense raised this issue again, and a DNA test was finally performed; the court held that test results were inconclusive. On July 6, 1989, the West Virginia Supreme Court of Appeals affirmed Woodall's conviction. Woodall continued to file motions to allow DNA testing of the evidence, filing several appeal petitions and habeas corpus petitions with both the trial court and with the West Virginia Supreme Court. The state supreme court finally allowed the evidence to be released to the defense for additional DNA testing; this evidence was forwarded to Forensic Science Associates (FSA). FSA conducted PCR testing of the semen samples from the vaginal swabs from the original rape kits. FSA concluded that the assailant in both cases had the same DQ alpha type and neither matched Woodall's type. These results were reviewed and confirmed in testimony by several laboratories and forensics experts, including Dr. Alec Jeffreys and Dr. David Bing of the Center for Blood Research (CBR). CBR also conducted its own PCR analysis and arrived at the same results as FSA.

Woodall submitted a habeas corpus petition based on the DNA test results. On July 15, 1991, the trial court held a hearing on the petition and vacated Woodall's conviction. Other relevant evidence included secret hypnosis of the two victims and a romantic relationship between one of the victims and an investigating officer. The court set bond at $150,000 for Woodall and ordered him placed on electronic home monitoring. CBR continued conducting RFLP analysis and eliminated three potential donors as sources of the sperm, to counter the prosecution's argument that the stains may have come from consensual partners. The RFLP analysis also excluded Woodall, and the state conducted its own DNA test; its results also excluded Woodall, as noted in a report of April 23, 1992. As a result of the additional testing, West Virginia moved to dismiss Woodall's indictment on May 4, 1992, and the trial court granted the motion. Woodall served four years of his sentence in prison and spent a year under electronic home confinement.

The state police chemist in this case, Fred Zain, was investigated by the West Virginia attorney general's office and the state supreme court of appeals for providing perjured testimony in criminal cases. Woodall was the first person whose conviction was overturned after Zain testified for the state. More than 130 cases in which Zain either performed lab tests or provided the testimony were being reviewed by the state attorney general's office, and an investigation was launched in several Texas counties where Zain worked and testified as a laboratory expert. (Fred Zain is discussed in Chapter 6.) Woodall was awarded $1 million from West Virginia for his wrongful conviction and false imprisonment.

Many commentators point to the work of Borchard (1932) and Bedau and Radelet (1992), which reviewed 65 cases and 416 cases, respectively, relating to erroneous convictions. These studies, more often than not, indicate the presence of a few common factors that explain wrongful convictions, including mistaken eyewitness identification, coerced confessions, unreliable forensic laboratory work, law enforcement misconduct, and ineffective representation of counsel.

With cases like Woodall's coming to the forefront, capital jurisprudence was placed under the microscope in a number of books and studies, including one of the more high-profile reports, Convicted by Juries, Exonerated by Science: Case Studies in the Use of DNA Evidence to Establish Innocence after Trial (Connors et al., 1996), which examined 28 cases of wrongful conviction that shared a number of similar characteristics. Most of the cases were adjudicated during the mid- to late-1980s, when forensic DNA technology was not readily accessible.

In each of the cases, a defendant was convicted of a crime and was serving a sentence of incarceration. While in prison, each defendant obtained, through an attorney, case evidence for DNA testing and consented to a comparison of the evidence-derived DNA to his own DNA sample. In each case, the results showed that there was not a match, and the defendant was ultimately set free. All 28 cases involved some form of sexual assault; in six of these cases, perpetrators also murdered their victims. All alleged perpetrators were male and all victims were female. All but one case involved a jury trial. Of the cases where the time required for jury deliberations was known, most had verdicts returned in less than a day. The 28 defendants served a total of 197 years in prison (with an average duration of almost seven years) before being released as a result of DNA testing. The longest time served was 11 years; the shortest was nine months. For myriad legal reasons, defendants in several cases remained in prison for months after exculpatory DNA test results. Many defendants qualified for public defenders or appointed counsel. Most defendants appealed their convictions at least once, and most of the appeals focused on trial error, such as ineffective counsel or new evidence.

In the report, Connors et al. (1996) demonstrated that the 28 cases shared several common themes in the evidence presented during and after trial, including the following:

- Eyewitness identification placing the defendant with the victim or near the crime scene
- Use of forensic evidence that substantially narrowed the field of possibilities to include the defendant
- Alleged government malfeasance or misconduct, including perjured testimony at trial, police and prosecutors who intentionally kept exculpatory evidence from the defense, and intentionally erroneous laboratory tests and expert testimony admitted at trial as evidence
- Evidence discovered after trial
- DNA testing, most frequently by private laboratories, conducted using blood from defendants, blood or blood-related evidence from victims, and semen stains on articles of the victims'

clothing or on nearby items (in more than half of the cases, the prosecution either conducted a DNA test independent of that of the defense or sent test results obtained by the defendant's laboratory to a different one to determine whether the laboratory used by the defense interpreted test results properly)

■ Problematic preservation of evidence, including evidence samples that had deteriorated to the point where DNA testing could not be performed, or that the chain of custody demonstrated having a lack of adherence to proper procedures

The report by Connors et al. (1996) discussed a number of issues relating to policy, including reliability of eyewitness testimony; reliability of non-DNA analyses of forensic evidence compared to DNA testing; competence and reliability of DNA laboratory procedures; preservation of evidence for DNA testing; training in DNA forensic uses; third-party consensual sex sources; multiple-defendant crimes; and posttrial relief. This report's findings, as well as the findings of a report by the National Research Council (NRC), have been interpreted by some as a license to indict forensic science. The NRC states, "There is no substantial dispute about the underlying (DNA) scientific principles. However, the adequacy of laboratory procedures and the competence of the experts who testify should remain open to inquiry."

There is considerable agreement in the suggestions of the report by Connors et al. (1996) and the NRC report; the suggestions also reflect much of what has been proposed by other reports and agencies that have been discussed throughout this book. On the issue of lab quality, within the context of preventing wrongful convictions, the reports by Connors et al. and the NRC agree that there must be standardization to ensure quality and reliability, and that every forensic laboratory engaged in DNA testing must have a formal, detailed program of quality assurance and quality control. The NRC states, "Quality-assurance programs in individual laboratories alone are insufficient to ensure high standards. External mechanisms are needed to ensure adherence to the practices of quality assurance. Potential mechanisms include individual certification, laboratory accreditation, and state or federal regulation."

The report by Connors et al. (1996) asserts that DNA testing for exculpatory purposes should be conducted in a qualified laboratory, and the results, if they exculpate the suspect, should be accepted by both parties. In some states, sentenced felons may experience difficulty obtaining access to evidence for DNA testing. With an increasing volume of criminal cases, some police agencies destroy evidence when defendants have exhausted their appeals. Even when defendants obtain access to the evidence, it may be too deteriorated for DNA testing. In some of the study cases, insufficient evidence prevented laboratories from conducting RFLP testing, but PCR testing was still possible. (This issue is also discussed in the discovery section, earlier in this chapter.)

The question of typing is a moot point, however, if biological evidence is compromised when the proper chain of custody of the evidence is not maintained. Connors et al. (1996) point out, "At the trial stage, however, the U.S. Supreme Court has ruled that unless a criminal defendant can show bad faith on the part of the police, failure to preserve potentially useful evidence does not constitute a denial of due process of law. After a defendant's conviction, prosecutors are not required by constitutional duty to preserve evidence indefinitely."

Equally important to the prevention of wrongful convictions is a solid understanding of the evidence and the scientific testimony provided by expert witnesses in court. Connors et al. (1996) comment, "The introduction of DNA technology into the criminal trial setting is likely to create uncertainty, spawned in part by the complexity of the technology, and also to possibly generate unrealistic expectations of the technology's power in the minds of some or all of the players: prosecution, defense, judges, and jurors. The scientific complexities of the technology may influence all parties to rely more heavily on expert testimony than on other types of evidence."

A byproduct of this is the expectation of jurors that DNA evidence will be available in every case they hear, which is erroneous. This expectation, such as it is, according to Connors et al. (1996), "will place more pressure on prosecutors to use the technology whenever possible, especially as the cost decreases. Prosecutors must be trained on when to use the technology and how to interpret results for the jury. When the prosecution uses DNA evidence, the defense will be forced to attack it through expert testimony. The defense must rebut the persuasiveness of the evidence for the jury." Citing the NRC report's comment that mere cross-examination by the defense attorney inexperienced in DNA matters is insufficient, Connors et al. (1996) add, ". . . defense counsel as well as the prosecution and judiciary must receive training in the forensic uses of DNA technology." This is in line with the NRC's strong recommendation that all stakeholders in the criminal justice process arm themselves with credible knowledge.

With this education process comes the realization that DNA technology sometimes is constrained in its ability to convict or exonerate. For example, Connors et al. (1996) comment, "Multiple-suspect crimes present a particular problem for use of DNA identification as a crime-solving tool. In multiple-suspect sexual assaults without eyewitnesses, such as a rape-murder, it is possible that only one of the suspects ejaculated in, or even raped, the victim. In such cases, DNA testing of semen would seem likely to exculpate one or more of the suspects. This type of situation presents a real dilemma for police and prosecutors. Because of exculpatory DNA tests on semen and possibly other exculpatory evidence (an alibi, lack of other physical evidence), pressure mounts on prosecutors to release one or more of the suspects. The only other evidence against them may be the testimony of a suspect who is matched to the crime by DNA analysis."

As for the future of DNA evidence, some say that its level of sophistication can serve to eliminate or substantially reduce the DNA war in the courtroom in the first place. Rowe (1996) comments, "The advent of DNA typing will go a long way toward preventing miscarriages of justice in the future. Most wrongly accused suspects will be exonerated during the initial testing of physical evidence, long before prosecution would even be considered. The quantity and quality of documentation required by laboratory quality assurance/quality control protocols preclude the wholesale falsification of test results. The minuscule quantities of DNA required for PCR-based typing procedures also allow the preservation of sufficient DNA for independent laboratory testing."

However, not everyone is convinced that DNA technology alone, without the requisite proper execution of this testing by competent forensic scientists and analysts, can be the silver bullet for wrongful convictions.

Neufeld and Scheck (1996) state, "Post-conviction DNA exonerations provide a remarkable opportunity to reexamine, with greater insight than ever before, the strengths and weaknesses of our criminal justice system and how they bear on the all-important question of factual innocence. The dimensions of the factual innocence problem exceed the impressive number of post-conviction DNA exonerations . . . indeed, there is a strong scientific basis for believing these matters represent just the tip of a very deep and disturbing iceberg of cases."

Neufeld and Scheck (1996) point to data collected by the FBI since the inauguration of forensic DNA testing in 1989. They charge that in approximately one-quarter of sexual assault cases referred to the FBI where results could be obtained, the primary suspect has been excluded by forensic DNA testing. They explain that FBI officials report that out of about 10,000 sexual assault cases since 1989, approximately 2,000 tests have been inconclusive, about

2,000 tests have excluded the primary suspect, and about 6,000 have matched or included the primary suspect. Neufeld and Scheck assert, "The fact that these percentages have remained constant for seven years, and that the National Institute of Justice's informal survey of private laboratories reveals a strikingly similar 26-percent exclusion rate, strongly suggests that post-arrest and post-conviction DNA exonerations are tied to some strong, underlying systemic problems that generate erroneous accusations and convictions."

Neufeld and Scheck (1996) rightly point out further that the sexual assault referrals made to the FBI ordinarily involve cases where identity is at issue (where there is no consent defense), the non-DNA evidence linking the suspect to the crime is eyewitness identification, the suspects have been arrested or indicted based on non-DNA evidence, and the biological evidence has been recovered from a place in the victim's body that makes DNA results on the issue of identity essentially dispositive. Neufeld and Scheck admit, "It is, of course, possible that some of the FBI's sexual assault exclusions have included false negatives. False negatives could occur, for example, because of laboratory error; situations where the victim of the assault conceals the existence of a consensual sexual partner within 48 hours of the incident and the accused suspect did not ejaculate; or multiple assailant sexual assault cases where none of the apprehended suspects ejaculated (the FBI counts the exclusion of all multiple suspects in a case as just one exclusion).

Nonetheless, even with these caveats, it is still plain that forensic DNA testing is prospectively exonerating a substantial number of innocent individuals who would have otherwise stood trial, frequently facing the difficult task of refuting mistaken eyewitness identification by a truthful crime victim who would rightly deserve juror sympathy."

"The extent of factually incorrect convictions in our system must be much greater than anyone wants to believe," assert Neufeld and Scheck (1996). "Post-arrest and post-conviction DNA exonerations have invariably involved analysis of sexual assault evidence, even if a murder charge was involved, that proved the existence of mistaken eyewitness identification. Since there does not seem to be anything inherent in sexual assault cases that would make eyewitnesses more prone to mistakes than in robberies or other serious crimes where the crucial proof is eyewitness identification, it naturally follows that the rate of mistaken identifications and convictions is similar to DNA exoneration cases."

Paul C. Giannelli, a law professor at Case Western Reserve University in Cleveland, Ohio, and co-author of *Scientific Evidence*, asserts there is a body of flawed science behind every wrongful conviction. He points to an assertion made most strongly in the 2000 book, *Actual Innocence*, which examined more than 60 DNA-based exonerations. Its authors, Barry Scheck, Peter Neufeld, and Jim Dwyer, assert that one-third of these wrongful convictions involved "tainted or fraudulent science," in addition to abuse of expert testimony. Giannelli says that the improved use of scientific evidence in criminal trials depends on the regulation of crime laboratories and the independent validation of scientific evidence, and adds, "In other words, forensic science needs more science."

DNA has been called the gold standard for its basis in the bio-chemical sciences and the rigorous validation process it has endured, and many commentators wonder aloud why other forensic disciplines used to adjudicate cases haven't been subjected to the same scrutiny and testing. Saks and Koehler (1991) comment, "Forensic scientists, like scientists in all other fields, should subject their claims to methodologically rigorous empirical tests. The results of these tests should be published and debated. Until such steps are taken, the strong claims of forensic scientists must be regarded with far more caution than they traditionally have been."

Giannelli points to molecular biologist Eric Lander, who observed, "At present, forensic science is virtually unregulated, with the paradoxical result that clinical laboratories must meet higher standards to be allowed to diagnose strep throat than forensic labs must meet to put a defendant on death row." Giannelli writes, "In the interim, there have been a number of voluntary attempts to improve the system, such as accreditation of laboratories by ASCLD/ LAB. Nevertheless, except for New York, there is no mandatory accreditation.

Jones (2002) observes, "Unfortunately, while the ASCLD/LAB program has been successful in accrediting over 200 laboratories, a large number of forensic laboratories in the U.S. remain unaccredited by any agency. A similar situation exists with death investigation agencies accredited by the National Association of Medical Examiners (NAME); 40 such medical systems have been accredited, covering only 25 percent of the U.S. population. The same dichotomy exists in certification programs for the practicing forensic scientist, even though forensic certification boards for all the major disciples have been in existence for over a decade. Why have forensic laboratories and individuals been so reluctant to become accredited or certified?"

Giannelli (2003) blames the situation on a lack of funding, and observes, "Meeting accreditation and certification standards costs money, and the underfunding of crime labs is chronic." He adds, "To improve scientific evidence in criminal cases, the nation's crime laboratories need to be improved. They need to be funded so they can be accredited and their examiners certified. The lessons learned from the DNA admissibility wars should not be forgotten. Valid protocols and proficiency testing are important."

Lander and Budowle (1994) comment, "The initial outcry over DNA typing standards concerned laboratory problems: poorly defined rules for declaring a match; experiments without controls; contaminated probes and samples; and sloppy interpretation of autoradiograms. Although there is no evidence that these technical failings resulted in any wrongful convictions, the lack of standards seemed to be a recipe for trouble."

THE POWER OF DNA: AN ANALYSIS OF NATIONWIDE FORENSIC DNA CAPABILITIES AND CAPACITY

Even as the detractors fire away at forensic science, the community must contend with its numerous infrastructure needs, as discussed in Chapter 5. One of the biggest challenges facing forensic laboratories that conduct DNA testing is the infrastructure needs and backlog issues. An in-depth forensic DNA assessment project was undertaken by Smith Alling Lane in partnership with the Division of Governmental Studies and Services at Washington State University (Lovrich et al., 2003). Employing a number of data-collection processes, including a nationwide mail assessment of local and state forensics laboratories and law enforcement agencies, the researchers attempted to bring to bear quantitative methodology and rigorous qualitative analysis on a question that has increasingly occupied public debate in both law enforcement and public policy circles. The research team recognized the renewed interest in DNA testing, fueled in part by newspaper headlines of wrongful convictions and the solving of cold cases.

Lovrich et al. (2003) observe that prior to the researchers' undertaking, questions of capacity and backlog at local law enforcement agencies and the corresponding impact, or potential for impact, at crime laboratories, had not be widely addressed. Lovrich et al. state, "While popular wisdom has acknowledged the existence of a backlog of cases that might benefit from the application of forensic DNA analysis, no clear insight into the extent of any such backlog has previously been available." The researchers' report was the first comprehensive attempt to make scientifically supportable estimates of the numbers of unsolved criminal cases in the U.S. that might benefit from DNA analysis, to assess both law enforcement and laboratory capacities for dealing with cases involving DNA, and to identify significant issues relating to the expansion of the use of DNA forensic analysis in criminal cases.

There were limitations placed on the study. Responses to the nationwide DNA survey were received from 1,692 law enforcement agencies, 70 local laboratories, and 50 state laboratories; the researchers acknowledged that smaller agencies did not respond at as high a rate as did the large agencies, and in light of this, the researchers took a conservative approach to the analysis of needs and in the estimation of backlogs. In follow-up questioning with non-responding agencies, the researchers discovered that a lack of resources was the primary reason given for failure to complete the survey; in fact, in many jurisdictions, case management systems were either nonexistent or so antiquated as to be of little help to the assessment process. The researchers also found that many agencies lacked the manpower needed to manually review old case files for open cases that may contain DNA evidence. These limitations notwithstanding, the report paints an interesting picture of the capacity of DNA units in U.S. forensic laboratories.

One significant shortcoming of FBI data is that its crime data summaries do not identify cases with biological evidence that could yield DNA findings. Using the data from the mail survey, it was possible for the researchers to extrapolate total numbers of backlogged cases. They calculated an average figure for each type of case for each of the six strata of law enforcement agencies; that average number was then multiplied by the total number of agencies of that size in the U.S. to obtain a national backlog subtotal for each stratum. Adding up these figures provides an estimated national total for each type of crime. This approach provided the researchers with an estimated backlog of unsolved murder cases of more than 170,000 cases—more than 60,000 of which involve DNA evidence. The same estimation approach yields figures of more than 593,000 total unsolved rapes and more than 430,000 unsolved rape cases featuring forensic DNA evidence. The researchers also acknowledged that these approaches were problematic, since the FBI's data did not include DNA information, and the numbers obtained from the mail survey skewed upward by the presence of the very large agencies. The researchers calculated estimates in a number of different ways to ensure they are not the artifacts of a single method of statistical estimation.

The researchers reported that many law enforcement agencies indicated they could not provide an accurate estimate on the number of unsolved rapes and homicides without a time-consuming, comprehensive review of their case records. Lovrich et al. (2003) explain, "Many jurisdictions are not able, or possibly were not willing, to venture a guess as to how many cases are still open, much less speculate as to whether or not there may be biological evidence associated with such criminal offenses." Refined educated guesses, coupled with FBI crime statistics and conventional statistical estimation techniques, helped the researchers determine an estimate of the backlog of cases involving forensic DNA evidence. Lovrich et al. estimate that as of January 1, 2002, there are at least 49,000 unsolved murder cases in the U.S. Because this method of backlog estimation does not assess cases older than 10 years, and because it does not include the immediately previous calendar years' figures, the researchers emphasized that this figure is, in all probability, a low estimate. The researchers added that applying the same cautious approach to the estimation of unsolved rapes leads to a figure of at least 470,000 unsolved cases.

The mail survey asked responding agencies to count unsolved cases dating back to 1982. With regard to unsolved rape and unsolved homicide cases, Lovrich et al. (2003) reported there were an estimated 96,141 unsolved homicide cases and an estimated 304,178 unsolved rape cases reported by local law enforcement agencies in the U.S. in 2002–2003. Upon combining these two estimates, researchers arrive at an extrapolated total of as few as 400,319 to as many as 432,179 unsolved homicide and rape cases nationally. Law enforcement agencies were also asked how many murder and rape cases contained possible DNA evidence that had not been sent to a laboratory for testing. These findings show that a substantial portion of the adjusted totals for rape (169,229) and homicide (51,774) cases had not been sent to a forensic laboratory for testing; using the adjusted totals, an extrapolated total of 221,003 cases may contain biological evidence that has not been sent to a forensic laboratory for DNA testing.

The researchers also determined that there were as many as 264,371 property offenses with possible biological evidence in the U.S. Adding to the aforementioned totals of rapes and homicides, property crimes and "other" cases with possible DNA evidence could number as high as 542,723 unsolved cases containing possible DNA analysis (Lovrich et al., 2003).

Issues relating to law enforcement that the researchers studied included where law enforcement agencies typically send cases for DNA analysis; biological evidence storage issues; the reasons why DNA evidence for either unsolved homicides or rapes is not sent to a crime laboratory for testing; and cold case squad reviews. With regard to the local and state crime laboratories, the capacity issues upon which researchers focused included those associated with the evidence typically compiled in backlogged cases; the cases that are currently within the statute of limitations; the expected backlog of cases estimated by the crime laboratories; the average time for analysis and the output capacity of the laboratories; the major barriers associated with processing DNA evidence, with particular attention to property offenses; the potential need for mitochondrial DNA testing; and cost/funding issues.

The researchers found that regarding general case processing, 80 percent of law enforcement agencies report that the primary location for sending DNA evidence for processing is state crime laboratories. Conversely, just about 12 percent of law enforcement agencies reported that local and regional crime laboratories are the primary places to which they send forensic DNA evidence for testing. Another 4 percent reported that their evidence is sent elsewhere.

Lovrich et al. (2003) determined that although a greater number of law enforcement agencies report that they send their cases to state laboratories for DNA analysis, a relatively significant proportion of the overall DNA casework in the U.S. is in fact conducted in local crime laboratories. They add that an estimated minimum of 80 million U.S. residents are being served by these local crime laboratories. Lovrich et al. explain, "With an estimated U.S. population of slightly more than 280 million according to the 2000 U.S. Census Bureau data, local laboratory DNA testing accounts for nearly 30 percent of all DNA testing being done in the country. Moreover, of the 25 U.S. cities with the highest crime rate per capita, more than half are being served by local crime laboratories."

It's an obvious truth that larger jurisdictions have greater needs for DNA testing; in addition to having a larger caseload of rapes and homicides in general, large law enforcement agencies reported a slightly higher estimate of the proportion of rape cases that are likely to contain DNA evidence. Fifty-three percent of large agencies estimated that between 75 and 100 percent of rape cases are likely to contain DNA evidence, relative to 47 percent of all other law enforcement agencies. With regard to homicides, roughly 58 percent of both large and all other law enforcement agencies estimated that between 75 and 100 percent of all homicides are likely to contain DNA evidence. It should be noted that these estimates reflect the expectations of law enforcement, and are not necessarily indicative of the percentage of cases that test positive for DNA at the crime laboratory.

Although it is true that the majority of forensic DNA analysis is performed by state laboratories, many local laboratories primarily serve major metropolitan populations that have high crime rates and therefore may generate a higher level of demand for DNA analysis. A number of law enforcement agencies outsource DNA analysis to either the FBI crime laboratory or to private forensic laboratories, but many more do not have the financial wherewithal to pay the fees associated with such forensic testing.

Of significant concern to law enforcement agencies, the researchers discovered, is the availability of proper storage space for unanalyzed evidence. Lovrich et al. (2003) explain, "Pressures on evidence storage space can result in degradable biological evidence being maintained under improper conditions—or worse yet, being discarded or not collected at all for a lack of space to store it safely. Lack of appropriate storage space can lead to valuable DNA evidence becoming degraded and requiring a more expensive and potentially less exact DNA analysis process to be employed."

In addition to the need to retain evidence from unsolved crimes in the event that new advances in forensic technology may identify a suspect in the future, researchers emphasized that law enforcement agencies are facing increasing statutory requirements to preserve evidence pertinent to cases considered solved. Lovrich et al. (2003) observe, "Cases where post-conviction DNA testing has resulted in extraordinary exoneration have led a number of state legislatures to impose requirements for the indefinite storage of evidence used in serious crime convictions. While such systematic storage activity is important to the enhancement of the criminal justice system's capacity to 'do justice' for its citizens, such requirements for evidence storage frequently take the form of an unfunded mandate passed down to local jurisdictions from their respective state governments."

The researchers noted that more than one-fifth of law enforcement agencies reported that some of their unanalyzed evidence is stored at the crime laboratory rather than in agency evidence repositories. At larger agencies, as much as 40 percent report this practice. The problem can be compounded by the fact that numerous forensic laboratories also are required to store evidence after analysis is completed, and therefore face many of the same unfunded mandates for evidence storage for solved cases as well as for unsolved cases. As a consequence many laboratories find they are responsible for storing not only their own cases—both unanalyzed backlog cases and analyzed evidence—but also those of the law enforcement jurisdictions they serve (Lovrich et al., 2003).

Lost evidence is an increasing concern for the law enforcement and forensic science communities, as the media seizes upon reports of large metropolitan law enforcement agencies discarding potential DNA evidence (such as rape kits) in an effort to create additional storage space for new evidence. Lovrich et al. (2003) observe, "Regardless of whether these reported actions were the result of honest mistakes or the consequence of faulty agency decision-making processes, the fact remains that this critical evidence is forever lost to future crime investigations." According to the survey, 79 percent of law enforcement agencies indicated that unanalyzed evidence usually is held in a centralized storage area; 61 percent of these agencies indicated that they currently have insufficient storage capacity for evidence retention needs relating to DNA evidence; and 75 percent of large law enforcement agencies indicated that gaining additional space for the effective preservation of evidence was either of "critical" or "highly critical" importance (Lovrich et al., 2003).

Contrary to what many laypersons may believe, not all DNA evidence has been sent to a forensic laboratory for testing. Lovrich et al. (2003) suggest that what may be driving these backlog numbers and storage capacity issues at local law enforcement agencies are the specific reasons behind why forensic DNA evidence from unsolved homicides and unsolved rapes have not been sent to a crime laboratory for testing. The primary reason for this, according to the researchers, is that a suspect has not yet been identified. Lovrich et al. comment, "Clearly, these 'no suspect' cases are exactly the types of crime scene evidence that need to be submitted in order for the DNA database to be effective. This finding is a strong indication that forensic DNA testing is not considered an investigatory tool by a significant portion of law enforcement agencies which have chosen not to send biological evidence to a crime laboratory for testing."

Other considerations for a lack of testing include the fact that a suspect has been identified but not yet charged, or that analysis was not requested by prosecutors. The researchers stated that these reasons given by law enforcement agencies "show the bias towards using DNA analysis as a tool for the prosecution but not necessarily as an aid to identifying a suspect," Lovrich et al. (2003) state. According to the researchers, an estimated 50 percent of respondents indicated that forensic DNA was not considered a tool for law enforcement criminal investigations. Rather, DNA evidence is considered a tool for the prosecution—evidence to secure a conviction after traditional police investigations have already identified the suspected criminal. Lovrich et al. comment, "This revelation is particularly important for the corresponding impact it has upon DNA databases—crime scenes in which there are no suspects are precisely the types of cases that need to be submitted in order for the DNA database to be effective. The purpose of the DNA database is to link known offenders to crimes with no known suspects, and to link unsolved crimes together, thereby providing detectives either with suspects or with new investigatory leads. The fact that law enforcement agencies are purposely not submitting these cases indicates that there is limited understanding as to the nature and purpose of DNA databases."

The researchers discovered that frequently, law enforcement officials were unaware of the fact that a DNA database has been established. Lovrich et al. (2003) observe, "This limited knowledge of the DNA database is troublesome, but it should not be construed as an accurate reflection of law enforcement's desire for such a tool. In fact, when asked if the law enforcement agency filling out the assessment would be interested in using forensic DNA databases more frequently if there was a reasonable expectation that an unnamed suspect could be quickly identified, an overwhelming 96.9 percent responded positively. Many of the agencies responding negatively indicated that they needed no access to the database since the state laboratory took care of database searches. However, a handful of agencies also explained that they believed DNA to be too expensive for their jurisdiction or they had too few crimes to justify DNA testing."

Law enforcement agencies also reported that cost and a lack of funding prevented them from submitting biological evidence for testing. The researchers reported that some agencies said that evidence is not sent to crime laboratories because of a lack of funding for DNA analysis (9.4 percent), because crime laboratories could not produce timely results (10.4 percent), or because crime laboratories did not process requests for DNA (3.8 percent). The researchers emphasize, "Timely results require the existence of adequate capacity on the part of crime laboratories to handle demand, and such capacity is limited by resources. Crime laboratories that may not be processing requests for DNA testing do so primarily as a fallback means of caseload management, which is limited by capacity, which is limited in turn by resources. So, taken together, an estimated 23.6 percent of agencies do not submit DNA cases for reasons relating to poor funding. This grouping represents the second most frequently indicated reason for not submitting evidence for DNA testing. In fact, the issue of lengthy delays in DNA analysis time was identified as a major concern by a significant number of respondents who chose to include comments with their assessment instrument responses. Police agencies throughout the country often face long delays in requested DNA analysis, which in turn limits the usefulness of DNA as an investigative tool for the police. Delays meanwhile are typically caused by crime laboratory resources that are inadequate to meet the demand for testing."

Lovrich et al. (2003) report that testing of DNA evidence is expensive and creates a financial burden for local police and state laboratories. In the survey, approximately 100 respondents felt strongly enough about the issue to add handwritten comments, including one agency that wrote, "If funding was not an issue, DNA would prove to be one of the most valuable tools in solving cases."

The researchers identified what they called a "disconnect" between local agencies that complain of one- to two-year delays on DNA testing, and laboratories that report average processing times of 23 to 30 weeks. Lovrich et al. (2003) observe, "These issues bring to bear a larger question relating to evidence collection. Specifically, if law enforcement officers do not see DNA as a primary part of their investigation, and those agencies which would like to use DNA for investigations are limited in doing so due to evidence analysis turnaround times that are not constructive to ongoing crime investigations, then what effect do these factors have on the likelihood that investigators will identify, collect and submit DNA evidence?"

The researchers asked themselves further, how much potentially valuable DNA evidence is simply not collected by law enforcement officials who have little hope that forensic analysis will be conducted in a timely manner? And when collected, how often is such evidence actually sent to the laboratory for testing? Comments from law enforcement agencies on the survey ranged from "I have just recently been trained in collection of DNA; before my training, I am unaware of any cases where DNA was collected," to "I am not familiar enough with DNA collecting to know how it affects my agency." Some agencies alluded to the fact that the good use of DNA testing required a cultural change that could prove to be difficult in their jurisdiction.

The news isn't all bad, the researchers said, adding, "By looking at the converse of this scenario, the potential value of a fully functional forensic DNA crime laboratory setting may be understood. Virginia's forensic DNA program is among the most mature in the nation and the state database has been averaging one cold hit per day for the last two years. Virginia's processing time for DNA evidence, while not ideal, is by far more efficient than the majority of other forensic crime laboratories in the country. Additionally, and perhaps most importantly, Virginia's crime laboratory does not limit (within reason) the type of case or the type of evidence that can be submitted. This means that the Virginia crime laboratory is just as willing to conduct DNA analysis in a murder case as it is for a breaking and entering case under investigation. These factors—short processing time, database successes, and liberal case submission policy—have resulted in a steady rate of growth every year in the number of cases submitted for biological testing. In fact the crime laboratory estimates that the amount of evidence submitted by law enforcement for DNA analysis grows by 30 percent every year."

The researchers said they believed the fact that crime investigators feel more encouraged to submit DNA evidence for analysis in Virginia likely accounts for the growth rate. Lovrich et al. (2003) explain further, "This encouragement, coupled with the positive reinforcement of frequent DNA database matches, has resulted in a cadre of crime investigators across the state who tend to view the processing of crime scene DNA evidence as an effective means of reducing their caseload."

Lovrich et al. (2003) found that many of the major obstacles associated with DNA analysis concern the costs/funding issues involved. The majority of funding for the local crime laboratories is derived from local sources. Accordingly, state crime laboratories receive most of their funding from state sources. Conversely, most state laboratories (91.6 percent) receive little to no funding from local sources, and 88.9 percent of local laboratories report a similarly low level of assistance from the state. The researchers also found that federal funding was not a significant portion of the overall DNA budgets of state and local crime laboratories; only 20.5 percent of state laboratories receive at least half of their funding from federal sources, a figure that drops to a mere 4.5 percent for local laboratories. Moreover, nearly half of all local laboratories reported that 10 percent or less of their DNA budget was attributable to federal sources. Conversely, only 23 percent of state laboratories reported this lowest level of funding.

When considering that many of the local laboratories handle extremely high volumes of forensic DNA cases, this difference in reliance on federal money is startling. However, there may be two plausible explanations for this difference. First, local crime laboratories are not permitted to apply directly for federal funding grants for DNA analysis. Instead, local laboratories must apply as a consortium through the state laboratory. Although this application process works well for a number of state and local laboratories, some local laboratories privately complain that they do not get a fair amount of this grant money. This situation also potentially leaves local laboratories at the mercy of a state's level of interest in applying for federal funding. Additionally, the process of coordinating a consortium application—particularly in those states where local laboratories are numerous—can be difficult. A second reason why these data show a higher degree of reliance at the state level on federal funding is because the question did not allow for a distinction between funding received for casework versus funding received for offender samples. Offender DNA samples are the sole responsibility of the state, and therefore local crime laboratories are not eligible to apply for federal grants for offender DNA analysis.

Lovrich et al. (2003) asked local and state crime laboratories to estimate the average cost of processing an unnamed suspect rape kit (assuming a vaginal swab with one perpetrator and one victim); state and local laboratories arrived at the same approximate cost of $1,100. The majority of local and state laboratories included the costs of reagents and salaries, but very few included costs associated with overhead and equipment. There are a variety of other factors that can significantly increase costs associated with DNA analysis, including the size, quantity, and condition of the evidence; the number of perpetrators involved; and contaminants. As forensic cases become more complex, the cost of analysis will quickly rise.

In determining where the biggest needs lie, laboratories indicated that reagents and analytical equipment were two big priorities on their lists. Lovrich et al. (2003) asked laboratories to rank the top three most significant priorities, in order of importance. Salaries were, by far, considered the single most significant need. Although a handful of laboratories indicated that current staff needed augmented salaries, the majority of laboratories indicated that the need was for new-hires. This issue of salaries is significant because federal grants for DNA analysis may not be used in this manner. Instead, DNA laboratories are solely dependent on state and local funding for salary needs. Two other personnel issues—training and overtime—also ranked among the top needs reported. Additionally, the fact that local laboratories ranked funding for no suspect casework as a mid-level priority, but state laboratories ranked it last, is a point for consideration.

Lovrich et al. (2003) say that in addition to the costs of equipment and reagents needed to complete DNA testing, "an ever-increasing demand for DNA testing means a corresponding increase in the need for more capacity. Increased capacity, in turn, means more personnel, more equipment, and occasionally more space. Personnel costs pose a considerable hurdle to DNA testing at many crime laboratories." Those needing training include professionals in criminal justice and law enforcement, medical professionals (such as nurses and physicians responsible for collecting forensic evidence from living forensic patients), criminal investigators, prosecutors and defense attorneys, and judges. Lovrich et al. state, "Beyond training is the cost of simply having additional cases to be investigated, prosecuted and defended in an already over-burdened criminal justice system."

As we discussed in Chapter 5, forensic laboratories face an astounding amount of case backlogs and evidence-analysis backlogs, a trend that has not been lost on legislators, the courts, law enforcement, and commentators in the media and from the legal and social science communities. Beaupre (1996) comments, "Evidence that could imprison the guilty or free the innocent is languishing on shelves and piling up in refrigerators of the nation's overwhelmed and underfunded crime labs. In one case a suspected serial rapist was released because it was going to take months to get the DNA results needed to prove the case. Weeks later, the suspect raped victim No. 4 as she slept in her home. When the DNA tests finally came back—18 months after samples first went to the lab—a jury convicted (the suspect) of all four rapes."

Lovrich et al. (2003) state that forensic laboratories reported at least 1,637 backlogged rape cases that were expected to exceed the statute of limitations for prosecution. A significant number of these cases were reported to be held by the local laboratories. Furthermore, this number was generally expected to increase in the coming six-month period rather than decrease, thereby furthering the possibility that additional cases could have expiring statutes of limitation before the backlog is eliminated. It should be noted that local jurisdictions were also asked to estimate the number of cases for which the statute of limitations may be a factor, but a very high number of agencies either did not respond to the question or indicated that an educated guess was not possible. This inability to track important information relating to cases points to a considerable deficiency in case management systems. Without such systems, the burden placed on law enforcement to review cases and respond to opportunities provided by advancements in forensic and other crime-fighting technologies is overwhelming.

Criminal justice professionals and legislators have been considering statute of limitations issues in conjunction with changes to forensic DNA policies. There are known instances where DNA backlogs—either in casework samples or offender samples—have resulted in DNA database matches that occurred after the statute of limitations for prosecution had lapsed for the alleged guilty individual. One state reported an estimated 150 such positive matches being made after the statutory period of exposure to prosecution had expired for repeat offenders in that state. Also, an abbreviated statute of limitations period negates the long-term effectiveness of the DNA database, in that the crime investigators making use of the database will not be given a full opportunity to succeed in matching across crimes and/or individuals.

DNA databases are effective tools to catch recidivists, since a known offender entered into the database can be identified at a later date when he or she commits a subsequent offense that leads to the collection of DNA evidence. Lovrich et al. (2003) state, "Even with a year-long backlog, DNA testing should still be completed in sufficient time for the prosecutors to bring forward legal charges. However, the reverse scenario is also equally important in making DNA matches. For example, a crime occurs, and at some later date when the offender commits a crime that requires a DNA sample for the database, a match is made retrospectively to the earlier unsolved crime(s). These 'backward' matches are those limited by short statute of limitations periods."

For example, in a state in which the statute of limitations is six years, an unknown rapist violates an individual in 2003, and eight years pass before the offender commits a crime that qualifies for the DNA database. Under the state's statute of limitations law, the 2003 rape cannot be prosecuted. While this limitation on prosecutorial exposure protects individuals from the natural tendency for most evidence to become increasingly less reliable over time, there is no opportunity for closure or for justice for the victim. However, Lovrich et al. (2003) point out, "The reliability of DNA testing is quite different; it is largely undamaged by the passage of time. DNA forensic evidence has been used quite frequently to convict criminals decades after the commission of their crime. It should also be noted that while a fingerprint may be found at a crime scene for a variety of legitimate and/or illegitimate reasons, a semen sample has very few legitimate reasons for being part of the evidence found in a rape examination of an unknown suspect assault. Many states have responded to this statute of limitations problem by enacting new legislation intended to extend or remove the statute of limitations for specific violent crimes." Some states have and are considering eliminating their statutes of limitations temporarily in sexual assault cases where DNA evidence is available. Once a match is made on the database, however, prosecutors have a set number of years to bring charges against the suspect in question. In this way, matches made on the DNA database can still be prosecuted, but prosecutors cannot indefinitely postpone a trial.

Processing Time and Output Capacity

Capacity levels at various forensic laboratories must be taken into consideration in any discussion of backlogs and evidence-processing delays. Lovrich et al. (2003) asked forensic laboratories about the approximate length of time required for the analysis of a typical, non-priority unnamed suspect case rape kit, assuming a vaginal swab with one perpetrator, one victim, and that the time runs from the date the rape kit is received by the laboratory until analytical results are reported. The researchers took into account the many factors that can affect processing times, including cases that have more than one perpetrator or multiple pieces of evidence, or where analysis must control for known consensual partners of the victim. Delays between the collection of evidence and actual submission of the evidence to the crime laboratory can also lengthen the overall turnaround time; conversely, cases that become a priority can be accelerated through the system at a much quicker rate.

Lovrich et al. (2003) report that state crime laboratories require an average of 23.9 weeks, and local laboratories average 30 weeks for DNA processing. In addition, state crime laboratories process an average of 1,284.5 samples per year, as opposed to the local laboratories, which average an output of 771.4 samples per year. Lovrich et al. explain that the reasons for this difference may lie in the fact that "state crime laboratories tend to be slightly more process-oriented because DNA evidence is generally submitted to the laboratory from remotely located agencies. In contrast, local laboratories are generally embedded in the law enforcement agencies they serve, and hence may have a more significant role in determining which evidence is of the most probative value. A thorough understanding of the scope of capacity problems must also consider the wide range in existing capacity at crime laboratories."

In August 2001, then-Attorney General John Ashcroft directed the National Institute of Justice (NIJ) to assess the existing delays of DNA evidence collected from crime scenes and develop recommendations to eliminate those delays. Specifically, Ashcroft requested that the assessment and recommendations address, among other matters, the following: resource requirements for laboratory equipment; resource, training, and education requirements for laboratory personnel; and the use of innovative technologies that could permit speedier analysis. He also directed NIJ to make recommendations for a national, comprehensive effort to eliminate the unacceptable delays currently occurring with the analysis of crime scene DNA evidence.

In response to this direction, NIJ convened a task force comprising a broad cross-section of criminal justice and forensic science experts. The DNA task force met in March and

October 2002; at these meetings, the task force and NIJ staff discussed extensively the nature of DNA backlogs, the causes of those backlogs, and possible strategies for reducing the backlogs. In "Report to the Attorney General on Delays in Forensic DNA Analysis," the NIJ in March 2003 published several recommendations relevant to the delays in DNA analysis in forensic laboratories nationwide:

- Improve the DNA analysis capacity of public crime laboratories.
- Help state and local crime labs to eliminate casework backlogs.
- Eliminate existing convicted offender DNA backlogs.
- Support training and education for forensic scientists.
- Provide training and education to police, prosecutors, defense attorneys, judges, victim service providers, medical personnel, and other criminal justice professionals.
- Support DNA research and development.

The 2003 NIJ report acknowledged the potential to solve serious crimes that could not be solved otherwise through traditional law enforcement techniques, adding, "DNA has also exonerated persons charged with or convicted of crimes they did not commit. However, DNA currently is not used to its full potential in the criminal justice system. Ideally, forensic DNA evidence would be collected from rape kits and crime scenes, properly stored, transmitted to a crime lab, analyzed, and compared against a suspect's DNA sample or a DNA database (populated with offender and crime scene DNA profiles). The results, then, would be used in a criminal prosecution. However, any weakness in one part of the system will delay or prevent the use of DNA evidence as a crime-fighting tool. There is a significant backlog of casework samples that has been caused by a massive demand for DNA analyses without a corresponding growth in forensic laboratory capacity. These delays pose substantial barriers to using forensic DNA evidence to its full potential."

Task force members discussed various reasons why the majority of these unanalyzed samples are in the custody of police departments and not forensic laboratories. Task force members reached some of the same conclusions that Lovrich et al. (2003) did, namely, that most crime labs lack sufficient evidence storage facilities that provide appropriate conditions to prevent degradation of evidence. Further, the retention of casework samples by police is usually due to the belief that the crime lab will not accept the sample or, even if it accepts the sample, that it will be unable to analyze it.

The NIJ task force identified a number of factors that contribute to laboratories' inability to accept and process casework samples in a timely manner. Task force members repeatedly emphasized that most state and local crime labs lack sufficient numbers of trained forensic scientists and identified a variety of causes for this personnel shortage. State and local governments with shrinking budgets lack adequate resources to hire trained scientists. Even when funds are available, there is an insufficient pool of qualified forensic scientists to hire. This is due in part to the fact that some colleges that offer degrees in forensic science do not have curriculums that include the basic science courses necessary for this occupation.

Even when a state or local crime lab can afford to hire a qualified college graduate, the newly hired scientist still requires extensive training before he or she is permitted to conduct DNA analyses. This training includes, for example, evidence-handling protocols, how to determine whether a particular item may contain probative DNA evidence, and the proper use of scientific equipment. This on-the-job training is usually handled one-on-one, with a more experienced analyst responsible for training the newly hired analyst. This is a very labor-intensive form of training that places substantial demands on the time of experienced analysts. However, even when all of these obstacles are addressed, public crime labs report that they face substantial staff retention problems. Public crime lab salaries are often below the salaries paid by the private sector.

In addition, existing forensic staff often must devote time to clerical and repetitive functions that do not make the most of their analytical skills. Although some crime labs lack basic analysis equipment, most public crime labs lack a sufficient infrastructure that would speed DNA analyses and maximize staff resources. Many state and local crime labs lack basic information management systems, automated equipment, high throughput analyzers, and quality assurance software. Some of this equipment is commercially available, but state and local crime labs lack the funds to purchase it. In addition, many public crime labs have insufficient space to accommodate additional equipment.

Because DNA casework analysis often requires comparisons with offender DNA profiles contained in local, state, and national DNA databases, the effectiveness of a DNA casework backlog reduction strategy is dependent upon well-populated offender databases. Currently, however, there are impediments to offender database collections. In addition to casework analysis backlogs, backlogs exist in analyzing convicted offender samples. While many states have statutes authorizing the collection of DNA evidence from a variety of convicted offenders, substantial numbers of authorized samples have not been collected.

Task force members also noted that forensic DNA evidence analysis ultimately is intended to produce evidence that is admissible in a judicial proceeding to determine guilt or innocence. They noted that training for prosecutors, defense attorneys, and judges is insufficient and urged that training materials and programs be developed for these key players in the judicial process. To address the problems identified by the task force, NIJ recommended the creation of a comprehensive, national DNA strategy that addresses DNA casework analysis backlogs.

To increase capacity of crime laboratories, the NIJ said that these facilities must be properly equipped and adequately resourced. The NIJ report (2003) states, "Crime laboratories face rapidly increasing workloads and lack the funds to purchase and maintain new equipment. All crime laboratories should have access to the latest technology for conducting standard DNA analysis." NIJ recommended that assistance be provided to those crime labs that are without basic equipment and materials to conduct the fundamental processes of DNA analysis—extraction, quantitation, amplification, and analysis.

The NIJ also recommended that crime labs possess laboratory information management systems (LIMS) with which to automate evidence handling and casework management. The NIJ report explains, "Certain portions of the DNA testing procedure are labor-intensive and time-consuming. A significant amount of staff time is devoted to tracking and managing evidence samples. Often, evidence tracking is accomplished through hand-written entries on forms." The report explains further that LIMS can improve the integrity and speed of evidence handling and help to demonstrate a proper chain of custody. These systems can provide the additional benefit of aiding public crime laboratories with the management of all casework, not simply DNA samples. LIMS are especially critical to efforts to maximize staff resources, as they can increase efficiency by freeing up analysts' time, and this increased staff time can then be devoted to testing procedures not amenable to automation. LIMS also can be part of a comprehensive laboratory strategy to improve communication with other criminal justice agencies. The DNA task force identified inadequate communication among law enforcement, crime laboratories, and the courts as one of the largest problems plaguing existing resources. Duplicate collections, case dispositions, suspect exclusions, incomplete data submission, and evidence location are all issues that contribute to wastes of time and expense.

Providing automation tools to public DNA laboratories was another key recommendation of the NIJ (2003) report, which comments, "To streamline aspects of the DNA analysis procedure that are labor- and time-intensive, crime laboratories should seek to use automated systems, such as robots, to perform DNA extraction. These systems increase analyst productivity, limit human error, and reduce contamination. Additionally, the DNA task force supported the development of a Web-based system that provides automation solutions for convicted offender and casework laboratories, and that evidence control (i.e., tracking and storage) be addressed.

NIJ emphasized the need to assist crime laboratories in meeting accreditation requirements, since federal law requires that all laboratories submitting DNA forensic and convicted offender sample profiles for inclusion in the National DNA Index System (NDIS) demonstrate annual compliance with the FBI Director's National Quality Assurance Standards for Forensic DNA and Convicted Offender Laboratories. Laboratories can demonstrate compliance through accreditation by the ASCLD's Laboratory Accreditation Board (ASCLD/LAB), certification by the NFSTC, or a combination of internal and external audits. Forensic evidence must be stored in a manner that ensures its integrity and maintains its availability while criminal investigations and judicial proceedings continue. Appropriate evidence storage conditions require costly equipment such as security systems, environmental control systems, ambient temperature monitors, and dehumidifiers. Evidence storage problems further complicate casework backlogs. To encourage appropriate retention and storage of forensic evidence, NIJ recommended the collection and dissemination of best-practice information about evidence retention and storage. Such information should identify cost-effective practices and facilitate the exchange of information among the law enforcement and forensic community about the value of particular equipment. A long-term-capacity building strategy could also provide support for the development of appropriate storage.

Eliminating casework backlogs, including existing convicted offender DNA backlogs, was another priority identified by NIJ (2003), which states in its report, "At the present time, state and local crime laboratory capacity is limited, especially in smaller jurisdictions. Because clearing casework backlogs requires more capacity than may be needed for the long-term, state and local crime laboratories need continued financial support that gives them the flexibility to contract with private laboratories or consultants." The report states further, "Although crime laboratories have made enormous progress in reducing the number of unanalyzed convicted offender samples for DNA databases, they continue to be deluged with analysis requests. This backlog will only increase as more states enact statutes authorizing the collection of samples from more categories of offenders and arrestees. An aggressive program to ensure the timely analysis and entry of offender DNA samples into DNA databases is essential to maximize the crime-solving potential of DNA casework analysis."

Therefore, the NIJ task force recommended the development of funding strategies to address growing convicted offender backlogs, as well as the encouragement of aggressive programs to collect DNA samples "owed" by convicted offenders. The NIJ report recommended that a national DNA strategy supporting innovative and cost-effective collection programs, such as mobile collection units, be developed, and that new research and development programs could provide state and local policymakers with additional information about the cost effectiveness, efficiency, and usability of collection methods.

Another overreaching NIJ recommendation was improving the training and education of forensic scientists. The NIJ (2003) report states, "Crime laboratory capacity is directly related to the number and quality of highly trained forensic DNA examiners and technicians. DNA task force members emphasized that the criminal justice system needs to ensure that enough qualified DNA analysts are available to conduct DNA analysis. The DNA task force members agreed that there is currently a growing need for more uniformly educated and trained analysts who can begin supervised casework once hired." To this end, the NIJ issued a slate of recommendations, including ensuring that newly hired forensic scientists have the necessary training and education, providing increased opportunities for intensive, "on-the-job" training for new forensic analysts; developing strategies to increase the pool of qualified forensic scientists who work in public crime laboratories; providing forensic DNA analysts with up-to-date training and continuing education; and providing training to all stakeholders in the U.S. criminal justice system. The NIJ report notes, "Key players in the criminal justice system should be trained in the proper collection, preservation, and use of forensic DNA evidence."

Finally, the NIJ identified the critical need to support DNA research and development. The NIJ (2003) report states, "Forensic DNA analysis, like other areas of biotechnology, is rapidly evolving. Research and development promises to open up new ways to assist crime labs. Smaller, faster, and cheaper analysis tools will reduce capital investments for crime laboratories while increasing their capacity. These tools also will facilitate the application of forensic DNA technology to more categories of evidence and enable investigative uses of DNA as close to the crime scene as possible."

To accomplish this, the NIJ recommended the funding of research and development programs in new and emerging DNA technologies. The NIJ (2003) report notes, "Advances in DNA analysis technologies will reduce the personnel hours normally required for more repetitive tasks, thus decreasing overall turn-around time of casework analysis. Research and development of new capabilities in automated short tandem repeats (STRs), single nucleotide polymorphisms (SNPs), mitochondrial DNA analysis (mtDNA), and Y-chromosome DNA analysis methods can significantly reduce turn-around times and permit examiners to focus on the customized aspects of DNA testing."

In Chapter 14, we will explore various advocacy efforts and the ongoing efforts to secure federal funding to meet the demands placed on the forensic science community. To increase the use of DNA technology in the criminal justice system, on March 11, 2003, President George W. Bush announced a five-year, $1 billion-plus initiative to improve the use of DNA in the criminal justice system. The initiative called for increased funding, training, and assistance to federal, state, and local forensic laboratories, to members of law enforcement, to medical professionals, to victim-service providers, and to prosecutors, defense lawyers, and judges, to ensure that this technology reaches its full potential to solve crimes, protect the innocent, and identify missing persons. The initiative, Advancing Justice Through DNA Technology, promulgated the following objectives:

- Eliminate the current backlog of unanalyzed DNA samples and biological evidence for the most serious violent offenses—rapes, murders, and kidnappings—and for convicted offender samples needing testing.
- Improve crime laboratories' capacities to analyze DNA samples in a timely fashion.
- Stimulate research and develop new DNA technologies and advances in all forensic sciences areas.
- Develop training and provide assistance about the collection and use of DNA evidence to a wide variety of criminal justice professionals.
- Provide access to appropriate post-conviction DNA testing of crime scene evidence not tested at the time of trial.

- Ensure that DNA forensic technology is used to its full potential to solve missing persons cases and identify human remains.
- Protect the innocent.

This initiative followed on the heels of the aforementioned NIJ assessment of criminal justice system delays in the analysis of DNA evidence. On Oct. 30, 2004, President Bush signed into law the Justice for All Act of 2004, which establishes enforceable rights for victims of crimes, enhances DNA collection and analysis efforts, provides for post-conviction DNA testing, and authorizes grants to improve the quality of representation in state capital cases. In both fiscal years 2005 and 2006, Congress appropriated $108 million to fund activities under the President's DNA Initiative.

REFERENCES

Beaupre B. Crime labs staggering under burden of proof. *USA Today,* August 20, 1996.

Bedau H and Radelet M. *In Spite of Innocence.* Northeastern University Press, 1992.

Berger MA. Raising the bar: The impact of DNA testing on the field of forensics. In: *Perspectives on Crime and Justice: 2000–2001 Lecture Series.* 2002.

Bieber FR. Science and technology of forensic DNA profiling: Current use and future directions. In: *DNA and The Criminal Justice System: The Technology of Justice,* Lazer D, Ed. MIT Press, 2004.

Borchard E. *Convicting the Innocent.* Garden City: Publishers Press, 1932.

Connors E, Lundregan T, Miller N, and McEwen T. *Convicted by Juries, Exonerated by Science: Case Studies in the Use of DNA Evidence to Establish Innocence after Trial Case Studies in Use of DNA Evidence.* NIJ Research Report. Washington, D.C.: National Institute of Justice, June 1996.

Department of Justice. *Report to the Attorney General on Delays in Forensic DNA Analysis.* Washington, D.C.: National Institute of Justice, March 2003.

Giannelli PC. The admissibility of laboratory reports: The reliability of scientific proof. *Ohio State Law Journal,* 49:671, 1988.

Giannelli PC. Scientific evidence. *Criminal Justice Magazine,* 18(1), Spring 2003.

Imwinkelreid EJ. Commentaries on DNA testing. In: *Convicted by Juries, Exonerated by Science: Case Studies in the Use of DNA Evidence to Establish Innocence After Trial Case Studies in Use of DNA Evidence.* NIJ Research Report, June 1996.

Jones GR. President's editorial: The changing practice of forensic science. *Journal of Forensic Science,* 47(3), 2002.

Kaye DH and Koehler JJ. Can jurors understand probabilistic evidence? *Journal of the Royal Statisticians Society* (Series A), 54:75, 1991.

Kaye DH. DNA evidence: Probability, population genetics, and the courts. *Harvard Journal of Law Technology,* 7:101, 1993.

Kaye DH. DNA, NAS, NRC, DAB, RFLP, PCR, and more: An introduction to the 1996 NRC report on forensic DNA evidence. *Jurimetrics Journal,* 37:395, 1997.

Kaye DH and Sensabaugh GF. Reference guide on DNA evidence. In: *Reference Manual on Scientific Evidence,* 2nd ed. Washington, D.C.: Federal Judicial Center, 2000.

Koehler JJ. Error and exaggeration in the presentation of DNA evidence at trial. *Jurimetrics Journal,* 34:21, 1993.

Koehler JJ. The psychology of numbers in the courtroom: How to make DNA match statistics seem impressive or insufficient. *Southern California Law Review,* 74:1275, 2001.

Kreeger LR and Weiss DM. *Forensic DNA Fundamentals for the Prosecutor.* Alexandria, Va.: American Prosecutors Research Institute, November 2003.

Kreeger LR and Weiss DM. *DNA Evidence Policy Considerations for the Prosecutor.* Alexandria, Va.: American Prosecutors Research Institute, September 2004.

Lander E and Budowle B. DNA fingerprinting dispute laid to rest. *Nature,* October 27, 1994.

Lovrich NP, Pratt TC, Gaffney MJ, Johnson CL, Asplen CH, Hurst LH, and Schellberg TM. *National Forensic DNA Study Report, Final Report.* Pullman, Wash.: Washington State University and Tacoma, Wash.: Smith Alling Lane, PS. December 2003. Available at: http://www.ncjrs.gov/pdffiles1/nij/grants/203970.pdf#search=%22National%20Forensic%20DNA%20Study%20Report%2C%20Final%20Report%22 Moriarty JC and Saks MJ. Forensic science: Grand goals, tragic flaws, and judicial gatekeeping. *Judges Journal,* 44(4) Fall 2005.

National Academies. *DNA Evidence in the Legal System: The Evaluation of Forensic DNA Evidence.* Washington, D.C.: National Academies Press, 1996.

National Academies. *The Evaluation of Forensic DNA Evidence. Committee on DNA Forensic Science: An Update.* Washington, D.C.: National Academies Press, 1996.

National Institute of Justice. *The Future of Forensic DNA Testing: Predictions of the Research and Development Working Group.* Washington, D.C.: U.S. Department of Justice. 2000.

National Research Council Committee on DNA Forensic Science. *An Update: The Evaluation of Forensic DNA Evidence,* 1996.

National Research Council Committee on DNA Technology in Forensic Science. *DNA Technology in Forensic Science,* 1992.

Neufeld P and Scheck BC. Commentary. In: *Convicted by Juries, Exonerated by Science: Case Studies in the Use of DNA Evidence to Establish Innocence After Trial Case Studies in Use of DNA Evidence.* NIJ Research Report, June 1996.

Reinstein RS. Commentary. In: *Convicted by Juries, Exonerated by Science: Case Studies in the Use of DNA Evidence to Establish Innocence After Trial Case Studies in Use of DNA Evidence.* NIJ Research Report, June 1996.

Saks M and Koehler J. What DNA fingerprinting can teach the law about the rest of forensic science. *Cardozo Law Review,* 13(361):372, 1991.

Thompson WC. Accepting lower standards: The National Research Council's second report on forensic DNA evidence. *Jurimetrics Journal,* 37:405, 1997.

Thompson et al. (2003) from Chapter 19.

Walsh JT. The growing impact of the new genetics on the courts. *Judicature,* 83(3), November/December 1999.

RECOMMENDED READING

Burk DL. DNA fingerprinting: Possibilities and pitfalls of a new technique. *Jurimetrics Journal,* 28(455):3, 1988.

Callahan J. The admissibility of DNA evidence in the United States and England. *Suffolk Transnational Law Review,* 19:537, 1996.

Deftos LJ. Daubert and Frye: Compounding the controversy over the forensic use of DNA testing. *Whittier Law Review,* 15:955, 1994.

Duceman BW. DNA analysis: Scientific and legal aspects. *Alb Law Journal of Scientific Technology,* 2:53, 1992.

Faigman DL. The tipping point in the law's use of science: The epidemic of scientific sophistication that began with DNA profiling and toxic torts. *Brooklyn Law Review,* 67:111, 2001.

Finch AMT. Note. Oops! We forgot to put it in the refrigerator: DNA identification and the state's duty to preserve evidence. *Journal Marshall Law Review*, 25:809, 1992.

Fisher M. Procedural issues surrounding post-conviction DNA testing. *New England Law Review*, 35:621, 2001.

Giannelli PC. Criminal discovery, scientific evidence, and DNA. *V Law Review*, 44:791, 1991.

Giannelli PC. Impact of post-conviction DNA testing on forensic science. *New England Law Review*, 35:627, 2001.

Gordon JM. DNA identification tests: On the way toward judicial acceptance. *Journal of Suffolk Academy of Law*, 6:1, 1989.

Imwinkelried EJ. The debate in the DNA cases over the foundation for the admission of scientific evidence: The importance of human error as a cause of forensic misanalysis. *Washington University Law B*, 69:19, 1991.

Kaye DH. The admissibility of DNA testing. *Cardozo Law Review*, 13:353, 1991.

Kaye DH. The Relevance of matching DNA: Is the window half open or half shut? *Journal of Criminal Law and Criminology*, 85:676, 1995.

Kaye DH. DNA typing: Emerging or neglected issues. *Washington Law Review*, 76:413, 2001.

Koehler JJ. What DNA fingerprinting can teach the law about the rest of forensic science. *Cardozo Law Review*, 13:361, 1991.

Koehler JJ. On conveying the probative value of DNA evidence: Frequencies, likelihood ratios and error rates. *University of Colorado Law Review*, 67:859–886, 1996.

Koehler JJ. Why DNA likelihood ratios should account for error. *Jurimetrics Journal*, 37:425, 1997.

Koehler JJ, et al. The random match probability in DNA evidence: Irrelevant and prejudicial? *Jurimetrics Journal*, 35:201, 1995.

Kreimer SF and Rudovsky D. Double helix, double bind: Factual innocence and post-conviction DNA testing. *University of Pennsylvania Law Review*, 151:547, 2002.

Lempert R. After the DNA wars: Skirmishing with NRC II. *Jurimetrics Journal*, 37:439, 1997.

Lindsey S, et al. Communicating statistical DNA evidence. *Jurimetrics Journal*, 43:147, 2003.

McCabe J. DNA fingerprinting: The failings of Frye. *Northern Illinois University Law Review*, 16:455, 1996.

Nakashima RA. DNA evidence in criminal trials: A defense attorney's primer. *Nebraska Law Review*, 74:444, 1995.

Neufeld P. Legal and ethical implications of post-conviction DNA exonerations. *New England Law Review*, 35:639, 2001.

Rango JT. Truth or consequences and post-conviction DNA testing: Have you reached your verdict? *Dick Law Review*, 107:845, 2003.

Scheck BC. DNA and Daubert. *Cardozo Law Review*, 15:1959, 1994.

Smith GB and Gordon JA. The admissions of DNA evidence in state and federal courts. *Fordham Law Review*, 65:2465, 1997.

Strom CM. Genetic justice: A lawyer's guide to the science of DNA testing. Ill B Journal, 87:18, 1999.

Thompson WC. Evaluating the admissibility of new genetic identification tests: Lessons from the DNA war. *Journal of Criminal Law Criminology*, 84:22, 1993.

Thompson WC. DNA Evidence in the O.J. Simpson trial. *University of Colorado Law Review*, 67:827, 1996.

Thompson WC. A sociological perspective on the science of forensic DNA testing. *UC Davis Law Review*, 30:1113, 1997.

Thompson WC and Ford S. DNA typing: Acceptance and weight of the new genetic identification tests. *Virginia Law Review*, 75:45, 1989.

Thompson WC, et al. Evaluating forensic DNA evidence: Essential elements of a competent defense review. *Champion*, 24, 2003.

Tyler PB. Fundamental misunderstandings about DNA contamination: Does it help or hurt the criminal defendant? *Beverly Hills Bar Association Journal,* 15, 1996.

Williams CJ. Note. DNA fingerprinting: A revolutionary technique in forensic science and its probable effects on criminal evidentiary law. *Drake Law Review,* 37, 1987.

Wright EE. DNA evidence: Where we've been, where we are, and where we are going. *Maine B Journal,* 10:206, 1995.

CHAPTER 12

THE EVIDENCE TRILOGY AND FORENSIC SCIENCE

The 1990s gave birth to three U.S. Supreme Court decisions that significantly altered the evidentiary landscape for scientific issues and experts and supplanted, in many states, a standard for admitting expert evidence into court that had been in authority since 1923. All three decisions sprung from toxic tort cases, and legal scholars still debate the ramifications of these decisions for the admittance of scientific evidence in criminal cases. Kennedy and Merrill (2003) state, "The Supreme Court has clarified the standards for expert testimony. Now the forensic sciences must demonstrate that they make the grade." This chapter examines each decision and the ramifications for forensic science.

Essential to any discussion about the admissibility of forensic evidence and the impact of the evidence trilogy is agreement on the role of forensic evidence in a legal setting. Kiely (2003) explains, "The aspect of the forensic sciences of interest to practitioners in the criminal justice system is their potential for the production of forensic evidence or facts that, when combined with probability assessments geared to the defendant's participation in a crime, aid in establishing one or more essential elements of the crime. Those elements, such as *actus reus* (affirmative act), intent, and causation must be proved beyond a reasonable doubt." Kiely further admonishes the court to remember that the reason forensic science disciplines exist is to generate information about forensic evidence: "All this carefully gathered information is generated to meet the goal of establishing material facts at or before trial, not to demonstrate the latest technological advances or most recent methodologies."

Inman and Rudin (2001) state, "The law places physical evidence in the category of circumstantial evidence. . . . Science, on the other hand, perceives physical evidence primarily as tangible evidence that we can detect with one of our five senses, and that is amenable to some analytical technique."[1]

Kiely (2003) explains that forensic evidence is introduced into court in two ways: class characteristic evidence that does not reference a particular suspect, and individual-linking testimony that inferentially associates a particular individual with the commission of a crime. Of critical importance, of course, is the potential testimony generated by a forensic analysis technique that is a matching statement serving to link evidence found at the crime scene to a particular defendant. Kiely observes, "Class characteristic statements garnered from forensic analyses illustrate the great value in a criminal investigation of statements drawing contextual lines for subsequent attempts to link a particular suspect to a crime scene, especially by excluding other potential suspects. The ultimate goal of all forensic science is the linking of a potential offender to a crime scene by way of testimony as to individual characteristics, connecting a physical sample obtained from the suspect, such as datum from the crime scene. The exclusionary potential of class or individual forms is equally important as it can eliminate a suspect or void a conviction based on lack of or sloppy forensic evidence."

Although judges had always been allowed to review and exclude expert evidence, not many exercised this power before the Supreme Court vested them with renewed authority. Some experts say the *Daubert* trilogy provides a stronger platform upon which to challenge unsound scientific and forensic evidence, although how much expert testimony is excluded under this "gatekeeping" power varies from court to court. The challenge is judges' capability to understand the scientific process and be able to reject patently false or misleading testimony masquerading as science. This issue will be explored further in Chapter 13.

The landmark cases are as follows:

- *Daubert v Merrell Dow Pharmaceuticals:* This 1993 decision essentially directs trial judges to reject unreliable or less-than-compelling scientific testimony. The *Daubert* test replaced the *Frye* rule in 1993 by stating that scientific evidence must pass four tests before it can be admitted into evidence for a trial. The four tests determine whether the theory or technique has been tested, whether it has been peer reviewed, its known or potential error rate and the existence and maintenance of standards controlling its operation, and whether it has been accepted within a relevant scientific community.
- *General Electric Co. v Joiner* and *Kumho Tire Co. v Carmichael:* Following after *Daubert* were *General Electric Co. v Joiner* in 1997 and *Kumho Tire Co. v Carmichael* in 1999. In *Joiner,* the court ruled that judges could exclude the testimony of experts if it might confuse jurors by being insufficiently relevant to what caused the injury at issue in a case. In *Kumho,* the court ruled that a judge could bar an expert from testifying if he or she used unusual criteria for interpreting data or events. During the *Kumho* case, the wording of the *Daubert* decision came into question. *Daubert* was limited to the scientific content of expert testimony in a courtroom when determining the relevance of admissibility. *Kumho* brought to question that not all testimony given by experts is scientifically based; instead it can be non-scientific technical evidence. It was determined that the text of the *Daubert* rule when determining reliability and relevancy can be "flexible" based on the occupation of the expert witness.

IN THE BEGINNING, THERE WAS *FRYE*

Long before the birth of the trilogy of *Daubert v Merrell Dow Pharmaceuticals Inc.* (1993), *General Electric Co. v Joiner* (1997), and *Kumho Tire Co. v Carmichael* (1999), one test was the standard for the admissibility of evidence: the venerable *Frye* test. The *Frye* rule determined that to have scientific evidence admitted into court the evidence must be generally accepted by the mainstream scientific community.

Kennedy and Merrill (2003) state, "For 70 years, U.S. courts relied on the standard enunciated in *Frye v United States t*o determine the admissibility of expert testimony. Under *Frye,* expert testimony is admissible only if it is generally accepted in the relevant scientific community. In *Daubert v Merrell Dow Pharmaceuticals,* the Supreme Court, relying on the new Federal Rules of Evidence, declared that scientific expert testimony must be grounded in the methodology and reasoning of science."

To determine whether expert testimony meets the *Daubert* standard, the U.S. Supreme Court provided trial courts with the following criteria:

- Whether the theories or techniques on which the testimony relies are based on a testable hypothesis
- Whether the theory or technique has been subject to peer review
- Whether there is a known or potential rate of error associated with the method
- Whether there are standards controlling the method
- Whether the method is generally accepted in the relevant scientific community

To fans of *Frye*, the criteria, with the exception of the last tenet, seemed excessive. Kennedy and Merrill (2003) state, "These criteria are flexible, and no single one alone would be dispositive. Indeed, the Court recognized that some would be inappropriate under certain circumstances. A few years later, in Kumho Tire, the Supreme Court extended the Daubert standard to apply to expert testimony based on a wide range of technical or specialized disciplines while also recognizing that criteria for admission may differ across areas of expert testimony."

The so-called *Frye* test stems from the 1923 federal case of *Frye v United States*, which involved the admissibility of polygraph evidence. *Frye* has been used in many federal courts, particularly in criminal cases, and is still used in populous states such as California, Illinois, and New York. In *Frye*, a federal appellate court held that expert opinion based on a scientific technique is admissible only if the technique is "generally accepted" in the relevant scientific community. However, this concept of general acceptance was occasionally determined on the basis of the testimony of what was considered to be a self-validating expert.

In contrast, the Supreme Court's evidence trilogy, handed down some 70 years after *Frye*, encourages trial judges to decide admissibility not solely on this standard of consensus or general acceptance, but on whether the testimony is grounded in the principles and methods of a particular field or discipline (National Academies, 2002).

Saks and Faigman (2005) write, "Most discussions of the admissibility of scientific expert testimony begin with Frye. This is an odd custom, first because judges had been screening expert evidence for centuries before Frye, and second because for decades after Frye was decided the case was ignored by both courts and scholars (Faigman et al., 1994). Its influence emerged only when the adoption of the Federal Rules of Evidence drew near, the very time when Frye should have become obsolete."

Frye's function as a marketplace test had its virtues, but it also had drawbacks. Saks and Faigman (2005) write, "The market does not always select for validity. Much that is false, junky, or harmful may nevertheless sell well. The marketplace test honestly applied is unable to distinguish between astronomy and astrology and thus would admit both. In addition, the marketplace test conflates the expert and the expertise. The body of knowledge and the people who purport to possess it tend to be treated as one. A final problem, which ultimately gave rise to the Frye test, is that some fields have little or no life in any commercial marketplace. In particular, there are fields that have no function outside of their possible courtroom utility. The courtroom is their marketplace. Where then were judges to look for evaluation help?"

The crucial issue in the evidence trilogy, according to many legal scholars, was causation, something that *Frye* couldn't offer. Berger (2005) writes, "To prevail, plaintiffs in each case, through the offer of expert testimony, had to discharge their burden of proving that the defendant's product had caused the plaintiffs' injuries. Because plaintiffs' expert testimony was excluded, plaintiffs lost. The lower courts hearing *Daubert* relied on the so-called *Frye* or general acceptance test to hold that the plaintiffs' expert testimony on causation was inadmissible and that, consequently, plaintiffs "could not satisfy their burden of proving causation at trial."[2]

As established at the beginning of this chapter, *Frye* demands that there be a general acceptance of the underlying theory in the relevant field in any novel scientific principle that seeks admissibility in court. While *Frye* has withstood the test of time, Berger (2005) says it has been criticized "on numerous grounds" because, for instance, "it fails to explain how to determine what is the relevant field, that it counts the noses of experts rather than looking at the validity of their opinions, and that it leads to self-validating experts who claim that their particular subspecialty is the relevant field."[2]

At worst, *Frye* can be considered to be ambiguous. Walsh (1999) writes, "Although adopted in pure or modified form in most jurisdictions, federal and state, the Frye standard posed a significant ambiguity: what is the relevant scientific community and who defines it?. . . . Courts wrestled with its application in technical areas lacking clear scientific underpinnings [such as psychological syndromes and voice printing]."

Perhaps the greatest barrier to Frye's continued viability, however, arose with the emergence of the Federal Rules of Evidence that became the model for evidentiary standards in many state courts. This chink in *Frye*'s armor was exploited in 1993 when the Supreme Court said that the *Frye* test was superseded by the Federal Rules of Evidence (which govern evidentiary questions in federal court); when enacted in 1975, the Rules did not refer to *Frye*. But as we will soon see, many jurisdictions are loath to reject *Frye* as its admissibility standard.

Rule 702 of the Federal Rules of Evidence, with its emphasis on the reliability of the expert, appears almost at cross-purposes to *Frye*'s focus on the subject matter of the expert's opinion. Similarly, Rule 703, which permits an expert to use data not necessarily admissible in evidence in formulating an opinion provided such data is "of a type" reasonably relied upon by experts "in the particular field," seems to suggest a *Frye*-like test without the general acceptance requirement.

Courts seeking to reconcile *Frye*'s general acceptance test with the more specific criteria imparted by Rule 702 and Rule 703 struggled to provide a consistent practical guide for practitioners. To the extent that *Frye* was viewed as unduly conservative, courts sought to relax its application to avoid the exclusion of evidence, particularly in criminal cases. Also, as more scientific studies and methodology were brought to bear in toxic- and pharmaceutical-based tort actions, courts struggled to permit the use of innovative science to establish causation.

In the period immediately preceding *Daubert,* some courts, lacking consistent doctrinal standards, opted to treat close questions of admissibility of scientific evidence as matters of weight to be resolved by the trier of fact, typically a jury. Some trial judges applied the highly subjective probative value/prejudice balance of Rule 403 to resolve contests over the admissibility of scientific evidence. This relaxed approach placed a premium on the securing of a favorable expert witness and led to the much-criticized emergence of the hired gun expert.

Regardless of one's view of the continued efficacy of *Frye,* the controversy engendered by the use of confrontational experts opining on unusual, and sometimes novel, issues of scientific evidence created a demand for clarification. Not only was there division among the federal circuits, but varying admissibility standards promulgated by state courts led to claims of forum shopping. Thus, the time was ripe for an authoritative pronouncement.

THE LEGACY OF *FRYE*

One of the confounding things in the 1920s was that when confronted with a fairly new technology such as the polygraph, the court could not identify a viable commercial marketplace to support it—the very underpinning of the resulting *Frye* decision. Saks and Faigman (2005) write, "To help it evaluate the admissibility of that testimony, the Frye court devised a variation of the marketplace test: it substituted an intellectual marketplace for the commercial one."

Saks and Faigman (2005) assert that *Frye* changed the law's perspective regarding experts in several substantial ways. They write, "Principally, by changing the marketplace from the consumers of the expertise to the experts themselves, Frye helpfully separated the expertise from the expert. This innovation divided the issue of admissibility more clearly into two parts: the credentials of the expert and the body of knowledge the expert sought to impart. But the Frye innovation also, and counterproductively, replaced buyers with sellers as the principal evaluators of the value of what was being offered." The trouble, Saks and Faigman point out, is that *Frye* forces the courts to adopt the standards of the very discipline under scrutiny. Therefore, rigorous scientific fields are judged using strict admissibility standards (because that is how they judge themselves), whereas fields lacking a rigorous tradition are judged using lax admissibility standards (Saks and Koehler 1991).

Frye, with its demand for general acceptance of particular expertise within its field, admittedly had its advantages and disadvantages. On the one hand, the *Frye* test seemed relatively easy to administer, required little scientific sophistication from judges, and was to be applied only to evidence that presented a novel scientific issue, allowing much expert evidence to be scrutinized minimally, if at all. On the other hand, the *Frye* test could be construed as vague and easily manipulated, capable of obscuring the relevant inquiry, imposing a protracted waiting period on the use of sound new evidence and techniques, and lacking any definition of when a theory has become generally accepted by the scientific community.

Saks and Faigman (2005) observe, "Some products of the most rigorous fields with the healthiest scientific discourse might fail the Frye test, while the work of shoddy fields with a great deal of uncritical internal acceptance would easily pass. Moreover, no standards defined what constituted the particular field to which a technique belonged. Although often criticized for being the most conservative test of admissibility, the Frye test could produce the most liberal standards of admission. The more narrowly a court defines the pertinent field, the more agreement it is likely to find. The general acceptance test degenerated into a process of deciding whose noses to count, as well as how many."

FRYE VERSUS *DAUBERT*

Cheng and Yoon (2005) call *Daubert* "the foundational opinion in the modern law of scientific evidence and arguably one of the most important decisions in the area of tort reform." Cheng and Yoon (2005) state, "Legal scholars have debated which test is more stringent, and which bastion of decision-making power is correct: Frye in the scientific community, and Daubert in the judiciary. Also, state supreme courts have struggled with deciding whether to adopt Daubert or maintain Frye. In federal courts, where the decision is legally binding, Daubert has become a potent weapon of tort reform by causing judges to scrutinize scientific evidence more closely. Tort reform debate but arguing that the issue of whether the Daubert standard is more strict than the Frye standard is a red herring."

Cheng and Yoon (2005) surmise, "Among some commentators, there has been growing suspicion that whether a state adopts Daubert or Frye does not ultimately affect how courts handle scientific evidence. . . . At the heart of Daubert was not creating a new doctrinal test, but rather in raising the overall awareness of judges, in all jurisdictions, to the problem of unreliable science. Therefore, whether a jurisdiction nominally follows Frye or Daubert, the practical results are essentially the same. This theory, if true, could have important ramifications for both the field of scientific evidence and for tort reform more generally. If courts are making scientific admissibility decisions based not on doctrinal tests but rather on other extralegal views, then the traditional focus on the merits of Frye vs. Daubert may be largely misguided. Instead of debating Frye vs. Daubert, perhaps research should concentrate on these 'softer' extralegal mechanisms that judges use in their decision-making process."

Going to the heart of the issue, whether *Frye* or *Daubert,* is the mandate that admissibility standards be the same when applied to any type of evidence: The evidence must be reliable and relevant. How that determination is made, however, has triggered disagreement as to the success of court scrutiny of scientific evidence, and the overall questioning of what the appropriate standards should be and who should be making that determination (Cheng and Yoon, 2005). Cheng and Yoon also echo the hopes of many in the legal community who assume that "the everyday practice of law suggests that a state's adoption of Frye or Daubert should make at least some practical difference." When all is said and done, however, Cheng and Yoon admit that "For the scientific evidence field, the results suggest that debates about the practical merits and drawbacks of Daubert vs. Frye may be largely superfluous, and that that energy should be refocused. Perhaps it is time to move away from debating the merits of Frye vs. Daubert and toward a broader focus on how judges actually make decisions about science. Sometimes the power of a court decision or even a piece of legislation comes more from its underlying idea than from its technical legal effect."

POST-*DAUBERT* CHALLENGES TO FORENSIC SCIENCE

While *Daubert* and its progeny sprung from toxic tort cases, the applicability of these decisions to criminal cases in general, and forensic science-related evidence in particular, is up for debate. Some argue that trial courts admit most forensic evidence, even if it is questionable by the most basic standards of reliability and sound scientific practice.

Shirley Abrahamson, chief justice of the Wisconsin Supreme Court, in remarks made during the opening session of the November 2005 symposium Forensic Science: The Nexus of Science and the Law, sponsored by the National Academies, commented, "The defense thinks a lot of junk science is still coming in, and defendants normally lose Daubert challenges more often than not. Popular wisdom says Daubert challenges are not prevalent in criminal cases, while the forensic science community disagrees. A lot of cases raised Daubert issues, but in seven years following this decision, there were only 211 reported challenges to prosecution experts in state courts."

Stephen Fienberg, Ph.D., the Maurice Falk University professor of statistics and social science in the Department of Statistics at the Center for Automated Learning and Discovery at Carnegie Mellon University, acting as chair of the aforementioned 2005 symposium, remarked that the *Daubert* standard has "generated controversy and ambiguity" for admissibility criteria. Fienberg added, "These criteria haven't been sufficient to those watching from the sidelines and those engaged in the field; fingerprinting evidence challenges have ignited the issue of admissibility and old challenges to forensic science. . . . The courts have been slow to adopt scientific procedures and slow to respond to novel ideas. It's fair to say that in some quarters, forensic science is under attack."

Berger (2000) asserts that post-*Daubert* challenges to forensic identification have been "largely unsuccessful if looked at solely in terms of rulings on admissibility," since Courts have largely refused to exclude prosecution experts. Berger adds, "For instance, although a number of scholars have challenged the ability of forensic document examiners to identify the author of a writing, courts have permitted such experts to testify even while expressing concern about the reliability of their methodology."

Prior to the *Kumho* decision, Berger (2000) argues, "some courts reached this result using an approach not unlike that of the court of appeals in Kumho: The courts concluded that handwriting analysis is not a science, and that, therefore, Daubert—and the need for empirical validation—is inapplicable."

At issue for legal scholars is the preservation of the reliability criteria's place in the adjudication of criminal cases in which forensic evidence is proffered. Few can argue that after *Daubert,* there was a push for greater scrutiny of technical evidence under the bright light cast by empirical evidence and the scientific method. Berger (2000) states, "It would be a great pity if such efforts cease in the wake of Kumho because trial judges have discretion to admit experience-based expertise. Even though the Court's opinion clearly relieves a judge from having to apply the Daubert factors in a given case, it does not eliminate the fundamental requirement of reliability."

In a post-*Daubert* world, techniques employed by forensic practitioners should regularly come under greater scrutiny, legal scholars say, and under the *Kumho* directive of examining the particular circumstances of the case, forensic expertise could be seen in a new light. Berger (2000) says issues may be recast in criminal cases, in that, "rather than appraising the reliability of the field, courts would instead question the ability of experts in that field to provide relevant, reliable testimony with regard to the particular contested issue."

In toxic tort cases, causation is usually the most critical issue, but with it comes immensely technical material used to explain and substantiate complex diseases or defects that are allegedly caused by the agent in question. Proof of causation, then, would entail establishing the chain of events that produced the injury in question. Causation then triggers a steady stream of scientific evidence from which an inference of cause and effect may be drawn, and through which a judge and jury must wade. In the evidence trilogy, the Court was more interested in the "how and why" factors of causation that could be gleaned from the particular evidence being proffered than in formulating per se rules about the admissibility or inadmissibility of categories of evidence to prove causation. In no small way, the Court could have been setting the stage for a greater scrutiny of forensic science–related evidence.

THE SUPREME COURT'S INTEREST IN SCIENTIFIC EVIDENCE

While most cases, both civil and criminal, are decided at the trial court level, some observers wonder why the U.S. Supreme Court took up the question of expert testimony. Berger (2005) notes, "Certainly, the growing dependence on technology and science in our society meant that more issues turning on expert testimony were entering the courtroom. . . . In addition, the revolutionary advent of forensic DNA technology, which was first introduced in an American courtroom just a few years before Daubert, undoubtedly drew the Supreme Court's attention to how science and law interact. In addition, numerous prestigious groups, including the Federal Courts Study Commission established by Congress, the Judicial Conference, and the Carnegie Commission on Science, Law and Technology, had begun actively calling for a reexamination of how courts handle complex scientific and technological issues."[2]

Risinger (2000a) points to Peter Huber's 1991 book, *Galileo's Revenge,* in which Huber popularized the phrase "junk science." Risinger comments, "Given the polemical success of that book, it seems unlikely to have been pure coincidence that the United States Supreme Court chose a civil case to review the appropriate threshold criteria of reliability for expert testimony, or that its two subsequent forays into these waters have also been in civil cases. Be that as it may, the pronouncements of the Supreme Court are given as trans-substantive constructions of the Federal Rules of Evidence, and so have application in criminal as well as civil cases."

Berger (2005) concurs, adding, "By the time the Supreme Court undertook to hear Daubert, plaintiffs' experts were being castigated with some frequency as the villains whose testimony, supposedly based on junk science, was responsible for huge unjustified verdicts in product liability and toxic tort actions. The phrase . . . quickly became a shorthand expression for referring to perceived problems with expert witnesses."[2] (See Chapter 10 for a discussion of junk science.)

THE EVIDENCE TRILOGY IS DISSECTED

In 2003, the 10-year anniversary of the *Daubert* decision, there was a groundswell of commentary from legal scholars pondering what a decade of *Daubert* had wrought upon the legal system. As Cecil (2005) points out, "Law professors and other scholars have filled the law library shelves with articles analyzing published cases following Daubert." It is an open book upon which many legal scholars will continue to write, and the impacts of the evidence trilogy may not be clearly understood before the end of this decade.

According to Saks and Faigman (2005), the federal courts have averaged about 500 decisions per year on *Daubert*-related issues. They add that states also are actively involved in this arena, with more than half the state courts now following *Daubert* (Bernstein and Jackson 2004), and many other state courts influenced by *Daubert* (Faigman et al., 2005). According to Saks and Faigman, some *Frye* states, especially New York and Florida, have occasionally interpreted their test in ways that bear a strong resemblance to *Daubert* criteria.

"The key issue related to Daubert is whether Federal Rule 702 superseded Frye," observes Victor Weedn, M.D., J.D., professor at Duquesne University School of Law. "There was increasing criticism of the Frye test; many saw it as a popularity contest of sorts. You could say that the world was flat would have met the general acceptance standard at some point in history, but it doesn't really address the veracity of the proposition proffered. About half of the circuit courts said that Daubert superseded Frye, while the other half seemed to say Frye helped one to understand Federal Rules—it was a basis by which you judged the helpfulness. So the Supreme Court said 702 does supersede Frye, and in doing so it points out that the purpose of the 1975 rules of evidence is to liberalize admissibility of evidence. So some of the thinking was in fact that there would be an opening of evidence to the jury, recognizing though there is some screening function and the judges would allow that."

Weedn continues, "I think the Supreme Court justices were liberalizing the standard, and declaring that general acceptance was just one of several bases for admissibility. However, most people looked at the case as tightening admissibility standards to keep out junk science, and admonishing judges by saying, 'You should be screening this.' Well, the truth is, that was in the Federal Rules of Evidence from the beginning; the Supreme Court justices were just emphasizing the point. There was then an expectation of higher scrutiny. It's not clear what people really thought it would do in terms of loosening or tightening. It has certainly given the criminal defense bar a leg to stand on when challenging things like fingerprint evidence. Prior to that you could say, 'Well, it's generally accepted.' Now there is something in Daubert with which you can say, 'Prove it—show me the scientific foundation.' That's key, but of course, the judges are reluctant to really rule evidence such as fingerprints inadmissible. Judge Pollak, in the Plaza case, said fingerprints were not admissible then took it back. What judges are faced with is, if they call it inadmissible, then thousands of cases in which people have been put in prison for just that, are in question."

THE IMPACT OF THE EVIDENCE TRILOGY

For the first time since the establishment of the *Frye* test, courts were scrutinizing anew the quality and reliability of expert testimony and scientific evidence, which are a fundamental component of the American adjudication process.

Saks and Faigman (2005) write, "The law of expert testimony provides a lens through which many aspects of modern legal practice can be studied. Every jurisdiction that confronts devising a rule of admission for expert evidence must resolve two basic matters. First, how strict should the rule be? Should it be liberal and allow testimony from virtually all who claim expertise, stopping short perhaps of astrologers and tea-leaf readers? Or should it be conservative and demand rigorous proof of experts' claims of expertise? The second matter that a jurisdiction must resolve is where the real axis of decision making will be. Should courts defer to the professionals in the field from which the experts come, or should they evaluate the quality of the expert opinion for themselves? Implicit in the answers that a particular jurisdiction gives to these two, largely independent, matters are numerous beliefs about legal process and beyond, including its faith in the adversarial process, its confidence in judicial competence, its trust of the jury system, and even its philosophy and sociology of science and empirical knowledge."

Saks and Faigman (2005) add, "Courts have long struggled to develop a test to guide their gate-keeping of expert testimony, scientific or otherwise. The task is easily framed: How is a judge to determine which kinds of opinions from which areas of asserted expertise are dependable enough to be permitted at trial? But the task presents what may be an insuperable dilemma: Courts need expert evidence to assist them in making decisions on issues about which they by definition know far less than the expert, yet for that very same reason courts are in a poor position to assess the expertise. The history of rules and procedures for screening expert witnesses represents successive responses to that dilemma."

GETTING TO THE HEART OF EACH DECISION

Daubert v Merrell Dow Pharmaceuticals held that the admissibility of scientific evidence depends mainly on its scientific merit, and instructs courts to consider whether the scientific basis has been tested empirically, the methodological soundness of that testing, and the results of that testing. Saks and Faigman (2005) write, "These were flexible criteria, so that if courts thought of more appropriate criteria they could use the alternatives. Lower courts were later cautioned, however, against taking flexibility as a license to scrutinize sloppily or not at all. In the Kumho opinion, Justice Antonin Scalia wrote, 'Though . . . the Daubert factors are not holy writ, in a particular case the failure to apply one or another of them may be unreasonable and hence an abuse of discretion.'"

General Electric Co. v Joiner held that appellate courts must review trial court admission decisions under *Daubert* deferentially and that the logic by which the expert traveled from principles and evidence to a conclusion also is subject to appraisal by the court. *Kumho Tire Co. v Carmichael* held that *Daubert*'s essential evidentiary reliability requirement applies to all fields of expert evidence, not only to science. *Daubert* retained the general acceptance criterion, though in downgraded status, and *Kumho* demoted it further.

In essence, although the evidence trilogy consisted of interpretations by the Supreme Court of the Federal Rules of Evidence, *Daubert, Joiner,* and *Kumho* triggered an amendment to the Rules in 2000 in order to better reflect trial courts' obligations to insure the soundness of expert evidence as prescribed in these cases. Rules 701, 702, and 703 were amended. According to Saks and Faigman (2005), "Rule 701, which permits lay witness opinions under certain circumstances, was strengthened to ensure that testimony that should be evaluated under Rule 702 did not slip in through the back door of Rule 701. Rule 702 essentially codified Daubert by adding three new numbered clauses. The rule now states: 'If scientific, technical, or other specialized knowledge will assist the trier of fact to understand the evidence or to determine a fact in issue, a witness qualified as an expert by knowledge, skill, experience, training, or education, may testify thereto in the form of an opinion or otherwise, if the testimony is based upon sufficient facts or data, the testimony is the product of reliable principles and methods, and the witness has applied the principles and methods reliably to the facts of the case.'"

In the past, Rule 703 had been used to introduce otherwise inadmissible hearsay statements into evidence; the amended rule states, "Facts or data that are otherwise inadmissible shall not be disclosed to the jury by the proponent of the opinion or inference unless the court determines that their probative value in assisting the jury to evaluate the expert's opinion substantially outweighs their prejudicial effect."

In *Daubert,* Berger (2005) explains, the Supreme Court established a new two-pronged test for the admissibility of scientific evidence, whose object was to ensure that expert testimony "is not only relevant, but reliable."[2]

In the majority opinion of the Court, Justice Harry Blackmun explained that to satisfy reliability, the expert must have derived his or her conclusion by the scientific method. Blackmun embraced the scientific method and its components, including hypothesis testing, peer review and publication, known or potential rates of error, and the existence of standards controlling the technique's operation. As a nod to *Frye,* general acceptance of the methodology in the relevant discipline also was mentioned as a factor to be considered.

Berger (2005) explains that the second prong of relevancy dictated that an expert's theory had to fit the facts of the case. Even if the expert's theory was completely scientific, it had no application if it dealt with a matter that was not at issue. Berger writes, "Perhaps of paramount importance, the Daubert opinion recast the role of the trial court. Trial judges had always had the power to exclude inappropriate expert testimony, but some preferred to leave this task to the jury, particularly when the expert proof related to complex scientific principles with which the judge was not very familiar or comfortable. But the Court now told trial judges that they were gatekeepers who were obliged to screen scientific expert testimony for relevancy and reliability before it could be admitted. The Supreme Court did not apply its new test for the admissibility of expert testimony in the Daubert case. Instead, it reversed the decision and remanded the case to the lower court."[2]

Berger (2005) writes, "In essence, the Daubert trilogy adopts a changed perspective and relocates the axis of decision. With the old commercial marketplace test, judges piggy-backed onto what consumers seemed to think about a proffered expertise and expert. Under Frye's general acceptance test, judges took a rough nose count and deferred to what the producers of knowledge thought about the knowledge they had to offer. Daubert finally places the obligation to evaluate the evidence where one might have expected it to be all along: on the judges themselves."[2]

Berger (2005) and Risinger (2000a) acknowledge that *Daubert* places a heavy responsibility on judges' shoulders; they must scrutinize scientific proffers from experts to find the core of their research findings and methods of the evidence, and the principles used to extrapolate from that research to the task at hand. Berger admits, "This obligation on the part of judges is daunting. It may be more apparent now than it was for centuries before why judges sought ways to avoid such responsibility [and why, notwithstanding the commands of Daubert, many of them still do]."[2] (An expanded discussion of judicial responsibilities is offered in Chapter 13.)

Berger (2005) emphasizes, "Daubert, in many respects, appeared to be a revolutionary decision. . . . The core principle of Daubert is its changed focus from Frye's deference to the experts to a more active judicial evaluation of a particular field's claims of expertise. Under

Frye, judges did not need to understand research methodology because it was sufficient to inquire into the conclusions of professionals in the pertinent fields. Daubert mandates that judges query which methods support the scientific opinions that experts seek to offer as testimony, and this requires that they understand those methods and data. . . . The revolutionary core of Daubert is in this call for judges to become knowledgeable about basic research methods. Daubert, in effect, brought the scientific revolution into the courtroom."[2]

Berger (2005) writes, "Revolutions inevitably produce partisans having widely varying views, including some who defend the old regime, others who seek to justify the new order, and still others on either side of the barricades, who determine its ultimate fate. Many of the battles over the Daubert revolution have been carried out in the law review literature, where the debate moved quickly from whether a revolution had occurred at all to the nature of that revolution, and, even more so, to the philosophical justifications for it. For instance, some commentators argue that in Daubert, 'the U.S. Supreme Court took it upon itself to solve, once and for all, the knotty problem of the demarcation of science from pseudoscience'" (Goodstein 2000), or that the Court adopted and imposed a specifically experimental or Newtonian or Popperian view of science. But, in the legal context in which the Daubert trilogy arose and to which it pertains, the Court can be seen as trying to solve more flexibly a more modest (though similarly enduring and knotty) problem of trial evidence, namely, how to filter proffered expert opinion testimony so that reliable evidence is admitted and unreliable evidence is not. Daubert confronted a particular type of expertise, empirical claims, that lends itself to evaluation by scientific methods. Daubert's answer, in essence, is that if the proponent of such evidence cannot supply good grounds for concluding that the expert opinion is sufficiently trustworthy—cannot supply appropriate validation—then the testimony should be excluded. It added that the obligation to test the soundness of expert proffers is applicable to timeworn as well as to novel testimony. Given that Daubert itself was a case about epidemiological (correlational) data, the charge that it wrongheadedly demands experimental data is hard to support. Still, one can debate whether the best filter has been chosen. In addition, one can debate the philosophical justifications for the revolution itself. How long this philosophical debate will endure only time can reveal, but it certainly occupied a prominent place in the Daubert era's first decade."[2]

Giannelli (2003) notes, "One unexpected development has been Daubert's disparate impact in civil and criminal cases. The notion that expert testimony in criminal and civil cases should be treated differently does not seem, at least to me, to be a remarkable proposition. The issues are very different. Instead of worrying about the hired gun phenomenon as in civil litigation, the criminal defense lawyer often lacks money for any gun. Moreover, the causation issues that loom so large in toxic tort cases are seldom an issue in criminal prosecutions, and the termination of the litigation before trial through summary judgment is not a concern. What is remarkable about the civil-criminal dichotomy is that civil litigants have far greater discovery rights than criminal practitioners even though it is well accepted that pretrial disclosure is critical. Not only are discovery depositions and interrogatories unavailable, but a defendant in a death penalty case involving DNA can be precluded from seeing an expert's lab notes before trial. What is also remarkable is that stricter admissibility standards would apply in civil cases than in criminal cases. It is difficult to imagine a federal court in a toxic tort case that would allow a plaintiff's attorney to admit evidence that passed for science in a recent fingerprint case. In *United States v Harvard*, the court accepted testimony by an FBI expert that there is a zero error rate in fingerprint examinations, peer review under Daubert means a second examiner looks at the prints, and adversarial testing is the equivalent of scientific testing. How can federal courts demand stringent epidemiological studies in toxic tort cases and then accept such vacuous reasoning in criminal cases?"

Berger (2005) asserts, "Much of the expert proof in criminal cases consists of forensic identification testimony; it would seem far easier to test whether a given technique can in fact match two tangible samples and to determine the frequency of such a match than to decide whether a substance can cause a particular disease. Clearly, however, except for a few cases excluding or limiting testimony about handwriting analysis, the courts are not applying Daubert stringently in the criminal context. The paramount example is fingerprint evidence that has never been validated. Although no one doubts that full sets of fingerprints can be matched, the fingerprint found at a crime scene is often a partial, latent, contaminated print. How much of a print is needed for a match under these circumstances has not been determined. Although a number of Daubert challenges have been made by defense counsel, they have to date been uniformly rejected. A federal judge who initially limited fingerprint experts to explaining similarities but barred them from expressing an opinion about identity changed his mind."[2]

The cases in question are *United States v Llara Plaza* and the appeal, United *States v Llara Plaza*. Berger (2005) writes, "Both cases acknowledge the lack of research into the validity of matching fingerprints; examiners have only been tested for proficiency. When it comes to expert testimony issues in criminal cases, the courts seem very conscious of the need to protect society against dangerous persons."

Studies by the Federal Judicial Center and the RAND Institute have stated that judges are much more likely since *Daubert* to scrutinize expert testimony before trial and then to limit or exclude expert testimony. But no one is making the claim that the evidence trilogy has produced improved expert testimony in civil or in criminal cases. Berger (2005) observes, "Nobody at this point has the data to support such a conclusion, because no one has as yet systematically compared proffered expert testimony that is excluded with that which is admitted."

What the trilogy has done, some experts say, is create a chilling effect on science, in that an increasing number of scientists are wary of testifying in court. Berger (2005) comments, "That a judge, who possibly has some incorrect or unsophisticated views about science, has the power to exclude the scientist as an expert witness and make some cutting remarks in print while doing so, may be enough to convince some scientists that they do not wish to be involved with the legal system. And they may also for similar reasons decline to undertake research related to litigation. On the remand of Daubert, Judge Kozinski of the Ninth Circuit added as a factor for courts to consider in assessing reliability whether the expert's research was conducted expressly for the purpose of testifying and suggested that unless science is conducted independently of litigation, it is not likely to amount to 'good science.' But often the need for research does not become apparent until litigation begins. Judge Kozinski's assessment puts another potential obstacle in plaintiffs' path by perhaps driving out of the courtroom good scientists who do not want to be castigated as hired guns."[2]

THE SCIENCE WARS AFTER DAUBERT: EVALUATING EVIDENCE

Saks and Faigman (2005) point out that Chief Justice William Rehnquist had complained that neither he, nor he supposed, most federal judges understood what falsifiability was. Moreover, the majority opinion, he complained, appeared to call upon judges to be amateur scientists, a role for which they were not trained and in which they were not likely to excel.

Saks and Faigman (2005) say that good science, according to the Supreme Court, follows certain methodological conventions, while bad science does not. "The vaunted Daubert four factors—testing, peer review and publication, error rate, and general acceptance—are essentially aspects of the ordinary conduct of scientific investigation. The Daubert Court, therefore, was engaged in the rather pedestrian activity of articulating a test by which lower courts could make decisions regarding the admissibility of expert evidence. The decision must be understood in those terms. Unlike philosophers of science, trial courts must make concrete decisions in particular cases. But in articulating this evidentiary standard, Justice Blackmun effectively entered the science wars."

Saks and Faigman (2005) explain that the basic challenge for trial courts in the area of expert testimony is to define the boundary between admissible and inadmissible evidence. "As the Kumho Tire Court understood, the definition of adequate science is only a subpart of this greater task. Expertise comes to court in myriad forms, ranging from the most traditionally rigorous fields, such as physics, to the most traditionally lax, such as clinical medicine. Some experts dress in the guise of science, such as forensic document examiners, whereas others claim expertise by virtue of experience alone, such as police officers. The one thing all these ostensible experts have in common is their claim to opinions that are relevant and sufficiently accurate to be helpful to the trier of fact."

As we have seen, *Daubert,* as reinforced by *Kumho,* applies to all expert testimony, holding simply that trial courts must determine whether the basis for proffered expert testimony is reliable and valid. But there are no absolutes. Saks and Faigman (2005) warn, "The four Daubert factors will often help courts make that determination, and sometimes they will not. In Kumho Tire, the Supreme Court declined any attempt to set forth a single set of criteria that might be useful in assessing the myriad kinds of expertise the courts hear. The point is that trial judges are obligated to carry out the gate-keeping function; how they do so is a separate question. Therefore, in the Daubert trilogy, the Court was engaged in the task of defining a rule of procedure that would apply to all forms of expertise. Philosophers and sociologists of science could offer insights into the difficulty of the task, but their views have limited relevance to whether the Court chose the correct rule for its purposes."

Saks and Faigman (2005) outline the ways courts can evaluate expert testimony and scientific evidence:

- Establish expectations regarding the rigor of the testing that should have been done: Should courts consider whether an opinion could be rigorously tested, or should they simply accept the standard practice of the particular field, which might include relying on experience as a basis of expertise?
- Determine how courts should evaluate the numerous expertises that rely on a wide variety of methods, from casual experience to controlled experiment.

Cecil (2005) observes, "Many federal judges were uncertain how the 1993 Supreme Court decision in *Daubert v Merrell Dow* Pharmaceuticals, Inc. would affect their work. But Judge Alex Kozinski, author of the Ninth Circuit appellate court decision that was vacated and remanded for further consideration by the Supreme Court, was worried. In reconsidering the case in light of the standards expressed in Daubert, Judge Kozinski wryly noted, 'Our responsibility, then, unless we badly misread the Supreme Court's opinion, is to resolve disputes among respected, well-credentialed scientists about matters squarely within their expertise, in areas where there is no scientific consensus as to what is and what is not 'good science,' and occasionally to reject such expert testimony because it was not 'derived by the scientific method.'"

In 1993, at the time of the *Daubert* decision, there was considerable uncertainty about its effect on admissibility of scientific evidence. It soon became clear that the interpretation of the decision was resulting in a more restrictive approach to admissibility of scientific testimony. Cecil (2005) reports that a Federal Judicial Center (FJC) survey of federal judges and attorneys confirmed this shift toward more demanding standards for admissibility of evidence. In 1998, both judges and attorneys indicated that judges were more likely to scrutinize expert testimony before trial and to limit or exclude proffered testimony compared with pre-*Daubert* litigation practice in 1991. Cecil also reports that the survey revealed that motions filed early in litigation have become a favored pretrial device for challenging the admissibility of expert testimony and that judges are focusing more attention in pre-trial proceedings on admissibility issues.

At the state court level, the picture becomes murkier. Gatowski's 1998 survey of state court judges found that judges were divided in their assessment of *Daubert*'s impact. Just about half of the judges from states that adhere to the Federal Rules of Evidence, and thus are far more likely to follow *Daubert*, expressed that their gatekeeping role had evolved due to *Daubert;* one-third of the judges said they thought Daubert was designed to raise the threshold for admissibility. In addition, Gatowski's study revealed that state court judges did not grasp firmly the meaning of *Daubert*'s scientific criteria and questioned the ability of state trial courts to apply these standards in a reasoned manner. According to the study, just a small number of judges could define the concept of falsifiability, as provided for in *Daubert*.

The FJC survey also examined judges' ongoing concerns about testifying experts' lack of objectivity. Cecil (2005) reports that according to the survey, both before and after the 1993 *Daubert* decision, the most frequent problem that federal judges encounter is "experts who abandon objectivity and become advocates for the side that hired them."

Cecil (2005) attributes this to several factors: "Experts are selected by the parties based on the extent to which their testimony will advance the parties' claims, a practice that may favor the selection of extreme viewpoints. Moreover, preparing an expert witness to offer testimony involves a socialization process that is likely to encourage the expert to identify with the interest of the party. It is reasonable that judges, who likely were exposed to such practices prior to their arrival on the bench, would be skeptical of testimony offered by expert witnesses who had undergone such selection and coaching."

One of the most important developments post-*Daubert* is that judges' gatekeeping role "has evolved beyond a device for reviewing only scientific evidence to include all types of expert testimony," according to Cecil (2005). One-third of the *Daubert* progeny, *Kumho Tire Co. v Carmichael,* extended the gatekeeping function to all types of expert testimony. Prior to the *Kumho* decision, the courts were divided on whether expert testimony based on experience should be subjected to the *Daubert* screening process. Cecil (2005) writes, "In extending the trial court's gate-keeping obligation to all expert testimony, the Supreme Court noted that 'no clear line' can be drawn between the different kinds of knowledge, and that 'no one denies that an expert might draw a conclusion from a set of observations based on extensive and specialized experience.'" The Supreme Court mandated that all expert witnesses should employ "in the courtroom the same level of intellectual rigor that characterizes the practice of an expert in the relevant field." Cecil (2005) comments, "In effect, this decision tethered the standard for admissibility of expert testimony to standards of professional practice. This reliability requirement has also been added as a recent amendment to Federal Rule of Evidence 702, strengthening the role of the court in assessing the foundation of all expert testimony proffered for litigation."

THE VARIABLE INTERPRETATIONS OF *DAUBERT*

That *Daubert* was open to interpretation may be a gross understatement. Following the *Daubert* decision, Risinger (2000) reports, "*The Washington Post* characterized it as a victory for those who wanted expertise more easily admitted, while *The New York Times* characterized it as a victory for those who wanted more expertise rejected. This schizoid characterization of the case has continued in both academic commentary and lines of judicial decision down to the present time."

Giannelli (2003) observed the difficulty many experienced in the interpretation of *Daubert* and its progeny. He writes, "In many ways, Daubert was a difficult opinion to interpret even at the time it was handed down. As one commentary observed, 'astonishingly, all parties expressed satisfaction with the Daubert decision—the lawyers for the plaintiff and defense, and scientists who wrote amicus briefs.' This alone should have raised red flags."

Risinger (2000) describes two schools of thought that have emerged regarding *Daubert*'s true meaning in reference to non-scientific expertise. He explains, "The first school saw Daubert as essentially a general construction of Rule 702 and the judge's systemic gate-keeping duties in regard to the sufficient reliability of all proffered expert testimony. To members of this school, Daubert's particular expositions about scientific evidence were important as guides to the kind of reliability that ought to be required of all expertise, even if the so-called Daubert factors . . . applied most powerfully to the products of the conventional sciences. People of this persuasion have, under the banner of Daubert, tended to call upon courts to examine proffered claims of expertise specifically and critically and have tended to advocate for generally rigorous standards of reliability as a condition of admissibility."

Risinger (2000a) adds that the other school of thought believes that *Daubert* should be read as "limited to scientific expertise, narrowly confined to the experimental sciences. As to all other forms of expertise, especially expertise with a claimed experiential component, this school of thought understood Daubert's broader references to Rule 702 as no more than restating the pre-existing understanding of the duty of the court under the helpfulness standard, without suggesting that this standard ought to be tightened up regarding reliability."

For proponents of the latter school of thought, Risinger (2000a) says, "To the extent some explicit approach to reliability was thought necessary for such testimony, people of this persuasion have tended to favor a more general or global examination of the claimed abilities of practitioners of the asserted expertise. They have advocated, at least where applicable, some version of either a sufficient experience test [relying on the expert's previous more or less similar experience, without further proof that the experience has resulted in any reliable skill], or a guild test, in which the existence of an organized group which supervises accreditation (and an expert's membership in it) is taken as a sufficient warrant to infer reliability for admissibility purposes."

Risinger (2000) asserts that "In the courts, these usually conflated approaches have been especially prevalent in regard to the products of forensic science in criminal cases. Unfortunately for their adherents, the Supreme Court's decision in Kumho Tire Co. v Carmichael has pretty much destroyed the tenability of these approaches." In *Daubert,* the Court held that Federal Rule of Evidence 702 imposes an obligation upon a trial judge to "ensure that any and all scientific testimony . . . is not only relevant but reliable." The question in front of the justices was whether the gatekeeping obligation applies only to "scientific" evidence or to all expert testimony. The Court ruled that it applied to all expert testimony.

Risinger (2000) asserts that post-*Daubert* decisions that depended on a clear distinction between scientific evidence and other expertise and applied a less rigorous standard of reliability to non-scientific testimony "have had their main rationale removed and their results at least called into question and put back into play." Risinger ponders, "Yet when these issues are put back into play, how is the game supposed to be played? A court must determine reliability, but does every kind of expert evidence in every context have to meet the same threshold level of reliability to gain admission? The Court does not address this question. I have argued that there ought to be varying levels of foundational reliability, with that required for prosecution-proffered expertise in criminal cases being very high, especially when it goes to issues of . . . guilt or innocence, such as the identity of the defendant as the perpetrator."

THE BOTTOM LINE

While legal scholars continue to debate the meaning of the evidence trilogy and its impact on judges' ability to separate the scientific and technical wheat from the chaff, Saks and Faigman (2005) emphasize that *Daubert* may have forever altered the behavior of lawyers, litigants, and expert witnesses, "either in anticipation of or in reaction to changes in judicial treatment of expert evidence—or the discussions that scholars and those in the legal system generally have about expert evidence."

The legal community learned that *Daubert* did not apply only to new and novel scientific evidence. The Court stated that "well-established propositions are less likely to be challenged than those that are novel, and they are more handily defended," and Saks and Faigman (2005) believe that "long veneration was no protection from scrutiny." Again, Saks and Faigman point to the Gatowski (2001) survey of judges, which revealed that 32 percent believed the intent of *Daubert* was to raise the threshold of admissibility for scientific evidence; 23 percent believed the intent was to lower the threshold, and 36 percent believed the intent was neither to raise nor to lower but instead to articulate a framework for admissibility. Saks and Faigman observe, "Numerous courts have expressed surprise to discover that their application of a supposedly more liberal test led them to the brink of excluding evidence that had never before appeared so excludable. The better answer probably is that 'it depends.'"

Saks and Faigman (2005) assert that when a scientific proposition is sound but not generally accepted, *Daubert* should admit while *Frye* should exclude. They explain, "This is the category of cases that most commentators and courts had in mind when they suggested that Daubert is more liberal than Frye. But when a scientific proposition has not been shown to be sound yet nevertheless has gained general acceptance in its field, then Daubert excludes even though Frye admits. This latter category is not a null set; it contains, perhaps most notably, many of the forensic sciences."

It is at this intersection that the art versus science debate emerges in the legal and forensic science communities. Saks and Faigman (2005) say that post-*Daubert*, some disciplines that did not have much of an empirical, scientific foundation engaged in a "dumbing-down" of their field. Saks and Faigman write, "For a time, some fields tried to evade scrutiny by redefining themselves as non-science or by emphasizing their art over their science." They state that a consortium of law enforcement organizations, "fearing that the expert testimony of forensic scientists and police officers would be excluded if they were to be required to prove that what they were saying had a sound basis," submitted an amicus brief to the Supreme Court in *Kumho* that petitioned the Court to exempt from *Daubert* scrutiny prosecution expert evidence that frequently offers opinions instead of scientific theory..

Envisioning the legal drubbing that pattern identification disciplines, such as fingerprinting, would take in court, there was a call for increased empirical research in the forensic sciences. The National Institute of Justice created several funding initiatives so that scientists could "fill the considerable gaps in the knowledge claims of these fields that they were sure the courts would now discover in the glare of Daubert and Kumho Tire scrutiny" (Saks and Faigman, 2005).

It was, however, a small first step, and some prosecutors worried about *Daubert* challenges to forensic evidence. In civil cases, there was a growing trend that *Daubert* was allowing judges to exclude more testimony than ever before. Dixon and Gill (2001) showed that challenged expert evidence had been excluded about half of the time prior to *Daubert*, and increased by 20 percent after *Daubert*. In addition, Krafka et al. (2002) showed that judges excluded or severely or limited expert evidence about 25 percent of the time before *Daubert*, compared with more than 40 percent of the time after *Daubert*. In criminal cases, however, challenges to scientific evidence were successful less than 10 percent of the time. Importantly, the prosecution's challenges to the defense's expert testimony succeeded about 75 percent of the time (Risinger 2000). Saks and Faigman (2005) suggest that data from Groscup et al. (2002) indicates virtually unchanged patterns of admission and exclusion from the pre-*Daubert* era.

That the quality of the science being proffered in civil cases varies from criminal cases is one reason for the difference between the two types of cases, suggest Saks and Faigman (2005). They also point to what they characterize as "systematic differences between the factual issues that arise in civil and criminal cases. Or, perhaps, the differential outcomes are attributable to differences in the quality of advocacy in the two realms."

Saks and Faigman (2005) take the social science aspects of the debate a step further when they suggest that differential treatment can be chalked up to social and political differences. They explain: "As a general proposition, judges disfavor civil plaintiffs and criminal defendants and are more likely to rule against them than against their opposites even when presenting equivalent evidence or arguments. A more definitive explanation of the pattern awaits future research."

Some legal experts suggest that courts assume erroneously that, instead of the Federal Rules of Evidence applying to all cases, the *Frye* test of general acceptance was applicable to criminal cases only, while *Daubert* primarily was for civil cases. Saks and Faigman (2005) observe, "A number of studies suggest that judges do not employ Daubert as the directive it seems by its terms to be; a directive to conduct meaningful and sincere analyses of the substance of proffered expert evidence, using rational criteria and following them to their logical destination. Instead, judges have taken Daubert to be a vague call to arms against junk science in civil cases while keeping hands off of the government's proffers in criminal cases."

Saks and Faigman (2005) say that even though some disciplines of forensic science are suspect under the *Daubert* decision, many judges continue to admit the related expert testimony. They point to the willingness of courts to embrace fingerprint identification, for example, even though the courts experienced difficulty locating empirical evidence that supported the tenets of this discipline of pattern identification. In fact, Saks and Faigman write, the courts "found the proffered testimony regarding fingerprint evidence not only admissible but often worthy of high praise" in the 2000 case of *U.S. v Harvard*, which called fingerprint identification "the very archetype of reliable expert testimony under [Daubert]." Saks and Faigman cite Cole (2001), who postulates that "fingerprint identification has been so effective in its public mythology that courts cannot suspend their belief long enough to examine the real basis of the claims."

In the 1999 case of *Alaska v Coon*, the Alaska Supreme Court adopted *Daubert* as its admission doctrine, and admitted voiceprint identification evidence (Faigman et al. 2005). In another 1999 case, *Johnson v Commonwealth*, the court evaluated the admissibility of microscopic hair comparison evidence and held that the evidence was fully admissible based on its assumption of general acceptance by past cases, even though no empirical evidence could be produced and no prior cases in that state had found the evidence to be generally accepted. Saks (2004) comments, "The Johnson court reasoned that silence bespoke general acceptance."

There exists no firm interpretation of the evidence trilogy. Saks and Faigman (2005) observe, "Daubert has had somewhat paradoxical effects. Judges overwhelmingly say they subscribe to the gatekeeper role and endorse Daubert's framework for analyzing scientific (and other) expert evidence. It has precipitated a great increase in judicial examination of expert evidence. Yet judges often appear to have little understanding of the basis of the expertise at issue, and all indications are that they invest little of their scrutiny and decision making in seriously applying Daubert or in bringing any other kind of thoughtful examination to bear."

The bottom line? According to Saks and Faigman (2005), *Daubert* had a lasting impact on the legal landscape: "Daubert has led to increased exclusion of expert evidence, mostly in civil cases, and most of that excluding plaintiffs' evidence. The questionable sciences of criminal cases, often among the weakest of the scientific evidence that comes to court, are by one device or another usually admitted [or perhaps it is more accurate to say they are granted exemption from serious scrutiny]. Daubert has precipitated a pattern of gate-keeping that is impossible to explain in terms of Daubert's doctrinal elements or the relative quality of the underlying science presented for scrutiny. Thus, Daubert's impact may have more to do with the sociology of judging than with the law of Daubert. The future of expert evidence will need to take into account these odd patterns of decision-making."

LEGAL PERCEPTIONS OF SCIENCE AND EXPERT KNOWLEDGE

While some critics complain that *Daubert* is conflicted in its view of science as well as in its conception of the relationship between science and law, Mueller (2003) states, "Daubert is not at fault. Indeed, one of the strengths of the opinion is that its vision is broad enough to embrace internal tensions and difficulties in science, and in the relationship between law and science, that cannot be avoided."

While Mueller (2003) concedes that *Daubert* could be accused of viewing science as an unchanging, static body of objective knowledge reflecting certainty, Mueller adds that *Daubert* also acknowledged, "science is a process and anything but static; scientific knowledge does not reflect certainty but is uncertain and contingent; and that scientific expertise is affected by the forces that generate litigation, hence subjective in some respects, and socially constructed." Critics of *Daubert* say that judges cannot adequately perform their gatekeeping role because *Daubert* charges them to apply static objective standards in appraising shifting subjective, contingent knowledge (Mueller).

Mueller (2003) proposes that the legal community look at the relationship between law and science as *Daubert* envisioned it: "On the one hand, Daubert affirms that it is the job of courts to appraise science, and courts are not simply to defer to the scientific community on the question whether evidence presented as science is valid and reliable. This role for courts is what we mean by gate-keeping. On the other hand, Daubert says courts are to judge science by the standards that scientists deploy in judging science." Mueller continues, "Kumho Tire adds an exclamation point in commenting that scientists are to bring to the courtroom 'the same level of intellectual rigor that characterizes the practice of an expert in the relevant field.' Again this incoherent view asks courts to do what they cannot do and fails to recognize that science and law have different agendas, goals and purposes, and operate under different constraints."

Sanders et al. (2002) assert that the evidence trilogy asks judges to "assume the role of scientific methodologists," and that these three opinions reflect a "realist-constructivist view of science." Sanders et al. continue, "Science is socially constructed both in the laboratory and in the wider community, but the construction is constrained by input from the empirical world. In the past half century, expert testimony has played an increasingly important role in American litigation. As the volume of expert testimony has grown, so have issues surrounding its admissibility into evidence. . . . The cases and the way their admissibility tests are being applied have proven to be remarkably contentious."

Sanders et al. (2002) observe, "At bottom, the Daubert revolution is about the relationship between judges and experts, between law and science. Frye asked judges to acquiesce to the judgment of the relevant scientific community. Daubert on the other hand, invites the trial court to make an independent inquiry. The judge should determine whether the proffered evidence is reliable by examining the reasoning and methodology underlying the expert's testimony. To be sure, the opinion allows judges to make use of surrogate indicia of reliability. Peer review and publication and general acceptance in the scientific community are factors judges may consider, but they are secondary to a direct assessment of the testimony's scientific validity. As Michael Saks recently noted, "perhaps the purpose of the rules is simply to hold up a target to the courts; call one the Frye target and the other the Daubert target.' The Frye ideal says: do whatever the experts tell you to do. The Daubert ideal says: figure out the science yourself."

THE SUPREME COURT'S CRIMINAL "DAUBERT" CASES

Even in states that still adhere to the *Frye* test of general acceptance, judges are using *Daubert* and its progeny to evaluate scientific evidence proffered in criminal cases. A good example of this trend can be found in *Ramirez v State*, in which the Supreme Court of Florida rejected expert testimony asserting that a knife belonging to the defendant's girlfriend was the weapon used to inflict a fatal stab wound in the victim, and holding that the expert's methods did not meet the *Frye* standard. A federal district judge, Louis Pollak, using the *Daubert* standard, granted a defense motion to preclude expert testimony that proposed to identify a specific individual on the basis of matching fingerprints. However, Pollak granted a motion for reconsidering his order and ultimately allowed the prosecution to present identification testimony based on the matching fingerprint. Kennedy and Merrill (2003) state, "Pollak's initial ruling, along with challenges to other kinds of forensic evidence, have increasingly led to suggestions that the scientific foundation of many common forensic science techniques may be open to question."

While many forensic techniques had in the past escaped much scrutiny in the courtroom, legal scholars were delighted that criteria used in civil cases were starting to be applied in criminal cases, despite the overwhelming evidence that most judges still were admitting shaky evidence into their courtrooms. Coupled with the *Daubert* criteria was the advent of DNA analysis, a scientific discipline that had endured extensive scientific validation; these two forces were changing the way courts viewed other forensic science identification techniques such as fingerprints, fiber analysis, hair analysis, ballistics, bite marks, and tool marks. Kennedy and Merrill (2003) state, "These techniques rely on the skill of the examiner, but since the practitioners have not been subjected to rigorous proficiency testing, reliable error rates are not known."

Forensic science is attempting to rise to these new challenges. Kennedy and Merrill (2003) observe, "Advances in the forensic sciences have generally emerged to address the needs of the criminal law community. Most of the research has been sponsored by federal agencies whose missions include law enforcement and prosecution, but relatively little science. Scant funding has been provided for competitive basic academic research, and very few, if any, doctoral programs in forensic sciences exist. The culture of academic research, with the free and open exchange of ideas, peer review of research findings, and rigorous disciplinary programs, has not been the norm for the forensic science community."

Having said that, Kennedy and Merrill (2003) add that *Daubert* encourages the legal and forensic science communities to ponder "how scientific principles can be appropriately applied throughout the forensic sciences, how academic research in the forensic sciences can be promoted, and what the research agenda in this area should be. In the wake of Daubert, the community of forensic scientists may well be pressed to answer these questions in order to maintain their prominent role in U.S. courts."

Kennedy and Merrill (2003) continue, "In assessing admissibility under the Daubert standards, courts are seeking a better understanding of the scientific bases of forensic analysis. Courts are inquiring into the relative frequencies at which the identifying traits occur in the general population and the probability of a coincidental match with a crime scene sample. Courts are questioning the standards to which the experts making the identification are held; whether identification is based on objective criteria; and whether standardized minimum criteria must be met for a positive identification. Recognizing that no science consistently produces certain results, courts are also questioning the error rates associated with forensic identification techniques. In these ways, courts are actively seeking an improved understanding of the scientific basis of forensic science and of the body of research required to support expert testimony. We hope the academic and law enforcement communities will do the same."

As all stakeholders in the criminal justice system try to understand each other and work toward greater competence on all sides, many experts say that *Daubert* will continue to have applicability to criminal cases as well as civil cases. The capital case of *Barefoot v Estelle* (1983) reflects the spirit of *Daubert*. Giannelli (2003) explains that in the penalty phase, prosecution offered psychiatric testimony concerning Barefoot's future dangerousness. Without actually examining the defendant, a psychiatrist testified that there was an "absolute" chance that he would commit future acts of criminal violence. The defendant then challenged the admission of this evidence on constitutional grounds due to its unreliability. The American Psychiatric Association (APA) stated in an amicus brief that "the large body of research in this area indicates that, even under the best of conditions, psychiatric predictions of long-term dangerousness are wrong in at least two out of every three cases." The brief also acknowledged that the "unreliability of [these] predictions is by now an established fact within the profession." The Court rejected Barefoot's argument, stating, "Neither petitioner nor the (APA) suggests that psychiatrists are always wrong with respect to future dangerousness, only most of the time." The Court also stated that it was "not persuaded that such testimony is almost entirely unreliable and that the fact finder and the adversary system will not be competent to uncover, recognize, and take due account of its shortcomings."

Giannelli (2003) is quick to point to the dissenting opinion penned by *Daubert* author Justice Harry Blackmun: "In the present state of psychiatric knowledge, this is too much for me. One may accept this in a routine lawsuit for money damages, but when a person's life is at stake . . . a requirement of greater reliability should prevail." Giannelli rightly points out that "Daubert required a far higher standard of admissibility for money-damages than

Barefoot required for the death penalty. Nor can Barefoot be distinguished from Daubert as a constitutional, rather than an evidentiary, decision."

As stated earlier, *Daubert* has had a far more significant impact in civil litigation than in criminal litigation. That is not to say its effect in criminal cases has been insubstantial. Giannelli (2003) asserts that courts see *Daubert* as "inviting a reexamination even of generally accepted, venerable, technical fields," scrutiny that would have not occurred under the *Frye* test of general acceptance. Giannelli claims that *Daubert* "closed a major loophole in the Frye rule" because numerous *Frye* courts recognized an exception for non-novel evidence, which exempts certain techniques from the general acceptance requirement. As an example, Giannelli points to the fact that some California courts apply this exception to bite mark comparisons or evidence based on narcotic detection dogs, while Arizona courts use this exception to exempt footprint evidence. Giannelli remarks, "Daubert explicitly rejected this free pass to admissibility, and Kumho reinforced this view by subjecting all expert testimony to the reliability requirement."

Daubert's effect on the *Frye* test has also been significant, according to Giannelli (2003), because it forced state courts to reexamine their admissibility standard for scientific evidence. Giannelli remarks, "Although numerous courts have rejected Frye in favor of Daubert, some jurisdictions have retained Frye, and many of these are populous states, in which many, if not most, criminal cases are tried. Some of these courts believe Frye offers greater protection for defendants than Daubert."

Barefoot v Estelle illustrated another important tenet related to *Daubert*'s effect on scientific evidence, specifically the relevancy approach, under which the act of qualifying the expert generally also qualifies the technique employed by that expert. Giannelli (2003) calls it a "lax" standard, which *Daubert* rejected by requiring reliability in addition to relevancy.

Giannelli (2003) says that one of the most important effects of *Daubert* on criminal cases is that the 2000 amendment to Federal Rules of Evidence Rule 702 can be traced to *Daubert* and extends beyond both *Daubert* and *Kumho*. In essence, DNA cases, which raised significant, complex questions and raised the stakes considerably in the minds of jurors, created the need for admissibility criteria more extensive than what the *Frye* test could offer. According to Giannelli, a trio of criteria was adopted: The underlying theory must have been generally accepted, the procedures implementing the theory must have been generally accepted, and the testing laboratory must have followed these procedures. Giannelli explains that the third criterion was referred to as "Frye plus." In addition, a few courts applied this requirement after *Daubert* was decided, referred to as the "Daubert plus" approach. Amended Rule 702 favors the more stringent approach, Giannelli states, adding, "The Advisory Committee's Note to Rule 702 specified a number of reliability factors that supplement the ones enumerated in Daubert. One is whether the field of expertise claimed by the expert is known to reach reliable results. This provides some official support for challenges to entire fields of forensic science."

Of all of the cases most discussed in an intense evidence-admissibility debate, DNA cases may take the prize. Giannelli (2003) acknowledges, "The advent of DNA evidence has also shaped the course of forensic science in significant ways. The DNA admissibility 'wars' highlighted the need for valid protocols and proficiency testing, and commentators soon began asking why such procedures were not applied in other forensic fields. More importantly, the research scientists who testified as experts in the DNA cases [for both the prosecution and defense] came from a 'scientific' culture, unlike the many forensic examiners who work in crime laboratories and are sometimes described as 'cops in lab coats.' The DNA scientists were comfortable with quality control procedures, demanded written protocols, viewed proficiency testing as a positive development, and believed in open science and not trial by ambush. All this was new to forensic science, which had grown to maturity in an adversarial environment. The spillover effect of DNA profiling on forensic science has been substantial."

WHERE DO WE GO FROM HERE?

While a crystal ball may be the only way to predict the future of admissibility of scientific evidence, Saks and Faigman (2005) make a few prophecies. First, they predict that it is unlikely that the U.S. Supreme Court will radically alter the existing body of thought on expert evidence, as "The Supreme Court rarely changes its mind shortly after making a grand pronouncement. But once the Court becomes aware of problems in the implementation of its earlier rulings, it might adjust the law in ways it thinks will solve those problems. This is especially so if the lower courts split in regard to how they handle certain kinds of evidence."

The bigger issue, say Saks and Faigman (2005), is the lower courts' ability to apparently apply the principles of *Daubert* equally in civil and criminal cases. Some commentators like Berger (2003) have observed that once the courts approve questionable science under *Daubert*, the chances of improvement in those fields, like the chance of judicial re-examination, are less than ever.

Saks and Faigman (2005) add to the list of trends the observation that "The deferential standard of review announced in *General Electric v Joiner* cannot survive in the long run. Courts will find ways to fudge, to slow the contradictory or repetitious examinations of the same evidence again and again." They also state, however, that "As the fraction of the population of lawyers and judges consisting of people with scientific training slowly grows—due as much as anything else to the advent of more technologies . . . or downturns in the market for scientists and engineers—there will be more lawyers and judges who are capable of understanding what Daubert is aiming to do and able to see where it has been failing most."

Moriarty and Saks (2005) argue that the *Daubert* factors will continue to "make good sense when evaluating the myriad forms of forensic evidence" when examining reliability.

As we saw in Chapter 10, evidentiary trustworthiness of forensic identification disciplines will continue to be called into question under the evidence trilogy. Moriarty and Saks (2005) say that early in the history of the forensic identification sciences "courts set aside their traditional caution and freehandedly admitted nearly every species of such testimony, asking little of the proponents, such as to establish the validity of their various claims. In their willingness to be less searching with forensic identification evidence than with other types of scientific evidence, courts opened their doors to a risk of error that today's courts are only beginning to recognize."

One of the main complaints about forensic science is that by and large it has escaped scrutiny by the courts, and only lately have members of the legal community challenged its validity. Moriarty and Saks (2005) comment, "Some proponents of admission have argued that the ready acceptance by early courts made many forensic sciences feel that continuing research and self-scrutiny were unnecessary and that, because the low threshold set by courts was responsible for these fields' weak foundations, it would now be unfair to the forensic sciences to be confronted with a more demanding test. However unavailing the argument, it does make an important point: The tests posed by courts affect the quality of some fields, especially those whose ultimate and often only audience is the courts. Why exert the effort to produce a product of better quality when the customer is satisfied with one of lower quality?"

The answer, Moriarty and Saks (2005) say, is errors. They explain, "DNA typing has revealed something quite surprising about the rest of forensic science: how common errors are in forensic science. Because DNA typing has convincingly exonerated numerous persons who had been wrongly convicted, it created an opportunity to reexamine trial evidence in an effort to discover what led to the erroneous convictions in the first place."

REFERENCES

Berger MA. The Supreme Court's trilogy on the admissibility of expert testimony. In: *Federal Judicial Center Reference Manual on Scientific Evidence*, 2nd ed. 2000.

Berger MA. Expert testimony in criminal proceedings: Questions Daubert does not answer. *Seton Hall Law Review*, 34:1125–1140, 2003.

Berger MA. What has a decade of Daubert wrought? *American Journal of Public Health*, Supplement 1, 95(S1 S64), 2005.

Bernstein DE and Jackson JD. The Daubert trilogy in the states. *Jurimetrics Journal*, 44:351–66, 2004.

Cecil JS. Ten years of judicial gate-keeping under Daubert. *American Journal of Public Health*, Supplement 1, 95(S1), 2005.

Cheng EK and Yoon AH. Does Frye or Daubert matter? A study of scientific admissibility standards. *Virginia Law Review*, 91:471, 2005.

Committee on Science, Technology, and Law. Science in Litigation: Post Daubert. A project of the National Academies. 2005. Available at: http://www7.nationalacademies.org/stl/STL_Projects. html

Dixon L and Gill B. Changes in the Standards for Admitting Expert Evidence in Federal Civil Cases Since the Daubert Decision. Rand Institute for Civil Justice. 2001.

Faigman DL, Porter E, and Saks ML. Check your crystal ball at the courthouse door, please: Exploring the past, understanding the present, and worrying about the future of scientific evidence. *Cardozo Law Review*, 15:1799, 1994.

Faigman DL, Kaye DH, Saks MJ, and Sanders J. Modern scientific evidence. *The Annual Review of Law in Social Sciences*, 1:105–130, 2005.

Gatowski S, Dobbin S, Richardson JT, Ginsburg G, Merlino M, and Dahir V. Asking the gatekeepers: A national survey of judges on judging expert evidence in a post-Daubert world. *Law and Human Behavior*, 25:433, 2001.

Giannelli PC. The abuse of scientific evidence in criminal cases: The need for independent crime laboratories. *Virginia Journal of Social Policy Law*, 4:439, 1997.

Giannelli PC. Expert admissibility symposium: Reliability standards—too high, too low, or just right? *Seton Hall Law Review*, 2003(a).

Giannelli PC. The science of wrongful convictions. *Criminal Justice*, 18(1), 2003(b).

Goodstein D. How science works. In: *Federal Judicial Center Reference Manual on Scientific Evidence*, 2000.

Groscup JL, Penrod SD, Studebaker CA, Huss MT, and O'Neil KM. The effects of Daubert on the admissibility of expert testimony in state and federal criminal cases. *Psychology, Public Policy and the Law*, 8:339–372, 2002.

Huber PW. *Galileo's Revenge: Junk Science in the Courtroom.* New York: Basic Books, 1991.

Inman K and Rudin N. *Principles and Practices of Criminalistics: The Profession of Forensic Science.* Boca Raton, Fla.: CRC Press, 2001.

Jasanoff S. *Science at the Bar: Law, Science, and Technology in America.* Cambridge, Mass.: Harvard University Press, 1996.

Jasanoff, S. Law's knowledge: Science for justice in legal settings. *American Journal of Public Health*, 95: S49–S58, July 2005.

Jonakait R. Forensic science: The need for regulation. *Harvard Journal of Law Technology*, 4:109, 148, 191, 1991.

Kennedy D and Merrill RA. Assessing forensic science. *Issues in Science and Technology*, online edition, Fall 2003. Available at: http://www.issues.org/20.1/kennedy.html

Kiely T. Forensic science and the law. In: *Forensic Science: An Introduction to Scientific and Investigative Techniques*, James SH and Nordby JJ, Eds. Boca Raton, Fla.: CRC Press, 2003.

Krafka C, Dunn MA, Johnson MT, Cecil JS, and Miletich D. Judge and attorney experiences, practices, and concerns regarding expert testimony in federal civil trials. *Psychology of Public Policy Law*, 8:309–332, September 2002.

Moriarty JC and Saks MJ. Forensic science: Grand goals, tragic flaws, and judicial gate-keeping. *Judges Journal*, Fall 2005.

Mueller CB. Daubert asks the right questions: Now appellate courts should help find the right answers. *Seton Hall Law Review*, 33:987, 2003.

National Academies Press. *The Supreme Court Trilogy: The Age of Expert Testimony: Science in the Courtroom, Report of a Workshop*. Washington, D.C.: National Academies Press, 2002.

Risinger DM. Defining the task at hand: Non-science forensic science after Kumho Tire Co. v. Carmichael. *Washington and Lee Law Review*, Summer, 2000(a).

Risinger DM. Navigating expert reliability: Are criminal standards of certainty being left on the dock? *Albany Law Review*, 64:99–152. 2000(b).

Risinger DM, Saks MJ, Rosenthal R, Thompson WC. The Daubert/Kumho implications of observer effects in forensic science: Hidden problems of expectation and suggestion. *California Law Review*, 90:1–56, 2002.

Saks MJ. Merlin and Solomon: Lessons from the law's formative encounters with forensic identification science. *Hastings Law Journal*, 49:1069–1141, 1998.

Saks MJ. Johnson v. Commonwealth: How dependable is identification by microscopic hair comparison. *Journal of Criminal Justice Education Research*, 26:14–23, 2004.

Saks MJ and Faigman DL. Expert evidence after Daubert. *Annual Review of Law and Social Science*, Vol. 1: 105–130. 2005.

Saks MJ, Faigman DL, Kaye D, and Sanders J. *Annotated Reference Manual on Scientific Evidence*, 2nd ed. Minneapolis: West Group, 2004.

Saks MJ, Koehler JJ. What DNA fingerprinting can teach the law about the rest of forensic science. *Cardozo Law Review*, 13:361–372, 1991.

Saks MJ and Koehler JJ. The coming paradigm shift in forensic identification science. *Science*, 309:892–895, 2005.

Sanders J. Kumho and how we know. *Law and Contemporary Problems*. 64:373–415, 2001.

Sanders J, Diamond SS, and Vidmar N. Legal perceptions of science and expert knowledge. *Psychology, Public Policy and Law*, 8(2):139–153, 2002.

Supreme Court of the United States, No. 92–102. William Daubert, etc., et al., Petitioners v. Merrell Dow Pharmaceuticals, Inc. June 28, 1993.

Supreme Court of the United States, No. 96–188. General Electric Company, et al., Petitioners v. Robert K. Joiner, et al. Dec. 15, 1997.

Supreme Court of the United States, No. 97–1709. Kumho Tire Company, Ltd., et al., Petitioners v. Patrick Carmichael, etc., et al. 1999.

Vidmar N and Diamond SS. Juries and expert evidence. *Brooklyn Law Review*, 66:1123, 2001.

Walsh JT. The growing impact of the new genetics on the courts. *Judicature Genes and Justice*, 83(3), November-December 1999.

RECOMMENDED READING

Black B. A unified theory of scientific evidence. *Fordham Law Review,* 56:595–695, 1988.

Breyer S. Science in the courtroom. *Issues in Science and Technology,* 52–56, 2000.

Cecil JS and Willging TE. *Court-Appointed Experts: Defining the Role of Experts Appointed under Federal Rule of Evidence 706.* Washington, D.C.: Federal Judicial Center, 1993.

Evett IW. Criminalistics: The future of expertise. *Journal of the Forensic Science Society,* 33:173–178, 1993.

Faigman DL. To have and have not: Assessing the value of social science to the law as science and policy. *Emory Law Journal,* 38:1005–1095, 1989.

Faigman DL. *Legal Alchemy: The Use and Misuse of Science in the Law.* New York: Freeman, 1999.

Faigman DL. Is science different for lawyers? *Science,* 197:339–340, 2002.

Faigman DL. *Laboratory of Justice: The Supreme Court's 200-Year Struggle to Integrate Science and the Law.* New York: Henry Holt (Times Books), 2004.

Faigman D, Kaye D, Saks M, and Sanders J. Modern Scientific Evidence: The Law and Science of Expert Testimony, 2nd ed. St. Paul, Minn.: West Group, 2002.

Giannelli PC. The admissibility of novel scientific evidence: Frye v. United States, a half-century later. *Columbia Law Review,* 80:1197–1250, 1980.

Graham MH. The expert witness predicament: Determining reliable under the gate-keeping test of Daubert, Kumho, and proposed amended Rule 702 of the Federal Rules of Evidence. *University of Miami Law Review,* 54:317, 2001.

Haack S. *Defending Science Within Reason: Between Scientism and Cynicism.* New York: Prometheus, 2003.

Imwinkelried EJ. The debate in the DNA cases over the foundation for the admission of scientific evidence: The importance of human error as a cause of forensic misanalysis. *Washington University Law Quarterly,* 69:19, 1991.

Imwinkelried EJ. The next step after Daubert: Developing a similarly epistemological approach to ensuring the reliability of nonscientific expert testimony. *Cardozo Law Review,* 15:2271, 2293, 1994.

Jasanoff S. What judges should know about the sociology of science. *Jurimetrics Journal,* 32:345–359, 1992.

Kovera MB and McAuliff BD. The effects of peer review and evidence quality on judge evaluations of psychological science: Are judges effective gatekeepers? *Journal of Applied Psychology,* 85:574–586, 2000.

Krafka C, Meghan A, Dunn MA, Johnson MT, Cecil JS, Miletich D. Judge and attorney experiences, practices, and concerns regarding expert testimony in federal civil trials. *Psychology of Public Policy Law,* 8:309–332, 2002.

Krimsky S. The weight of scientific evidence in policy and law. *American Journal of Public Health,* 95: S129–S136, July 2005.

Kuhn T. *The Structure of Scientific Revolutions,* 3rd ed. Chicago: University of Chicago Press, 1996.

Leiter B. The epistemology of admissibility: Why even good philosophy of science would not make for good philosophy of evidence. *Brigham Young University Law Review,* 1197:803–819, 1997.

Lloyd D and Gill B. Changes in the standards for admitting expert evidence in federal civil cases since the Daubert decision. *Psychology of Public Policy Law,* 8:251–308, September 2002.

Maletskos CJ and Spielman SJ. Introduction of new scientific methods in court. In: *Law Enforcement, Science & Technology,* Yefsky SA, Ed. Washington, D.C.: Thompson, 1967.

Michaels D and Monforton C. Manufacturing uncertainty: Contested science and the protection of the public's health and environment. *American Journal of Public Health,* 95:S39–S48, July 2005.

O'Connor S. The Supreme Court's philosophy of science: Will the real Karl Popper please stand up? *Jurimetrics Journal,* 35:263–276, 1995.

Shuman DW and Sales BD. The impact of Daubert and its progeny on the admissibility of behavioral and social science evidence. *Psychology of Public Policy Law,* 5:3–15, 1999.

ENDNOTES

1. *Principles and Practice of Criminalistics: The Profession of Forensic Science* by Inman and Rudin. Copyright 2007 by Taylor & Francis Group LLC—Books. Reproduced with permission of Taylor & Francis Group LLC—Books in the format Other Book via Copyright Clearance Center.
2. Berger, Margaret. "What has a decade of *Daubert* wrought?" *American Journal of Public Health*, July 2005, Volume 95, Number S1, S59–S65. Reproduced with permission of the American Public Health Association.

CHAPTER 13

THE STAKEHOLDERS IN COURT: JUDGES, JURIES, EXPERTS, AND ATTORNEYS

The various stakeholders in the U.S. criminal justice system lean heavily on forensic science in the adjudication of criminal cases, as forensic evidence is depended upon to help reconstruct events of the crime at the focus of the case to be adjudicated. It is a tall order, as Kiely (2003) describes it: "Increasingly, circumstantial proof comes in the form of forensic evidence. The long history of proof of crime always depended more on the experience of jurors than any startling analysis developed in a laboratory. Logic and common sense always had and will continue to have as great, if not greater, force than probabilistically based forensic facts. The marshaling of facts that comport with the life experiences of triers of fact remains the bedrock of the criminal justice system."

We now explore the roles and interaction between four key stakeholders: Judges, jurors, expert witnesses, and attorneys, as they relate to the notion that forensic science is both under siege and yet used as a powerful tool to advance the agendas of each stakeholder.

JUDGES AS GATEKEEPERS OF FORENSIC EVIDENCE

As we saw in Chapter 12, the U.S. Supreme Court bestowed upon trial judges the mantel of "gatekeeper" of technical and scientific evidence that can be admitted into the courtroom. While some commentators have said this is an appropriate use of judges' powers of legal discretion, others wonder aloud whether a gatekeeper is needed in the first place. Mueller (2003) states, "Daubert is the right standard because it asks directly the question that Frye put only indirectly, and thus puts courts in a better position to arrive at satisfactory answers. The central issue is scientific 'validity,' and the criteria suggested by Daubert are useful in resolving that issue. Here it is worth pausing to ask some pragmatic questions: Why have a validity standard to begin with? Why not simply approach science with the kind of openness suggested by Federal Rule of Evidence (FRE) 702 on its face? In other words, why not simply admit scientific evidence if it seems relevant and helpful and the witness is qualified?"

FRE 702 requires science to satisfy a validity standard, therefore courts will acquiesce by scrutinizing the evidence. Mueller (2003) asserts it is an unsatisfactory arrangement because "it does not emerge from the 'plain meaning' of FRE 702 or even a reasonable interpretation of the rule's language. The court has acknowledged that the rules did not displace all prior evidence doctrine." Mueller says this leads to a second important assumption; he explains, "The conclusion in Daubert rests on the notion that the word 'scientific' as used in FRE 702 is a rich or deep normative term that implies a standard of legitimacy. It is of course astonishing, if we suppose that this meaning really is to be found in FRE 702, that nothing in legislative background supports this reading (in fact the term seems merely descriptive). In truth, the rules provide no compelling basis for discarding the old Frye standard. What we now call the Daubert standard is in reality judge-made law disguised as something else. That is not to say that I disapprove of the decision, for the opposite is true: I think Daubert represents an advance, that it is at least consistent with the elastic contours of FRE 702, and that it good law-making, even if disingenuous in its logic."

Mueller (2003) says there are three factors that suggest the need for a validity standard: "First, we ask courts to resolve difficult technical and scientific issues. Second, much scientific knowledge is fluid and contestable, inaccessible to laypeople, hard to understand, and qualified in ways that elude ordinary experience and intuitions. Third, our adversary system places primary responsibility for gathering and presenting evidence in the hands of the parties, and creates incentives that lead to risks." Mueller recognizes the quandary courts are in, and suggests, "Courts can suppose that the data and conclusions presented by qualified experts reflect valid science, upon which our system can reasonably allow a jury to rely in rendering a verdict for or against recovery in some very substantial amount."

Mueller (2003) suggests there is another, more realistic possibility: "We can make the judgment that not all evidence that is presented as science, even by qualified witnesses, is of such quality that it can be relied upon to make serious decisions of the sort required for civil judgments. We can believe that such evidence varies in quality, and that sometimes it is not reliable enough. We can suppose that gaps in scientific understanding create room for interpretive disagreement, and that financial incentives, whether arising from the involvement of scientists in commercial or other funded projects or from their involvement in litigation, can compromise expert testimony. We can believe that science, like law, leaves room for principled intellectual disagreement that reflects differences in technical understanding or personal philosophy. We can also suppose that these differences sometimes lead to errors or to conclusions that cannot be defended or would be condemned by most others of similar training. Obviously, Daubert reflects the latter view of science, and I think that is the more realistic view."

As we saw in Chapter 12, the U.S. Supreme Court expanded the scope of the trial judge's role as the gatekeeper of the evidence in its opinion in *Kumho Tire Co. v Carmichael*. Walsh (1999) summarizes, "The plaintiffs' proof of causation rested exclusively on the testimony of its expert; the trial court, applying its view of Daubert, excluded the expert's testimony because it found insufficient indications of reliability. The court of appeals reversed, ruling that the subject of the expert's opinion . . . fell outside Daubert's scope and its rigorous standards for the admissibility of scientific evidence."

The Court emphasized that FRE 702 makes no distinction between two types of specialized knowledge, whether "technical" or "scientific," but it does impose a reliability finding as a prerequisite for all expert testimony in areas beyond the knowledge and experience of lay jurors. The Court said the *Daubert* criteria used to guide trial judges' discretion was not exclusive. Walsh (1999) states, "In discharging its duty to determine reliability and relevancy, the trial court is extended considerable latitude, not only in the acceptance or rejection of the expert's opinion, but also in the evaluation of the factors leading to that conclusion."

But how competent are judges in exercising their gatekeeping responsibilities? Walsh (1999) comments, "The controversy over the merits of Daubert continues in academia with some critics questioning whether trial judges possess a sufficient level of scientific sophistication to assume the gate-keeping role in determining complex scientific issues. Protagonists on both sides of the tort reform debate also dispute whether Daubert places too much power in the hands of the trial judge, whose rulings to exclude expert opinions, particularly in products liability cases, may deprive a plaintiff of redress at the hands of a jury. Even in the federal system, where Daubert's general application is not open to question, appellate courts, in particular, continue to struggle with the enormous power of a trial court to foreclose submission of a party's case to a jury on the basis of a threshold determination of non-reliability of opinion evidence."

Ronald Singer, M.S., supervisor of the Forensic Criminalists Laboratory of the Tarrant County (Texas) Medical Examiner's Office, speaking at the November 2005 symposium Forensic Science: The Nexus of Science and the Law, presented by the National Academy of Sciences, stated, "I am concerned about Daubert and all of the decisions that followed, from the standpoint of making the judge the gatekeeper of science. I think it is a good idea to have a gatekeeper, and I am not defensive about any criticism for forensic science, as much is well deserved in all areas of science and academia, but lawyers and judges tend not to have science backgrounds. While Federal Evidence Rule 706 says that a judge can appoint an independent expert to advise on matters of admissibility, I think that flies in the face of the adversarial system."

Shirley Abrahamson, chief justice of the Wisconsin Supreme Court, also speaking at the 2005 symposium, commented, "Are judges in over their heads? Judges have prevented plenty of qualified experts from testifying. Daubert has become a verb these days—people say they have been 'Dauberted' if they are excluded from providing testimony. Judges are confused about how to put Daubert in effect. Chief Justice Rehnquist warned that we don't want to make judges amateur scientists. Others say they need experts to educate judges on science. Daubert was supposed to relax the barriers to experts but it doesn't appear to be working that way. One-third of judges say they admit less evidence under Daubert."

"When Daubert was decided, and even more so when Kumho Tire was decided, I think it did put the fear of God into forensic scientists," remarks Michael Saks, Ph.D., M.S.L., a member of the faculties of the Sandra Day O'Connor College of Law and the Department of Psychology, as well as a faculty fellow of the Center for the Study of Law, Science & Technology at Arizona State University. Saks continues, "There was a lot of discussion among judges, and a lot of angst among expert witnesses in the forensic science community about how they are going to survive in a post-Daubert world. And then there was a rush of government agencies falling over themselves to conduct research in a field that had, up until then, pretty much been enjoying itself in terms of easy admissibility. And then they discovered that, well, the courts didn't really care. The courts were not going to police criminal cases the way the courts were policing civil cases. And so I think the community relaxed."

Saks adds, "So, we have judges who also relaxed, and who seem to apply very different standards in criminal cases when the government is offering the pseudo-expert than they do in civil cases where a plaintiff may be offering the pseudo-expert. A few judges get it, but most of them, especially if it's the government in a criminal case offering the suspect evidence, just let it in. Forensic scientists could see what was happening in the courts and they could tell they didn't have to worry anymore. So, I think Daubert hasn't had the impact some thought it would have. Having said that, however, there are some judges who actually obtain some education in scientific issues and forensic science, and they are the ones who are better engaged in admissibility issues."

Some see the evidence trilogy as an unrestricted license to exclude evidence. Mueller (2003) writes, "*Daubert* is one of the more important decisions of the 20th century because it changed fundamentally the relationship between law and science. Prior to Daubert, the law deferred to the scientific community on the question of whether answers that scientists provide are sufficiently grounded in theory and practice to be trusted and acted upon by courts. After Daubert, judges are charged independently to appraise what science has to offer, in effect screening out evidence offered as science if it is invalid or unreliable. To put it another way, a pre-Daubert judge who might have hesitated to exclude what seemed to be testimony on a matter of science could say, in effect, 'it is not the court who rejects what you say, but other experts in your field.' A judge fearful of criticism for admitting such testimony could say, in effect, 'It is not the court who endorses what this expert has to say, but credentialed people in a recognized discipline.'" Mueller suggests further that a post-*Daubert* judge has less room to hide: "If he excludes evidence proffered as science he is expected to say 'the court finds that what you say is not sufficiently grounded in theory or practice,' or 'lacks sufficient basis in fact' or 'lacks sufficient connection to the case at hand.' A post-Daubert judge who admits such evidence is expected to say 'the court finds that indeed this testimony is properly grounded in theory and practice, and adequately based on the facts and sufficiently related to the task at hand.'"

Still, Mueller (2003) asserts, *Daubert* and its progeny leave room to hide: "Factors like peer review and general acceptance provide opportunities, as does the possibility of invoking FRE 403, and a judge can also distance himself by casting his decision in terms of 'adequate assurances' or 'inadequate assurances' of validity. The basic point, however, is that Daubert puts judges into the position of judging science. That makes Daubert revolutionary."

The determination of legal admissibility is a long road pocked with potholes that can swallow both good and bad evidence. Wagner (2005) observes, "Both science and law depend on rigorous review and penetrating critiques to legitimate and perfect work done in their respective fields. Science and law differ dramatically, however, in whom they trust to conduct this review. Scientists insist that this vetting be done by disinterested scientists whose only aim is to establish objective fact. Law, by contrast, favors input from persons who have a strong stake in the outcome. The more affected the parties, the more important their participation. Science thus strives to obtain the most objective advice; the legal system seeks input from those who are the most aggrieved."

Up until the 1990s, judges determined whether scientific testimony and evidence was reliable based largely on whether this testimony and its scientific underpinnings were generally accepted by the technical and scientific community, as established by the *Frye* test. Some commentators, as we saw in Chapter 12, state that *Frye* was flawed because it forced the courts to become dependent upon external sources to tell them what was generally accepted by the scientific community, with the expectation of complete deference to expert consensus. If an accurate consensus could be reached, there still was no guarantee, commentators say, that the courts were able to understand the issues at hand and had the right criteria for making this evaluation. Some commentators add that the *Frye* test was prejudiced against novel research that had not had sufficient time to be generally accepted, even though it might be reliable and probative.

With the emergence of *Daubert v Merrell Dow Pharmaceuticals*, judges were faced with the revised Federal Rules of Evidence and the decision that *Frye* was no longer the appropriate test for assessing the reliability and validity of expert testimony. Instead, FRE 702 created a different scientific screening test that positioned litigants as the informants on the quality of science and the judge as the arbiter of quality, rather than looking to the scientific community for primary guidance. The U.S. Supreme Court allowed lesser courts to still consider whether the research underlying expert testimony was peer reviewed and accepted in its field, but it held that the parties to the litigation would provide the primary, if not exclusive, source of information on whether scientific testimony met this "testability" test (Wagner, 2005).

Wagner (2005) explains that the shift from *Frye* to *Daubert* "involves less deference to the scientific community with regard to what constitutes valid and reliable science and greater reliance on the judge's non-expert assessment, informed by the litigants." Wagner explains that *Daubert* revises the basis for the decision about scientific reliability "from one that relies on experts' collective judgment (albeit filtered through the litigants) to one that demands a judge's independent assessment of the reliability of the proffered scientific testimony, ultimately moving away from the expert model implicit in Frye."

Wagner (2005) enumerates the challenges that positioning judges as the primary assessors of scientific quality presents: ". . . litigants have little interest in ensuring scientific quality and are instead primarily concerned with striking testimony that is unfavorable to their position. The information they provide the judge on scientific quality and reliability, then, is likely to be skewed to the tails of scientific opinion and may omit scientific mainstream views. Yet the judges must still rule on whether the proffered scientific testimony is reliable based on their non-expert assessment of the testimony's faithfulness to the scientific method, rather than looking to the scientific community for assistance. In fact, in high-stakes mass litigation, some judges have found the parties so unhelpful in informing their assessment of scientific reliability that they switch back to an expert review model and empanel independent scientific advisors . . . to assist them in making decisions on scientific evidence challenged under Daubert. This occasional retreat to the expert model suggests that judges are not always comfortable presiding over disputes about scientific quality when the primary sources of information are provided by the affected parties." This retreat to safer harbors by judges "violates one of the fundamental tenets of science, namely that scientific research, as well as peer review of that research, should be unbiased, objective, and disinterested," Wagner asserts.

Commentators have expressed concern over judges' ability to identify and reject questionable science, shady expert witnesses, and exaggerated statements, as they attempt to assess scientific reliability. Wagner (2005) observes, "Judges . . . are not typically scientists, and we know from a large body of critical literature and a growing number of published opinions that they sometimes make decisions about science that are wrong. The literature on judicial review of agency technical decisions is perhaps the most negative about the capacity of judges to review the science used by agencies in rulemakings. But scientific errors committed by lay persons who preside over challenges to the quality of scientific studies arise throughout the science-policy literature, with documented problems arising in scientific misconduct hearings, discovery disputes, and evidence determinations. To the extent that errors emerge from these frailties in the system, the most serious error is the possibility that good studies will be excluded from the policymaking process." At stake, Wagner explains, is an already short supply of research in numerous areas of scientific and public health–related policy; Wagner comments, "The probability that good science will be erroneously excluded seems most likely when an affected party has a great deal to lose from a research study and has the resources to invest in discrediting it. Indeed, one would expect Daubert and the 'good-science' challenges to be used only when a party is adversely affected by scientific knowledge and has the resources to mount an expensive technical attack against it. Research on Daubert's effects in erroneously excluding good research is ongoing, although preliminary evidence suggests that this is a problem in some cases."

"Daubert put some meat on the bones of admissibility issues," declares defense expert Richard Saferstein, Ph.D., a forensic science consultant and author. "But there has been some back-and-forth discussion about the criteria that must be met. I believe Daubert merely added more substance to Frye, and gave trial judges a few points to examine; however, at the same time, Daubert said you don't have to have all these criteria every time because they may not be relevant. So, you are right back to where you started, in a sense. Essentially it is left up to the judge. Daubert has generated a lot of papers and seminars, and it has become a cottage industry of sort, giving attorneys something to do and something upon which to hang their hats. But there doesn't seem to be any hue and cry on the part of the forensic science community that Daubert has represented a major call for change. It's a complicated set of issues, there are problems here and there; some judges are unequipped to deal with these issues as I would like to see them deal with it, while others are."

ADMISSIBILITY AND FORENSIC EVIDENCE: KEEPING THE FAITH

Critics of forensic science assert that too much unsound evidence that lacks empirical research and scientific rigor is admitted by judges who have foresworn this directive because of an undying allegiance to forensic science. Moriarty and Saks (2005) assert, "There is virtually no expert testimony so threadbare that it will not be admitted if it comes to a criminal proceeding under the banner of forensic science. (Handwriting and voiceprint identification are the chief exceptions to this generalization.) Some forensic sciences have been with us for so long and judges have developed such faith in them that they are admitted even if they fail to meet minimal standards under Daubert. Faith, not science, has informed this gate-keeping."

Critics continue to point to the longevity of fingerprint testimony in the courts. Moriarty and Saks (2005) represent this cadre of critics when they state, "Through dozens of Daubert challenges, no judge has been presented with conventional scientific evidence capable of persuading a rational gatekeeper, yet at the same time no court has excluded the opinions of fingerprint examiners. Various judges have found various paths around Daubert."

Not that the standards established by *Frye, Daubert, Joiner,* or *Kumho* have posed much of an obstacle, critics add. Moriarty and Saks (2005) state, "The maverick who is a field unto him- or herself has repeatedly been readily admitted under Frye and the complete absence of foundational research has not prevented admission in Daubert jurisdictions. As noted above, there are exceptions both historical and contemporary, such as asserted handwriting and voiceprint identification, but these are exceptions that prove the rule."

Judges are assigned this gatekeeping function as a means to shield jurors from questionable expert testimony. Moriarty and Saks (2005) say that the gate can be reinforced through the following: partial or limited admission of evidence, renewed focus on the task at hand, limiting or disallowing overpowering and misleading terminology, allowing competing opinions to be admitted into evidence, and providing limiting jury instructions.

For example, fingerprint examiners should be acknowledged for their training and their experience, which are assumed to help the practitioner hone his or her craft. The examiner can point out similarities and differences in a fingerprint to a jury, but legal scholars say the judge should closely examine the interpretation of those findings. "Thus, the most expedient fix to the problem of missing data supporting these individualization specialties," according to Moriarty and Saks (2005), "is to allow the examiner to discuss the points of comparison but to disallow the examiner from declaring a match or asserting conclusions." This is an example of limited admissibility.

Focusing on the task at hand is another attempt to ferret out unsound science or exaggerated testimony. In the *Daubert* and *Kumho* decisions, the U.S. Supreme Court mandated that testimony must be reliable and relevant "to the task at hand," meaning that the testimony must fit tightly and appropriately with the issue under discussion. Or, stated another way, the expertise should be tied to the facts of the case and assist jurors in their resolution of the case.

Another attempt at gatekeeping is to disallow misleading testimony that is filled with overstatement, exaggeration, and industry-related jargon that creates a stronger probability than is warranted by the underlying science. A classic example is the terminology of an absolute match, used by pattern evidence examiners. Moriarty and Saks (2005) explain: "Some fields use terms that do not readily convey to laypersons what the examiner intends. For example, if a forensic dentist states that in his opinion a match has been found between the bite mark in a victim and the defendant's dentition, the jury is likely to infer that means that the defendant is the biter. But, for forensic dentists, the actual meaning of a match is some concordance, some similarity, but no expression of specificity intended; generally similar but true for a large percentage of the population." In other words, while a forensic practitioner uses the word *match* to convey an irrefutable probability of common origin, jurors may interpret it to mean an absolute linkage.

Moriarty and Saks (2005) add, "Sometimes expert witnesses and fields have developed terms that are conceived to be defensible as literal truth but that are likely to induce the jury to think a more inculpatory opinion has been offered than the witness has (or could) actually assert given the evidence. 'Consistent with' is one such example. Witnesses should be confined to meaningful language that accurately conveys inferences that genuinely can be supported by the field's methods. In short, overreaching and exaggeration should be banned from the witness box. Thus, any expression of absolute certainty by forensic identification experts, or any term likely to be understood by the fact finder as conveying such a strong and unjustifiable meaning, should be prohibited."

One aid to the gatekeeping role, legal scholars insist, is the increased use of court-appointed experts, in addition to the experts offered by the prosecution and the defense. Federal Rule of Evidence 706 provides for the trial court's ability to "procure the assistance of an expert of its own choosing," as well as an expert who can assist in pre-trial admissibility decision making.

Gatekeeping can also be facilitated by the allowance of competing expert opinions. Moriarty and Saks (2005) state, "The most obvious reason for this is a lack of funds to pay for them. In addition, many criminal defense lawyers do not know they need an expert, assuming all forensic evidence will be reliable or that they can expose all of the weaknesses they need to on cross-examination. . . . Greater access to and use of competing expert evidence in criminal cases involving forensic identification testimony would dovetail with Daubert's recognition that 'presentation of contrary evidence' is one appropriate method of attacking shaky but admissible evidence."

Moriarty and Saks (2005) add that "for the adversary process to work, both advocates need the resources to present their strongest case. Courts can help make the adversary process work as it should by making such appointments more regularly. In the long run, it would also lead to improvements in forensic science because, ironically, the weaknesses in forensic science are in considerable part the result of a lack of adversarial testing of forensic science throughout most of the 20th century."

Saks and Faigman (2005) suggest that the call for increased use of court-appointed witnesses, however, will go unheeded to a large extent. They state, "Although the net use of court-appointed experts and, possibly more so, technical advisers is likely to rise over time, this reform is unlikely to be as transforming as its advocates hope." Saks and Faigman chalk it up to courts' commitment to the adversarial process or to their disinclination to become more managerial, and point to Gross (1991), who offered the suggestion that a certain number of experts should be court-appointed, and then require that all meetings with these experts be open to all parties (and forbid any contact outside of those open meetings). This suggestion has not been followed, Saks and Faigman say.

ALL JUDGES ARE NOT CREATED EQUAL

Not everyone is in favor of surrendering total control over admissibility issues to judges. "I am not a big fan of the trend toward giving trial judges this powerful gate-keeping role," says forensic pathologist and law professor Cyril Wecht, M.D., J.D., clinical professor at the University of Pittsburgh Schools of Medicine, Dental Medicine, and Graduate School of Public Health; adjunct professor at the Duquesne University School of Law, School of Pharmacy, and School of Health Sciences; and former coroner of Allegheny County in Pennsylvania. "All trial judges were lawyers at one time, and the overwhelming majority of them stayed as far away from science courses in college as they could. They were all pre-law, so they hated chemistry, biology, and physics. Then they went to law school and had no exposure to science. In fact, I would bet that a bright junior or senior high school student who has a bent toward science knows more about it than a graduate of law school does. College seniors who are pre-med know more about science than they do."

Wecht continues, "So, now the trial judge is a gatekeeper of science; are they qualified for this simply because they wear a black robe? They don't know a damn thing about forensic science. However, this concern about junk science has caught on like wildfire, and people don't stop to think that there is a difference between junk science and forensic science. But do these judges know that? I say that they don't."

Wecht says that judges should not expect to see absolutes in forensic science, since there is ongoing debate in every scientific discipline. Wecht explains, "In the biggest and best hospitals in the country, for example, you will hear world-renowned physicians disagreeing about conclusions and diagnoses. It tells you that medicine is far from an absolute science. Look at the medical journals and read the numerous letters to the editor in which people argue about everything. Now just because you are in the courtroom and there is a difference of opinion, it makes everything suspect. It's disgusting. It's intellectually dishonest. And it's totally ridiculous. So, with Daubert, you get into the expert's credentials and so forth, looking for ways to discredit the person because he or she didn't do original research to support a conclusion. It's ridiculous; I think Frye was adequate and withstood the test of time."

Wecht continues, "I am strongly opposed to the tremendous power that has been given to trial judges, because after all, who are they? Sometimes they are experienced attorneys and other times they are simply people who are well connected. In an elected system, we've had people elected judge who had essentially no legal experience as a lawyer and now they are on the bench. All of a sudden by virtue of a popular election and the donning of a black robe, this individual now will make a decision as to whether or not a medical person or scientific person can give testimony? It is so absurd as to make one laugh."

There is little argument that some judges are more suitable to the gatekeeper role than others, whether it comes down to training and education, experience with particular kinds of criminal cases, or time spent on the bench, or even other less tangible factors such as personality, temperament, or the willingness to do one's homework. Saks and Faigman (2005) state, "Although there have been efforts to teach judges to become better students of natural and social science as well as statistics, crash courses and checklists will probably not accomplish much. To ensure that courts have judges with scientific acumen, the best method is to recruit scientifically educated lawyers to the legal profession and then to the bench . . . more such persons are becoming lawyers. Perhaps the process could be accelerated."

"The reality is that most judges, lawyers, and law students have very little science in their backgrounds," says Carol Henderson, J.D., director of the National Clearinghouse for Science, Technology and the Law, and law professor at Stetson University College of Law. "I recall a survey of incoming law students which found that only 5.3 percent had any hard science backgrounds. As lawyers, what we do, and what we are good at, is gathering information and trying to figure out where the truth lies, and judges are trying to do that too. We don't normally incorporate science into that equation."

"Daubert is flawed because judges cannot be gatekeepers when they themselves don't understand science," says author and forensic science media consultant Lawrence Kobilinsky, Ph.D., a professor and associate provost of John Jay College of Criminal Justice. "There is a real need for the education and training of judges. How can judges make a smart decision about whether evidence is admissible when they have no concept of the science or the technology underlying that evidence?"

"Most judges are not people of science," says Mary Fran Ernst, a medico-legal death investigator for the St. Louis County Medical Examiner's Office, and director of medico-legal education at St. Louis University School of Medicine. "They didn't become lawyers because they were brilliant in science, and I suspect that forensic science scares them a little. Very few judges have any kind of scientific background, and in terms of admissibility of evidence, I think they probably just don't want to have to deal with it. They have so much on their plate, they don't have time to look deeper into forensic science. They think if forensic evidence is important in only 5 percent or 10 percent of the cases they hear, they probably won't spend the time it takes to be aware of issues related to forensic evidence. I think judges need more training in forensic science, and I think the community has tried to facilitate that learning process."

Ernst continues, "When I talk to judges I will say to them, 'Check out these so-called forensic experts; don't let some of these people pull the wool over your eyes. Make sure they really are experts before you let them testify.' Their answer always is, 'It's not my job,' or 'It's the jury's job to decide who is an expert and who isn't.' Right there, you see that it comes down to who is the powerhouse in the courtroom, the prosecutor or the defense, and who has the biggest ammunition. I think judges are afraid to find out about forensic science and are afraid to be gatekeepers, and so taking that stance, it's very easy for them to say forensic evidence or a forensic discipline is no good."

Henderson believes that education in evidence issues should begin in law school so that attorneys (and potential judges) are better prepared to face admissibility issues. She recalls a course from her law school days that made a big impression: "I took a course at George Washington that focused on the forensic laboratory, with Jim Starrs as the professor," Henderson says. "Jim would bring in terrific guest speakers like medical examiners and crime lab managers, and I was fascinated by what they shared with us. I thought, 'Why don't more law schools have this?' After I graduated I became a federal prosecutor and went out to crime scenes as a part of my job. It stuck with me when I became a professor; I conducted a survey and discovered that only about 30 schools out of 180 or so had a course addressing science and the law. I'm glad to say there has been an increase in these kinds of courses because forensic science and expert witnesses are featured more prominently in many more cases than ever before. However, there still are not as many hands-on, skill-based courses, which is something for which I advocate. I teach a course like this, where we are very hands-on; I bring in expert witness guest speakers, we process a crime scene with a crime scene technician, my students do a pretrial evidentiary motion on a cutting-edge issue, they have to depose an expert, they have to do a direct and cross, and that helps prepare them for the rigors of court and exposes them to issues pertaining to evidence. These kinds of courses are just one small step toward educating lawyers and judges."

It takes a discerning judge to spot unsound scientific evidence or shaky expert testimony, especially when, as some commentators assert, forensic science tries to be something it isn't. Saks (2000) writes, "Some forensic identification scientists looked for ways to evade Daubert scrutiny. The solution to this problem for those judges and for pseudo-scientists was to reclassify those fields as non-science. But *Kumho Tire Co. v Carmichael* patched that hole, so to say, at least by its apparent terms. That is to say, hauling down the science flag and hosting the non-science flag does not exempt expert evidence from Daubert scrutiny."

While *Daubert* and *Kumho* instructed judges to scrutinize science, Saks (2000) observes, "One can never underestimate the ingenuity of judges in finding ways to evade rules that tell them to do something that would lead to a result contrary to the one suggested by their intuitions. The post-Daubert, pre-Kumho Tire period was telling: Obeying the letter and spirit of Daubert would lead to significant exclusion of a type of evidence that the courts welcomed for most of the twentieth century. On the other hand, a ruling to admit these fields would be both a rejection of conventional science as the criterion for admission of empirical claims and a ruling in the teeth of repeated unanimous Supreme Court opinions declaring the conventional scientific method to be the touchstone for evaluating empirical claims of all kinds."

That many judges are uncomfortable with the gatekeeping role is no surprise to those who study human behavior and recognize man's discomfort with the unfamiliar. Kesan (1997) states, "Many judges have expressed discomfort at having to review methodologies and techniques that undergird scientific evidence presented in courts. One look at the range of scientific theories, opinions, and results presented in civil and criminal cases indicates that the concerns of the judiciary regarding scientific evidence are amply justified."

Judges' actual comprehension of the evidence trilogy has been the subject of much debate and scrutiny. Saks and Faigman (2005) state, "The limited attention actually paid in judicial opinions to the vaunted (or reviled) Daubert factors is less surprising once one realizes that judges do not understand what they mean."

Gatowski et al. (2001) surveyed a large number of state court judges who almost unanimously said they supported the gatekeeping responsibility and who also claimed they were making evidence-admissibility decisions under *Daubert's* criteria. The survey revealed that only 5 percent of respondents could define or explain each of the *Daubert* factors; 5 percent demonstrated a working understanding of falsifiability, and 4 percent demonstrated an understanding of error rate. Gatowski et al. also showed that when presented with examples of expert testimony to evaluate, the criterion relied upon most heavily was general acceptance. Gatowski et al. suggested that judges' responses "reflected more of the rhetoric of Daubert than the substance." Saks and Faigman (2005) comment, "Whether excluding or admitting expert evidence, judicial opinions displaying sophisticated application of Daubert or other thoughtful focus on the validity of the proffered expertise are few and far between."

One of the byproducts of the gatekeeping role of judges is the constraints placed on new and novel scientific techniques and information. Saks and Faigman (2005) state, "Judicial gate-keeping has unavoidable effects on the creation of new knowledge. We believe the courts should act in ways that promote the growth of knowledge that is important to resolving major or frequent disputes that come before the courts. For example, some fields will do no more research than is required of them. If the courts set a low threshold of admission, some fields will develop little or no fundamental new knowledge. They can remain in business with what they already have and, indeed, risk setting themselves back in the eyes of courts by producing real data that can never show them to be as flawless as they have long claimed themselves to be. For these fields, most often seen on the criminal side of the docket, the courts should set higher thresholds, or set time limits (a period of years) for the production of research on fundamental questions about the field. If nothing else, courts should require parties to remain within the bounds of the knowledge they have, forbidding wishful exaggerations, and requiring statements of the limits of what is known, whether those statements are informed by data showing error rates or by the absence of data on error rates. A court could ask parties for briefs on these matters and issue its own instruction to the jury on the limits of expertise."

Another emerging byproduct of courts' decisions on admissibility of evidence is the perils of "litigation science," or science that has been developed for the express purpose of adjudication in a court of law. Cecil (2005) writes, "The skepticism of courts toward expert testimony in general and scientific testimony in particular seems rooted in a view of science and litigation that has caused the courts to be extremely cautious in acknowledging the value of some scientific methodologies in providing an informed assessment of causal relationships. Consequently, courts often declare common methods of professional assessment based on animal research or clinical inference to be so lacking in scientific rigor that they fail to meet a suitable standard for consideration by the jury."

Judge Alex Kozinski, writing in the decision of *Daubert v Merrell Dow Pharmaceuticals*, commented, " One very significant fact to be considered is whether the experts are proposing to testify about matters growing naturally and directly out of research they have conducted independent of the litigation, or whether they have developed their opinions expressly for purposes of testifying. . . . In determining whether proposed expert testimony amounts to good science, we may not ignore the fact that a scientist's normal workplace is the lab or the field, not the courtroom or the lawyer's office."

The issue of litigation science has become so pronounced that the Science, Technology & Law Panel of the National Academies developed a proposal to examine the characteristics of this phenomenon. According to Cecil (2005), the panel will examine the litigation circumstances that brought about the research; the extent to which the participants in litigation participate in the design, analysis, and interpretation of the research; and the extent to which the research finds an audience beyond the participants in the litigation. In addition, the panel will be applying the same examination to the scientific foundation of forensic science testimony submitted in criminal cases. Cecil states, "This topic has been generally neglected by the broad scientific community, but it has grown in importance after the Kumho decision with the extension of evidentiary standards of reliability to all areas of expert testimony. An empirical analysis of appellate decisions in criminal cases by Groscup et al. indicates that the Daubert factors have been rarely used outside of forensic areas that are clearly scientific." Cecil says that following *Kumho* and amendments to the Federal Rule of Evidence 702, the panel has identified the need to formulate a research agenda for forensic science disciplines related to the forensic identification disciplines "to strengthen the scientific methodology underlying these areas of forensic science and to promote academic research in forensic sciences."

Risinger and Saks (2003) suggest that the very culture of science, with its required mental discipline and adherence to the scientific method, tends to "keep human motivation-produced threats to validity within acceptable bounds in individuals." However, where "partisanship is elevated and work is insulated from the normal systems of the science culture for checking and canceling bias, then the reasons to trust on which science depends are undermined." They say this can occur in a litigation-driven research setting "because virtually no human activity short of armed conflict or dogmatic religious controversy is more partisan than litigation. In litigation-driven situations, few participating experts can resist the urge to help their side win, even at the expense of the usual norms of scientific practice. Consider something as simple as communication between researchers who are on different sides of litigation. Although there is no formal legal reason for it, many such researchers cease communicating about their differences except through and in consultation with counsel. What could be more unnatural for normal researchers? And what purpose does such behavior serve other than ensure that scientific differences are not resolved but exacerbated?"

Risinger and Saks (2003) assert that one form of litigation science is flying under the radar in most courts: "law enforcement-sponsored research relevant to the reliability of expert evidence in criminal cases, evidence that virtually always is proffered on behalf of the government's case." They add, "Of primary concern is research directly focused on the error rates of various currently accepted forensic identification processes, which have not been subject to any formal validity testing." Risinger and Saks say that for police and prosecutors, any such research "can result only in a net loss" because of a "carefully fostered public perception of near-infallibility." They explain, "Research revealing almost any error rate under common real-world conditions undermines the aura. In addition, data that can show deficiencies in individual practitioners threaten that individual's continued usefulness as an effective witness. The combined effects of these two kinds of findings can potentially result in increased numbers of acquittals in cases where other evidence of a defendant's guilt is weak."

Some commentators like Risinger and Saks assert that prosecutors who are secretly convinced of the defendant's culpability will resort to any device allowable by law to persuade the jury. "Consequently," Risinger and Saks (2003) state, "research results calling into question the validity of such expertise, or defining its error rates, is threatening because it undermines a powerful tool for obtaining convictions and also threatens the status and livelihood of the law enforcement team members who practice the putative expertise." They continue, "It is not surprising, therefore, to discover that until recently, such research was rare, especially in regard to forensic science claims that predated the application of the Frye test. Such evidence had never been considered 'novel' and therefore had never been confronted with any validity inquiry in any court. Even in regard to expert evidence that had been reviewed as novel, the review often consisted of little more than making sure that there was at least some loosely defined 'scientific' community that would vouch for the accuracy of the claimed process."

A number of initiatives are under way to foster better and more research to support the claims of various forensic disciplines, as will be discussed more fully in Chapter 15. However, some commentators fear that some of this research will be, in fact, litigation driven. Risinger and Saks (2003) assert that much new research could be skewed to favor the prosecution; they comment: "Various strategies appear to have been adopted to ensure that positive results will be exaggerated and negative results will be glossed over, if not withheld. These include the following: placing some propositions beyond the reach of empirical research, using research designs that cannot generate clear data on individual practitioner competence, manufacturing favorable test results, refusing to share data with researchers wishing to conduct re-analyses or further analyze the data, encouraging overstated interpretations of data in published research reports, making access to case data in FBI files contingent on accepting a member of the FBI as a coauthor, and burying unfavorable results in reports where they are least likely to be noticed—coupled with an unexplained disclaimer that the data cannot be used to infer the false positive error rate that they plainly reveal."

To address the problem of litigation science, commentators like Risinger and Saks insist that this issue must be part of any larger inquiry into scientific research, and that efforts to recruit truly independent researchers should be encouraged. Risinger and Saks (2003) note, "As to the judicial consumers of such research, it is unlikely that, in an adversarial system, anything official can or will be done about the phenomenon, especially when the research enters the legal process during pretrial hearings, where the usual rules of evidence are themselves inapplicable. And thus until fundamental changes occur in the research environment that creates litigation-directed forensic science research, courts would be well advised to regard the findings of such research with a large grain of salt."

Just how influential expert witnesses, their testimony, and the research-driven underpinnings of their opinions are, should be the topic of further scrutiny, some commentators observe. Cecil (2005) suggests, "More research is needed in the manner in which attorneys identify, recruit, and prepare experts for testimony. Most difficult will be identifying the manner in which consulting experts who are not designated to testify at trial are used to shape the claims and defenses, because such activities are protected by attorney work-product privilege. Finding a similar opportunity to explore these issues with those who have served as experts will also be difficult. Finally, more research is needed on the extent to which courts conduct pretrial inquiries into the reliability of expert testimony. We do not know the extent to which judges engage in the screening of expert testimony as part of a routine pretrial process and how this screening process varies across areas of expert evidence."

In a similar vein, Sanders et al. (2002) comment, "This increased sensitivity to social, political, and economic pressures that impinge on expert judgment is reflected in a fifth admissibility factor frequently cited in post-Daubert opinions: whether experts are proposing to testify about matters growing naturally and directly out of research they conducted independent of the litigation. This criterion now is very frequently mentioned in federal admissibility opinions. The 'non-judicial uses' test is a judicial acknowledgment that external pressures may bias expert testimony and the self-reflecting observation that the legal system itself imposes significant pressures on the parties and their experts. Kumho Tire also reflects a concern for the pressures that impinge on expert judgment. The court's focus on whether an expert has applied the 'same intellectual rigor' as people in her field implicitly recognizes that the pressures of litigation and party witnessing may influence expert testimony. Daubert and Kumho Tire implicitly accept the notion that expert knowledge is influenced by the social, economic, and political situation of the expert and expert communities. Nevertheless they reject a radical social constructionist perspective that would argue that expert opinion is solely the result of such influences. The opinion directs judges to become sufficiently knowledgeable about scientific methods so that they can fairly assess the validity of evidence."

In subsequent chapters, we more fully explore the relationship between judges and jurors, but there is some concern that judges can actually usurp the role of jurors in the trial process, given *Daubert*'s "conferral of excessive power on judges," according to Saks and Faigman (2005). While opinions differ, some may advise that judges should wield their power to exclude expert evidence with restraint. Jasanoff (1992) comments, "When judges exclude experts, they help shape an image of reality that is colored in part by their own preferences and prejudices about how the world should work. Such power need not always be held in check, but it should be exercised sparingly. Otherwise, one risks substituting the expert authority of the black robe and the bench for that of the white lab coat—an outcome that poorly serves the causes of justice or of science." Saks and Faigman note, however, "But the more that science is socially constructed, the less the black robe should defer to the white lab coat. Judges have the institutional and, in most respects, the constitutional obligation to ensure due process and fair and balanced trial procedures. To the extent that expert testimony is infused with preferences and prejudices, they should be those of the judge and not the expert. The responsibility to exercise such preferences and sometimes impose such prejudices devolves upon judges in our constitutional system."

While some favor putting the most control elsewhere, Saks and Faigman (2005) emphasize, "If anyone's preferences and prejudices are going to infuse the trial process, it should be those of the judges, whose biases (such as they are) are imposed with political legitimacy. And, if we hope to limit the effect of bad, biased, or seriously misleading testimony, judicial gate-keeping is our best hope." Mueller (2003) asks whether judges should continue as evidence gatekeepers, or whether this power should be coupled with the fact-finding responsibility vested in juries.

Some commentators appear disillusioned by both judges and juries. "Judges are political animals," asserts Brent Turvey, senior partner of Forensic Solutions LLC, and a forensic scientist in private practice, "They can be very political about their own agendas, especially if they want to be an appellate court judge someday. Not to say that all judges are this way; some judges are doing very well as gatekeepers and are paying attention to the kind of evidence that attorneys are proffering. Others are married to prosecutors and police officers, and literally make their decisions about the admissibility of evidence based on whether or not they will have to sleep on the couch."

Mueller (2003) observes, "As for juries, we have indications that they have trouble with complex cases, and with scientific evidence, and we have reason to believe that better-educated juries do better in these areas. We have indications that juries approach expertise with skepticism. We have indications that juries appraise expert testimony not by grappling with technical issues, but by counting extraneous factors like qualifications, the number of arguments (rather than quality), and personal attractiveness. We understand that jurors give more credence to messages framed in simple language, less to those framed in complex language, and they pay close attention to demeanor. As for experts, we have confirmation of what we have long suspected: They tailor their testimony to please whoever pays them. They learn to perform in court. As for judges, we have some mixed news: Data on state judges suggest that many do not understand the 'testability' concept (can the evidence be falsified) or error rates, although they do better with criteria of peer review and general acceptance. Surveys of federal opinions, however, suggest that judges are achieving a better understanding of science. As for alternatives, we have some indications that cross-examination does little to affect jury appraisals of expert testimony."

There is debate on how well judges actually manage evidence and testimony proffered by experts, considering the acceleration of the complexity of much of the technical information presented in court. Schwarzer and Cecil (2000) explain, "Scientific evidence is increasingly used in litigation as science and technology become more pervasive in all aspects of daily life. . . . Scientific evidence encompasses so-called hard sciences (such as physics, chemistry, mathematics, and biology) as well as soft sciences (such as economics, psychology, and sociology), and it may be offered by persons with scientific, technical, or other specialized knowledge whose skill, experience, training, or education may assist the trier of fact in understanding the evidence or determining a fact in issue."

Management of expert evidence is a thorough process to which judges must adhere. An initial conference is held to determine the breadth and depth of expert evidence in the case. Schwarzer and Cecil (2000) say that the court should use this conference to "explore in depth what issues implicate expert evidence, the kinds of evidence likely to be offered and its technical and scientific subject matter, and anticipated areas of controversy. The court will also want to inquire into whether the science involved is novel and still in development, or whether the scientific issues have been resolved in prior litigation and whether similar issues are pending in other litigation."

The objective of the initial conference is to define and narrow the issues in the litigation. Schwarzer and Cecil (2000) explain, "In cases presenting complex scientific and technical subject matter, the court and parties must focus on the difficult task of defining disputed issues in order to avoid unnecessarily protracting the litigation, generating confusion, and inviting wasteful expense and delay." Regarding expert discovery, judges consider the discovery of testifying experts, non-testifying experts, non-retained experts, court-appointed experts, and use of videotaped depositions.

Schwarzer and Cecil (2000) state that objections to expert evidence relating to admissibility, qualifications of a witness, or existence of a privilege should be raised and decided in advance of trial whenever possible, and that the exclusion of evidence may sometimes remove an essential element of a party's proof, providing the basis for summary judgment. In other cases, the ruling on an objection may permit the proponent to cure a technical deficiency before trial, such as clarifying an expert's qualifications. When expert evidence offered to meet an essential element of a party's case is excluded, the ruling may be a basis for summary judgment. A final pretrial conference further frames the issues and defines the structure of the case, as well as helps formulate a plan for the trial, including a program for facilitating and streamlining the admission of evidence.

"Trials involving scientific or technical evidence present particular challenges to the judge and jurors to understand the subject matter and make informed decisions," Schwarzer and Cecil (2000) state. They point to a number of techniques used to facilitate presentation of such cases and enhance comprehension of the facts.

Judges are advised to lighten the jurors' load, by giving preliminary instructions that explain what the case is about and what issues the jury will have to decide. Some judges have found it helpful to ask a neutral expert to present a tutorial for the judge and jury before the presentation of expert evidence at trial begins, outlining the fundamentals of the relevant science or technology without touching on disputed issues. Consideration should also be given to having the parties' experts testify back-to-back at trial so that jurors can get the complete picture of a particular issue at one time rather than getting bits and pieces at various times during the trial.

Schwarzer and Cecil (2000) state, "Attorneys and witnesses in scientific and technological cases tend to succumb to use of the jargon of the discipline, which is a foreign language to others. And to facilitate the comprehension of technical language, judges are encouraged to insist that the attorneys and the witnesses use plain English to describe the subject matter and present evidence so that it can be understood by laypersons. Schwarzer and Cecil add, "They will need to be reminded from time to time that they are not talking to each other, but are there to communicate with the jury and the judge."

Acknowledging that most members of the judiciary do not have a scientific background, the Supreme Court recommended that judges obtain outside expertise to guide them in their gatekeeper responsibilities. The Court suggested that judges ask organizations such as the National Academy of Sciences and the American Association for the Advancement of Science for assistance in identifying experts to review scientific testimony before it is presented to juries. In addition, the Federal Judicial Center publishes and distributes to federal judges a *Reference Manual on Scientific Evidence* that contains chapters on how science works, statistics, survey research, several aspects of medical science, and engineering (Federal Judicial Center 2000).

EXPERT WITNESSES: A JUDGE'S FRIEND OR FOE?

Almost as powerful as the judge acting as gatekeeper is the expert witness whose testimony can make or break a criminal case. Much has been written about the clash of these titans in the courtroom, the high-profile, big-dollar, star witnesses who do battle in the presumed name of justice. While not designed to be a comprehensive treatment of the subject, this section endeavors to familiarize the reader with pertinent observations about expert witnesses related to their relationship with judges.

Although each state has its own definition, an expert witness is usually an individual who has been shown to the court to be qualified by his or her special knowledge, skill, or experience, and who can competently testify as an expert in a specific field; from the law's standpoint, an expert witness can give his or her opinion based on demonstration of this special knowledge or skill.

Testimony is the verbal statement of a witness, under oath, to the trier of fact (the judge and/or jury). A fact witness can testify only on the basis of personal knowledge of a situation gained through the use of his or her five senses and may not express opinions formed on any other basis. An expert witness may testify not only on the basis of personal knowledge, but also in the form of opinion based on his informed evaluation of the evidence presented and scientific tests performed and interpreted within the bounds of his or her skills, experience, and ability. Four criteria are used to generally qualify an individual as an expert witness: educational degrees received, number of years of occupational experience in the field, membership in professional organizations, and professional articles or books published.

Most importantly, an expert witness must state the truth, free from prejudice and subjectivity. The American Academy of Forensic Sciences (AAFS) notes, "The forensic scientist must be impartial and unbiased. The forensic scientist must tell . . . the whole truth, no matter what it is or whom it hurts or helps. An expert opinion can be offered only if there are scientific facts upon which to base it. In court, the work of the forensic scientist is carefully examined to find any flaws, whether in the test performed, the interpretation of the results, or the science upon which opinion is based. Whether the forensic scientist expert is hired by the prosecution or defense, the opposing attorney will try to undermine or discredit testimony which is against his client. The forensic witness must be qualified and knowledgeable of both his special area of scientific knowledge and expertise and the rules of evidence that govern the admissibility of opinions and conclusions. The forensic scientist often spends long hours testifying clearly and concisely in judicial proceedings concerning scientific information and what it means. Throughout he must maintain a posture of impartial professionalism."

The emphasis on objectivity among expert witnesses was not lost on Bashinski (1984), who notes, "A basic ethical tenet of forensic scientists is that as witnesses they are not advocates in the trial—that their analytical results and conclusions should not be swayed or biased by the party who calls for their testimony. It is accepted that it is the duty of the forensic scientist to avoid misleading the jury by his testimony." Bashinski recognizes, however, that an expert can be led during cross-examination, for example, putting the expert in an unenviable position and opening the margin for error or misstatements: "Given the fact that the testimony is being elicited by an advocate, however, it is not uncommon to encounter a courtroom situation in which the scientist is unable to present his results in what he considers to be a fair and impartial manner. Although it is possible for an experienced witness to control his own testimony to some extent, the scientist is often confined to limited responses to carefully constructed questions and is somewhat at the mercy of the attorney examining him. This situation can limit the witness' ability to be as clear or specific as he would like. Including clear-cut statements of conclusions in written laboratory reports can help prevent manipulation or misstatement of those conclusions by the advocates (attorneys) in the adversarial atmosphere of the courtroom."

Some commentators suggest that forensic scientists make poor expert witnesses because of a supposed lack of adherence to scientific principles, an allegation discussed in Chapter 10. "Because they don't know what the scientific method is, they don't apply it," Turvey asserts, "because that takes time, money and education, and almost no one in forensic science has that in sufficient quantities. And the ones who do are just keeping their heads down. Forensic scientists who work as expert witnesses examine and interpret evidence in the image of law enforcement, to confirm the theories of law enforcement, and there is no science in that."

Turvey explains, "When I consult for the defense, I am in a position to see everything in the case. But when you are working for the prosecution, you are only shown a tiny bit of the case—the part they care about. So, when you go into court to testify, you are often at a massive disadvantage. But you don't know it because you haven't seen it all—yet you think you are getting it all because you think you work for the prosecution, and you think the cops are all your buddies. It comes down to the fact that forensic scientists are essentially invited to make this false choice between law enforcement and defense work. That's not a real choice. The issue is if you are an actual scientist, it's a question of whether or not the evidence can support a particular conclusion. But the problem is the immense political pressure and financial pressure brought to bear, the golden handcuffs they have on you when you work for the state."

It is the responsibility of the trial judge to determine the legitimacy of the expert witness, says William Webster, former director of the CIA and the FBI, and co-chair of the American Judicature Society National Commission on Forensic Science and Public Policy. "It goes to the heart of the credibility of expert testimony," Webster says. "The judge must ensure that the expert witness is not some snake oil peddler from off the streets, providing testimony that has no validity or reliability. The judge has to take into account the qualifications of the witness, the nature of the testimony, whether it is relevant, whether it is reliable, and whether his background and experience and his reputation makes him an appropriate vehicle for communicating that information to a jury. The judge must also ensure that the expert is telling the truth as he sees it. I think the trial judge has always had that responsibility of a gatekeeper, but perhaps more so now because the U.S. Supreme Court has told him he is to do that."

Webster continues, "Another crucial aspect is that the judge be able to determine whether or not the testimony is relevant to what is at issue in the case being adjudicated, or is the testimony simply throwing mud on something? That's what we don't need or want in any courtroom. And I think that the trial judge knowing his exercise of authority as a gatekeeper is reviewable in a higher court is healthy. I believe most judges accept their role as gatekeeper and try to do the very best that they can to serve justice."

In Chapters 9, 10, and 12 we discussed the uneasy alliance between science and the law. This relationship was studied in 2002 by the National Academies, which held a workshop to discuss expert testimony and science in the courtroom. For scientists, the courtroom is a foreign, intimidating place. One veteran scientific witness attending the workshop stated that this arena "is a challenge that used to frighten me and continues to worry many of my colleagues as they consider whether to step into the courtroom." Common concerns of scientists are that they will be embarrassed publicly, their results may be misunderstood or used out of context, and that they may be branded as a "hired gun" for either the defense or for the prosecution (National Academies, 2002).

The workshop report stated, "One reason scientists are uncomfortable in the courtroom is that they are neither trained in nor comfortable with the formalism of the legal adversary proceeding as a mechanism to resolve scientific differences. One scientist discussed the modes of debate in science, which traditionally lead to consensus, not victory or defeat. When a group of scientists is asked to address a question, the group eventually recognizes the value of the strongest evidence and opinions. At that point, even if one or a few members of the group are at extreme ends of the bell-shaped curve of opinion, the custom is for all to join in a 'consensus truth'" (National Academies, 2002).

In the courtroom, the goal is not a consensus truth but a definitive decision. According to the National Academies (2002), "Although there may be a consensus in the scientific community about a particular question, this consensus is unlikely to appear in the courtroom. Instead, opposing attorneys search out experts from the tails of the bell-shaped curve so as to strengthen their particular arguments."

Because the law and science can be viewed as social constructs, there are professional myths surrounding each file that are perpetuated with time and each new courtroom experience. According to the National Academies (2002), "Participating in resolving legal disputes is one way for the two cultures to untangle those myths and learn to communicate better."

The stigma of being seen as the proverbial "hired gun" is reason enough for many scientists to want to avoid serving as an expert witness. Hansen (2000) remarks, "Not long ago expert witnesses were considered to be friends of the court, people whose willingness to take time out of their busy professional lives and participate in the judicial process entitled them to absolute immunity from civil liability for anything they said on the witness stand. But somewhere along the way, we stopped viewing them as the courts' friends and started seeing them as hired guns, people who were willing to testify on just about anything for a buck. And short of a vigorous cross-examination, the risk of professional sanctions, and the threat of a criminal prosecution for perjury, there was virtually nothing anybody could do to hold them accountable for the consequences of their testimony."

Rothstein (2005) notes, "Even after Daubert, scientists might still agree that the law endorses a somewhat peculiar form of knowledge. In almost all cases scientific testimony is presented by experts chosen by the parties based on the extent to which their arguments further the party's interests. Expert testimony is revealed in response to questions by attorneys who may not wish to explore the limitations of the testimony. Truth is thought to emerge from the opportunity for cross-examination by the opposing attorney, sometimes a bruising and confusing process. Most importantly, the courts must answer scientific questions and resolve disputes based on the current state of knowledge. Unlike scientists, judges cannot suspend judgment until research studies have addressed their sources of doubt." Rothstein adds, "Scientists may still shake their heads in dismay when judges attempt to engage in scientific discourse, and judges may still wonder why it is so hard for scientists to answer a straightforward question. But the two professions are much closer today than ever before."

In some cases, the expert witness can be seen as a necessary evil, mandated by the presumed ignorance of judges and juries. Kesan (1997) states, "Although the veracity of expert testimony is highly controversial, it has been a mainstay of English and American courts for several centuries. Juries in civil and criminal trials, often lacking the training to assess expert scientific testimony on its merits, give overwhelming deference to it." Kesan points to this paradox presented by expert testimony, as seen through the eyes of Judge Learned Hand, who commented, "The whole object of the expert is to tell the jury, not facts . . . but general truths derived from his specialized experience. But how can the jury judge between two statements each founded upon an experience confessedly foreign in kind to their own? It is just because they are incompetent for such a task that the expert is necessary at all."

Expert witnesses' believability, of course, has been called into question by numerous commentators, including Kesan (1997), who reports, "In a nationwide survey of 800 people who served on civil and criminal juries, 89 percent of the jurors reported that paid experts were believable. Among criminal jurors, 68 percent thought experts were very believable and 50 percent of the civil jurors found experts to be very believable. Yet a significant fraction of this expert testimony invites lay jurors to reach conclusions not grounded in any scientific theory or methodology."

The more things change, the more they stay the same. A 1932 report from the National Research Council observed the following about the reliability of expert witnesses, "The criteria for determining expertness leave much to be desired. Expert medical witnesses are of two types. The first type embraces those who are truly expert but who often make poor witnesses. . . . The second type of expert medical witnesses includes those who make excellent witnesses but may be sadly deficient in expertness. They have no hesitation in expressing very definite and decided opinions, which they are able to maintain upon cross examination. Every large city has its 'professional' medical experts of this type who may be well thought of by those lawyers who make use of that kind of expert testimony, but who are less well thought of by their medical colleagues. Some form of official licensing of experts might remove some of the pseudo-experts, but not many of them. Licensure can do no more than set up minimum standards. What the administration of justice needs is the highest possible standard of expert service, such as would be rendered by a properly organized institute of legal medicine."

As early as this 1932 report, scholars were asking themselves about the problems posed by expert witnesses. The report comments, "Three important and fundamentally different problems appear to be involved in this matter of expert medical testimony. The first relates to the establishment of a method or organization through which scientific medicine may be applied in an impartial and nonpartisan manner in the interest of justice. . . . The second problem relates to the ability of the medical profession to furnish the necessary scientific information . . . there can be little question of the existence in the United States of a store of medical knowledge adequate for the needs of justice and capable of great development if properly utilized. The third problem concerns the actual utilization of medical science, if the medical profession is able to furnish the scientific facts and if government can establish agencies for making the facts available."

The rise of the expert witness was meteoric in some cases. Risinger (2000) asserts that there has been the development of an "unbridled expansion of asserted expertise in civil and criminal courtrooms, limited only by the imagination of an attorney with a point to prove and a hole in her more conventional evidence." The impetus for this groundswell, he says, includes questionable levels of sufficiency of evidence, coupled with "decidedly lax threshold standards of admissibility for expertise." Risinger comments, ". . . the stage was set for the acceptance of some fairly questionable practices in the utilization of expertise by litigants. Consequently, although all sides were free to play the game, the result was generally much more favorable to parties with the proof burdens (generally civil plaintiffs and the prosecution in criminal cases, though criminal defendants were substantial players in regard to various affirmative defenses)."

"I have seen experts give testimony that appears to be rehearsed because they have it down pat," Kobilinsky says. "You can tell because there is a particular sequence to the things they discuss. There are certainly people who will testify because they are getting paid and they will say whatever the prosecutor or the defense bar asks them to say. It's a slippery slope because we are in an adversarial legal system and it is tempting to stray from what the evidence tells you. I believe that if someone is foolish enough to sit on the witness stand and say something detrimental because they are getting paid for it, there must be some kind of safeguard against this. Someone must be there to say, 'Hey, this expert is giving you nonsense, and it's not science.'"

ATTORNEYS PREPARE FOR BATTLE

As the stakes are raised in criminal cases, especially in capital cases, defense attorneys are beginning to realize that they must gain a better grasp of how forensic science works, most notably the inner working of the forensic laboratory and how forensic evidence is examined, analyzed, and interpreted. Of special concern for defense attorneys is the representation of indigent clients who may not be able to afford expert witnesses who can help poke holes in the forensic evidence presented by the state against the defendant. Kelly and Wearne (1991) comment, "The vast majority of defendants in criminal courts in the United States do not have access to forensic expertise, even though they will almost certainly face forensic evidence from the prosecution. . . . The prosecution's access to crime laboratories, the latest technology, and an unlimited range of expertise in the most serious cases means that, of all the disparities between defense and prosecution in the criminal justice system in the United States, that in the forensic field may be the greatest. The impact on the outcome of a case, where a defendant's life or liberty is on the line, can be equally disproportionate."

Kelly and Wearne (1991) point out that according to U.S. discovery and disclosure rules, defendants have no right to know if a forensic expert is going to testify against them in federal court, and they also have no right to confront the analyst who performed the tests that might incriminate him or her. Their one important right, provided by way of Rule 16 of the Federal Rules of Criminal Procedure, is to see all results and reports of scientific tests discoverable to the defense. Kelly and Wearne also emphasize that Rule 16 does not mention lab bench notes or test findings, adding, "Court after court has ruled that these are not discoverable, despite the fact that it is these, rather than the reports, which are often deliberately perfunctory and conclusory, that allow other experts to assess and check the scientific work carried out."

The process of pre-trial discovery is usually when much of the debate of any lawsuit takes place. Discovery is defined as the entire efforts of a party to a lawsuit and his/her attorneys to obtain information before trial through demands for production of documents, depositions of parties and potential witnesses, written interrogatories, written requests for admissions of fact, examination of the scene, and the petitions and motions employed to enforce discovery rights. The theory of broad rights of discovery is that all parties will go to trial with as much knowledge as possible and that neither party should be able to keep secrets from the other (except for constitutional protection against self-incrimination).

From the start, many experts have advocated for a strong suspicion of forensic science, especially during discovery. Arvizu (2000) advises attorneys, "Never stipulate to forensic evidence. If you stipulate to a forensic report, you are buying into the big lie: that forensic laboratories are infallible." Instead, defense attorneys are advised to start looking for the figurative skeletons in forensic laboratories' closets.

Attacking the forensic science-related findings of the prosecution's case involves a number of quality issues, including determining the fallibility of the lab and any errors analysts may have made, including mislabeling, misrepresentations, case mix-ups, possible contamination of samples, various interpretive errors, false positives and false negatives, use of nonspecific testing methods, problems with instruments, problems with methods of analysis, and faulty conclusions.

A common concern among legal scholars is that many defense attorneys do not question the validity of the prosecution's claims and the scientific and/or forensic evidence it presents. They add that reports from the forensic laboratory that state the analyst's conclusions about the test findings falls far short of providing the bigger picture and do not address key issues such as the basis for the conclusion; procedures that the technician used to reach the conclusion; what tests were performed; the protocols by which the technician reached valid conclusions; how the evidence was collected or handled; if the chain of custody and all transfers of evidence were complete; what safeguards against contamination were used; technical procedures in effect at the time the test was performed; data reporting and instrument operation; documentation of standards and reference materials used during analysis; copies of bench notes, logbooks, and other records pertaining to case samples or instruments; records documenting observations; measurements regarding testing; records reflecting of internal review; and much more that will be discussed in this section.

This kind of scant pre-trial discovery, defense experts say, does not provide adequate information about quality issues. They add that attorneys must be provided with these materials during discovery, especially since most defense attorneys do not have science backgrounds and do not know what to ask for. Thus, defense attorneys should be proficient in cross-examining forensic laboratory analysts and other scientific experts regarding their education, training, and experience, as well as quality issues relating to the analysis and interpretation of forensic evidence.

One of the key components of discovery is the case file, including copies of bench notes, logbooks, and any other records pertaining to case samples or instruments; and records documenting observations, notations, or measurements regarding case testing. A laboratory case file is the repository for records generated during the analysis of evidence from a case. Arvizu (2000) admonishes, "A forensic laboratory's report is never enough information for due diligence. Neither is it sufficient to rely on trial testimony from the laboratory's expert. There are simply too many ways that quality can be compromised, and too much information for any individual to remember."

Arvizu (2000) advises that the case file "should be an internally consistent, unbroken chain of records that document all activities, observations, measurements, and results relating directly to evidence from a given case. It should provide sufficient detail, so that someone who is versed in the technique, but not involved in the laboratory's work, can understand what was done and the basis for the reported conclusions." Arvizu adds that if the reported results on the quality of the laboratory, the test method(s), and the case file cannot be supported by laboratory records, "the credibility and defensibility of the laboratory's report can be undermined."

Defense attorneys are zeroing in on this as a weak link in the prosecution's chain. Whitehurst (2004) observes, ". . . this is one of the weakest areas in trial preparation where review is required of a forensic scientist. Generally crime labs provide one-liner reports, short, to the point, and hiding all the data. There is nothing for the reviewing scientist to review. In a post-conviction review, the forensic scientist with only the lab report with none of the supporting data must say to counsel that there is essentially nothing he can do."

Barring any objections, it may or may not be easy to gain access to all of the information that is needed to assess the quality of forensic evidence. Arvizu (2000) states, "Given the historical tendency to accept forensic reports at face value, forensic laboratories have only rarely been asked to produce complete sets of supporting documentation. As a result, the systems necessary for controlled generation, storage, maintenance, and retrieval of laboratory records may not be fully developed or implemented. Even those laboratories that generated all the requested materials may be unable to retrieve them on request. From a quality assessment perspective, if the records can't be found, it is as if they never existed."

Another necessary piece of information for defense attorneys is the evidence collection form, which provides descriptions of the evidence, its packaging, the identification of specimens, the identification of individuals collecting the samples, and the sample collection procedures. Whitehurst (2004) asserts, "If we think about this it becomes obvious that very often those individuals who have acquired the samples in the field are not trained scientists, have no forensic training at all, and very seldom are even college-educated individuals. Police officers who have not received forensic training can contaminate evidence, package it improperly, not preserve it in an appropriate environment, essentially make more mistakes than we can imagine."

While there are many highly trained crime scene investigators who collect, preserve and document evidence at crime scenes, in some jurisdictions, there are less experienced individuals to whom this responsibility falls. Defense attorneys must also be aware of the fact that evidence collected at crime scenes can be less than optimal in quality, and that analysts in forensic laboratories have little, if any, control over the way evidence is collected, stored, packaged, and transported to the lab. Whitehurst (2004) adds, "A scientist who is reviewing a scientific work product for counsel must know everything about the collection, preservation, transportation and handling of the evidence before the evidence was ever analyzed in the crime lab."

Chain-of-custody records, including field-to-lab transfers, and all transfers of evidence and associated analytical samples within the laboratory, are another important piece in the pretrial discovery puzzle. Whitehurst (2004) says that the chain of custody is critical not only for forensic practitioners, law enforcement, and prosecutors, but increasing numbers of defense attorneys are inquiring about the details of what has happened to the evidence from the time it was collected at the scene of the crime, to the point where it is analyzed, and beyond." Defense attorneys are reminded that mix-ups and mislabeling of evidence can occur in the lab, and that thorough determination of the chain of custody and verification of the evidence analyzed is an important safeguard against error.

Arvizu (2000) observes, "Evidence collection and management are often a weak link in the quality chain of forensic evidence. At best, a forensic laboratory test is only representative of the evidence as received by the laboratory. If evidence was compromised in the field, there is nothing the laboratory can do to correct the problem. The degree to which the test results can be interpreted within the context of a case depends on many things that may be outside a crime laboratory's direct control, such as: evidence collection equipment and techniques; statistical validity of evidence sampling; evidence transportation and storage conditions; skill and proficiency of evidence technicians; and ambient weather conditions at the collection site. It is impossible to observe evidence collection practices for every case. However, it is possible to evaluate the quality of law enforcement's field operations through an on-site quality audit of field evidence practices. Such an audit would include reviews of operating procedures, training records, and field records, as well as in-field inspections of operational compliance with procedures and good field practices. An independent audit of field practices is one of the most effective means of determining whether effective contamination control procedures have been implemented."

Defense attorneys are reminded to ask for laboratory receiving records that document the date, time, and condition of receipt of the evidence, as well as laboratory-assigned identifiers and the storage location. Whitehurst (2004) discloses that when he worked as a forensic scientist in the 1980s and 1990s in the FBI crime laboratory, on many occasions he "was forced to return evidence to contributors due to leaking containers, improper packaging, and cross-contamination." Whitehurst adds, "Forensic lab technicians who document evidence which must be returned due to improper packaging may find the same evidence re-shipped to them later repackaged with no concern about possible contamination during the first shipment."

Many defense attorneys know to question the techniques employed by the forensic scientist, as well as inquire about the procedures used to secure test findings. Tarantino (1988) summarizes that the analyst or chemist must follow particular steps in any analysis, in keeping with scientific protocol. These steps are as follows: Isolate and identify the chemical substance using the appropriate scientific technique; determine the presence or absence of other potentially related chemical substances in the specimens taken; quantitatively measure any identifiable chemical substance found in the specimen; use appropriate corroborative tests to confirm the identity and amount of any chemical substance found in the specimen; maintain appropriate measures to secure the collection, storage, and analysis of the specimen to guarantee that no contamination, spoilage, interference, or loss occurs; and issue a report that details the specificity, sensitivity, and reproducibility of each test.

In that vein, defense attorneys frequently request copies of standard operating procedures of the forensic laboratory that were in effect at the time the evidence testing was performed, including sample preparation, sample analysis, data reporting, and instrument operation. Whitehurst (2004) notes, "Testing laboratory procedures/protocols are very specific. Each step of a protocol is spelled out completely. For instance for a laboratory to simply note that in an analysis a mass spectrometer is utilized gives the reviewer nothing to work with. The mass spectrometer, though simple in theory, is a complex instrument. In order to properly utilize it to analyze chemicals one must be sure not only that it is functioning correctly but that all the parameters are set at valid values established by validation studies. In other words, all the buttons and knobs need to be set right. When the instrument is functioning correctly for the analysis at hand, there will be a read-out of all the parameters. A reviewer needs those printouts to determine if the analysis is being conducted correctly. And parameters which are correct for one type of analysis may not be correct for another." Whitehurst explains that if a forensic laboratory is constrained to the use of only a few mass spectrometers for a number of different analyses, one analyst may set the instrument correctly to detect the presence of cocaine, while the next analyst to use the machine may not change the parameters correctly to detect the presence of alcohol. Whitehurst states, "When analyses are complex requiring a variety of analytical instruments, the complexity requires in-depth review of all instrumental parameters as well as comparison to established procedures found in the scientific literature. If at the end of the review one finds that instrument settings are different from those which the crime lab itself notes are necessary for a valid work product, then counsel can point to the crime lab's own standards as proof of reasonable doubt."

Whitehurst (2004) recommends that defense attorneys request copies of proficiency test results for each analyst responsible for the preparation or analysis of samples, explaining, "To determine if an examiner is conducting analyses correctly, that examiner is tested. Most crime labs test using internal proficiency exams. A more proper method of testing is through the use of external proficiency tests where results are not reviewed by anyone associated with the crime lab." The lab should also engage in proficiency studies, legal experts claim, to validate its methods for ascertaining false positive rates and to ensure that analysts are proficient in performing the tests.

Many defense attorneys do not ask for a copy of the laboratory's quality manual, the laboratory's ASCLD/LAB application for accreditation and its most recent annual accreditation review report, a copy of the laboratory's ASCLD/LAB onsite inspection report, or a copy of internal audit reports generated during the period subject samples were tested. The reasoning is that validation and accreditation are two important safeguards against quality problems and deficiencies in test methods in forensic laboratories. Arvizu (2000) states, "Even though evidence from a particular test method has been determined to be reliable and admissible under the applicable legal standard, method quality remains an issue for forensic evidence. Despite the fact that the scientific community accepts a given measurement technique, it doesn't mean that every laboratory and every analyst is capable of successfully performing the method."

Experts say that a forensic laboratory should demonstrate and document its ability to successfully perform any method using the appropriate equipment in its facility before it uses any method to analyze forensic evidence. Arvizu (2000) explains, "This is accomplished by performing a validation study to determine the performance characteristics of the method. In the absence of a validation study, a laboratory that performs a test method does not have an objective basis for assigning uncertainties to its reported results. Even if performance data for a method are reported in the literature, they are not necessarily applicable to any individual laboratory's performance. If a laboratory has not determined a method's performance characteristics, it should not use the method to analyze forensic samples. Without a validation study, a laboratory doesn't know whether or not a method is working as it should."

Assurance that the proper instrumentation was used by analysts is garnered in part through the lab's instrument run log, as well as record of instrument operating conditions, initial calibration, continuing calibration checks, and calibration verification. Whitehurst (2004) comments, "Instruments in forensic crime labs are seldom, if ever, dedicated to one task. Crime labs are generally severely underfunded, understaffed, and underequipped. A mass spectrometer that is used for drug analysis today may be used for explosives or paint analysis tomorrow. Parameters are changed and rechanged. Different operators sit before the instruments and can make mistakes that the next operator will not detect. An instrument may be contaminated by the previous operator analyzing for the presence of cocaine and the technician who analyzed evidence in your case may detect cocaine but that cocaine was actually from the previous case." In addition, defense attorneys are instructed to ask for the lab's record of instrument maintenance status. All lab equipment should be properly maintained and calibrated for optimum testing results.

Issues related to quality in the forensic laboratory are numerous and have been discussed elsewhere in this book. Arvizu (2000) recommends that defense attorneys inquire if the laboratory's testing procedures are scientifically valid; if the methods as performed were compliant with approved and validated procedures; if the laboratory's activities, observations, and results can be reconstructed solely on the basis of the available records; if the laboratory complied with applicable elements of the quality assurance program; if all measurement systems and instruments were in statistical control at the time of analyses; if there were any reported uncertainties consistent with validation and quality control results; and if measurements are traceable through the appropriate use of calibration, standards, and reference materials. Two big issues for defense attorneys become evident during the quality assessment process: sample quality and the integrity and qualifications of analysts. By now, most defense attorneys have heard or read various accounts of mistakes made by laboratory personnel. Attorneys are reminded that laboratory testing does not always run smoothly, and that false positives and false negatives are not unusual. Legal scholars have pointed to misrepresentations or misinterpretation of test results by the analyst or examiner caused by carelessness or lack of experience.

Arvizu (2000) states, "The quality of a forensic measurement is limited by the quality and integrity of the evidence subject to analysis. It can be a daunting prospect to select, collect, package, label, transport, store, maintain, distribute, and prepare evidence in such a manner that the quality and integrity of the evidence are not compromised for any of the subsequent tests." Opportunities for introduction of contaminants abound in the laboratory, including inexperienced crime scene technicians and analysts who contaminate samples through poor practices in the field and in the laboratory, or in poorly designed and maintained labs with environmental factors that can help spread contaminants via air-handling systems, traffic patterns, or operating practices. Arvizu adds, "Many laboratories do not have formal procedures to identify contaminant carryover between samples on analytical systems. It is worth remembering that unless you look for contamination, chances are you won't find it."

Sometimes, if the evidence appears to be sound, defense attorneys will go after the qualifications of the individual examiner or analyst. Key areas for defense cross-examination include the levels of education, training, experience, and ethics of laboratory personnel. Legal scholars recommend that defense attorneys determine the extent of the education of analysts, to see if it is appropriate and relevant to the analyst's task at hand, as well as ask about any research the individual may have undertaken to further his or her career and standing in the field. Also worthy of inquiry is the analyst's duration of time on the job, pursuit of in-service training and continuing education, and certification of particular skills. Defense attorneys are instructed to prohibit the analyst to testify in areas outside of his or her universe or outside the scope of the questioning. Savvier defense attorneys are also cognizant of the effects of analyst bias; they are advised to determine how frequently an analyst has testified in court proceedings or has prepared for court proceedings on behalf of the state.

Arvizu (2000) reminds defense attorneys not to feel overwhelmed by the task of sorting through tons of paperwork and recommends they seek an independent assessment of the quality of reported results. Arvizu states, "Depending on the types of testing protocols required for a case, testing laboratories may generate lots of information. Don't be intimidated by the amount of material you receive. Despite the large quantities of paper and electronic information that may be provided, disciplinary and quality assurance experts know how to review the material and find the relevant information."

Arvizu (2000) states that defense attorneys must determine whether the laboratory's reported results are technically valid, and whether the quality and uncertainty of these results can be defended on the basis of the laboratory's records. Arvizu states, "If the supporting documentation provided by a laboratory is incomplete or inconsistent, the pedigree of the reported results is questionable, and the defensibility of the reported results can be compromised." To assist with this determination, defense attorneys may opt to hire the services of an independent auditor. Arvizu states, "Despite the fact that documentation can be a useful tool for assessing a laboratory report, only an on-site laboratory audit can provide a complete picture of a laboratory. It is one thing to have acceptable written procedures for a laboratory's activities. It is quite another to comply with the procedures on a daily basis. A laboratory quality audit is a systematic, independent investigation to determine whether a laboratory's activities and reported results comply with planned arrangements, and whether the activities are suitable to achieve the desired quality of results. An audit is not necessarily directed toward an assessment of laboratory performance on a particular case, although it is certainly possible. An effective on-site quality audit should be performed by trained and experienced quality auditors who have laboratory testing experience. In order to avoid a conflict of interest or inadvertent bias, a forensic quality audit should be performed by auditors who are completely independent of laboratories with a prosecutorial affiliation. As independent parties acting on behalf of the users of forensic reports, the auditors should report not to the laboratory, but to the sponsoring entity that receives forensic reports."

Above all else, Arvizu (2000) advises defense attorneys to know the strengths and limitations of forensic laboratories. She states, "You need to understand the strengths and weaknesses of the relatively small number of forensic laboratories that provide forensic services in your geographic area. In many locations, forensic laboratories are operated in substandard facilities by civil servants who are paid a fraction of the prevailing wage scale for trained scientists. A stellar record in one area of testing is no guarantee that all a laboratory's work is of comparable quality; a laboratory that excels in drug testing may do a dismal job on DNA.

Laboratory management may be completely unaware that evidence is subject to serious contamination during laboratory operations. Laboratory examiners may be drawn from the ranks of law enforcement, and may lack any academic foundation or formal training in science. And in far too many cases, neither management nor the laboratory staff understand the type of quality assurance program that is necessary to consistently generate results that can withstand rigorous scrutiny and challenge."

SPECIAL CONSIDERATIONS FOR DNA CASES

DNA is one arena in which both the prosecutor and the defense attorney must stay abreast of current technology in order to accurately evaluate the scientific evidence presented in court and conduct efficient cross-examination.

"The ability of prosecutors to understand how forensic science and how DNA works, and to be able to prosecute successfully using knowledge of these technologies and scientific disciplines, is of utmost importance," remarks Joseph Polski, chief operations officer for the International Association of Identification (IAI). "I have talked with folks at the National District Attorneys Association who acknowledge that DNA cases especially are receiving a lot of attention, and that necessitates further education and training of prosecutors and courts on how to successfully prosecute and understand cases containing a great deal of forensic evidence. It wasn't that long ago when prosecuting attorneys presented with cases that involved DNA, looked at them with trepidation, and knew they had to be knowledgeable on the subject. Nothing is scarier than prosecuting a case where a well-informed defense attorney cuts the prosecution's argument to shreds due to the lack of knowledge of forensic science."

One of the prosecutor's allies is the forensic laboratory, and nowhere is this forensic laboratory's documentation more important than in DNA-related cases. Thompson et al. (2003) explain, "The report should state what samples were tested, what type of DNA test was performed, and which samples could (and could not) have a common source. Reports generally also provide a table of alleles showing the DNA profile of each sample. The DNA profile is a list of the alleles (genetic markers) found at a number of loci (plural for "locus," a position) within the human genome."

The proper understanding of DNA evidence relies on the understanding of alleles and the process of DNA typing and the estimates of the statistical frequency of the matching profiles in various reference populations (which are intended to represent major racial and ethnic groups). Forensic laboratories compute these estimates by determining the frequency of each allele in a sample population, and then compounding the individual frequencies by multiplying them together. For example, if 10 percent (1 in 10) of Caucasian Americans are known to exhibit the 14 allele at the first locus, and 20 percent (1 in 5) are known to have the 15 allele, then the frequency of the pair of alleles would be estimated as 4 percent among Caucasian Americans. The frequencies at each locus are simply multiplied together, producing frequency estimates for the overall profile that can be staggeringly small: often on the order of one in a billion to one in a quintillion, or even less.

According to Thompson et al. (2003), when the estimated frequency of the shared profile is very low, some laboratories will state "to a scientific certainty" that the samples sharing that profile are from the same person. Thompson et al. comment, "Labs use different cut-off values for making identity claims. All of the cut-off values are arbitrary: there is no scientific reason for setting the cut off at any particular level just as there is no formally recognized way of being 'scientifically certain' about anything. Moreover, these identity claims can be misleading because they imply that there could be no alternative explanation for the match, such as laboratory error, and they ignore the fact that close relatives are far more likely to have matching profiles than unrelated individuals. They can also be misleading in that the DNA tests themselves are powerless to provide any insight into the circumstances under which the sample was deposited and are generally unable to determine the type of tissue that was involved."

Thompson et al. (2003) charge that too many defense attorneys accept on face value forensic laboratories' reports without determining if the actual test results fully support the laboratory's conclusions: "This can be a serious mistake. In our experience, examination of the underlying laboratory data frequently reveals limitations or problems that would not be apparent from the laboratory report, such as inconsistencies between purportedly 'matching' profiles, evidence of additional unreported contributors to evidentiary samples, errors in statistical computations and unreported problems with experimental controls that raise doubts about the validity of the results." Thompson et al. add that forensic DNA analysts report that they receive discovery requests from defense lawyers in no more than about 15 percent of cases in which their tests incriminate a suspect.

What commentators such as Thompson et al. fear most is subjectivity on the part of forensic examiners; although DNA typing relies on computer-automated equipment, interpretation of the results frequently requires human judgment skills. Thompson et al. (2003) assert, "When faced with an ambiguous situation, where the call could go either way, crime lab analysts frequently slant their interpretations in ways that support prosecution theories. Part of the problem is that forensic scientists refuse to take appropriate steps to 'blind' themselves to the government's expected (or desired) outcome when interpreting test results. We often see indications, in the laboratory notes themselves, that the analysts are familiar with facts of their cases, including information that has nothing to do with genetic testing, and that they are acutely aware of which results will help or hurt the prosecution team."

Commentators point to the context effect explored in greater depth in Chapter 10, a phenomenon summarized as the tendency for individuals to see what they expert to see when interpreting and evaluating ambiguous data. Thompson et al. (2003) observe, "This tendency can cause analysts to unintentionally slant their interpretations in a manner consistent with prosecution theories of the case. Furthermore, some analysts appear to rely on non-genetic evidence to help them interpret DNA test results. Backwards reasoning of this type (i.e., 'we know the defendant is guilty, so the DNA evidence must be incriminating') is another factor that can cause analysts to slant their reports in a manner that supports police theories of the case. Hence, it is vital that defense counsel look behind the laboratory report to determine whether the lab's conclusions are well supported, and whether there is more to the story than the report tells."

Even as the defense launches a campaign to undermine the evidence, the prosecution is quickly learning how to confront an expert witness hired by the defense to call into question evidence such as DNA. Kreeger (2002) states, "The prosecutor focuses, organizes, and controls the evidence presentation to ensure that the fact finders will reach the correct result. Treat the defense DNA expert accordingly (i.e., as a witness whose testimony is controlled by preparatory research, anticipatory pre-trial motion work, motions-in-limine regarding trial testimony, and focused cross-examination)."

Prosecutors first assess the strength of the DNA evidence in the case to determine if it is ironclad and whether or not the defense could mount a credible attack on it in court. Kreeger (2002) advises, "When your DNA analysts provide a report to you, ask if there are any foreseeable criticisms, attacks, concerns, or problems. Do your analysts believe any issue was created in the seizure, storage, submissions or handling of the evidence? Do the analysts believe there is any procedure, policy, or practice of the lab that could be criticized for failing to meet appropriate scientific standards? Did anything different or unusual happen with the evidence or the analysis in this case? Confirm that the analysts are confident in finding a match between crime scene evidence and the defendant, their analysis of a mixture and the major or minor contributors, and about the statistical conclusions that can be drawn from the analysis. Review with the analysts all of the other evidence in the case to make sure that the DNA evidence is consistent with all of the facts. Examine whether your analyst will testify to the absence of DNA evidence in certain aspects of your case. Learn from your expert witness whether a defense expert's testimony would be a good faith challenge and not misleading to the fact finder. When there are no identifiable issues relating to the DNA (or lack thereof), focus on preparing your case as a whole."

Anticipation of the defense in the case is another important step for prosecutors, as Kreeger (2002) notes, "The better in command you are of all the facts and all the plausible defenses, the better positioned you are to successfully exclude or limit the defendant's expert." Kreeger adds, "Challenge the defense's ability to call an expert whose testimony will be a general criticism of science or statistics." Limiting the defense expert witness is key, as is challenging the defense to articulate the need for and the testimony of the expert in the case so that this expert can be held to those specific limits.

Prosecutors are advised to learn as much as they can about the experts called by the defense. Kreeger (2002) recommends, "Learn who the defense expert is in the forensic science community. Is this person a forensic DNA examiner, a non-forensic scientist, an academic, or a population geneticist? Has the expert worked in a lab? If so, when, where, doing what and for how long? Examine the witness's résumé, biography, or curriculum vitae for what is and is not there. . . . Call or contact resources to confirm the credentials and qualifications of the expert. Ask your analyst and others in your lab to use their professional resources, including neighboring labs or the FBI, to gather information about the expert. Compare what the expert's testimony has been to what the defense purports to be the expert's role in your case. If the expert's credentials are inconsistent with the purported defense challenge to your evidence, move to exclude the expert."

Cross-examination is where the prosecutor can do the most damage to the defense's expert witnesses and change the course of the trial. Zeroing in on the expert's experience in forensic science-related cases is important, as Kreeger (2002) points out: "Which expert works on forensic science cases, solely, in a lab that is accredited or working towards accreditation? Which expert is in a lab every working day of the year? Who works daily with other qualified scientists available to review the expert's work? Who has examined the evidence in the case? When did the defense expert learn about the case?"

Kreeger (2002) advises, "DNA evidence is just one form of identification. It is not the determinant of guilt. DNA is, however, an easily validated and trustworthy science. Similarly, statistics is not new or fuzzy math. Consequently, a defense expert cannot attack the fields of science and statistics credibly. To be relevant, experts should challenge facts in a case. Put the defense expert's criticism in proper context. Understanding the purpose and consequent import of the defense expert's testimony, given all of the evidence, enables you to control it. The background of a defense expert is most meaningful in a context of comparison to your case. Move to exclude or to limit the expert's testimony as completely as possible. If the expert cannot testify to case-specific, fact-specific issues relating to the evidence, the analysis, or the conclusions of your witness, then the expert's testimony really is irrelevant, a waste of judicial money and time."

Hogan and Swinton (2003) assert that prosecutors need not fear cross-examination, especially when the expert witness testimony involves molecular biology, population genetics, or laboratory quality assurance protocols: "What is most frustrating in forensic DNA cases is that the prosecutor knows that good science is being portrayed incorrectly as bad science. Never before have prosecutors had a more powerful tool at their disposal for determining the identity of persons who commit crime. Today, scientists develop DNA profiles from minute amounts of crime scene evidence. The use of PCR-based testing of short tandem repeat (STR) locations on the DNA molecule has revolutionized forensic science." Hogan and Swinton explain further, "The STR DNA tests now used in crime laboratories across the country are highly discriminating. The resulting profiles often allow for random match probability estimates that are less than 1 in a quadrillion."

Hogan and Swinton (2003) also assert, "There are few, if any, techniques in the history of forensic science that have been more thoroughly scrutinized, validated, and tested than forensic DNA testing. The underlying science of DNA testing is virtually unassailable, and the techniques that apply the scientific principles have survived intense scrutiny. For this reason, few defense experts will dare to challenge the validity of DNA amplification or the detection of genetic variation using electrophoresis."

However, as we explored in Chapters 10 and 11, they recognize that prosecutors will face defense challenges to the population statistics associated with a DNA match. Hogan and Swinton (2003) note, "Some of these attacks will focus on issues such as the use of the product rule to calculate profile frequency statistics; others will focus on the database size and/or the populations that were either included, or not included, in the database. A final issue is misstating the meaning of the statistics."

Prosecutors face the argument that the product rule should not be used, while the defense will push for use of the counting method or the ceiling principle. The product rule is a concept in which the frequency of occurrence of several independent events is equal to the product of their individual frequencies. Hogan and Swinton (2003) explain, "For example, if you flip a coin, the probability of getting 'heads' is one half. The probability of getting 'heads' three times in a row is one half multiplied by one half multiplied by one half, or 1 in 8. Since a person's profile at one DNA locus has no bearing on the person's profile at another locus, the frequency of occurrence of the entire profile equals the product obtained by multiplying the frequencies at each individual locus."

A defense objection to use of the product rule is frequently countered by the prosecutor pointing to the stamp of approval provided by the National Research Council (NRC) of the National Academy of Sciences; in a 1996 study the NRC endorsed the product rule to calculate DNA random match probability, and according to Hogan and Swinton (2003), this study "is considered by most scientists in the field to be the definitive pronouncement on the issue of DNA match statistics." In the study, experts also rejected numerous alternative methods of calculating DNA random match probabilities. Hogan and Swinton observe, "Prosecutors today often have the benefit of outstanding DNA testing technology when attempting to prove the identity of persons who commit crimes. These suggestions can help frontline prosecutors fend off even sophisticated attacks on DNA match evidence and help fact finders reach just verdicts.

Kreeger and Weiss (2003) advise prosecutors to consider the following tactics when formulating a trial strategy:

- Establish identity with every form of available evidence, including direct testimony, direct physical evidence, and circumstantial evidence, and ensure that the proof reflects that DNA was merely one of several sources of identity evidence.

■ During cross-examination of the prosecution analyst, identify the defense issues with the DNA evidence, such as the collection process, potential contamination of the sample, and interpretation of the statistics, and respond with detailed redirect testimony of the government's analyst to explain why retesting would not be a remedy.

■ During cross-examination of the defendant or defense witnesses, elicit a concession that identity is not in issue.

■ When the defense is not identity, but rather consent or the justified use of force, discuss these defenses in argument for judgment of acquittal or in closing. Conversely, when identity is the issue, discuss all of the evidence that proves identity in argument for judgment of acquittal or in closing.

As the fight over forensic science in the courtroom escalates, a growing number of law schools offer courses in scientific evidence and the law, in an attempt to prepare lawyers on both sides of the courtroom for the rigors of adjudication of cases.

"There is plenty of education in science evidence to be had for lawyers," says Paul Ferrara, Ph.D., director of the Virginia Department of Forensic Science, and co-founder of the Virginia Institute of Forensic Science and Medicine. "The key is to understand who is teaching these courses. Many of the professors also serve as experts for the defense, and they will concentrate on teaching students how, for example, to attack forensic laboratories' testing results, including instruction on what to look for and what to ask for, and how to poke holes in the case, regardless of its overall bearing on the accuracy of the conclusions."

Ferrara continues, "The criminal law process is adversarial, of course; you put any two good attorneys together and they can argue either side of the case, especially to a jury of laypersons, and make an argument stick. Attorneys are taught first to look at the underpinnings of the forensic evidence in the case, especially newer technology such as DNA, to see if there are any admissibility issues to challenge. For years and years, relevancy hearings have been held on evidence, and finally in the early 1990s, the National Academy of Sciences' National Research Council basically gave its blessing to DNA and declared, 'This is good science.' So then, for the defense, the argument becomes one of statistics used in association with the technology. Instead of the DNA wars, you have the statistics wars. The National Research Council basically gave us the green light to use the appropriate mathematical formulae associated with DNA, so when defense attorneys are finished with that, what's left? Well, that's when they are instructed to attack the competency, the education and training levels, or the objectivity of the people who conduct the tests in crime labs."

Ferrara says he takes issue with defense attorneys who cross the line, and judges who allow it in their courtrooms. "I think many judges bend over backward for the defense bar, giving them so much latitude in reviewing the evidence so that the defense can argue about the labs' competence. I think many judges are too liberal in granting motions relating to defense attorneys who think evidence is suspect and who want review by external experts. These law professors don't teach students about the science, but about manipulation."

On the other hand, experts for the defense assert that the prosecution does not provide for adequate opportunity to scrutinize the forensic evidence, especially if green defense attorneys don't know to ask for it. "A lot of the issues that have arisen in terms of misleading testimony on the part of experts or incorrect findings, stem from the inability of the defense to have ready access to experts who can examine the evidence that is being presented by the opposing side to ensure that the evidence is proper, and also to prepare the defense for examining bad evidence," says Saferstein. "Nine times out of 10, when you look at these situations, you realize that the defense was the victim of bad forensic science, or because they weren't prepared to deal with the issues that came up in court—whether it was because the experts weren't made available to the defense, or because the defense attorney was incompetent and didn't seek external assistance. I believe that the defense attorney has the responsibility of securing experts to evaluate the evidence being presented and controlled by the state. I especially believe that if the defendant is indigent, appropriate funds should be made available to pay for these services."

Saferstein points to a recent case to make his point: "In a DNA case that I just evaluated, I found the evidence to be incorrect," he says. "Now, if the defense attorney hadn't taken the initiative to contact my office for a review and to also seek funding for this review, this error would have never been discovered. It's that simple. More cases fall through the cracks because of lack of review. The presence of defense experts is probably the best quality control program we have for forensic science today."

When he is hired to review a case, Saferstein explains, he essentially examines the forensic and technical evidence put forth by the state and determines whether or not analysis, testing, and interpretation were conducted by forensic laboratories correctly. "The role of a defense expert is not necessarily to poke holes in the case, but to make sure everything is done properly," Saferstein says. "Once it is determined that, through omission or commission, as both do happen, that problems exist, then you help the defense attorney point out the weaknesses of the state's case. How you do that depends on the nature of the case. It may be a question of an overstatement of the significance of a comparison, for example, or maybe it's a case of not stating a statistic sufficiently and misleading the jury as to how significant the comparison is. In one of my recent cases, there was an out-and-out error. If I as a defense expert find either through omission or commission that there is a problem, I will do my utmost to help the defense attorney point the problems out to the jury."

Saferstein acknowledges that defense attorneys and defense experts face an uphill battle when it comes to interacting with jurors. "I think it is very difficult, even under the best of circumstances, for a defense expert to try to convince the jury that an error has been made," Saferstein says. "Most jurors have a very high regard for the crime labs and the people who work in them. It's tough for a defense expert such as myself to say to the jury, "Perhaps the forensic laboratory or the forensic practitioner were wrong. All I want to do is make a record of this error for the appeal process, if nothing else. I know that as a defense expert, I am going in with two strikes against me, but that doesn't prevent me from doing my job for the defense attorney and for the defendant."

As an advocate of case review, Saferstein says there are limited mechanisms that allow the defense attorney to secure impartial examination of the forensic evidence. "In the Brandon Mayfield case, the cross examiner was brought in and incorrectly identified the fingerprints, so even the court examiner can fail," Saferstein notes. "My feeling is that cases that include things like fingerprint evidence are very subjective, so there should be a vehicle put into place to allow for the evaluation of findings by either a defense expert of the defense's choosing, or by a court-appointed impartial expert. There must be some mechanism besides what is in our courts today where a judge can automatically appoint an impartial examiner of the evidence for admissibility purposes, or allow for a defense expert to be funded. There has to be some better mechanism in the system for review. And this review must be conducted on a case-by-case basis because every case is different. What's missing in forensic science today is the ability to define those areas that are particularly in need of review, such as latent fingerprints and document examination especially, and once those areas are defined, there should be some mechanism in the system that requires a court-appointed expert to review the findings of the state with respect to admissibility. It's the only logical way to do it, and we have to make the time and spend the money to do it."

For Allan Sobel, J.D., former president of the American Judicature Society and director of the Arlin M. Adams Center for Law and Society at Susquehanna University, everything takes a backseat to the need to look out for indigent defendants, the most vulnerable participants in the legal system. Sobel says, "We conduct our judicial business in an adversarial setting and that traditionally has required defense counsel to challenge the admissibility of evidence to protect the client's right to a fair trial. When attorneys failed to challenge the admissibility of evidence, judges have generally sat on their hands and let the offered evidence come into the proceedings. In my view, you can't talk about the admissibility of evidence and the gate-keeping function of judges without talking about the state of indigent defense in the United States. I would guess that well over 90% of criminal defense work is done by attorneys representing indigent clients. There are some who can afford counsel, but only a small percentage of those charged. And when I speak of indigent defense, I am not just talking about the attorney, but rather the whole package of resources that is made available to an indigent defendant, which should include experts as needed. The indigent defense system is in a horrible state virtually everywhere, severely underfunded in most jurisdictions, and the right kinds of challenges supported by the right kinds of resources, are often not made given the Daubert-related issues that might be pressed."

THE JURY AND THE "CSI EFFECT"

It is difficult to pinpoint the exact origins and time frame of the general public's fascination with forensic science, as we saw in Chapter 1. Perhaps it was in 1995 with the O.J. Simpson case and every major televised criminal case since then. Or perhaps it has been with the onslaught of dozens of television programs offered on both network and cable that have followed the real and fictional exploits of detectives, criminal profilers, forensic pathologists, and crime scene technicians. Mirsky (2005) quotes trace evidence analyst Max Houck, director of West Virginia University's Forensic Science Initiative, as stating, "The 'CSI effect' is a term that came into use around 2003, when the show really started to become popular. It represents the impossibly high expectations jurors may have for physical evidence."

Essentially, the "CSI effect" supposedly describes the impact that television programming has had on the behavior of jurors. Commentators assert that the unrealistic version of forensic science that people watch on dramatized television shows causes them to raise their expectations of the forensic evidence presented in real criminal trials, which often bears little resemblance to its Hollywood counterpart. As a consequence, these commentators charge, jurors are more likely than not to acquit defendants based on their possibly flawed perceptions of the criminal justice system.

The phenomenon that has been dubbed the "CSI effect" has been named after a wildly popular television show about crime scene technicians' exploits in Las Vegas, debuting in 2000, which spun off into two additional permutations of CSI whose fictional characters were based in Miami and New York. The CSI: Crime Scene Investigation trilogy has proven to be the flashiest of the forensic shows, creating the greatest impression on the collective psyche of its viewers in terms of how scientists in lab coats catch crooks.

CSI is simply one of a number of attempts throughout history to explore the realm of forensic science through the eyes of a readily identifiable individual or cast of characters, according to Victor Weedn, M.D., J.D., professor at Duquesne University. "The first major dramatization of a forensic science-related figure was Sherlock Holmes, accompanied by his sidekick Dr. Watson, who brought an interesting medical component to crime detection and forensic science. That's not surprising, since Sir Arthur Conan Doyle had medical training in his background." Weedn continues, "Now fast-forward a great number of years to the 1970s to the ground-breaking show, 'Quincy, MD.' Actor Jack Klugman took a lot of pride in trying to make the show very realistic, although you can argue about how realistic it actually was. Klugman battled with the show's writers to try to keep the science and the medicine on track, but in the end, the writers got their way and ratings fell. One of the shows actually mentioned the very new (at the time) 'Christmas tree stain' for spermatozoa in rape cases. We fast-forward even more and now suddenly there are all of these forensic programs. A guy named Anthony Zuiker noted that his wife was glued to these shows, but they were non-fiction documentaries. Zuiker thought that what television needed was a dramatization of forensic science, and 'CSI' was born. In part, 'CSI' was a nod to the fascination of all of these forensic programs as well as the broadcasts of the sensationalistic O.J. Simpson trial and other high-profile criminal cases that have triggered media frenzies. Quite soon after 'CSI' debuted in 2000 it was on its way to becoming the No. 1 show on TV in the United States. I believe that it has truly achieved a whole new level of 'forensic speak' at home and at the dinner table."

CSI, which has consistently placed in the Nielsen top 10 for several years, is watched by more than 60 million people every week, meaning that millions of potential jurors are being exposed to Hollywood's interpretation of forensic science and forensic pathology. Throw in a few more viewing hours of *Law & Order*, and individuals have the entire criminal justice process down cold. McRoberts et al. (2005) observe, "The runaway popularity of TV shows that make heroes out of forensic scientists has produced a spin-off of its own. Authorities have dubbed it the 'CSI effect.' The script for this phenomenon, written by prosecutors across the country and dutifully repeated by newspapers in recent months, is simple and compelling: Having watched hour after hour of 'CSI: Crime Scene Investigation' and other legal dramas, jurors nationwide are demanding forensic evidence and acquitting defendants en masse when prosecutors don't deliver. The truth, it turns out, is more complicated than this TV-inspired fiction."

Legal scholars, commentators, and members of the forensic community each have their own concerns about the prevalence of this so-called "*CSI* effect." While it has certainly created new interest in forensic science principles that could translate into a supply of forensic scientists for the future, it has begun to alter the way jurors view the evidence in criminal cases, as well as the way attorneys present that evidence, whether it is physical, trace evidence, or opinions expressed in the testimony of forensic science experts. Or has it? That seems to be the power of the myth of the "*CSI* effect"; anecdotal evidence appears to point to cases in which the "*CSI* effect" acted as the tipping point for an acquittal, yet some assert there is an abysmal lack of proof that the "*CSI* effect" is real. Instead, some say the "*CSI* effect" points to systemic problems within the criminal justice system.

McRoberts et al. (2005) comment, "A few anecdotes and the complaints of prosecutors aside, there is no definitive evidence to prove that jurors' TV-watching habits are uniformly hurting the prosecution rather than the defense. The raft of crime-lab scandals across the country—revealing the shoddy and sometimes fraudulent work of forensic analysts—suggests broader problems in American courts: how easily some prosecutors have brought unproven forensic theories or unchallenged forensic experts into the courtroom and how some jurors are willing to believe them. Judges note the keen interest jurors have in forensic evidence, but some reject the notion that jurors punish prosecutors whose cases aren't ready for prime time."

Does the "*CSI* effect" even exist? Experts seem to ponder that very question themselves. "If the CSI effect indeed is true, it's going to make the jurors more sensitive to issues I will raise in the courtroom, and I think that's great," says Saferstein. "But I don't know if that phenomenon exists, quite frankly." Tyler (2006) observes, "The CSI effect has become an accepted reality by virtue of its repeated invocation by the media. Although no existing empirical research shows that it actually occurs, on a basic level it accords with the intuitions of participants in the trial process."

Taking the place of substantial empirical data is the conjecture on the parts of legal scholars and attorneys, much of it based on anecdotal information. Cole and Dioso (2005) observe, "To argue that CSI and similar shows are actually raising the number of acquittals is a staggering claim, and the remarkable thing is that, speaking forensically, there is not a shred of evidence to back it up. There is a robust field of research on jury decision-making but no study finding any CSI effect."

"I decided to do a panel on this topic with the American Bar Association recently," Henderson reports. "We pulled 104 articles about the CSI effect and we realized that these were all anecdotal situations. There are a few individuals who are currently trying to get their arms around whether or not the CSI effect exists and the impact it is having on cases; I found two studies, but neither researcher talked to jurors; instead, they talked to prosecutors and judges to get their perspectives. There is one study being done by Dave Khey at the University of Florida which is currently surveying the membership of the American Academy of Forensic Sciences (AAFS) and the International Association for Identification (IAI) about their perceptions of the CSI effect. He is then surveying jurors in several jurisdictions. There have been a few more studies done and everyone likes to talk about this phenomenon, but we need many more studies to determine if there is any actual evidence of the impact of the CSI effect."

So while researchers are trying to pin down this phenomenon within a more scientific or statistical context, true believers are quick to point to the concept as a symbol of what is wrong with forensic science, expert testimony, and the legal system in general. "The essence of the CSI effect is that more people are expecting this wonderful forensic science and this competent technology, and trustworthy experts," says Turvey. "But what they are getting are either these schlubs with no expertise at all who are trying to tell them something about the case, or a guy who is trying to tell them things they know from watching shows like 'CSI' can't be true. People are confused. They are asking, what do you mean you can't get DNA from eyeglasses? Yes you can. I remember hearing a cop say in court that you couldn't lift a fingerprint off of a car because the surface was not amenable to it. And everybody in court believed him. And they had to bring me in to explain the truth. There's a battle for people's beliefs."

"In the past, criminal defense attorneys would take jurors off a jury panel on *voir dire* if they watched these forensic shows or had some scientific background," Weedn says. "If jurors were too smart, they could read through the confusion in the courtroom. Now, with the CSI effect, prosecutors take off the list of potential jurors those same people because they tend to say in deliberations, 'Where is the fingerprint evidence? Where is the DNA?' And then these jurors vote for an acquittal because that evidence wasn't present in the case. After all, they think, 'If there was that kind of evidence, then they'd show it to us, right?'"

Ferrara observes, "I remember when I first heard about DNA technology in the mid-1980s. I thought to myself, 'If this technology is out there, how do you argue why it was not used in a particular case?' And now, prosecutors have a hell of a time when they don't have or need DNA evidence. The first thing the jurors want to know is, 'Where is the DNA?' Perhaps they have it, perhaps they don't; perhaps it was inconclusive; maybe they think, 'We have a good enough case, we don't need the DNA.' It's becoming so problematic."

It has been several years since commentators and journalists first embraced and perpetuated the term "*CSI* effect" to indicate the influence that television shows have had on jurors who have unreasonable expectations of forensic science and its practitioners based on unrealistic depictions of the field. On television, crimes are solved in 60 minutes (minus commercials) by sexy, crime-fighting scientists in even sexier locales, using seductively sophisticated equipment. In reality, there's little sex appeal attached to the sometimes dilapidated or outdated labs, the people unglamorous but dedicated, and the science that requires much more time for analysis to be effective in solving cases. Botluk and Mitchell (2005) ask, "Can you really solve a crime in an hour while not messing up your hair or designer suit? Do forensic technicians drive Hummers to crime scenes? Can a prosecutor still try a case when forensic scientists can't discover that rare element in the trace evidence that eliminates all suspects but one?"

Stephen Fienberg, Ph.D., the Maurice Falk University professor of statistics and social science in the Department of Statistics at the Center for Automated Learning and Discovery at Carnegie Mellon University, notes, "Some have said that CSI is to forensic science as science fiction is to science."

Perhaps the allure of these kinds of shows is the opportunity to participate in the investigation of crime, an element of modern society that surrounds us, threatens us, maybe even titillates us because it reaches into the deep, dark places inside humans that have fascinated us for centuries. Hayes (2004) comments, "Movies and TV shows let people look at death and not turn away; prime time on many nights is wall-to-wall death. Increasingly though, that death is mediated through the lens of forensic science, a mediation that sanitizes and protects. The new forensic shows owe less to 'Quincy' than they do to the 1995 O.J. Simpson trial, which focused unprecedented public attention on forensics."

"There's nothing wrong with 'CSI' as long as people are able to discern fact from fiction, and that's where they get into trouble," says Ernst. "The positive aspect is that it does raise the profile of forensic science, but we in the forensic science community have to do what we can to counter this fiction with the facts. I give a presentation called 'The Real World of Forensic Science: Not CSI' and I explain to people how 'CSI' or 'Crossing Jordan' differ from real-life criminalistics. For example, 'Crossing Jordan' employs a forensic entomologist full-time in the medical examiner's office. In reality there are something like fewer than 10 board-certified forensic entomologists in North America and no office in this country can boast of having the luxury of a full-time forensic entomologist at their service. However, because that's what people see on television, that's what people think happens in real life. I try to explain to people how much time it takes to conduct DNA analysis, or how long it takes to conduct an autopsy when there are seven bullets in the body. They will see that it's not 60 minutes, like in the television shows."

There are two critical issues relating to the impact of the CSI effect; the first issue is that forensic television shows raise the profile and awareness of forensic science, triggering renewed interest in the field by students; the second issue is the way in which putting forensic science on a pedestal is affecting case verdicts.

Linville and Liu (2002) observe, "The reality of forensic science does retain many of the traits that make the field so appealing in this fictional setting. In the real world, scientific analysis of physical evidence does play a role in the prosecution of criminals. However, popular media rarely exposes the public and, more importantly, prospective forensic science students to actual forensic work. When considering a career in forensic science it is important to have a clearer picture of what forensic science is, and is not, and what it demands of its practitioners."

Degrees in forensic science are now offered by educational institutions ranging from community colleges to Ivy League universities, and schools across the country have been reporting skyrocketing interest in undergraduate- and graduate-level programs. Willing (2004) reports that at West Virginia University, forensic science is the most popular undergraduate major, attracting 13 percent of incoming freshmen, while Lovgren (2004) reports that there are now at least 90 forensic science programs at universities across the United States. For example, it has been reported that 180 people applied for 20 openings in the forensic science master's program at Michigan State University. Many of these would-be forensic scientists have stars in their eyes about their career prospects, pursuing dreams fueled by what they see on *CSI*, but there is a rude awakening when the line of demarcation between education and entertainment is crossed. Linville and Liu (2002) state, "Hollywood focuses on the most interesting aspects of the forensic investigation. Science becomes a gimmick—a technological toy that the hero uses to find evidence the criminal surely hoped was undetectable. In reality, forensic scientists spend a great deal of time in the laboratory, working with evidence collected from crime scenes. For the forensic scientist, the goal is to objectively analyze submitted evidence and return an interpretation to the investigator. Although there are opportunities for investigative field-based work, most forensic scientists work in laboratories processing evidence. The work is just as demanding as the work in any other analytical laboratory, but rarely requires the scientist to outsmart or chase down nefarious evil doers."

With heightened awareness and visibility of forensic science comes increased scrutiny by jurors of forensic practices and the results they produce for the adjudication of criminal cases. Botluk and Mitchell (2005) comment, "The legal community finds itself in constant debate as to whether the CSI effect positively or negatively influences juries. Regardless, prosecutors and defense attorneys agree that an effective trial strategy can no longer ignore the influence of pop culture on jury decision-making."

At the heart of the "*CSI* effect" is the "glorification," Botluck and Mitchell (2005) say, of the use of scientific principles to assist in crime solving. The popularity of shows such as the three *CSI* shows, as well as *Crossing Jordan, Law & Order,* and *Forensic Files,* to name a few, fuels America's fascination with forensics. Botluck and Mitchell comment, "The television viewing public can turn to either network or cable television on any given night and find a variety of forensic based programs. These programs showcase stylish technicians using state-of-the-art technology to piece together a crime scene's unknown variables in less than 60 minutes. Viewers are repetitively exposed to episodes where DNA test results are reported in 15 minutes or less and fingerprints are matched to prints in law enforcement databases almost immediately. In the rare instance where the suspect does not confess to the crime, the viewers are exposed to these same stylish technicians as expert witnesses. The experts use visual aids and hands-on experiments to demonstrate the scientific techniques to the jury members. The courtroom drama is just as entertaining as the investigation."

Botluk and Mitchell (2005) add, "As television educated America about the role of forensic evidence in the law enforcement/justice system, the legal community found itself adapting as juries began finding reasonable doubt when the state did not produce 'sufficient' forensic evidence. 'The CSI effect' placed the legal community under a new burden of helping jury members distinguish the fictional aspects of television from reality. Additionally, expert witnesses must now explore new ways of presenting testimony that captivates the jury's desire to be not only entertained, but also convinced that law enforcement properly collected evidence and that crime scene technicians properly performed all of the relevant types of forensic analyses."

Essentially, *CSI* depicts everything about forensic science, from the technology, to the pace of the evidence analysis, to the sophistication of the equipment employed, as being representative of the average forensic laboratory or medico-legal office; this is a damaging portrayal because, as we saw in Chapters 5 and 8, television in no way mirrors reality at the majority of these facilities in the United States.

"Some jurors are expecting that some of the technology used on the shows is real, and it's not," says Henderson. "In fact, they're sometimes disappointed if some of the new technologies that they think exist are not used. This is causing quite a bit of concern for prosecutors trying the cases, as well as some of the jurors. They want evidence that may not exist. Unrealistic expectations are harming the jury system."

On television and in real life, investigations involve assembling the pieces of the puzzle that will assist law enforcement, aided by forensic scientists and technicians, to construct vital facts about the crime. Hayes (2004) writes, "There is a forensic saying that 'there is only one honest witness to every murder—the victim.' And we talk about those five questions, 'Who are you? How did you die, when did you die, where did you die, and who killed you.'"

Uncovering the right answers to these questions is a process facilitated by the use of sophisticated equipment such as DNA sequencers, mass spectrometers, photometric fingerprint illuminators, and scanning electron microscopes; the important thing for laypersons to bear in mind is that these pieces of equipment are exceedingly expensive and can be cost-prohibitive for many forensic laboratories and medico-legal offices to obtain. Because of the wide variability of infrastructure and budgets in forensic facilities across the country, some forensic laboratories may not be able to purchase the latest and greatest piece of equipment that costs $100,000, and so not every laboratory is created equal. This becomes a concern when members of the general public assume that the whiz-bang technology they see on television doesn't translate to their local forensic laboratory that must decide between buying a new mass spectrometer or offering raises to its overworked staff. So while the technology is real in many cases, not every laboratory will have the grandness of the Las Vegas Police Department crime lab shown in *CSI*, nor will it be able to achieve the kind of results using the specific forensic techniques depicted on television.

"Thanks to what people see on 'CSI' each week, people think every lab has state-of-the-art technology at their fingertips," says W. Earl Wells, president of the American Society of Crime Lab Directors (ASCLD) and director of the Forensic Services Laboratory of the South Carolina Law Enforcement Division. "'CSI' can push the envelope beyond what is possible from a technology standpoint; so much of even the more routine technology is not available to many labs because of budget restrictions. I consider myself fortunate in that my lab has a lot of state-of-the-art technology, but we still struggle with our budgets."

Lovgren (2004) comments, "While the cool technology in the 'CSI' crime lab sometimes seems lifted out of 'Star Trek,' real-world experts say the equipment used on the shows is firmly rooted in reality." Lovgren then quotes Dean Gialamas, director of the forensics laboratory at the Orange County Sheriff-Coroner Department in Santa Ana, California, as remarking, "The gadgetry that you see on TV is very close to what we have in real life. The major difference is the application of some of that technology." Lovgren adds, "For example, on 'CSI,' a computer automatically matches fingerprints to those in its database. But in real life, scientists must perform such detailed work. And while DNA testing on the show is instant, in real life it takes at least a week. There have been some obvious errors. In one episode during the first CSI season, scientists put a casting material into a stab wound and let it harden. When they pulled it out, the cast was in the shape of a knife." According to Gialamas, this technique was completely unrealistic.

While there are some techniques in real life that can dazzle, viewers must understand that there are limitations to forensic science practices. Willing (2004) observes, "Some of the science on 'CSI' is state-of-the-art. Real lab technicians can, for example, lift DNA profiles from cigarette butts, candy wrappers, and gobs of spit, just as their Hollywood counterparts do. But some of what's on TV is far-fetched. Real technicians don't pour caulk into knife wounds to make a cast of the weapon. That wouldn't work in soft tissue. Machines that can identify cologne from scents on clothing are still in the experimental phase. A criminal charge based on 'neurolinguistic programming,' detecting lies by the way a person's eyes shift, likely would be dismissed by a judge."

That the forensic techniques shown on the *CSI* shows are highly stylized is obvious to practitioners, but many viewers don't realize that Hollywood has interpreted these practices through the use of special effects; while producers say they are trying to educate viewers, members of the forensic science community assert that this continues to perpetuate misperceptions about how scientists process evidence.

Hayes (2004) notes, "One of my favorite 'CSI' moments involved a badly decomposed body. Since there's no tissue left, (television character) CSI Warrick Brown must take maggots for analysis; this makes for a great scene as actor Gary Dourdan, face grim as Socrates gripping his mug of hemlock, places a single maggot under the microscope and begins to dissect. I found that hilarious; I'll spare you the details, but suffice it to say that, in real life, the procedure involves a cupful of maggots and a blender."

Mirsky (2005) reports that Houck says he finds it challenging to watch his television counterparts "use analytical tools that don't quite exist," and as Houck adds, "We joke that we need to get one of those—that's a damn fine instrument. The amazing databases employed on some episodes prompted a friend of mine to ask, 'Why don't they just ask the computer who did it?'" Mirsky adds, "Another show convention that annoys Houck is investigators wandering around dark indoor crime scenes. 'They always use flashlights,' Houck notes. 'I don't know why. I usually just turn the lights on.'"

Producers of forensic-related television programming insist they must take some liberties with the capabilities of forensic science in order to progress story lines. Hayes (2004) adds, "I'm a lot more willing . . . to give the producers artistic license. I like to be entertained, and I find the aestheticized approach that TV and movies bring to my field highly entertaining; 'CSI' works not so much as forensic science but as forensic science fiction. And at its heart, the show really nails the true nature of forensic investigation—the elimination of false leads, the winnowing down to the provable conclusion. Basically, though, I enjoy seeing my profession sexed-up; it's a bit like the ending of 'Pee-Wee's Big Adventure,' where Pee-Wee watches himself, played by James Brolin, in a Hollywood version of his life."

"I have talked to some of the 'CSI' folks and they tell me they really try to engage technical advisers," Weedn says. "But of course they also have to please their viewing public and get their ratings. My biggest problem with 'CSI' is that it tends to mix the science, and by that I mean the neutral and objective lab science, with investigation and interrogation of witnesses. I think that biases the science. They talk a lot about not being biased, but if you are part of the investigation then you are biased. Also, I dislike that on shows like 'CSI' and 'NCIS' the forensic pathologist appears to work for the crime lab, which is simply not the case in all but the exceptional jurisdiction. On 'Crossing Jordan,' the medical examiners will go to the crime scene and then they talk to witnesses; that doesn't really happen in real life; I have, in fact, called people on the phone, but that's not our primary gig because that's the territory of the medico-legal death investigator or the police. We talk to people, but we're not doing it in that criminal 'whodunit' sort of way you see on television."

Weedn continues, "Another problem with TV dramatizations is that they create the illusion that in forensic science, there is no sense of uncertainty or other plausible alternative explanations in a case; on television it's always, 'This is the answer definitively,' with little room for other conclusions, and that's not realistic. The grayness of what happens in real life simply doesn't come across on 'CSI' and that's problematic."

Another complaint is that the *CSI* shows and their ilk erroneously depict the pace of the criminal investigation, evidence analysis, and arrest process. Hayes (2004) comments, "Most of the show's distortions involve quickening the pace, from the fast turnover of lab results to the fact that each CSI performs the real-life work of many specialists." One common depiction on television is that an investigator focuses on one case at a time. In real life, they must juggle numerous cases due to frantic workloads; Lovgren (2004) reports that the L.A. County Sheriff's Office, the largest sheriff's office in the United States, handles more than 50,000 cases involving forensic evidence per year. There are a few exceptions; Lovgren notes that two scientists spent two years solely on the case of Richard Ramirez (dubbed "the "Nightstalker" by the media), a serial killer who stabbed, shot, raped, and tortured dozens of victims in Southern California in the mid-1980s.

The success and popularity of the *CSI* franchise is likely to continue for a number of years, or until the general public tires of the ubiquitous nature of forensic and criminal justice television programming. Until then, commentators are prepared to live with the presence of a Hollywood alter ego.

"Most members of the forensic science community don't watch shows like 'CSI' and they pooh-pooh it," Weedn comments. "Even when there was 'Quincy, MD,' most of the forensic pathologists pooh-poohed it, although there were some proponents. I am in the proponent category because I believe television shows like these help make our profession relevant—and therefore valuable—to society and to lawmakers. I think people tend to neglect that side of the CSI effect argument. Yes, these shows do raise people's expectations of forensic science above what scientists can really do, and yes, our cynical community bemoans that fact greatly. But it's not fair to completely dismiss these shows, again, because they raise the profile of forensic science."

Hayes (2004) comments, "Unexpected natural deaths, accidents and suicides fill up the roster; homicides, the purring engine of the forensic drama, are in the minority. It takes junior pathologists a while to grasp that, no matter how thorough we are, the question 'Who killed you?' is rarely answered in the morgue. In real life, we accept the limitations of the evidence, acknowledge the ambiguity of what we are seeing; the moments of heroic insight are relatively few. On 'CSI,' in contrast, the lab machines are fetishized—in the precise movement of a sampling pipette through a cohort of vials, the whir of a mass spectrometer spitting out its verdict, there is an implication that the yield is perfect truth. That's very much the way we want the world to be—clean, neat, unambiguous. And to an extent we are moving toward that ideal; the 21st century will be the century of DNA. At the New York Medical Examiner's Office, the original 1959 facility occupies eight cramped floors, while our DNA department is to be rehoused in a new, ultramodern seventeen-story building, allowing for four times the space. The science is difficult, but the promise is immense."

There is a darker side to the "*CSI* effect." While the debate rages about the reality of the phenomenon's impact on jurors, one last question must be asked: Does *CSI* teach criminals how to get away with murder? An Associated Press (2006) story reported that a few members of the law enforcement community believe that forensic programming is a crib sheet for criminals. For example, according to the Associated Press (AP), a man charged with a double homicide in Ohio was a known fan of *CSI* and used the techniques depicted in the show to help him cover his tracks. Prosecutors said the 25-year-old male defendant burned the bodies of his two victims as well as his own clothing containing traces of DNA; he also used bleach to remove blood from his hands. According to the AP report, an increasing number of law enforcement agencies across the country are seeing suspects attempt to cover up or destroy potential trace evidence at crime scenes.

This doesn't trouble some prosecutors, however; the AP report quoted Larry Pozner, former president of the National Association of Criminal Defense Lawyers (NACDL), as remarking that sophisticated planning of a crime and concealment of destruction of evidence are aberrations and not the norm: "Most people who commit crimes are not very bright and don't take too many precautions. CSI and all the other crime shows will make no difference."

Mirsky (2005) quotes trace evidence expert Max Houck, who says, "When they try to escape detection from what they see on 'CSI,' they're actually leaving more evidence. A good example of that is instead of licking an envelope (for fear of providing DNA in their saliva) they'll use adhesive tape. Well, they'll probably leave fingerprints on the tape, and it'll pick up hairs and fibers from the surroundings. So, the more effort you put into trying to evade detection, honestly, the more evidence you leave behind."

" 'CSI' is a double-edged sword," comments Wells. "Certainly the show has educated the general public and jurors about the basic tenets of forensic science. I can remember a time when I had to explain what forensic science was to jurors because they had no idea. Now they do. Unfortunately, I think we have educated the criminal element as well. At a crime scene in South Carolina in which one of the units in my laboratory provided processing services, we found bleach all over the place; the perpetrator tried to destroy any and all DNA evidence. The use of bleach had been discussed in a recent 'CSI' episode, so it makes me wonder to what extent people are being educated."

Some science experts assert that the science community should relax about the impending doom that dramatized forensic programming supposedly is bringing to the legal arena, because the media itself is not an impenetrable monolith. In fact, some commentators say the media isn't everything it's presumed to be, and this chink in the armor represents an important opportunity for the forensic science community to challenge the media instead of being cowed by it. Crichton (1999) reviews some truths about the mass media: "Mass media isn't mass. If Letterman cracks an anti-science joke, does it matter? He's a famous guy with an audience of 3 million people. But wait: that's 1.2 percent of the U.S. population. How about a nasty article in *Time* magazine? Four million circulation; say two people read each issue. That's 3 percent. *The New York Times* is critical of science? The article is seen by perhaps 1 percent of the population. Of course, we can always count on a good word from *Nova*, but that's only reaching 8.5 million, or 3.3 percent. Internet, you say? Only 18 percent of homes wired. And how they use the 'Net is hard to assess. . . . The perception of an all-pervasive media that reaches everybody is simply not accurate. No media speaks directly to the majority of Americans."

Crichton (1999) asserts that the mass media is neither respected nor influential, and that the scientific community must keep this in mind as it struggles with the media's betrayal of science: "For the last decade, an increasing majority of Americans say that the media isn't responsive to their concerns, that it is focused on trivia, that it is sensationalistic, unreliable and unbelievable. As a result, they have turned away. . . . All traditional media are viewed less often, and more skeptically, with each passing year. . . . The media has lost its power. All the more reason for science to stop worrying about how it is portrayed. What then should scientists be concerned about? I want to advance the radical notion that what really matters is not the image, but the reality. Adopting this attitude has the advantage of turning your focus from things you can't do anything about, like scientists in the movies, to things you can."

Crichton (1999) advocates for changing the prevailing culture of science and for addressing several critical issues that will hamstring science more surely than the byproducts of the "*CSI* effect" ever could. He asserts, "There's a problem about the number of Americans drawn to technical and scientific careers. We are a technological society that can't fulfill its own needs. And I don't know anyone who thinks that scientific education is as good as it should be. But if it were up to me, I'd put particular emphasis on introductory courses. First, because you want to attract talent. And perhaps more important, most students aren't going to become scientists, so the introductory course is your only direct chance to work on them."

Most importantly, Crichton (1999) advises scientists to "start using (the media) instead of feeling victimized by them. They may be in disrepute, but you're not. The information society will be dominated by the groups and people who are most skilled at manipulating the media for their own ends." For example, Crichton suggests that science organizations establish service bureaus for reporters: "Reporters are harried, and often don't know science. A phone call away, establish a source of information to help them, to verify facts, to assist them through thorny issues. Don't farm it out, make it your service, with your name on it. Over time, build this bureau into a kind of good housekeeping seal, so that your denial has power, and you can start knocking down phony stories, fake statistics, and pointless scares immediately, before they build. And use this bureau to refer reporters to scientists around the country who can speak clearly to specific issues, who have the knack of being quotable, and who can eventually emerge as recognizable spokespeople for science in areas of public concern, like electromagnetic radiation scares, cancer diets, and breast implant litigation. Convince these scientists that appearing on media isn't an ego trip, but is part of their job, and a service to their profession. Then convince their colleagues. Because this pool of scientists will eventually produce media stars, and you need the profession to respect them, instead of making their lives hell. Carl Sagan took incredible flak from colleagues, yet he performed a great service to science. . . . I am sure there are scientists today who might become media figures but don't because they correctly foresee professional scorn. All this must change. Science has dealt with its disdain of the press by turning media work over to popularizers. But popularizers can't do what needs to be done, because people see they aren't really scientists, they're just well-informed talkers."

Crichton advises the scientific community to cultivate a few well-spoken individuals to fly the flag for the rest of the community, a tactic that has worked for the forensic science community in many respects (see Chapter 14). Crichton (1999) suggests, "You need working scientists with major reputations and major accomplishments to appear regularly on the media, and thus act as human examples, demonstrating by their presence what a scientist is, how a scientist thinks and acts, and explaining what science is about. Such media-savvy people are found in sports, politics, business, law, and medicine. Science needs them too." Crichton says that while other professions have realized the value of interaction with the press, "It's my impression that science has not kept pace with other professions. Scientists retain the old disdain for the press. To do interviews badly may even be a point of pride, establishing your intellectual bona fides. You are above the fray. But the truth is, the world has really changed and science is now suffering."

The forensic science community understands this, yet it is struggling with ways in which it can both communicate its issues and improve its image without conceding weakness or being perceived as hostile and defensive as it looks inward to address its demons. Crichton (1999) believes the community can achieve this by raising the overall profile of scientists, but it is a tall order: "If you say 'scientist' to most people, they draw a blank. Perhaps Stephen Hawking, because of his dramatic illness. . . . But mostly, a blank. This is not good. I recognize that to build a pool of media stars is going to take a minor revolution in professional attitudes. But you have no choice. I hope I have convinced you that you can never convey a sense of real science through movies or TV shows. You can only do that by exposing real scientists, with wit and charisma, to the waiting public in the media, and in the classroom."

Crichton (1999) urges scientists to "stop the self-flagellation" and work in new and infinitely more productive directions in the advancement of scientific knowledge: "Science is the most exciting and sustained enterprise of discovery in the history of our species. It is the great adventure of our time. We live today in an era of discovery that far overshadows the discoveries of the New World 500 years ago. In a stunningly short period of time, science has extended our knowledge all the way from the behavior of galaxies to the behavior of particles in the subatomic world. Under the circumstances, for scientists to fret over their image seems slightly absurd. This is a great field with great talents and great power. It's time to assume your power, and shoulder your responsibility to get your message to the waiting world. It's nobody's job but yours. And nobody can do it as well as you can."

THE LEGACY OF THE "CSI EFFECT"

As we have seen, the "CSI effect" may simply be the product of a media storm that has a lot of thunder and lightning but little rain. The jury is still out on the "CSI effect," but for many the phenomenon crystallized in 2004 and 2005 during the trial of actor Robert Blake, accused of fatally shooting his wife. Despite more than one witness testifying that Blake had asked them to kill his wife, jurors demanded a stronger source of proof, the kind of forensic evidence that was unavailable in the case; after nine days of deliberation, the jury of seven men and five women voted 11 to 1 in favor of acquittal on March 16, 2005. Although prosecutor Shellie Samuels called more than 70 witnesses against Blake, she could not produce blood evidence or conclusive gunshot residue. A juror later remarked that if that particular kind of evidence had been presented, it would have indicated guilt. Interestingly enough, it was reported widely that as many as half of the jurors in the Blake trial regularly watched forensic television shows.

The Blake trial begs the question, to what degree is an individual influenced by the mass media? Tyler (2006) observes, "If people's reactions to crime and criminals are generally shaped by the mass media, then it seems reasonable to assume that public reactions to criminal cases are shaped by shows like CSI." Tyler focuses on several potential factors in the fallout of the CSI effect, and points to a body of literature on pre-trial publicity's ability to shape verdicts. According to Tyler, "These studies directly address the key concern underlying the discussion of the CSI effect in the popular press—that media exposure shapes the threshold of reasonable doubt and, through that mechanism, changes verdicts." Of concern to many commentators is the often-debated fact that jurors bring with them information outside of the trial, and this knowledge may affect their deliberations. Tyler observes, "Preconceptions are only a problem if jurors are unable to set them aside. . . . If jurors can clear their minds, then the biasing influences of watching CSI could be counteracted merely by a judge urging jurors to set aside any information they had learned from watching crime shows on television."

During the course of a trial, it is common for a judge to instruct jurors to disregard a witness's last statement, but some commentators fret that they are unable to compartmentalize the data and mentally sequester themselves from the undue influence of inadmissible material. Tyler (2006) states, "Studies by psychologists have repeatedly shown that admonitions to disregard inadmissible evidence are ineffective (Lieberman and Arndt, 2000). . . . Some studies have found that calling attention to inadmissible evidence actually increases the influence that evidence has on jurors. This effect might occur because jurors resent having their impartiality called into question, or it may be that making a particular type of information the focus of attention heightens its role in decision-making. Like the CSI effect itself, this argument suggests that when an issue—such as the probative value of evidence—is made salient, the importance of that issue in decision-making is increased."

Defense attorneys have caught on to the "*CSI* effect," and are taking this phenomenon into account when rejecting or accepting potential jurors during the jury selection process. Willing (2004) reports that in a high-profile murder case against a millionaire real estate tycoon, a jury consultant was hired to assist defense attorneys in selecting jurors for the trial. That, of course, is a practice that happens all of the time; of particular interest, however, is that the jury consultant wanted jurors who were familiar with television shows such as *CSI* and who could identify gaps in the presentation of forensic evidence that might serve the interest of the defense. Willing writes, "That wasn't difficult; in a survey of the 500 people in the jury pool, the defense found that about 70 percent were viewers of CBS' 'CSI' or similar shows such as Court TV's 'Forensic Files' or NBC's 'Law & Order.'" Willing reports that the defendant was acquitted, adding, "To legal analysts, his case seemed an example of how shows such as 'CSI' are affecting action in courthouses across the U.S. by, among other things, raising jurors' expectations of what prosecutors should produce at trial."

Altering standards of reasonable doubt is at the crux of the issue, and Tyler (2006) argues that it is "equally plausible to hypothesize the opposite of the CSI effect; that is, that CSI potentially lowers the standards used by jurors, making conviction more likely, rather than less. The argument is that jurors want to resolve the tensions associated with an uncorrected injustice, and that tension is best resolved by a conviction. Thus, jurors are motivated to search for and find arguments that will legitimate their desires to convict. We know that jurors overweigh the probative value of science, putting greater weight on such evidence than its statistical value warrants. CSI's presentation of science encourages this mystification and may, therefore, lead juries to accord inflated probative value to the evidence they see in trials. Jurors would then rely on that evidence to justify convictions."

The desire to convict may be rooted in the "belief in a just world" (BJW), the psychological concept used to describe the belief that people get what they deserve and deserve what they get in life, a theory further studied and documented by Lerner (1980). Andre and Velasquez (1990) explain, "The need to see victims as the recipients of their just deserts can be explained by what psychologists call the 'just world' hypothesis. According to the hypothesis, people have a strong desire or need to believe that the world is an orderly, predictable, and just place, where people get what they deserve. Such a belief plays an important function in our lives since in order to plan our lives or achieve our goals we need to assume that our actions will have predictable consequences. Moreover, when we encounter evidence suggesting that the world is not just, we quickly act to restore justice by helping the victim or we persuade ourselves that no injustice has occurred. We either lend assistance or we decide that the rape victim must have asked for it, the homeless person is simply lazy, the fallen star must be an adulterer. These attitudes are continually reinforced in the ubiquitous fairy tales, fables, comic books, cop shows, and other morality tales of our culture, in which good is always rewarded and evil punished. . . . If the belief in a just world simply resulted in humans feeling more comfortable with the universe and its capriciousness, it would not be a matter of great concern for ethicists or social scientists. But Lerner's 'just world' hypothesis, if correct, has significant social implications. The belief in a just world may undermine a commitment to justice."

The BJW concept may have ramifications for the adjudication of criminal cases. Tyler (2006) observes, "If this hypothesis is correct, it is particularly significant for our understanding of the CSI effect. Just as CSI is popular, at least in part, because it satisfies our longing to see justice prevail in social relations, these instincts may motivate jurors to try to resolve the cases before them by identifying the perpetrator and bringing him to justice. Achieving the finality of conviction is surely the most psychologically satisfying resolution because an acquittal leaves the crime unsolved. While there is a cognitive motivation to acquit the innocent, the emotional need to achieve justice for the victim is incomplete until someone is identified and punished for the crime." Tyler further promulgates the notion of individuals' struggles to balance their need for closure with the responsibility for restoring the moral balance following the crime act: "When it is uncertain or unknown who has caused harm, people seek the closure that comes from seeing the guilty party identified and punished, but they lack the ability to take actions that satisfy this desire. This frustration is most palpable when perpetrators are never identified, but even lingering doubts about whether justice has been served trigger this sentiment. In reality, truth is seldom certain. As recent high-profile criminal trials make clear, the evidence available at trial can rarely put to rest all doubt as to the guilt or innocence of a defendant. Smoking guns are typically elusive at trials, which are more often characterized by collections of contradictory assertions and fallible evidence."

While much research has focused on the many factors affecting juror decision making, there exists is a gray area relating to how jurors process their feelings about reasonable doubt and the verdicts they hand down. Tyler (2006) notes, "In terms of resolving uncertainty, then, guilty and not-guilty verdicts are not equivalent. A guilty verdict identifies someone responsible for a crime and provides a sense of psychological completeness and closure. A not-guilty verdict prevents an injustice to a potentially innocent person but does nothing to resolve the psychological desire to see justice done, either for the victim or the population at large. Finally, irrespective of the verdict they render, jurors often remain uncertain about their decision, leaving any verdict shrouded in a mist of doubt." Tyler adds further, "As portrayed by the media, the CSI effect causes jurors to maintain high standards for assessing reasonable doubt. From a psychological perspective, this reasoning is suspect because it runs contrary to the motivation that leads people to watch CSI—the desire to see enactments of certain truth and justice. Fiction, like CSI, is reassuring because it takes viewers to a place where wrongs are righted and those who break rules are punished. But if viewers respond to this stimulus by raising the bar and acquitting the wrongdoers, then reality fails to match fiction. There is no closure, no feeling that justice has been restored."

While some prosecutors are alarmed by acquittals that may have been influenced as a result of the presumed "*CSI* effect," many defense attorneys are delighted that what used to be seen as dry and mundane is now the object of great fascination and interest. The flip side of the coin is that some jurors may be too willing to accept forensic evidence on face value, seeing it as infallible and resistant to the effects of human or technical errors that can compromise the value of this crucial evidence. Also in the mix is that prosecutors may encounter increased difficulty in winning convictions if forensic evidence is missing or irrelevant in some cases, and in addition, there is concern on the part of some commentators that jurors overestimate the probative value of forensic evidence in response to their unconscious psychological desires to convict or acquit.

On the inability of jurors to correctly assess the value of evidence Tyler (2006) notes, ". . . The motivation to distort evidence and create confidence in one's verdict would be strongest when jurors are faced with weak evidence such as an eyewitness with low credibility. If the jurors want to convict and have strong evidence, they face no psychological conflict.

However, if they want to convict but the evidence is weak, they are motivated to distort the evidence by seeing it as more probative than it actually is. And, it is in fact when evidence is weak that the overbelief effect is found. The fact that people do overestimate the probative value of scientific evidence does not, in and of itself, show that they are motivated to distort the probative value of evidence. However, the finding that people overestimate the accuracy of evidence is consistent with the psychological argument that people's reaction to harm and the need to resolve harm are motivated, in part, by their desire to see justice done. In order to fulfill their need for certainty and closure, people need to be comfortable that they have identified the guilty party and that he has been appropriately punished."

As if the act of adjudicating a case were not enough, attorneys must consider that judges and jurors determine a defendant's innocence or guilt in different ways, which could also be construed as a byproduct of the presumed "*CSI* effect." Kalven and Zeisel (1966) report that trial judges agreed with juries in criminal cases about 75 to 80 percent of the time, adding that fewer disagreements occurred in cases in which the evidence was clear. Tyler (2006) notes, "Recently, Theodore Eisenberg and others used a sample of 300 trials in four locales to partially replicate the findings of Kalven and Zeisel; this study also found juries less likely to convict than judges when reacting to the same cases. Kalven and Zeisel attribute this difference to the jurors applying a higher threshold for proof beyond reasonable doubt (rather than judges applying a lower one). Likewise, in the Eisenberg replication, the authors concluded that 'juries require stronger evidence to convict than judges do.' Where could this leniency come from? The highly salient mass media culture of crime and criminal justice is only one of many possible explanations."

Tyler (2006) adds further, "Although the inflated-expectations explanation is consistent with classic and recent findings about judge-juror differences in verdicts, it does not address the perception among prosecutors that juries are increasingly likely to acquit. Researchers have not systematically tracked the judge-jury discrepancy over time, so we do not know if the relative tendency to convict between judges and juries is constant or changing. Thus, it is impossible to determine whether this explanation is suitable for understanding the CSI effect. However, the similarity of the findings in the classic Kalven and Zeisel study and the more recent work by Eisenberg suggests constancy over time."

"I think prosecutors are improving in their response to things like the CSI effect," says Henderson. "They realize, especially after the advent of DNA, they must be up to speed on issues impacting how jurors respond to the evidence in a case. Prosecutors realize they have to fight the CSI effect, whether it is real or imagined; they know that if they don't explain why certain types of evidence aren't present in the case, or why certain forensic tests were not conducted, jurors' expectations will not be met and they will get the wrong ideas about the case. I have been around long enough to observe that jurors always have had certain expectations, but it is more pronounced because it's all over the television these days. You cannot discount the sway that the popular media has over the general public, and prosecutors are realizing that."

As commentators debate the reality of the "*CSI* effect," cases are unfolding in courtrooms across the United States that may point to some subtle influence of *CSI*. In California, Arizona, and Illinois, prosecutors are employing expert witnesses to explain to jurors why forensic evidence such as DNA or fingerprints is absent in cases, while in some states, prosecutors are querying prospective jurors about their television-viewing proclivities. In one case in Virginia, jurors inquired if a cigarette butt collected at the crime scene could be tested for the defendant's DNA profile; as it turned out, DNA testing exonerated the defendant and the jury acquitted him. In another case in Arizona, jurors questioned whether a bloodied article of clothing had been subjected to DNA testing.

So, it's the television franchise forensic practitioners love to hate. But whatever the emotion, the forensic and legal communities acknowledge that the three shows in the *CSI: Crime Scene Investigation* franchise are bringing to light issues that have been discussed within the tighter confines of the legal and forensic worlds but that remain unresolved. For example, frequently jurors expect the presence of testable DNA evidence at every crime scene and in every case; however, trace evidence such as fingerprints or biological evidence such as blood or semen is not always present, nor would it always be conclusive even if it were.

"Given the uncertainties of physical evidence, the 'CSI' shows would have you believe that at every crime scene numerous pieces of evidence exist that will lead straight to the bad guy," says Polski. "But that's not always the case. Oftentimes the quality of the evidence is such that a conclusion cannot be reached; you can't rule it out, but you can't rule it in, and so it's inconclusive. A shoe print may have the class characteristics of a sneaker worn by the bad guy, but you can't say it's definitely the person, and you can't say that it's not because it certainly could be. If it had a different sole pattern, it could perhaps be excluded; an analyst could say, 'Well we know this to be a Nike sole pattern and it can be matched from a database, and this other one is an Adidas and they are not even close.' But on the other hand, if you have Nike tennis shoes and they appear to be about the same size, you can say, 'The defendant had a Nike tennis shoe, this pattern is consistent with the shoe,' but we can't say it's the same one. Because an inconclusive conclusion is reached doesn't mean it can indict or exonerate. It's just inconclusive." Polski continues, "Jurors also need to understand that there may not be usable evidence in any given case. For example, if there are problems with the chain of custody of certain evidence, it could render the evidence unusable. Or perhaps viable evidence is not found at the crime scene in the first place. These are realistic scenarios that jurors must understand."

McRoberts et al. (2005) observe, "Given the crime lab scandals and the exoneration of scores of wrongly convicted inmates in recent years, perhaps these jurors simply are bringing healthy skepticism to cases that don't meet the burden of proof. Prosecutors are complaining that jurors are insisting on forensic evidence. But isn't the justice system all about providing proof? The same prosecutors almost always demand DNA before releasing a wrongly convicted inmate, even when the rest of their case has fallen apart. What's more, the CSI effect argument assumes that most jurors can't distinguish fantasy from reality. By the same logic, jurors who have watched reruns of 'Perry Mason' would be ready to acquit anytime the defendant doesn't break down and confess under the withering cross-examination of the prosecutor." McRoberts et al. add, "Experts cloaked in the white lab coat of science have extraordinary sway with jurors. It is this special influence that makes the misuse of forensic testimony and evidence particularly troubling. A Kane County jury convicted a man in 1997 largely based on a lip print taken from a piece of duct tape found at the murder scene. Though the theory that lip prints can uniquely identify individuals is unproved, jurors cited it in convicting (the defendant)."

Tyler (2006) asserts that in addition to healthy skepticism about certain forensic science disciplines, distrust in law enforcement, government, and the criminal justice system might be the fire fueling the "*CSI* effect": "Another explanation for increasing jury acquittals, and one that is linked to change over time, is that jurors, like members of the general public, are becoming less trusting of legal authorities. Acceptance of the case put forward by the prosecution during a criminal trial is heavily dependent upon a juror's willingness to trust the honesty and the competence of the state, including the police (who investigate crimes) and the prosecutors (who manage criminal trials). Conducting a trial is an exercise in persuasion in which the authorities need to convince the jury that someone is guilty beyond a reasonable doubt.

Persuasion research indicates that people are less persuaded by others when they regard them as less competent, less trustworthy, or both. Other studies establish that trust is a central dimension against which members of the public evaluate legal authorities."

Sherman (2002) reports, "What is known about public trust and confidence in the criminal justice system is both limited and sobering, and no clear definition of terms guides a consistent approach to measurement. No data about 'trust' or 'confidence' in criminal justice were gathered in recurrent national polls before the 1990s, although similar data existed for selected institutions (see the following discussion). The clearest, most recent data available compare public confidence in criminal justice institutions—without defining the term—with confidence in non-criminal justice institutions. Those data give criminal justice overall very poor marks." Sherman points to a 1999 Gallup poll that revealed that public ratings of confidence in the criminal justice system ranked far below ratings of confidence in other institutions, such as banks, the medical system, public schools, television news, newspapers, big business, and organized labor. The criminal justice system was the third lowest in the level of public confidence among the 17 institutions examined, with only Internet news and health maintenance organizations ranking lower. Sherman says that the poll's 23 percent confidence level for criminal justice was actually a 50 percent increase from the 15 percent confidence level in 1994 and was almost identical to the ranking of the U.S. Congress.

Tyler (2006) asserts that this kind of research into public confidence and trust in the criminal justice system suggests "the possibility that juries are less likely to convict because they increasingly lack trust in the legal authorities who are responsible for investigating and prosecuting criminal cases. If that is the case, the question is what might reinforce the credibility of these authorities? One possibility is an increase in the perceived reliability of scientific evidence. From this perspective, the CSI effect is two-sided. CSI may raise the standards for assessing guilt, but the use of scientific evidence may also increase the credibility of the state. At least, the scientific community seems to have higher credibility than does the state, suggesting that the association of the prosecution with science ought to increase trust and confidence in the state. As noted above, the investigators in CSI always get their perpetrator, conveying an image of competence that may influence juror views of authority. Hence, CSI may counter increasing distrust and skepticism regarding the law and legal actors." Tyler adds further, "If jurors are less inclined to accept prosecutorial arguments due to general distrust and lack of confidence, the criminal justice system can respond in two ways. First, individual prosecutors can build personal trust and confidence through their actions. Second, the state can build general trust and confidence in its authorities and institutions. A judge or prosecutor can draw upon a reservoir of trust from the general legitimacy of the law and the legal system. Based upon such legitimacy, he can anticipate that the jury will be inclined to trust his reasons for acting rather than question his credibility and integrity. Because such institutional trust has declined—leading jurors to be more skeptical of the state and state actors—legal authorities must increasingly create their own legitimacy through personal actions."

Some members of the criminal justice community, however, wax philosophic about the "CSI effect." William Webster, former director of the CIA and the FBI, observes, "I remember years ago, when a case didn't really involve forensic elements, people would invariably ask, 'Where are the fingerprints?' because that's what people associate most with any kind of criminal wrongdoing and evidence. These days, people still expect more from evidence. There is a tendency for members of the general public to depend on what they are taught in school or what they hear or read, to help them interpret the world around them. It doesn't bother me that the scientific methods employed by forensic science practitioners become so impressive that jurors want to know what happened to 'the rest of the evidence.' It tells me they at least are thinking about the process."

Those who remain bothered by the longevity of *CSI* and the hold it has over the general public may simply be jealous, asserts Hayes (2004), who comments, "At the end of the day, I suspect that what irks forensic professionals who are 'CSI' naysayers is some vague sense of jealousy that they weren't involved in creating the program, a proprietary feeling toward their field."

That protectiveness includes the desire for their field to be portrayed as realistically as possible, and that includes the possibility that forensic science is not perfect. Willing (2004) asserts that real scientists find fault with *CSI* because it depicts forensic science as being above reproach at all times. Willing quotes Dan Krane, president and DNA specialist at Forensic Bioinformatics in Fairborn, Ohio, as remarking, "You never see a case where the sample is degraded or the lab work is faulty or the test results don't solve the crime. These things happen all the time in the real world."

There is no doubt, however, that jurors lean heavily on forensic science to help them reach verdicts. Jonakait (1991) states, "Forensic science is significant. A recent survey found reports from crime laboratories present in about a third of all criminal cases. Forensic science enhances the accuracy of fact-finding. It certainly affects verdicts. Jurors believe that they comprehend scientific evidence as well as or better than other evidence. Furthermore, about one quarter of jurors who were presented with scientific evidence believed that had such evidence been absent they would have changed their verdicts—from guilty to not guilty."

Saks recalls a conversation he had with a judge recently: "There was a criminal trial in which he (the judge) had been trying to read the jury's nonverbal behavior," Saks says. "The jurors would look concerned, tense, and uncertain as the evidence was coming in, until the forensic scientist got on the stand and said, 'It's a match.' The judge told me it seemed to him that the jurors appeared to lean back in their seats, more relaxed, as if to say, 'It's over now . . . we have the answer.' Depending on the forensic science presented and what that knowledge really tells you about the case, maybe that's the right response. But, from the prosecution's viewpoint, it's the job of the expert witness to seduce the jury into that sense of confidence."

This leads us to consider just how gullible jurors supposedly are; if the basic premise of the "*CSI* effect" is correct and jurors cannot differentiate art from life, are they fit to serve as determiners of a defendant's guilt or innocence? And are juries the best way to adjudicate criminal cases? In the words of historian Alexis de Tocqueville: "The jury . . . may be regarded as a gratuitous public school, ever open, in which every juror learns his rights . . . and becomes practically acquainted with the laws, which are brought within the reach of his capacity by the efforts of the bar, the advice of the judge, and even the passions of the parties . . . I look upon the [jury] as one of the most efficacious means for the education of the people which society can employ."

The foundation of the American jury system is vested in the Sixth Amendment in the Bill of Rights of the U.S. Constitution, which guarantees, among other tenets, speedy and public trials; that defendants will be informed of all charges against them; and that they will be tried by a jury of their peers. While most members of the general public assume that all trials are decided by a jury, many cases are dismissed, settled out of court, reduced to guilty pleas, or are bench (non-jury) trials. Juries determine the facts in a trial, the truth or falsehood of testimony, the guilt or innocence of criminal defendants, and the liabilities in a civil trial. In the United States, juries are still considered by many to be the best tool for ensuring that the law will be upheld and justice will be served in any case. Assembling a jury of peers is a concept rooted in the legal systems of the ancient Egyptians, Greeks, Romans, and Europeans, while most believe that the way the English conduct their jury system has influenced the American system the most. Juries fulfill three purposes: to serve as an arbiter regarding the conflict of facts and evidence as presented at criminal and civil trials; to provide a means by which community values and sentiments are injected into the judicial process; and to help to increase the public's acceptance of legal decisions.

"Our modern-day jury system is our heritage from our English legal forebears," says Wecht. "I would be tempted to side with Winston Churchill, who once commented that democracy is a terrible form of government, but there's just nothing better out there. The jury system is a ridiculous form of dispensation of justice, but is there anything better out there? Is it better simply to go before a judge? Yes, if you can pick your judge, that is. In America, with its politicization of the appointment of judges, you cannot comfortably say one judge will dispense justice you can count on. The argument is that 12 people coming together can better decide a man's fate and that they can figure it all out. It's ridiculous, but what else are you going to do? If you are the plaintiff and the judge is a former plaintiff's attorney, that's great. If the judge is a former defense attorney with a particular point of view, do you suddenly want to argue your case before this particular judge? Or if the judge was a prosecutor for 25 years and now in a murder case you are arguing for the defendant, do you think you might get a fair shake? And that's before you even get to the jury."

Vidmar (2005) remarks, "In the United States, many highly visible and contentious disputes are decided by a jury, a group of randomly conscripted laypersons chosen to hear evidence and render a verdict. From its inception in England to the present day, praise of the basic wisdom and good sense of juries has been countered by critics who charge them with incompetence and irresponsibility. In particular, critics level charges that juries are confused or otherwise led astray by the testimony of scientific and medical experts. Much of the criticism has been based around anecdotal accounts. Claims about 'junk science' in the courtroom have helped fuel this perception."

Earlier in this chapter, we explored the question of whether judges are competent in their ability to serve as gatekeepers in terms of the admissibility of complex scientific information. Here, at issue is the jury's ability to comprehend difficult technical material presented in court. Angell (1997) says that while expert medical and scientific testimony is difficult for judges, "For a jury it is especially difficult, because its members usually have no competence in the area. They are often left to make judgments largely on the basis of emotional appeals of the lawyers and their expert witnesses."

Some experts believe that the most incompetent judge is better than the most competent juror when it comes to making sense of complicated issues presented before the court. Vidmar (2005) observes, "While meticulous Daubert inquiries may bring judges under criticism for donning white coats and making determinations that are outside their field of expertise, the Supreme Court has obviously deemed this less objectionable than dumping a barrage of questionable scientific evidence on a jury, who would likely be even less equipped than the judge to make reliability and relevance determinations and more likely than the judge to be awestruck by the expert's mystique."

This train of thought leads Vidmar (2005) to then ponder: "Are juries confused by expert opinions and do they surrender their fact-finding function by uncritically accepting experts' opinions? Do they rely on superficial characteristics of the expert witness rather than analyzing the reliability and validity of the testimony? How do juries fare in comparison to trial judges, who are the main alternative to the jury? Even if the jury is confused on some issues involving expert evidence, to what degree and how often does it make a difference in the ultimate verdict rendered?" Ivkovic and Hans (2003) state, "Jurors are laypersons with no specific expert knowledge, yet they are routinely placed in situations in which they need to critically evaluate complex expert testimony."

Vidmar (2005) suggests that the very nature of a trial in the United States lends itself to the difficulties jurors face in upholding their duties to weighing contested facts and bringing closure to a dispute as opposed to seeking truth in the scientific sense. For example, information in trials is primarily delivered in an auditory fashion, and jurors are frequently prohibited from seeing printed data, prohibited from asking questions, and prohibited from taking notes during the course of the trial. They are, however, instructed as to the nature of the case; according to Vidmar, "The judge instructs the jurors on what is and what is not evidence, about evidence that can be used only for a limited purpose, about the distinction between direct and circumstantial evidence, and about the guidelines to be used in assessing credibility of witnesses, including experts. At the end of the trial, the presiding judge instructs jurors on the law they should apply in rendering their verdict. Thus, in deference to legal policy goals of promoting autonomy for the disputing parties and other fairness issues, jurors are placed in a unique role that is different from decision-makers in almost any other setting. They are forced to be passive decision-makers, exclusively dependent on others for the evidence on which they must make their decision and the rules under which they operate."

Another challenge for jurors is comprehending the testimony of expert witnesses, deciding whether it is scientifically sound or flawed, as well as relevant, and using it to understand the disputed facts in the case. Gross (1991) outlined the "essential paradox" of expert testimony: "We call expert witnesses to testify about matters that are beyond the ordinary understanding of lay people (that is both the major practical justification and a formal legal requirement for expert testimony), and then we ask lay judges and jurors to judge their testimony."

Vidmar (2005) acknowledges the varying importance of an expert's testimony, and how it inadvertently can serve to obfuscate the facts: "Debate about juries and experts often centers on examples of instances in which the expert evidence is asserted to be of great import with respect to guilt or liability, such as when a defendant's DNA matches with semen samples taken from a murder victim. In many cases, however, expert testimony is only one piece of evidence among many others that need to be weighed by the jury. Lawyers sometimes introduce expert evidence to attempt to substantiate peripheral issues in the dispute. In other instances, an expert's opinion may be contradicted by much more compelling evidence."

Relevance of the expert's testimony is often revealed in the cross-examination process, and as Vidmar (2005) explains, "Recognition of what the law expects and instructs jurors to do is central to evaluating claims about juror responses to experts. This is particularly true with regard to the assertion that jurors give undue attention to expert credentials and disregard other evidence." When considering the testimony of an expert witness, according to Vidmar, jurors frequently are instructed to take into account the following: the opportunity and ability of the witness to see or hear or know the things testified to; the witness's memory; the witness's manner while testifying; the witness's interest in the outcome of the case and any bias or prejudice; whether other evidence contradicted the witness's testimony; the reasonableness of the witness's testimony in light of all the evidence; and any other factors that bear on believability.

The factors that influence jurors' decision-making skills have been of particular interest to social scientists and legal scholars in recent years. The National Science Foundation (1997) observes that there is an ever-growing body of social science research proving what attorneys already know: Factors other than facts influence jurors' decisions. NSF-sponsored researchers are discovering that factors such as the credentials of expert witnesses, the confidence of eyewitnesses, or the comprehensibility of judges' instructions can sway jurors in the courtroom. At issue are some of the preconceived notions that jurors bring with them into the courtroom, and the ways attorneys must conduct themselves in order to best communicate their side of the case, and how they employ the testimony of expert witnesses.

Ivkovic and Hans (2003) state, "Some of the sharpest attacks on the jury as an institution center on jurors' difficulties with expert evidence." Cecil, Hans, and Wiggins (1991) point out that Peter Huber's argument that the courts have fallen victim to "junk science" is based on his view that when juries and judges attempt to evaluate expert scientific testimony, many are incapable of separating "sound science from fanciful fiction." Cecil et al. add, "Few jury scholars would go so far as Huber to agree that jurors are unable to evaluate scientific evidence. But surveys of judges and jurors themselves indicate that jurors find the task of evaluating expert evidence to be challenging."

The rise of the expert witness has prompted social scientists to study jurors' responses to expert testimony and complex technical material. Much of the research focuses on whether or not jurors are able to critically assess and evaluate the claims and technical information provided by experts. Kalven and Zeisel (1966) studied criminal trials in the 1950s and discovered that experts testified relatively infrequently; one in four cases offered an expert, typically a medical doctor and usually a prosecution expert witness. Compared to jurors from the 1950s, jurors in the 2000s face an increasingly complex array of scientific and technical evidence offered by expert witnesses for the prosecution and for the defense.

Researchers have attempted to determine if jurors' comprehension of a case is negatively impacted by a large quantity of expert testimony or increased complexity of the testimony. Goodman et al. (1985) interviewed judges and jurors about the issues raised in complex cases. When jurors encountered difficulty in comprehension, judges usually pointed to problems in understanding the evidence, as well as teasing out fact from fiction in conflicting expert testimony from highly qualified witnesses.

Researchers have long debated jurors' comprehension of statistics in complex cases. Thompson and Schumann (1987) examined (in mock criminal trials) how jurors evaluate statistical evidence. They concluded that the respondents were susceptible to fallacious statistical reasoning, and had difficulty detecting flaws in arguments based on statistics. They found that jurors frequently underestimated or overestimated the value of statistical evidence.

Goodman et al. (1985) outline ways jurors could resolve the problem of contradictory expert testimony, including ignoring all expert testimony and evaluating the case based on other grounds. Goodman et al. found that, instead, jurors were more likely to attempt to uncover the factors leading to the contradictory testimony, or to reach their own conclusions about the content of the testimony. In some cases, according to Goodman et al., jurors tried to determine which expert was the most credible and then relied on that expert's testimony for a final disposition of the case.

In an in-depth study of jury decision making during several complex cases, the American Bar Association Special Committee of Jury Comprehension (1989) discovered that jurors rejected experts who appeared to be "hired guns," and accepted as the most influential those individuals who tended to be directly involved with the parties and those who presented comprehensive testimony.

Champagne et al. (1992) found that most jurors thought that expert testimony was critical to the outcome of their cases, but many studies have revealed some surprises about what does—and does not—influence jurors. Champagne et al. and Shuman et al. (1994) found that very few jurors said an expert's pleasant personality or physical appearance influenced their decision, but that they were impressed by an expert's ability to convey technical information in an easy-to-comprehend fashion, the expert's willingness to draw firm conclusions, the expert's reputation as a leading expert, and the expert's impressive educational credentials as more influential. Shuman et al. suggest that an expert's occupation and jurors' demographic characteristics played no significant role in jurors' assessments of credibility. Conversely, the party who retained the expert was important, as was the expert's qualifications, familiarity with the case, quality of reasoning, and impartiality (Shuman et al.).

Jurors tended to be turned off by perceived underhandedness by attorneys or expert witnesses, and any "dirty tricks" during cross-examination destroyed an expert's credibility. Kassin et al. (1990) discovered that insinuation about an expert's reputation during the cross-examination in a simulated rape trial diminished the credibility of an expert witness. Conversely, Kovera et al. (1994) suggest that the strength of cross-examination was unrelated to the credibility of the expert witnesses.

Cooper et al. (1996) found that personal characteristics of experts, such as their credentials, played a significant role only when the evidence was complex and the mock jurors had difficulty evaluating it. Cooper et al. also hypothesized that mock jurors confronted with difficult testimony would shift from central processing of the evidence, which involves careful critical analysis of the content and quality of the argument, toward peripheral processing, in which jurors rely on shortcuts to assess the validity of the testimony. Cooper and Neuhaus (2000) undertook three additional experiments to examine that hypothesis. In the first, mock jurors who heard testimony of a highly paid expert with high credentials—fitting the profile of a hired gun—rated the expert as less likable, less believable, less trustworthy, less honest, and more annoying, compared to the mock jurors in any of the remaining three conditions (experts with low pay, high credentials; low pay, low credentials; high pay, low credentials). In a second study, Cooper and Neuhaus varied the pay and the frequency of testimony by an expert with high credentials. Mock jurors showed more trust in the novice experts than in the experts who testified frequently. In particular, they were the least convinced by, and least likely to trust, the experienced expert with high pay. The third in the series of experiments examined the effect of the pay and the complexity of testimony on the mock jurors' perceptions of trustworthiness and believability of a frequently testifying expert with high credentials. The results suggest a significant interaction between the pay and the complexity of testimony. While in the case of simple testimony the expert's pay induced no differences in the degree of expert's trustworthiness, when the testimony was complex, the expert who received the highest pay was evaluated as the least trustworthy.

Ivkovic and Hans (2003) state, "While providing important insights into the phenomenon of expert testimony and its impact on jurors, mock jury research takes place in a controlled environment, and it typically uses only one or two experts in each study. The differences between the conditions in mock jury research are seldom so exaggerated in real life. Depending on the study design, mock jurors, unlike actual jurors, may make individual decisions, may not engage in group deliberation, may not see and hear experts in person, may receive no judicial instructions, and lack the overall sense of finality that accompanies a verdict and the pressures and motivations associated with real jury service. Samples are relatively small and the subjects used in such studies—often college students—have frequently been non-representative of typical jury pools in terms of age, education, class, race, and experience."

Myers et al. (1999) suggest that as judges and attorneys prepare themselves for an onslaught of scientific evidence, "one principal justice system decision-maker is largely unprepared . . . the trial juror. . . . The ability of juries to adequately understand genomic evidence, distinguish between and resolve contradicting opinions of expert witnesses, and properly apply the law to the evidence, is being called into question. Some court watchers believe juries are not competent to resolve scientific evidence issues, and matters of complex scientific evidence should be removed from them. Others argue that the societal values represented by both criminal and civil juries are too important to forego, and that the common sense approach jurors bring to disputes equip them in a unique, capable manner to comprehend novel and complex scientific evidence. In reality, the truth likely lies somewhere in between."

"A juror can be very easily swayed," asserts Ferrara. "When you get into technical or scientific minutia, it's very difficult for jurors to follow; they tend to shut down and tune out. But even if you try to dumb it down, you still have to explain concepts such as allele drop-out or drop-in, or differential extractions, or random-match probability statistics. And then you get into the stats wars in the courtroom, with each side's experts quibbling about the millions, billions and trillions, losing sight of the science itself. Or experts get into a situation where they discuss DNA, presumably the end-all and be-all of the evidence of any case; these kinds of issues have been resolved in the scientific community, but that doesn't mean these same issues and resolutions are going to be brought up to jurors who don't know that this has all been settled recently in the latest issue of the *Journal of Forensic Science*."

"I think jurors are more competent than a lot of people think they are," comments Saks, "but I am aware of a number of studies testing the ability of jurors to make sense out of epidemiological data, and the picture does not appear to be a good one. On the other hand, sometimes they seem to get it right. The reason I go back and forth on this topic of jury competence is I can think of studies that sometimes find juries looking pretty good and others that don't. I guess what that means is that sometimes information is provided in just the right way that jurors get it, and other times, it's a confusing mess. Or sometimes some jurors are simply smarter than others. And we shouldn't blame juries completely because we also know there are plenty of judges and attorneys that are confused, too, because of lack of any kind of scientific training. I always want to mention judges when we talk about juries because if we got rid of the juries, we'd still have the judges, and there is no assurance that judges will be better when it comes to technical fact-finding."

Terrence Kiely, J.D., L.L.M., professor of law and director of the Center for Law and Science at DePaul University, also looks to judges, but to come to the aid of jurors. "Because of all of the talk about the CSI effect, the public has become aware of a lot of so-called science involved in criminal cases and are demanding more of it," Kiely says. "Although they are not quite sure what they are demanding, it keeps everyone on their toes. I think it's up to the judges to help jurors know what they should be looking for. Judges should caution jurors, for example, about giving the testimony of an expert witness' more credence than it deserves. It's the classic white-coat-and-resume problem that you encounter in expert witnesses; it's all very impressive for ordinary people—the jurors—to see; why wouldn't they believe this person who appears to have all of the necessary credentials? He's got experience, he went to school to earn degrees that you didn't, he made a clear presentation and came to a conclusion, and the other camp's witness didn't do much to him on the stand . . . so why not take his testimony at face value? It's a problem."

Saks says that a more enlightened system of jury duty could help boost the quality of the selection process. "In Maricopa County, Arizona, there is a one-day, one-trial jury system where everybody has to serve, with very few exemptions, and therefore you get an increased number of jurors who have adequate backgrounds to serve, even if it's just based on greater odds and bigger pools of potential jurors," Saks explains. "Arizona is one of the leading states in adopting jury trial reforms. In this one-day, one-trial jury selection system, you ask people to come in one time, one day; if they don't get picked for jury duty, they say, 'Fine, we won't call you again for another few years.' If you do get picked, you just do the one trial. This is in contrast to the traditions of the past where you'd be on call for a month or several months and it would disrupt your life a lot more. When jury duty disrupts people's lives more, many more potential jurors were exempted, and those would usually be people who have responsible jobs and are better educated. In a traditional system, you end up with juries made up of retirees, the unemployed, or housewives; again, nothing against these people, but many of them don't have the backgrounds you would find in the people who usually seek exemption. If jury duty only takes a very short amount of time, it is easier to justify saying that everyone has to participate in it, and that raises the quality of the juries on average."

An increasing number of legal scholars insist that the courts must embrace new ways to assist jurors in their heady responsibility of convicting the guilty or freeing the innocent. Myers et al. (1999) suggest turning courtrooms into classrooms in which active learning environments are created. This new approach was pioneered by Arizona in 1995 when the state began allowing jurors to ask questions and take notes, and (in civil cases) permitting jurors to discuss the evidence during the trial. The goal of the initiative was to improve jurors' decision-making skills by transforming their role from passive observers to active participants, using proved adult-learning methods, as well as allowing pertinent information to unfold during the trial in more meaningful and understandable ways.

Myers et al. (1999) observe, "As research on Arizona's jury reform experience progresses, there is growing evidence that the courtroom, turned juror-friendly classroom, is more conducive to juror comprehension and promotes ease in understanding complex concepts and data. If such is the case, must others wait for statewide system changes? The simple answer: no. Courts and lawyers already possess the means and discretion to enable juries to better carry out their vital roles. Judges and lawyers can independently recognize their roles as educators by embracing ground breaking jury reforms and introducing them in their own courts. These reforms will become increasingly important as (DNA) evidence appears ever more routinely in America's courtrooms."

The competence of jurors has been roundly criticized, as commentators pondered if a jury of inexperienced individuals could serve as adequate or even skilled fact finders and decision makers in trials offering immensely difficult scientific, technical, or statistical evidence, as well as address the testimony of contradictory expert witnesses. Myers et al. (1999) state that critics assume "jurors who are untrained in science and technology are ill-equipped for sound fact finding. As a result, critics allege, jurors will base their decisions less on the evidence and a careful consideration of the reliability of expert testimony, than on external cues, such as the perceived relative expertise and status of the expert witnesses, and will be more susceptible to junk science and emotional appeals."

Some legal scholars have called for the widespread establishment and greater use of special science courts and blue-ribbon panels; however, an increasing number of studies are demonstrating that, based on case studies or experimental studies, jurors, "rather than giving up in the face of voluminous evidence and conflicting expert opinions, take their fact-finding and decision-making responsibilities seriously." Myers et al. (1999) continue, "The research shows that while certain elements of complex trials do tax jurors' comprehension and understanding, there is no firm evidence that their judgments have therefore been wrong. Jurors are in fact capable of resolving highly complex cases . . . the research shows that jurors, rather than being passive participants in the trial process, are active decision makers and want to understand. Jurors actively process evidence, make inferences, use their common sense, have individual and common experiences that inform their decision making, and form opinions as a trial proceeds."

In a report, "Jurors: The Power of 12," the Committee on More Effective Use of Juries cited an "unacceptably low level of juror comprehension of the evidence" as one of the motivating factors in encouraging the Arizona Supreme Court to adopt its proposed jury reform rules. The reforms encompassed note taking by jurors, pre-deliberation discussions of evidence during civil trials, and the right of jurors to ask written questions—processes designed to make jurors active participants during trials. The reform agenda included giving judges greater freedom to provide jurors with preliminary and final written instructions, as well as permission to open up dialogue between the jurors, the judge, and attorneys when a jury believes it is deadlocked or needs assistance. The result, according to Myers et al. (1999) "has been increased satisfaction with the judicial process by judges, lawyers, jurors, and litigants."

Arizona's success is significant because traditionally, jurors' note-taking and queries were denied on the assumption that jurors would miss critical evidence or assume the role of advocate rather than neutral fact finder. Myers et al. (1999) state, "The empirical evidence collected thus far, however, overwhelmingly indicates that such opportunities do not adversely affect the pace or outcome of trials."

Myers et al. (1999) add, "It is intellectually arrogant for those in the legal system to assume that lay jurors are incapable of processing complex information. We have all been thrust into a technologically advanced world, and lawyers and judges are hardly better prepared for the task of sifting through scientific evidence than the jury. But common sense suggests that jury reform measures will aid understanding, and jurors themselves support reforms.... We should recognize that it makes little sense to oppose practices that make jurors more comfortable with complex scientific information. To drive the point home, we have often made the observation that it is difficult to imagine an academic setting in which taking notes and asking questions would not be permitted."

While a number of studies do seem to indicate that particular elements of complicated trials test jurors' comprehension, Myers et al. (1999) assert, "There is no firm evidence that their judgments have therefore been wrong. Jurors are in fact capable of resolving highly complex cases. These studies have also shown that factors such as length of trial, and evidentiary complexity in itself, are not necessarily the critical factors in jury performance in complex matters. The problem presented by conflicting testimony of experts hired by the respective parties, for example, is present in simple as well as complex cases. Finally, the research shows that jurors, rather than being passive participants in the trial process, are active decision-makers and want to understand. Jurors actively process evidence, make inferences, use their common sense, have individual and common experiences that inform their decision making, and form opinions as a trial proceeds."

Myers et al. and Vidmar seem to agree that the trial process itself may be as significant an impediment to jury comprehension as the complexity of the evidence or the competency of jurors. Myers et al. (1999) explain, "Many factors, including failure to follow instructions, confusing instructions, non-sequential presentation of evidence, 'dueling' expert witnesses, evidentiary admissibility rulings, and attorney strategic errors, affect the jury's ability to follow and comprehend complex evidence. Researchers, and increasingly many progressive courts, suggest that reforming and improving the decision-making environment can improve not only jury comprehension and performance, but juror satisfaction with their trial experience."

While a number of states are beginning to look into jury reform, Myers et al. (1999) suggest that a complete overhaul of state and local jurisdictional rules is not necessary. "These reforms can often be implemented, consistent with existing rules, at the discretion of the trial judge.

Of course, when local rules conflict, those rules control, but most judges possess the inherent power to implement reforms in complex cases."

Instead, what some advocate for is a common-sense approach to reform. Myers et al. (1999) suggest that, instead of attempts to "dumb down" the jury, jurors be empowered; they state, "In complex cases . . . it is in the best interest of all concerned to select educated jurors and not strike persons based on the extent of their education. While there is little empirical evidence to demonstrate that more educated jurors are struck more often than less educated jurors, there does seem to be an unwritten rule of practice that professionals should be struck when possible . . . Perhaps lawyers fear that highly educated individuals will dominate in the jury room and be able to persuade the jury to their side during deliberations. However, preliminary data suggest . . . that jurors take their job seriously and will not be easily persuaded to a position with which they do not agree. Those lawyers who believe in 'dumbing down' juries should adjust their views accordingly, and recognize the important role of jurors as fact finders and decision makers. Of course, both lawyers and judges must still attempt to detect jurors with prejudices or preconceived ideas, but they should also seek to empanel the best jurors available from the pool."

Some attorneys and judges are pushing for a lift on the ban against jurors taking notes during the trial, suggesting further that jurors in complicated cases should be given a notebook containing simplified jury instructions, layouts of the courtroom with the names and locations of lawyers and parties, as well as learning aids such as glossaries of scientific terms, scientific diagrams, photographs, charts, and other appropriate background data. Myers et al. (1999) comment, "Research indicates that note-taking does not distract jurors, nor does it create an undue influence on those jurors who choose not to take notes. The vast majority of courts recognize that it is within the sound discretion of the trial judge to permit jurors to take notes. Judges need to thoughtfully exercise their discretion and allow juror note-taking in complex cases, and lawyers must urge judges to do so. Jurors need to be encouraged to take an active role in the trial. Allowing the jury to keep track of parties, witnesses, testimony, and evidence by taking notes will empower juries to improve their recall and understanding of all issues, simple and complex."

A number of advocates of jury reform also propose that judges do a better job of providing instruction to juries. For example, Arizona judges provide juries with pre-trial instructions that define the elements of the alleged crime or define terms such as *negligence* and *fault*, thus helping jurors to comprehend fundamental legal standards from the very beginning of the case, refer to them during the trial, and then concentrate on the presentation of the evidence.

Note-taking and improved jury instructions should be accompanied by jurors' ability to ask written questions, according to Myers et al. (1999), who observe, "When it comes to issues of scientific evidence, lawyers and judges collaborate to understand and narrow the issues before the court. They ask each other questions to clarify misunderstandings prior to trial, and will confer even during the trial. Yet, once the trial begins, jurors traditionally are not permitted to ask questions. It is time to end this nonsensical practice." A 1996 study found that questions assisted jurors in understanding the facts and issues of the case; the study also revealed that jurors neither asked inappropriate questions nor drew inappropriate inferences when their questions, due to counsel's objection, were not asked. Attorneys have noticed that the ability to ask questions keeps jurors engaged in the trial and actually improves attorneys' presentations in court because jurors' questions "often reveal areas of confusion or concern, enabling us to adjust our presentation accordingly."

Some advocates of reform propose the use of independent court-appointed experts to assist jurors; the idea has merit since in most jurisdictions, trial judges have the authority to appoint experts as technical advisers to assist the court in general under Rule 706 of the Federal Rules of Evidence. However, Myers et al. (1999) point out, "The use of court-appointed experts to serve as a jury tutor on the basics of, for example, DNA evidence, is an under-utilized tool." Myers et al. explain further, "Unlike fingerprint or ballistic evidence, where it is easier to understand the samples juries are asked to compare, genetic evidence requires juries to sit through conflicting scientific interpretations from expert witnesses presented by the opposing parties."

For example, Myers et al. (1999) report that "a case involving the admissibility of DNA evidence using a particular type of analysis was recently before the Arizona Superior Court. Both parties agreed to the appointment of a neutral court expert to testify about the procedures used in this analytical method. Substantial saving, in time and money, were realized by the appointment of the court expert. Judicial economy and fairness demand the use of innovative techniques in dealing with admittedly complex scientific issues."

While not every court tends to use independent experts to assist in complex cases, "Independent experts present an opportunity to not only improve juror comprehension and performance, but also decrease the substantial costs of expert witnesses, and increase judicial economy," Myers et al. (1999) state. "The adversarial nature of the trial may be diminished, but that is actually a benefit, not a cost, according to independent experts considering jury reactions to lawyer cross-examination of opposing party witnesses. It is the judge's responsibility to be proactive in ensuring that the trial is a search for the truth, and that it is not about lawyers setting up roadblocks to that search."

Sometimes jurors are not given enough credit for their comprehension of the material and their discernment of the quality of the content of expert testimony. Vidmar and Diamond (2001) point to the conclusion reached by Schuman and Champagne in their research: "We did not find evidence of a 'white coat syndrome' in which jurors mechanistically deferred to certain experts because of their field of expertise. Instead, we found jurors far more skeptical and demanding in their assessments."

Vidmar (2005) asserts that overall, "Regardless of difficulties and complexity of evidence, jurors, as a group, take their tasks seriously. They clearly understand the nature of the adversary system and recognize the potential bias in testimony that may result from it. Most of the evidence suggests that jurors attempt to evaluate the testimony on its merits rather than deferring to an expert's credentials, likeability, or other peripheral factors. Furthermore, jurors' responses to experts appear to be complex and nuanced."

"The predominance of the literature says that the average juror, who has a high school education, is remarkably able to deal with the issues at hand in a courtroom," says Weedn. "It is the job of the attorney and the experts to explain the technical material in simple enough language so that it is understood. Now, it's not that they fully understand the inner working of DNA or all kinds of vagaries of gas chromatography technique, but rather they only need to know the issue at hand, which is a narrow issue in any case before a jury. While there is a big body of literature saying that the level of education of jurors is very low, and that the level of recall and comprehension of what is presented is rather low; however, jurors usually grasp the point in question, which is remarkably high given the other two factors."

Some in the community are reserving judgment. Sobel comments, " 'CSI' is having a short-term effect on case adjudication from what people are saying, but it remains to be seen what the long-term effect is, and whether it is advantageous or detrimental for society. We simply don't have that answer yet. I can't imagine that 'CSI' is going to be that different from all the other fad programs we have seen come and go in popular culture. Five years from now there probably won't be a 'CSI' and people will be on to something else. But the question is, what will be the legacy of those programs? Will the legacy be to permanently establish in the minds of a good percentage of the public a false impression of what forensic science is all about? Or will the legacy be to heighten the awareness of Americans to the importance of science and to make them understand that we need to embrace the knowledge of science? Will it be the impression that these shows are not necessarily reflective of the state of knowledge in forensic science? People can speculate but I don't think they know the answers to those questions. Personally, I am glad that these shows are on television, for the sole reason that it raises the profile of forensic science, and it is getting students interested in the field. Educators are reporting that enrollment in forensic science programs is off the charts; that's a good thing in my mind because we need more forensic scientists to meet the demands of the future."

REFERENCES

American Bar Association Special Committee of Jury Comprehension, Litigation Section. Jury comprehension in complex cases. Chicago: American Bar Association, 1989.

Andre C and Velasquez M. The just world theory. *Issues in Ethics,* 3(2), Spring 1990.

Angell M. *Science on Trial: The Clash of Medical Evidence and the Law in the Breast Implant Case.* W.W. Norton & Co., 1997.

Arvizu J. Forensic labs: Shattering the myth. *The Champion,* May 2000.

Associated Press. TV crime drama is how-to guide for killers. January 30, 2006.

Botluk D and Mitchell B. Getting a grip on the CSI effect. *Law Library Resource Xchange,* online issue. Accessed May 15, 2005, at http://www.llrx.com.

Cecil JS, Hans VP, and Wiggins EC. Citizen comprehension of difficult issues: Lessons from civil jury trials. *American University Law Review,* 40:727–774, 1991.

Cecil JS. Ten years of judicial gatekeeping under Daubert. *American Journal of Public Health,* 95(July): S74-S80, 2005.

Champagne A, Shuman DW, and Whitaker E. Expert witness in the courts: An empirical examination. *Judicature,* 76:5–10, 1992.

Cole SA and Dioso R. Law and the lab. *The Wall Street Journal,* May 13, 2005.

Cooper J, Bennett EA, and Sukel HL. Complex scientific testimony: How do jurors make decisions? *Law and Human Behavior,* 20:379–394, 1996.

Cooper J and Neuhaus IM. The hired gun effect. *Law and Human Behavior,* 24:149–171, 2000.

Crichton M. Ritual abuse, hot air, and missed opportunities: Science views media. Presentation at the American Association for the Advancement of Science, Anaheim, California, January 25, 1999.

de Tocqueville A. *Democracy in America.* Sever & Francis. 1945, pp. 295–296.

Gatowski SI, Dobbin SA, Richardson JT, Ginsburg GP, Merlino ML, and Dahir V. Asking the gatekeepers: A national survey of judges on judging expert evidence in a post-Daubert world. *Journal of Law and Human Behavior,* 25(5), 433–458. October 2001

Gross SR. Expert evidence. *Wisconsin Law Review,* 1113:232, 1991.

Hans VP, Hannaford PL, and Muntersman G. The Arizona jury reform permitting civil jury trial discussions: The views of trial participants, judges, and jurors. *University of Michigan Journal of Law Reform,* 32:349, 1999.

Hansen M. Experts are liable, too. *American Bar Association Journal,* November 2000.

Hayes J. Exquisite corpses. *New York* magazine, Sept. 27, 2004.

Hogan S and Swinton S. Meeting defense challenges to DNA evidence. *Silent Witness,* 8(1), 2003.

Huber P. *Galileo's Revenge: Junk Science in the Courtroom.* New York: Basic Books, 1991.

Ivkovic SK and Hans VP. Jurors' evaluations of expert testimony: Judging the messenger and the message. *Law Social Inquiry,* 28:441–482, 2003.

Jasanoff S. What judges should know about the sociology of science. *Jurimetrics,* 32:345–359, 1992.

Kalven H and Zeisel H. *The American Jury.* Chicago: University of Chicago Press, 1966.

Kassin SM., Williams LN, and Saunders CL. Dirty tricks of cross examination. *Law and Human Behavior,* 14:373–384, 1990.

Kesan JP. A critical examination of the post-Daubert scientific evidence landscape. *Food and Drug Law Journal,* 52, 1997.

Kreeger L. Preparing for defense experts. *Silent Witness,* 7(2), 2002.

Kreeger L and Weiss D. Keeping a conviction secure. *Silent Witness,* 8(2), 2003.

Lerner MJ. *The Belief in a Just World: A Fundamental Delusion.* New York: Plenum Press, 1980.

Linville J and Liu R. Forensic science: Fact and fiction. 2002. Accessed at http://www.sciencecareers .org.

Lovgren S. CSI effect is mixed blessing for real crime labs. *National Geographic News,* September 23, 2004, online issue. Accessed at http://news.nationalgeographic.com/news/2004/09/0923_040923_ csi.html.

McRoberts F. et al. Fact or fiction? The jury is still out on the CSI effect. *The Chicago Tribune,* June 5, 2005.

Mirsky S. Crime scene investigation: TV super scientists affect real courts, campuses and criminals. *Scientific American,* online issue, May 2005. Accessed at http://www.scientificamerican.com.

Mueller CB. Daubert asks the right questions: Now appellate courts should help find the right answers. *Seton Hall Law Review,* 987, 2003.

Munsterman G. A brief history of state jury reform efforts. *Judicature,* 216, 1996.

Myers RD, Reinstein RS, and Griller GM. Complex scientific evidence and the jury. *Judicature,* 83(3), November/December 1999.

National Academies Press. *The Age of Expert Testimony: Science in the Courtroom,* Report of a workshop. Washington, D.C.: National Academies Press, 2002.

National Science Foundation. Has the jury decided? What juries use to make up their minds. October 1997.

Risinger MD and Saks M.J. (2003). A house with no foundation. *Issues in Science and Technology,* 20, 35–39, 2003.

Risinger MD. Defining the task at hand: Non-science forensic science after Kumho Tire Co. v. Carmichael. *Washington and Lee Law Review,* Summer 2000.

Rothstein BJ. In bringing science to law. *American Journal of Public Health,* 95(S1), 2005.

Saks MJ. Banishing ipse dixit: The impact of Kumho Tire on forensic identification science. *Washington and Lee Law Review,* Summer 2000.

Saks MJ and Faigman DL. Expert evidence after Daubert. *Annual Review of Law and Social Science,* Vol. 1, 105–130. 2005.

Sanders J, Diamond SS, and Vidmar N. Legal perceptions of science and expert knowledge. *Psychology and Public Policy Law,* 8:139–153, 2002.

Schklar J and Diamond SS. Juror reactions to DNA evidence: Errors and expectancies. *Law and Human Behavior,* 23:159–184, 1999.

Schwarzer WC and Cecil JS. *Management of Expert Evidence.* Reference Manual on Scientific Evidence. Washington, D.C.: Federal Judicial Center, 2000.

Sherman LW. Trust and confidence in criminal justice. *National Institute of Justice Journal,* March 2002.

Shuman DW and Champagne A. Removing the people from the legal process: The rhetoric and research on judicial selection and juries. *Psychology of Public Policy Law,* 3:242–258, 1997.

Shuman DW, Champagne A, and Whitaker E. Assessing the believability of expert witnesses: Science in the jury box. *Jurimetrics Journal,* 37:23–33, 1996a.

Shuman DW, Champagne A, and Whitaker E. Juror assessments of the believability of expert witnesses: A literature review. *Jurimetrics Journal*, 36:371–382, 1996b.

Tarantino JA. Chapter 8. In: *Strategic Use of Scientific Evidence*. New York: Kluwer Law Books, 1988.

Thompson WC, Ford S, Doom T, Raymer M, and Krane DE. Evaluating forensic DNA evidence: Essential elements of a competent defense review. *The Champion,* April 2003.

Thompson WC, Ford S, Doom TE, Raymer ML, and Krane DE. Evaluating forensic DNA evidence, part 2. *The Champion,* May 2003.

Thompson WC and Schumann EL. Interpretation of statistical evidence in criminal trials: The prosecutor's fallacy and the defense attorney's fallacy. *Law and Human Behavior*, 11:167–187, 1987.

Tyler TR. Viewing CSI and the threshold of guilt: Managing truth and justice in reality and fiction. *Yale Law Journal*, 115:1050, 2006.

Vidmar N. Are juries competent to decide liability in tort cases involving scientific/medical issues? Some data from medical malpractice. *Emory Law Journal*, 43:885–911, 1994.

Vidmar N. Expert evidence, the adversary system, and the jury. *American Journal of Public Health*, 95: S137–S143, 2005.

Vidmar N and Diamond SS. Juries and expert evidence. *Brooklyn Law Review*, 66:1121–1180, 2001.

Wagner W. The perils of relying on interested parties to evaluate scientific quality. *American Journal of Public Health*, 95:S99–S106, 2005.

Walsh JT. The growing impact of the new genetics on the courts. *Judicature Genes and Justice*, 83(3), November–December 1999.

Whitehurst F. Forensic crime labs: Scrutinizing results, audits and accreditation, part I. *The Champion*, April 2004.

Willing R. CSI effect has juries wanting more evidence. *USA Today*, Aug. 8, 2004, online issue. Accessed at http://www.usatoday.com/news/nation/2004-08-05-csi-effect_x.htm.

RECOMMENDED READING

Amarelo M. Pathologists say TV forensics creates unrealistic expectations. American Association for the Advancement of Science, news archives, Feb. 21, 2005. Accessed at http://www.aaas.org/news/releases/2005/0221csi.shtml.

Cooley CM. Forgettable science, forensic science, and capital punishment: Reforming the forensic science community to avert the ultimate injustice. *Stanford Law Policy Review*, 15:381, 2004.

Cray D, et al. How science solves crimes from ballistics to DNA, forensic scientists are revolutionizing police work: On TV and in reality. *Time,* October 21, 2002.

DeWitt JS, Richardson JT, and Warner LG. Novel scientific evidence and controversial cases: A social psychological examination. *Law and Psychology Review*, 21:1–23, 1997.

Hansen M. The uncertain science of evidence. *American Bar Association Journal,* July 2005.

Heuer and Penrod. Increasing juror participation in trials through note taking and question asking. *Judicature*, 79:256, 260–261, 1996.

Myers RD, Reinstein RS, and Griller GM. Scientifically complex cases, trial by jury, and the erosion of adversarial processes. *DePaul Law Review*, 48:355, 378–379, 1998.

Roane KR and Morrison D. The CSI effect. *U.S. News & World Report.* April 25, 2005, online issue. Accessed at http://www.usnews.com/usnews/culture/articles/050425/25csi.htm.

Rowlands T. "CSI effect cuts both ways." CNN. Air date: February 15, 2006.

Smith BC, Penrod SD, Otto AL, and Park RC. Jurors' use of probabilistic evidence. *Law and Human Behavior*, 20:49–82, 1996.

Vidmar N. The performance of the American civil jury: An empirical perspective. *Arizona Law Review*, 40:849, 1998.

CHAPTER 14

THE CHAMPIONS OF FORENSIC SCIENCE: ADVOCACY AND FUNDING EFFORTS

As we saw in Chapter 13, popular culture and the mass media have had considerable influence on members of the general public and their expectations of forensic science. And because media is consumed by laypersons who also serve as jurors, judges, and lawmakers, a little bit of the wrong kind of information can be dangerous, especially in terms of decisions made on Capitol Hill that can alter the destiny of the medico-legal community. So it is in Washington, D.C., where much of the future of forensic science is determined.

The needs of the forensic science community are many, but the opportunities to petition for assistance from local, state, and federal governments are too few. That is, until Beth Lavach entered the picture. For the last five years, Lavach has represented the Consortium of Forensic Science Organizations (CFSO), an association of six forensic science professional organizations: the American Academy of Forensic Sciences (AAFS), the American Society of Crime Laboratory Directors (ASCLD), the American Society of Crime Lab Directors/Laboratory Accreditation Board (ASCLD/LAB), Forensic Quality Services, the International Association for Identification (IAI), and the National Association of Medical Examiners (NAME).

"The good news is that 'CSI' is the No. 1 show on television, so you have lots of visibility and everyone loves you," Lavach says. "The bad news is you have the 'CSI effect' where jurors have certain expectations of forensic evidence. And the forensic laboratories have more cases than they can handle because even if someone gets their pocketbook stolen, people want to know, where's the forensic evidence to solve the case? How do we ever catch with that kind of expectation?"

"Tremendous progress has been made with technology used to collect and evaluate evidence at a crime scene," says Joseph Polski, chair of the CFSO and chief operating officer for the IAI. "However, what people see on television is not the real world. Turnaround time for forensic testing isn't completed in an hour and almost every lab has huge backlogs. Equipment shown on TV is financially out of reach for most crime labs. We want to change this."

While the CFSO member groups together represent more than 12,000 forensic science professionals across the United States, this robust community was largely unrepresented on Capitol Hill. Barely out of its infancy (the group formed in 2000), the CFSO hired Lavach to advocate in Washington, D.C., on its behalf, at a time when forensic science was beginning to make a name for itself independent of an increasing awareness among the general public. However, the forensic science community was becoming polarized with the advent of DNA technology; Congress was learning about this high-powered, high-profile weapon in the forensic arsenal, but to the detriment of other forensic disciplines overshadowed by DNA. In the late 1990s, the National Institute of Justice (NIJ) had created the National Commission on the Future of DNA Evidence to provide the U.S. attorney general with pertinent information about the potential of this evolving technology to inculpate and exonerate individuals accused of committing crimes.

Even as legislators jumped aboard the DNA bandwagon, many believed that the importance of non-DNA forensic disciplines was being eclipsed, ignored, and unfunded. Essentially, the current federal fiscal picture does not allow for funds to be used for anything other than DNA analyses and backlog reduction, which represents only about 5 percent of the overall forensic workload in the United States. During the 106th Congress, the U.S. House of Representatives and the U.S. Senate passed the Paul Coverdell National Forensic Sciences Act of 2000. That bill was signed into law by President George Bush on Dec. 21, 2000, but has yet to be fully funded; rather, Congress has provided funding strictly for DNA technology. The Paul Coverdell Act is a critical mechanism for the forensic science community, in that it is the only funding vehicle that ensures that much-needed money is available to all state and local forensic laboratories, which analyze more than 90 percent of all forensic cases in the United States. In addition, only the Coverdell Act allows funding to go to medical examiners, where money is most desperately needed. The current funding mechanisms are earmarked so heavily that many states do not receive funds and thus are shutting down forensic laboratories and medical examiners' offices.

According to the CFSO, its mission is to "speak with a single forensic science voice in matters of mutual interest to its member organizations, to influence public policy at the national level, and to make a compelling case for greater federal funding for public crime laboratories and medical examiner offices." Lavach is a conduit to Capitol Hill decision makers and plays a vital role in getting the CFSO's voice heard when and where it counts most. For Lavach, it's all in a day's work, but it is also very much a labor of love. "I tease the members of the consortium all the time about how if they ever decide to fire me, I'll keep going because I am so committed to their cause," Lavach says, laughing. "They are such a joy to work with, and they are so easy to work for in terms of message development."

For many forensic lab directors, the CFSO is a way to lend a voice to managers who frequently have no time or ability to petition lawmakers on their facilities' behalf. "Just a small number of people have the ability to get to Capitol Hill because they would have to take time out from their jobs and do this on their own," says Don Wyckoff, director of the Idaho State Police Laboratory, chair of ASCLD/LAB, and a member of the board of directors of the National Forensic Science Technology Center. "They are hamstrung by time and financial constraints. But the CFSO is able to represent us and that's a good thing for everyone. Most scientists aren't good publicists because we're introverts—that's why we're in science in the first place."

Playing the political game is distasteful for many members of the forensic science community, and that's why a select group of individuals finds itself on the frontline. "The CFSO is trying to act as a lightning rod and an agent for change for the forensic science community," says Barry A.J. Fisher, director of the Los Angeles County Sheriff's Department's forensic laboratory, past president of the American Academy of Forensic Science, past president of the American Society of Crime Laboratory Directors, and past president of the International Association of Forensic Sciences. "We must remain diligent about raising our issues and keeping them in front of the decision-makers. What I just said sounds really nice, but the real problem is that everything on Capitol Hill is personality-driven. People see problems in different ways and want to do different things about them. For example, some CFSO members have long-established, close relationships with the FBI, so they tend to defer to the FBI in a number of areas when it comes to advocacy and reform issues. I personally think the FBI is no different from any other crime lab in terms of what its role is. The FBI lab is bigger, has more people and resources, but they have a lot of the same issues as the rest of us. They ought not to be dictating what state and local labs do." Fisher continues, "The FBI is very effective in obtaining forensic science research funds which should be directed through the NIJ. Further, research should be distributed more to universities which support graduate programs in forensic science and help to grow the next generation of forensic scientists at the masters and PhD levels. Instead, much of the FBI lab's research is conducted in-house or in a limited number of universities. The FBI likes to tell state and local labs that 'We are doing this to help you out.' However, there is a very limited vetting process to find out what is wanted by the crime lab community, which includes practitioners and lab managers."

Fisher bemoans the lack of a critical mass of practitioners who can agitate for change for the benefit of all forensic laboratories and medico-legal offices. "There are very few advocates who are championing our issues," Fisher says. "For all of the attention that forensic science gets on television and in the print media, you'd think there would be a groundswell of advocacy and information. You'd also think that the U.S. attorney general or some other high-level person at the federal level would take this up as a cause celebre, but it's barely on anyone's radar screen. The only time anyone pays attention is when there is one of these crime lab meltdowns like in Houston, and then there's a lot of hand-wringing. People are consumed by the finger-pointing and they fail to examine the root causes, the systemic issues, and what really needs to be done about it."

Fisher acknowledges that not every forensic lab or medical examiner's office has the time it takes to work as an industry advocate: "Many crime labs are severely constrained by a lack of manpower, money, and resources and are unable to do any kind of advocacy work. It's very difficult for many of us to pick up the phone and talk to our elected representatives, deal with the media, and get out in front of these issues to talk about them openly and honestly. For those who work for elected officials, you can't necessarily say that we are starving for resources because that reflects badly on the boss. So you have to be circumspect. But many crime lab managers are skittish about speaking up. It's a challenge for crime lab managers to get up in front of the media and speak their minds, even if we want to. So therein lies a very significant problem—there are not enough of us in the forensic science community talking about it."

The challenge comes, Lavach says, in bridging the knowledge gap between where science ends and politics begins. "Because they are scientists, and rightfully so, they don't understand the budget process and budget prioritization in Washington. I tease them about how far they have come. When I first met them, they were so excited that the Paul Coverdell Act had passed. I had to be the unfortunate bearer of bad news that while it was incredibly exciting that it *had* passed, it really was the first of many steps because it was only an authorization bill—there was no money in it."

Lavach likens the process to a consumer going to a bank and opening a new checking account with a line of credit for overdraft protection. "So you have a line of credit but that doesn't mean you can write checks, because you don't have any money in your bank account," Lavach says. "You have to put money in the account and once you do, you can spend that money. You don't have any money in the bank when an authorization bill is passed; you only have the authorization for the agency to spend the money, but you don't have the money yet. So we embarked on an education process."

It has been an interesting journey for Lavach and the CFSO, with an equal number of victories and disappointments as the dynamic duo continues to advocate for its concerns, its issues, and its infrastructure and funding needs. "So much of their success has been a combination of skill and luck, and frankly I'll take luck over skill any day," Lavach comments. "The sudden popularity of the TV show 'CSI,' while it has been a mixed blessing for the forensic science community, has been wonderful in that it has raised the visibility of this profession. The show made it sexy and interesting, and while forensic science always has been an exciting and rewarding field, its members were the unsung heroes. People didn't know who they were or what they did. So next, we embarked on an education process on Capitol Hill; we were not lobbying as much as we were saying to anyone who would listen, 'Do you know who we are? 'Do you know what we do?' And 'this is why we need funding put into the Paul Coverdell Act.'"

Lavach recalls that at that point, there had been some acknowledgement of the CFSO within the various congressional committees and existing programs, since many of the CFSO's individual associations for years had been visiting Washington and meeting with legislative staff. "So there was some small knowledge of the forensic science community, but it was not brought together in a strong enough manner to effect change. So the end result was public policy that again was not comprehensive."

A turning point occurred for the group when a legislator's staff person leveled with Lavach. "This staff was very honest with us and said, 'Listen, this is great stuff but what you are giving me is all anecdotal; I need facts and numbers.' As a former staffer myself I knew that, so we did some internal surveys and looked at what we have done and where we were. We knew there was more to forensic science than DNA, and that while DNA was absolutely critical, it shouldn't be to the exclusion of other forensic disciplines because the whole of forensic science is important. [Los Angeles Sheriff's Department crime lab director] Barry Fisher was interviewed by 'Good Morning America' and he provided a wonderful soundbite. He said, 'If you have a car and you wake up one morning and it has four bald tires, have you fixed the problem if you only replace one bald tire? You haven't.' I thought that was brilliant of him to say because it describes the situation perfectly."

The CFSO began to cultivate friends in high places, as its message began to be received and digested on Capitol Hill. One such champion was Alabama Senator Jeff Sessions, who is a member of the Senate Judiciary Committee. "We became truly lucky and fortunate beyond comprehension in that Sen. Sessions has the background, as a former attorney general and prosecutor, to really appreciate and understand what crime labs do," Lavach says. "So he decided to become a proponent of the cause of forensics as a whole, and I don't know where we'd be without him. He was essential to our cause."

Another champion is Senator Richard Shelby of Alabama. "The CFSO has made a lot of inroads into the Senate Appropriations Committee thanks to the assistance of Sen. Shelby, who chairs the Subcommittee on Commerce, Justice, and Science," says Fisher. "He listens to what we have to say, and we are hoping he is able to help bring our issues to the table. How everything will ultimately play out is anybody's guess at this stage, but we are glad to have a willing ear on the Hill." Shelby was recognized in April 2006 at the CFSO's annual Forensic Science Technology Fair for his role in securing congressional support for the forensic science community with the Friend of Forensics Award. Sessions was the first recipient of the award and sponsor of the event for the past four years. "Sen. Shelby is a great supporter of the forensics community," says Polski. "He understands that it is critical that funding support all aspects of forensic science, because major crimes are solved by a broad spectrum of forensic disciplines."

"Our two major benefactors are Sens. Sessions and Shelby, and it's fortunate that they are both well connected, on important committees, and have taken a great interest in forensic science and crime lab issues," Fisher continues. "Sen. Sessions, with whom we have been working a little longer, was able to put in a good word for us with Sen. Shelby, and we have been working closely with his staff on a number of these issues. Because the leadership of these key committees tends to be somewhat stable, it increases our chances of moving our issues ahead."

A watershed moment for the forensic science community came on September 14, 2000, when Sessions introduced a bill to advance the work of Senator Paul Coverdell, called the Paul Coverdell National Forensic Sciences Improvement Act of 2000. Making a statement on the Senate floor, Sessions acknowledged that on June 9, 1999, Coverdell had introduced legislation aimed at addressing backlogs in state crime labs: "Sen. Coverdell's National Forensic Sciences Improvement Act of 1999 (S. 1196) attracted broad bi-partisan support in Congress, as well as the enforcement of national law enforcement groups. Unfortunately, before Sen. Coverdell's bill could move through Congress, he passed away. As a fitting, substantive tribute to Sen. Coverdell, I am today introducing the Paul Coverdell National Forensic Sciences Improvement Act of 2000 to eliminate the crisis in forensics labs across the country. This was an issue he cared a great deal about, and I am honored to have the opportunity to carry on his efforts to address this problem."

Sessions indicated that an "acute" crisis existed in the country's forensic laboratories, pointing to a report issued by the Bureau of Justice Statistics indicating that as of December 1997, 69 percent of state crime labs reported DNA backlogs in 6,800 cases and 287,000 convicted offender samples. Sessions commented, "The backlogs are having a crippling effect on the fair and speedy administration of justice."

Sessions observed, "For example, *The Seattle Times* reported . . . that police are being forced to pay private labs to do critical forensics work so that their active investigations do not have to wait for tests to be completed. 'As Spokane authorities closed in on a suspected serial killer, they were eager to nail enough evidence to make their case stick. So they skipped over the backlogged Washington State Patrol crime lab and shipped some evidence to a private laboratory, paying a premium for quicker results. A chronic backlog at the State Patrol's seven crime labs, which analyze criminal evidence from police throughout Washington state, has grown so acute that Spokane investigators feared their manhunt would be stalled.' As a former prosecutor, I know how dependent the criminal justice system is on fast, accurate, dependable forensics testing. With backlogs in the labs, district attorneys are forced to wait months and years to pursue cases. This is not simply a matter of expediting convictions of the guilty. Suspects are held in jail for months before trial, waiting for the forensic evidence to be completed. Thus, potentially innocent persons stay in jail, potentially guilty persons stay out of jail, and victims of crime do not receive closure."

In his testimony, Sessions also referred to a 1999 story in the Alabama newspaper, *The Decatur Daily*, which reported, "The backlog of cases is so bad that final autopsy results and other forensic testing sometimes take up to a year to complete. It's a frustrating wait for police, prosecutors, defense attorneys, judges and even suspects. It means delayed justice for the families of crime victims." Sessions commented further, "Justice delayed is justice denied for prosecutors, defendants, judges, police, and, most importantly, for victims. This is unacceptable. Given the tremendous amount of work to be done by crime labs, scientists and technicians must sacrifice accuracy, reliability, or time in order to complete their work. Sacrificing accuracy or reliability would destroy the justice system, so it is time that is sacrificed. But with the tremendous pressures to complete lab work, it is perhaps inevitable that there will be problems other than delays. Everyone from police to detectives to evidence technicians to lab technicians to forensic scientists to prosecutors must be well-trained in the preservation, collection, and preparation of forensic evidence."

Sessions explained to his fellow senators that the bill he was introducing was essentially a reintroduction of Coverdell's National Forensic Sciences Improvement Act of 1999 (S. 1196), which expanded the use of grants to include improving the quality, timeliness, and credibility of forensic science services, including DNA, blood, and ballistics tests. Sessions added, "It requires states to develop a plan outlining the manner in which the grants will be used to improve forensic science services and requires states to use these funds only to improve forensic sciences, and limits administrative expenditures to 10 percent of the grant amount."

Sessions' bill also added a reporting requirement so that the backlog reduction could be documented and tracked.

Sessions' bill, when introduced in 2000, had received early support from both parties, including senators Trent Lott, Orrin Hatch, Richard Shelby, Phil Grams, Richard Durbin, William Frist, Jessie Helms, Arlen Specter, James Jeffords, and others, including Representative Sanford Bishop, the primary sponsor of Senator Coverdell's bill in the U.S. House of Representatives. Sessions' bill also delighted the forensic science community and received support from the American Society of Crime Laboratory Directors, the American Academy of Forensic Sciences, the Southern Association of Forensic Sciences, the National Association of Medical Examiners, the International Association of Police Chiefs, the Fraternal Order of Police, the National Organization of Black Law Enforcement Executives, the Georgia Bureau of Investigation, the National Association of Attorneys General, and the National Association of Counties.

In his testimony Sessions commented, "These members of Congress and these organizations understand, as I do, that crime is not political. Our labs need help, and after 15 years as a prosecutor, I am convinced that there is nothing that the Congress can do to help the criminal justice system more than to pass this bill and fund our crime labs. To properly complete tests for DNA, blood, and ballistic samples, our crime labs need better equipment, training, staffing, and accreditation. This bill will help clear the crippling backlogs in the forensics labs. This, in turn, will help exonerate the innocent, convict the guilty, and restore confidence in our criminal justice system."

The Coverdell bill passed, of course, but the CFSO is not resting on its laurels any time soon. Fisher says that the consortium has been active and successful in working with Congress, taking staff members on tours of local forensic laboratories and medical examiner offices to show them the realities of the forensic community's needs. "They have been very, very receptive to us and these efforts to help them understand the challenges we face," Fisher adds. "But it's a far cry from receptivity to actually making something happen, and we realize that. Many things must line up before we are able to get where we need to be. I'm guardedly optimistic that we're making progress. They are certainly calling us up and talking to us and asking what our opinion is on a number of issues, and our lobbyist is talking regularly with senators' staffers. Yes, it can be frustrating because you keep saying the same things over and over again, but by saying it over and over again, you get very good at what you are saying, and it increases the chances of your message being heard."

Lavach says it is difficult to pinpoint one overriding reason for the success that the CFSO has had so far; instead, it is a combination of factors working together to shore up the luck and skill to which Lavach refers. "It's the process that people like Barry have gone through in growing through the congressional process and getting to the point where he has become so good at knowing that when you are on TV, that's the time to advocate. It's also the absolute utter luck we have had that Sen. Sessions understands us and is such a strong proponent of our issues. Yes, I have gone in and developed a relationship and put the message together, but on the other side are brilliant staff people who are willing to listen, and do their homework to make sure I am telling them the truth, and who are willing to tour crime labs and see for themselves. It's all of that together and more."

"I think Congress has been made aware of our situation, and we have the CFSO to thank for taking our message to Congress," says W. Earl Wells, president of ASCLD and laboratory director of the South Carolina Law Enforcement Division. "They do a good job of highlighting the problems and showcasing our needs, and both the good and the bad that the profession faces right now. We are making some inroads, I think."

Lavach says she believes the CFSO's agenda of issues will be moved forward even further upon completion of the comprehensive study of forensic science being undertaken currently by the National Academies (see Chapter 16). "I think the surveys of crime labs conducted by the Bureau of Justice Statistics were some of the first documents that put the issues out there, but much of it is still anecdotal evidence. Regardless, it's information from the trenches and its gives people something to point to. But that merely scratches the surface because it is a survey, not an analysis. NIJ has done a wonderful job but let's face it, they have asked only DNA questions so they only have DNA answers. I don't fault them on that; DNA is a science that is sexy, it does amazing things, it has moved forward at such an extraordinarily rapid pace, so it deserves the limelight and the visibility, but the problem is, it is at the exclusion of other forensic disciplines."

"The hot button continues to be efforts to fund DNA to the exclusion of all other forensic sciences," says Wells. "I will speak for ASCLD as an organization when I say that while that has good intentions, it's just not practical. DNA typing represents a very small percentage of work conducted in most crime labs—probably 5 percent or less on average. That means you are looking at 95 percent of the total forensic casework and a majority of criminal cases that have no DNA evidence involved. You can't ignore 95 percent of the problem and concentrate on just the 5 percent. We would like to see funding for both the DNA initiative and for other forensic science disciplines. I think that message has been put forth to Congress as well and hopefully they will react appropriately." Wells refers to the 2003 survey—conducted by the University of Illinois, Chicago and ASCLD for the Bureau of Justice Statistics and the Department of Justice—of state and local forensic laboratories that found that DNA evidence accounted for only 5 percent of the total backlog in those facilities. Fingerprint analysis, drug analysis, questioned documents, and other forensic discipline work comprised the other 95 percent of the laboratory backlog.

For 2006, Lavach and the CFSO will remain focused on funding issues, especially since it is the year in which the Paul Coverdell Act expires and reauthorization is a top priority. At the time of this writing, the issue of forensic science funding was being debated in Congress as part of the federal government's criminal justice budget for fiscal year 2007. The U.S. Senate Appropriations Committee has approved $18 million for the Paul Coverdell Forensic Science Act in the Senate Commerce, Justice, and Science Appropriations bill, and an additional $175 million for DNA (see Table 14–1). "In Washington state, we have experienced a massive increase in the number of forensic cases. Adequate crime lab funding is a constant battle," says Dr. Barry Logan, of the Forensic Science Laboratory Services of the Washington State Patrol. "Forensic funding is a government responsibility at all levels." "Funding for our crime labs is a national issue at a critical stage. What you see on television is not reality," Fisher

Table 14–1

Coverdell/DNA/CLP Funding Per Year (in millions)

	2003	2004	2005	2006	2007
Coverdell	5	10	15	18.5	18
CLP	35	30	0	0	0
DNA	40	100	110	108.5	175.6

Note: 2003 DNA includes $5 million for Coverdell.

notes. "Crime labs are running large backlogs and simply don't have resources to get results out in a timely basis. This federal money will be a great help."

Lavach explains that any bill reauthorization usually entails revisions made to the language of the bill itself, with some back-and-forth work until it represents what the forensic science community needs. "Within that process, I may become aware of other things that need to be modified or addressed in the bill," Lavach says. "For example, when the original bill was first introduced by Sen. Coverdell, it did not come from the forensic community; instead, it came from the Coalition of States, and when I read that bill, one of the things that struck me was that it did not call for funding of local units, only federal units. So I performed some modifications of the language."

Lavach says, "It's an education process on all sides regarding funding, for the forensic community to understand the budget and how it works and the role Congress and the administration plays, the limitations, and how long it really takes. I ask everyone who ever comes to me for help on Capitol Hill: 'Do you have the perseverance to do this?' Because everything requires more time than anyone realizes. Everyone has to fight for funding, no matter who you are or how much time you spend on the Hill or how many friends you make when you are there. You are always in a competition to maintain attention on your issues. It's a matter of making sure you are in front of staffers."

One of the most effective strategies used by the forensic science community to demonstrate its needs is a tour of a forensic laboratory or a medico-legal office. Lavach explains, "The crime lab directors and medical examiners have lived their situations day in and day out, and when they go forward and speak on this, they are the experts and what they say can have a great impact."

One of the issues that crime labs are battling is the emphasis on DNA to the exclusion of other forensic disciplines, and its overabundance of funding. In this case, too much of a good thing may not be what the community needs. Lavach says, "We have crime lab directors coming forward to members of Congress to say, 'I am fully in support of DNA because it is incredibly important, however, it is only 1 percent or 5 percent, or whatever it may be, of what I do in my crime lab; there are so many other disciplines and there are so many other crimes where DNA is not involved and fingerprints are, tire tracks are, or drug analysis is—I have so much DNA money I can't spend it.'"

Lavach recalls the time when, touring a crime lab, the difference between the laboratory "haves" and the "have nots" became clear for legislative staff members. "I had some staff with me on a tour of a crime lab; we visited the DNA section of the lab which was pristine and state of the art. To see the other units of the facility, we had to go to another building. At the time of the tour I was pregnant, and when we got to the drug analysis section of the lab, an analyst said I couldn't enter the section because the lab didn't have funding to provide the proper equipment and storage facilities. The reason was there were fumes that while they were not dangerous to the average person, the analyst didn't want to take a chance with a pregnant woman. I turned to the staff person and said, 'I swear I did not script this!' The point being, the DNA section was state of the art, while other sections were sub-par. It's situations like that where you see the lack of parity between labs or between sections of labs, especially when so much money is thrown at DNA and very little else. When things like that happen on a crime lab tour, we have reality on our side. If I was trying to lobby or change policy for something that was merely a figment of someone's imagination, I would have been caught a long time ago. But the great need for infrastructure in crime labs is very real. These are such amazing people who do such incredible things, and we need to make sure they have what they need to do their jobs and do them well."

Lavach says the hard work and advocacy will continue, as will the push for the reauthorization of the Coverdell legislation. "We're in a bit of a coast mode right now, maintaining the status quo on major policy issues until the National Academies study is done. That will create new detailed knowledge about the issues in forensic science, and we will know what needs to be fixed, what role the federal government can and should play, what role the states can play, and what roles the crime labs and medico-legal offices have to play to get where they need to be."

In the meantime, there is one member of the CFSO who is happy about what the CFSO has accomplished so far in its six-year lifespan. "I'm pretty pleased with what we have been able to do on Capitol Hill," remarks Polski. "Especially when you look at where we were five or six years ago. The forensic science community wasn't even a blip on the radar screen of most decision-makers, by coming together to form the consortium, we've been able to gain the attention of Congress to an extent that would have been unheard of if the consortium had not gotten off the ground. One thing I have learned about the political process is that it just takes time. It's like the old cartoon about breeding elephants—it happens in high places and takes forever," Polski says, chuckling. "There are many who are impatient and ask, 'What have you done for me lately?' Well, it just doesn't happen like that. We must be patient as we move forward, remembering our successes, including Coverdell funding, and now getting the National Academies to take a closer look at forensic science. It's reassuring to know we are at the point when issues relating to forensic science come up in Washington, we are going to be involved."

Polski continues, "Beth has become known as the go-to person on forensic science issues, and through her things get channeled back to us. It's made a significance difference in our level of visibility in Washington, and I think it's all good because we're to the point where we are being consulted on issues. I can't envision five years ago the NIJ or anyone else coming to us. As I said to the consortium members not long ago, we have pretty much been like the dog chasing the car, but now we have caught up with the car, and now it is important not to become arrogant or complacent. We can no longer complain that no one on the Hill recognizes us and no one gives us any funding or anything else, because that really isn't true anymore. Now we have to start operating from a different perspective, knowing that we are more visible, and have an opportunity to help shape the decision-making process."

Polski emphasizes that consortium members must realize it is just one of a very large number of entities lobbying for its interests. "One of the things I have learned over the years is that depending on your perspective, whatever you happen to be doing or whatever cause you happen to be representing, is the most important thing in the whole world. On a recent flight to Washington, D.C. I was sitting next to a nurse who was the representative of a national organization; we chuckled as we figured at least 90 percent of the 129 people on the plane were going to Capitol Hill with their hand out. We have to be realistic about our approach to funding requests." Polski continues, "We received $108 million for DNA, and crime labs have received a great deal of benefit from that. Plus we received $18.5 million for Coverdell; given where we started from five years ago, we have accomplished a great deal and were instrumental in obtaining considerable funding for the forensic community. There are huge inequities in funding, but on the other hand, you can only do what you can do, and it takes time. The political reality is that the landscape is constantly changing and the consortium has been consistent with its message. Unexpected events occur over which the forensic community has no control so we take the high road, continue to speak the truth, and keep going."

"While the crime labs have received much of the limelight, and accordingly when most legislators think of forensic science, they think of the crime lab, not the medical examiner offices," remarks Victor Weedn, M.D., J.D., the former representative of the National Association of Medical Examiners (NAME) to the CFSO. "However, as part of police systems, the forensic scientists in the crime labs are often not permitted to lobby. So, independent medical examiners have turned out to be quite valuable allies to criminalist forensic scientists and vice versa. This has really happened in only recent times, when the major forensic science organizations got together by forming the CFSO to lobby Washington."

On July 31, 2003, forensic pathologist Michael Baden, M.D., director of the Medico-legal Investigations Unit of the New York State Police, traveled to Washington, D.C., where he testified before the Senate Committee on the Judiciary regarding myriad relevant issues affecting the medico-legal community. He made an impassioned plea for lawmakers to not lose sight of the immense contributions made by medico-legal professionals. Baden stated: "There will be 45 murders today in this country. More than one-third will not be solved. Most of the autopsies will be performed by hospital pathologists who are well-trained in the examination of natural diseases and not by forensic pathologists who are specifically trained to investigate trauma, homicide and unnatural death—as it was with President Kennedy where serious autopsy mistakes were made. Our Select Committee urged in 1979 that it was necessary that medico-legal investigation offices and crime labs be improved nationally so that murders and violent death could be more accurately, effectively and fairly investigated. Nothing was done to this end. Today, of 800,000 physicians in this country, less than 400 are full-time forensic pathologists. Some states have no forensic pathologists." Baden continued, "Today, medical examiner offices and crime labs are also the early warning agencies for any death from acts of terrorism or from chemical or biological weapons. It is the medical examiner and forensic scientists who must determine if a death is from anthrax, smallpox, SARS, saran gas, cyanide; who must recover identifying bullets or bomb fragments from the body."

Baden also addressed the role of DNA in modern criminal investigations, encouraging senators to consider the needs of all forensic disciplines and offices: "During the past 15 years the development of DNA technology has been a wondrous addition to the medical community and to the ability of the forensic scientist and police to investigate sex crimes, and to identify the unknown dead. But less than 1 percent of all murders involve sexual assault. In less than 10 percent of murders the perpetrator leaves DNA evidence behind. The ability to properly investigate crimes such as murder, robbery, illicit drug possession, assaults, arson and rape requires teamwork: properly trained police, medical examiners, forensic scientists, district attorneys, defense attorneys, and judges. Medical examiner offices and crime labs require properly trained forensic pathologists, crime scene investigators, criminalists, toxicologists, ballistics experts, odontologists, etymologists, anthropologists, as well as expertise in DNA analysis. The criminal justice system requires teamwork among all of the forensic sciences to function properly. Please consider all of the members of the team in your deliberations. To paraphrase Voltaire, we owe truth to all of the dead."

"What the CFSO has done for medical examiners," Weedn observes, "is supported the Coverdell legislation and to ensure that bill includes the medical examiner component. They have allowed us to get out in front of Congress to some point, so we are a little more visible than we were before."

"There is very low interest about medical examiners on the part of legislators and administrators," asserts Randy Hanzlick, M.D., chief medical examiner for Fulton County, Georgia, and professor of forensic pathology at Emory University School of Medicine. "It goes back to the old cliché about how dead people don't vote, but they don't realize that family members do. It's hard to convince them of the need to support us when they have the attitude that these people are dead and there is a basic system in place to take care of it. It's not as urgent of a problem to them as some other things are, and it pales when you have to try to allocate money for services for the living. So, medico-legal issues relating to the dead are placed on the back burner." Hanzlick continues, "Thanks to television and the proliferation of forensic science shows, they have a better understanding of at least what they *think* we do. But the entertainment industry shovels little, if any, funds into the real world that practices the science they portray on television. Legislators know about forensic science but I guess they want someone to convince them how pumping money into the medico-legal system is going to make it any better."

Art did imitate life on May 15, 2001, when actor William Petersen, who plays a crime lab director in the hit television series *CSI: Crime Scene Investigation,* testified before the U.S. Senate Judiciary Committee on the realities faced by today's forensic laboratories. Petersen stated: "As a result of my role in the CBS dramatic series, 'CSI,' I began to research the field of forensic science and became fascinated with it. Weekly, 23 million viewers find forensic science just as fascinating. What motivates these viewers to tune in to 'CSI' is the belief that, as Americans, our criminal justice system is about the truth, and they find comfort in the fact that the evidence is, ultimately, the essence of that truth. The forensic laboratory that my character, Gil Grissom, inhabits is one that knows no budget constraints or budget cuts, that has adequate space for every technological advance imaginable, that has sufficient employees to solve every crime that we encounter, and has no backlogs. The CSI lab processes evidence and solves crimes in a mere 44 minutes allotted to a network program. My character's lab is a technological wonder and state of the art. But, we all know that this is not the reality of the approximately 450 crime labs and coroners' labs across our country. Their reality is quite different than the manufactured world of my character and 'CSI.'"

Petersen continued, "Labs across the country are faced with a myriad of problems. Caseloads have grown faster than funding and backlogs are expanding. Many labs have outdated facilities and equipment and an insufficient number of qualified personnel to conduct the analyses that are so vital to our criminal justice system. For every 44 minutes that CSI spends solving crime, 44 days, 44 weeks, or 44 months are spent by victims and suspects waiting to receive the truth. CSI restores people's belief in the criminal justice system before they go to bed at night, but in reality it is frequently weeks, months, and sometimes years, that the innocent are held hostage and the guilty roam free, while evidence sits untouched in overburdened labs. Recently the media has focused some attention on the failures of several in the forensic community. These scientists are the exception, rather than the rule. As I am sure you would agree, we cannot let the behavior of any one taint the whole profession. The forensic scientists that I have met are dedicated professionals committed to objectivity—they are advocates for the truth. They recognize the consequences that their analyses and decisions can have on both the accused and the victim—they need and want the tools and training that are so vital to keeping the scales of justice level. In conclusion, let me say that I am deeply committed to this issue and recognize the needs of the laboratories doing this important work. I support the efforts of the forensic scientists and the funding of the Paul Coverdell National Forensic Sciences Improvement Act."

Petersen's real-life counterparts, crime lab directors across the country, received a vote of confidence by another group of showbiz-related supporters in the creation of The Crime Lab Project (CLP), a group of writers, producers, and concerned members of the public who are working together to increase awareness of the problems facing the country's severely underfunded crime labs. The group is urging our local, state, and federal representatives to provide better funding for crime labs for all aspects of the scientific examination of evidence, including DNA, fingerprints, trace evidence, firearms examination, tool mark evidence, toxicology, and pathology, as well as promoting the needs of the forensic science community through various Web sites and mailing lists, and at speaking engagements.

The CLP is the brainchild of best-selling author Jan Burke, past president of the Southern California Chapter of Mystery Writers of America and a vocal advocate of forensic laboratories. A veritable "Who's Who" list of writers and producers form the ranks of the CLP membership, and Burke says these individuals didn't require a lot of coaxing to join the crime lab cause. "Crime writers have the deserved reputation of being, on the whole, a friendly and cooperative community of writers," Burke says. "Their response to this project has been gratifying and increases my regard for them. The first four people I talked to about the project all gave me an immediate and enthusiastic 'yes.' That was on the basis of a loose set of ideas I proposed in brief conversations. Later, I sent out an e-mail request and literally hundreds of other people responded and persuaded others to do the same. One of our first members was William Link, who, with his late partner Richard Levinson, created 'Columbo,' 'Murder She Wrote,' and many other famous programs. Soon we were joined by the producers of 'The Forensic Files,' and John Langley, the producer of 'COPS.' Producer Stephen J. Cannell also joined."

The origins of the CLP can be traced back to Burke's collaboration with several individuals in the law enforcement and forensic science communities in Los Angeles County. "In 2003, I co-taught a class for writers of crime fiction at UCLA with Barry Fisher of the Los Angeles Sheriff's Department's labs, and with Elizabeth Smith, a homicide detective with that department," Burke recalls. "People asked how long it took for DNA samples to be processed, and the answers that Barry and Beth gave made it clear that in the majority of cases, DNA was not being used as an investigative tool; everyone hoped the tests would be finished by the time a case was being brought to trial. And the problem was not isolated to Los Angeles County."

"This was shocking and appalling," Burke continues. "It was so shocking and appalling that when I spoke in public after that, and said that in many labs—because of backlogs—DNA was not being used to solve rapes and murders, fans of 'CSI' and other forensic science dramas in my audiences clearly thought I had to be crazy or misinformed. Additionally, I didn't have specific actions to recommend to them. Not much later, I was asked to be the dinner speaker at the annual ASCLD meeting in Florida. I attended the meeting, and heard more about backlogs and funding cuts. I learned that pork barrel-free Coverdell grants for forensic science had received minimal funding."

Burke explains that she was surprised by how little of the authorized monies actually reached the forensic science community. For example, $35 million had been authorized, but zero dollars had been appropriated in 2001 and funded only at a level of 5 percent of what was authorized in 2002. "It seemed to me that the amount of money needed to change the sad state of affairs in the U.S. was not, in a budget of billions (now trillions) of dollars, much to ask for, given what forensic science could do," Burke comments. "It was equally clear that forensic scientists were very often in a position in which prohibited them from speaking out about their difficulties. Besides, they were already overburdened with work. Not long before I was to speak, I talked to Michael Connelly, Laura Lippman, William Link, and a few other writers. I proposed what was to become the Crime Lab Project. At the dinner that night, I pledged to the members of ASCLD that we would help. To be honest, while they appreciated the thought, I don't think those lab directors believed anything would come of it!"

Within the past year, Burke reports, the CLP earned the endorsement of the Mystery Writers of America and Sisters in Crime, the two largest organizations of crime writers in the

United States; each organization has more than 3,000 members, and both groups encouraged their members to join the CLP. "Best of all," Burke adds, "the writers and producers have been spreading the word to the general public, which has also responded eagerly. We stopped being a writers-only organization very early on.

As for the impetus to join, Burke explains, "Many see an opportunity to 'pay it forward,' or a way to acknowledge the generous help we've had from experts in forensic science."

For example, Burke has worked with crime lab manager Barry Fisher to get a better understanding of day-to-day challenges that forensic laboratories face, and not only uses that inside information to promulgate the CLP but also incorporates it into her crime novels. "For writing my books, I try hard to get the forensic science right," Burke emphasizes. "I have a number of friends in the forensic science community who have patiently helped me out with those passages, and I try to stay abreast of changes in the field. Please don't blame anyone who has tried to help me for my inability to grasp a concept, though. I want to make clear that I don't believe I'm a forensic scientist. I am a writer, and I hope I'm suited to help communicate your needs to others. But let's face it, there are a few people out there who think that reading textbooks at home, attending courses designed for laypeople, and rubbing shoulders with their local coroner makes them an expert. That's as insulting to forensic scientist as it is ludicrous."

Still, many of the same creative types that embrace the CLP are engaged in the profession of dramatizing forensic science and criminalistics for the big screen, the small screen, and the printed page—with mixed regard for technical accuracy. "Some writers are scrupulous about realism where forensic science is concerned, and believe drama and realism can work together to make a better, more interesting and involving book," Burke says. "They acknowledge that there may be a need for a suspension of disbelief by the reader in fiction, but that doesn't require creating a fantasy world; in fact, believability is necessary to the suspension of disbelief. Others take the opposite view: to hell with realism, let me entertain you. This is more a starburst configuration than a continuum as far as where opinions may fall. Likewise, in television, there is a variety of crime-related programming. Can we put 'The Forensic Files,' which dramatizes cases to some slight extent, but mostly works to present real stories and science, in a basket with a show in which a psychic works backward looking for evidence to convict based on what she saw in a dream? I don't think so."

As we saw in Chapter 13, while *CSI* has served as the lightning rod for criticism and concern about its impact on the criminal justice system, Burke says she believes it might be a tempest in a teapot. "CSI gets a certain amount of criticism from some members of the forensic science community, but on the whole, I think the show has been beneficial to forensic science," she notes. "I believe one reason we're hearing more about backlogs in crime labs is because newspaper editors, and subsequently, politicians, are aware that millions of viewers are interested in forensic science. A dozen years ago, DNA baffled a jury and most of the people watching the O.J. Simpson trial on television. Today a jury would ask why veterinary DNA testing, fingerprinting, and fiber analysis wasn't done in a dog-theft case. That presents other problems, but the concern for forensic science is there, and CSI has done a lot to foster it."

Burke continues, "As for what the CLP can do, we always urge our members to consider writing passages which present the problems facing forensic scientists. If you write about a lab, don't make it the forensic science equivalent of Buck Rogers' space ship. We point out what a handy dramatic device a crime lab backlog can be if you need [for the sake of your story] an amateur sleuth or police detective to solve the case in other ways. And we remind them that drama is a product of what goes wrong, not what goes perfectly, so make use of that. The truth that is at the heart of all good fiction is, in the case of forensic science, one that can provide both hope and heartbreak. Readers like to be in the know, to learn something. You can do this without hitting the reader over the head. So in my next book, when a young reporter gets excited about the possibility of a killer's DNA being in a shoe he or she left behind in a dash away from the scene, a homicide detective explains that the lab is backed up, and even if the test is rushed, a DNA sample doesn't automatically mean a DNA database match will be found. Other writers tell me they have added similar scenes to their books."

Burke believes that the CLP can help foster a more realistic portrayal of the forensic science disciplines by improving communication and interaction with the scientists themselves. "The more we hear from forensic scientists about their pet peeves, the better!" she enthuses. "We'd love to make writers (and readers) more aware of these. Post something on the CLP Forum about it, or e-mail me and I'll post it for you. When we get writers involved in the struggle for better funding for labs, they seem almost automatically to become more sensitive to how they are writing about forensic science. Also, as the CLP raises public awareness of the problems, writers respond out of self-protection. No one wants readers to think to themselves, 'That would never happen!'"

Regarding any lasting impact of the "*CSI* effect," Burke waxes philosophical. "People use the term CSI effect to describe several possible effects of the show. If we're talking about unrealistic views of the work (and workplaces) of forensic science, that's real, but this is, after all, a drama meant to entertain. Trust me, few homicide detectives, let alone newspaper reporters, work on as many interesting cases as my series protagonist does—but that's not the point of my books. Dramas and stories, including CSI, are heroes' tales that are aimed at something other than being career guides. If you want the world to see your real work day, get a Web cam."

Burke continues, "Can these imaginative television portrayals be damaging? Yes, if the public believes what it's seeing is real life and that all is well. More and more is being done by the CLP and others to counter that impression, and I don't believe the false impression should be laid entirely at the doorstep of the show. After all, if law enforcement agencies aren't willing to be honest about the problems of their labs and medical examiners' offices, won't let their workers publicly discuss these difficulties, who is to blame for presenting a picture that all is well? Another use of the term CSI effect is to indicate unrealistic juror expectation. CSI, of course, never has to do the 'forensic' part of forensic science, so viewers don't see what can happen in court. The defense attorney side of this is that forensic scientists are viewed as infallible gods because of the CSI effect. Prosecutors complain that jurors expect physical evidence in every case, and may refuse to convict if they believe the prosecution is 'hiding something' from them that would exonerate the defendant. Both sets of attorneys complain that jurors believe they know more about forensic science than they really do, I've seen some this first hand in my own experience on a jury, and there is a lot of anecdotal evidence that it exists elsewhere. But we are a long way from seeing rigorous and convincing studies on this phenomenon. Once those are in place, I think we'll have a better idea of how to prevent it. One other use of the term CSI effect I've heard is that students are flocking into science courses, wanting to work in forensic science. I have mixed feelings about this one. More students, especially young women, in science courses . . . that's great. That they have a mixed-up notion of the job, no problem, they'll soon learn and maybe if they dislike forensic science they'll stick with science itself and go on to find a cure for cancer—or at least wise up about TV. But I'm deeply concerned that every college that wants increased enrollment is offering forensic science coursework, and it's being taught by people who have no experience or expertise. This is also true at the high school level, where I've been horrified by some of the stories I'm hearing. Again, not the show's fault; it's the fault of people who hold themselves out as qualified teachers when they are barely acquainted with the subject."

With an ambitious agenda ahead of the CLP, Burke says she is very pleased with what the CLP has been able to accomplish so far. "We've seen our members respond quickly to calls for action that have sent letters to Congress across the country," Burke explains. We're told by the Consortium for Forensic Science Organizations that this has been a great help in obtaining more funding for the Coverdell grants. Without any formal structure until very recently, we have an informative Web site, and we've distributed more than 1,000 calendars at book signings and speaking engagements that keep the site's URL in mind for our audiences. And our mailing list for that site continues to grow. Our members have been mentioning the problems facing public forensic science in media interviews and when they speak before audiences. They've written letters to editors and talked to their legislative representatives. They've blogged about the issues. We've also just established a blog (http://crimelab-project.blogspot.com). We have two lists that provide a twice-weekly sampling of news stories about forensic science, and have heard repeatedly from both members of the forensic science community and the public that these lists are useful to them. For a group that really only got underway in 2004, I think we've made good progress. Now we've incorporated and created a foundation as well, so I believe we'll be able to create an even greater base of support for forensic science."

Burke believes it is absolutely essential to seek the guidance of forensic professionals as she steers the CLP into future endeavors. "We want to deliver what forensic scientists themselves tell us they need," she says. "We don't want to second-guess the people who are on the front line. That's why from the start we have taken our cues from the Consortium of Forensic Science Organizations. Most crime writers believe in what they write about—the importance of working toward [if not always achieving] justice, especially on behalf of those who cannot attain it on their own. Others have long felt frustrated by what they knew to be a gap between the reality and the public perception of conditions in crime labs and other public forensic science venues. Those in the CLP who write about crime and its impact on individuals and society quickly grasped that we pay a high price for the neglect and lack of support forensic science receives."

Maintaining the current power of the advocacy machine and continuing the kind of grassroots initiatives launched by the CLP and other groups is vital, according to Burke, who adds, "It's one thing for a writer to say we need this or that; it carries much more weight when a professional who has had to face these problems speaks up. I know some people believe they are forbidden to do so, but they may not be as limited as they believe. I think we also need to get students of forensic science involved in this early on it their careers, which is one reason we are hoping to help establish more forensic science student associations. I have spoken to students about these issues, and have been astounded to see how unaware most are of the basics. I ask, 'Who will decide whether or not the agency you want to work for will have the funds to hire you? Where will the money for your job come from?' They look back at me like deer caught in headlights. By the end of the session, they are ready to ask all their relatives to e-mail their legislators. That's what we must do everywhere. Education about the political and funding realities should be a part of forensic science education. They also need to know about forensic science organizations. How many students know why they should join professional associations or what to do if they want to attend a meeting of the American Academy of Forensic Sciences?"

Burke's respect for the forensic science community spills over onto her personal and professional hopes for the future of the field. "What I want first and foremost is to ensure that I am listening to forensic scientists and those they serve, and remaining clear about their real needs, advocating from a solid connection to that community. I know there is disagreement (healthy, for the most part) between the members of that community on a number of subjects, but I'm convinced we can agree on some goals. So far, this is what I've seen and heard. Go ahead and call me a dreamer, but I'm not just dreaming. Here's what I'm working toward: A public that understands the great many ways in which it benefits from good forensic science. A public that demands its government meet its obligations to provide justice, public safety, national security, protection of property, protection of public health, product safety, and all the other public good that forensic science can help to provide."

Also on Burke's list for the future is a 30-day turnaround for analyses: "Not just in big cities, but throughout the U.S. I want the staffing, equipment, and facilities to achieve 30-day turnaround in every crime lab, coroner's or medical examiner's office, in every fingerprint processing unit. Then I want us to improve on that, so that all that is required is the time it takes to process the evidence in and run the test itself. No one waits in a jail a day longer than necessary if a test could exonerate him. No guilty person released from prison because no one got to the test in another case. No rape victim suffering the knowledge that an earlier, unprocessed test, might have taken her attacker off the street. No family of a missing person left not knowing that the John Doe waiting in a morgue is their son. No courts backed up because of delays in testing."

Increased funding for forensic science research and education is another priority on Burke's wish list: "Make it a field the top scientists in this country long to work in, not only for the money, but for the gratification it can bring." Other desires include: "facilities that are safe for forensic science workers and which are designed to meet their needs . . . secure and reliable evidence tracking systems throughout the U.S. . . . support for labs so that they may meet the public's need for assurance of the quality, reliability and independence of their work . . . uniform death investigation protocols throughout the country—there are more national laws governing cars than there are for the investigation of unexpected deaths . . . a unified national system for death investigation in mass fatality situations that respects the needs of families of victims . . . better communication between labs, and across databases— for example, a unified latent prints system," and finally, "adequate federal funding for the immediate collection and processing of DNA samples from John and Jane Does in every jurisdiction in the country, and a widespread public advertising campaign to increase the number of families of missing persons to participate in this program." Burke adds with a purposeful grin, "And when we've done that, there's the international list. . . ."

> The Crime Lab Project can be found at http://www.crimelabproject.com; the CLP Forum can be accessed at http://crimelabproject.blogspot.com/, and interested individuals may sign up for the CLP Morgue by sending an e-mail message to subscribe@yahoogroups.com/.

Lest it appear to be one big love fest, there *is* much admiration for the hard-working individuals who labor on behalf of the entire forensic science community. "The CFSO is fabulous," exclaims Mary Fran Ernst, a medico-legal death investigator for the St. Louis County Medical Examiner's Office, director of medico-legal education at St. Louis University School of Medicine, and past president of the American Academy of Forensic Sciences. "It has taken a few years to get all of the forensic science organizations to talk in one voice, and the consortium has achieved that important goal. If it hadn't been for people like Barry Fisher and Joe Polski, so much might not have happened in such a short time. I remember in the early days of the

CFSO seeing both of them working hard and doing so much to try to get everyone else on board; it was a struggle because of the debate in the community and everyone trying to get their own issues to the political forefront. The CFSO is the best thing that ever happened, but it was a struggle; Fisher and Polski were phenomenal in making it happen." Ernst continues, "The CFSO has made it a one-for-all-and-all-for-one situation, and that has helped bring us together and move us forward. Barry was the No. 1 person who said if we don't get the federal government to understand our problems, nothing is going to happen. He has been saying that for six years, and no one has worked harder than he has."

THE BOTTOM LINE: SHOW ME THE MONEY

As Lavach explained previously, authorization, appropriations, and actual funding are very different things. While the promise of improved funding of forensic laboratories and medico-legal offices is there, it's anyone's guess just how much money will actually reach forensic service providers. And one of the main initiatives of the Crime Lab Project is to encourage members of the forensic science community to become more knowledgeable about the funding process and to petition their lawmakers to renew the Coverdell Act.

It is critical for both forensic practitioners and laypersons to understand the basics of the congressional budget process, a complex journey that begins with the U.S. Constitution giving Congress the power to spend money provided by the U.S. Treasury. The federal government cannot fund any program or agency without first securing proper authorization from Congress. However, while an authorization bill clears the way for money to be spent, it does not provide funding. Authorization bills establish or continue a program or agency, set policies concerning it, and recommend spending levels, but these levels are not binding. The Paul Coverdell National Forensic Sciences Act of 2000 was an authorization bill, passing both the U.S. House of Representatives and the U.S. Senate unanimously, and was signed into law in 2000. However, authorization does not ensure that Congress will actually vote to spend any money on a particular item, as funding is allocated only through appropriation bills.

The fiscal year runs from October 1 to September 30. In February, the president submits his budget request to Congress for the next fiscal year. The budget is then sent by each house of Congress to its own appropriations committee. Each appropriations committee has 13 subcommittees; these subcommittees draft the 13 annual appropriations bills that fund the federal government. The Coverdell Act falls under the jurisdiction of the Subcommittee on Commerce, Justice, and Science in the Senate, and the Subcommittee on Science, State, Justice, Commerce, and Related Agencies in the House of Representatives. When each subcommittee finishes its work, it votes to send its bill on to the full Appropriations Committee, which then votes on the bill, sometimes adding amendments. Once the bill passes the Appropriations Committee, it goes to the floor of that committee's house (the House of Representatives or the Senate); amendments may also be added at that time. After each house of Congress passes the bill, it goes to conference with the other house. Conference is where the two houses reconcile on a final version of the bill. When the House of Representatives and the Senate agree on final legislation, it goes to the president to be signed into law.

The forensic science community is calling on lawmakers for the support of full funding for the Paul Coverdell National Forensic Sciences Act of 2000 at the authorized level of $135 million. Previous bills giving funds for labs were often heavily earmarked, which means that relatively few labs benefited from them. The Coverdell Act makes funds available to all state and local labs. Of the total amount authorized for the Coverdell Act, little has been appropriated, according to the Crime Lab Project. The funds authorized and appropriated (with information collected from the National Institute of Justice) are as follows:

- *2001:* Authorized: $35 million. Actually appropriated: zero.
- *2002:* Authorized: $85.4 million. Actually appropriated: $5 million.
- *2003:* Authorized: $134.7 million-plus. Actually appropriated: $5 million.
- *2004:* Authorized: $128 million-plus. Actually appropriated: $10 million.
- *2005:* Authorized: $56.7 million-plus. Actually appropriated: Information not provided by the NIJ; approximated to be $15 million.
- *2006:* Authorized: $42 million-plus. Actually appropriated: Information not provided by the NIJ; approximated to be $18 million.

These amounts are divided among all 50 states, five U.S. territories, and the District of Columbia through a grant process.

With curiosity about forensic science at an all-time high, coupled with more scrutiny from critics than ever before, the CFSO and the forensic science community must launch a proactive outreach campaign to answer ongoing questions from the media about lab scandals and the "*CSI* effect," as well as dig deeper to address issues of quality improvement, backlogs, infrastructure needs, and of course, funding challenges. Even as the CFSO has identified this list of actionable issues, it is developing a cohesive message for its member organizations so that forensic professionals are able to better articulate their positions. The consortium has adopted the goal of convincing local, state, and federal representatives to provide better funding for forensic laboratories and forensic service providers for all aspects of the scientific examination of evidence, and now more than midway through the decade, it must communicate its message.

In order to achieve its goal of increasing awareness of the issues relating to forensic science, the CFSO is looking to build credibility, maintain a level of high visibility in the news media, and leverage its various alliances to create improved understanding by stakeholders in the criminal justice process. To accomplish this, the CFSO is currently discussing a media relations campaign, including issuing press releases and public service announcements, to encouraging influential members of the forensic science community to interact with broadcast and print journalists to help convey the message that forensic science is a field in need of attention, resources, and funding if it is to continue to provide its services in a timely, capable fashion.

REFERENCES

Crime Lab Project. Accessed at http://www.crimelabproject.com.
U.S. Department of Justice. Advancing justice through DNA technology. Executive summary, accessed at http://www.usdoj.gov/ag/dnapolicybook_exsum.htm/. Full document accessed at: http://www.whitehouse.gov/infocus/justice/dna_initiative-toc.html.

RECOMMENDED READING

Willing R. Forensic specialists want funding beyond DNA. *USA Today*, August 10, 2005.

CHAPTER 15

THE ROAD TO REDEMPTION:
AN AGENDA FOR REFORM

As we saw in Chapters 4 and 7, forensic science conducted in both forensic laboratories and in medico-legal offices is under siege by various stakeholders of criminal justice, as well as commentators and the media, for alleged breaches in technique leading to errors and wrongful convictions and to accusations of malfeasance and fraud, and for various shortcomings related to a lack of resources, manpower, education and training, funding, and infrastructure.

In this chapter, we review current thought, writings, research, and initiatives related to the reform of forensic science. The allegations and indictments are varied; for example, Saks et al. (2001) assert, "As it is practiced today, forensic science does not extract the truth reliably. Forensic science expert evidence that is erroneous (that is, honest mistakes) and fraudulent (deliberate misrepresentation) has been found to be one of the major causes, and perhaps the leading cause, of erroneous convictions of innocent persons."

The outcome of forensic science reform, then, is to achieve accuracy, reliability, and validity in all forensic laboratory examinations and analyses, as well as in all medico-legal death investigations and autopsies. Feldman et al. (2001) state that the overarching goal of forensic science reform is to "Reduce the adversary influences on, and emphasize science, in forensic science." Thomson (1974) calls for a suite of reforms: Consolidation of forensic facilities, placing forensic labs under the supervision of the courts, accreditation, instituting a mandatory regime of proficiency testing, provision for open access for all parties in a criminal action, and use of separate facilities by the antagonists in a criminal process.

Reformers may differ in their approaches to reform, but Jonakait (1991) seems to sum it up: "All available information indicates that forensic science laboratories perform poorly. Logic, justice, and concern for the wise expenditure of money require improvement in forensic science performance. Current regulation of clinical labs indicates that a regulatory system can improve crime laboratories. Lack of manpower, money, experience, and an appropriate institutional superstructure make comprehensive regulation of crime labs infeasible. However, forensic facilities should at least be required to undergo mandatory, blind proficiency testing, and the results of this testing should be made public. The testing would be an important first step in correcting inherent problems in the forensic science system."

Reform requires more than just testing and mandatory reporting, as we shall see. In August 2004, the American Bar Association adopted a set of principles it believed that if adopted by federal, state, local, and territorial governments, would help prevent the incidence of wrongful convictions; these principles are reduced to their most elemental natures and represent much of what both the legal and the forensic science communities agree should occur within the U.S. criminal justice system:

■ Crime laboratories and medical examiner offices should be accredited, examiners should be certified, and procedures should be standardized and published to ensure the validity, reliability, and timely analysis of forensic evidence.

■ Crime laboratories and medical examiner offices should be adequately funded.

■ The appointment of defense experts for indigent defendants should be required whenever reasonably necessary to the defense.

■ Training in forensic science for attorneys should be made available at minimal cost to ensure adequate representation for both the public and defendants.

■ Counsel should have competence in the relevant area or consult with those who do, where forensic evidence is essential in a case.

Of particular interest to the legal community, DiFonzo (2005) asserts that there is a "current disconnect between the public perception of DNA and the reality of forensic testing" and suggests the retention of reasonable statutes of limitations: "The traditional rationales for statutes of limitations continue to supply persuasive evidence for caution before shifting the balance between the state and the individual. Especially in the age of DNA, the risk of an erroneous verdict is great and is generally related to the endemic human factors of evidentiary mismanagement and mendacious witnesses. Ascertaining the perfect balance among the extraordinarily public policy concerns in sexual offense cases is an impossible task. But the goal should be to allow prosecutions in a timely—and thus not unlimited—manner, in order to minimize the risk of erroneous convictions."

There are a number of common planks for the reform of forensic science, reflecting specific areas of the discipline needing improvement. In this chapter we present a summary of the criticisms of forensic science and offer suggestions for improvement.

Critics charge that practitioners working in forensic laboratories and medico-legal offices at all levels—county, state, and federal—are subjected to undue influence of and pressure by law enforcement agencies under which these labs and offices operate. High on commentators' list of issues to be remedied is the alleged bias and subjectivity of forensic service providers. Scheck and Neufeld (2001) comment, "Laboratories need to control the flow of information from police to the forensic scientist. They can continue to assist law enforcement and prosecutors without performing as subordinates. In some jurisdictions, the office of medical examiner serves this purpose. But unfortunately, all too frequently, the medical examiner also sees itself as a member of the prosecution team."

Saks (1998) says that the creation of an independent, statewide forensic science service center would provide forensic science services to police, prosecutors, defense counsel, judges, and even defendants. Giannelli (1997) suggests that laboratories should be transferred from police control to the control of medical examiner offices, agencies that are already independent of the police. Giannelli states, "This step will eliminate potential undue influence from law enforcement and prosecutors, possibly controlling or eliminating context bias on the part of lab analysts." Koppl (2005) cites Saks et al. (2001), who say this measure "provides forensic science expertise to both the prosecution and the defense on equal terms." Bourke (1993) observes, ". . . Independence in forensic science institutions avoids commercial concerns, promotes adherence to scientific principles, avoids bias, and permits unrestricted free speech."

DiFonzo (2005) observes, "The pro-prosecution bias of forensic examiners has been repeatedly documented. It seems unlikely to end until law enforcement no longer employs and supervises the same forensic examiners from whom society expects complete neutrality and fealty only to scientific norms. Crime labs today are an arm of law enforcement, funded with criminal justice dollars, and often physically located in police buildings. But this linkage to law enforcement is the very one which taints the evidence. In order to remove this attachment, we will have to decide whether DNA matching and other forensic procedures are truly scientific, and thus objectively neutral, or are tools of the law enforcement team, and pressured to achieve results suitable for the prosecution. I propose that DNA testing be segregated from the adversary system. Public crime labs should be funded and administered independently from the police and prosecutor, and forensic analysts and lab directors should not be subject to review by law enforcement personnel. Further, defense attorneys should have access to DNA testing on the same basis as the prosecution. Only in this way will the crime labs achieve independence, and with it the freedom to engage in true science."

The separation of forensic laboratories and medico-legal offices from law enforcement agencies has other benefits; this move could also liberate their budgets from the overzealous reach of the police. Giannelli (1997) comments, "Crime laboratory budgets are currently part of the law enforcement or prosecutorial agency's overall budget. This severely restricts forensic scientists since law enforcement or prosecutorial priorities come first. As Saks et al. argue, 'By freeing the crime laboratory from police management, police funding, police personnel, and police culture, forensic scientists would be freed to concentrate on the job of scientific investigation.'" In addition, Giannelli states, "Having scientists dictate direction and policy will create an atmosphere where science is the No. 1 priority."

Risinger et al. (2002) observe, "The establishment of freestanding government forensic laboratories, though occasionally advocated, would require such a revolution in thinking and organization, and diminish so many established bureaucratic empires, that it would take a generation of patient lobbying to have a chance of success. The winds of change are beginning to blow, however, for reasons independent of any explicit calls for reform. The biggest single factor contributing to this change appears to be the increased forensic use of academic science disciplines which cannot be adequately taught to law enforcement personnel as 'technicians,' such as forensic chemistry, forensic anthropology, and DNA analysis. Some time over the past quarter century, the percentage of trained personnel in the larger forensic science laboratories with advanced degrees in science appears to have begun to grow." Risinger et al. add, "While some desirable structural changes seem unrealistic, and other desirable changes are happening by evolution and infusion, the serious problems of observer effects can only be solved, or at least ameliorated, by intentionally embraced changes in forensic practice. These changes will be neither tremendously complex nor excessively expensive; fortunately, many of these problems already have solutions that are in routine use in most scientific fields, and that can be found in the standard research methodology textbooks of those fields."

To that end, the researchers call for a greater awareness of the phenomenon of observer effects, followed by action. They state, "Forensic scientists have no less need, and no less ability, than so many other serious scientists around the world to institute procedures to protect their findings against avoidable sources of error." Risinger et al. (2002) note, "An examiner who has no domain-irrelevant information cannot be influenced by it. An examiner who does not know what conclusion is hoped for or expected of her cannot be affected by those considerations." The action steps include preventing distortions due to expectation and suggestion through the implementation of blind testing, what Risinger et al. describe as "the simplest, most powerful, and most useful procedure to protect against the distorting effects of unstated assumptions, collateral information, and improper expectations and motivations." They add, "A wall of separation must be created between forensic science examiners and any examination-irrelevant information about a case. That means properly controlling information flowing to examiners from external investigators, from laboratory managers, and from fellow examiners."

Some commentators have suggested that the most contentious issues, such as subjectivity or disagreements over statements of certainty, could be addressed by increasing the overall scientific foundation of forensic science. It has been a common refrain on the part of commentators and forensic service providers throughout this book that increased scientific research would benefit all of the forensic disciplines and medico-legal death investigation, as would a partnership with the academic scientific community. Some observers have also noted that the field could benefit greatly from improved rigor in daily responsibilities in both forensic laboratories and in medico-legal offices.

Giannelli (2001) observes, "In many areas (of forensic science) little systematic research has been conducted to validate the field's basic premises and techniques, and often there is no justification why such research would not be feasible."

The U.S. Department of Justice (DOJ), through the National Institute of Justice (NIJ), regularly seeks applications for funding of appropriate research projects related to forensic science, but many members of the forensic science community grouse that they are frequently not the ones participating in this opportunity due to time constraints and prohibitive caseloads. Instead, social scientists are the typical grantees, and most of the research does not directly involve or benefit the field. Commentators insist that forensic scientists and medico-legal professionals need to step up to the plate and pursue these valuable opportunities to contribute to the body of literature on forensic science. As an example of the desire to boost academic rigor in the forensic disciplines, in June 2006, the DOJ promulgated applications for social science research on the role and impact of forensic evidence on the criminal justice process, noting, "Forensic evidence is an integral part of many criminal investigations, however there has been limited research on the impact of forensic evidence on the criminal justice system through the collection, analysis, and subsequent investigative and adjudicative processes. Findings from this study could influence policies on such issues as the allocation of resources and the training of laboratory and crime scene personnel." The DOJ adds further, "With advances in technology, forensic evidence has become an increasingly powerful tool in criminal investigations. The advent of DNA technology has revolutionized forensic science, and DNA's ability to identify criminal offenders and exonerate the innocent has helped solve crimes that would not have been solvable 20 years ago. Similarly, advances in other forensic disciplines, such as impression evidence (e.g., shoeprints and firearms/tool marks) and trace evidence (e.g., fibers, paint, glass), have provided increasingly valuable information about the source of the physical evidence or the circumstances surrounding a criminal act."

Prospective grantees were asked by the DOJ to describe how the research would accomplish four primary objectives: Estimate the percentage of crime scenes from which one or more types of forensic evidence is collected; describe and catalog the kinds of forensic evidence collected at crime scenes; track the use and attrition of forensic evidence in the criminal justice system from crime scenes through laboratory analysis, and then through subsequent criminal justice processes; and identify which forms of forensic evidence contribute most frequently (relative to their availability at a crime scene) to successful case outcomes. The DOJ instructed applicants to consider and discuss definitions of successful case outcome beyond identifying a suspect or successfully prosecuting (i.e., guilty verdict or plea agreement) a case. Successful case outcomes include arrests made, suspects eliminated, and forensic evidence introduced in court proceedings. A number of variables must be accounted for to determine how forensic evidence contributes to case outcomes. The probative value of certain types of forensic evidence will vary by the type of crime scene. For example, forensic evidence may be more probative in violent offenses involving strangers or property crimes than in violent offenses perpetrated by acquaintances. The quality of forensic evidence will vary from scene to scene (e.g., partial fingerprint vs. full fingerprint). Thus, rather than simply measuring the quantity and identifying the types of evidence at crime scenes, proposed research should include some measure of the quality of the evidence obtained."

Perhaps picking up on the current discord regarding traditional, rigorous research in forensic science, the DOJ emphasized that scientific methods be utilized for this research: "It is anticipated that a multi-site approach will be required. Data could be gathered in a sample of jurisdictions varying by size, location, population demographics, etc., in two principal ways: in-depth, cross-sectional data surveys describing forensic evidence found at the crime scene, applied to police investigations, analyzed by the crime laboratory, and used in the adjudicative process; and longitudinal data surveys in which criminal offenses are tracked from beginning to end so as to trace the flow and filtering of evidence as the case proceeds though the criminal justice system." The forensic science community will eagerly await the news of a recipient of this $600,000 grant as this book goes to press.

Increased scientific rigor is complimented by improvement in documentation quality, specifically a paper trail that indicates how tests were conducted and what led examiners and analysts to the conclusions they made. Reformers embrace this idea of enhanced documentation, especially in forensic reports issued by analysts and examiners. Commentators suggest that all forensic reports must not only include any and all conclusions and inferences, but they must also include the limitations placed upon those conclusions and a sufficiently detailed statement of the hypothesis being tested and the reasoning process by which the conclusions were reached. Reformers such as Bourke (1993) suggest further that the following data be incorporated into every report: a preliminary background section, highlighting the hypotheses being tested; a chain-of-custody section, outlining the inventoried evidence that underwent testing; a descriptive section where the examiner thoroughly describes the evidence to be tested and what presumptive testing methods were relied upon during the examination; a descriptive section describing the various scientific procedures utilized; and a results section where the examiner lists all results, including their significance and limitations.

Upgraded documentation may also assist with the creation of a common forensic language that could cross discipline borders and foster better communication in the courtroom. Reformers frequently suggest that forensic service providers develop this uniform language so that forensic practitioners are able to express complicated conclusions in similar terms. Conversely, some critics argue that forensic practitioners express divergent conclusions using the same terms; the most illustrative examples are *match* and *consistent with*. Reformers advocate the establishment of a standardized language that minimizes any potential for juries to be misled. Reformers also suggest that the expression of the degree of certainty on the part of practitioners be addressed. Reformers assert that examiners attempt to embellish their opinions with probability ratios. Rudram (1996) states, "The tendency to express probability in the form of racing odds can overemphasize the strength of some conclusions and there have been extensive arguments over what every small probabilities actually mean." Accordingly, reformers say language standards must be developed to enable forensic practitioners to convey their conclusions, and that forensic service providers must agree among themselves what their probabilistic phrases indicate.

A common language would further support efforts toward validation and reproducibility of forensic tests and analyses, another bedrock upon which reformers hope to build. Inman and Rudin (2001) observe, "Validation establishes the capabilities and limitations of the system, and builds a body of work from which practitioners can learn when variations are explainable and when they indicate a real difference. The greatest utility of validation studies is in providing the practitioner doing the work with information that will assist in the interpretation of difficult samples. Validation studies are essential—for the field, for individual laboratories, and, in the form of proficiency testing, for individuals. This is simply good science and contributes to a solid foundation for performing work and interpreting the results."[1]

The issue of standards for forensic science has generated intense dialogue within the forensic science and legal communities. Lee (1993) notes, "Perhaps the most important issue in forensic science is the establishment of professional standards. An assessment is needed of standards of practice in the collection, examination, and analysis of physical evidence."

Reformers are calling for standardization of the accreditation and certification process for all forensic analysts and examiners, as well as for continued standardization of techniques and protocols. However, under the tightening vise of suggested reforms, Rudin and Inman (2005) lament the loss of freedom that criminalists once had: "The core of criminalistics has been lost, and analysts are no longer willing, or even allowed, to consider evidence in the context of the case and to interpret it appropriately. The collateral damage from this approach is that someone else will. That someone else is typically an attorney . . . or a crime scene reconstructionist, typically a retired detective, or perhaps a criminal profiler who likes to use bits of physical evidence analyzed by some lowly lab technician to flesh out his view of the crime event. By abdicating a part of our responsibilities as forensic scientists, we open the door to far less qualified people who are more than willing to opine on the significance of physical evidence to a crime event. This all too often leads to unsupported extrapolation and blatant speculation, neither of which ultimately assist the criminal justice system in understanding the relevance of the physical evidence analysis to the case."

Rudin and Inman (2005) suggest further that the system currently in place "has resulted from an over-reaction to some of the 'cowboy' forensic science that has been practiced over the last century or so. Forensic science has historically been developed separately from clinical medicine and science, hence was not part of the movement of standards, certification and accreditation that evolved in those disciplines. No unified framework of fundamental concepts for forensic science existed and few professional standards were promulgated. Clearly, the creation of basic guidelines and minimal standards was necessary to establish a framework for oversight as well as to provide the forensic consumer with a set of criteria by which to judge the veracity of the product they were receiving. However, we have now gone overboard. Analysts have been effectively demoted to technicians while those establishing standards appear to have become so disconnected from the everyday practice of criminalistics that their recommendations (which we somehow accept as directives) have become irrelevant to the real-world practice of criminalistics."

Scheck and Neufeld (2001) advocate for a national institute to validate technologies and methodologies, and set standards for interpretation of data, explaining that while medical research for medicine is underwritten by the National Institutes of Health, for example, no such comparable vehicle exists for forensic science: "Truly independent forensic research does not exist. Most of the studies are commissioned by the Department of Justice and carried out by the crime labs with a significant bias in the outcome. For most forensic science, there are no enforceable standards for individual interpretation of data." Scheck and Neufeld continue, "These problems could be remedied by the creation of an institute of forensic science, jointly operated by a medical school and law school or as a necessary extension of the National Academies of Science. It could provide the necessary conflict-free environment augmented by rigorous academic policies and procedures. Federal grants to the institute could finance objective research, necessary validation studies, and peer review. Moreover, the synergy of law and medicine would enhance the development and implementation of appropriate standards and controls for reporting scientific results in writing and in court. The effort will fail, however, unless it is managed jointly by scientists and legal scholars who are independent of as well as those who work with law enforcement."

Many commentators and forensic practitioners agree that forensic laboratories and medico-legal offices must maintain strong programs of quality assurance and quality control to facilitate standardization. Quality assurance guidelines define the minimum standards of operation, and should be based on external and internal validation studies that garner specific information about proper procedures and protocols. Quality control programs are designed to enumerate ways that quality assurance can be implemented in forensic facilities through day-to-day operational activities. Other safeguards include standards (a measurement system against which an unknown sample is compared) and controls (a sample whose result is unknown). Inman and Rudin (2001) observe, "For the science in forensic science to be taken seriously, each analytical test must be accompanied by the appropriate standards and controls. These will differ depending on the kind of analysis, but their conspicuous absence is unacceptable."[1] Inman and Rudin add further, "Quality assurance guidelines and quality control procedures are neither merely an encumbrance nor a panacea. When implemented thoughtfully and with intelligence, they are simply another tool used to demonstrate the high quality of a work product."[1]

Critics charge that there are too many individuals working in forensic science who are committing intentional and accidental mistakes that result in egregious consequences such as wrongful convictions or errors that lead to distress for decedents' families. Another important plank of proposed reform of forensic science involves a better system of checks and balance, as well as more frequent and more independent reviews of casework. Reformers are calling for mandatory quality control measures, including enacting certification requirements for forensic scientists and examiners; accreditation standards for forensic laboratories and medico-legal offices; mandating routine double-blind proficiency testing for any labs desiring to obtain accreditation; and requiring random external scientific assessments. They are also calling for the results of proficiency testing of forensic practitioners being made public, as well as for standardized protocols for all areas of forensic science, based in science and empirically validated before it can be utilized in practice.

DiFonzo (2005) states, "The experiment of voluntary accreditation and haphazard analyst certification has failed. As a baseline proposition, states and the federal government should hold forensic science to professional standards. DNA samples should be processed exclusively in nationally accredited laboratories, whose certification procedures, employee training, and evaluation records, and laboratory error rates are made public."

Commentators are pushing for a broader system of independent external audits to investigate instances of alleged misconduct or gross negligence on the part of forensic service providers. Scheck and Neufeld (2001) assert, "Congress has provided generous support for forensic DNA typing, but experts estimate that only 20 percent of violent crime investigations will benefit from evidence suitable for DNA testing. Because other forensic disciplines lack the heightened scientific dimension of DNA, measures are needed to raise their standards of performance. There is simply no better way than external audits to investigate the scope of a problem and to remediate, thus reducing the risk of it happening again."

Scheck and Neufeld (2001) observe further, "Congress might require independent external investigations into allegations of serious negligence or misconduct committed by employees or contractors of the forensic laboratory, as a condition of federal funding to state and local crime labs. Ultimately, the audit function should illuminate what went wrong and how to make it right, thereby reducing the risk of future mishaps." According to Scheck and Neufeld, the essential elements of the certification would include the following:

- Investigators must be independent of the entity being investigated; investigators do not report to or depend on the laboratory for any resource or benefits, and they do not rely on the results of the laboratory in a professional capacity.
- Investigators must have adequate experience and qualifications and be trained in conducting similar reviews.
- Resources must be adequate to conduct a professional and thorough investigation.
- Protocols must be established for conducting investigations.
- Adequate quality control for the investigation must be established.
- Public disclosure of the results of these audits is assumed.

Scheck and Neufeld (2001) say that this kind of investigatory responsibility should be delegated to the states rather than centralize it with the Department of Justice's inspector general (IG): "The expansive and extensive oversight necessary to monitor adequately all forensic disciplines in all state and local laboratories receiving federal funding could overwhelm the IG. The load is lightened considerably if spread among the states. Moreover, there is broad concern that state criminal justice systems should have the freedom and flexibility to implement their own integrity controls. A concern for federalism can be satisfied if Congress delegates to the states the responsibility of creating or identifying a pre-existing independent investigative mechanism but at the same time requires that the state system be certified by the Department of Justice IG."

Some commentators point out that the Justice for All Act signed by President George W. Bush in November 2004 provided that, as a condition of receiving Coverdell federal grant money to aid state and local crime labs, states are required to certify that ". . . a government entity exists and an appropriate process is in place to conduct independent external investigations into allegations of serious negligence or misconduct substantially affecting the integrity of the forensic results. . . ."

In a July 31, 2003, hearing before the Senate Judiciary Committee, Peter Neufeld, co-director of the Innocence Project, testified that an overriding issue facing forensic science and criminal justice was oversight. Neufeld noted, "One of the things in the federal government that most states lack is oversight through the Office of the Inspector General. We all know about how the IG has oversight over the FBI Laboratory, and they can decide when it is appropriate to commence a forensic audit. We know how important forensic audits are in everything in life. When the space shuttle crashed, you didn't want it to be an in-house investigation by NASA; Congress demanded that it be an independent external audit. When the Enron scandal happened, people said, no, it can't be Enron or Arthur Andersen that looks into this; it has to be an independent external audit. Well, the same thing applies when there is some major mishap at a crime laboratory." Neufeld continued, "Our suggestion is very simple and very inexpensive: Allow the IG to set up some guidelines, some parameters, and then allow each state . . . come up with its own type of IG. It could be a different agency in each state, but there must be some external, independent auditing mechanism in place, which means certain minimum federal criteria, chosen by the states so that when there is a scandal, and in the last year there have been more crime lab scandals in America, and you read about them in the newspapers, than in the preceding five years. In those scandals, it wasn't just about innocent people being wrongly prosecuted or convicted. More often than not, it was about guilty people going free because of laboratory sloppiness. So we need to have somebody who can look into it when it happens, not to point the finger, but to make recommendations so this doesn't happen in the future."

Neufeld and other commentators have suggested that accreditation by the American Society of Crime Laboratory Directors/Laboratory Accreditation Board (ASCLD/LAB) is not sufficient. Speaking at the 2003 Senate Judiciary Committee hearing, Neufeld added, "Obviously, the internal audit that goes on through an ASCLD accreditation is very, very important. The FBI Laboratory is ASCLD/LAB-accredited, but nevertheless there was a small scandal in that laboratory recently when it turned out that one of the scientists was consistently not utilizing a certain control which was essential in all the forensic DNA tests. So the IG of the DOJ commenced an audit [because] they wanted to see the scope of the problem, where the traditional controls failed, and what changes should be made in their protocols to make it more likely that that won't happen again. So it can even happen with accredited laboratories."

Reviews consist of external reviews conducted by a third party such as ASCLAD/LAB, as well as internal reviews performed by senior members of the forensic laboratory or medico-legal office. Review and oversight is the cornerstone of the accreditation, a process that seems to be the center of great debate in the forensic science and legal communities.

Commentators suggest that the U.S. needs a national system of accreditation and quality assurance independent from law enforcement and any other politically charged entities, and that a model can be found in how clinical laboratories conduct themselves. Scheck and Neufeld (2001) state, "Forensic science is to criminal justice what clinical laboratory science is to healthcare. Health and public safety depend on the integrity of the product. The consumer of clinical medicine receives a measure of protection through government-imposed and regulated quality assurance and quality control. Defendants, victims, and the public would derive comparable protection from government-imposed oversight to ensure the integrity of forensic science before it gets to court. But whereas a national regulatory scheme has been in place for clinical laboratories since 1968, there is simply no national or, with one exception, meaningful state regulation of forensic science. Instead, the protections to avoid compromised evidence are few, and the measures to investigate and address abuses once they are discovered are virtually nonexistent."

Much of the confusion over accreditation stems from accusations that the forensic science community does not want this kind of a system. Scheck and Neufeld (2001) assert, "Most of the crime laboratories are resistant to any oversight. Additionally, in an effort to fend off a clinical laboratories improvement act-type regulatory approach, some public crime lab directors have urged their colleagues to voluntarily seek accreditation through their private professional organization, ASCLD/LAB. . . . Although unquestionably, ASCLD/LAB fulfills a critical role in the overall improvement of the delivery of forensic services, they cannot be the final arbiter."

Arguing that the assertions of Scheck and Neufeld are off the mark is Barry A.J. Fisher, director of the Los Angeles County Sheriff's Department's forensic laboratory, past president of the American Academy of Forensic Science, past president of the American Society of Crime Laboratory Directors, and past president of the International Association of Forensic Sciences. "Crime labs should be regulated in some fashion," Fisher emphasizes. "Certainly there are problems, but they are not as widespread as some claim. The real problem is that many crime labs and medical examiner offices are underfunded. There has to be a mechanism to set out requirements not only for the facilities but for personnel as well. These requirements should be written into law. Today, only a handful of states require labs to be accredited. Police departments with crime scene units or fingerprint units have no regulation. Practitioners ought to be certified. Model legislation would be helpful to set forth accreditation and certification requirements, and to tie these requirements to federal funding for crime labs and medical examiner/coroner offices. Consider the medical model; the big hook in health-care in the United States is that the federal government provides funding through the Medi-care program; if a medical service provider does not follow the rules, they may not receive reimbursement for services provided. This is not done in the forensic arena, and as a result, we have significant differences in how labs are operated throughout the country. In some areas labs are very well funded; in other areas, the level of resources, the quality of the facil-ity, staff, and equipment is marginal. Standards would help to improve this situation. Some form of oversight would help maintain quality in crime labs."

As we saw in Chapter 5, many members of the forensic science community do not resist accreditation and, in fact, support it heartily. However, there is some debate about the finer points of accreditation, as well as how accreditation may or may not strip analysts and examin-ers of certain degrees of self-determination.

Rudin and Inman (2005) observe, "An ASCLD/LAB inspection sometimes feels like a season of the TV reality series 'Survivor'; between us we have 'survived' a number of accredi-tations in different laboratories over more than a decade. While we support the general idea of basic standards and reasonable oversight, we fear that both the process and goals of the current iteration of the program may sometimes be counterproductive. Has the science in forensic science become just a trivial and disposable obstacle in the way of a new hyperspace bypass on the highway of accreditation?"

Rudin and Inman (2005) assert that unlike individual certification, laboratory accredita-tion may be undermining their abilities: "Some have stated that although professional certi-fication of individuals has worked well to encourage improvement of the expertise and knowledge base of criminalists who choose to undergo the rigorous process, laboratory accreditation has strayed from its original intended ideals and has had far-reaching, if unin-tended, consequences. Expected is a strict adherence to protocols and procedure manuals that some say leads to the "stultification of the scientific analysis of evidence, reducing it to a cookbook of 'acceptable' tests. The investigative world is far too complex to expect all answers to be found in a cookbook (no matter how comprehensive that cookbook can be made)."

Some forensic practitioners are fearful that the accreditation's requirement to use only protocols existing in the laboratory's procedures manual removes both the requirement and ability of an analyst to use science to think his/her way through an analysis for which no published protocol exists. Rudin and Inman (2005) introduce the concept of "children of accreditation," explaining, "Many young analysts that enter the crime laboratory system today are immediately shunted into a particular specialty and indoctrinated into the accreditation lifestyle, or at least lab-style. They are taught a limited spectrum of methods that are pre-scribed by the laboratory manual. Rather than being encouraged to pose a relevant question and seek a method of scientific inquiry to answer it, they are implicitly taught to look for questions that can be answered by the available tests. Not only does everything look like a nail waiting to be hammered, they don't even have a choice of a ball peen hammer or a sledge hammer. By limiting the tools available, the risk of providing an answer to an irrelevant or useless question increases. However, these children of accreditation seem satisfied that, as long as they've done what it says in the protocol checked off the little boxes and filled in the lot numbers, they've performed the analysis correctly, and their analysis is unassailable. They have, however unintentionally, acquired a mentality that requires the safety net of cookbook procedures. The idea of performing and defending original scientific work has become a foreign concept."

Conversely, Simms (2005) states that rather than "being stifling and prohibitive, accredited environments can offer the analyst just as much opportunity for flexibility and creativity as is needed for any situation." Simms also cautions that the forensic laboratory community must be cautious about rushing to embrace the new or novel: ". . . Should it not be an important premise that we don't want to rush into some new wild test that may yield an unproven answer? Accreditation makes certain that if we do have to use a new test not in our established protocol, we have carefully worked through those appropriate controls and standards to ensure that the new or unusual method is working properly, even before we test the evidence. This is, in fact, the time to be even more careful because we are in new territory." Simms adds, "If a laboratory environment truly prohibits creativity and flexibility, it is the fault of the laboratory rather than ASCLD/LAB or the process of accreditation."

Rudin and Inman (2005) say that accreditation's goal was to establish a set of standards for infrastructure and organization. The problem, they say, "is that those criteria were seen as an end rather than a beginning. The manual of common methods became the manual of permitted methods. Rather than a resource, we are now stuck with handcuffs that restrict us from posing questions if they cannot be answered by a specific method already in the manual." To which Simms (2005) replies, "They may be describing a few labs out there, but this hardly describes the system in general. If a laboratory has self-imposed a restriction to the use of only its documented technical procedures, then that laboratory, not ASCLD/LAB, applied the handcuffs."

Some members of the forensic science community believe that the accreditation process is uneven and possibly lacking parity among the forensic facilities inspected. Rudin and Inman (2005) assert, "It has not yet been possible to achieve consistent and intelligent application of accreditation requirements, even as they exist today. One of the more pervasive problems has been uneven interpretation of the standards and worse, the interjection of the personal opinions of individual auditors. Some auditors seem limited by the scope of procedures in their own laboratories—they cannot conceive that another way might be equally as good, or even better, than the ones they employ. In some cases, they are fundamentally unqualified to perform the audit to which they have been assigned. Of even greater concern are the auditors who take it upon themselves to legislate the use of particular protocols."

Simms (2005) disagrees, commenting, "Through the years, I have heard the following complaint many times from various labs . . . what was acceptable in one lab with one inspection team was not acceptable for another lab with a different team." Simms explains that as quality assurance managers began to network, inconsistencies in the accreditation process became more apparent and were addressed, and adds, "ASCLD/LAB listened to the complaints, and, as a result, restructured themselves and the inspection process." What is needed, Simms says, are specific system improvements, including a greater number of appeals to findings that are not justified, as well as better feedback from ASCLD/LAB. Simms explains, "Many times lab directors acquiesce to the findings of the inspection team when they should be fighting a bad call. These are missed opportunities by the lab directors to improve the process. Caving in to a bad interpretation of an inspection criterion is unfair to the labs yet to be inspected, as bad precedent is set. . . . If ASCLD/LAB has an ineffective inspector in the field, they need to be told about it so they can either retrain or remove that inspector from service."

Accreditation serves the dual purpose of improving casework and assuring end users that testing results are accurate; however, Rudin and Inman (2005) ask, "Have we actually accomplished either of these goals? We seem to have convinced the public that accreditation is the answer to assuring quality casework, in spite of several high-profile examples to the contrary. However, those of us who independently review casework understand very well that accreditation is no barrier to poor quality, indeed even poorly documented, casework. Conversely, laboratories that remain unaccredited by any outside agency may be perfectly capable of turning out excellent work. Certainly, we have also seen egregious examples of laboratories so incompetent and insular that only public humiliation has been able to force a systemic change. It is clear to us that the best use of an accreditation program is to provide an infrastructure within which quality casework can be performed. But that begs the question of what criteria we use to assess casework and whose responsibility is it. . . . We must insist on rigorous academic programs that teach students how to think, not just how to do. We must encourage active debate and discussion, not only in the general community, but within the laboratory about specific case interpretations."

Rudin and Inman (2005) propose that the forensic laboratory community alter its expectations of the accreditation process: "Accreditation should focus on providing an environment in which analysts are not only free, but encouraged to concentrate on quality case work. Requirements should focus on infrastructure (both physical plant and administrative support), safety, security, funding, and providing for continuing education. They should not stray into legislating acceptable protocols."

Quibbling aside, accreditation is an important reinforcement of compliance with guidelines from ISO and ILAC, which provide international standards for forensic laboratories. We now review the essence of these standards, which reformers and forensic laboratory personnel agree must be observed to protect the integrity of forensic test results presented in court.

Forensic laboratories should have defined processes that ensure that all analysts and examiners are competent to perform the work required, and labs' policies should include procedures for the maintenance of their skills and expertise. Laboratories must also have clear statements of the competencies required for all jobs, and records should be maintained to reflect personnel's ability to keep pace with the demands of their jobs.

Stam (2005) comments, "Quality work is the responsibility of every single employee in the laboratory from the clerical staff to the management staff. There is no substitute for the proper supervision, review of reports, and review of work in the crime laboratory. In the broadest sense quality assurance/control is the maintenance of the degree of excellence or superiority of your product or service. Controlling the quality of your product requires putting into place systems to achieve desired results."

Regarding the physical plant, great care is needed in forensic laboratories when handling trace levels of materials, and physical separation of high-level and low-level work is required for the preservation of evidence integrity. Access to these areas should be restricted, and the work undertaken controlled carefully. Another critical area focuses on test and calibration methods and method validation; standards dictate that all methods should be fully documented, including procedures for quality control, and, where appropriate, the use of reference materials. All technical procedures used by a forensic laboratory should be fully validated before being used on casework; where a laboratory introduces a new (validated) method, it should first demonstrate the reliability of the procedure in-house against any documented performance characteristics of that procedure.

Stam (2005) notes, "The implementation of quality assurance programs has made crime labs take a long look at their practices and procedures. Analytical methods must be validated, proper controls must be run, appropriate blanks must be run, work must be technically reviewed, and reports must be technically and administratively reviewed. In a nutshell, any process or analysis must be evaluated for the specific areas that could be affected by a variable. If the specific task does not require rigid specifications or guidelines, or isn't affected adversely by slight variations, then general good practice should prevail."

As part of a quality system, all forensic laboratories are required to operate a program for the maintenance and calibration of equipment used in the facility. General-service equipment not directly used for making measurements should be maintained by visual examination, with safety checks and cleaning as necessary; calibration or performance checks are necessary where the equipment setting can significantly affect the test or analytical result. Microscopes should be cleaned and serviced periodically, and they should be checked for proper setup and use. Volumetric equipment should be maintained by visual examination and cleaning, with performance checks carried out before initial use and at intervals depending on the type and frequency of use. Measuring instruments such as densitometers, chromatographs, spectrometers, and spectrophotometers should receive periodic servicing, cleaning and calibration. However, because these safeguards do not necessarily ensure that a measuring instrument or detection system is performing adequately, periodic performance checks should be carried out and predetermined limits of acceptability assigned. The frequency of such performance checks is determined by need, type, and previous performance of the equipment.

Stam (2005) observes, "The calibration of instrumentation that provides quantitative results is a crucial area and must meet strict requirements in order to maintain accurate results. In the case of instruments that are used qualitatively and not quantitatively, the requirements can be relaxed to documenting the operation of the instrument. The requirement of analyzing standards for an instrument of this type on some arbitrary time schedule does not improve the quality of the results for this instrument."

Regarding evidentiary samples, guidelines state that the selection, recovery, prioritization, and sampling of materials from submitted test items and from crime scenes are important parts of the forensic process. For legal purposes, forensic science laboratories should be able to demonstrate that the samples examined and reported on were indeed those submitted to the laboratory. A record of the chain of custody should be maintained from the receipt of samples, which details each person who takes possession of an item or alternatively the location of that item (if in storage). Forensic laboratories must follow documented procedures that describe the measures taken to secure exhibits in the process of being examined, which must be left unattended.

In addition, analytical performance should be monitored by quality control vehicles, including the following: reference collections, certified reference materials and internally generated reference materials, statistical tables, positive and negative controls, control charts, replicate testing, alternative methods, repeat testing, spiked samples, standard additions and internal standards, and independent verification by other authorized personnel. The quality control procedures necessary in any particular area of work should be determined by the laboratory responsible for the work, based on best professional practice. The procedures should be documented and records should be retained to show that all appropriate quality control measures have been taken, that all results are acceptable or, if not, that remedial action has been taken. An effective means for a forensic laboratory to monitor its performance, both against its own requirements and against the performance of peer laboratories, is to participate in proficiency testing programs. Proficiency testing records should include full details of the analyses/examinations undertaken and the results and conclusions obtained; an indication that performance has been reviewed; and details of the corrective action undertaken, where necessary. The laboratory should also follow a documented process whereby the testimony of each examiner and analyst is monitored regularly.

Stam (2005) comments, "The technical review and administrative review of reports are good quality checks on the performance of an analyst to help ensure that the results reported are accurate. The practice of requiring second opinions is also an extremely good way to find mistakes and ensure that the conclusion is defendable when an identification is made. Even the court testimony evaluations help make sure the laboratory is producing quality work. These things go directly to the elimination of honest errors by an analyst and give us a chance to locate dishonest errors."

Accreditation is not a perfect system of quality control, and some members of the forensic laboratory community say that accreditation must be combined with a practitioner's own system of checks and balances as well as his or her suggestions on how to improve the process. Stam (2005) observes, "ASCLD/LAB inspectors' interpretations of the original ASCLD guidelines . . . have become very subjective, inconsistent, and in many cases unrealistic. I propose that the ASCLD/LAB guidelines be reviewed periodically by the criminalists doing the work and that these reviewers should suggest changes. The changes should not be made by the laboratory managers, who may or may not have ever done casework, or if they did, it probably was several years ago. I am very concerned that the quality assurance process has become a charging horse and the criminalists are in the way and about to be flattened by an overburdensome and unrealistic set of quality assurance guidelines. Completing casework will become secondary to the paranoia of meeting all of the quality assurance rules."

Many forensic practitioners embrace the concept of self-checks; Rudin and Inman (2005) propose a casework checklist:

- Has the analyst read, understood, and summarized the case?
- Has the analyst formulated relevant questions?
- Has the analyst posed alternative hypotheses?
- Do the examinations and analyses specifically address the questions posed?
- Has the analyst considered the limitations of the sample (the nature of the evidence)?
- Has the analyst considered the limitations of the test?
- Do the data support the reported conclusions?
- Has the significance of the conclusions within the context of the case been articulated?

Despite a variety of review opportunities available, they are not a silver bullet. Rudin and Inman (2005) comment, ". . . No matter how many people review a case, and even agree that the results and conclusions are correct, there is no a guarantee of infallibility; we can still be dead wrong. This is a very difficult concept for both scientists and the public to accept. We can regulate and review all we want, but forensic casework . . . does not operate in an arena of absolutes."

Another critical plank in the reform platform, for commentators and forensic practitioners equally, is the improvement of the education and training opportunities for all levels of personnel. Reformers advocate a standardized educational and training curriculum for all individuals wanting to enter the field, with a focus on the traditional sciences of biology, chemistry, and physics, rather than law enforcement and criminal justice protocols.

Linville and Liu (2002) observe, "A misconception about the work of forensic scientists leads to misconceptions about forensic education. Students weary of the 'hard' sciences may think they can pursue a career in forensics and avoid the stringent training required for more traditional science disciplines. This is not the case. Prospective students should be aware that the forensic scientist is a scientist first. Forensic scientists are chemists and biologists with supplemental training on applying their science to forensics and the criminal justice system. It would indeed be unjustifiable if the forensic scientists that are called on to help resolve issues in the criminal justice system had less scientific knowledge or skill than those working in equivalent analytical laboratories."

Reformers also push for an emphasis on the scientific method and how it relates to forensic science, as well as mandatory practical experience within a laboratory or medico-legal office environment. They explain that learning how to incorporate the methods of scientific investigation in the laboratory or medico-legal setting will benefit forensic practitioners, since knowing the limitations and powers of the scientific method will enable them to conduct their own research in the various forensic disciplines. Linville and Liu (2002) add, "The excitement of today's forensic science is the continuous grappling with the most advanced knowledge and technologies to provide definitive interpretations of criminal acts. The mission of a forensic science program is to advance a student's knowledge and skill in problem solving by emphasizing basic science and new technologies. The work of a forensic scientist is unique in that the scientist will collect samples under many adverse conditions. Each sample possesses a unique challenge to the analyst. The forensic scientist must have knowledge of the current practices in the field, understand the underlying scientific principles behind these practices, and be equipped with advanced scientific knowledge and skill. Only when both the basic science and the nature of forensic science is understood, will the forensic scientist have the ability to determine the best method for analyzing varying types of evidence."

As noted in Chapter 13, the "*CSI* effect" is continuing to spark interest in forensic science among students, but the needs of the educators and veteran practitioners is the story that is not making the headlines. There exists a great need to provide education and training for novices and veterans and everyone in between who works in forensic science and medico-legal death investigation. According to the NIJ (2004), "To be competent to analyze evidence, forensic examiners need both basic scientific education and discipline-specific training. To be in compliance with widely accepted accreditation standards, scientists in most of the disciplines must have, at a minimum, a baccalaureate degree in a natural science, forensic science, or a closely related field of study. Education and training are also needed to maintain expertise, update knowledge and skills, and keep up with advances and changes in technology."

When a new analyst or examiner is hired, that individual requires initial training to build competency. The length of the initial training also depends on the laboratory specialty area. For example, controlled substances analysts may require only six to 12 months of training. Thus training in experience-based disciplines such as latent print examinations, firearms and tool marks analyses, and questioned documents examinations may require up to three years of training before being permitted to perform independent casework. Requirements for continuing professional development training may vary by forensic discipline. Linville and Liu (2002) suggest, "Although the bulk of forensic work is laboratory based, many students expect their education in forensic science to take the form of a job-training program. It is common for prospective students to expect forensic science education to be centered on the standard operating procedures used in crime laboratories. Crime laboratory protocols are important to forensics work and can be more effectively taught in the crime laboratory during the probationary employment period. These protocols, along with classes on courtroom proceedings and evidence handling, are commonly addressed in a forensic science program to create an environment that is not available in traditional scientific programs. However, they are not often the core of the forensic program."

Prior to conducting analysis on evidence, forensic scientists require both basic scientific education and discipline-specific training. To be in compliance with widely accepted laboratory accreditation standards, forensic scientists working in crime laboratories must have, at a minimum, a baccalaureate degree in a natural science, forensic science, or a closely related field of study. Each examiner must also have successfully completed a competency test (usually after a training period) prior to assuming independent casework. Education and training also are needed to maintain expertise, update knowledge and skills, and keep up with advances or changes in technology. According to the NIJ (2004), these needs can be addressed by collaborations, innovative approaches, and alternative delivery systems for forensic analysts and manager training. Regional centers based on established programs could also be used for expanded training. Professional models for training and establishing competency should be developed.

Although the number of forensic science programs at colleges and universities has recently increased, the Council on Forensic Science Education (COFSE) has noted that many forensic educational programs have been established with very limited resources, insufficient personnel, laboratory space, and support. NIJ's Technical Working Group on Education (TWGED) has recommended guidelines for forensic science education programs. It provides minimum curricula guidelines for undergraduate and graduate science programs. TWGED also recommends that academic forensic science programs establish a working relationship with forensic science laboratories and that forensic science educational programs seek accreditation.

In 2002, the American Academy of Forensic Sciences (AAFS) established the Forensic Educational Programs Accreditation Commission (FEPAC) to establish a program for formal evaluation and recognition of college-level academic programs based on the TWGED guidelines. With financial assistance from AAFS and NIJ, FEPAC established standards, policies, and procedures to accredit university forensic science programs. The program includes a self-study completed by the university applying for accreditation and an onsite assessment by trained FEPAC assessors. In 2003, a pilot test of the FEPAC accreditation program resulted in the accreditation of forensic programs at five colleges/universities. Pilot testing of this program continues.

AAFS and NIJ provided financial assistance for pilot accreditations. As a result, costs for these accreditations are reduced during the pilot stage of this program. Many members of the forensic science community are pushing for the continued support of FEPAC in order to ensure that future forensic scientists are adequately educated and equipped. This support will assist the community by keeping the costs of the program affordable for universities and colleges that seek recognition for their forensic science programs. Additionally, FEPAC is currently focused on university programs with traditional delivery systems. The forensic science community believes that the program should be expanded to consider less traditional program delivery mechanisms, including distance learning.

The TWGED guidelines recommend that institutional support for forensic science programs be comparable to other natural science programs. Graduate education in forensic science has not received dedicated criminal justice funding, although educational loans and other forms of financing are well established for other graduate programs throughout the country. The NIJ has traditionally supported graduate programs by providing research funding for the forensic sciences. A program to eliminate or forgive student loans for those graduates who obtain full-time employment in public forensic science institutions would be one such alternative source and should be considered, many in the forensic science community suggest. Any support provided would need to ensure that it is directed to those who would be employed in the public criminal justice sector.

In addition to research and student support, the forensic science community seeks support for the acquisition and maintenance of equipment, for major research instrumentation, and for laboratory renovation. Institutions offering forensic science programs should address the ongoing costs associated with the important practical laboratory components of their programs. The typical cost for the research component for a master's degree thesis, a requirement to meet FEPAC accreditation standards, is between $15,000 and $20,000 per student, in addition to other tuition and educational costs each student will incur. In order to ensure the integrity of forensic science educational programs nationwide, the forensic science community believes that any government resources that support university forensic science programs and students should be linked to FEPAC accreditation.

Regarding training needs within the forensic science community, to be in compliance with widely accepted accreditation standards, scientists in each of the disciplines must have, at a minimum, a baccalaureate degree in a natural science, forensic science, or a closely related field of study. However, to be competent to analyze evidence, forensic scientists need both basic scientific education and discipline-specific training. Hands-on training is needed to develop and maintain expertise, update knowledge and skills, and keep pace with advances in technology.

When a new analyst or examiner is hired, that individual requires initial training to build competency and proficiency with standard operating procedures. The length of the initial training provided to an analyst depends on the discipline the trainee will enter, and operating procedures may vary from laboratory to laboratory within a specific discipline. For example, controlled-substance analysts may require only 6 to 12 months of training. Those training in experience-based disciplines such as latent prints examinations, firearms, and tool marks analyses, as well as questioned-documents examinations, may require up to three years of training before being released to perform independent casework. During their training period, individuals in experience-based disciplines serve much like an apprentice to a senior examiner.

Initial training remains largely on-the-job and is labor intensive. The laboratory manager must first identify an existing member of the staff with appropriate expertise and experience who can serve as the trainer. Often, this is an individual with significant casework experience whose casework productivity is reduced or lost to the laboratory during the training period. Laboratory accreditation standards require the training to be documented and to contain a demonstration of competency prior to assuming casework responsibilities. The salary cost of an analyst in a one-year training program is between $30,000 and $40,000, but the cost to the laboratory is equally significant, as laboratories can realize up to a 30 percent reduction in productivity during that training interval.

Some visiting-scientist and intern programs are available that can be used to augment or abbreviate initial onsite training, but costs are high and funding remains scarce. Some laboratories have initiated collaborations with universities to offer their initial training programs to students enrolled in the university's graduate program. Other forensic laboratories have made attempts to collaborate on initial training, sending the individuals to be trained to a single site. For example, the National Forensic Science Technology Center (NFSTC) has developed an academy program as part of its cooperative agreement with the NIJ. NFSTC academies typically run for 16 weeks and provide intensive programs of study for new recruits to forensic laboratories.

Training also is required on a continuing basis for qualified analysts to maintain and update their knowledge and skills in new technology, equipment, and techniques. Almost all scientific and technical working groups, certification programs, and accreditation programs for the forensic science community recommend or require continuing professional development training, but the requirements vary by discipline. Symposia, workshops, and short courses are offered on a number of topics by an array of service providers, including professional societies and associations. The costs of continuing professional development vary, depending on the requirements of the specialty. The TWGED recommends that between 1 and 3 percent of the total forensic science laboratory budget be allocated for training and continuing professional development. Preliminary data reported by the BJS from its forensic laboratory census showed that the training and continuing education budgets of the largest 50 laboratories in the United States were actually less than one-half of 1 percent of their total budgets. In lieu of time requirements or a percentage, some agencies specify a budget amount for each analyst per year. Considering that the funds support travel and fees, $1,000 to $1,500 per analyst per year is typical. For a laboratory with 25 analysts, the annual cost of continuing professional development would be an estimated $25,000.

In addition to technical training (either initial or continuing), analysts need ongoing professional development training in a wide range of topics, including ethics, courtroom testimony, quality assurance, and safety. Some agencies, such as the Virginia Division of Forensic Sciences, include this type of training as part of agency training programs. Organizations such as the AAFS and some regional forensic science societies also offer training opportunities that may include presentations or workshops on these topics. Supervisors and managers often are educated in the sciences, but the forensic community also urges instruction in basic business and personnel management, fiscal procedure, and project management, and annual management symposia are held by the FBI and ASCLD.

While alternate delivery systems for forensic science training, such as electronic media, are increasingly being used, certain kinds of training require hands-on participation and evaluation. For these types of training, regionally based programs would reduce travel costs. Illinois, Virginia, New York, Florida, and California have operational laboratories/systems with well-developed training programs that also have strong collaborations with universities. Such established programs are ideally suited for expansion to provide training on a regional basis, if sufficient funding is provided. The FBI's traditional, on-site, forensic training classes have been popular within the forensic science community, and for many agencies these opportunities provide the only technical training available within their budget constraints. As expectations grow within the judicial system and technology continues to advance, there will be an increasing demand for these types of training opportunities. The forensic community urges that funding be provided so that technical training can be expanded to meet the demand for on-site training. It should be noted that in fiscal year 2003, the FBI provided 1,311 law enforcement training opportunities of various types to non-FBI personnel. In fiscal year 2004, it provided 2,857 such opportunities. In addition, FBI Laboratory personnel provided presentations to more than 5,000 attendees of meetings and more than 2,000 attendees of workshops or road show schools.

Grooming and growing future forensic scientists is a compelling component of any conversation about the education and training needs of the forensic science community. As we discussed in Chapter 13, the "*CSI* effect" has triggered renewed curiosity about and interest in forensic science as a vocational choice. However, many students entertain mistaken assumptions about the nature of the work and the specific training and education demanded of them.

"Students will get very excited about crime scene work, they'll call me and say, 'I want to go into your program, tell me what I need to do,'" says author and forensic science media consultant Lawrence Kobilinsky, Ph.D., a professor and science advisor to the president of John Jay College of Criminal Justice. "Then you explain to them what the work really involves, the science component required, and suddenly they realize that they have misunderstood the occupation and its rigors. Forensic science is science, not the soft side of things. It is not about interrogations or criminal justice theory, it is the kind of work that is based on the fundamental principles of science. When students discover this, it throws them. Most of them are not prepared for it."

Kobilinsky says the key to grooming prospective forensic scientists is starting early: "We in the forensic science community must reach out to the elementary schools and the high schools, introducing kids to forensic science as part of the traditional science curricula. Then, when they graduate from high school, they are better prepared to pursue a higher education in the sciences. We also need to do a better job of communicating to young people what an education and a career in forensic science really entails, and that it's not like what they see on television."

Education and training of forensic practitioners is more critical today, even as commentators argue that forensic scientists are scientists in name only and not practice. Moriarty and Saks (2005) inquire, "Where are the scientists? 'Forensic scientist' is a misleading title. In the world of conventional science, academically gifted students spend at least four years after college in doctoral training where much of the socialization into the culture of science, as well as specialized education, take place. That culture emphasizes obsessive methodological rigor, openness, relentless criticism of methods and findings, and cautious interpretation of data. Science proceeds by testing hypotheses using double-blind, controlled, repeatable studies that are published only after careful review of methods and logic. . . . By contrast, those who routinely testify under the appellation of forensic scientist operate in a much different world. In the forensic sciences, where 96 percent of practitioners hold bachelor degrees or less, 3 percent master's degrees, and 1 percent doctoral degrees, it is hard to find the culture of science."

Moriarty and Saks (2005) assert further that members of the forensic community would not fare well when compared with their counterparts in academia: "Most forensic 'scientists' have little understanding of scientific methodology, do not design or conduct research (and do not know how to), often do not read the serious scientific literature beginning to emerge in their fields (often conducted by doctoral level scientists from other fields), and would be unable to critique these studies sufficiently for the standards of conventional peer-reviewed scientific journals. Scientific findings relevant to a given forensic science often are ignored in the conduct of everyday casework."

Having said that, Moriarty and Saks (2005) favor the use of the title of forensic science "technician" to better reflect the backgrounds of the average forensic practitioner: "Yet, the nominal upgrading of title to forensic 'scientist' has obvious advantages in the world of litigation, where appearance often can serve as well as reality. If hard questions are asked about the underlying science, typical forensic science witnesses can explain that they cannot be expected to respond to such questions because the work they do, and the training they receive, is really that of a technician. Sometimes a genuine scientist (not infrequently from a different field than the forensic discipline at issue) can be brought in to try to defend it." While other nations are employing many more "real" scientists to conduct forensic science research, Moriarty and Saks observe that the United States might be able to set a course for correction: "There is also a small but growing cadre of serious American forensic scientists thinking deeply and conducting research, both in academic settings and in some crime laboratories. Given that they often must swim against a complacent tide, these American forensic scientists deserve considerable praise. But it is clear that the numbers, the culture, the support, the research, the deepest thought, and the improved techniques are more often found among scientists working outside of the United States."

Infusing forensic science with more science, as argued in Chapter 10, and elevating forensic practitioners beyond the aforementioned concept of the technician, will require professionals with advanced levels of education, training, and experience. The advent of DNA fingerprinting and the polymerase chain reaction (PCR) amplification of DNA, for example, represent the evolving sophistication of technology used in forensic science and indicate an ongoing need to refine educational criteria for its practitioners. Many individuals who want to pursue a career in forensic science mistakenly enroll in criminal justice programs instead of programs that are rich in the sciences, including biology, chemistry, or genetics.

Almirall and Furton (2003) state, "Over the years, surveys have repeatedly indicated that lab directors have a preference for applicants with a strong chemistry background. Results of a survey published in the *Journal of Forensic Science* in 1999 reinforced that the majority of crime lab directors require applicants to have B.S. degrees with a preference for chemistry/ biochemistry, followed by biology and forensic science with a requirement for a substantial number of chemistry and other natural science courses. Crime lab directors generally expected applicants to have 'hard' science degrees with a preference for the B.S. in chemistry, followed by biology and forensic science degrees with significant chemistry components."

The survey included a summary of degrees required for all positions combined: 63 percent B.S.; 27 percent B.A.; 6 percent none; 3 percent M.S.; and 1 percent Ph.D. The degree specialty required was 41 percent chemistry (including biochemistry), 24 percent biology (including genetics and molecular biology), 22 percent forensic science, 7 percent medical laboratory science, and 6 percent other (including 2 percent physics and 1 percent criminal justice). Of significance are the specific courses suggested by the respondents of the survey; the minimum course requirements were nine to 11 semester courses (or 36 to 44 credit hours) of chemistry and biology, with three main tracks: chemistry/trace track, biochemistry/DNA track, and firearms/document/fingerprint track.

Almirall and Furton (2003) report, "Overall, there has been a steady requirement of a significant scientific background for applicants, with an increasingly high expectation for areas such as criminalistics. On the issue of internships, the crime laboratory directors responded that internships were not a requirement, for the most part, for a new hire. For example, in the past, crime scene investigators and firearms examiners routinely were sworn officers with A.A. degrees; current successful applicants are now more likely to have B.S. or M.S. science degrees. While individual professional aspirations will determine the level of education a student will pursue, it is apparent that the trend in forensic science practice includes graduate studies, especially for those practitioners interested in advanced technical positions."

A recent survey of academic programs in forensic science revealed that 89 colleges and universities in the U.S. and 43 colleges and universities outside the U.S. offered a program of study in forensic science. Almirall and Furton (2003) comment, "While the list of programs generated from the survey may not be exhaustive, it does hint to the growing need and/or interest to offer degrees in forensic science around the world. Much of the growth in this interest has occurred over the last decade."

In 2001, the American Academy of Forensic Sciences (AAFS), the American Society of Crime Laboratory Directors/Laboratory Accreditation Board (ASCLD/LAB), and the American Society of Crime Laboratory Directors (ASCLD) encouraged the National Institute of Justice (NIJ) to establish a technical working group to examine education- and training-related issues for the forensic science community. A 10-member panel was created, and members represented forensic science laboratory directors, educators, and trainers; these members were key stakeholders in the future of education and training in forensic science.

The panel was charged with developing an outline for a guide for education and training in forensic science, as well as identifying experts to serve as members of the technical working group. Forty-nine experts (20 forensic science educators and trainers, 22 forensic science laboratory managers, two attorneys, and 5 experts from other organizations) from 20 states were invited to be members of the working group.

In 2004, the NIJ published a report outlining recommendations for the education and training of forensic practitioners. The report's working group stated that a "solid educational background in natural sciences with extensive laboratory coursework establishes the groundwork for a career in forensic science. Strong personal attributes, professional skills, certification, and professional involvement also are critical to the professional growth of prospective and practicing forensic scientists" (NIJ, 2004).

The NIJ report states that undergraduate forensic science degree programs are expected to deliver a strong and credible science foundation that emphasizes the scientific method and problem-solving skills. It stated, "Exemplary programs would be interdisciplinary and include substantial laboratory work, as most employment opportunities occur in laboratory settings. Natural sciences should dominate undergraduate curriculums and be supported by coursework in specialized, forensic, and laboratory sciences and other classes that complement the student's area of concentration."

In regard to graduate programs, the NIJ report emphasizes that they can move students from theoretical concepts to discipline-specific knowledge. The report adds, "Exemplary curriculums can include such topics as crime scenes, physical evidence, law/science interface, ethics, and quality assurance to complement the student's advanced coursework. Graduate programs should be designed with strong laboratory and research components. Access to instructional laboratories with research-specific facilities, equipment, and instrumentation and interaction with forensic laboratories are required to enhance the graduate-level experience. By emphasizing written and oral communication and report writing, graduate programs can prepare students for future courtroom testimony."

Continuing education was designated as being crucial to the professional development of forensic practitioners. The report emphasized, "Forensic scientists have an ongoing obligation to advance their field through training and continuing professional development. Training programs should include written components (e.g., instructor qualifications, student requirements, performance goals, and competency testing), and their content should contain several core and discipline-specific elements guided by peer-defined standards. Continuing professional development—mechanisms through which forensic scientists remain current or advance their expertise—should be structured, measurable, and documented."

The NIJ report (2004) also outlines the qualifications for a career in forensic science, explaining, "Forensic science plays a crucial role in the criminal justice system. As an applied science, it requires a strong foundation in the natural sciences and the development of practical skills in the application of these sciences to a particular discipline. A forensic scientist must be capable of integrating knowledge and skills in the examination, analysis, interpretation, reporting, and testimonial support of physical evidence. A properly designed forensic science program should address these needs and strengthen the student's knowledge, skills, and abilities in these areas."

Forensic scientists must have a strong fundamental background in the natural sciences. For example, new-hires who analyze drugs, DNA, trace, and toxicological evidence in forensic laboratories typically have a degree in chemistry, biochemistry, biology, or forensic science from an accredited institution. Although forensic scientists involved in the recognition and comparison of patterns (such as latent prints, firearms, and questioned documents) historically may not have been required to have a degree, the trend in the field is to strengthen the academic requirements for these disciplines and require a baccalaureate degree, preferably in a science.

A variety of skills are essential to an individual's effectiveness as a forensic science professional, including critical thinking (quantitative reasoning and problem solving), decision making, good laboratory practices, awareness of laboratory safety, observation and attention to detail, computer proficiency, interpersonal skills, public speaking, oral and written communication, time management, and prioritization of tasks.

A model career path for a forensic scientist begins with formal education and continues with training, postgraduate education, certification, and professional membership. According to the NIJ (2004), a forensic scientist's career path should demonstrate continued professional development that is documented by credentials, which are a formal recognition of a professional's knowledge, skills, and abilities. Indicators of professional standing include academic credentials, professional credentials, training credentials, and competency tests. While casework is the primary focus of a forensic scientist, he or she can also strive to advance the profession. This may be accomplished through professional involvement in research, mentoring, or teaching and by participating in professional organizations, community outreach, publishing, or other professional activities.

Forensic science is an applied science that covers an array of disciplines. Regardless of the area of forensic science pursued, an undergraduate degree in forensic science should be interdisciplinary, combining a strong foundation in the natural sciences with extensive laboratory experience. A model undergraduate forensic science degree program should provide a strong and credible science foundation that emphasizes the scientific method and the application of problem-solving skills in both classroom and laboratory settings.

An undergraduate degree in forensic science provides an educational foundation that meets the current hiring requirements of forensic laboratories. This curriculum emphasizes the strong natural science foundation that is essential to prepare a student for a successful career in forensic science. This curriculum is not designed to produce case-ready forensic scientists; laboratory managers, educators, and students may realize that prior to beginning casework, additional on-the-job training and possible postgraduate studies may be necessary to meet the specific needs of the individual employer. Peer-based working groups have promulgated specific education requirements. Forensic science laboratories and graduate programs may require more than the recommended credit hours of specific coursework.

Certain natural science courses are required for any student in forensic science. Unlike other criminal justice professionals, a forensic scientist requires a foundation in chemistry, biology, physics, and mathematics. In addition to a strong foundation in the natural sciences, forensic science professionals are expected to recognize concepts integral to forensic science, such as individualization, reconstruction, association, and chain-of-custody of evidence. Because the work product of a forensic scientist is used by the justice system, it is expected to meet legal as well as scientific standards.

The best academic program is only as good as the support it receives to keep it afloat; significant additional funding is necessary to bolster existing forensic science undergraduate programs and to create new programs. Funding can create an incentive for programs to provide students with the highest quality forensic science education.

According to the NIJ (2004), there are several factors that are essential for the proper implementation of a successful undergraduate academic program in forensic science, including the following:

- The program provides documented, measurable objectives, including expected outcomes for graduates, and regularly assesses its progress against its objectives and uses the results to identify areas for program improvement.
- The program receives institutional support equal to other natural science programs, with funding coming from federal sources, other public and private sources, and the host institution.

- The program has an adequate number of full-time faculty members to ensure continuity and stability to cover the curriculum, and to allow an appropriate mix of instruction and scholarly activity.
- The program has an adjunct faculty of practicing forensic scientists, who are expected to have the knowledge and experience appropriate to the course being taught.
- The program has adequate and appropriate laboratory facilities to enable students to complete their coursework and support the teaching needs and scholarly activities of the faculty.
- The program has sufficient support for faculty to enable the program to attract and retain high-quality faculty capable of supporting the program's objectives.
- The program is accredited by an accrediting body recognized by the U.S. Department of Education.

The NIJ (2004) also outlines recommendations for a graduate program in forensic science, admonishing, "A graduate-level forensic science program is expected to do more than educate students in theoretical concepts. It should provide the student with critical thinking ability, problem-solving skills, and advanced discipline-specific knowledge." The NIJ also identifies the need for an increased number of doctoral programs in the natural sciences with an emphasis on forensic science research: "Advanced education is necessary to prepare forensic scientists, academicians, and researchers for leadership roles in public and private laboratories and academic institutions."

Existing graduate programs in North America include a master of science in forensic science/criminalistics and a master of science in a natural science, such as chemistry or biology, with a track in forensic science. Program and other considerations have led to a wide variation in the content and structure of these programs; according to the NIJ (2004), an exemplary program encompasses forensic science subject matter, rigorous academic coursework in a specialized area, a research component, a laboratory component, interaction with forensic laboratories and professional societies, qualified faculty with appropriate forensic science experience, sufficient faculty-to-student ratio and support personnel, adequate academic resources, and fellowships.

The NIJ (2004) notes that an exemplary graduate forensic science curriculum also will address crime scene processing, physical evidence concepts, law/science interface, ethics and professional responsibility, quality assurance, and specific courses covering analytical chemistry and instrumental methods of analysis, drug chemistry/toxicology, microscopy and materials analysis, forensic biology, and pattern evidence. While all forensic science programs may offer specializations, tracks, or concentrations in different areas such as analytical chemistry or molecular genetics, the NIJ (2004) emphasizes that these programs are expected to offer "rigorous graduate-level academic coursework in appropriate subjects."

Coupled with education and training issues is the credentialing of forensic practitioners. While accreditation certifies forensic facilities such as laboratories and medico-legal offices, certification allows individuals to demonstrate high levels of competency and professionalism. What stands in the way, frequently, is individuals' ability to pay for the various credentials they seek.

"The federal government must give the organizations representing the different forensic disciplines the financial resources to be able to get their people certified," says Mary Fran Ernst, a medico-legal death investigator for the St. Louis County Medical Examiner's Office, director of medico-legal education at St. Louis University School of Medicine, and past president of the American Academy of Forensic Sciences. "For us to even apply to the specialties accreditation board, it's something like $2,000. They have to have that to survive. Analysts in the pattern identification fields, for example, have many boards and there isn't enough money to get everybody in line and to test. If the feds could provide this kind of financial assistance, it would be a huge help."

Ernst points to the creation of the Forensic Specialties Accreditation Board (FSAB) as a means to improve the way standards for certification were implemented. In a 1995 report, the Strategic Planning Committee of the AAFS reported that the quality and standards applied by different forensic boards for granting certification varied widely. The committee recommended that AAFS should assume a role in establishing a formal mechanism whereby the different credentialing processes of the various certifying boards can be objectively assessed. During the review of this issue, the AAFS recognized that an important aspect of professional oversight is monitoring the quality and consistency of credentialing of forensic specialists by the various forensic boards, or essentially accrediting the certifiers.

Groundwork was laid to accomplish this in 1996 by the AAFS's Professional Oversight Committee, as well as the Mini-Task Force on Criteria for Specialist Certifying Boards. The Accreditation and Certification Task Force, now known as the Forensic Specialties Accreditation Board (FSAB), with grant assistance from the National Institute of Justice, was formed to develop a voluntary program to objectively assess, recognize, and monitor the various forensic specialty boards that seek accreditation. The FSAB was incorporated as an independent organization in June 2000. "I have been fortunate to serve on the board of the FSAB since its inception, and I am thrilled to see that the organization has made a difference in the standardization of the credentialing process," Ernst adds. "That was a huge advancement for the forensic science disciplines. I think the secret for forensic scientists is to be certified. However, many specialties have standards but they aren't enforced. Until we start enforcing these standards, we won't see change. First of all, standards must be maintained in every discipline, and then those standards have to be promulgated. And finally, they must be enforced so that they are truly observed and put into practice."

The FSAB has created a set of standards to be applied by the organization for the accreditation of programs that certify individuals practicing forensic science. The standards address the process by which such knowledge, skills, and abilities are assessed, documented, and maintained. Of note, the general provisions of the FSAB standards establish that certification should be awarded only to applicants who meet or exceed the criteria set by the certification body, and that these criteria should include at minimum appropriate credentials, successful examination completion, and agreement to abide by defined ethical and professional standards. In addition, the standards are clear that the certification body must require periodic recertification and that grandfathering is not an acceptable method of certification.

Mandatory proficiency testing has become a contentious issue among practitioners and reformers. Jonakait (1991) suggests that a limited form of regulation, while a departure from an ideal program, could find middle ground with critics and with practitioners: "A certification program that only required labs to participate in proficiency testing could be a significant step towards achieving better crime lab quality. Such a program would not impose personnel standards, require in-house quality control measures, prescribe methods of analyses, or mandate a certain level in proficiency testing accuracy." Jonakait adds, "Limited regulation avoids the difficult problem of creating institutions to devise and implement a thorough, mandatory quality control program. The institution of good proficiency examinations alone will be much easier than the imposition of an entire quality control program. Of course, the creation of a comprehensive proficiency testing program will take effort, but it can draw upon the knowledge gained from past and continuing forensic testing programs. Similarly, the proficiency component will require fewer people and less money than an entire quality control program."

Jonakait (1991), along with other reformers, insists that mandatory proficiency testing can significantly raise the quality of forensic science: "Voluntary proficiency testing is not sufficiently effective. Particularly, noncompulsory testing for forensic facilities is undersubscribed. The starting point for improving forensic laboratory performance is fuller knowledge about the problems. Complete proficiency testing of all laboratories is essential to gain that knowledge."

Blind testing is the preferred method of proficiency examination by many commentators. Hoeffel (1990) observes, ". . . Passing a battery of blind tests should be required before a crime laboratory (analyst) is allowed a license to make determinations that affect an individual's freedom." Jonakait (1991) emphasizes, "The important issue for criminal justice is not how accurately laboratories perform when they are aware of being tested, but how well they do on actual cases. We can draw few useful inferences about real casework by administering trials that the analysts know to be tests. Studies indicate that performance will be better on known examinations than on either blind tests or real casework. To learn about the accuracy and reliability of lab work, forensic facilities must be subjected to blind testing that simulates real cases as much as possible."

Reformers also insist that the results of the proficiency testing be made public. Jonakait (1991) explains, "The true state of forensic science will not be known until the testing results from all laboratories are disclosed. This information will not only reveal the extent of the problems, but also how, for example, education and training of analysts, size of budgets, and kinds of equipment correlate with performance. Such data is essential for determining the necessary steps for improvement. The dissemination of such information should also serve as a direct spur to improvements."

Benchmarking is as good a reason for public reporting of proficiency testing as any, since forensic laboratories would be able to see how other forensic facilities are performing. Jonakait (1991) states, "Widespread dissemination of the test results will allow all scientists to examine the data to see where further studies would be most fruitful. This would improve use of resources, which is particularly important in a field where so little research is done. A thorough examination of findings may reveal that errors consistently occur in certain analyses, identifying important areas for investigation where present procedures are not particularly precise. . . . Wide dissemination of proficiency testing data will enable as many people as possible to scrutinize the information, find possible problems, and seek solutions."

Public reporting would also facilitate the determination of the admissibility of forensic evidence, as the reliability of a forensic analysis technique is essential to the process. Jonakait (1991) observes, "The criminal justice system needs to know about the quality of individual laboratory performances, both to spur more accurate and reliable performance and to dispense justice. Just as physicians and consumers with appropriate information can produce a greater number of correct analyses by choosing the better clinical facilities, consumers of forensic analyses can similarly affect quality when they know how individual laboratories and analysts perform." Judges are not the only stakeholders who could benefit from mandatory public reporting of proficiency testing; jurors should be able to determine what weight to give scientific evidence, and this testing data could even help secure improved verdicts.

Reformers suggest that the legal community should share in the commitment to improved outcomes within the criminal justice system. It is a given that forensic science must assist the criminal justice in reliably convicting the guilty and exonerating the innocent. Reform efforts must never lose sight of the tenets of the proper adjudication of cases: policing the threshold for expert testimony; ensuring defense counsel has access to competent forensic experts; mandating that prosecutors who wish to introduce scientific evidence should be required to disclose all underlying documentation used to construct a final report; expanding pretrial discovery of expert testimony; increasing the educational opportunities for attorneys to become aware of the capabilities and limits of forensic science; and requiring that every public defender office have at least one attorney who acts as a full-time forensic science specialist who can assist other attorneys with their cases.

Koppl (2005) acknowledges that there may be resistance to reform, or that some may be quick to point to problems in the legal system: "Good lawyering, one might argue, is the cure for bad forensics. This argument overlooks a basic scarcity consideration: High-quality counsel is not a free good. Without constraints on their time or energy, skilled and intelligent lawyers could learn enough about the limits of forensics to persuade judges and juries in those cases in which the forensic evidence presented by the prosecution was deficient; no innocents would be jailed because of forensic error. Good lawyering is a scarce good, however. Most criminal defendants are indigent and must rely on public defenders, who generally lack adequate incentives to perform well (Schulhofer and Friedman 1993) and may also be less skilled than private-practice lawyers specializing in criminal cases. Even a scientifically well-informed defense lawyer may be ineffective. . . . Presumably the difficulty is that even a skilled lawyer has no metaphorical white lab coat creating an aura of scientific authority. Uninformed and boundedly rational jurors and judges may be driven to rely on the scientific credentials of a speaker as a proxy for scientific validity of the speaker's argument."[2]

A FEW WORDS ABOUT ETHICS AND PROFESSIONALISM

That forensic science promulgates a sense of lawlessness is absurd to the practitioners who work within the confines of a number of codes of ethics. However, there is little dispute by the forensic science community that it could use increasing opportunities to strengthen its core level of professionalism. Inman and Rudin (2001) observe, "Because the early forensic scientists were more or less lone practitioners of a yet-to-be-recognized discipline, each felt a pioneer of sorts. While this was certainly true a century or even half a century ago, this trail-blazing mentality is no longer appropriate. The profession has survived a rather tumultuous adolescence and has achieved young adulthood, if not quite maturity. . . . With increased exposure comes scrutiny. Although the movement toward acquiring the accoutrements of professionalization began around the middle of the century, it was not until the 1990s that it really gained momentum. . . . While the acceptance of the need for accountability has been slow, the community has finally come to grips with the reality of that necessity."[1]

Some commentators have stated that forensic science lacks formal codes of ethics and standards for its practitioners, but there are a number of professional organizations that promulgate codes of professionalism. There is debate, however, among some critics who charge that these codes are not enforced; otherwise, they say, how could the Fred Zains of the world escape detection and sanctions for so long? Some argue that it is an honor system, others say it is a formality, while others say the only safeguard in place, as a last resort, is the criminal justice system that enacts when a member of the field has crossed the line. Just like any organization, a code of ethics may be only as good as the individual swearing to uphold it. It is an issue being taken up by the American Judicature Society's new institute, which will be discussed in Chapter 16.

Inman and Rudin (2001) state, "In every group, one or more individuals will inevitably decide that the end supersedes the means. At this juncture, even a code of ethics is insufficient to prevent the actions that follow from this decision. Whatever the agenda may be—convict-ing those we 'know' are guilty, discrediting DNA analysis wholesale, or simply monetary profit—these people play by their own rules. Sometimes they act from maliciousness, sometimes from their perception of a greater good, sometimes from coercion or confusion. Whatever the intent, whatever the motivation, we know that unethical behavior occurs and, like laboratory contamination, we must do what we can to prevent it and, failing that, to detect and correct it."[1]

Nordby (2003) observes, "Forensic scientists . . . may look to professional organizations' codes of conduct to illuminate correct conduct for scientists. Sadly, much of what passes for professional ethics embodied in codes of professional conduct reduces to lists of permissible and prohibited conduct designed to prevent professional heresy, or simply avoid troublesome litigation. Matters become even worse when professional ethics reduces to conduct designed to avoid embarrassing some specific agency or organization that supplies the code. Even if we developed explicit and robust codes, their usefulness remains doubtful at best. The ethical conduct of forensic science involves much more than a list of do's and don'ts. Professional ethics is not some random, extraneous thing that attaches to forensic practices as an afterthought. It must remain an essential element of doing science, or it is simply nothing at all."

Inman and Rudin (2001) observe that forensic science must share with academic sciences the basic ethical considerations, which include accurate representation of qualifications; true and accurate representation of data; clear and complete documentation; and reporting of colleagues who violate the profession's ethical code. Inman and Rudin add to this list another set of considerations more specific to forensic science, including maintaining the integrity of the evidence; impartiality of the examiner; limitations on conclusions as well as on the examiner's expertise; confidentiality and disclosure; exculpatory evidence; and testimony.

The ASCLD's Guidelines for Forensic Laboratory Management Practices provide instruction on a number of issues encountered by forensic service providers:

- *Managerial competence:* Laboratory managers should display competence in direction of such activities as long-range planning, management of change, group decision making, and sound fiscal practices. The role(s) and responsibilities of laboratory members must be clearly defined.
- *Integrity:* Laboratory managers must be honest and truthful with their peers, supervisors, and subordinates. They must also be trustworthy and honest when representing their laboratories to outside organizations.
- *Quality:* Laboratory managers are responsible for implementing quality assurance procedures that effectively monitor and verify the quality of the work product of their laboratories.
- *Efficiency:* Laboratory managers should ensure that laboratory services are provided in a manner that maximizes organizational efficiency and ensures an economical expenditure of resources and personnel.
- *Productivity:* Laboratory managers should establish reasonable goals for the production of casework in a timely fashion. Highest priority should be given to cases that have a potentially productive outcome and that could, if successfully concluded, have an effective impact on the enforcement or adjudication process.
- *Meeting organizational expectations:* Laboratory managers must implement and enforce the policies and rules of their employers and should establish internal procedures designed to meet the needs of their organizations.
- *Health and safety:* Laboratory managers are responsible for planning and maintaining systems that reasonably assure safety in the laboratory. Such systems should include mechanisms for input by members of the laboratory, maintenance of records of injuries, and routine safety inspections.

- *Security:* Laboratory managers are responsible for planning and maintaining the security of the laboratory. Security measures should include control of access both during and after normal business hours.
- *Responsibility to the employee:* Laboratory managers understand that the quality of the work generated by a laboratory is directly related to the performance of the staff. To that end the laboratory manager has important responsibilities to obtain the best performance from the laboratory's employees.
- *Qualifications:* Laboratory managers must hire employees of sufficient academic qualifications or experience to provide them with the fundamental scientific principles for work in a forensic laboratory. The laboratory manager must be assured that employees are honest, forthright, and ethical in their personal and professional life.
- *Training:* Laboratory managers are obligated to provide training in the principles of forensic science. Training must include handling and preserving the integrity of physical evidence. Before casework is done, specific training within that functional area shall be provided. Laboratory managers must be assured that the employee fully understands the principles, applications, and limitations of methods, procedures, and equipment they use before beginning casework.
- *Maintaining employees' competency:* Laboratory managers must monitor the skills of employees on a continuing basis through the use of proficiency testing, report review, and evaluation of testimony.
- *Staff development:* Laboratory managers should foster the development of the staff for greater job responsibility by supporting internal and external training, providing sufficient library resources to permit employees to keep abreast of changing and emerging trends in forensic science, and encouraging them to do so.
- *Environment:* Laboratory managers are obligated to provide a safe and functional work environment with adequate space to support all the work activities of the employee. Facilities must be adequate so that evidence under the laboratory's control is protected from contamination, tampering, or theft.
- *Communication:* Laboratory managers should take steps to ensure that the employees understand and support the objectives and values of the laboratory. Pathways of communication should exist within the organization so that the ideas of the employees are considered when policies and procedures of the laboratory are developed or revised. Communication should include staff meetings as well as written and oral dialogue.
- *Supervision:* Laboratory managers must provide staff with adequate supervisory review to ensure the quality of the work product. Supervisors must be held accountable for the performance of their staff and the enforcement of clear and enforceable organizational and ethical standards. Employees should be held to realistic performance goals that take into account reasonable workload standards. Supervisors should ensure that employees are not unduly pressured to perform substandard work through caseload pressure or unnecessary outside influence. The laboratory should have in place a performance evaluation process.
- *Fiscal:* Laboratory managers should strive to provide adequate budgetary support. Laboratory managers should provide employees with appropriate, safe, and well-maintained and -calibrated equipment to permit them to perform their job functions at maximum efficiency.
- *Responsibility to the public:* Laboratory managers hold a unique role in the balance of scientific principles, requirements of the criminal justice system, and the effects on the lives of individuals. The decisions and judgments that are made in the laboratory must fairly represent all interests with which they have been entrusted. Users of forensic laboratory services must rely on the reputation of the laboratory, the abilities of its analysts, and the standards of the profession.

- *Conflict of interest:* Laboratory managers and employees of forensic laboratories must avoid any activity, interest, or association that interferes or appears to interfere with their independent exercise of professional judgment.
- *Response to public's needs:* Forensic laboratories should be responsive to public input and consider the impact of actions and case priorities on the public.
- *Legal compliance:* Laboratory managers shall establish operational procedures in order to meet constitutional and statutory requirements, as well as principles of sound scientific practice.
- *Accountability:* Laboratory managers must be accountable for decisions and actions. These decisions and actions should be supported by appropriate documentation and be open to legitimate scrutiny.
- *Disclosure and discovery:* Laboratory records must be open for reasonable access when legitimate requests are made by officers of the court. When release of information is authorized by management, all employees must avoid misrepresentations and/or obstructions.
- *Work quality:* A quality assurance program must be established. Laboratory managers and supervisors must accept responsibility for evidence integrity and security; validated, reliable methods; casework documentation and reporting; case review; testimony monitoring; and proficiency testing.
- *Responsibility to the profession:* Laboratory managers face the challenge of promoting professionalism through the objective assessment of individual ability and overall work quality in forensic sciences. Another challenge is dissemination of information in a profession where change is the norm.
- *Accreditation:* The Laboratory Accreditation Board (ASCLD/LAB) provides managers with objective standards by which the quality of work produced in forensic laboratories can be judged. Participation in such a program is important to demonstrate to the public and to users of laboratory services the laboratory's concern for and commitment to quality.
- *Peer certification:* Laboratory managers should support peer certification programs that promote professionalism and provide objective standards that help judge the quality of an employee's work. Meaningful information on strengths and weaknesses of an individual, based on an impartial examination and other factors considered to be important by peers, will add to an employee's abilities and confidence. This results in a more complete professional.
- *Research:* When resources permit, laboratory managers should support research in forensic laboratories. Research and thorough, systematic study of special problems are needed to help advance the frontiers of applied science. Interaction and cooperation with college and university faculty and students can be extremely beneficial to forensic science. These researchers also gain satisfaction knowing their work can tremendously impact the effectiveness of a forensic laboratory.
- *Ethics:* Professional ethics provide the basis for the examination of evidence and the reporting of analytical results by blending the scientific principles and the statutory requirements into guidelines for professional behavior. Laboratory managers must strive to ensure that forensic science is conducted in accordance with sound scientific principles and within the framework of the statutory requirements to which forensic professionals are responsible.

The AAFS demands that its members and affiliates "refrain from exercising professional or personal conduct adverse to the best interests and purposes of the Academy, refrain from providing any material misrepresentation of education, training, experience or area of expertise, refrain from providing any material misrepresentation of data upon which an expert opinion or conclusion is based, and refrain from issuing public statements that appear to represent the position of the Academy without specific authority first obtained from the board of directors." Those who violate the Academy's code "may be liable to censure, suspension or expulsion by action of the board of directors."

The California Association of Criminalists (CAC) mandates that "It is the duty of any person practicing the profession of criminalistics to serve the interests of justice to the best of his ability at all times. In fulfilling this duty, he will use all of the scientific means at his command to ascertain all of the significant physical facts relative to the matters under investigation. Having made factual determinations, the criminalist must then interpret and evaluate his findings. In this he will be guided by experience and knowledge which, coupled with a serious consideration of his analytical findings and the application of sound judgment, may enable him to arrive at opinions and conclusions pertaining to the matters under study. These findings of fact and his conclusions and opinions should then be reported, with all the accuracy and skill of which the criminalist is capable, to the end that all may fully understand and be able to place the findings in their proper relationship to the problem at issue. In carrying out these functions, the criminalist will be guided by those practices and procedures which are generally recognized within the profession to be consistent with a high level of professional ethics. The motives, methods, and actions of the criminalist shall at all times be above reproach, in good taste and consistent with proper moral conduct."

The CAC incorporates the scientific method into its code of ethics by requiring that the criminalist has a "truly scientific spirit" and should be inquiring, progressive, logical, and unbiased, and will make adequate examination of his materials, applying those tests essential to proof. The criminalist is expected not to "utilize unwarranted and superfluous tests and attempt to give apparent greater weight to his results merely for the sake of bolstering his conclusions." The CAC code says that the "modern scientific mind is an open one incompatible with secrecy of method. Scientific analyses will not be conducted by 'secret processes,' nor will conclusions in case work be based upon such tests and experiments as will not be revealed to the profession." It adds that "a proper scientific method demands reliability of validity in the materials analyzed. Conclusions will not be drawn from materials which themselves appear unrepresentative, atypical, or unreliable." The CAC supports a "truly scientific method" that requires that no generally discredited or unreliable procedure will be utilized in the analysis. The code also states that "the progressive worker will keep abreast of new developments in scientific methods and in all cases view them with an open mind. This is not to say that he need not be critical of untried or unproved methods, but he will recognize superior methods, if and when, they are introduced."

The CAC code also addresses ethics relating to opinions and conclusions, and makes the following statements:

- Valid conclusions call for the application of proven methods. Where it is practical to do so, the competent criminalist will apply such methods throughout. This does not demand the application of standard test procedures, but, where practical, use should be made of those methods developed and recognized by this or other professional societies.
- Tests are designed to disclose true facts and all interpretations shall be consistent with that purpose and will not be knowingly distorted.
- Where appropriate to the correct interpretation of a test, experimental controls shall be made for verification.
- Where possible, the conclusions reached as a result of analytical tests are properly verified by retesting or the application of additional techniques.
- Where test results are inconclusive or indefinite, any conclusions drawn shall be fully explained.

- The scientific mind is unbiased and refuses to be swayed by evidence or matters outside the specific materials under consideration. It is immune to suggestion, pressures and coercions inconsistent with the evidence at hand, being interested only in ascertaining facts.
- The criminalist will be alert to recognize the significance of a test result as it may relate to the investigative aspects of a case. In this respect he will, however, scrupulously avoid confusing scientific fact with investigative theory in his interpretations.
- Scientific method demands that the individual be aware of his own limitations and refuse to extend himself beyond them. It is both proper and advisable that the scientific worker seek knowledge in new fields; he will not, however, be hasty to apply such knowledge before he has had adequate training and experience.
- Where test results are capable of being interpreted to the advantage of either side of a case, the criminalist will not choose that interpretation favoring the side by which he is employed merely as a means of justifying his employment.
- It is both wise and proper that the criminalist be aware of the various possible implications of his opinions and conclusions and be prepared to weigh them, if called upon to do so. In any such case, however, he will clearly distinguish between that which may be regarded as scientifically demonstrated fact and that which is speculative.

The CAC code is mindful of a criminalist's courtroom duties, and provides for the following:

- The expert witness is one who has substantially greater knowledge of a given subject or science than has the average person. An expert opinion is properly defined as "the formal opinion of an expert." Ordinary opinion consists of one's thoughts or beliefs on matters, generally unsupported by detailed analysis of the subject under consideration. Expert opinion is also defined as the considered opinion of an expert, or a formal judgment. It is to be understood that an expert opinion is an opinion derived only from a formal consideration of a subject within the expert's knowledge and experience.
- The ethical expert does not take advantage of his privilege to express opinions by offering opinions on matters within his field of qualification which he has not given formal consideration.
- Regardless of legal definitions, the criminalist will realize that there are degrees of certainty represented under the single term of expert opinion. He will not take advantage of the general privilege to assign greater significance to an interpretation than is justified by the available data.
- Where circumstances indicate it to be proper, the expert will not hesitate to indicate that while he has an opinion, derived of study, and judgment within his field, the opinion may lack the certainty of other opinions he might offer. By this or other means, he takes care to leave no false impressions in the minds of the jurors or the court.
- In all respects, the criminalist will avoid the use of terms, and opinions which will be assigned greater weight than are due them. Where an opinion requires qualification or explanation, it is not only proper but incumbent upon the witness to offer such qualification.
- The expert witness should keep in mind that the lay juror is apt to assign greater or less significance to ordinary words of a scientist than to the same words when used by a lay witness. The criminalist, therefore, will avoid such terms as may be misconstrued or misunderstood.
- It is not the object of the criminalist's appearance in court to present only that evidence which supports the view of the side which employs him. He has a moral obligation to see to it that the court understands the evidence as it exists and to present it in an impartial manner.
- The criminalist will not by implication, knowingly or intentionally, assist the contestants in a case through such tactics as will implant a false impression in the minds of the jury.

- The criminalist, testifying as an expert witness, will make every effort to use understandable language in his explanations and demonstrations in order that the jury will obtain a true and valid concept of the testimony. The use of unclear, misleading, circuitous, or ambiguous language with a view of confusing an issue in the minds of the court or jury is unethical.
- The criminalist will answer all questions put to him in a clear, straightforward manner and refuse to extend himself beyond his field of competence.
- Where the expert must prepare photographs or offer oral background information to the jury in respect to a specific type of analytic method, this information shall be reliable and valid, typifying the usual or normal basis for the method. The instructional material shall be of that level which will provide the jury with a proper basis for evaluating the subsequent evidence presentations, and not such as would provide them with a lower standard than the science demands.
- Any and all photographic displays shall be made according to acceptable practice, and shall not be intentionally altered or distorted with a view to misleading court or jury.
- By way of conveying information to the court, it is appropriate that any of a variety of demonstrative materials and methods be utilized by the expert witness. Such methods and materials shall not, however, be unduly sensational.

According to the CAC, "In order to advance the profession of criminalistics, to promote the purposes for which the association was formed, and encourage harmonious relationships between all criminalists of the state, each criminalist has an obligation to conduct himself according to certain principles."

- It is in the interest of the profession that information concerning any new discoveries, developments or techniques applicable to the field of criminalistics be made available to criminalists generally. A reasonable attempt should be made by any criminalist having knowledge of such developments to publicize or otherwise inform the profession of them.
- Consistent with this and like objectives, it is expected that the attention of the profession will be directed toward any tests or methods in use which appear invalid or unreliable in order that they may be property investigated.
- In the interest of the profession, the individual criminalist should refrain from seeking publicity for himself or his accomplishments on specific cases. The preparation of papers for publication in appropriate media, however, is considered proper.
- The criminalist shall discourage the association of his name with developments, publications, or organizations in which he has played no significant part, merely as a means of gaining personal publicity or prestige.
- The C.A.C. has been organized primarily to encourage a free exchange of ideas and information between members. It is, therefore, incumbent upon each member to treat with due respect those statements and offerings made by his associates. It is appropriate that no member shall unnecessarily repeat statements or beliefs of another as expressed at C.A.C. seminars.
- It shall be ethical and proper for one criminalist to bring to the attention of the Association a violation of any of these ethical principles. Indeed, it shall be mandatory where it appears that a serious infraction or repeated violations have been committed and where other appropriate corrective measures (if pursued) have failed.

The ASCLD code of ethics states that it "recognizes that laboratory managers bear additional ethical responsibilities beyond those expected of forensic scientists involved in analytical casework. Ethical issues can arise from activities unique to managers, such as hiring, training and supervising subordinates; establishing policies and procedures for evidence handling and analysis; providing quality assurance; budgeting and expenditure of authorized funds; and proper handling of agency property and supplies. While laboratory managers might not be involved directly in the analysis of evidence and presentation of courtroom testimony, their actions as managers can have a profound impact on the integrity and quality of the work product of a crime laboratory.

ASCLD's code forbids any member of ASCLD to engage in any conduct that is harmful to the profession of forensic science, including, but not limited to, any illegal activity, any technical misrepresentation or distortion, or any scholarly falsification; nor can an ASCLD member impose undue pressure on an employee to take technical shortcuts or arrive at a conclusion that is not supported by scientific data. The code also forbids members to misrepresent his or her expertise or credentials in any professional capacity; offer opinions or conclusions in testimony, which are untrue or are not supported by scientific data; and misrepresent his or her position or authority in any professional capacity.

ONE LAST THOUGHT

As the numerous planks of forensic science reform fall into place in the coming years, it may be helpful to consider the need for improved leadership of forensic science at the national level. Forensic pathologist Michael Baden, M.D., in testimony given July 31, 2003, before the Senate Judiciary Committee, expressed his desire to see leadership at the federal level for the forensic science community: "It struck me as a physician that we have a Surgeon General who has been a bully pulpit over the years for doing research and for improving natural diseases—heart disease, cancer—and it has been a very effective bully pulpit. Maybe the time has come to have some kind of a national bully pulpit, like a forensic science general, who can have authorization to be a bully pulpit and to help set up programs."

MODELS FOR IMPROVEMENT

Two commentators have proposed sets of solutions for the reform of the forensic science. We explore each of these.

Jonakait

Jonakait (1991) proposes that forensic laboratories take a cue from the Clinical Laboratory Improvement Act (CLIA) for a successful model to emulate. The Centers for Medicare & Medicaid Services (CMS) regulate all laboratory testing performed in the United States through the CLIA, and all clinical laboratories must be properly certified to receive Medicare or Medicaid payments. The CLIA program, implemented by the Division of Laboratory Services within the Survey and Certification Group, under the Center for Medicaid and State Operations (CMSO), covers approximately 189,000 laboratory entities. Jonakait reports four major components to the program: maintenance of a quality assurance and quality control program by the laboratory; maintenance of appropriate records, equipment, and facilities; personnel standards; and proficiency testing. According to Jonakait, "proficiency testing is the central element in determining a laboratory's competency, since it purports to measure actual test outcomes rather than merely gauging the potential for accurate outcomes. A lab must undergo quarterly testing for each type of analysis that it performs. Most importantly, the testing must be done in a blind fashion 253 with the results made available to the public."

In addition, the Department of Health and Human Services can suspend, revoke, or limit a clinical laboratory's certification, as well as invoke fines to induce compliance.

Jonakait (1991) comments, "Congress concluded that this rigorous, mandatory quality control program was necessary after studying the performance of clinical laboratories and the positive effects regulation can have on the quality of those labs. If such a regime is necessary for clinical labs, a similar regulatory scheme—involving inspections, personnel standards, quality control, and external proficiency testing—seems in order to improve the endemic poor quality of forensic laboratories. However, regulation of crime laboratories raises several difficulties not present with the regulation of clinical facilities."

Going to the heart of the debate is the question of who, precisely, would be in charge of devising, implementing, and enforcing a forensic laboratory quality control program built in the image of the CLIA. As Jonakait (1991) points out, the CLIA has benefited from decades of national regulation and has a history stemming from mandatory state programs, and federal regulators are experienced in determining appropriate standards relating to the program's operation. Conversely, would-be regulators of a national forensic laboratory program lack this kind of data and experience. Jonakait comments, "Little thought has been given to forensic personnel standards and quality control programs. Consensus does not even exist over such basic matters as protocols for routine analyses. Regulation of forensic labs truly must start from scratch. The imposition of a rigorous, comprehensive, mandatory scheme will require extensive study and effort. . . . Since no institutions currently regulate crime laboratories, the source of potential forensic regulators is not clear. New organizations would have to be created or significant new duties would have to be given to existing organizations."

The deep pockets required for such a program on the level of the CLIA was not lost on Jonakait (1991), who observes, "Besides a workforce, experience and knowledge, money will be necessary for forensic laboratories to be well regulated. For clinical regulations, congress found a politically expedient, if somewhat disingenuous, method of funding. Laboratories are charged fees for certification. This allows the regulation of clinical laboratories without the use of tax money, although the public ultimately pays for the regulatory scheme. A legislature, however, will not find such a convenient method of funding forensic regulations. Overwhelmingly, crime labs are public agencies that cannot pass additional costs on to insurance companies or consumers. Public money must be directly allocated if forensic facilities are to be regulated."

Could a CLIA-like program for forensic science even sustain itself? Jonakait (1991) identifies several challenges associated with such an ambitious endeavor to regulate forensic laboratories: "Fines imposed on crime laboratories would almost always have to be paid out of the public till. It is unlikely that a regulator would so sanction a governmental crime lab. Even if this occurred, the penalty would probably not have much deterrent or rehabilitative effect on an organization that does not make money. Regulators are also unlikely to suspend or revoke an accreditation necessary for a forensic laboratory to operate or present its results in court. Proficiency testing has taught that accreditation on the basis of adherence to certain standards of accuracy would apparently mean that a good number of laboratories would be shut down. Often, a major city may be dependent on a single crime lab, and its forced closing would have a huge effect on criminal justice. It would take great political will to enact and enforce such regulation even if it improved the accuracy of forensic science."

In the end, Jonakait (1991) seems to bemoan the fact that such challenges could eliminate all chances for a CLIA-like program to get off the ground: "While the pervasive poor quality of forensic science cries out for regulation like that imposed on clinical facilities, the difficulties in devising and implementing such regulations, as well as the fierce resistance by the forensic science community to any kind of enforced quality control, may make needed regulation politically infeasible. Nevertheless, less rigorous regulations may present fewer difficulties and still provide beneficial results."

SIDEBAR 15.1 A REFORMER SPEAKS OUT

Randolph Jonakait, a professor of law at New York Law School, has written extensively about forensic science and its impact in the courtroom, as well as on the intersection of criminal procedure and evidence. He says his interest in the quality of forensic science was rooted in early appeals work, which led him to write one of the earlier treatises on forensic science, evidentiary issues, and reform.

"I think there has been improvement in forensic science (since the paper was published in 1991)," Jonakait says. "DNA changed everything; one of my criticisms of forensic science was that the field was in its own world, separated from mainstream science in many ways. DNA at least partially changed that because at the beginning of the DNA technology revolution, scientists who were outside the forensic community got involved, and that tended to elevate this new discipline. The DNA community people conducted extensive research, and that helped DNA pass the test of validity and reliability." Jonakait adds, "I think there have been some positive changes in the quality of crime labs over time; however, quality control is still an issue to some degree, and that's one of the big deficits in the field."

Jonakait's paper elicited a strong response from the forensic science community, and he says he received "a lot of criticism" for it. He recalls an invitation to speak at the American Academy of Forensic Sciences, where the reception was a bit chilly, but as time went on, he says he did hear from individuals who agreed with his premises. Jonakait remarks, "I received calls from renegade scientists in support of the paper who would tell me, 'You got it right,' during a time when there was a fairly active movement of trying to challenge forensic science, especially DNA. Interestingly enough, no one who went through the paper issue by issue said that I was wrong. They proposed reasons why quality control testing that couldn't be done, and lots of assurances about how good crime labs were, but no data ever showing that."

Jonakait says his goal for the paper was to launch a dialogue about the issues facing forensic science, especially the debate about junk science: "I believe there have been aspects of forensic science that represent junk science in the sense that there have been assertions made without the data to back it up. The field is so separated from real science, as are the testing and quality control procedures. It doesn't mean forensic science isn't right, it's just that we don't really know if it is, and can we trust it? Their answer, and there is a lot of merit to this, is that it is incredibly hard to test real-life stuff. But it doesn't mean you should make claims without the science to support it. I think it is trusted, but whether it should be, I'm not sure. I think that when we talk about reforming forensic science, we need to talk about whether or not scientists can really do what they claim to be able to do, is there data to back it up, and can the procedure be subjected to quality control." Jonakait continues, "What is most important to me is that independent audits of crime labs be conducted, and that the results be made public. So many crime labs are not accredited and there do not seem to be many requirements to become a forensic scientist. I think we need to take a look at that for the future."

Koppl

Koppl (2005) says that reforms such as independence of forensic labs from law enforcement agencies (Giannelli 1997), improved documentation of forensic work (Kaufman, 1998), double-blind proficiency tests (Risinger et al., 2002), and the use of evidence lineups (Miller, 1987; Risinger et al., 2002) have limited impact without further reform in the institutional structure of forensic work. Koppl therefore proposes a system of "competitive self regulation" for police forensics to address the current institutional structure that "gives each lab a monopoly in the analysis of the police evidence it receives" and provides "inadequate incentives to produce reliable analyses of police evidence."[2] Under Koppl's vision, each jurisdiction would have several competing forensic labs: "Evidence would be divided and sent to one, two, or three separate labs. Chance would determine which labs and how many would receive evidence to analyze. Competitive self regulation improves forensics by creating incentives for error detection and reducing incentives to produce biased analyses."

Koppl (2005) observes that the current institutional structure of forensic science is "an important source of forensic error, insufficiency and, sometimes, malfeasance," and that "past calls for reform seem to have neglected both the role of industrial organization in discouraging high-quality forensics and the importance of competition in the supply of forensic services."[2]

Going to the heart of Koppl's (2005) proposal is "breaking up the forensic worker's monopoly" by instituting this system of competitive self-regulation, which he says would "put forensic labs into a competition similar to the competition characterizing pure science. Each forensic lab becomes a check on every other forensic lab. This system of checks and balances would reduce the errors committed by forensic scientists. It would even work to reduce the conscious and unconscious abuses committed by some forensic workers. . . . Under competitive self regulation, forensic science would finally become 'forensic' in the truest sense."[2]

If the underlying problem of forensic science is the unchecked power of the forensic practitioner that leads to what Koppl (2005) calls "substandard forensics," the solution lies in "fixing the problem by making that power divided and contested," Koppl states. "As long as such a monopoly is enjoyed, the forensic worker has an incentive to shirk and to act on any biases he may have. To render power divided and contested, it is necessary to establish competition among forensic workers. Competitive self regulation would not, of course, magically cure all forensic ills. It would, however, induce significant improvements in the quality of forensic work."[2]

A tenet of Koppl's (2005) theory of competitive self-regulation is the practice of "strategic redundancy," in which evidence should be selected at random for duplicate analysis at other forensic laboratories: "This strategic redundancy gives each lab an incentive to find the truth and apply rigorous scientific standards. Strategic redundancy should be accompanied by statistical review. For example, if a given lab produces an unusually large number of inconclusive findings, its procedures and practices should be examined. Competitive self regulation creates checks and balances."[2] Koppl adds, "Strategic redundancy works best if errors and biases are not correlated across labs. If all labs share the same biases, then strategic redundancy is less able to root out error and bias. Indeed, if competing labs all share the same strong bias, then strategic redundancy may make things worse by increasing the seeming legitimacy of what are, in fact, bogus results. It is necessary to create incentives for the discovery of error. The stronger such incentives are the more they will mitigate or overwhelm any biases. Without such incentives we have mere redundancy. When such incentives are in place, however, we have rivalrous redundancy."[2]

The difference between mere redundancy and rivalrous redundancy, as Koppl (2005) explains it, is that the laboratory that produces the most accurate results is rewarded monetarily: "If the labs disagree, there is an infallible adjudication procedure to determine who is right. The lab that told the truth will collect two money payments, one for performing the test, and one for discovering the other lab's error. The erroneous lab gets nothing. This situation creates an incentive to perform a careful and objective analysis. Each lab would prefer the other to play along by supporting the police theory. On the other hand, each lab always has an incentive to be truthful, either to avoid forfeiting its payment or to get a double payment if the other lab provides a false analysis. . . . Mere redundancy will not produce a truth-seeking system, but rivalrous redundancy will. This is a particularly likely outcome under a regime of information hiding."[2] Koppl adds, "It seems perfectly possible to create monetary penalties for deficient laboratories and to create, thereby, a reasonable real-world version of rivalrous redundancy."[2]

Koppl (2005) explains, "Competitive self regulation would create conditions of forensic science similar to the conditions of pure science. In pure science, research results are subject to the discipline of review and reproduction. I propose subjecting forensic scientists to the same discipline of review and reproduction. . . . New techniques will not solve the problem that forensic scientists do not operate in the sort of environment that encourages good science. They face the wrong set of incentives and pressures. New technologies or scientific advances will not solve this problem. The problem and its solution are not a matter of lab science, but of social science. Competitive self regulation puts forensic workers in the right environment to do the right thing."[2]

In order to facilitate a program of competitive self-regulation, Koppl (2005) says, an evidence control officer is needed to coordinate tasks among forensic examiners and to serve as a liaison between the prosecution or defense and the forensic laboratory. This individual would "serve as the filter between each examiner and any information about the case, whether it originated from without or from within the lab," as well as "decide not only generally what kinds of tests were needed, but what information about the case was needed to perform those tests, and the primary duty would be to maintain appropriate masking between the examiners and all sources of domain-irrelevant information."[2]

Koppl (2005) acknowledges that this evidence control officer could fall victim to the same behaviors he or she was trying to prevent: "The evidence control office may look every bit as monopolistic as the forensic worker in the current system. Several considerations suggest, however, that it is easy to structure the job . . . so that the position involves a low incentive to cheat, high costs to being discovered cheating, and a high probability of being caught if cheating is attempted."[2] Koppl explains that as he envisions the position, the functions are fairly mechanical, and if they are carried out in as a public of a fashion as possible, "they are less likely to be improperly carried out." Koppl also indicates that, "In the face of competition among labs, the evidence control officer has an incentive to adopt an above-the-fray attitude that helps maintain objectivity and discourage cheating. Moreover, if the officer should exhibit bias or share inappropriate information, the fact is more likely to be revealed if there are several labs observing the problem. Thus, strategic redundancy is a palliative limiting abuse in the function of the evidence control officer."[2] In addition, Koppl says that imposing stringent sanctions could ward off potential malfeasance on the individual's part.

In Koppl's (2005) proposal, forensic laboratories would undergo periodic statistical review, consisting of counting the number of cases falling into various categories: "In how many cases was a lab's findings found to be deficient when compared to the contradictory results of competing labs? How many cases led to conviction? How many to exoneration? In how many cases did a lab find the evidence to be inconclusive? And so on. If a lab is found to have an unusually high or low number of cases in any category, it should be investigated to learn why," Koppl explains, adding, "It might seem that there is no reason to look at the number of convictions. The question is how the lab does its work, not who goes to jail. But if the analyses of a given lab correspond to an anomalous number of convictions (whether large or small), then we have reason to inquire if there has been a breach in the wall of separation between the forensics lab and the prosecution or defense."[2]

A major tenet of Koppl's concept of competitive self-regulation is the division of labor among forensic examiners and the use of vouchers to address the problem of the perception that these forensic professionals work for law enforcement or for the prosecution, which potentially triggers bias. Koppl (2005) states, "This bias is combined with rules of discovery that make it hard for defense attorneys to challenge the supposed results of forensic tests. The consequence is that the sloppiest work may easily satisfy a jury, who cannot be expected to know about the difficulties of practical forensic science today."[2]

Koppl (2005) maintains that the interpretation of forensic test results should be separated from the task of performing the test: "Dividing test from interpretation and providing separate forensic interpreters for both sides would bring forensic evidence into the adversarial system of the courts. The common law system is based on the idea that the truth comes out best in an adversarial process. But, as we have seen, forensic evidence is largely excluded from the adversarial process. This exclusion from the adversarial system is a profound, needless, and inappropriate compromise of one of the most fundamental principles of our common law system. Separating out the task of interpretation could also be combined with the creation of standardized reports such that every expert having an ordinary knowledge in the field would be able to reproduce the test and interpret the results. Standardized reports would tend to reduce the unfortunate element of idiosyncrasy that still characterizes much forensic work."[2]

Koppl (2005) also espouses the voucher system embraced by Schulhofer and Friedman (1993), which would give public defenders an incentive to act in the interests of their clients. Koppl believes that indigent defendants should be provided with similar forensic vouchers and that they would "likely reduce the costs of police forensics."[2] If anything, this result would tend to increase the spending on defense lawyers. Stuntz (1997) argues that legislators may reduce funding of defense attorneys to "get tough on crime." My proposals would reduce this incentive by increasing the ability of the system to distinguish the guilty from the innocent. Indeed, improved forensics would tend to break the vicious circle Stuntz identifies. Court-mandated procedures make procedural arguments more attractive at the margin than material arguments, producing more acquittals on technicalities. Such acquittals induce reduced funding to defense spending, as well as increases in mandatory sentencing and in the number of crimes defined. Improved forensics would reduce the relative price of arguing the facts. Finally, it should be noted that Stuntz does not provide a clear mechanism establishing the links he claims to exist between legislation and the results of criminal procedure. In other words, as Stuntz admits (p. 5), his argument is speculative.

What may be the most controversial plank in Koppl's (2005) proposal is the privatization of competing forensic laboratories to turn them into "profit-making enterprises" that could potentially provide cost savings. Koppl asserts that the literature supports the idea of privatization: "As Megginson and Netter (2001) note, 'privatization tends to have the greatest positive impact...in competitive markets or markets that can readily become competitive.' Forensics is such an industry." Koppl explains, "The current situation is almost the reverse of a natural monopoly. Currently, a forensic lab's scale of operation is dependent on the size of the jurisdiction it serves. It is thus unable to exploit economies of scale. Under privatization, the same lab may serve many jurisdictions and thus enjoy economies of scale."[2]

Koppl (2005) says that privatization would "improve the ability of national governments to intervene in the operation of forensics labs, as least in the U.S.," adding, "Forensic labs are currently under the jurisdiction of local governments, which may adopt policies different from those the national government might choose. Privatization would open the way for national regulations. Privatization would reduce the cost of national regulation and, therefore, of intervention at the national level. Interventions that impose national standards and protocols would be easier under privatization. If interventions at the local level are undesirable in the forensics industry, whereas national regulations are desirable, then privatization would help create the right set of government regulations of forensic practice."[2]

According to Koppl (2005), the advantages of converting forensic laboratories into private entities include the benefits of increased competition, such as quality drivers and incentive for the development of new technology that can simultaneously lower costs. Koppl also believes that because private entities have a reputation to protect, they will strive for the highest level of service: "If demanders insist on a high-quality product, the market will provide just that."[2]

The fatal flaw of proposals such as Koppl's may lie in the costs required to execute this kind of an extensive reform effort. Koppl (2005) asserts that competitive self-regulation would add less than $300 to the costs incurred by the criminal justice system in each investigation and possible trial, based on annual laboratory budgets and including the expected value of time spent in court as an expert witness. Koppl explains further, "The Bureau of Labor Statistics reports that the average hourly and weekly earnings of production or non-supervisory workers on private payrolls in February 2003 was $15.34. At this value of time, the extra forensic analysis required by competitive self regulation would correspond to less than 20 working hours, or the opportunity cost of a day in jail for the average worker. The exaggerated sum of $300 is a small fraction of trial costs for the cases that go to trial. A small improvement in the quality of forensic analysis would induce compensating reductions in the social cost of the further crimes of guilty persons not convicted and of the loss of social output from innocent persons wrongly convicted. I believe it is fair to conclude that competitive self regulation is cost effective."[2]

Koppl (2005) advocates the implementation of fees to subsidize costs associated with analysis, citing work by Saks et al. (2001), who propose that "fees be charged to parties requesting tests and examinations" and that the "schedule of fees shall apply equally to all parties requesting tests and examinations." Koppl observes, "Right now, the marginal cost of a forensic test is often zero for the party requesting the test. The government has a third-party payer, the taxpayer. Thus, it is likely that needlessly wasteful tests are being conducted today. Saks et al. say, 'Because the tests are not without cost to the parties, the requesters will be more thoughtful about the knowledge expected to be obtained from the costs associated with testing.' Thus, the overall result of competitive self regulation might well be a reduction in the costs of forensic testing . . . competitive self regulation would require little or no additional overhead. Improved forensics would produce fewer costly appeals. The modest increases in the average cost of an individual trial would be more than compensated by a reduction in total number of proceedings."[2]

To further justify the added expense, Koppl (2005) invokes the high cost of the potential failure of forensic science: "We have no adequate measure of the costs of forensic mistakes today. A forensic mistake can put the wrong person in jail. When that happens, we may have one innocent person removed from a productive role in society and another guilty person left free to commit crimes. Each such failure of forensics has a high social cost. It may be that a very small increase in the reliability of police forensics will produce a very large decrease in the social cost of forensic mistakes. Unfortunately, we have no measures of the costs of forensic mistakes in the current system. Given our ignorance in this area, it would be a mistake to dismiss competitive self regulation as costly when we have no reliable measure of the costs of the mistakes produced under the current system."[2] Additionally, Koppl points out that competitive self-regulation could curtail unforeseen costs triggered by lawsuits stemming from faulty forensics.

Koppl and Kobilinsky

Koppl and Kobilinsky (2005), working from Koppl's earlier theory, outline a more specific approach to the implementation of the concept of forensic science administration; the impetus for this new doctrine of thought lies all around us: "The environment of forensic science has changed with DNA typing, the Daubert decision, the CSI effect, and other factors. The new environment has led to calls for higher standards of professionalism, verifiability, and scientific rigor in forensic science. The forensics community must answer such calls. In so doing, it should have the benefit of a clear scientific vision of forensic science as a social, legal, and political phenomenon. The emerging academic discipline of forensic science administration provides precisely such a scientific understanding of forensic science. Since the advent of fingerprints at the beginning of the last century, dramatic progress has been made in the forensic sciences. Surprisingly little effort, however, has been devoted to the scientific study of how to organize forensic science, including how to run our crime labs. Our knowledge of forensic technique is running ahead of our knowledge of how to manage forensic labs and workers. Forensic science administration fills this gap. Forensic science administration studies the organization of forensics labor in the criminal justice system, using the tools of social science and business administration. Forensic science administration studies forensic science within its legal and political context."

As one of its key tenets, Koppl and Kobilinsky (2005) assert that "Forensic science administration studies the link between the organization of forensic work and error rates in forensic science. They say that forensic science administration fills a void of knowledge created by the ambiguous intersection of advancing technology, evolving techniques, challenging human resources issues, and legal challenges to forensic evidence. Koppl and Kobilinsky explain that forensic science administration is a branch of social science that "studies the organization of forensics labor in the criminal justice system, using the tools of social science and business administration." They add, "Forensic science administration studies forensic science within its legal and political context. Forensic science tells us how an alert, skilled, unbiased, and conscientious expert can perform a useful test. It tells us nothing, however, about what arrangements best ensure that forensic scientists are alert, skilled, unbiased, and conscientious. Forensic science administration addresses that issue. Almost nothing has been done in this field of study and its very existence has been only dimly perceived in the past."

Indeed, the need for forensic science administration seems to spring from what Koppl and Kobilinsky (2005), as well as Saks and Koehler (2005), describe as a new national attention to previously invisible issues plaguing the forensic science community. A handful of highly publicized cases, such as those discussed in Chapters 4 and 7, appears to have unnerved some commentators who have resorted to anxious hand-wringing as they contemplate the impact on forensic science. Koppl and Kobilinsky state, "These cases and others like them seem to be attracting increasing public attention. Such negative attention may reduce the prestige and perceived reliability of forensic science. They also suggest that error rates in forensic science may be needlessly high. Both the loss of reputation and needlessly high error rates have the same consequence, namely, a tendency to reduce the actual and perceived value that forensic science adds to the American justice system. Here we have a case in which perception is reality in at least some degree. The perception that forensics is unreliable weakens its evidentiary force, which, in turn, reduces the real value it really adds to the judicial system." Koppl and Kobilinsky observe further, "Recent changes in the environment of forensic science have led to calls for higher standards of professionalism, verifiability, and scientific rigor in forensic science administration. At present there is little coordinated effort directed to studying forensic science administration and how it might respond to changes in its legal and social environment."

As if to mount an early offense to address their concept's detractors, as well as to build buy-in from the forensic science community, Koppl and Kobilinsky (2005) insist, "The new environment of forensics matters. Newspaper stories of 'faulty forensics' abound (McRoberts et al., 2004), defense attorneys are learning new strategies for questioning forensic evidence (Giannelli, 2003; Saks, 2003), political organizations such as the Innocence Project are publicizing (real or imagined) flaws in the system, and jurors are demanding higher standards of performance. These environmental factors put pressure on lab managers to adopt new and higher standards of professionalism, verifiability, and scientific rigor. The forensics community must meet the challenge of these environmental changes."

According to Koppl and Kobilinsky's (2005) vision, forensic science administration would promote improved understanding of forensic science as a legal, social, and political phenomenon, as well as improved forensic science administration within the criminal justice system. However, there is a catch: "We need dedicated scholars of forensic administration providing research, education, outreach, and policy espousal," they emphasize, adding, "Action on several fronts is required to meet this challenge. First, we need research on the principles of forensic science administration. Second, we need to create a separate academic discipline of forensic science administration. Just as we have the distinct academic discipline of public administration, we need a distinct academic discipline of forensic science administration. Third, we need outreach programs through which criminal justice practitioners could keep abreast of current developments in forensic science administration. Fourth and finally, we need policy espousal; we need experts in forensic science administration who will propose new laws, regulations, and government policies aimed at continuous improvement of forensic science administration. Such research, education, outreach and policy espousal would help the forensic science community meet the challenges facing forensic science today."

Few in the forensic science community would dispute Koppl and Kobilinsky's wish list, as it reflects what these professionals have been expressing as their needs for some time. However, these needs and issues have not been assembled comprehensively nor given a name by which to call any vehicle that serves to address them, until now. Where some controversy may spark is the way in which this vehicle operates, how it is driven, and by whom. For example, Koppl and Kobilinsky (2005) advocate for a far more aggressive research agenda within forensic science, with this research "closely related to the field of 'science studies.'" The forensic professional reading this text may very well identify with the need for improved research to shore up the scientific rigor of the field; however, he or she may next question why this research must then be divided into two traditions, Merton and Mannheim, as outlined by Koppl and Kobilinsky, in the fashion of traditional science studies. The forensic professional in the trenches is looking for real-world traction where the rubber meets the road, while theorists may delight in the chance to remove forensic science from the lab and encase it in an academic ivory tower. According to Koppl and Kobilinsky, "The broadly Mertonian tradition might be labeled 'conservative' in that it tends to support the view that science is relatively objective and truth-driven. In this tradition, the relative rationality and objectivity of science is not a product of any supposed virtues of individual scientists; it is the product of the social structure of science. Important representatives of this tradition today include Kitcher (1993) and Goldman (1999). Kitcher is explicitly engaged in a rearguard defense of science against its critics. The broadly Mannheimian tradition is 'radical' in that it tends to support the view that science is ideological and value-driven. Important representatives of this tradition today include Bloor (1976) and Fuller (1988); Butos and Koppl (2003) are Mertonians in the broad sense of the term." They add, "We declare ourselves fully for the broadly Mertonian tradition. Simon Cole seems to work within the broadly Mannheimian tradition. In our judgment, this difference makes a difference. It seems difficult to imagine that outside criticisms of forensic science could produce constructive change if the external critics are generally Mannheimian. On the other hand, useful suggestions for institutional improvement are not likely to emerge from within forensic science unless we take seriously the Mertonian principle that the relative rationality and objectivity of science is the product of the social structure of science."

Before forensic professionals scramble for their college science and philosophy texts to wage war against an unfamiliar concept, it should be emphasized that Koppl and Kobilinsky are attempting to represent the interests of both camps—those in the field and those in the academic arena. However, it remains to be seen how their theory about forensic science administration will translate into practice, given the current challenges within academia and especially related to instruction in forensic science.

Koppl and Kobilinsky (2005) call for the creation of a separate academic discipline of forensic science administration, akin to current programs in public administration, healthcare administration, and business administration. Specifically, this new discipline would "provide a way for forensic scientists and the managers and directors of forensics laboratories to receive training in the established principles of forensic science administration," they say, adding, "Presumably, the preponderance of such training would be through continuing education vehicles such as seminars and certification programs. Such training would be provided by recognized specialists in forensic science administration. It might be appropriate to consider adding such training to the requirements of university programs in forensic science. Forensic scientists would be educated on the nature of the environment in which forensic science is practiced and the challenges thereby created for forensic science; and they would be given training in how to meet the challenges facing forensic science."

As we will see in an upcoming section, training and education of forensic practitioners has not been a priority for the community until very recently, when the Department of Justice established recommendations for a curriculum for undergraduate and graduate levels of study in forensic science. Education is at the top of the agendas of most of the professional associations representing the forensic science disciplines, and it is one of the foci of a number of new studies and initiatives we will explore in Chapter 16. Within this discourse on forensic science education, Koppl and Kobilinsky's concept of forensic science administration may be a welcome way to organize this sudden upwelling of attention on the lifelong training of new and veteran forensic scientists and managers.

Training in forensic science administration, according to Koppl and Kobilinsky (2005), would serve the needs of individual forensic scientists, as "Training would be aimed in part at helping forensic scientists prepare for testimony in open court. For example, it would help them defend the scientific integrity of fingerprint analysis in a Daubert hearing." In addition, training in forensic science administration would serve the needs of forensic labs, as it would "help crime labs to adapt scientific protocols to the contingencies of daily practice of high throughput lab work." Koppl and Kobilinsky explain further, "PCR DNA analysis, for example, is extremely reliable if all scientific protocols are followed scrupulously. These protocols, however, are hard to follow (Teichroeb, 2004). Merely greeting a co-worker may cause contamination of a sample from minute bits of saliva, phlegm, or mucus released when speaking. Forensic science administration can design and test protocols that reflect not only the scientific requirements of PCR DNA analysis, but also the contingencies of daily crime-lab work. Training in forensic science administration will then allow forensic scientists to understand and implement such protocols."

In general, the overall institutional needs of the forensic science community would be served by the new discipline's attention to fostering long-term improvements, Koppl and Kobilinsky (2005) say, mandated by ever-evolving technology and new demands on the forensic workforce. Specifically, they add, the discipline of forensic science administration could address what Koppl (2005) outlines as the eight features of the organization of forensic science that needlessly reduce the quality of work performed by forensic scientists: monopoly on forensic evidence; lab dependence on law enforcement; poor quality control systems; questionable information sharing; a lack of division of labor between forensic analysis and interpretation; lack of forensic counsel for indigent defendants; lack of competition among forensic counselors; and public ownership of forensic laboratories. In addition, forensic science administration embraces the concept of competitive self-regulation (Koppl, 2005) outlined earlier.

As forensic science administration is explored by the various stakeholders in the larger criminal justice community, Koppl and Kobilinsky (2005) remain confident that it represents a sound approach to reformation. They emphasize, "Forensic science has enjoyed a presumption of validity and reliability for decades. New demands for professionalism, verifiability, and scientific rigor ushered in by DNA typing and other events have weakened that presumption and threaten to create the disastrous presumption that forensic science is junk science. The forensic science community has two choices. It can hide from this sea change in the social, political, and legal environment of forensic science or it can meet new challenges with new strategies. It hardly needs saying that the first strategy will produce no good and will lead, ultimately, to the complete discrediting of the most vitally scientific element of our justice system. The second path is our only viable option. That second path is the path of forensic science administration, a new discipline filling a vital need."

HAS ANYONE ASKED THE FORENSIC COMMUNITY?

As we did in Chapter 2, we again ask, has anyone asked the forensic community what it needs? Commentators are quick to ascribe to the community a list of fast fixes, but it is critical to see where the community itself believes time, money, and attention most need to be diverted. In a 2004 report produced by the NIJ, the forensic science community identified the following recommendations springing from their issues, concerns, and needs:

1. Manpower and equipment needs:
   - Certain forensic disciplines have significant manpower shortfalls, including crime scene processing, digital evidence analysis, latent fingerprint examination, firearms examination, document analysis, and toxicology, and these should be addressed.
   - An organized attempt should be made to determine the quantity of forensic service providers outside crime laboratories.

- There should be outreach to all forensic service providers, including non-crime lab providers, to advise them of professional and governmental assistance programs.
- The needs of the forensic community should be monitored on an ongoing, systematic basis.
- Government support of the Automated Fingerprint Identification System (AFIS) should be contingent on interoperability between AFIS systems of different manufacturers, allowing an "enter once, search many" capability. This interoperability must address not only a seamless exchange of fingerprint data among states and among state and local systems; that same seamless interoperability must be developed among all state and local systems and the latent print search capability of the FBI's International Automated Fingerprint Identification System (IAFIS).
- A quality medico-legal death investigation system should be encouraged. Professional death investigation systems should examine the need for fully trained and qualified forensic pathologists with competent investigative and support staffs. Specifically, states should reexamine their current medico-legal death investigation systems to determine whether they can conduct appropriate, timely, and reliable death investigations.

2. Training and education:
   - Professional models for training and establishing competency should be encouraged.
   - Minimum standards should be established for each forensic discipline for equipment, techniques, training, and documentation, including testing of personnel to confirm minimum competency.
   - Collaborations, innovative approaches, recognized training centers, and alternative delivery systems for forensic analyst and manager training should be considered to reduce training costs.
   - Quality graduate education in forensic science programs should be encouraged. A program to eliminate or forgive student loans for graduates who obtain full-time employment in public forensic science institutions is one alternative that should be considered.
   - The FBI should increase the number of Universal Latent Workstation systems to state and local law enforcement so that the full capacity of the IAFIS may be utilized.
   - Forensic science training programs at the FBI should be reinstated or expanded.
   - Tuition assistance should be provided to encourage enrollment in university forensic science degree programs.

3. Professionalism and accreditation standards:
   - The forensic community supports accreditation of organizations and certification of practitioners.
   - Crime laboratories need dedicated staff to support quality assurance programs.

4. Collaboration among federal, state, and local forensic service providers:
   - A formal mechanism, such as an advisory board or focus group, should be established to facilitate coordination and collaboration between federal laboratories and the forensic community.
   - The forensic science organizations support the creation of a national forensic science commission to assess the needs of the forensic science community and to stimulate public awareness of and interest in the uses of forensic technology to solve crimes. The commission should be asked to undertake a comprehensive review of the role of forensic science in the criminal justice system, cost/benefit analysis of the value of forensic science to the administration of justice, needs of forensic science providers, and policy issues with respect to forensic science.
   - Information sharing and coordination with federal agencies should be supported.
   - The federal government must strengthen the support given to crime labs and other crime scene/disaster scene first responders with respect to terrorism or other events that might result in mass casualties, including support for training, equipment, and coordination of activities.

Of particular concern is the training of crime scene responders in the safe handling of evidence that may be contaminated with biological, chemical, or radiological material.

■ Forensic science providers need greater awareness of state and federal assistance and programs, especially those outside the traditional crime laboratory.

■ The federal government should conduct scientific research to improve the practice of forensic science and address emerging technology challenges from criminals, particularly in the area of electronic crime.

A MODEL MEDICAL EXAMINER SYSTEM

Up to this point, far more attention has been focused on reforming forensic laboratory science and criminalistics than on reforming the medico-legal death investigation system. Much of the push for reform of medico-legal offices has come from within the community, by individual practitioners who are advocating for a transition to a more uniform, all-medical examiner system. As we saw in Chapters 6 and 8, the medico-legal death investigation community is a patchwork quilt of jurisdictions with varying standards and levels of expertise, as determined by whether it is a coroner-led, medical examiner-led, or dual-practitioner system. The concept of an all-medical examiner system has been championed by small numbers of medico-legal practitioners, but the idea has not gained traction on a national level. Proponents say it's simply a matter of time before the idea gains momentum, while detractors say there are too many financial, administrative, and manpower barriers.

"On paper, and intuitively, that concept makes sense," says Randy Hanzlick, M.D., chief medical examiner for Fulton County, Georgia, and professor of forensic pathology at Emory University School of Medicine. "It's a no-brainer because this concept ensures that there are experienced physicians trained in pathology and sub-specializing in forensic pathology, who are investigating deaths in this country. The problem right now is the manpower issue; if we converted to a national all-ME system, however, we would need great numbers of forensic pathologists, and we simply can't meet that need currently—there are just not enough to go around. So, in promoting the conversion to an all-ME system, one must also promote the training of forensic pathologists. There is a glaring need for more forensic pathologists in this country."

"Personally, I think the all-medical examiner system is impractical—not because it isn't a great idea, but because of the logistics involved," says Mary Fran Ernst, a medico-legal death investigator for the St. Louis County Medical Examiner's Office, director of medico-legal education at St. Louis University School of Medicine, and a past president of the AAFS. "There are fewer than 500 board-certified forensic pathologists currently working in the United States, yet there are more than 3,100 counties in the country. The concept is to eliminate coroner system and replace it with an all-medical examiner system; I definitely think that 95 percent of the time, a system run by a board-certified forensic pathologist is superior, but how can you ever have enough of these highly skilled professionals to make the concept a reality? What are you going to do about the counties that don't have a forensic pathologist willing to run the medico-legal office? Yes, I would like to see a board-certified forensic pathologist make every call related to cause and manner of death for every decedent, but we physically can't do it. At least not until we train more people and ensure that these professionals receive the salary and respect equal to their colleagues who are general pathologists or other physicians. So, an all-medical examiner system is a wonderful goal, but until we have our ducks in a row, it won't happen."

Ernst adds, "I'm not saying we shouldn't strive toward it, however. I would like to see board-certified forensic pathologists stationed strategically across the country to run the medico-legal offices and determine cause and manner of death, but then utilize those coroners who are very, very good at their jobs as chief investigators for their jurisdictions, working with the death investigators to bring information back to the pathologists. That way, these former coroners are under the guidance of the forensic pathologists, and they know what the rules, standards, and expectations are."

The most vocal supporter of the all-ME system is Victor Weedn, J.D., M.D., a professor at Duquesne University. "I believe passionately that the system can be made right again, and fashioned into something that is outstanding. There are some great people in forensic pathology and they are doing a yeoman's job; it's not always understood or appreciated. It seems clear to me that the most progressive systems in the country are all medical examiner systems; however, most people outside the field have a harder time recognizing there is a problem."

Weedn says he has approached the National Conference of Commissioners on Uniform State Laws (NCCUSL) in hopes that they may write model medical examiner legislation. NCCUSL is a bipartisan organization that writes model legislation and promotes its adoption in the legislatures of the 50 states and provides research, technical assistance, and opportunities for policy makers to exchange ideas on the most pressing state issues. Weedn says the reputation of the NCCUSL can help get the issue in front of state legislators.

"The NCCUSL formed a formal committee to consider the proposition," Weedn reports, "and that committee is recommending going forward to actually draft model ME legislation. The NCCUSL is made up of a group of two representatives from every state. Generally the people who act as commissioners work for the state's legislative reference bureau, which is the group that drafts legislation for the state. So when the NCCUSL drafts legislation, it immediately goes back to the states for consideration. There are model laws and uniform laws. A uniform law is a law to be adopted among the states without change, meaning it is adopted verbatim, exactly as drafted. Uniform laws are needed when it is important that all states have the same kind of law; for example, so that businesses can act across state borders with confidence that they are meeting the same legal criteria for a financial transaction. Model laws will not necessarily be adopted whole and unchanged; rather, states will change the law or adopt only what they want to fit their particular jurisdictional needs and philosophy. So essentially, the NCCUSL will say, 'This is what we think you ought to do,' and states are then free to make changes to the law, and to adopt or not to adopt." Weedn continues, "I believe that if this model legislation is drafted, then, there is a real possibility for movement. I think there are many people and agencies who want qualified, credentialed people working in death investigation."

"I expect resistance to come from three major pockets, the first being existing lay coroners," Weedn explains, "because they see their jobs going away. I don't think they have a great argument for their preservation. For a long time the National Research Council has been saying, 'Replace the coroner system with the medical examiner system.' Well, every one of those coroners is entrenched. They like what they are doing; it's a little bit of extra money on the side, they get some publicity in the newspaper from time to time, and they are part of the political machinery. They think, 'Hey, this is a pretty good gig. I have the title of coroner and I can do my funeral home directing,' or whatever they do in their day jobs. So when proposed legislation to do away with the coroners comes up, they fight it. In coroner systems, of course, there is no medical examiner present to say, 'We really ought to change this system.' If it's a mixed system, the coroners will probably outnumber the medical examiners. Politics has been the biggest impediment to the progress of the U.S. medico-legal death investigation system. I have suggested that all coroners be immediately hired as medico-legal death investigators for medical examiner offices so their positions can be saved at least for the short term. That may help to allay some resistance." Weedn continues, "When you have all these coroners throughout the country, there are two ways to approach the transition; either let them fail so that they have to come to the medical examiners for assistance, or you can try to train them so they function better. They may not be great, but they at least make the system work at some level. Most medical examiners work with the coroners around them, training them and getting them sufficiently up to speed enough so that the medico-legal system limps along. People on the outside see that it's 'working' but do not recognize problems."

A second pocket of opposition is represented by the states that may not want an all-medical examiner system because they may not want to pay for it. "If the change is to go to a state system, then it is a new cost to that government. I recognize that's a problem, but quality death investigation ought to be available throughout a state and most counties simply can't afford it," Weedn says.

The third area of resistance, according to Weedn, is incumbent medical examiners. "The all-medical examiner system rocks the boat," he says. "Some medical examiners are for it until they think, 'Wait a minute, you mean I won't be chief of my operation anymore? I have to respond to someone at the state capitol?' So local medical examiners may object, and if these local medical examiners *and* the coroners object, *and* the states say they don't want to spend the money, well, that's a pretty big hurdle."

Forensic pathologist, attorney, and medical-legal consultant Cyril Wecht, M.D., J.D., clinical professor at the University of Pittsburgh School of Medicine, and adjunct professor at the Duquesne University School of Law, comments, "There's no question there are big defects in the elected coroner system; however, that is not the same as saying we should have an appointed medical examiner system universally and forever to ensure a greater degree of professionalism. Some of the biggest problems and some of the most controversial cases have involved medical examiner systems. Just because someone is a good forensic pathologist, does not mean that he or she is going to be a good administrator and be able to run the medico-legal office properly. Additionally, to say that the medical examiner system is an independent, autonomous office, is an oxymoron if it has been appointed by someone other than God. To begin with, if you are appointed by somebody, are you truly independent? You say well, there are protections such as removal for cause only, there are specified terms, certain qualifications; those things are safeguards, I realize, but I don't think you can ever truly ensure a significant degree of independence."

Weedn says a significant source of inertia is the cynical defeatist attitude that many in the community have: "'I have been in the business for 30 years and things never get better.' I believe that the forensic pathology community in general has a Depression-era mentality. In the Great Depression, people were trying just to survive and as a result, an entire generation was so starved and deprived, it essentially became a risk-averse generation—a significant body of sociology literature confirms this. It was hard for people to see the bigger picture because they were too busy surviving. If you look at the medical examiner community, it has been starved to death. There seems to be a generation of pessimists who do not believe that the government will ever come to its aid to increase its capacity and facilities. That group may have to die off, and a new generation must rise up behind it to embrace new ways of thinking. It has been decades since the first National Research Council report advocated attempts to create physician-run organizations. It may be that we will have to wait for yet another generation in order to see change take place."

Forensic pathologist Michael Dobersen, M.D., Ph.D., coroner for Arapahoe County in Colorado and president of the Colorado Coroner Association, says that an all-medical examiner system would have its advantages, provided it is executed properly. "I suspect that every state that is a coroner state has had some experience with a citizen who is unhappy with the coroner, goes to his or her legislator, and then the legislator tries to turn the state into a medical examiner state without getting input from the coroners or from anyone else," Dobersen says. "Having said that, I think an all-medical examiner system would be good, but because the coroners are so politically active, it would encounter resistance. I know that Victor Weedn has been pushing hard for this model legislation. I am on the CAP committee for forensic pathology, and Victor used to be part of this committee, made up of 12 forensic pathologists; some are medical examiners and some are coroners. We were in near-unanimous agreement that we would not endorse Victor's idea simply because we didn't really agree with the way he painted the picture of the medico-legal system being in dire straits. I think there are problems, but I think we all do the best we can and in some ways the model medical examiner system would not really solve these problems. We thought it was too simplistic of a fix. It's similar to the healthcare system; we all agree that it needs to be fixed, but no one really has a good idea about how to do it."

Members of the forensic pathology community say they are frustrated by the need for improvement within the medico-legal system yet they are frequently shackled by the impediments to progress.

"I am not optimistic about anything changing significantly on the national level, outside of individual states recognizing that they have a problem and they need to address it," Hanzlick comments. "Unfortunately, that level of realization is sometimes achieved only when there is a major screw-up in a case; only then will people be convinced that the system needs fixing, or that we at least need more funding for better training and education, and improved infrastructure. I'm not optimistic that any assistance like that is going to come any time soon. When the Model Post-Mortem Examinations Act of 1954 was established, there was a sort of rush toward the conversion of coroner systems to medical examiner systems for a couple of decades; a number of states and counties converted, and then the effort slowed down and died for the most part. I believe what's happened is that in most areas of the country, the geographical and financial dynamics are such that the jurisdictions that could make the conversion have done so, and the rest don't have the population, the tax base, or the funding to do it, so they stay the way they are."

Hanzlick explains that when it comes to funding, local jurisdictions are reluctant to combine their resources with larger surrounding regions: "County officials have their pride, and they seem reluctant to relinquish control of their county-based operations—that can be an obstacle to progress in some ways. Although local death investigation services are highly desirable, in many areas of the country, regionalization and pooling of resources is the only way they are going to be able to effect change in the quality of medico-legal death investigation. I think the funding will have to come at the state level; whether that is achieved with some kind of federal assistance, I don't know. I would be cautious, however, to go the route of the health departments, for example. They receive funding from the federal Centers for Disease Control and Prevention (CDC) to do various things, and then the states end up controlling that money and it doesn't necessarily get down to the local level where it may be needed the most. In some areas, funding may even have to come from the local jurisdictions, which is going to be tough."

Marcella Fierro, M.D., chief medical examiner for the commonwealth of Virginia and co-director of the Virginia Institute of Forensic Science and Medicine, says she supports an all-medical examiner system but emphasizes that federal support is critical. "It needs a federal sponsor, whether it is supported by the U.S. Department of Health and Human Services, or the U.S. Department of Justice, or the U.S. Department of Homeland Security," Fierro explains. "With a federal sponsor and the funding that accompanies it, I think you might see something happen. If only the medical examiner community supports this model legislation, I don't think we'll get much traction, because it will appear as if it is only in our own best interests, even though it will benefit the entire death investigation system."

Fierro continues, "I don't think county administrators have bought into the all-medical examiner system for several reasons; first of all, they are always wary of new programs because they don't know how much they will cost. Secondly, they don't know what they don't have, meaning, if it's not broken, don't fix it. If there are no obvious problems with their coroners, they have no inspiration to fix the system. I think if it can be demonstrated that an all-medical examiner system is more economical than a coroner system or a mixed system, you can get their attention. If it appears that an all-medical examiner system would improve criminal prosecution or public health and safety, they might become even more interested. In Iowa, the medical society took an active interest in establishing a medical examiner system; the medical school got on board, and finally the system was changed. It takes time, and it takes interested partners."

Fierro adds, "For example, the medical examiner system in Virginia was actually put in place by the General Assembly with the assistance of the Virginia Bar Association and the Medical Society of Virginia. It was an incredible act of cooperation. These groups joined together to promote the medical examiners. So, if you can get the folks who receive the services and the people who provide the services to agree that something is worthwhile, and then make it an important plank in their political platform, you might get somewhere. We must get the public health sector on board because they need medical examiners' assistance with bioterrorism and homeland security-related issues. And we must get law enforcement on board with the promise that more competent forensic pathologists mean better testimony in court." Partnerships are one thing, but funding is at the crux of any collaboration. "You must always scrutinize the funding component," Fierro maintains. "The state might have to bear some of the costs so that counties are not bearing the full brunt of the expenses related to cases."

Hanzlick says the model medical examiner legislation would be beneficial because it lays out the basic principles of an optimized system, but he adds that conflict would arise between a national law and existing state laws. "You must decide whether or not coroners are or are not constitutional officers, and I think there is reluctance to take away local authority" Hanzlick explains. "Just like the feds, in theory, don't like to intervene with what states are doing; states don't necessarily like to intervene with what local cities and jurisdictions are doing, and whenever you have that kind of a split, you get into complicated funding issues. A small county can't really support a full-blown system. That to me is the major obstacle. But that aside, you still have to deal with abolishing elected offices, which is a difficult thing to do. You also have to remember that there are good coroners and not-so-good medical examiners just like as there are good medical examiners and not-so-good coroners. The best way to go about it is to ensure that the coroner (and medical examiner) systems which are underfunded or not well developed at least have resources and access to services they need. This may be a feasible interim measure until we can figure out what will work best. Personally, I don't foresee a federalized system, and I don't think we need a federal death investigation system."

Hanzlick says that whether or not an all-medical examiner system comes to fruition in the United States anytime soon, a critical step toward increased professionalism and reform for the community was the adoption by the National Association of Medical Examiners (NAME) of forensic pathology performance standards (see Chapter 8). "While they admittedly may not really be standards, they represent a goal to shoot for, and they define what is considered to be suitable set of professional practices for death investigation. It creates a framework for any jurisdiction contemplating a revamping of its system." Hanzlick isn't ruling out an eventual move toward an all-medical examiner system, but notes, "Governments are slow on the uptake, and they need data to reassure them. That's why I think everyone is anxiously awaiting some kind of national report that examines the true state of forensic science and forensic pathology. Many see the establishment of some kind of national forensic science commission as an important first step toward system improvement."

The future of model medical examiner legislation remains unclear for now. "No model legislation is perfect for every state, but generally, the core elements are good for everybody," Fierro states. "It's a big disappointment that we have not seen more movement on this concept. To implement any concept, you need a constituency that desires it and supports it. Governments are responsive to constituents' needs, but they also won't put something in place that isn't perceived as being needed urgently. It ties back into the fact that most jurisdictions' death investigation systems, even if they are medical examiner systems, don't rank high as a priority for many state officials. After all, the dead have no constituency. Many of the people we take care of have even less of a constituency. In violent deaths, many of them are criminals, and they have no constituency. No one is out there saying, 'Yes, John Doe was a criminal but he deserves to have a decent autopsy and a competent person to testify in court about it.' We need to rethink our attitudes toward death investigation for the betterment of the living and the dead."

RECOMMENDATIONS FOR IMPROVEMENT OF THE MEDICO-LEGAL DEATH INVESTIGATION SYSTEM

As we saw in Chapter 8, a symposium was held in 2003 by the National Academies to address issues pertaining to the quality of the U.S. medico-legal death investigation system. Participants suggested that the system could be improved by doing the following:

- *Creating a referral-based medical examiner system:* A county-based (local) system would be best with regard to the need for communication, travel, and investigative response time but may be impossible because of an insufficient population or tax base. A referral-based medical examiner system could improve the function of coroner systems that do not have ready access to qualified pathologists and needed services.
- *Ensuring that death investigation systems are headed by trained and qualified medical professionals:* The qualifications of those in charge of and working in death investigations need to be raised at virtually all job levels in many areas of the United States. Inspection and accreditation of systems should eventually be required.
- *Increasing the investment in personnel and facilities:* Increases in medical examiner salaries and incomes are essential, as current salaries are substandard and need to be higher to attract qualified people. Increasing the level of education, training, and qualifications of death investigators, and in modernization of facilities, is also critical.
- *Revisiting of the Model Post-Mortem Examinations Act of 1954:* This model legislation was developed by the National Association of Counties to promote the shift from coroners to professional medical examiners trained and credentialed in medicine. Death investigation statutes in various states should be more uniform and modernized.

Regarding reform of the U.S. medico-legal death investigation system, Hanzlick (2003) offered the following opinions, which he said a proper study might be able to turn into solidified conclusions:

- A county-based system makes the most sense when communication, travel, investigative response, and data are considered but may not be possible due to insufficient population or tax base to support it.
- A referral-based medical examiner system is a reasonable system to improve the function of coroner systems that do not have ready access to qualified pathologists and needed services.
- If medical examiner systems are to replace coroner systems completely, population distribution and tax base will require a district or regional system in many areas of the country.
- If medical examiner systems are to replace coroners systems throughout the country, investigative personnel will be needed locally to perform investigative functions formerly done by the coroner; this will cost considerable money if death scenes are to be adequately investigated and autopsies are to be done when indicated.
- Qualifications for those who are in charge of a death investigation system and for those who work in it need to be elevated at virtually all job levels in many areas of the country.
- Death investigation offices should be independent administrative units that are independent of law enforcement and other government bodies and should be funded at a level to operate professionally and competently.
- Measures should be taken to promote and eventually require the inspection and accreditation of medico-legal death investigation systems.
- The expansion of medical examiner systems has stalled primarily because of geopolitical factors related to population distribution, tax base issues, and a need for cooperation among governments, combined with an inadequate pool of qualified professionals who could manage and operate such systems.
- Accredited training in forensic pathology needs to be expanded, and all training positions should be funded.
- Medical examiner salaries and incomes are substandard and need to improve to attract qualified individuals.
- Measures should be in place to permit medical examiners to augment their salaries, especially when they are low.
- Death investigation systems should be funded at an adequate and more uniform and adjusted per capita level.
- County systems seem to be better funded than state systems, and state systems should be brought in line with these.
- There are not enough forensic pathologists to conduct all medico-legal investigations of death, and evolving trends may impose even greater demand for forensic pathologists.
- The demand for forensic pathologists seems disparate with typical salaries.
- The Model Post-Mortem Examinations Act of 1954 needs to be revisited, and death investigation statutes in the states could be more uniform and modernized.
- Evolving trends will create a need fore more educated, trained, and qualified death investigators; plans are needed to address this.
- Death investigation routinely involves analysis of medical information, medical findings, and the performance of medical procedures, so it only makes sense that death investigation systems be run by trained, qualified medical professionals.

The 2004 NAME report says that to address the deficiencies within forensic death investigation services, "the federal government should act to ensure that the nation is blanketed by forensic pathologist-based medico-legal death investigation to ensure adequate competent medico-legal death investigation no matter where a murder is committed or a public health threat is posed." Specifically, NAME recommends the following:

- Congress should fully fund the Paul Coverdell (National Forensic Science Improvement) Act.
- The federal government should develop an active interest in medico-legal death investigation and should designate lead agency assignment.
- The federal government should ensure medico-legal death investigation by adequately supported and professionally staffed forensic pathologist–based death investigation systems.
- The U.S. Department of Health and Human Services should establish policies and programs to encourage and enable more physicians to enter the field of forensic pathology and pursue their employment within medical examiner systems, and to retain currently practicing forensic pathologists.
- The federal government should support the NAME accreditation program and NAME's development of professional performance parameters for medico-legal death investigation.
- Medical examiners should be designated as homeland security first responders, eligible for first responder funds.
- The federal government should establish a federal medical examiner's liaison office within the Department of Homeland Security.
- The federal government should develop and fund a system of information sharing between medical examiners' offices and relevant federal government agencies.
- The federal government should sponsor research and policy discussions on forensic pathology and medico-legal death investigation issues.

Members of the forensic pathology community cultivate wish lists for their field; however, as Dobersen says, "We often don't think about it because we don't think it's going to happen. At the top of my wish list is that every state would have a regional medico-legal center, and the states would be connected at the federal level so activities are coordinated and practices are standardized. States would have a regional medical examiner, with the coroners and death investigators reporting to one central place. I realize that initially, it would require a big outlay of money, but in the long run I think there would be inherent efficiencies and overall, the system would be more efficient and more uniform."

Hanzlick says he would like to see every state assemble a group that could examine the specific medico-legal issues and determine how various jurisdictions could work together to resolve them. "After they identify the possibilities at the state level, they could then start planning what kind of federal assistance is necessary to improve the system. The states must identify the problems, the funding issues, the training and education challenges, and come up with a report for the governor addressing what they think they need. I think that approach would be a lot more successful than trying to attack it on the federal level. As an example, when the child-fatality review panels were being established under the Juvenile Justice Act, the feds essentially said, 'You have to put these things into place in your state by a certain year or you are not going to receive certain federal funding. Sure enough, over the years, states—at least to some degree—have developed those types of programs. That type of incentive would help here, at least to bring our needs to a national level of attention, and the feds would be more willing to support some kind of initiative if the states demonstrated their interest and commitment to the issues. The feds can help, but they need not control the systems.'"

"I don't expect that the feds will wave a magic wand and provide everything that we need," remarks Kurt Nolte, M.D., assistant chief medical investigator for the New Mexico Office of the Medical Investigator, and professor of pathology at the University of New Mexico School of Medicine. We won't see medical examiner systems supplanting all coroner systems immediately, but the feds could create a system of inducements so that over time, we make that transition. That effort would have to be coupled with increased manpower, training, and better salaries for forensic pathologists. There are some real issues that serve as barriers to this conversion, including statutory and constitutional changes, organizational changes, training changes, but that doesn't mean it can't be done."

Fierro says she hopes for the day when medical examiners are recognized for their contributions to the medico-legal system. "We have been such a quiet component of the infrastructure for so long that no one pays attention to us," she says. "I hope that our interests will be represented on Capitol Hill by the Consortium of Forensic Science Organizations (CFSO), and that our issues will be heard. Our needs aren't met, I suspect, because we are taken for granted. We're like clean air and fresh water—people expect it to be there, and unless we have mass failures of the system, there is no realization there should have been something there but wasn't. Our breakdowns constitute a multi-level failure, from the local level up through the state level, straight to the federal government, so our reform efforts have to be likewise."

Fierro continues, "I'd like to see further evolution into a model where we have groups of counties serviced by a forensic pathologist within a medical examiner system, maybe headed up by a commissioner, or have a chief medical examiner responsible for handling administration of the system. I think it's possible to evolve and it's possible to do it economically, and it's possible to generate a better product . . . but only if the end users of the system help us demand more for the system and for its service providers. It has to come from the people who receive the service. I am guardedly optimistic about the future of medico-legal death investigation, but going it alone only gets you so far; you must have buy-in from partners who will assist you in seeking the funding, the infrastructure that you need. No major changes for the better will happen without buy-in from public health, from prosecutors and defense attorneys, from law enforcement, and from anyone else who interfaces with the death investigation system. I've always got my hand out, ready to grab anyone and pull them in as a partner for change, because I won't get anything if I don't. It does require spunk, but I don't know any better," she says, laughing. "If I want something for my medico-legal office, I first figure out how I am going to get it, and if I have to make 10 friends to do it, well, line them up!"

Predicting the future of forensic science is tenuous at best. Inman and Rudin (2001) observe, "Especially in the current climate, where technology is advancing at warp speed, it is sometimes all one can do is to hang onto the trailing edge, never mind forecast future directions."[1]

SIDEBAR 15.2 FORENSIC SCIENCE SCRUTINY AND REFORM ACROSS THE POND

The desire to improve forensic science knows no borders; countries other than the United States are wrestling with the same issues that face the American criminal justice system. England and Australia are two countries long considered to be on the leading edge of forensic science; however, like the United States, they are also in the process of conducting serious scrutiny and reform of the field.

Magnusson (1996) observes, "Forensic scientists in Australia are watched more carefully and the profession has been made more accountable than ever before, but it is still agonizingly difficult to judge the quality of

Continues on next page

forensic science's contribution to justice. Apart from strong reactions to sensational cases in which science played a major role, it is hardly ever evaluated, certainly not in any systematic way." Magnusson undertook an unscientific survey of forensic scientists in four Australian states, hoping to extract their views about science in the Australian legal process, and reports, "The results were rather alarming. Alongside the ethics, professionalism, detachment, and skill was a large dose of cynicism. Few thought that science was serving the community up to its potential and none thought that courts were using scientific evidence scientifically. None had any confidence that a court would find the truth if they unexpectedly found themselves facing incriminating scientific evidence, charged with a crime they did not commit. So, at least one group of knowledgeable people believes that science in courtrooms needs some reform." Magnusson notes further, "The agenda for reform is easy to state. How hard will it be to produce it?"

Magnusson (1996) is quick to point to the improvements in the quality of the laboratory science and its courtroom presentation in Australia over the past two decades: "Robust systems have been introduced to assure the community that most of the laboratory science is of high quality, and that the practitioners are ready for change about as quickly as the changes in science and technology demand.... In Australia, as in other democracies with similar justice systems, science can still fail in the courtroom. However, human failure is now much more likely to be the cause than a scientific failure in the laboratory. Automated equipment and better methodologies solve some human problems but others are less easy to mechanize. Scientists worry most about the way the evidence will be dealt with in court, but there is potential for failure at every stage."

Magnusson enumerates a short list of desired reforms not dissimilar to that proposed by reformers in the United States; hot-button issues include the separation of powers, issues relating to admissibility of forensic evidence, and the contamination of forensic evidence. Regarding the need for a separation of powers, Magnusson (1996) observes, "Some errors result from the way the evidence was handled while still on its way to the laboratory. Others derive from an inadequate attention to the separation of powers. The rule for investigators must be different from the rule for experts. The former must look for evidence that will incriminate but scientists must test the evidence hard to see if it might exonerate. They should only claim value for a report if all alternative explanations have been rigorously excluded. Science loses its special value if it is owned by only one side. The aim must be to install proper, even-handed practices in all the sub-disciplines and, as well, control the pre-laboratory part of the process." Magnusson bemoans a similar lack of support of forensic science by stakeholders: "Science is science whatever its use in the community and, of all the uses, the service of justice should surely entitle a scientist to the full support of the scientific professions. Sadly the professions have never offered their help to the courts in the difficult job of assessing an increasingly complex science. And the courts have never let slip the suggestion that they need any. Now, maybe, it is time for courts to receive help from the independent scientific authorities, apply the standards of accuracy developed by the professions and forego the old idea of hearing only what happens to be presented to the court."

Admissibility issues seem to be somewhat universal. Australian researcher Magnusson (1996) states, "Admissibility calls for a yes-or-no answer: is the science well enough done to be safe for the jury to hear? If not it should not be admitted. Of course, but the primary question is 'How could a non-technical court know what's safe and what's not?' to which the answer is 'Don't let science into the court without the information needed to give it a proper scientific assessment.' If it isn't scientifically assessable, it should not be admissible." Magnusson continues, "If judges in pre-trial hearings were provided with the criteria that scientists would use they could easily become competent in ruling scientific evidence admissible or inadmissible. The jury can then decide its weight. Otherwise, the jury has to do two incommensurable tasks together: determine the validity of the science to count as evidence and estimate the reliability of the evidence to be used to convict. The second, not the first, is where their real competence lies. The two tasks can easily contaminate each other. The danger is especially severe when the strength of a strong item of evidence leads a jury to disregard the sloppiness with which it was gained. Similarly, the weakness of weak evidence could easily be ignored if the highly competent manner in which it was obtained attracts too much attention. The possibility of contamination has to be considered because science is complex and juries can be easily confused. Even if they postpone asking for professional assistance in assessing science now, courts eventually will be forced to seek it by exploding technology. The jury can then return to the job they were called to do." For the British, *Daubert* criteria may fit the bill; the House of Commons and Technology Committee (2005) observes, "The absence of an agreed protocol for the validation of scientific techniques prior to their being admitted in court is entirely unsatisfactory. Judges are not well-placed to determine scientific validity without input from scientists. We recommend (the development of) a gate-keeping test for expert evidence. This should be done in partnership with judges, scientists and other key players in the criminal justice system, and should build on the U.S. Daubert test."

The British also wrestle with statistical evidence the way Americans do; the House of Commons and Technology Committee (2005) notes, "We are of the view that there is significant room for improvement in the way that statistical evidence, including risks and probabilities, is presented to juries. In order for this to occur, there needs to be a better understanding of the forms of wording and presentation that are easiest to understand, and least misleading, to members of the general public. We do not make a judgment about which form of wording is most apposite for the presentation of DNA evidence but recommend that the decision be informed by research."

In England, the House of Commons and Technology Committee (2005) tackled the subject of expert witnesses, observing, "We are disappointed to discover such widespread acknowledgement of the influence that the charisma of the expert can have over a jury's response to their testimony, without proportional concomitant action to address this problem. If key players in the criminal justice system, including the police and experienced expert witnesses, do not have faith in a jury's ability to distinguish between the strength of evidence and the personality of the expert witness presenting it, it is hard to see why anyone else should. There is clearly no easy answer to this problem . . . ." This British entity observes further, "The training of expert witnesses in the general principles of presentation of evidence to courts and the legal process is essential." It also remarks, "Expert witnesses have been penalized far more publicly than the judge or lawyers in cases where expert evidence has been called into question. These cases represent a systems failure. Focusing criticism on the expert has a detrimental effect on the willingness of other experts to serve as witnesses and detracts attention from the flaws in the court process and legal system which, if addressed,

Continues on next page

could help to prevent future miscarriages of justice."

And when it comes to juries' comprehension of complex material, as well as experts' testimony, the House of Commons and Technology Committee (2005) adds, "Jury research is vital to understand how juries cope with highly complex forensic evidence. Jury research would also be instructive for understanding differences in the way that jurors respond to oral and written reports by experts, and how easy they find interpretation of these reports.

While the United States and the United Kingdom seem to split on their views of who should provide education and training to forensic scientists, both countries seem to agree that there are a lack of learning opportunities and the provision of educational services. The House of Commons and Technology Committee (2005) notes, "The two largest employers of forensic scientists in the United Kingdom are the police and the Forensic Science Service, responsibility for which falls within the remit of the Home Office. It is disappointing that, in view of the concerns expressed to us by the police and the wider forensic science community over standards in forensic science education, the Home Office has taken no action to communicate the existence of these problems." The British also focus on the education of attorneys and judges; the House of Commons and Technology Committee (2005) states, "While we have no particular complaints about the quality of the guidance available to lawyers on the understanding and presentation of forensic evidence, it is of great concern that there is currently no mandatory training for lawyers in this area. In view of the increasingly important role played by DNA and other forensic evidence in criminal investigations, it is wholly inadequate to rely on the interest and self-motivation of the legal profession to take advantage of the training on offer. We recommend that the Bar make

a minimum level of training and continuing professional development in forensic evidence compulsory . . . . We recommend that judges be given an annual update on scientific developments of relevance to the courts. We also recommend that the Home Office issue a consultation on the development of a cadre of lawyers and judges with specialist understanding of specific areas of forensic evidence. An additional benefit to this would be the creation of a small group of judges and prosecution and defense lawyers with the ability and current knowledge to act as mentors to their peers when required."

The British also seem to be seizing upon the opportunity to promulgate forensic science among the student population, for the future benefit of science in general and forensic science in particular. The House of Commons and Technology Committee (2005) observes, "There is an opportunity to harness the excitement surrounding forensic science to promote interest in science more generally. Academically rigorous and scientifically sound joint honors degrees in forensic science, chemistry, and biology could build on the appeal of forensic science while providing students with the analytical skills and scientific background required by employers. These degrees need to be developed in close collaboration with the main employers in order to ensure that graduates would be well qualified for the roles for which these organizations recruit . . . . We recommend that the Forensic Science Society . . . and the main employers work together with the Royal Society of Chemistry to promote an understanding of the value of chemistry as a route into forensic science. This could be done, for example, through visits into schools by practicing forensic scientists."

The United States is not the only country contemplating the merits of a central commission that could lead improvement efforts related to forensic science. In the United Kingdom, the House of Commons and Technology Committee (2005) notes, "At this time of transition in the forensic services market, the need for an independent regulator is becoming ever more critical. We recommend that the government establish a Forensic Science Advisory Council to oversee the regulation of the forensic science market and provide independent and impartial advice on forensic science. The Council would also be ideally placed to review, or to commission inspections of, the use of forensic science across the whole of the criminal justice system, and to propose improvements where necessary." The agency states further, "The absence of formal and permanent channels for forensic scientists and experts to give feedback on their courtroom experiences seems to us to represent a serious flaw in the criminal justice system. We recommend that the Home Office establish a forum for Science and the Law,

which meets at least every six months. If the recommendation to set up a Forensic Science Advisory Council is adopted, the forum should be subsumed into this body."

Magnusson (1996) observes, "Used professionally, science is ready to offer much more to the justice system than it can now. The participants in the process will be acting within their competence. The merits of the evidence will start to count more than the merits of its presentation. The risks of misunderstood science will be minimized. Control of the court process will pass back to the court. The justice system will be able to take advantage of improvements in the practice of forensic science and simultaneously be less vulnerable to the possibility of bad science being used in prosecutions. Finally, the justice system will become less vulnerable to people who mislead or confuse the court by capitalizing on the complexities which forensic science unavoidably carries with it."

REFERENCES

Almirall JR and Furton KG. Trends in forensic science education: Expansion and increased accountability. *Anal of Bioanalytical Chemistry*, 376:1156–1159, 2003.

Bourke J. Misapplied science: Unreliability in scientific test evidence. *Australia Bar Review*, 123:196–197, 1993.

DiFonzo JH. The crimes of crime labs. *Hofstra Law Review*, 34(1), Fall 2005.

Feldman S, Constantine L, Dolezal M, Garcia J, Horton G, Leavell T, Levin M, Muntz J, Pastor R, Rivera L, Stewart J, Strumpf F, Titus C, VanderHaar H, and Saks MJ. Model prevention and remedy of erroneous convictions act. *Arizona State Law Journal*, 33:665, 699; 2001.

Giannelli PC. The abuse of evidence in criminal cases: The need for independent crime laboratories. *Virginia Journal of Social Policy Law*, 4: 439–478, 1997.

Giannelli PC. Scientific evidence in civil and criminal cases. *Arizona State Law Journal*, 103:112, 2001.

Goodstein D. How science works. *Federal Evidence Manual*, 2000.

Hanzlick R. Coroner training needs: A numeric and geographic analysis. *Journal of the American Medical Association*, 276:1775–1778, 1996a.

Hanzlick R. On the need for more expertise in death investigation. *Archives of Pathology Lab Medicine*, 120:329–332, 1996b.

Hanzlick R and Combs D. Medical examiner and coroner systems: History and trends. *Journal of the American Medical Association*, 279:870–874, 1998.

Hoeffel JC. The dark side of DNA profiling: Unreliable scientific evidence meets the criminal defendant. *Stanford Law Review*, 42:465, 494; 1990.

House of Commons Science and Technology Committee. *Forensic Science on Trial: Government Response to the Committee's Seventh Report of Session 2004–2005.* July 20, 2005.

Inman K and Rudin N. *Principles and Practices of Criminalistics: The Profession of Forensic Science.* Boca Raton, Fla.: CRC Press, 2001.

Jonakait RN. Forensic science: The need for regulation. *Harvard Journal of Law Technology,* 4:109, 1991.

Kitcher P. *The Advancement of Science.* Oxford: Oxford University Press, 1993.

Koppl R. How to improve forensic science. *European Journal of Law and Economics,* November 2005.

Koppl R and Butos WN. Science as a spontaneous order: An essay in the economics of science. In: *The Evolution of Scientific Knowledge,* Jensen HS, Vendeloe M, and Richter L, Eds. Cheltenham, UK: Edward Elgar, 2003.

Koppl R and Kobilinsky L. Forensic science administration: Toward a new discipline. November 2005. Accessed at http://alpha.fdu.edu/~koppl/fsa.doc.

Magnusson E. Making forensic science work. *Reform,* online issue No. 69, Winter 1996.

Accessed from the Australian Law Reform Commission at http://www.austlii.edu.au/au/other/alrc/publications/reform/reform69/ALRCR69MAKIN.

Mannheim K. *Ideology and Utopia: An Introduction to the Sociology of Knowledge.* New York: Harcourt, Brace & World, 1936.

McRoberts F, Mills S, and Possley M. Forensics under the microscope: Unproven techniques sway courts, erode justice. *The Chicago Tribune,* Oct. 17, 2004.

Merton RK. *Science and the Social Order.* New York: The Free Press, 1957.

Miller LS. Procedural bias in forensic science examinations of human hair. *Law of Human Behavior,* 11:157–163, 1987.

Mills S, McRoberts F, and Possley M. When labs falter, defendants pay: Bias toward prosecution cited in Illinois cases. *The Chicago Tribune,* October 20, 2004.

National Institute of Justice (NIJ). *Science Laboratories, Educational Institutions, and Students' Education and Training in Forensic Science.* Washington, D.C.: U.S. Department of Justice, June 2004.

National Institute of Justice (NIJ). *Status and Needs of Forensic Science Service Providers: A Report to Congress.* Washington, D.C.: U.S. Department of Justice, May 2004.

Nordby JJ. Countering chaos: Logic, ethics, and the criminal justice system. In: *Forensic Science: An Introduction to Scientific and Investigative Techniques,* James SH and Nordby JJ, Eds. Boca Raton, Fla.: CRC Press, 2003.

Risinger MD, Saks MJ, Thompson WC, and Rosenthal R. The Daubert/Kumho implications of observer effects in forensic science: Hidden problems of expectation and suggestion. *California Law Review,* 90(1), January 2002.

Rudin N and Inman K. A hitchhiker's guide to accreditation. *CAC News,* third quarter 2005.

Rudram DA. Interpretation of scientific evidence. *Science Justice,* 133, 1996.

Saks MJ. Merlin and Solomon: Lessons from the law's formative encounters with forensic identification science. *Hastings Law Journal,* 49:1069–1141, 1998.

Saks MJ. Reliability standards: Too high, too low, or just right?: The legal and scientific evaluation of forensic science (especially fingerprint expert testimony). *Seton Hall Law Review,* 33(49):1167–1187, 2003a.

Saks MJ. The legal and scientific evaluation of forensic science. *Seton Hall Law Review,* 23(4):1167–1187, 2003b.

Saks MJ et al. Model prevention and remedy of erroneous convictions act. *Arizona State Law Journal,* 33:665–718, 2001.

Saks MJ and Koehler JJ. The coming paradigm shift in forensic identification science. *Science,* 309:892–895, 2005.

Schulhofer SJ and Friedman DD. Rethinking indigent defense: Promoting effective representation through consumer sovereignty and freedom of choice for all criminals. *American Criminal Law Review,* 31:71–122, 1993.

Simms J. Guest editorial. *CAC News,* fourth quarter 2005.

Stam J. QA/Q much? *CAC News,* fourth quarter 2005.

Stuntz WJ. The uneasy relationship between criminal procedure and criminal justice. *Yale Law Journal,* 107:1–75, 1997.

Teichroeb R. Rare look inside state crime labs reveals recurring DNA test problems. *Seattle Post-Intelligencer,* July 22, 2004.

Teichroeb R. They sit in prison but crime lab tests are flawed. *Seattle Post-Intelligencer,* March 13, 2004.

Thomson MA. Bias and quality control in forensic science: A cause for concern. *Journal of Forensic Science,* 19: 504–517, 1974.

RECOMMENDED READING

De Forest PR, Gaensslen RE, Lee HC. *Forensic Science: An Introduction to Criminalistics.* New York: McGraw-Hill, 1983.

Furton KG, Hsu YL, and Cole MD. What educational background is required by crime laboratory directors? *Journal of Forensic Science,* 44:128–132, 1999.

Higgins KM and Selavka CM. Do forensic science graduate programs fulfill the needs of the forensic science community? *Journal of Forensic Science,* 33:1015–1021, 1988.

Kelly JF and Wearne P. *Tainting Evidence: Inside the Scandals at the FBI Crime Lab.* New York: The Free Press, 1998.

Peterson JL, Ryan JP, Houlden PJ, and Mihajlovic S. The uses and effects of forensic science in the adjudication of felony cases. *Journal of Forensic Science,* 32(6):1730–1753, 1987.

Reforming the Forensic Science Community. Accessed at http://www.law-forensic.com/final_VI.htm.

Siegel JA. The appropriate educational background for entry-level forensic scientists: A survey of practitioners. *Journal of Forensic Science,* 33:1065–1068, 1988.

Thompson WC. Subjective interpretation, laboratory error and the value of forensic DNA evidence: Three case studies. *Genetica,* 96:153, 1995.

Thompson WC. Accepting lower standards: The National Research Council's second report on forensic DNA evidence. *Jurimetrics,* 37:405, 1997.

ENDNOTES

1. *Principles and Practice of Criminalistics: The Profession of Forensic Science* by Inman and Rudin. Copyright 2007 by Taylor & Francis Group LLC—Books. Reproduced with permission of Taylor & Francis Group LLC—Books in the format Other Book via Copyright Clearance Center.
2. Koppl, Roger. "How to improve forensic science." Springer/Kluwer Academic Publishers *European Journal of Law and Economics*, Volume 20, Number 3, pgs. 255–286, 2005. With kind permission of Springer Science and Business Media.

CHAPTER 16

NEW INITIATIVES AND THE FUTURE OF FORENSIC SCIENCE

Just like the haphazard nature of the U.S. medico-legal death investigation system and the polarity inherent within the tiered U.S. forensic laboratory system, the attempt to characterize, assess, and study the forensic science community has lacked discernable substance, structure, and staying power. As we have seen, a handful of studies, reports, and surveys have attempted to put the finger on the pulse of these two parallel systems over the years, but no definitive agenda has been established to address their overwhelming needs. Until now, that is. The forensic science community is the focus of several significant efforts currently under way to gauge the quality of the infrastructure and to determine the direction of future endeavors to support these two pillars of the criminal justice system.

Action in merely words and not deeds will do a disservice to the forensic science community, which has long awaited the attention it so richly deserves and mandates in return for its contributions. Studies, however, have their distinct advantages and disadvantages. Schultz (1932), speaking from a much different era, provides some timeless advice for proceeding with caution: "If the administration of justice is to be improved permanently, the task must be conceived as a continuous process and not as a flash-in-the-pan survey. Surveys have their place—a useful place. But their best service is rendered when they have their setting in a more comprehensive plan. In our rapidly changing civilization there is no possibility of 'solving' once for all, the defects of the administration of justice. A continuous but flexible campaign must be waged against a permanent resourceful foe. What is said about the futility of sporadic surveys and spasmodic studies of judicial administration in general, applies with equal force to the problems of administration of criminal justice considered in this report. Studies such as this can do no more than scratch the surface. Having been presented, they're soon forgotten without having produced much more than a slight superficial agitation. The problems concerned involve so many distinct aspects of law and medicine and so many interrelated aspects of the two domains that prolonged and continuous study is necessary."

Schultz (1932) continues, "The bench and the bar, and the medical academicians and practitioners must first of all be educated. Both professions must be educated to an understanding of what legal medicine should be; what it should be when properly developed as an important correlative field of scientific medicine, and what it should be in its practical application to the needs of justice. Certainly the laity, who must make the changes in law that will be necessary if any reform is to come about, cannot be expected to see the need of change if the two professions most vitally concerned do not see the light." Schultz advocates for the study and education to be undertaken by a philanthropic agency, but acknowledges, "The problems of the adequate future development of legal medicine in the United States in its university aspects and it its practical application are tremendous. The more thought one gives to them, the less easy do they appear of solution. . . . Not until the shortcomings and the factors upon which they are based are known will it be possible to correct them in an intelligent manner."

As we saw in Chapters 5 and 8, the Bureau of Justice Statistics has undertaken several surveys of forensic laboratories since 1998, and in 2005, it undertook the first major survey of medical examiner offices. While these surveys have gone a long way toward serving as a useful head count and catalogue of the components of these systems, they fall short in providing anything akin to a comprehensive study that ultimately leads to policy recommendations for the improvement of forensic science and forensic pathology. In 2003, the National Institute of Justice (NIJ) recommended the formation of a forensic science commission. Its DNA task force had been a helpful advisory group in identifying the DNA needs of state and local crime labs and had highlighted the relationship of DNA evidence to other forensic sciences. Although this advisory group has reached its objectives, it reminds the criminal justice community and the current administration that there is a continued need for a body to guide the future of technology, policy, and program development. Accordingly, the NIJ recommended the creation of a national forensic science commission to keep abreast of rapidly evolving scientific advances in all areas of forensics and to make recommendations on technology investments to improve public safety. According to the NIJ, "Such a commission could also serve as an ongoing forum for discussing strategy and policy to help ensure that existing forensic technologies are maximized to aid the criminal justice system. It could also serve as a clearinghouse for the thorough and thoughtful exchange of information and ideas." When the DNA task force was active, its members had emphasized that the success and productivity of such of a commission would be dependent on those appointed to it. The NIJ recommended that commission members be drawn from professional forensic science organizations, accreditation bodies, and key components of the criminal justice community.

Legislation was passed during the 2005–2006 term of Congress to create a forensic science committee under the National Academies to examine the state of publicly funded forensic science laboratories. " Barry A.J. Fisher, director of the Los Angeles County Sheriff's Department's forensic laboratory, past president of the American Academy of Forensic Science, past president of the American Society of Crime Laboratory Directors, and past president of the International Association of Forensic Sciences notes,. "About a year ago, the International Association of Chiefs of Police formed a forensic committee comprised of 10 crime lab directors and 10 chiefs of police to examine some of the issues. There is a greater realization among chiefs of police in law enforcement agency crime labs, that there are potential time-bombs, like the Houston crime lab, and that their careers could be cut short if something terrible happened. Police chiefs are major stakeholders in the criminal justice system, and they ought to be concerned about what happens in crime labs. A few years ago I served on an American Bar Association criminal justice committee to look into innocence-related issues. One of the components studied was crime labs and medical examiner offices. They examined a number of forensic-related issues and made recommendations. I believe that if enough people and organizations press these issues, eventually something will happen."

THE AMERICAN JUDICATURE SOCIETY

In November 2005, the American Judicature Society (AJS), a national, non-partisan organization dedicated to promoting the effective administration of justice, announced the formation of a new institute that will research and educate on issues at the nexus of science and law, including those that have led to wrongful convictions. The American Judicature Society Institute of Forensic Science and Public Policy was launched simultaneously with a bipartisan commission to assist the institute in establishing its research agenda and national forensic science standards, which can offer guidance to members of the legal and forensic science communities, as well as to help inform legislative and other public policy decisions. This new body, the American Judicature Society National Commission on Forensic Science and Public Policy, is led by three co-chairs: former U.S. Attorney General Janet Reno, former FBI and CIA director William Webster, and statistician Dr. Stephen Feinberg of Carnegie Mellon University. Dr. Donald Kennedy, president emeritus of Stanford University and editor-in-chief of *Science*, is serving as honorary chair. The launch of the institute and the commission was announced at the National Academy of Sciences, which is collaborating with the institute on one of its first research projects, a study of the economic costs of wrongful convictions.

"There's a real need for this kind of research and education because throughout the history of American law, knowledge of science has all too frequently been ignored by the judicial system," says Talbot D'Alemberte, chair of the AJS board. "Advances in science today come at an incredibly rapid pace, potentially benefiting every segment of society. With (the) launch, we have the opportunity to bring the certainty of science to our judicial system so that it produces the most reliable results possible. Our ultimate goal is to build and maintain the highest level of trust and confidence in our justice system."

Founded in 1913, the AJS is comprised of judges, lawyers, and concerned citizens who are interested in and support the improvement of the administration of justice in the United States. The AJS maintains that its mission is to ensure a fair, impartial, and independent judiciary. "We focus on developing public trust and confidence in the criminal justice system," explains Allan Sobel, former president of the AJS. "When the advent of DNA evidence gave rise to a series of widely reported exonerations, we became concerned about the impact of those revelations on public trust and confidence in the justice system, which includes the courts, the prosecutors and law enforcement. Our justice reform committee, which was largely inactive for many years because we hadn't done much in this arena, began to monitor the situation and think about what, as an organization, we could do to respond to help restore any public trust and confidence that was lost. Ultimately, we concluded that we needed to hold a national conference to discuss the issue much in the same way that AJS conducts business generally."

Sobel says that during its 93-year history, the AJS has served as a catalyst for directing public attention to issues of concern about the U.S. criminal justice system, and has provided the mechanism by which these issues can be addressed in a meaningful way. "We strive to achieve buy-in for how these needs might be remedied. The way we do that is to hold conferences and meetings with all interest groups represented. We share at the outset a common view, such as the fact that we don't want innocent people being convicted of and punished for crimes they did not commit, and at the same time and equally importantly, we don't want people who commit serious crimes to avoid responsibility. So we ask that people rally around common goals and start from a place we all agree is important."

Sobel explains that at a recent AJS-sponsored conference, 11 teams were assembled, whose members gathered and presented information about the root causes of a large percentage of the wrongful convictions. "We explored ways that different jurisdictions had started to address the problem without promoting one particular reform over another or suggesting to any jurisdiction what it needed to do, but instead just laid out the information. At the AJS, we try to educate as opposed to browbeat people. We facilitated conversations of two types: one was a conversation among peers, and another dialogue was comprised of separate conversations that were based on jurisdictions. Each jurisdiction sent a team to the conference, made up of a prosecutor, a defense attorney, a judge, a law enforcement official, a legislator, a crime victim advocate, and in some cases, a journalist. They worked as teams and then they met with peers from other jurisdictions to discuss the issues and share information."

Sobel emphasizes that the meeting was attended by individuals with a longstanding interest in the criminal justice system but who did not identify with any particular partisan interest group. "We avoided the appearance that the conference was somehow leaning in any one direction," Sobel says. "And a lot of good came out of that conference, which we attribute to action plans put together during the team meetings; if attendees concluded that there was a need for reform in their jurisdictions, they came up with ideas about what they should be doing at home to address those needs. The good news is, a number of those ideas became reality."

It was at such an AJS conference that the seeds of the institute and the commission were planted. "The impetus for so much was the keynote speech by Janet Reno, who is a long-time friend of AJS," Sobel says. "She was on our board before she became U.S. attorney general [during the Clinton administration] and has now returned to our board. In her speech she essentially said the overarching problem is that the law has failed to embrace the knowledge of science, especially in considering what would be the most reliable procedures that would yield the least number of mistakes. She urged the creation of a multi-disciplinary approach to reviewing the needs of the U.S. criminal justice system." Sobel recalls, "Unlike most keynote speakers, Janet stayed for the duration of the conference, and at the end of three days she came up to me and said, 'If there's anything I can do to help you in this area, let me know.' I said, 'I have an idea. Why don't we explore this great thought that you shared with us; let's look into the feasibility of creating a multi-disciplinary institute through the AJS.' She immediately agreed to help."

"I am delighted to be working with AJS on this important initiative," says Reno, a member of the AJS board of directors. "Wrongful convictions are blights on any system of justice, especially in a country where freedom is considered a basic right. The work to be undertaken by the institute is a significant step towards ensuring that we learn from our prior mistakes and purge the system of errant convictions. We can all agree that innocent people should not be incarcerated while the guilty remain free."

Sobel says that since late 2003, the AJS explored the idea, with active work to bring the concept to life since late 2005. "Along the way we met with every conceivable group that we thought might be interested in this project and willing to share with us an opinion about whether it was a good or a bad idea," Sobel says. "Every response we received was very supportive; people expressed a sincere desire to work with us. A number of universities wanted us to locate on or near their campus and work with their faculty, and individual faculty members who were engaged in forensic science research were all very excited about the prospect of the formation of a multi-disciplinary entity."

One of the greatest strengths of the institute since the time the idea was on the drawing board, Sobel says, is its objectivity in an age of increasing partisanship. "What I think excited them about us is that we are an organization that can rightfully claim neutrality and integrity are our absolute foundational characteristics. We have no partisan agenda. We have liberals and conservatives, people of every belief on our board and in our membership and staff because our view is that you have to bring disparate minds together; you cannot accomplish anything meaningful through a partisan agenda. That was attractive to people for a number of reasons; one is that it suggests we can actually accomplish something, and two, it doesn't scare anybody. We eventually got to the point where we said we are going to do this, we need to get funding and space, and then things came together in Greensboro, N.C. We have fabulous rent-free space for five years that can accommodate up to 20 staff, although we are not going to be up to that level for some time, and we have financial grants that cover a good part of our overhead expenses for quite a while. We also are working with very prestigious scientific organizations like the National Academy of Sciences to develop grant propos-als to get busy on conducting appropriate research."

With these kinds of advantages on its side, Sobel says the institute is poised to create real and lasting reform for the benefit of all stakeholders. "The commission is comprised of some extraordinary people from all aspects of criminal justice, forensic science, and the judiciary; this entity will add two things to our work: one, it will be the advisory committee for the institute, functioning as the body that provides the institute help in drafting its research agenda. Secondly, when it is appropriate and the evidence has been gathered, it will consider whether research that has been performed or commissioned by the institute reasonably allows for the formulation of standards or guidelines that should be implemented nationwide on specific forensic science issues. This body will help determine, based upon the science that is known, whether a standard the institute proposes should be adopted or not. If they do adopt it, this will allow the institute in its educational phase to say whether something is advisable or not from the perspective of our researchers."

One issue on which the institute will focus is the advancement of forensic science in areas such as DNA analysis. The availability of DNA evidence has led to the disclosure of numerous wrongful convictions and has proven to be an effective tool in solving crimes. In some juris-dictions, nonetheless, thousands of DNA samples collected from criminal cases remain untested simply because there are not enough qualified scientists capable of processing these important pieces of evidence. "Handled correctly, DNA evidence is extremely valuable, but there is more demand for testing today than there are qualified analysts, and there are few regulations governing labs and procedures," says Sobel. "The challenge today is to make certain that important evidence is tested promptly by well-qualified analysts. Unfortunately, today we have neither adequate facilities nor a sufficient number of analysts to effectively maximize the use of DNA evidence."

As a former U.S. attorney general, Janet Reno knows the value of DNA testing to the criminal justice system; it was during her tenure in the Bill Clinton administration that the National Commission on the Future of DNA Evidence was created by the NIJ in the late 1990s to provide recommendations on the use of current and future DNA methods, applications, and technologies in the operation of the criminal justice system, from the crime scene to the courtroom. Over the course of its charter, the NIJ commission reviewed critical policy issues regarding DNA evidence and provided recommended courses of action to improve its use as a tool of investigation and adjudication in criminal cases. Reno reflects on what has changed since the time of the NIJ commission: "It's an evolving effort on the part of the people in the system, and the scientists who are using technologies that are new and applicable to the criminal justice system. But it is also an evolving science. What we have learned from DNA testing prepares us for the future; it has given us an important new perspective as well as the opportunity to review cases and determine why a wrong occurred and use that information to build a process that passes scientific muster. It is a process that will enable us to use the law and science in the widest way possible."

The power of DNA to fight wrongful convictions is not lost on a particular representative of the law enforcement community and a member of the commission, Hubert Williams, who is president of the Police Foundation, an independent, nonprofit research and technical assistance organization dedicated to the improvement of policing. "Police officers are on the front lines of the criminal justice system every day, and no one is more committed to getting criminals off the streets," Williams says. "Wrongful convictions put innocent people in jail and allow the real perpetrators to remain free. Research that helps ensure that the real criminals are caught, prosecuted and put behind bars is good for law enforcement, good for crime victims and good for the entire system of justice."

The issue of wrongful convictions is high on the priority list of the new AJS institute and the commission, with its members highly aware of the rift developing within the criminal justice community. Sobel says it is necessary to get back to basics to begin to unravel this knotty problem, and notes that the debate itself has shifted with the passage of time and increased usage of DNA testing. "The debate before DNA that was commonly heard centered on the question of whether people were ever wrongfully convicted, and we now know that people have been," Sobel says. "We can prove that to an absolute certainty. So the question today is how many people have been wrongfully convicted, and I don't think we know the answer. We can speculate, and some speculate with higher numbers than others; some refuse to speculate and simply say the ones we know about are the only ones out there and they assume that there are no others. This debate has changed the landscape of the criminal justice system, and I am concerned about the public's trust of and confidence in it. We must demonstrate to the owners of the system—the public—that to the extent we are able to eradicate error, we're going to do it, and the only way to demonstrate that in good faith is to canvas all of these issues and ensure that we are handling them correctly." Sobel points to other examples of oversight and investigation, and the importance of an exhaustive inquiry into a problematic scenario: "If a plane crashes, the National Transportation Safety Board doesn't assume that it's not going to happen again. They go in and review the entire situation with a fine-toothed comb, looking for causation to make sure it doesn't happen again to the extent that is humanly possible. We need to do the same thing with the criminal justice system."

For Reno, serving as the co-chair of the AJS commission is a natural extension of her career commitment to furthering the advancement of the criminal justice system. Reno was the first woman U.S. attorney general, nominated by President Bill Clinton in February 1993 and again appointed by Clinton in 1997. Reno has served as staff director of the Judiciary Committee of the Florida House of Representatives and also worked as a prosecutor in the Dade County State's Attorney's Office before working in private practice. She was appointed State Attorney General for Dade County and then elected to the Office of State Attorney and was returned to office by the voters four more times. Reno says her interest in serving on the AJS commission stems from her many years in service as a prosecutor in Dade County, watching the system at work and then seeing the number of individuals who were exonerated through post-conviction DNA testing.

"This was a marvelous moment of learning, if you will, an opportunity to look at wrongful convictions, to see why they take place, and to determine the reoccurrence of such situations in the future," Reno says. "We will be able to examine cases in which DNA testing is not available to serve as a system of checks and balances. I think it is very important that we understand the application of science to the criminal justice system as well as the entire court system, and that we apply science according to the prescribed scientific methods and the facts as they exist. In many instances, what has been taken to be science has not been fully explored from the scientific perspective. I think it is important that lawyers work with scientists to come up with standards that will enable us to seek the truth."

Using new research developed by the institute and its partners, the commission intends to develop organizational and operating standards for laboratories that conduct analysis of forensic evidence such as DNA, ballistics, and pathology.

"I think we need to support an agenda which brings lawyers and scientists together to enable them to speak the same language to understand the application of the scientific method and to use law and science together to seek the truth," Reno says. Regarding the commission's ability to tackle the ambitious agenda it has established for itself, Reno comments further, "I think it has the capacity to do so and I hope and trust it will and that its ultimate goal will be the truth—truth assumes different forms for different people depending on language and processes and it is important that we understand the processes that both law and science use and how we apply it together to seek the truth. It is an ambitious agenda, and one that we are moving to address in as thorough a manner as possible. What we hope to achieve is the utilization of science and the law together in a manner that is consistent with scientific methods."

Other areas of focus for the institute within the fields of civil and criminal justice include channels to transfer knowledge from the scientific community to the forensic and courtroom communities; mechanisms to improve juror comprehension of scientific testimony; independence of crime laboratories and the need to equalize access to laboratory findings for all stakeholders in the criminal justice system; human memory and its effect on eyewitness identification; and causes and methods of avoiding tunnel vision in the investigation and prosecution of criminal activity. The commission will advise on the institute's research agenda and will periodically consider standards for forensic science proposed by the institute, such as those used for the collection, testing, preservation, and admissibility of evidence.

This research will come at a time when, as we have seen, forensic science is under an intense amount of scrutiny. Sobel acknowledges the presence of detractors of forensic science and comments, "A number of people have made a lot of statements and I can't endorse or refute anything in totality, but I hope it is in the attempt to create a shared vision of making our criminal justice system as reliable as possible and to never stop working toward improving the system so that it yields the most accurate results."

While Sobel is clearly not a scientist, and he says he leaves it to the scientists to determine the field's current state of knowledge, as a long-standing member of the legal community he believes those outside of the scientific realm have an important stake in how forensic science operates. "I think that if some of the current practices under attack should be changed, that will come to light. But if these practices are scientifically valid and reliable and there are no improvements that need to be made to them, that's good to know, too. I think it's a great benefit for the public to know we are doing things properly, the same as if we are doing things incorrectly. Widely distributed media reports have raised, in the minds of the public, concerns about the criminal justice system. You can't read in the newspaper about people being convicted of murder who are innocent without scratching your head and saying, 'If the justice system can't get it right in a case like this, where so much is at stake, what kind of a job is it doing when there are less serious matters that are being resolved?'"

Sobel says he believes it is essential to determine, through meticulous research, the validity, reliability, and error rates of various forensic science disciplines, to lay the controversy to rest. He adds, "At this point, I don't think we know as much as we should about certain areas of forensic science. It may turn out that scientists are doing it right and if so, we need to validate what they are doing, again, to maintain public confidence. On the other hand, if they are not doing it right, or if it turns out you simply cannot do it right because it is really not science, we need to know that, too. And the only way we are going to make these kinds of determinations is with the help of qualified researchers." Sobel adds that the scientific foundation for certain areas of forensic practice must be clarified: "We need to know more than we currently know. I pass no judgment at this point on anything; if others do, it needs to be done by those with informed opinions; we need the feedback of the world's best scientists and input from individuals who have no agenda and are not associated with any particular point of view. That will put the issues to rest, hopefully."

While that resolution is a long way off, there are already big hopes for what can be achieved in the interim. The AJS commission held its first meeting in late March 2006 and set in motion a solid plan for research and policy implementation. Calling it a "symbiotic gathering bringing together the finest minds in the fields of law and science," Sobel adds, "This meeting is the first of its kind. Never before have all interested parties—sheriffs, judges, defense attorneys, prosecutors, scientists and others—come together to find the best practices and see those practices implemented." The weekend retreat included presentations by some of the commission's members, including DNA technology expert Dr. Marcia Eisenberg, and outside experts such as Dr. Gary Wells, a psychologist specializing in eyewitness identification.

"There is a greater awareness than ever about the power of forensic science in criminal justice," Sobel says. "But until now there has not been a single source of experts from all corners of science and criminal justice for the public, the press, and policy-makers to call on when determining how to best use the tools that forensics brings to solving crime. This commission will be that source." Sobel continues, "The need for a greater understanding of the promise and limits of science in criminal justice is real. Over the course of three days, national leaders from all areas touched by the criminal justice system had frank conversations about what we know, what we have to learn, and how we can work together to improve the use of forensic science in the courts."

The commission established five initial areas for the focus of its work: ensuring the preservation, scientific testing, and access to evidence; improving the quality of eyewitness testimony; promulgating standards for, and the systematic evaluation of, the nation's forensic labs; encouraging research and evaluation of pattern recognition techniques associated with forensic evidence to help solve crimes; and developing mechanisms to improve science education for the legal profession.

The AJS commission is targeting a number of mechanisms of the criminal justice system that have been subjected to criticism by commentators, including erroneous eyewitness identification, which has been cited as a leading cause of wrongful convictions. "I am disturbed about the number of innocent people who have been sent to prison for something they did not do," Webster says. "I, like many others, grew up believing that the claims of people who said they were innocent were overstated, that our system with all of its protections for the accused, very rarely would let someone be wrongfully convicted. Many people also grew up thinking that the most important kind of evidence that could be developed in a case was eyewitness identification. My confidence in eyewitness identification has plummeted to the bottom of the heap. I think eyewitness identifications are not scientific; instead, I think it is someone's best subjective effort to tell the truth as they know it or to lie about it. A person's memory will be affected by things that will influence their thinking, they will forget important details, and they will remember things that didn't happen—that has been revealed in a number of scientific studies. But before we knock all the scientific evidence, we better realize that we are very vulnerable to what someone like an eyewitness chooses to say; we need the scientific techniques that have been developed and refined over the years to support anything like eyewitness identifications."

To this end, Webster says the AJS commission shares a commitment to using forensic science to help advance the cause of justice. "This initial research agenda will get us started down a path of learning from each other, and helping improve the accuracy of, and trust in, our nation's judicial system," Webster adds.

Reno says she feels very encouraged by what transpired at the commission's first meeting and adds, "Everyone who was at the meeting that I talked to was excited about the ability to sit down and talk it out, to discuss the issues that confront us, and for scientists and lawyers to be in the same room. I had scientists telling me it's so exciting to be here and to have the opportunity to participate. It was a very interesting and very encouraging time for everyone. We defined the issues as much as we could, based on the conversations we had with the people who have joined the commission. Now, it is a matter of determining how we address the issues that have arisen, and how we apply law and science in a cooperative way."

"The commission's next step is to turn our agenda into a plan of action," says Feinberg. "We have already begun to identify the research that has been done and to articulate where the need to learn more is the greatest. By bringing the nation's best science to bear on the problem of the evaluation of forensic and other scientific evidence, we hope to provide improved and useable tools to enhance the objectivity and fairness of our criminal justice system."

Sobel acknowledges the tension that exists between law and science and attributes it to the different roles each discipline plays in society and in this system. He says it's a matter of understanding how each discipline approaches its responsibilities, the inherent characteristics of each, and taking into account the viewpoints of each stakeholder. "If science discovers a mistake was made, it becomes very motivated to find the right way to fix the mistake and find news ways to avoid making the same mistake," Sobel explains. "It's viewed as an opportunity to reexamine the way scientific conclusions are reached. Scientists understand that one may never know for sure that the absolute, right conclusion has been reached because science constantly changes. So scientists have this never-ending search for the truth because their sole objective is to get at the truth and do it right. The law certainly has that same objective, but at some point, the concept of finality enters into the picture. The law doesn't want to keep every file in the courthouse open in perpetuity, so there is this interest in bringing matters to a conclusion. The law also is interested in precedent, with the thought that 'we're going to set up a rule so everybody can rely on it.' So rules are put into place and exist for hundreds of years; nobody says, 'Wait a second, do we know more about things today than we did when this rule was formulated, that would tell us there is a better rule?'" He continues, "So everyone is interested in seeking the truth, but for science, I think, that search shall never end. For the law, to the contrary, there is an element of finality. I try to remind people, as we talk about the work of the institute, that what we think is true today, may turn out not to be true tomorrow. Even if we canvass all of the knowledge of science and come to what we consider to be a brilliant, impeccable conclusion about what needs to be done, we have to realize that tomorrow morning, something could be discovered which is going to change everything as we know it. We have to be willing to rethink everything whenever new knowledge surfaces. So we can only speak to what appears, as of this moment in history, to be the best practice. We cannot say what will be the best practice tomorrow or next week or a year from now because knowledge is an ever-evolving entity."

Webster knows a thing or two about the needs of the criminal justice system and the services it requires from forensic science. Webster, a consulting partner in the law firm of Milbank, Tweed, Hadley & McCloy since 1991, served as director of both the CIA and the FBI and, prior to that, served as a judge in the U.S. Court of Appeals for the Eighth Circuit; in addition, in Missouri Webster was a judge for the U.S. District Court, and he served as a U.S. attorney.

Webster says he joined the AJS commission as co-chair because of his long-standing belief in equipping criminal justice and forensic science personnel with the tools and resources they need to do their jobs well—a necessary component of the adjudication of cases.

"Much of my thinking goes back to the time somewhere in 1980 when I was director of the FBI and I accepted an invitation to talk to the Lincoln scholars at their annual meeting in Springfield, Ill.," Webster recalls. "I thought to myself, what do I know about Lincoln that they don't possibly know? I thought it might be interesting to deliver a talk on the investigation of Lincoln's assassination, and how that contrasted with the modern investigation of a presidential assassination or attempt at assassination. What struck me was what people do when they have no forensic science supporting the investigation effort, and in Lincoln's case, they had nothing, really . . . people observed a man jump out of the theater box and run across the stage and disappear. Investigators had a name and they tracked him down, but the fact of the matter was, they didn't have any forensic tools at their disposal. They arrested 2,000 people, including the whole cast of the play My American Cousin. To fast forward through time since then, it seems to me that in the years as we have progressed as a nation and as a society, our laws have imposed responses to emerging standards of decency. This is a U.S. Supreme Court term, and what is meant by it is that there are a lot of things you can't do now that you might have done before in order to carry out your investigative responsibilities."

Webster explains that when he joined the FBI as director in 1978, a priority for the bureau was improving its level of professionalism. "That meant utilizing forensic skills that were there and developing better ways of doing things," Webster says. "We simply had to do better at what we were doing within the framework that our society defines as protecting the privacy of citizens and other rights. At that point in the FBI we were starting to computerize fingerprints; in the past, every fingerprint investigated required manual retrieval. There were issues about the reliability and accuracy of fingerprinting, which was probably considered to be our most accurate tool. We went through computerization and we were no longer dependent on the system of 10 fingerprints on a card on file somewhere; we could search for latent fingerprints found at the scene of a crime via the computer in a short matter of time and come up with the right answers. It didn't mean you necessarily had the guilty person, but you had the person you were looking for. So it is important to have the right reliable tools and know how to use them properly for the good of society."

Webster continues, "To go to the other extreme, we were just beginning to think about DNA testing, and now DNA has altered the entire forensic, law enforcement, and legal landscape. Forensic science can tell us so much, but it doesn't mean it answers all of our questions. We are in pursuit of certainty, and we are in pursuit of truth, but without damaging the principles of individual liberty and protection of rights against self-incrimination and all of those basic constitutional rights we want to keep intact; we try to do that by improving the quality of our expertise and developing a more certain level of confidence in the investigation."

Webster acknowledges the changing times, when even members of the lay public expect a higher degree of certainty from law enforcement, forensic scientists, and prosecutors. "One of the earliest forms of evidence analysis that became very useful was ballistic sciences to help identify bullets and determine which firearm had been used," Webster comments. "It wasn't always enough to make a case that would satisfy a modern jury which expects to have everything from DNA to fingerprints to solve the case. It's important that the public have confidence in forensic science, and that the people who do this for a living are operating under stringent standards that will hold up in court. Ultimately, it's all about balancing order and liberty. Part of the AJS commission's efforts will focus on establishing standards in the forensic sciences, especially for pattern evidence analysis, to try to test out what we can about them." Webster laughs when he describes how at the first AJS commission meeting, there was a discussion about lip print science. "I didn't know there was such a thing as lip print science," he says, chuckling. "Ear prints I can believe, but lip prints I am not too convinced about."

But it is precisely evidence such as ear prints, lip prints, and other novel forms of identification that are coming under fire for being junk science. Webster acknowledges that the reliability and validity of certain forensic disciplines have been questioned but believes the public's faith in forensic science has not been destroyed by it. "I don't think their trust is shaken by the use of science that is relatively new and has not been in existence for a long time; however, I do think that from time to time, the public's confidence has been shaken by reports of evidence that was not properly collected, preserved or stored, and that has to be addressed. That cannot be allowed to undermine forensic science."

Webster also believes in the importance of going beyond merely settling for educated guesswork. "When I was at the FBI I reminded everyone not to go beyond what the evidence demonstrates, and to let the scientific method help them in their determinations. Hunches are fine, and all the better if they lead to other evidence that would be admissible in court, but they should never take investigators away from the solid science. We don't want people opining beyond what the evidence under our standards of admissibility will permit."

While some commentators expect a standard of science akin to Newtonian physics, Webster scoffs at the notion. "The world wouldn't function if we waited for everything to reach that level of certainty and absoluteness and purity," he says. "We are in the business of trying to identify wrongdoing where it has occurred, and of matching evidence to people or to crime scenes, and I don't think it serves any useful purpose to complain about forensic science being too 'soft' and saying you can't use it; the courts provide some direction here, and they are the ones that decide admissibility issues. That's the issue the Supreme Court took on in the Daubert decision."

Instead, Webster says the attention should be focused on sub-par work by practitioners, adding, "I think we should be far more concerned about sloppy work rather than the science being not rigorous enough. Sloppy work by an analyst has the potential of sending someone to prison erroneously. It is unacceptable if someone does a few tests and makes a pronouncement about a conclusion without meeting scientific standards; that's human error, not scientific error."

Webster is adamant when he says forensic science is not a broken system, and he adds that members of the AJS commission will approach the matter with open minds. "I don't think we need to go in thinking that things are in terrible shape because I don't think that's the case. I just think we need to improve our confidence in the evidence that is being used, and we can do that by scrutinizing the methodology, imposing standards for the professionals who apply that methodology, and then testing what they did to see what we are getting as a result of the methodology. I don't think we're dealing in junk science at all; however, the modern world requires a good deal more science than it did 25, 50 or 100 years ago to be convinced of its reliability and validity."

THE NATIONAL ACADEMIES

A separate effort is a comprehensive report on the status of forensic science being undertaken by the National Academies. According to Anne-Marie Mazza, Ph.D., as of spring 2006 the director of the Committee on Science, Technology, and Law in the Policy and Global Affairs Division of the National Academies, the first steps are being taken in a committee selection process. Mazza says that a number of organizations have begun to submit to the National Academies names of individuals to consider as potential committee members. "We are talking to different people but nothing has officially begun because we do not have an assigned grant yet, and it takes time to get through the pipeline. The first thing we will do is assemble a committee and establish the schedule of meetings. There will probably be five or six meetings, most will be open to the public, while some meetings will be closed so the committee can conduct its analysis, engage in its deliberations, and make its recommendations."

A typical National Academies study requires anywhere from 16 to18 months before a report can be issued, according to Mazza. An impetus for this study on forensic science, she adds, was members of Congress identifying gaps in the understanding of forensic disciplines other than DNA testing, as well as gaps of knowledge regarding the needs of the forensic science community in general.

"I heartily support the efforts of the National Academies to take a closer look at forensic science to determine, among other things, what kind of research must be conducted to further solidify the various forensic disciplines," says Joseph Polski, chief operations officer of the International Association for Identification (IAI) and chair of the Consortium of Forensic Science Organizations (CFSO). "It will be a significant step toward elevating forensic science, especially at a time when many disciplines are very much under the gun. I believe it will be a process similar to what occurred with DNA, when a new discipline secured a more solid footing within the scientific community."

Polski continues, "DNA went from zero to 60 in a very short time. Although DNA had a very rocky start, it quickly captured the attention of the scientific and legal communities. The National Research Council finally said, 'We need to look at this,' and at that point, DNA was elevated to the scientific world; that community looked at DNA and reached the same conclusions about it that the National Research Council did. Essentially, they announced that DNA works, case closed. When a DNA analyst testifies in court and there's a doubt about that testimony, all that needs to be said is a reference to the National Research Council's opinion on DNA and suddenly all the doubt goes away. Why? Because the scientific community agreed on the reliability of DNA. Not because it had been around for 100 years, like fingerprinting, but because DNA typing evolved through traditional science. But a discipline like fingerprinting, for example, is perceived as coming out of a process of trial and error and conjecture; certainly it has never been found to be wrong, but to some extent it doesn't have that scientific pedigree that DNA has. So a strong research agenda for forensic science is a very good idea."

For more than 140 years, the National Academies have been advising the nation on issues of science, technology, and medicine. The 1863 congressional charter signed by President Abraham Lincoln authorized this non-governmental institution to honor top scientists with membership and to serve the nation whenever called upon. Today, the National Academies—comprising the National Academy of Sciences (NAS), the National Academy of Engineering (NAE), the Institute of Medicine (IOM), and the National Research Council (NRS)—continue that dual mission by enlisting the country's foremost scientists, engineers, health professionals, and other experts to address the scientific and technical aspects of some of society's most pressing problems. Each year, more than 6,000 of these experts are selected to serve as volunteers on hundreds of study committees that are convened to answer specific sets of questions.

The Academies' work is primarily funded by federal agencies, with additional projects supported by state agencies, foundations, other private sponsors, and the National Academies endowment. In pursuit of neutrality, the Academies provide independent advice; the external sponsors have no control over the conduct of a study once the statement of task and budget are finalized. Study committees gather information from many sources in public meetings, but they deliberate in private in order to avoid political, special interest, and sponsor influence. The forensic science endeavor is just one of the 200 to 300 authoritative reports produced annually that can influence policy decisions, facilitate new research programs, or provide program reviews.

According to the National Academies, its reports are perceived as being credible because of the institution's reputation for providing independent, objective, and non-partisan advice with high standards of scientific and technical quality. Checks and balances are applied at every step in the study process to protect the integrity of the reports and to maintain public confidence in them. The study process consists of four stages. In the first stage, the study is defined. Before the committee selection process begins, National Academies' staff and members of their boards work with sponsors to determine the specific set of questions to be addressed by the study in a formal "statement of task," as well as the duration and cost of the study. The statement of task defines and bounds the scope of the study, and it serves as the basis for determining the expertise and the balance of perspectives needed on the committee. The statement of task, work plan, and budget must be approved by the Executive Committee of the National Research Council Governing Board. This review often results in changes to the proposed task and work plan. On occasion, it results in turning down studies that the institution believes are inappropriately framed or not within its purview.

The second stage in the process involves committee member selection and approval. All committee members serve as individual experts, not as representatives of organizations or interest groups. Each member is expected to contribute to the project on the basis of his or her own expertise and good judgment. A committee is not finally approved until a thorough balance and conflict of interest discussion is held at the first meeting, and any issues raised in that discussion or by the public are investigated and addressed. Careful steps are taken to convene committees that meet the following criteria:

- *An appropriate range of expertise for the task:* The committee must include experts with the specific expertise and experience needed to address the study's statement of task. One of the strengths of the National Academies is the tradition of bringing together recognized experts from diverse disciplines and backgrounds who might not otherwise collaborate. These diverse groups are encouraged to conceive new ways of thinking about a problem.
- *A balance of perspectives:* Having the right expertise is not sufficient for success. It is also essential to evaluate the overall composition of the committee in terms of different experiences and perspectives. The goal is to ensure that the relevant points of view are, in the National Academies' judgment, reasonably balanced so that the committee can carry out its charge objectively and credibly.
- *Screening for conflicts of interest:* All provisional committee members are screened in writing and in a confidential group discussion about possible conflicts of interest, including any financial or other interest that conflicts with the service of the individual because it could significantly impair the individual's objectivity or create an unfair competitive advantage for any person or organization. The term *conflict of interest* means something more than individual bias. There must be an interest, ordinarily financial, that could be directly affected by the work of the committee. Except for those rare situations in which the National Academies determines that a conflict of interest is unavoidable and promptly and publicly disclose the conflict of interest, no individual can be appointed to serve (or continue to serve) on a committee of the institution used in the development of reports if the individual has a conflict of interest that is relevant to the functions to be performed.
- *Other considerations:* Membership in the three academies (NAS, NAE, IOM) and previous involvement in National Academies studies are taken into account in committee selection. The inclusion of women, minorities, and young professionals are additional considerations.

The National Academies follows a specific series of steps in the committee member selection and approval process. First, staff solicits an extensive number of suggestions for potential committee members from a wide range of sources, and then it recommends a slate of nominees. Nominees are reviewed and approved at several levels within the National Academies; a provisional slate is then approved by the president of the National Academy of Sciences, who is also the chair of the National Research Council. The provisional committee members complete background information and conflict of interest disclosure forms. This committee balance and conflict of interest discussion is held at the first committee meeting, where any conflicts of interest or issues of committee balance and expertise are investigated; changes to the committee are proposed and finalized. The committee is then formally approved.

The third stage in the overall study process encompasses committee meetings, the task of information gathering, deliberations, and then the actual drafting of the report. Study committees typically gather information through meetings that are open to the public and that are announced in advance through the National Academies Web site, the submission of information by outside parties, reviews of the scientific literature, and the investigations of the committee members and staff. In all cases, efforts are made to solicit input from individuals who have been directly involved in, or have special knowledge of, the problem under consideration. In accordance with federal law and with few exceptions, information-gathering meetings of the committee are open to the public, and any written materials provided to the committee by individuals who are not officials, agents, or employees of the National Academies are maintained in a public access file that is available for examination. The committee deliberates in meetings closed to the public in order to develop draft findings and recommendations free from outside influences. The public is provided with brief summaries of these meetings that include the list of committee members present. All analyses and drafts of the report remain confidential.

The final stage of the process entails the report review. As a final check on the quality and objectivity of the study, all National Academies reports—whether products of studies, summaries of workshop proceedings, or other documents—undergo a rigorous, independent external review by experts whose comments are provided anonymously to the committee members. The National Academies recruit independent experts with a range of views and perspectives to review and comment on the draft report prepared by the committee. The review process is structured to ensure that each report addresses its approved study charge and does not go beyond it; that the findings are supported by the scientific evidence and arguments presented; that the exposition and organization are effective; and that the report is impartial and objective. Each committee must respond to, but need not agree with, reviewer comments in a detailed "response to review," which is examined by one or two independent report review monitors responsible for ensuring that the report review criteria have been satisfied. After all committee members and appropriate National Academies officials have signed off on the final report, it is transmitted to the sponsor of the study and released to the public. The names and affiliations of the report reviewers are made public when the report is released.

Congress, in Senate Report 109–088 issued on June 23, 2005, set the stage for the upcoming forensic science study, or a "DNA and Forensics Initiative" by the National Academies. Much of the impetus was due to the lack of infrastructure for forensic laboratories as portrayed by two recent surveys of the field. According to the report, "The Committee recommends $89.5 million to assist in forensics and DNA. Within the amounts provided, OJP may apply up to 5 percent of the total funds to support the continuation of the development of standards and Standard Reference Materials at the NIST OLES, to maintain quality and proficiency within federal, state, and local crime laboratory facilities. The Committee has reviewed the Bureau of Justice Statistics (BJS) Census of Publicly Funded Forensic Crime Laboratories and the NIJ Status and Needs of Forensic Science Services: A Report to Congress. The report identifies that the backlog in forensic science labs is not limited to DNA. In fact, these studies demonstrate a disturbing trend of increased cases and increased backlog in all disciplines of forensic science. According to the BJS Census, a typical lab finished the year with a backlog of about 650 requests, which was an increase of 73 percent from 2001 and 73 percent of the total backlogged requests at year end 2002 were attributable to controlled substances (46 percent), latent prints (17 percent), and DNA analysis (10 percent). Further, the study concluded that only 2 percent of all new requests were in the area of DNA analysis. The budget request proposes to allocate 100 percent of the federal funds for forensic science to DNA even though it represents only 2 percent of the workload identified in the study. Further, these data do not include the nation's medical examiners and coroners who are responsible for investigating all homicides. Based on the study's findings, the budget should allocate funds to all disciplines as opposed to just one. The results of these studies are indicative of a larger problem within the forensic science and legal community: the absence of data. While a great deal of analysis exists of the requirements in the discipline of DNA, there exists little to no analysis of the remaining needs of the community outside of the area of DNA. Therefore, within the funds provided for the DNA and Forensics Initiative the Committee directs the Attorney General to provide $1.5 million to the National Academy of Sciences to create an independent Forensic Science Committee. This Committee shall include members of the forensics community representing operational crime laboratories, medical examiners, and coroners; legal experts; and other scientists as determined appropriate."

According to the Senate report, the National Academy of Sciences committee will be expected to accomplish the following:

- Assess the present and future resource needs of the forensic science community, to include state and local crime labs, medical examiners, and coroners
- Make recommendations for maximizing the use of forensic technologies and techniques to solve crimes, investigate deaths, and protect the public
- Identify potential scientific advances that may assist law enforcement in using forensic technologies and techniques to protect the public
- Make recommendations for programs that will increase the number of qualified forensic scientists and medical examiners available to work in public crime laboratories
- Disseminate best practices and guidelines concerning the collection and analysis of forensic evidence to help ensure quality and consistency in the use of forensic technologies and techniques to solve crimes, investigate deaths, and protect the public
- Examine the role of the forensic community in the homeland security mission and interoperability of Automated Fingerprint Information Systems
- Examine additional issues pertaining to forensic science as determined by the committee.

The National Academies was requested by Congress to issue its report to the Committees on Appropriations no later by June 1, 2006. The committee recommendation provides $22 million for the Paul Coverdell Forensic Sciences Improvement Grants.

As the study process picks up steam, the forensic science community will continue to advocate for its voice to be heard. As we saw in Chapter 14, the CFSO has been the strongest show of force on Capitol Hill. "The Consortium has been very active in talking to legislators and bringing their needs and concerns to the attention of the Hill so that the study would be requested," says Mazza. "They have been very helpful and it seems there is a genuine desire to ensure the science related to their techniques and practices are sound and up to date, and that they have the appropriate resources to support this endeavor. They have been on the leading edge of continuing to move their field forward."

It remains to be seen how these new efforts and initiatives will play out. For now, Sobel remains philosophical. "From my perspective, the methods the AJS has used for 93 years have proved to be outstanding ways of bringing about reform. I'm confident that our method will prove to be successful in this set of issues as well. Any time something has gone under the auspices of an organization that has any sort of agenda or it's done by government, reflects obviously to a large extent the attitudes of the administration that is in control. It is less likely to lead to reform because there will be people who are suspicious or resistant to the work product. The more research that is done and the more people pay attention to these issues, hopefully the better it will be for society. As far as how all of this shakes out, with different organizations and government involved, it's very difficult to say." Sobel adds, "I think some of the other efforts out there are somewhat disjointed in the sense that they either involve research or they involve the concept of a commission, but they don't tie the two ideas together. I don't fully understand how any research institute will ultimately be involved or how their work will then get translated into a reform effort. Somebody's going to have to do the hard job of educating the people who are in a position to make policy decisions about what the processes in the justice system ought to look like. I don't see how the researchers do that. On the other hand, these commissions, how will they get the information they need to determine what the standards ought to be—so aside from the philosophical difference between us and a lot of other organizations in government, I think what we bring here is a package that enables us to do both ends of something that has to be done to bring about reform."

The subject of reform is contentious because of the desire on the part of the forensic laboratory and the medico-legal communities to be self-determining, contrasted with the desire of reformers to show these communities the errors of their ways. If approached correctly, reform is a streamlined process of building consensus and achieving mutually beneficial goals; if not, it is a torturous, unproductive, ill-fated undertaking. Fisher says that the forensic science community wants to improve, but reformers must pick their battles, do their homework, and be respectful of forensic practitioners' perspective. "While crime labs have their faults, they have a strong desire to do what is expected of them," Fisher says. "There is a serious disconnect out there; crime lab managers are put off by the do-gooders who are trying to save us from ourselves. People constantly tell us we are 'cops in lab coats' or mere technicians, and then they expect us to embrace them when they offer to 'help' us. Critics have been so strident with their criticism in the past that it makes me wonder why we would ever want to talk to them; they bad-mouth us, tell us we're dumb, we're biased. So why do they expect us to willingly work with them? We do, because we have to ultimately bring people together on the issues. Crime lab personnel want to improve their profession, and they want to do what's right."

Fisher continues, "Crime labs don't need unwarranted or misinformed criticism. Critics who want to reform forensic science don't understand the issues, and they don't understand what it is like to be in the trenches. In various meetings people will make statements that the problem with forensic science is that it is completely unregulated, which isn't true; yes, some things are voluntary, like accreditation, but for DNA testing facilities and in some states for all labs, accreditation is mandatory. But those are the details people tend to overlook when they make these big pronouncements."

BUILDING NEW BRIDGES

Reflecting a renewed interest in studying and improving forensic science is the creation of two separate ventures designed to build new bridges between forensic science and the law.

The Institute for Studies in Science and the Law (ISSL) at Hastings College of Law at the University of California is on the drawing board, according to law professor David L. Faigman. "It's a completely independent venture, with the objective of creating a place where a meeting of the minds can occur," Faigman explains. "We are creating a board comprised of people like Joe Peterson, Michael Saks, and Barry Fisher, to help the institute navigate through the issues as we endeavor to create a bridge between mainstream academic scientists and the legal community with the ultimate goal of coming together to support forensic science research."

Faigman continues, "Once we have established an operating budget with which to run the institute, we then want to approach private foundations and convince them to dedicate a certain amount of funding that will go directly to scientists and statisticians around the country so that they may engage in research benefiting forensic science. For example, the law and forensic science look at soft-tissue injuries differently; the law looks at soft tissue analysis for the purpose of human bite mark determination. We'll approach a scientist and say, 'Hey, keep doing what you are doing, but if you expand your research to also look at bite mark analysis and its statistical aspects, we'll help you write the grant to secure the research funding.'"

"It's all in an effort to engage mainstream academic scientists in forensic science and medico-legal issues," Faigman explains. "We are hoping to be the Johnny Appleseeds of forensic science research in the academic scientific community, getting these scientists interested in conducting forensic science research as a component of mainstream academic science. So, the board of directors of the ISSL will help shape forensic science issues in a way that will make them academically interesting to mainstream scientists. If the courts are going to continue to say, 'You need to do research,' then we have to find the scientists to do the research. Hopefully we will provide the infrastructure to allow forensic science to move into what Michael Saks and Jonathan Koehler refer to as the new scientific paradigm."

Faigman says his frustration about the lack of academic research in forensic science helped propel him to pursue the institute idea. "In 2002 I published an article in *Science* magazine calling for forensic scientists to just do the research, and when I speak at conferences, I say, just do the research. This spring, two things came together that gave me the inspiration for the creation of the ISSL. I read a *Science* article reporting that less than 1 percent of scientists have research-level degrees; then I read a wonderful article in *The New York Times* about a philanthropist who gives tremendous amounts of money to non-mainstream scientific efforts. He discussed the need to provide support for research which is somewhat visionary; I put down the paper and thought to myself, I have been yelling forever for scientists to do the research, and they never do the research, but if you create a bridge between mainstream science and the forensic community, that could happen. So, the idea of the ISSL was born. It's an entity that will be able to translate what is needed from the law to what is interesting to academics and help provide the funding to get there. Even though forensic scientists get really frustrated with people like me, I really want to see forensic science proved correct, I think a lot of it will be, and I think traditional science can help forensic science. I don't see myself at all as the nemesis of forensic science, as I think I am on their side, actually, I am just trying to drag them into the 21st century, just like what was done with DNA profiling. The technological advances that are possible with good research are astounding, and that's where forensic science should be headed. Apply good research techniques to technology and these efforts will likely validate a good deal of what forensic scientists already do. And with any luck, they will also produce all sorts of wonderful new inventions for medico-legal use in the future."

Faigman emphasizes his belief in collaboration. "I think we ought to be working together in a bi-partisan effort to say, 'Look, if innocent people are being convicted, then we have made two mistakes: we locked up someone who has not done anything wrong, and we failed to lock up someone who is a bad person who is likely to be out there committing more crimes.' So we are not just working for the defendant when we say that we want good forensic science; we are working for all of forensic science and the criminal justice system. Science can really bring to forensics a fresh perspective and new technology, and that can really help avoid mistakes in the future." Faigman continues, "I understand that some members of the forensic science community feel defensive about what I say, but I try very hard not to make it personal. I am simply saying, let's fix this problem, and I do understand their perspective, that they are under assault, and in response, they are going to circle the wagons and fight back. At a 2005 conference held by the National Academies it was really clear that separate communities of forensic scientists and mainstream scientists existed, and that's what we are trying to bridge."

Forensic science may very well be poised on the threshold of a new era of communication, dialogue, and information sharing. The National Clearinghouse for Science, Technology, and the Law (NCSTL) at Stetson University College of Law was created to help bridge the chasm between these disciplines, according to its director, Carol Henderson, J.D., a professor at Stetson University College of Law. The clearinghouse, funded by a grant from the National Institute of Justice, is the embodiment of Henderson's vision of a one-stop shop for judges, lawyers, scientists, and law enforcement officials who seek data within the nexus between law, science, and technology.

"My personal goal, in putting together the database, is to level the playing field and help people understand what the issues and concerns are of law enforcement, lawyers, judges, scientists, and others involved in the criminal justice system," Henderson says. "I think it is imperative that we engage in the kind of dialogue that will enable us to communicate these issues and concerns, to see that we are not adversaries, and to realize that we must work together, even if we are on opposite sides of a case, toward greater understanding of truth and justice. Right now, it's more about winning at all costs, and there's a high price to pay for that approach."

The NCSTL offers educational programs and a database of relevant information, focusing on fostering communication and understanding, as well as raising awareness, within the context of the promotion of justice based on sound science and technology. One of the primary purposes of the NCSTL is to provide a resource that collects and tracks the majority of available sources related to forensic science and technology. The vast expanse of the targeted information gap prompted the NCSTL to scrutinize and disseminate useful information in order to reconnect jury expectations with the realities of the justice system, as well as to assist expert witnesses in ethically testifying and avoiding liability. The NCSTL database, which was first offered to the public in February 2005, collects and distributes bibliographic information on thousands of court decisions, pieces of legislation, legal and scientific publications, news and media features, Web sites, and educational opportunities.

"We must continue to look at how and why scientific evidence is being called into question and challenged," Henderson adds. "And we must look at why we have reports of faulty forensic science. I mean, you see the headlines about the bad stuff, and you ask yourself, is it the fault of the forensic scientist? Was the science not up to snuff? Is it the fault of an overzealous prosecutor or a lazy defense lawyer? You can't point the finger at one group, as there may be many causes, and that's what we have to explore."

Henderson continues, "Some people who are pointing out the flaws in the system are disliked by some in the forensic science community, but there is value in what they are saying; we need to come together to address the problems instead of being defensive. And at the same time we might be able to show the critics why things aren't broken. If we want a solid relationship between the law and forensic science, we need better communication between the two disciplines. I think all of these new efforts to bring the law, forensic science, and technology together is terrific. Let's share perspectives and see what we can learn from each other for the benefit of all."

Fisher says that solutions are in reach, but they will require cooperation and like minds throughout the reform process. "You can't have a democracy if forensic science and the criminal justice system are not working as they ought to," Fisher states. "If everyone with a stake in forensic science could sit down together, have an open mind, get rid of the pejorative thoughts and talk through the problems in order to get a firm grip on them, we'd have a decent chance at solving our issues. It's too important not to reach a consensus and move forward to make forensic science the best it can be."

REFERENCE

Schultz OT. Possibilities and need for development of legal medicine in the United States. *Bulletin of the National Research Council.* Washington, D.C.: National Research Council, October 1932.

LOOKING OUT FOR DECEDENTS AND DEFENDANTS: TAKING A CUE FROM HEALTH CARE

We have discussed the various ways in which forensic science is under siege, and we have looked to the future, where new challenges and opportunities await. It may be helpful to remind ourselves that forensic science is not alone in its struggle to identify and address perceived and actual systemic flaws. For years, the health-care industry has wrestled with its own systemic problems, especially medical errors. A 1999 report, "To Err Is Human: Building a Safer Health System," from the Institute of Medicine (IOM) of the National Academies, asserts that reducing one of the nation's leading causes of death and injury—medical errors— would require rigorous changes throughout the U.S. health-care system, including mandatory reporting requirements. The report laid out a comprehensive strategy for government, industry, consumers, and health-care providers to reduce medical errors, and it called on Congress to create a national patient safety center to develop new tools and systems needed to address persistent problems. The report, based on the findings of one major study, asserts that medical errors kill approximately 44,000 people in U.S. hospitals each year, while another study puts the number as high as 98,000.

I believe that some important parallels may be drawn between the efforts to improve forensic science and the efforts to revamp health care. In the same way that medical errors have captured headlines, so too have the mistakes made by medico-legal professionals. In each case, there must be a system in place that makes it easy to do things right and difficult to do things wrong, and the right amount of accountability when this system fails. I agree with the IOM report when it states, "It may be part of human nature to err, but it is also part of human nature to create solutions, find better alternatives, and meet the challenges ahead." System failures result from a complex interaction of people, technology, work processes, and working conditions; when identified and caught before they become fatal, they can be vehicles for remarkable transformation.

The IOM report states that the majority of medical errors do not result from individual recklessness, but from basic flaws in the way the health-care system is organized. Medical knowledge and technology advance so rapidly that it is difficult for health-care practitioners to keep pace, and the health-care system itself is evolving so quickly that it can leave its professionals unprepared for the rigors of practice. The same clearly may be said for forensic science; its practitioners also must contend with staying abreast of technological developments, evolving technical thought, and ever-increasing demands and expectations from end users and stakeholders.

The IOM report states that health care is a decade or more behind other high-risk industries, such as aviation, in its attention to ensuring basic safety. Forensic science has been a neglected field, from an academic standpoint, and requires similar attention to help safeguard accuracy of analyses and cultivate new empirically based techniques with which to conduct scientific experiments.

The IOM report also advocates the creation of a center for patient safety within the U.S. Department of Health and Human Services (HHS) in order to establish national safety goals, track progress in meeting them, and invest in research to learn more about preventing mistakes. The center also would act as a clearinghouse, an objective source of the latest information on patient safety for the nation; for example, if a health-care organization improves safety, its practices should be shared with a broad audience, and the center, working with others, would help provide the needed channel. Similarly, as we saw in Chapter 16, there is movement within the criminal justice system to launch new initiatives, studies, and institutes through which forensic practice may be deconstructed, studied, analyzed, reconstructed, and improved.

It is fascinating to take the IOM's recommendations and align them with those proposed for the forensic science community. The IOM report defines *error* as the failure to complete a planned action as intended or the use of a wrong plan to achieve an aim, and notes that not all errors result in harm. To learn about medical treatments that lead to serious injury or death and to prevent future occurrences, the IOM recommends the establishment of a nationwide, mandatory public reporting system for U.S. health-care institutions. Currently, about one-third of states have mandatory reporting requirements for adverse events and medical errors. As we have seen, there is a growing number of individuals who are advocating for similar transparency within the forensic laboratory system. While some believe that accreditation, certification, and licensure are adequate safeguards, only time will tell if more aggressive, involuntary approaches to quality assurance will be pursued for a greater number of medico-legal practitioners.

Interestingly, the pressure for transparency is similar in both health care and forensic science. Public and private consumers of health care are expecting their practitioners to make safety a priority at the same time that the stakeholders in the criminal justice system expect a zero-tolerance policy on errors from forensic scientists and criminalists and medico-legal professionals. And for the commentators who claim that forensic science is the only field lax about the professionalism of its practitioners, the IOM report notes that for many health-care professionals, there is no assessment of clinical performance once they earn their licenses to practice, and that licensing and certifying bodies should implement periodic reexaminations of doctors, nurses, and other key health-care providers, based on both competence and knowledge of safety practices.

It is as essential for forensic science to build a culture of continued accuracy and integrity as it is for the health-care field to construct a culture of safety. The IOM report emphasizes that health-care organizations must create an environment in which safety will become a top priority. This culture of safety means designing systems geared to preventing, detecting, and minimizing hazards and the likelihood of error—not attaching blame to individuals. The report stresses the need for leadership by executives and clinicians, and for accountability for patient safety by boards of trustees. I suggest that the same is true for forensic science, without exception, by simply swapping the word *safety* for *accuracy*.

There are no magic bullets, the IOM report emphasizes, as no single action is sufficient to bring about the degree of change needed. Additionally, and most critically, the IOM report says that responsibility for taking action should not be borne by any single group of providers, but must be addressed by all parts of the health-care enterprise. Many in the forensic science community agree with this statement and accept it as a credo for their field. It is time to end this destructive, fatalistic blame game and replace it with a new agenda of constructivism. In health care, preventing adverse events before they occur is the imperative; it is the very same in forensic science, and we have an incredible opportunity to explore how we can create a culture of constant quality improvement.

Significant progress in improving the stature of the U.S. medico-legal death investigation system and the U.S. forensic laboratory system will be achieved only when all members of the criminal justice system, the academic community, and the government are fully engaged in and committed to this most challenging and rewarding process. The initiatives noted in Chapter 16 are encouraging, but so much more must be achieved to break down the barriers that prevent forensic service providers from optimizing their contributions to the system. One significant barrier is the frustration and fear that forensic practitioners experience when engaging in dialogue about the needs of their profession; frustration, because they might not be heard, and fear, because they may be heard and face retribution as a result. Yes, it is a contradiction in terms, but it is a reality for the thousands of practitioners who work for the government and are nervous about speaking up, rocking the boat, and risking their futures. As I said before, we need a system that does not punish honest dialogue but encourages and rewards it. Many forensic practitioners are wary of discussing their needs, their issues, and their concerns in a public forum because of the criticism and skepticism that will rain down upon them from commentators who are slow to understand and even slower to empathize, but quick to judge. There must be an environment imbued with good faith in which forensic practitioners and the decision makers can meet to exchange perspectives without fatal repercussions for themselves, their staff, their constituents, and most importantly, those who depend on forensic science the most—decedents and defendants.

I said it in the preface and I say it again here: The vast majority of forensic professionals in both the medico-legal death investigation system in the forensic laboratory system are profoundly dedicated, conscientious individuals who toil long hours under exceedingly difficult circumstances. They deserve our utmost respect, and they should be supported, not attacked. Forensic science is our first responder to death scenes, terrorism attacks, and public health challenges, and it should be recognized as such. It must be built up, not torn down with careless, unfounded accusations, so it is imperative that the siege mentality be transformed into a mindset of reasoned, tempered suggestions for the advancement and improvement of forensic science.

ABOUT THE AUTHOR

Kelly M. Pyrek is an award-winning journalist and editor who has worked in the newspaper and magazine industry for 25 years. She is a graduate of the University of Southern California and is the author of the textbook *Forensic Nursing* (CRC Press, 2006).